The *Family* Communication Sourcebook

Provided By

Grizzly Riders International

We would like to dedicate this book to our students and teachers of family communication (many of whom are represented in this collection).

Lynn dedicates this book to her husband, Ted, who continues to explore lessons of family communication with her.

Rich dedicates this book to his mother, Beverly, who has been a constant source of support for him.

The *Family* Communication Sourcebook

Lynn H. Turner
Marquette University

Richard West
University of Southern Maine

EDITORS

SAGE Publications
Thousand Oaks ▪ London ▪ New Delhi

For information:

Sage Publications, Inc.
2455 Teller Road
Thousand Oaks, California 91320
E-mail: order@sagepub.com

Sage Publications Ltd.
1 Oliver's Yard
55 City Road
London EC1Y 1SP
United Kingdom

Sage Publications India Pvt. Ltd.
B-42, Panchsheel Enclave
Post Box 4109
New Delhi 110 017 India

Printed in the United States of America

Library of Congress Cataloging-in-Publication Data

The family communication sourcebook / [edited by] Lynn H. Turner, Richard West.
      p. cm.
Includes bibliographical references and index.
ISBN 1-4129-0991-0 (cloth)—ISBN 1-4129-0992-9 (pbk.)
     1. Communication in the family—Research—United States. 2. Interpersonal communication—Research—United States. I. Turner, Lynn H. II. West, Richard L.
HQ536.F3645 2006
306.870973—dc22   2005031044

This book is printed on acid-free paper.

06   07   08   09   10   10   9   8   7   6   5   4   3   2   1

Acquisitions Editor:	Todd R. Armstrong
Editorial Assistant:	Sarah K. Quesenberry
Production Editor:	Laureen A. Shea
Copy Editor:	Gillian Dickens
Typesetter:	C&M Digitals (P) Ltd.
Proofreader:	Kevin Gleason
Indexer:	Jeanne Busemeyer

Contents

PART III: INTERNAL FAMILY DYNAMICS

PART IV: EXTERNAL STRUCTURAL FRAMEWORKS

MEDIA-FAMILY INTERFACE

WORK-FAMILY INTERFACE

RELIGION-FAMILY INTERFACE

SCHOOL-FAMILY INTERFACE

HEALTH CARE–FAMILY INTERFACE

Preface

Lynn H. Turner

Marquette University

Richard West

University of Southern Maine

A s we write this, issues from the public sphere (e.g., the war in Iraq and related protests at Camp Casey, echoes of September 11, 2001, the devastation of Hurricane Katrina, and the global fight against crippling diseases such as AIDS and malaria) resonate deeply and remind us of the importance of examining the influences of the private sphere called "family" (however it is defined). These events and ongoing challenges—despite their time in history—remain etched in our hearts and minds forever. The family, we contend, is inherently and explicitly situated in these public proceedings. For instance, we cannot think about war without simultaneously considering the toll it exacts on loved ones and family members. The tragedies on September 11, 2001, cannot be framed without reflecting on the grief experienced by the families of the victims. Hurricane Katrina devastated more than buildings and levees; family units were permanently altered. Disease knows no boundaries, and families frequently experience disruption because of the effects and availability of diagnosis and treatment.

The pervasiveness of family, however, is unquestionable, whether events are tragic, joyful, or mundane. For instance, the family is situated clearly in wedding announcements, anniversary celebrations, and the birth of a child. Happy moments such as winning a lottery, buying a home, surviving cancer, and going on vacation also require us to consider the role of family. Groundbreaking legal decisions on same-sex marriage in Massachusetts and successful same-sex adoptions across the country prompt us to further commit ourselves to discussions about the family. The topic of family is inescapable as we read our daily newspaper, surf Web sites, chat with work colleagues, and live our lives, thereby illustrating how deeply intertwined the public and private spheres are (Coontz, 2000).

We cannot think of any relationships more fundamental to people's lives, their communication patterns, and overall psychological, emotional, and physiological development than those found in family. Family relationships school us in how to communicate, how to relate to others, and whether and how to commit ourselves to significant others. As we learn these lifelong lessons, we construct family in a recursive cycle of communication. Thus, communication reflects and creates family experience, and family experience is grounded in communication (Turner & West, 2006a).

Yet, these fundamental relationships are complex and various. They are incapable of formulaic description, and the diversity of family life must be acknowledged by students and scholars of family communication. We have written elsewhere (Turner & West, 2003) that forming an expansive ideology of family is both necessary and important to scholarship in family communication. First, U.S. census figures suggest that family households are now more diverse than ever. Second, given that "the family has been forced to renegotiate not only the structure of family life but the familiar roles within that structure" (Dickson, 2006, p. 135), the intersection between diversity and communication in the family cannot be ignored or devalued.

We write at a time when the area known as family communication is clearly burgeoning in scholarly and practical ways. The Family Communication Commission of the National Communication Association (NCA) was founded in 1989. At the time, a core group of family communication scholars was trying to assemble enough interest to achieve "divisional status" in the association. Today, the Family Communication Division is one of the largest units in the NCA. A journal dedicated to the topic (*Journal of Family Communication*) has been publishing quality scholarship for several years, and family communication courses proliferate in schools across the country.

Communication researchers, over the past 30 years, have described how families are created, shaped, and sustained through social interaction (e.g., Callan & Noller, 1986; Fitzpatrick, 1988; Jorgenson, 1989; Noller & Fitzpatrick, 1993). Furthermore, as Kathleen Galvin (2001) notes, family communication is now a familiar and important part of the communication research landscape, although 30 years ago, it only had meaning for a small number of professionals whose interest in interpersonal communication focused on long-term committed relationships. Furthermore, today, this landscape of family communication scholarship must necessarily include a number of gatekeepers, including journal editors, publishers, and granting agencies (Turner & West, 2006b).

Thus, we believe the time is auspicious for presenting this book: *The Family Communication Sourcebook*. The book offers a collection of both fundamental and cutting-edge research on the family, grounded in communication theory. We had two basic goals in compiling this book: First, we wished to present a communication perspective on the family, and second, we wanted to show how family is more than simply another context for communication. Our concern to explicate family as a multidimensional concept unites these two goals.

Underlying Themes of the Collection: Our Organizational Pattern

We envisioned the book divided into four sections, mirroring our thematic approach to the topic. First, we founded the book on definitional issues. Part I: Defining and Interpreting the Family consists of two chapters approaching the definition of family in two different ways. Kathleen M. Galvin's chapter (Chapter 1) argues that "as families become increasingly diverse, *their definitional processes expand exponentially, rendering their identity highly discourse dependent.* Family identity depends, in part, on members' communication with outsiders, as well as with each other regarding their familial connections" (p. 3). Galvin's approach is consistent with a great deal of research in the family communication field, contending that the definition of family is dependent on the communication that the members engage in both inside and outside of family boundaries.

Chapter 2 by Kory Floyd, Alan C. Mikkelson, and Jeff Judd reviews what they call three lenses for the purpose of defining family: "We distinguish among defining familial relationships based on their emotional attachment and patterns of interaction (role lens), their legally sanctioned status (sociolegal lens), and their shared genes and/or reproductive potential (biogenetic lens)" (p. 26). They explain the strengths and weaknesses of each lens, concluding that it is important to distinguish clearly between relationships that are familial and those that are not. Taken together, these two chapters present a comprehensive and provocative introduction to the problem of mapping the conceptual terrain of family.

Part II consists of theoretical and methodological reviews, providing foundational information for any student of family communication. Teresa C. Sabourin (Chapter 3) overviews an extensive repertoire of theories that have been frequently used to frame studies of family communication. In Chapter 4, Deborah S. Ballard-Reisch and Daniel J. Weigel distinguish between theories and models and review important models of family functioning. They include a model they have created, focusing specifically on family communication. Finally, Sandra Metts and Emily Lamb organize the myriad methods researchers employ in examining family communication. In total, this part of the book presents a coherent guide to a variety of approaches to thinking theoretically and conducting research in family communication.

The third section of the book, Internal Family Dynamics, examines communication practices that are integral to families, making families unique among settings for interpersonal communication and more than simple contexts for interpersonal communication. These communication practices include storytelling (Chapters 6 and 7), conflict (Chapters 8 and 9), intimacy (Chapters 10 and 11), discipline (Chapters 12 and 13), and rituals (Chapters 14 and 15). Each topic is addressed in two chapters; the first chapter provides a conceptual framing and literature review of the topic, and the second chapter presents a data-based study of the topic (or a specific aspect of the topic). In the area of storytelling, Kristin M. Langellier and Eric E. Peterson (Chapter 6) illustrate how storytelling is communication practice for families. In Chapter 7, Theresa L. Hest, Judy C. Pearson, and Jeffrey T. Child present a study based on a specific type of story, cover stories, that they collected from married couples.

Michael E. Roloff and Courtney Waite Miller (Chapter 8) review the literature on family and marital conflict, providing a rich overview of the critical concepts in this area. In Chapter 9, Patricia Noller, Sharon Atkin, Judith A. Feeney, and Candida Peterson illustrate the topic with two studies about conflict between adolescents and their parents. In these studies, their aim was to shed light on what adolescents and parents perceive as typical in conflict as well as to examine the effects of different conflict styles.

The intimacy section begins with a chapter (Chapter 10) by Megan K. Foley and Steve Duck that clarifies the term *family intimacy,* which they note is a slippery term in need of definition. Chapter 11, by Sandra Petronio and Susanne M. Jones, reports on a specific aspect of this term in their study of unwanted advice given to pregnant couples. Chapter 12 by Thomas J. Socha offers a look at how discipline has been treated in the family literature and then argues for enlarging our thinking about discipline by adopting "orchestration" as a new frame. Steven R. Wilson, Xiaowei Shi, Lisa Tirmenstein, Alda Norris, and Jessica J. Rack (Chapter 13) present a meta-analysis examining parental negative touch, noting that "parents do not strike their children at random but rather at predictable moments that arise out of larger interactions usually involving discipline" (p. 238).

Leslie A. Baxter and Dawn O. Braithwaite (Chapter 14) overview the area of family ritual by bringing together research and theory from the interdisciplinary fields of ritual studies and family studies, as well as from family communication. They are specifically interested in the following questions: "How can we conceptualize 'ritual' in the family context? What theoretical approaches do scholars use to understand rituals? How have researchers studied rituals? How do families ritualize? What are possible directions for future research by family communication scholars who study rituals?" This chapter is followed by Leah E. Bryant's study (Chapter 15) on rituals in the context of stepfamilies. Bryant asks, How do family rituals function after the death of a parent?

The fourth and final section of the book is called External Structural Frameworks. In this section, chapters address the interface between the family and another important social institution. Again, chapters are paired to provide conceptual overviews and data-based studies at each interface. Chapters 16 and 17 examine the interface of the family and media. J. Alison Bryant and Jennings Bryant (Chapter 16) consider the implications of living in a wired family and suggest new directions for family and media research. In Chapter 17, Alison Alexander, Seok Kang, and Yeora Kim present the results of a study surveying both parents and children about Internet concerns, attitudes, and use. Their discussion of "cyberkids" helps us to understand the new technological world of young people.

Other interfaces examined include work and family (Chapters 18 and 19), religion and family (Chapters 20 and 21), school and family (Chapters 22 and 23), and health care and family (Chapters 24 and 25). In Chapter 18, Kristen Lucas and Patrice M. Buzzanell present discourses pertaining to the work-family framework and problematicize some antiquated notions pertaining to family. Caryn E. Medved and Elizabeth E. Graham (Chapter 19) examine gendered messages pertaining to work and family. They present research findings that support (and refute) the notion that women and men are socialized differently about work, family, and balance. Religion and religious identity are articulated in Chapter 20; Patrick C. Hughes and Fran C. Dickson explain the nuances associated with interfaith marriages. In Chapter 21, Helen Sterk and Rebecca Kallemeyn present a study examining Southern Baptist women preachers. In Chapter 22, Pamela Cooper presents a theoretical overview of family-school relationships, identifying the importance of looking at the family, arguing that "education is everyone's business." Scott A. Myers, Paul Schrodt, and Christine E. Rittenour help us to better understand whether hurtful messages affect a student's academic progress (Chapter 23). In Chapter 24, Loretta L. Pecchioni, Teresa L. Thompson, and Dustin J. Anderson embrace a life span perspective and examine family talk about health, sexuality, and substance use and abuse, among other topics. In Chapter 25, Donna R. Pawlowski researches the dialectical tensions pertaining to stroke survivors. Pawlowski explores the onset of stroke through the rehabilitation process and establishes that despite medical setbacks associated with a stroke, participants still see their quality of life overall as positive.

In addition to these four sections, the book is introduced by L. Edna Rogers, who provides a chapter reflecting on the development of family communication as a field of study. Rogers offers a brief history of the field, which sets a context for the rest of the material in the book. Finally, Mary Anne Fitzpatrick concludes the book with an epilogue summarizing the current state of the field.

Expressing Our Appreciation

We are grateful for the outstanding scholarship of all the authors in this collection. Each time we read a chapter, we found ourselves learning something new about family communication. We appreciated the authors' willingness to revise and reconsider as we worked toward completion of this volume. Working with this distinguished group of scholars was a great pleasure for us, and we are very happy to have had the opportunity to do so. We also appreciate the historical framing provided by having two founders of the field, L. Edna Rogers and Mary Anne Fitzpatrick, introduce and conclude the book. Lynn extends her thanks to her research assistant, Mei Jia, who has helped her check references and copy edit and is always cheerful and smiling when she comes into the office to work. She also appreciates the support she has received from the College of Communication and Marquette University, enabling her to work on this project. Rich is indebted to the Department of Communication and Media Studies for providing him ongoing support. He also remains grateful to be able to work with such supportive students, colleagues, and administrators. We both extend a sincere thank you to Todd Armstrong, who is the very definition of a perfect editor. His support, friendship, and unwavering good humor make him a joy to work with, and we both value Todd's skills as an editor and his delightful personality as a friend. We also thank Camille Herrera and Deya Saoud and the entire Sage team for all their help in facilitating the publication of our book.

References

Callan, V. J., & Noller, P. (1986). Perceptions of communicative relationships in families with adolescents. *Journal of Marriage and the Family, 48,* 813–820.

Coontz, S. (2000). Historical perspectives on family diversity. In D. H. Demo, K. R. Allen, & M. A. Fine (Eds.), *Handbook of family diversity* (pp. 15–31). Oxford, UK: Oxford University Press.

Dickson, F. C. (2006). Commentary on Part B. In K. Floyd & M. T. Morman (Eds.), *Widening the family circle: New research on family communication* (pp. 129–134). Thousand Oaks, CA: Sage.

Fitzpatrick, M. A. (1988). *Between husbands and wives.* Newbury Park, CA: Sage.

Galvin, K. M. (2001). Family communication instruction: A brief history and call. *Journal of Family Communication, 1,* 15–20.

Jorgenson, J. (1989). Where is the "family" in family communication? Exploring families' self-definitions. *Journal of Applied Communication Research, 17,* 27–41.

Noller, P., & Fitzpatrick, M. A. (1993). *Communication and family relationships.* Englewood Cliffs, NJ: Prentice Hall.

Turner, L. H., & West, R. (2003). Breaking through silence: Increasing voice for diverse families in communication research. *Journal of Family Communication, 3,* 181–186.

Turner, L. H., & West, R. (2006a). *Perspectives on family communication* (3rd ed.). New York: McGraw-Hill.

Turner, L. H., & West, R. (2006b). Understudied relationships in family communication research: Expanding the social recipe. In K. Floyd & M. T. Morman (Eds.), *Widening the family circle: New research on family communication* (pp. 93–206). Thousand Oaks, CA: Sage.

Introduction

A Reflective View on the Development of Family Communication

L. Edna Rogers

University of Utah

The family has been a central domain of study in the social sciences from the early institutional view of the family as a primary social unit to the more recent communication view of the family as a dynamic, socially constructed system of relationships. The movement toward the development of family communication had its beginnings in the 1970s as a special area of interest within the broader arena of interpersonal communication. Over the past three decades, we have seen this interest of a small group of scholars unfold, blossom, and take on a life of its own. The present volume speaks "volumes" to the progressive development and value of applying a communication perspective to the study of the family.

For those of us entering the newly established discipline of communication in the late 1960s, there were, however, few "footholds" within the discipline from which to build a research program focusing on family communication. During these early years, the field was heavily weighted toward mass communication, with an emphasis on the study of message effects, speaker credibility, persuasion, compliance gaining, and related issues using a strategic, actor, or action-oriented approach. In similar fashion, research in interpersonal communication drew largely on psychological models, and thus the majority of the work was primarily focused on the individual, particularly the study of perceptual and cognitive processes. Given this research orientation, few solid guidelines were available for studying relationships, especially those most personal: family relationships.

As a result, the two most promising research literatures on which to draw were, first and rather obviously, the broad area of family sociology and, second, the general area of system theory and related writings in family therapy. Although the volume of work by family sociologists provided a wealth of information on marriage and the family, the accumulated research clearly indicated an analytical preference for either an individual or larger social unit focus over an interaction focus. Nye and Bernardo's (1966) edited text outlined 11 conceptual frameworks for family analysis, ranging from the structure-functional, psychoanalytic, social-psychological, developmental, to an economic approach. Of the approaches covered, the most relevant for communication scholars was the conceptual framework based on symbolic interaction. Although not included by Nye and Bernardo, system theory as applied to the family provided the other main resource for forming a communication perspective on the family. The theoretical foundations of both symbolic interaction and system theory offered a potentially rich grounding for the development of family communication. Each perspective, albeit in different ways, centered on key communication aspects of human relationships—namely, interaction processes, the interconnection of self and other, socially constructed realities, and mutually created patterns of relationship.

In thinking back on symbolic interaction and the influence of the Chicago school, a host of prominent writings comes to mind with only a few mentioned here. The work of the school's early founders—Park, Burgess, Thomas, and Mead, among others—fundamentally reshaped how we viewed human behavior and social relationships. This was also the case with the family. Prior conceptions of the family were fully redefined with Burgess's (1926) well-known definition of the family as "a unity of interacting personalities." This reframing shifted the focus of family study from the more traditional social institution, or structure-functional approach, to a view of the family based on the interaction processes of family members (Burgess & Locke, 1945). Waller (1938), in his early family text, was the first to incorporate Burgess's ideas. In applying this approach, Waller provided fresh insights on the dynamics of the family; for instance, in his discussion of power differentials, he first introduced the "principle of least interest." This text and a later revision (Waller & Hill, 1951) were instrumental in expanding the social implications of symbolic interaction from the original focus on the self to the study of the family, as well as relationships in general.

Two writings, founded on the central premise of this perspective, have become classic readings in exemplifying the social construction of meaning. Hess and Handel's (1959) extensive case study of five families is noted for its methodological approach providing an in-depth analysis of how families construct their lives through interaction. In a complementary manner, the essay by Berger and Kellner (1964) provides a richly layered conceptual understanding of everyday communication processes by which marital partners coconstruct the evolving reality of their relationship.

While symbolic interaction formed an early and well-established foundation for developing studies of the family, the original 1930s formulation by Bateson of a system-based approach for studying relationships lay hidden and unrecognized until much later. The initial awareness of Bateson's early work came largely through the writings of the Palo Alto research group, particularly through the publication of Watzlawick, Beavin, and Jackson's (1967) *Pragmatics of Human Communication.*

A 30-year time gap existed between Bateson's first publications and knowledge of his work by communication scholars. The Watzlawick et al. volume opened a window to a large set of readings that offered a systemic, process view of communication, a view that significantly influenced the field in general, particularly the study of family communication. Among these readings were Bateson's (1951, 1972) foundational writings that introduced what are now basic concepts in the field (e.g., levels of message meaning, metacommunication, schismogenesis, symmetry, and complementarity), along with Jackson's (1957, 1965) view of the family as a cybernetic system, Sluzki and Beavin's (1965) typology of dyads, Haley's (1963) communication control strategies, and many others. This work prompted further reading in family system therapy and the burgeoning area of clinical research on the family. For example, communication-centered writings—such as Lennard and Bernstein's (1969) focus on patterns of human interaction; Laing's (1969) politics of the family; Raush, Barry, Hertel, and Swain's (1974) communication in marital conflict; and Kantor and Lehr's (1975) model of family process—were important resources for how to conceptualize and design communication research. Bochner (1976) provides an extensive review of this large volume of early work in an influential essay outlining the conceptual frontiers of family communication. Two dissertations, credited with initiating family communication research, were completed during this period: Rogers's (1972) relational communication perspective for studying marital interaction patterns and Fitzpatrick's (1976) typological approach to the study of marital couple types. Since that time, the research accomplishments of an increasing number of family scholars have greatly enlarged our knowledge and understandings of marital and family relationships.

The breadth and depth of family communication research continues to expand and benefit from the application of different theoretical approaches. The formulation of the dialectic perspective by Baxter and Montgomery (1996) and the related approach of Petronio (2002) on communication privacy management are of particular note. With the development of these approaches and the wealth of research generated from their application to the context of the family, dialectic thinking forms an additional foundational perspective for the field of family communication. Based on the "both/and" relational quality of dialectic tensions continually in flux within the unity of opposites, this perspective offers an alternative way of conceptualizing and investigating the dynamic interplay of the communication processes underlying family relationships.

Family research has also been influenced by the increased practice of studying relationships from an interdisciplinary perspective. With additional conceptual approaches and multiple methodologies from which to draw, we have seen the scope of family study expand over the past two decades far beyond earlier research boundaries. Movements in the field have spread out over a large terrain of family-related topics with the investigation of different family forms; lifestyles; issues of diversity, health, and aging; violence and abuse; mass media and the Internet; family rituals; social support; attachment; and feelings and emotions—and the list goes on. Many of these current issues are addressed in subsequent chapters in this volume.

A point to keep in mind, however, is that while the variability of family topics covered has increased, the variability of the family units and populations studied has not kept pace. Family research continues to focus primarily on the marital dyad and relatively young, educated, European American study participants. Based on a content analysis of nearly 1,000 family articles published in six mainstream family and personal relationship journals from 1994 to 1999, Fingerman and Hay (2002) found the marital relationship to be the most frequently studied family unit, with the majority of participants drawn from college student samples within an 18 to 44 age range. The authors did not track race or ethnicity, but given the sample base, it is not unlikely that a large proportion of the participants were European American. The overuse of college student samples clearly limits the diversity of our research. A call to move beyond the classroom is essential to widen the sampling lens for investigating many understudied arenas of family life. Likewise, although not diminishing the importance of studying marital relations, "family" research will take on new meaning and insights with the investigation of larger, multimember units of the family, as well as the full family unit. These issues are not to take away from present achievements but to further enhance the development of family communication research.

A different mode for viewing the field's development is to reflect on the progressive movement toward solidifying family communication as an established field of study. A number of events, representing important first accomplishments, serve as "markers" in tracing this development. A beginning move in this direction was the first convention program devoted to family communication, titled "Studying Family Communication: Prospects, Problems and Research Methods." This program, organized by Art Bochner, was presented at the 1974 Speech Communication Association meeting in Chicago. Bochner's promotion of this area of study and his formative papers (Bochner, 1974, 1976) on communication in families were influential in the initial identification of family communication as a separate research area. Also during this time period, the first college courses on family communication were being offered at a few universities: Michigan State, Temple, Cleveland State, University of Denver, Northwestern, and Wisconsin. By the 1980s, family communication courses were being taught across U.S. campuses. These first offerings used a variety of text materials, articles by the Palo Alto group, family sociologists, communication researchers, Satir's (1972) *Peoplemaking,* and Kantor and Lehr's (1975) *Inside the Family.* The first textbook on family communication was published in 1982 by Galvin and Brommel. Several other texts appeared in the late 1980s and early 1990s and, since that time, many more, all giving evidence of the growth of the field. No doubt many of the second and third generations of family scholars were first introduced to the field via these texts.

The recognition of the field began to be more formally solidified in 1989, with the formation of the Commission of Family Communication within the National Communication Association. Six years later, with increasing members of the association identifying with family study, the Family Communication Division was established. Another step in establishing the visibility and identity of the field was taken with the publication of the first issue of the *Journal of Family Communication* in 2001, under the editorship of Tom Socha. And a recent capstone to the series of events marking the progress of the field is the 2004 *Handbook of Family Communication,* edited by Anita Vangelisti. With these past accomplishments, although only briefly sketched here, the progressive development of the field has established a strong momentum for future advances, with many of these unfolding at the present time.

By continuing to build on the centrality of communication and the basic premise of its constitutive qualities, the theoretical perspective of family communication offers a particularly powerful approach for integrating family relationship research. The communication perspective holds the potential for bringing together two traditional arenas of family study, one giving primary attention to the individual members of the family and the other to the larger social unit and contextual aspects of the family. This approach provides an essential connective link between the two areas by focusing on the communicative processes of family relations in which the interrelated influences of the individual members and the larger social system are played out.

From the early foundational work, the interwoven connection between communication and relationship has been central to the family communication perspective. In offering a reflective view on the development of the field, I see the continuing importance of the theoretical and practical implications of a communication perspective on the family reflected in this basic principle.

References

Bateson, G. (1951). Information and codification: A philosophical approach. In J. Ruesch & G. Bateson (Eds.), *Communication: The social matrix of psychiatry* (pp. 168–211). New York: Norton.

Bateson, G. (1972). *Steps to an ecology of mind*. New York: Ballantine.

Baxter, L. A., & Montgomery, B. M. (1996). *Relating: Dialogues and dialectics*. New York: Guilford.

Berger, P., & Kellner, H. (1964). Marriage and the construction of reality: An exercise in the microsociology of knowledge. *Diogenes, 46*, 1–25.

Bochner, A. P. (1974, December). *Family communication research: A critical review of approaches, methodologies and substantive findings*. Paper presented at the annual convention of the Speech Communication Association, Chicago.

Bochner, A. P. (1976). Conceptual frontiers in the study of communication in the family: An introduction to the literature. *Human Communication Research, 2*, 381–397.

Burgess, E. (1926). The family as a unity of interacting personalities. *The Family, 7*, 3–9.

Burgess, E., & Locke, H. (1945). *The family from institution to companionship*. New York: American Book Company.

Fingerman, K., & Hay, E. (2002). Searching under the streetlight? Age biases in the personal and family relationships literature. *Personal Relationships, 9*, 415–433.

Fitzpatrick, M. A. (1976). *A typological approach to communication in relationships*. Unpublished doctoral dissertation, Temple University, Philadelphia.

Galvin, K., & Brommel, B. (1982). *Family communication: Cohesion and change*. Glenville, IL: Scott Foresman.

Haley, J. (1963). *Strategies of psychotherapy*. New York: Grune & Stratton.

Hess, R., & Handel, G. (1959). *Family worlds: A psychological approach to family life*. Chicago: University of Chicago Press.

Jackson, D. (1957). The question of family homeostasis. *Psychiatric Quarterly Supplement, 31*, 79–90.

Jackson, D. (1965). The study of the family. *Family Process, 4,* 1–20.

Kantor, D., & Lehr, W. (1975). *Inside the family: Toward a theory of family process.* San Francisco: Jossey-Bass.

Laing, R. D. (1969). *The politics of the family and other essays.* New York: Random House.

Lennard, H., & Bernstein, A. (1969). *Patterns in human interaction.* San Francisco: Jossey-Bass.

Nye, F. I., & Bernardo, F. (1966). *Emerging conceptual frameworks in family analysis.* New York: Macmillan.

Petronio, S. (2002). *The boundaries of privacy: Dialectics of disclosure.* New York: State University of New York Press.

Raush, H., Barry, W., Hertel, R., & Swain, M. (1974). *Communication, conflict and marriage.* San Francisco: Jossey-Bass.

Rogers, L. E. (1972). *Dyadic systems and transactional communication in a family context.* Unpublished doctoral dissertation, Michigan State University, East Lansing.

Satir, V. (1972). *Peoplemaking.* Palo Alto, CA: Science and Behavior Books.

Sluzki, C., & Beavin, J. H. (1965). Simetria y complementaridad: Una definicion operacional y una tipologia de pardjas [Symmetry and complementarity: An operational definition and typology of couples]. *Acta Psiquiatrica y Psicologica de America Latina, 11,* 321–330.

Vangelisti, A. L. (2004). *Handbook of family communication.* Mahwah, NJ: Lawrence Erlbaum.

Waller, W. (1938). *The family: A dynamic interpretation.* New York: The Cordon Company.

Waller, W., & Hill, R. (1951). *The family: A dynamic interpretation.* New York: Dryden.

Watzlawick, P., Beavin, J. H., & Jackson, D. (1967). *Pragmatics of human communication.* New York: Norton.

PART I

Defining and Interpreting the Family

CHAPTER 1

Diversity's Impact on Defining the Family

Discourse-Dependence and Identity

Kathleen M. Galvin

Northwestern University

Contemporary families represent a world of "normative instability and definitional crisis" (Stacey, 1999a, p. 489), making it more difficult for members to keep order in their personal lives and maintain family stability (McCracken, 2004). Although all societies and cultures have webs of kinship relationships, the structures of which change across time and cultures (Garey & Hansen, 1998), U.S. families represent the forefront of familial redefinition due to the multiplicity of changing kinship patterns. As families become increasingly diverse, *their definitional processes expand exponentially, rendering their identity highly discourse dependent.* Family identity depends, in part, on members' communication with outsiders, as well as with each other, regarding their familial connections.

Even though all families engage in some level of discourse-driven family identity building, less traditionally formed families are more discourse dependent, engaging in recurring discursive processes to manage and maintain identity. A growing number of U.S. families are formed through differences, visible or invisible, rendering their ties more ambiguous to outsiders as well as to themselves. Many other cultures such as those in the Middle East or Asia still identify families by similarities. Circumstances such as ongoing connections to a birthmother and adoptive parents, visual differences among members, siblings' lack of shared early childhood experiences, same-sex parents, or ties to ex-step relatives create ambiguity, necessitating active management of family identity. These definitional concerns surface as members face outsiders' challenges regarding the veracity of their claims of relatedness or as members experience a need to revisit their familial identity at different times. The greater the ambiguity of family form, the more elaborate the communicative processes needed to establish and maintain identity.

Highly discourse-dependent families engage regularly in external and internal boundary management practices. Times of stress and/or boundary ambiguity challenge families because expectations of inclusion and support are less clear in self-ascribed or ambiguous relations than in families formed and maintained through traditionally recognized biological and adult legal ties. Clarification, explanation, and negotiation of identity become commonplace.

My own experience, unique but not extraordinary, may make this clearer. I was born into a traditional, biological family as an only child; both my parents reflected an Irish Catholic heritage. This rather uncomplicated family experience lasted until I was 17, when my father died and my mother became ill and died a few years later. At that time, another family (Norwegian-German, Methodist with three younger biological children) to whom I was emotionally attached informally adopted me, incorporating me into a familial relationship that continues to this day. Eventually I married, bore a son and daughter, and adopted another daughter from Korea, making us a family formed through "visible adoption" with extended biological relatives of Irish and Korean descent and adoptive relatives of Norwegian and German descent.

When my first child was born, my informally adopted mother and I discussed what she and her husband should be called; we agreed on Grandma Mae and Grandpa Arnold. Today, I have three young adult children; a daughter-in-law; a set of informally adopted siblings; current and, due to divorce, former in-laws; nieces, nephews, step-nieces, and step-nephews, to whom I am "Aunt Kathy"; a whole extended set of in-laws; plus a set of "fictive kin" or extremely close friends who also serve as my extended family. Consequently, my family cannot be explained easily through traditional familial titles; my family requires naming, explaining, legitimizing, and, occasionally, defending. It is held together internally through discussions, narratives, and rituals, as well as some legal and biological ties. Today, family life is like that.

What serves as the basis of family? Minow (1998) identifies the key question as, "Does this group function as a family?" arguing that the issue is not whether a group of people fits the formal, legal definition of a family but "whether the group of people function as a family; do they share affection and resources, think of one another as family members, and present themselves as such to neighbors and others?" (p. 8). Communicative practices contribute to family functioning, especially in families formed, fully or partly, outside of traditional means. Before addressing these communicative processes, it is necessary to describe briefly the current diversity of U.S. families.

Family Diversity

Families in the first half of the 21st century will alter irrevocably any sense of predictability as to what "being family" means. These families will

1. Reflect an increasing diversity of self-conceptions, evidenced through structural as well as cultural variations, which will challenge society to abandon historical, nucleocentric biases, unitary cultural assumptions, traditional gender assumptions, and implied economic and religious assumptions.

2. Live increasingly within four and five generations of relational connections. Escalating longevity, changing birth rates, and multiple marriages or cohabitations will reveal long-term developmental patterns, ongoing multiple intergenerational contacts, generational reversals, and smaller biological-sibling cohorts.

3. Continuously reconfigure themselves across members' life spans as members' choices create new family configurations through legal, biological, technological, and discursive means, affecting family identity (Coontz, 1999; Galvin, 2004a).

Further examination of these claims provides a picture of contemporary family life. Fewer families can be depicted validly by discrete categories or unitary terms, such as stepfamily, biological family, single-parent families, or adoptive families, due to overlapping complexities of connections. An overview of contemporary patterns of family formation reveals the following:

People continue to marry across their life spans. The 2000 census reveals that more than half of people age 15 and older were married, although the majority of those younger than 24 were single. Many of these are second or third marriages. In 2000, 9.7% of males and 10.8% of females reported that they were currently divorced, with the 45- to 54-year-old age group reporting the highest percentage of divorces (Kreider & Simmons, 2003).

Stepfamilies, formed through remarriage or cohabitation, generally reflect divorce and recommitment, although an increasing number are formed by single mothers marrying for the first time. In 2000, married or cohabiting adults reported parenting 4.4 million stepchildren (Kreider, 2003). These blended families exhibit a wide range of trajectories leading toward family identity (Braithwaite, Olson, Golish, Soukup, & Turman, 2001). Far more is understood about mutual obligations among biologically related family members than among step-kin (Coleman, Ganong, & Fine, 2000). Even less is known about ex-stepfamily relationships, although increasing numbers of individuals live in second or third stepfamilies.

Single-parent families continue to increase. In 2000, 22% of children lived with only their mothers, and 4% lived with only their fathers (Simmons & O'Neill, 2001). Today, women younger than 30 who become pregnant for the first time are more likely to be single than married. Increasingly, single women and men become parents through adoption and new reproductive technologies.

Gay and lesbian committed couples and families are becoming more visible due, in part, to a greater willingness of same-sex partners to identify their lifestyle. Census data do not include gay and lesbian partners, although the 2000 data on unmarried partner households indicated that over half a million households were headed by same-sex partners, representing 1% of all coupled households (Simmons & O'Connell, 2003). According to the 2000 census, 33% of women in same-sex partnerships lived with children, as did 22% of men in same-sex partnerships (Simmons

& O'Connell, 2003). Lesbian and gay families are not easily categorized because they "come in different sizes, shapes, ethnicities, races, religions, resources, creeds, and quirks, and even engage in diverse sexual practices" (Stacey, 1999b, p. 373).

More families are being formed, in part, through adoption. In 2000, 2.5% of children younger than 18 were adopted; a total of 2.1 million children were recorded as adopted, approximately 200,000 of whom were foreign born (Kreider, 2003). Many of these families become transracial through the adoption process. Open adoption is emerging as the common domestic form, creating an ongoing adoption triangle—the adoptee, the birth parent(s), and the adoptive parent(s)—with variable contact among members. The triangle may involve multiple individuals because the biological parent(s) may have partners and other children and the adoptive parent(s) may have other children (Elmhorst, 2003).

Intentional families, families formed without biological and legal ties, are maintained by members' self-definition. These "fictive" or self-ascribed kin become family by choice, performing family functions for one another. The next-door neighbors who serve as extended kin, the best friend who is considered a sister, other immigrants from the same homeland, or occasionally an "urban tribe" or intricate community of young people who live and work together in various combinations (Watters, 2003) function as family. Major tragedies create a need for such families; families of the International Service Workers 32BJ who lost relatives in 9/11 meet together regularly, expanding each others' definition of family (Imber-Black, 2004). The processes by which intentional families are formed reflect a transactional definition of family, that is, "a group of intimates who generate a sense of home and group identity and who experience a shared history and a shared future" (Koerner & Fitzpatrick, 2002, p. 71).

Currently, fewer people report membership in families fully formed through lifelong marriages and biological offspring; many experience multiplicities of connections. The complexities are captured in a discussion of the label *gay and lesbian families:* "Should we count only families in which every single member is gay? . . . Or does the presence of just one gay member color a family gay?" (Stacey, 1999b, p. 373). The same question must be asked about labeling families as adoptive, blended or step, single parent, and so on.

Other factors, such as ethnicity and religion, affect family structure. According to 2000 census data, Asians report the lowest proportion of separation or divorce, Black men and women report the lowest percentage of marriage (42% of Black men were married and 31% of Black women were married), and Alaska Indians and Alaska natives report the highest percentage of divorce (Kreider & Simmons, 2003). Ethnicity interacts with parenthood; in 2000, 77% of white non-Hispanic children, 65% of Hispanic children, and 38% of African American children lived with two parents, not necessarily biological. Mixed-race families are growing. In 2000, 7% of married couples and 12% of unmarried male/female partners reflected different races (Simmons & O'Connell, 2003). More than 4% of children are of mixed race; overall, 2.4 million persons report a heritage of two or more races (Jones & Smith, 2001).

Religious identification adds to familial complexity. Recent research reports a growing increase in interfaith marriage among several denominations as the majority of young adults indicate that shared religion is not significant in a partnership.

Yet interfaith marriages are less stable and more likely to end in divorce than same-faith marriages (Hughes, 2004).

As the population ages, families face increased involvement in managing and renegotiating their identities over decades and across generations. Multigenerational bonds are becoming more important than nuclear family ties for well-being and support over the life span (Bengston, 2001). The average life expectancy for an individual born in the United States in 2000 is 76.9 years: 74.1 years for males and 79.5 years for females (National Center for Health Statistics, 2004), but these figures are further complicated by race. For example, White male life expectancy is 74.8 years, while Black male life expectancy is 68.2 years; White female life expectancy is 80 years versus 74.9 years for Black females.

Families are characterized increasingly by elongated generational structures. Due to increases in longevity and decreases in fertility, the population age structure in most industrialized nations changed from a pyramid to a rectangle, creating "a family structure in which the shape is long and thin, with more family generations alive but with fewer members in the generation" (Bengston, 2001, p. 5). This portends shifts in interaction patterns as family members share more years together.

Grandparenting, as well as its great or great-great variations, is becoming a more predictable familial role; more grandparents assume child care functions, although involvement varies by race and ethnicity. More than half of the African American, American Indian, and Alaska Native grandparents were "coresident grandparents" responsible for their grandchildren (Simmons & Dye, 2003). Elder generations will compete with each other for the attention of their few grandchildren and great-grandchildren.

Longevity implies increased generational reversals as middle-aged business owners hire their parents (Leland, 2004), senior citizens are coaxed online by younger family members, parents learn how to use the Internet from their children (Allen & Rainie, 2002), and middle-aged adults confront elderly divorcing parents. Dissonant acculturation of certain immigrant families places children in positions of significant responsibility, thereby undercutting parental authority and putting young people at risk (Pipher, 2002). Young children assume the burden of translating medical, social services, and educational information for their parents or siblings. Their elders may not recognize the children's involvement in unsafe or unhealthy activities.

Family change is inevitable. Technological advances transform family life as fertility treatments result in increasing multiple births, infertile individuals become first-time parents, highly premature infants survive, terminal diseases leave aging relatives existing indefinitely on life support systems, and gender identity and presentation are changed surgically. Such circumstances necessitate serious discussions about the meaning of family as well as negotiations among members.

A tangible lag time exists between institutional definitions of "family" and the rapidly changing composition of household living arrangements and socially constructed relations. Lived practices outpace familial identity building, which outpaces the discourse, which outpaces societal acknowledgment or acceptance. Increasingly, diverse families are dependent on discourse for their identity development.

Discourse and Family Identity

As a nation built extensively through immigration, the United States is a key site for exploring constructed family identity. Waves of immigrants have created nonbiological familial structures for psychological and practical survival because most of their biological relatives remained in "the old country." In a metaphorical sense, many persons with strong nonbiological family ties have immigrant familial identities, an identity that "ever occupies a border position, temporarily divided between the self that was formed in the old world and the forming self of the new. Displacement, not security, is the immigrant's lot; construction of reality is ongoing" (Goodnight, 2004, n.p.). The lack of biological or adult legal ties creates a sense of displacement for some family members who regularly engage in constructing their familial identity.

We need richer concepts and tools both to make sense of increasingly complex family forms as well as to address questions such as the following: "How are we to characterize the most important relationship processes in such families? When do we need to expand our lexicon to address the new relationships and issues challenging such families?" (Grotevant, 2004, p. 12). From a social construction standpoint, "our languages of description and explanation are produced, sustained, and/or abandoned within processes of human interaction" (Gergen, Hoffman, & Anderson, 1996, p. 102). Discourse processes are relevant to families because, through interaction and language, individuals, within their family context, collectively construct familial identity (Stamp, 2004). Although all families rely on discourse to some extent to construct their identities, the increasing diversity of family forms is accompanied with increasing involvement of discursive processes. Thus, these families may be considered discourse dependent.

In this treatment of the social construction, the focus is on the constitutive formation of families in which there is a desire for an authentic, committed, and substantive feel of family. This discussion does not include the more loosely socially enacted families that serve a time- or place-bound function, performing roles, acknowledging the special nature of the connection, but understanding that it is a situation made up as one goes along without commitment or focus on authenticity. For example, some neighbors serve as fictive kin, finding pleasure in their connections, but do not anticipate a substantive and deep sense of family; when circumstances change, the definition of family changes also. Some informal adoptions, urban tribes, cohabiting pairs, cohabiting stepfamilies, and open adoption triangles represent deeper levels of commitment and perceived future investment. The following pages address the experiences of the consciously committed constitutive family experience.

Family communication scholars claim families are based on, formed, and maintained through communication, or "our families, and our images of families, are constituted through social interaction" (Vangelisti, 2004, p. xiii), necessitating studies that "employ definitions of the family that depend on how families define themselves rather than definitions based on genetic and sociological criteria" (Fitzpatrick, 1998, p. 45). Over time, as diversity increases, communicative definitions of family will be privileged over structural definitions, requiring new models for talking about and studying families (Whitchurch & Dickson, 1999). Discourse dependency is not new; what is new is that discourse-dependent families are becoming the norm.

The following analogy may highlight this point. The joining of unlike entities occurs through the process of *adhesion,* whereas like entities are joined through the process of *cohesion.* Adhesion refers to how particles of different substances are held together; cohesion refers to how particles of the same substance are attached. Increasingly, families are formed and maintained through processes of *adhesion* rather than *cohesion* as individuals create a family life outside of the traditional biological and/or legal processes (Galvin, 2004b). In biologically formed families, members tend to *cohere* to one another, reflecting the tendency of units of the same substance to hold together with minimal discourse about identity and belonging. In families not fully formed through biological and legal connections, members *cohere* and *adhere* to each other. Finally, in families formed outside biological or legal connections, members *adhere* to each other, reflecting the tendency of entities of different substances to bind together. In the second and third cases, elaborated discourse serves as the primary adhesive or substance supporting family members' efforts to establish and maintain their identity. Thus, families formed wholly or partly without biological and/or legal ties depend heavily on discourse processes to create their "stickiness," or bonding, to provide members with an internal sense of identity as well as an identity presented to outsiders.

The question emerges: What discourse practices do family members use to build an internal as well as an external identity? A review of the academic and popular material on complex families reveals a range of communicative practices used to construct and maintain family identity. Usually, the necessity for such practices depends on the degree of difference reflected within the family form. For example, in discussing adoptive families, Kaye and Warren (1988) suggest that the extent of communicative management depends on the degree to which the adoptive circumstances present intrinsic reminders that the child's biological roots are different.

External Boundary Management Practices

When families appear different to outsiders, questions and challenges arise. Family members manage the tensions between revealing and concealing family information on the assumption that they control access to their private information (Petronio, 2002). Yet, little is specifically known about how families with differences manage their boundaries. For example, researchers have not yet examined the strategies that gay and lesbian parents use "to shelter their children from negative experiences, to help children cope with instances of prejudice, to build resilience in their children" (Peplau & Beals, 2004, p. 244). And the practices of families built through new reproductive technologies remain unexplored. The following set of communication strategies for boundary management includes labeling, explaining, legitimizing, and defending.

Labeling

Labeling frequently involves identifying the familial tie, titles, or positions when introducing or referring to another person, for example, "This is my sister." The constitutive approach invites questions such as the following: What is the intent of a familial title? What questions are believed to be answered by that familial title? What do we want a familial label to communicate? To whom? How will others view labeling?

Labeling orients familial relationships such as "brother" or "mother." When transitions occur, the specific meaning of certain names must be linked to the person-in-relationship. For example, among the many communicative tasks a man faces in becoming a stepfather is negotiating a definition of the stepfather-stepchild relationship (Jorgenson, 1994). Frequently, this involves overt or covert negotiations about whether to refer to him as "my mother's husband," "Brad," "my stepfather," or "my other Dad"; each choice reveals a different sense of connection (Galvin, 1989). Because language serves as a constituent feature of cultural patterns embedded within a relationship, changing the language alters the relationship (Gergen et al., 1996).

Labeling establishes expectations. When a stepmother looks the same age as her stepson, two siblings represent different races, or "Grandma Carl" is male, creating a relational definition becomes challenging. Today's families are confronted with labeling circumstances unimaginable to earlier generations: How does one name his sperm donor or the surrogate mother who carried her?

Explaining

Explaining involves making a labeled family relationship understandable, giving reasons for it, or elaborating on how it works. When someone's nonhostile curiosity seems to question the stated familial tie, explanation is a predictable response. Remarks such as, "How come your mother is White and you're Asian?" or "How can you have two fathers?" seem to require explanation. An explanation for an international adoptee's lack of facility in her native language may include "My parents are Irish, so I didn't learn any Korean" (Galvin & Wilkinson, 2000, p. 11). When a playmate challenged her young son because he did not have a "Daddy," Blumenthal (1990–1991) explained the concept of a Seed Daddy to the boys—"a man who is not really a parent, but one who helps a woman get a baby started" (p. 185). Negotiating parenthood within a heterocentric context creates issues for same-sex partners faced with educating others about their family but who are often frustrated by the task (Chabot & Ames, 2004). In her study of lesbian and gay stepfamilies, Lynch (2000) found that many of the biological parents had not come out prior to being involved in this relationship, creating a need to explain their new family identity as a lesbian/gay stepfamily to unsuspecting friends and extended family.

Legitimizing

Legitimizing invokes the sanction of law or custom: It positions relationships as genuine and conforming to recognized standards. Legitimizing occurs when one's relational ties are challenged, creating a need to provide information that helps another recognize the tie as a genuine, familial link. Adoption agencies regularly prepare parents of families formed through transracial and/or international adoption for questions such as, "Is she your real daughter?" Adoption Learning Partners (2004), an online adoption education community, provides new parents with alternative responses to such an intrusive question. These include "No, she's my fake daughter," "Yes, she's really mine," or "Yes, we're an adoptive family." The response is chosen on the basis of the parent's interaction goals and/or the child's age and ability to understand the interaction. Gay or lesbian parents make reference to outside sources that legitimate their family, such as books that depict their family as genuine (*Heather Has Two Mommies* or *Daddy's Roommate*) or well-known figures who represent gay male or lesbian parents. Those in families created by benefit of a gestational carrier may refer questioners to books, such as *Conceiving Luc* (Freilicher, Scheu, & Wetanson, 1999).

Defending

Finally, defending involves shielding oneself or a familial relationship from attack, justifying it, or maintaining its validity against opposition. Defending is a response to hostility or a direct challenge to the familial form. For example, Garner (2004), the daughter of a gay father, depicts the difficulty of listening to constant messages from media, politicians, religious leaders, teachers, and neighbors claiming gay people are bad or sinful. She describes the specific complications for her nephew when a teacher or friend asserts, "That's impossible. You can't have two grampas in the same house. Which one is REALLY your grampa?" (n.p.). Parents who adopt transracially must be prepared for questions such as, "Couldn't you get a White child?" or "Is she one of those crack babies?" (Adoption Learning Partners, 2004). Defending responses may arise from sheer frustration. Annoyed by hearing the question, "How can you two be sisters?" a pair of Asian and Caucasian teenage sisters decided, "When we got the question . . . we would respond 'The Mailman' and walk away" (Galvin & Fonner, 2003, p. 1).

Children in cohabiting stepfamilies face challenges such as, "He's not your real stepfather if your Mom didn't marry him." Members of families formed through assisted reproductive technology encounter comments such as "Where is the Daddy?" or "She can't be your real mother if that other woman was pregnant with you." Advice columnists regularly respond to questions about how to deal with similar invasive comments or questions. Defending responses tend to reflect strong feelings. They may be straightforward ("That's not something that concerns you"), or they may be indignant ("That's a totally inappropriate question to ask").

Internal Boundary Management Practices

Members of families formed through differences engage in ongoing communication practices designed to maintain their internal sense of family-ness. These practices include naming, discussing, narrating, and ritualizing.

Naming

"Names entitle situations" (Kauffman, 1989, p. 273). Naming plays a significant role in the development of internal family identity as members struggle to indicate their familial status. Sometimes, names are decided and never revisited; in other cases, names become a source of ongoing negotiation. Naming a child, especially an older child, or a child adopted internationally and/or transracially, presents a challenge. Children arrive with names reflecting their birth family and/or birth culture. An international adoptee captures the loss involved when her Korean name was replaced by an American one, saying, "That was really all I had when I came to this country: that name. And my parents overlooked it and chose another one" (Kroll, 2000, p. 18). A married Korean adoptee reviewed her multiple name options, settling on "Jane, Jeong, Trenka: one name from each family" (Trenka, 2003, p. 208).

Open adoption provides a unique set of linguistic challenges, given the lack of terminology for any extended family members in the adoption triangle. For example, a birthmother reports preparing her younger birth children to meet her oldest child who would have been their older sister by telling them, "It's hard to explain how I feel when I see her as to why it doesn't bother me that she calls me [first name] rather than, you know, her mom. Because I'm not" (Fravel, McRoy, & Grotevant, 2000, p. 429).

Stepfamily members confront the question, "What do I call you?" Answers are confounded by the "wicked stepmother" myth, conflicting loyalties between biological parents and stepparents, and the lack of conventional names for a stepparent's extended family. Stepchildren may choose a name honoring a stepparent's parental role, such as a hyphenated last name or using biological terms such as "Pop" or "Moms," dissimilar from their name for the biological parent. A study of stepfathers reinforces the importance of naming, indicating that the child's use of the "*daddy* or *dad* label can intensify the child's feelings for an attachment to a stepfather" (Marsiglio, 2004, p. 31) and encourage a stepfather to claim the child. Conversely, some stepfathers reported feeling like a dad but were reluctant to be called by such a title. Gay and lesbian parents confront the issue of how they wish to be referred to by their children because linguistic labels do not include the nonbiological parent easily. For lesbian couples, name choice for a nonchildbearing partner may reflect that partner's cultural heritage (Chabot & Ames, 2004). For example, one Jewish couple decided on *Mommy* and *Ima*, the Hebrew word for *Mommy* (Balka & Rose, 1989). Some lesbian pairs consider taking a hyphenated last name, giving the child the coparent's name or creating a new name. Those who changed names report that it was to establish a public family identity or to strengthen their presence as a couple or family (Suter & Oswald, 2003). Some who did not change names believed keeping separate names would promote equality in their relationships.

Discussing

The degree of difference among family members affects the amount of discussion about their family situation. If individuals see few role models for their family form, they have to identify the issues and then attempt to resolve them. Gay or lesbian partners may find themselves discussing how to represent their relationship to each other's extended family because parents and siblings function as gatekeepers to a sense of family belonging. For such partners, a supportive climate is key to a feeling of inclusion (Oswald, 2002). Lesbian parenting partners encounter decisions regarding how to become parents, who will be the biological mother, and how to decide on a donor (Chabot & Ames, 2004). In many cases, donors are chosen because of their physical appearance since "looking related suggests family, which helps communicate a shared family identity" (Suter, Bergen, Daas, & Parker, 2004, p. 15). It also reduces the number of challenges to relatedness faced by the family members. Gay male parents experience variations on these issues.

A blended family must develop its identity and "create a shared conception of how their family is to manage its daily business" (Cherlin & Furstenberg, 1994, p. 370). A study of blended family development found that some of the families "used direct communication, such as regular family meetings, to air issues surrounding the adjustments to becoming a family" (Braithwaite et al., 2001, p. 243). Schrodt (2004) identified five types of stepfamilies that varied in discussions of stepfamily issues. Concerns regarding belonging result in conversations ranging from grandparent gift giving, designated space for noncustodial children, signing official school papers, or rights to discipline. As a stepfamily undergoes divorce, members hold conversations about their future identities and ties.

A child's entrance into a family through adoption or new reproductive technologies necessitates an ongoing series of talks across years as the child's ability to comprehend information results in greater depths of discussion. Currently, sequential, age-appropriate discussions of adoption have replaced the earlier "one big talk" because children's informational needs change as they reach new developmental milestones (Wrobel, Kohler, Grotevant, & McRoy, 2003). Transracially adopted children begin to question the physical differences between themselves and other family members at an early age. Parents in families formed through assisted reproductive technology raise questions about how to discuss their children's origins.

Sometimes, the practices used to manage external boundaries are a source of internal family conversation. In certain cases, parents need to prepare all their children for racial derogation although they never experienced it. After interviewing 20 young adult Korean adoptees, Fujimoto (2001) reported that a persistent message from adoptees is "the need for parents to understand that their children are likely to face racist and racialized experiences that the parents will not face" (pp. 15–16) and to discuss how to respond to the challenge. In a list of strategies for transracial families, Bamberger (2004) suggests, "Get ready for the ugly words. . . . Better to hear them first from you, in the context of preparing responses" (p. 45). Such discussions, although painful, are necessary.

Narrating

Every family tells stories; however, families formed through differences experience more complex storytelling processes (see Chapters 6 and 7, this volume). McAdams (1993) suggests that a person's story "brings together the different parts of ourselves and our lives into a purposeful and convincing whole" (p. 12). By extension, as family stories emerge, they represent the family's definition of itself. Personal and family stories are recursive in that they influence how lives move into the future (Yerby, 1993). Over time, "we tell and retell, to ourselves and to others, the story of who we are, what we have become, and how we got there, making and remaking a story of ourselves that links birth to life to death" (Jorgenson & Bochner, 2004, p. 516). Because family stories are "laced with opinions, emotions, and past experiences, they can provide particularly telling data about the way people conceive of their relationships with family members" (Vangelisti, Crumley, & Baker, 1999, p. 337). Everyday narratives create a powerful scaffold for a family's identity.

Creation or entrance stories answer the question, "How did this family come to be?" They include accounts of how the adult partners met or how an individual chose to become a parent, as well as birth and adoption narratives. In cases of adoption, the entrance story sets the tone for a family's adoption-related communication; it is the beginning of an ongoing dialogue between parents and their children (Wrobel et al., 2003). In addition, "How the (adoption) story is told and retold in the family can have lasting consequences for the child's adjustment and well-being" (Friedlander, 1999, p. 43). In their study of adoptive parents' entrance narratives, Krusiewicz and Wood (2001) identified the themes of fortune versus misfortune and desire versus rejection. Their stories also included references to issues of destiny, compelling connection, rescue, and legitimacy. Cooper (2004) depicts the development of her stepfamily through three types of stories—stepfamily, blended family, and bonus stories—each reflecting a stage in the family's move toward deeper joining. In all cases, sensitivity to narrative language is critical. Consider the impact of, "Then, when my sister ran off with that jerk, we took you in" versus "Then, you joined our family when your Mom was unable to care for you." Or, "When you were abandoned . . ." versus "When your birthmother made an adoption plan. . . ."

Many families formed through differences suppress or lose their narratives. Just as many divorced families and stepfamilies lose the original parental love stories, certain adoptive parents struggle with the extent to which an adopted child's painful birth family background should be told to family members. Uncertain parents may fabricate some pieces of the story to avoid discussing infertility or donor insemination. To provide his 2-year-old foster daughter with a missing piece from her childhood after she left his home, her foster father wrote Sierra a story of their time together, hoping she would read it when she grew older (Grady, 2004).

Ritualizing

Families accomplish their "emotional business" as they enact rituals (Bossard & Boll, 1950; see also Chapters 14 and 15, this volume). A typology of family rituals includes major celebrations; traditions such as reunions, vacations, and birthdays; and mundane routines (Wolin & Bennett, 1984). Although most families develop rituals, families formed through differences struggle with what to ritualize and which rituals from previous family experiences should be continued.

Family rituals provide opportunities for stepfamilies to define family membership on multiple levels of connection, although they require sensitivity and negotiations. Yet traditions for special occasions "generate a feeling of closeness providing fuel for weathering the more difficult times" (Whiteside, 1989, p. 35). In their study of blended families, Braithwaite, Baxter, and Harper (1998) found that members engaged in rituals or "important communicative practices that enable blended family members to embrace their new family while still valuing what was important in the old family environment" (p. 101). Family members described enacting new rituals, not imported from a previous family; rituals that were imported unchanged; and rituals that were imported and adapted. Respondents also reported that some new rituals lasted and some failed, demonstrating that becoming a family is an ongoing process.

Adoptive families may celebrate arrival or "gotcha" days as well as birthdays; in families formed through international adoption, members may adopt some celebrations from a child's birth culture. Birth family members may be invited to share a holiday or a tradition. Some children report rituals of pulling out adoption papers and looking at them or attending a summer culture camp (Fujimoto, 2001).

Conclusion

Families and their individual members experience multiple identities. As noted earlier, most families cannot be described in unitary terms; they are formed through multiple differences. For example, White lesbian mothers of two African American boys reported the following common (nonhostile) questions from the boy's preschool peers: "Why are you Black and she White?" or "Why is he Black and you White?" As the boys aged, they encountered variations on the question, "Why do you have two moms?" (Fine & Johnson, 2004). These authors detail the multiple objectified identities ascribed to them as parents in a family created across race and gender borders. Black lesbians experience "triple jeopardy" by virtue of race, gender, and sexual orientation, with racism as the most stressful challenge (Bowleg, Huang, Brooks, Black, & Burkholder, 2003).

The concept of family is changing visibly, invisibly, and irrevocably. When family identity is involved, language follows lived experience. This language, managed within and across boundaries, reflects and shapes family experience. Contemporary families, living in a world of normative instability and definitional crisis, depend increasingly on discourse to construct their identities.

References

Adoption Learning Partners. (2004). Retrieved March 8, 2005, from http://www.adoption learningpartners.org

Allen, K., & Rainie, L. (2002). *Parents online.* The PEW Internet and American Life Project. Retrieved November 17, 2004, from www.pewinternet.org

Balka, C., & Rose, A. (1989). *Twice blessed.* Boston: Beacon.

Bamberger, J. C. (2004). Ready for the world: When you form a transracial family, you must build in a system to combat racism. *Adoptive Families, 36,* 45–46.

Bengston, V. L. (2001). Beyond the nuclear family: The increasing importance of multi-generational bonds. *Journal of Marriage and the Family, 63,* 1–16.

Blumenthal, A. (1990–1991). Scrambled eggs and seed daddies: Conversations with my son. *Empathy: Gay and Lesbian Advocacy Research Project, 2,* 185–188.

Bossard, J. H. S., & Boll, E. S. (1950). *Ritual in family living: A contemporary study.* Philadelphia: University of Pennsylvania Press.

Bowleg, L., Huang, J., Brooks, K., Black, A., & Burkholder, G. (2003). Triple jeopardy and beyond: Multiple minority stress and resilience among black lesbians. *Journal of Lesbian Studies, 7,* 87–108.

Braithwaite, D. O., Baxter, L. A., & Harper, A. M. (1998). The role of rituals in the management of the dialectical tension of 'old' and 'new' in blended families. *Communication Studies, 49,* 101–120.

Braithwaite, D. O., Olson, L. N., Golish, T. D., Soukup, C., & Turman, P. (2001). "Becoming a family": Developmental processes represented in blended family discourse. *Journal of Applied Communication Research, 29,* 221–247.

Chabot, J. M., & Ames, B. D. (2004). It wasn't "let's get pregnant and go do it": Decision making in lesbian couples planning motherhood via donor insemination. *Family Relations, 53,* 348–356.

Cherlin, A. J., & Furstenberg, F. F. (1994). Stepfamilies in the United States: A reconsideration. *Annual Review of Sociology, 20,* 359–381.

Coleman, M., Ganong, L. H., & Fine, M. (2000). Reinvestigating remarriage: Another decade of progress. *Journal of Marriage and the Family, 62,* 1288–1307.

Coontz, S. (1999). Introduction. In S. Coontz (with M. Parson & G. Raley) (Eds.), *American families: A multicultural reader* (pp. ix–xxxiii). New York: Routledge.

Cooper, P. J. (2004, April). *Step? Blended? Bonus? Looking back to look forward: Legacies, myths and narratives of stepfamilies.* Paper presented at the annual convention of the Central States Communication Association, Cleveland, OH.

Elmhorst, J. (2003, February). *Communication privacy management theory and international adoption.* Paper presented at the annual Western States Communication Association, Salt Lake City, UT.

Fine, M., & Johnson, F. (2004). Creating a family across race and gender borders. In A. Gonzalez, M. Houston, & V. Chen (Eds.), *Our voices: Essays in culture, ethnicity, and communication* (pp. 240–247). Los Angeles: Roxbury.

Fitzpatrick, M. A. (1998). Interpersonal communication on the Starship *Enterprise:* Resilience, stability, and change in relationships for the twenty-first century. In J. Trent (Ed.), *Communication: Views from the helm for the 21st century* (pp. 41–46). Boston: Allyn & Bacon.

Fravel, D. L., McRoy, R. G., & Grotevant, H. D. (2000). Birthmother perceptions of the psychologically present adopted child: Adoption openness and boundary ambiguity. *Family Relations, 49,* 425–433.

Freilicher, L., Scheu, J., & Wetanson, S. (1999). *Conceiving Luc: A family story.* New York: Morrow.

Friedlander, M. L. (1999). Ethnic identity development of internationally adopted children and adolescents: Implications for family therapists. *Journal of Marital and Family Therapy, 25,* 43–60.

Fujimoto, E. (2001, November). *South Korean adoptees growing up in White America: Negotiating race and culture.* Paper presented at the annual convention of the National Communication Association, Atlanta, GA.

Galvin, K. M. (1989, March). *Stepfamily identity development.* Speech presented at the annual van Zelst Lecture, Northwestern University, Evanston, IL.

Galvin, K. M. (2004a, March). *Discursive construction of identity: Adoptive family processes.* Paper presented at the annual convention of the Central States Communication Association. Cleveland, OH.

Galvin, K. M. (2004b). The family of the future: What do we face? In A. L. Vangelisti (Ed.), *Handbook of family communication* (pp. 675–697). Mahwah, NJ: Lawrence Erlbaum.

Galvin, K. M., & Fonner, K. (2003, April). *"The Mailman" as family defense strategy: International/transracial adoption and mixed siblings.* Paper presented at the annual convention of the Central States Communication Association, Omaha, NE.

Galvin, K. M., & Wilkinson, K. M. (2000, November). *That's your family picture?! Korean adoptees' communication management issues during the transition to college.* Paper presented at the annual convention of the National Communication Association, Seattle, WA.

Garey, A. I., & Hansen, K. V. (1998). Analyzing families with a feminist sociological imagination. In A. I. Garey & K. V. Hansen (Eds.), *Families in the U.S.: Kinship and domestic policies* (pp. xv–xxi). Philadelphia: Temple University Press.

Garner, A. (2004). Families like mine. Retrieved November 16, 2004, from http://www.familieslikemine.html

Gergen, K. J., Hoffman, L., & Anderson, H. (1996). Is diagnosis a disaster? A constructionist trialogue. In F. W. Kaslow (Ed.), *Handbook of relational diagnosis and dysfunctional family patterns* (pp. 102–118). New York: John Wiley.

Goodnight, G. T. (2004, April 24). Rhetorical criticism goes public: Goodnight's last lecture at Hardy House. E-mail distribution.

Grady, D. (2004). Sierra's story. In K. M. Galvin, C. L. Bylund, & B. J. Brommel (Eds.), *Family communication: Cohesion and change* (5th ed., pp. 130–134). Boston: Allyn & Bacon.

Grotevant, H. D. (2004, Spring). Comments. *Relationship Research News: International Association for Relationship Research, 2,* 12.

Hughes, P. C. (2004). The influence of religious orientation on conflict tactics in interfaith marriages. *Journal of Communication and Religion, 27,* 245–267.

Imber-Black, E. (2004). Editorial: September 11, 2004: The third anniversary. *Family Process, 43,* 275–278.

Jones, N. A., & Smith, A. S. (2001, November). The two or more races population: 2000. Census 2000 brief (C2KBR/01–6). In *Census 2000 special reports.* Washington, DC: U.S. Census Bureau, U.S. Department of Commerce. Retrieved February 1, 2005, from http://www.census.gov/prod/ 2001pubs/c2kbr01–6.pdf

Jorgenson, J. (1994). Situated address and the social construction of "in-law" relationships. *The Southern Communication Journal, 59,* 196–204.

Jorgenson, J., & Bochner, A. P. (2004). Imagining families through stories and rituals. In A. L. Vangelisti (Ed.), *Handbook of family communication* (pp. 513–538). Mahwah, NJ: Lawrence Erlbaum.

Kauffman, C. (1989). Names and weapons. *Communication Monographs, 56,* 273–284.

Kaye, K., & Warren, S. (1988). Discourse about adoption in adoptive families. *Journal of Family Psychology, 1,* 406–433.

Koerner, A. F., & Fitzpatrick, M. A. (2002). Toward a theory of family communication. *Communication Theory, 12,* 70–91.

Kreider, R. M. (2003, October). Adopted children and stepchildren: 2000 (C2KBR-30). In *Census 2000 special reports.* Washington, DC: U.S. Census Bureau, U.S. Department of Commerce. Retrieved February 1, 2005, from http://www.census.gov/prod/2003pubs/censr-6.pdf

Kreider, R. M., & Simmons, T. (2003, October). Marital status: 2000 (C2KBR-30). In *Census 2000 special reports.* Washington, DC: U.S. Census Bureau, U.S. Department of Commerce. Retrieved February 1, 2005, from http://www.census.gov/prod/2003pubs/censr-30.pdf

Kroll, M. L. (2000). My name is. . . . In M. W. Lustig & J. Koester (Eds.), *Among us: Essays on identity, belonging, and intercultural competence* (pp. 18–23). New York: Longman.

Krusiewicz, E. S., & Wood, J. T. (2001). 'He was our child from the moment we walked into that room': Entrance stories of adoptive parents. *Journal of Social and Personal Relationships, 18,* 785–803.

Leland, J. (2004, August). Need help at work? Mom and Dad are for hire. *New York Times,* pp. A1, A19.

Lynch, J. M. (2000). Considerations of family structure and gender composition: The lesbian and gay stepfamily. *Journal of Homosexuality, 40,* 81–95.

Marsiglio, W. (2004). When stepfathers claim stepchildren: A conceptual analysis. *Journal of Marriage and the Family, 66,* 22–39.

McAdams, D. P. (1993). *Stories we live by: Personal myths and the making of the self.* New York: Guilford.

McCracken, G. (2004). A look at 2020. *American Demographics, 26,* 39.

Minow, M. (1998). Redefining families: Who's in and who's out? In K. V. Hansen & A. I. Garey (Eds.), *Families in the U.S.* (pp. 7–19). Philadelphia: Temple University Press. (Originally published in 1991 *University of Colorado Law Review, 62,* 269–285)

National Center for Heath Statistics. (2004). *Life expectancy* (Table 11). U.S. Department of Health and Human Services, Centers for Disease Control and Prevention Web site. Retrieved August 10, 2004, from http://www.cdc.gov/nchsfastats/lifexpec.htm

Oswald, R. F. (2002). Inclusion and belonging in the family rituals of gay and lesbian people. *Journal of Family Psychology, 16,* 428–436.

Peplau, L. A., & Beals, K. P. (2004). The family lives of lesbians and gay men. In A. L. Vangelisti (Ed.), *Handbook of family communication* (pp. 233–248). Mahwah, NJ: Lawrence Erlbaum.

Petronio, S. (2002). *Boundaries of privacy: Dialectics of disclosure.* Albany: State University of New York Press.

Pipher, M. (2002). *The middle of everywhere: Helping refugees enter the American community.* Orlando, FL: Harcourt Inc.

Schrodt, P. (2004). *A typological examination of stepfamily communication schemata.* Unpublished dissertation, University of Nebraska–Lincoln.

Simmons, T., & Dye, A. L. (2003, October). Grandparents living with grandchildren: 2000 (C2KBR-31). In *Census 2000 brief.* Washington, DC: U.S. Census Bureau, Department of Commerce. Retrieved February 1, 2005, from http://ww.census.gov/prod/2003pubs/c2kbr-31.pdf

Simmons, T., & O'Connell, M. (2003, February). Married-couple and unmarried partner households: 2000. In *Census 2000 special reports.* Washington, DC: U.S. Census Bureau, Department of Commerce. Retrieved December 18, 2004, from http://www.census.gov/prod/2003pubs/censr-5.pdf

Simmons, T., & O'Neill, G. (2001, September). Households and families: 2000 (C2KBR/01–8). In *Census 2000 brief.* Washington, DC: U.S. Census Bureau, Department of Commerce.

Retrieved December 18, 2004, from http://www.census.gov/prod/2001pubs/ck2br01-8.pdf

Stacey, J. (1999a). The family values fable. In S. Coontz (with M. Parson & G. Raley) (Eds.), *American families: A multicultural reader* (pp. 487–499). New York: Routledge.

Stacey, J. (1999b). Gay and lesbian families are here; All our families are queer; Let's get used to it. In S. Coontz (with M. Parson & G. Raley) (Eds.), *American families: A multicultural reader* (pp. 372–405). New York: Routledge.

Stamp, G. H. (2004) Theories of family relationships and a family relationships theoretical model. In A. L. Vangelisti (Ed.), *Handbook of family communication* (pp. 1–30). Mahwah, NJ: Lawrence Erlbaum.

Suter, E. A., Bergen, K. J., Daas, K. L., & Parker, J. H. (2004, November). *Communicative construction of lesbian family through rituals and symbols.* Paper presented at the annual convention of the National Communication Association, Chicago.

Suter, E. A., & Oswald, R. F. (2003). Do lesbians change their last names in the context of a committed relationship? *Journal of Lesbian Studies, 7,* 71–83.

Trenka, J. J. (2003). *The language of blood.* Minneapolis: Borealis Books.

Vangelisti, A. L. (2004). Introduction. In A. L. Vangelisti (Ed.), *Handbook of family communication* (pp. xiii–xx). Mahwah, NJ: Lawrence Erlbaum.

Vangelisti, A. L., Crumley, L. P., & Baker, J. L. (1999). Family portraits: Stories as standards for family relationships. *Journal of Social and Personal Relationships, 16,* 335–368.

Watters, E. (2003). *Urban tribes: A generation redefines friendship, family, commitment.* New York: Bloomsbury.

Whitchurch, G. G., & Dickson, F. C. (1999). Family communication. In M. Sussman, S. K. Steinmetz, & G. W. Peterson (Eds.), *Handbook of marriage and the family* (2nd ed., pp. 687–704). New York: Plenum.

Whiteside, M. F. (1989). Family rituals as a key to kinship connection in remarried families. *Family Relations, 38,* 34–39.

Wolin, S., & Bennett, L. (1984). Family rituals. *Family Processes, 23,* 401–420.

Wrobel, G. M., Kohler, J. K., Grotevant, H. D., & McRoy, R. G. (2003). The family adoption communication (FAC) model: Identifying pathways of adoption-related communication. *Adoption Quarterly, 7,* 53–84.

Yerby, J. (1993, November). *Co-constructing alternative stories: Narrative approaches in the family therapy literature.* Paper presented at the annual convention of the Speech Communication Association, Miami Beach, FL.

CHAPTER 2

Defining the Family Through Relationships

Kory Floyd

Arizona State University

Alan C. Mikkelson

Whitworth College

Jeff Judd

Arizona State University

The family may be the most ubiquitous of all human relationships, and for good reason. Humans' psychologically ingrained need for belonging and attachment (Baumeister & Leary, 1995), coupled with our protracted period of infant dependence, give the familial unit, in whatever form, a host of vital roles to play in human well-being. Despite its importance—or perhaps, in part, because of it—the family is a challenging institution to define. As Galvin (Chapter 1, this volume) rightly notes, contemporary family life is fraught with definitional insta-bility, and as diversity in family forms increases, so too does uncertainty about where the boundary around the concept of *family* should be drawn. The family may therefore have become the type of social phenomenon that is pervasive but difficult to define.

We begin by noting some of the many reasons why the definition of family is consequential. Next, we describe three definitional "lenses" through which scholars might view the family: role, sociolegal, and biogenetic. Finally, we caution against excessive definitional breadth and advocate more concrete definitions of family in scholarly practice.

On the Importance of Definition

One need only peruse the scholarly or popular literatures on family communication to arrive at the conclusion that, although the family is widely researched, it is far from consistently defined. Diversity in definitions of family can be appreciated on a variety of levels, one of which involves the gap between the scholarly community and the lay public. As Jorgenson (1989) argued, "There are serious discrepancies between families' self-definitions and the definitions of 'family' embodied in theoretical constructs used by researchers and clinicians" (p. 35). Another involves diversity within the lay public in the way families are defined. In a 1990 study, Trost found considerable variation in the forms of relationships people would characterize as *family*. Spousal, opposite-sex cohabitational, parent-child, and sibling relationships were most likely to be characterized as familial, but a host of other relational forms, including friends or same-sex cohabitants, were considered by various percentages of the respondents as examples of family.

A third level of substantial variation in the definition is within the scholarly community itself. As Settles (1987) remarked, "It is not likely that the job of specifying what is meant by *family* will progress rapidly. Consensus would be . . . improbable for scholars" (p. 308). We suggest that, despite its challenges, the issue of how scholars define family is consequential for at least three reasons.

The Special Importance of Scholarly Definitions of Family

First, and most pragmatically, how scholars define family provides guidance regarding who should be observed in research purporting to study families. That is, definitional issues set boundary conditions around research, informing decisions about which relationships should be considered the purview of family scholarship, whom should be recruited as informants, and in which manner observations, stories, self- and other-reports, and other forms of data should be interpreted. Of course, the broader and more inclusive the scholarly definition of family, the more tautological its relationship with research becomes: On one hand, the definition provides boundary conditions for research; on the other, the relationships studied by family researchers serve to comprise the definition of family in the first place. *Family* becomes whatever family scholars study.

A second reason why the scholarly definition of family is consequential is that it can inform clinical practice. Many therapeutic approaches, particularly those therapies that are structural in nature (e.g., Minuchin, 1974, 1981), stress the importance of the therapist knowing how the client defines family (Nichols & Schwartz, 2003). As Jorgenson (1989) reported, however, clinical literatures avoid addressing familial definitions explicitly, which is problematic because "family therapists cannot avoid facing the recurring problem of how best to define the family systems they will treat" (p. 29). As she notes, the important question of whom to invite for inclusion in treatment presumes some measure of judgment on the part of the clinician about who "belongs" to the family and who does not (see also Madanes, 1991).

The third, and perhaps most far-reaching, reason why the scholarly community's definition of family is consequential is that it defines the scope of knowledge generation in areas that can inform policy and intervention. Just as definitions demarcate appropriate areas of study for researchers, they also, therefore, dictate which family relationships or family processes are going to be studied and which are not. In other words, how scholars define family has a necessary relationship with *what society learns about family*. If communication in postdivorce relationships, gay and lesbian relationships, or godparental relationships is not well understood, for instance, it may partly be because of disagreement over whether to consider these relationships familial.

On the Inherently Problematic Nature of Defining the Family

The question of how best to define family conceptually is an inherently problematic one, contaminated with tensions far surpassing those related to scholarly validity. Indeed, the apparent distinction between conceptual definitions and operational definitions might be understood as representing the difference between extant and aspirational approaches—that is, between how family *has been* defined and how researchers now want it *to be* defined.

One way to appreciate the distinction between these two approaches is to examine the conceptual and operational definitions offered in family communication textbooks. For illustrative purposes, we conducted an informal content analysis of six textbooks (Galvin, Bylund, & Brommel, 2004; Noller & Fitzpatrick, 1993; Pearson, 1993; Segrin & Flora, 2005; Turner & West, 2002; Yerby, Buerkel-Rothfuss, & Bochner, 1998). Our analysis focused on each book's explicit definition of family (if one was provided) and also on the types of family relationships that were addressed in the text. Most instructive in this exercise was the tension between these two; our analysis suggested that, whereas explicit definitions tended toward a focus on *families as constituted in communication*, most of the topics covered in the books related to *families as constituted in discrete relationships*.

The texts' explicit definitions of family placed heavy emphasis on families' transactional, interdependent, and longitudinal aspects. Pearson (1993), for instance, defined a family as "an organized, relational transactional group, usually occupying a common living space over an extended time period, and possessing a confluence of interpersonal images that evolve through the exchange of meaning over time" (p. 14). Yerby et al. (1998) provided a similar, but expanded, definition of the family as "a *multigenerational* social *system* consisting of at least two *interdependent* people bound together by a common living *space* (at one time or another) and a common *history*, and who share some degree of emotional *attachment to or involvement with* one another" (p. 13). Perhaps the broadest definition was that provided by Turner and West (2002), who defined the family as "a self-defined group of intimates who create and maintain themselves through their own interactions and their interactions with others; a family may include both voluntary and involuntary relationships; it creates both literal and symbolic internal and external boundaries; and it evolves through time: it has a history, a present, and a future" (p. 8).

There is little question that these explicit definitions are unabashedly reflective of the notion that we constitute families in communicative processes. This is certainly an understandable feature, given the disciplinary focus undergirding these texts. What is perhaps most striking about these explicit definitions, however, is not their heavy focus on the family as an interpersonal phenomenon but their near dismissal of families' structural elements and processes. For example, none of the definitions mentions either genetic associations or legal ties as a component of family relationships. Neither are processes such as reproduction, power, or child development—perhaps central to family life—included as part of the definition of families. Indeed, apart from Pearson (1993) and Yerby et al.'s (1998) mention of shared living space, the definitions give nearly exclusive dominion to the concept that families are constituted and maintained through interaction and interdependence. We considered Turner and West's (2002) definition to be the broadest because it defines the family as a "self-defined group," generating the possibility that any group of intimates who considers itself a family would be, therefore, a family (Galvin et al.'s [2004] definition also emphasized the notion of self-identification). Perhaps most important, none of the explicit definitions made mention of a single discrete relationship type (marriage, parent-child, sibling, etc.). As we will argue later in this chapter, this degree of breadth in scholarly definitions of the family—although defensible in the service of inclusion and acknowledgment of familial diversity—entails at least two significant risks for family researchers and consumers of their work: the risk of conceptual obfuscation and the risk of ignoring socially or genetically ingrained motivations for behavior.

With respect to the topics actually covered in the texts we analyzed, however, we found more of a focus on discrete, identifiable relationships. Pearson (1993) took the broadest approach, addressing family types (including, among others, cohabiting couples, single-parent families, blended families, and extended families) but focusing primarily on family communicative processes, such as conflict, intimacy, power, roles, and support (an approach mirrored by Segrin & Flora, 2005). Yerby et al. (1998) discussed both models of family organization as well as discrete relationships (marriage, parent-child, stepfamily relationships), whereas Turner and West (2002), Galvin et al. (2004), and Noller and Fitzpatrick (1993) provided fairly extended focus on discrete relationships, including many that are historically understudied (e.g., gay/lesbian relationships, grandparental relationships, siblings, adoptive relationships; see Fingerman & Hay, 2002).

We believe that the tension between conceptual and operational definitions reflected in this informal analysis of family communication textbooks is illustrative of larger pervasive problems surrounding the definition of a concept such as *family*. To illuminate the inherently problematic nature of familial definitions, we submit, first, that the family is a historically revered concept. As Mencius (372–289 B.C.) wrote, "The root of the kingdom is in the state. The root of the state is in the family."

Many centuries later, Havelock Ellis (1859–1939) offered that "a life is beautiful and ideal, or the reverse, only when we have taken into our consideration the social as well as the family relationship." As we argued at the start of this chapter, the family is perhaps the principal relationship in the human experience—its centrality, therefore, raises the stakes when it comes to defining individual relationships as either familial or not. Social scientists may define a host of other concepts (e.g., arousal, attachment, humor), including other relationships (e.g., doctor-patient, employer-employee) with relative indifference to potent social or political interests. Not so with the family, which is perhaps so revered a concept in the human social agenda that decisions about whom to include or exclude are inherently (and heavily) value laden. Specifically, for the family communication researcher, we will suggest here that several forces converge on an inherent tension between *defining the family as it is* (if an external standard exists, as in the cases of genetic or legal relationships) and *defining the family as it should be* (relative to a specified moral, political, economic, or religious value).

An illustrative example of just such a tension involves the Texas Board of Education's 2004 ruling that middle school and high school health textbooks sold in that state must explicitly define marriage as a union between a man and a woman (ABC News, 2004). From the vantage of scientific validity, this was a defensible move. Marriage is a legally sanctioned relationship, and under Texas law, only opposite-sex partners are allowed to marry; therefore, marriage is, *by definition,* an opposite-sex union. Setting aside the moral, political, and religious questions surrounding whether marriage *should be* limited to opposite-sex pairs, a scientifically valid approach must (under laws current at the time of this writing) treat all other significant romantic unions as nonmarital (including those of opposite-sex cohabiting couples who have the option to marry but elect not to). In other words, when one is studying any legally defined relationship, it is a clear threat to validity to include in one's research those who do not meet the legal criteria for that relationship (this would be akin to studying "doctors" who have no medical license; whereas they may be skilled and valued health care providers, they are not, by definition, doctors).

That some will take offense to these remarks only underscores our point that it is practically impossible to define the family *without* reference to the moral, political, and religious ramifications of one's definition. Indeed, on the other side of the scientific validity coin are those who point out that academic research confers (or withholds) a manner of moral propriety; therefore, when researchers define a human relationship in a particular way, they are implicitly granting *social* legitimacy (rather than merely scientific legitimacy) to that relationship. This necessarily invokes the interests of those with a stake in what the relationship should be (which often includes the researchers themselves) and makes it understandable why the Texas Board's decision was met with such a measure of public outrage ("Taking the Sex," 2004).

Paradoxically, however, taking into consideration the social ramifications of a scholarly definition of family can lead the communication researcher *either* toward a more inclusive *or* a more exclusive definition, depending on the social and political interests the researcher elects to serve. The politically liberal orientation can certainly lend itself toward the development of broadly inclusive definitions of the family, which help ensure that no significant attachments, no matter how nontraditional their form, are marginalized by their exclusion from the scope of family research. This cuts both ways, though; researchers with a politically conservative orientation may craft definitions of the family that are intentionally exclusive, granting legitimacy to some relationships while withholding it from others. Importantly, proponents of neither of these approaches can claim scientific superiority over the other (except in cases wherein an objective, external criterion exists to define a relationship as familial). We would contend that, once definitional issues are removed from the realm of what is and imbued with questions of what should be, no one can claim a monopoly on the *validity* of a definition, but only on its *value.*

We believe that the energies of family communication researchers need not be spent in the service of resolving this inherent tension, and neither will we attempt to do so in this chapter. Rather, we acknowledge that defining family, even for scholarly purposes, involves managing social and political interests in a way that defining, say, persuasion does not. This is, perhaps, one reason why explicit definitions of the family currently in use in course texts place such a strong emphasis on the family as an interpersonal *process,* whereas the research surveyed in those same texts evidences such a strong focus on discrete familial relationships (particularly those with a legal and/or genetic association).

We do not intend to try to solve the definitional tensions discussed here; we offer instead a broad overview of three approaches communication researchers might employ when crafting definitions of the family. We refer to these approaches as *lenses* to emphasize that they each involve bringing certain aspects of the family experience into focus while leaving others blurred. These perspectives are neither mutually exclusive nor exhaustive; rather, each highlights the importance of a particular criterion or set of criteria of use to communication scholars when establishing boundary conditions for research.

Three Conceptual Lenses for Defining Family Relationships

In explicating these lenses, we distinguish among defining familial relationships based on their emotional attachment and patterns of interaction (role lens), their legally sanctioned status (sociolegal lens), and their shared genes and/or reproductive potential (biogenetic lens). Of course, some relationships (e.g., marriage) would be considered familial according to all three perspectives, but others will vary from lens to lens in whether they would be considered familial. We do not advocate the exclusive use of any of these perspectives but instead recommend that family communication researchers consider the significant merits of each.

A Role Lens

One vantage from which researchers can define and understand family is offered by the role lens. This perspective takes a dynamic approach to defining familial relationships by focusing attention on emotional attachments and patterns of interacting. Viewed through a role lens, relationships are familial to the extent that relational partners feel and act like family; this can involve behavioral patterns of interdependence and the provision of support, as well as emotional attachments of love and intimacy. This lens therefore constitutes family relationships in social behavior and emotion, rather than in external criteria such as legal or genetic links. Via the role lens, researchers define family by how people feel and behave; therefore, nearly any significant attachment can be considered familial so long as people communicate with one another in a manner characteristic of families. Contrariwise, the role lens allows that even genetic or legally sanctioned relationships may not necessarily be considered familial in the absence of emotional attachment or supportive, interdependent behavior (e.g., a child with an estranged father).

Under the role lens, family relationships are specifically constituted in communication (Baxter, 2004). A constitutive approach argues that communication "defines, or constructs, the social world, including our selves and our personal relationships" (Baxter, 2004, p. 3). Role perspective definitions, as discussed below, are not separable from the communication that creates them. As noted, principles inherent in a role perspective are apparent in several definitions of family relationships. Researchers using a role lens include Fitzpatrick and Caughlin (2002). Their psychosocial definition of family argues that people who perform instrumental tasks, such as providing nurturance, caregiving, and support, are family. Similarly, Wamboldt and Reiss (1989) define family as a group of intimates who, through communication, create a sense of home and group identity, included in which are strong ties of loyalty and emotion. Moreover, Fitzpatrick and Caughlin's (2002) transactional process definition argues that families are understood as a group of intimates characterized by strong ties of interdependence and commitment. Although these examples of the role perspective are different in their conceptualization of families, they share the common idea that family relationships are defined by the way people *act* and *interact.*

The role lens allows researchers to include those who feel and behave like family to be counted as such even though they might not share genetic ties or enjoy legal recognition. For instance, cohabiting couples can be considered familial, due to the fact they live together and often share finances, transportation, and other pragmatic concerns indicative of interdependence and commitment. Similarly, nearly 12 million U.S. children now live with stepparents (Fields, 2001), who routinely provide nurturance, caregiving, and support. Such relationships would clearly be recognized as familial from the role lens, although other perspectives may fail to recognize them as such, as stepparents share no genetic material with stepchildren and have no legal obligation to them unless they adopt them (Engel, 2000). Generally speaking, then, working from a role lens allows researchers to classify nearly any significant attachment—including those with close friends, neighbors, or pets—as familial and worthy of the attention of family communication scholars.

Importantly, although the role lens holds much appeal for family researchers, adopting this cognitive representation of family may well lead people to experience some pronounced tensions during extraordinary circumstances, when the importance of legal and/or genetic ties may overshadow the feelings and behaviors on which role-defined relationships are founded. For instance, when confronting their own mortality, people overwhelmingly tend to will their assets to those with whom they share genetic and/or legally sanctioned relationships rather than to close friends or others with whom they may have had a quasi-familial relationship (Smith, Kish, & Crawford, 1987). Correspondingly, when a person dies intestate, the assets are typically given to genetic or legal relatives such as children, spouses, parents, or siblings (this tends to be true even if the deceased was in a significant nonmarital cohabiting relationship). Similarly, in times of grave crisis, people are most likely to seek and receive support from genetic relatives (Burnstein, Crandall, & Kitayama, 1994; Essock-Vitale & McGuire, 1985). It may be the case in these and similar circumstances that, even though a close friend or neighbor has been thought of and treated as family (and perhaps even referred to as family), humans are conditioned by their nature and/or by their cultural socialization to recognize in extraordinary situations that the person "isn't *really* family."

A second example of a potential tension between role-derived definitions of family and others based on external criteria involves instances wherein a person is in need of medical attention but is unable to give informed consent (e.g., intoxication, altered mental status or mental illness, brain injury, or in the case of a minor). In these situations, decisions about medical care and informed consent tend to fall on relatives defined by genetic relatedness and/or legal recognition. In the case of a nonmarital cohabiting couple, one partner would generally not be able to make medical decisions for the sick or injured other, as state laws overwhelmingly give priority to spouses or genetic relatives in such instances. That is, although a cohabiting pair might be considered familial to the people involved, it often is not recognized as such under the law, creating an ongoing tension that may, itself, be a subject of interest for communication researchers.

Advantages of the Role Lens

For many researchers, the role perspective might be the most appealing approach to defining family, given its relative breadth and inclusiveness. As we noted, family communication textbooks tend to prefer a role-oriented approach when explicitly defining families and familial relationships. This approach may be particularly useful for those who study less traditional forms of family relationships, such as gay and lesbian couples (Kurdek, 2003), nonmarital cohabiting couples (Stafford, Kline, & Ranking, 2004), post-divorce relationships (Graham, 1997), and others who may not be characterized by genetic or legal ties.

In addition, the role perspective may correspond most with people's lived experience of family, in that the experience of family can and often does include people outside of genetically defined and legally recognized relationships. To the extent that people think of families with respect to the roles they fulfill, this lends external validity to studies that take this approach to defining the family.

Disadvantages of the Role Lens

Although the role perspective is appealing for many family communication scholars and corresponds with many of the ways people like to think about family, it also invites liabilities. One is that its breadth, inclusiveness, and the variance in specific role definitions necessarily entail a lack of specificity. It is relatively simple to apply an external criterion, such as a genetic or legal tie, to a relationship to determine if the relationship "counts" as family. By contrast, the greater ambiguity inherent in the role approach can make it challenging for researchers to determine for themselves which relationships are familial, much less to come to agreement with each other on this issue.

The clash between the role lens and legal precedent as discussed above is directly related to the second liability, which is that the role lens may be more useful in studying some family communication practices than others. For instance, the role lens has clear utility for the examination of family secrets or family rituals, which are directly constituted in communication; it may be less applicable to issues surrounding inheritance or biological health, which necessarily engage externally oriented referents.

Of the three perspectives we detail here, the role lens is, at once, the most conceptually broad and the most widely embraced by scholars in the area of family communication. Its principal benefit is that it allows family relationships to be defined by their behavioral and emotional characteristics, instead of by genetic relatedness or legal recognition, which may hold less personal relevance for people, at least in ordinary times. There is merit, however, in considering the implications of legal sanction and genetic relatedness when working to understand the family; we address these issues in the subsequent sections.

A Sociolegal Lens

A second definitional perspective gives primacy to the legal sanction afforded certain relationships and denied to others. This lens conceives of family relationships as constituted in social behavior, but unlike the role lens, it focuses on a specific category of social behavior, the enactment of laws and regulations. From this perspective, then, family relationships are those that carry legal recognition of their familial status (and its attendant privileges and obligations). Relationships not formally sanctioned by law would be considered nonfamilial from this point of view, making this a more conceptually narrow lens than the role lens. We refer to this approach as "sociolegal" to acknowledge that the enactment and enforcement of laws are inherently social behaviors.

For purposes of this discussion, we define a legally sanctioned familial relationship as one that, at the very least, enjoys recognition as a family relationship in either common, statutory law, or both. Such relationships need not necessarily involve civilly or criminally enforceable obligations or privileges (siblings, for instance, usually have no legal obligations toward each other) but must be recognized as being familial, as opposed to some other type of legally sanctioned relationship (e.g., employer-employee). Of course, privileges and/or obligations are typical features of many legally sanctioned familial relationships, of which one of the best examples is marriage. Marriage is perhaps the most socially significant of all human relationships, engaging people, as it does, physically, emotionally, sexually, reproductively, financially, and in terms of individual and relational identity (Floyd & Haynes, 2005). Indeed, data from national surveys indicate that marital happiness contributes far more to ratings of overall happiness than does any other variable, including satisfaction with careers or friendships (Glenn & Weaver, 1981). A robust literature finds that married people are happier and healthier, and live longer, than never-married people (e.g., Lillard & Waite, 1995; Pinquart, 2003) and that the termination of marriage, either through divorce (Kiecolt-Glaser et al., 1988) or death (Irwin, Daniels, Smith, Bloom, & Weiner, 1987), is associated with pronounced declines in physical health. It is unsurprising, then, that marriage is perhaps the most heavily regulated of all familial relationships, at least in the United States. An internal survey conducted by the General Accounting Office (GAO) following enactment of the Defense of Marriage Act[1] produced a preliminary list of well over a thousand U.S. federal laws involving a distinction based on marriage. These laws covered a broad spectrum of human interests, from taxation, Social Security, and veterans' benefits to employment, family violence, immigration, intellectual property, and the use of natural resources (GAO, 1997).

That marriage is so heavily regulated is significant from the vantage of the sociolegal lens because this lens assumes that legislative and/or judicial laws will proffer the greatest privilege and levy the greatest obligation on those relationships that are the most important to human viability and fertility. That is, the sociolegal lens contends that *societies enact and modify family laws fundamentally to serve their own survival and procreation, without which other motivations to create family laws are irrelevant at best.* This perspective advances that, to the extent that marital, parental, or other relationships are important human pair bonds helping ensure safety and healthy reproduction, societies will exercise pronounced legal oversight regarding their definition. Conversely, relationships that contribute less directly to survival or procreation (e.g., siblings, cousins) will be less heavily regulated (and indeed they are; most state laws relevant to siblings or cousins refer only to prohibitions on marriage, which in itself serves the purpose of protecting healthy reproduction; see Krause, 2003).

The law being a socially constructed and enforced entity, however, practically ensures that it will evolve over time as the social significance of a familial relationship develops. This may happen, among other reasons, because a relationship is significant in the role sense—that is, because people have engaged each other in emotional and behavioral ways that mimic other significant family relationships—and the law evolves to recognize and protect that relationship. Three examples of relationships that reflect this evolution are adoptive parent-child relationships, common-law marriages, and same-sex romantic unions.

Adoptive Relationships

As Galvin (2006) points out, adoption is a centuries-old practice that has seen substantial changes in its legal status in the United States since the first modern adoption law was passed in Massachusetts in 1851. As the practice of adoption became more open and socially legitimate, particularly in the early part of the 20th century, adoption laws likewise evolved to regulate the process, providing more standardized oversight regarding who can adopt and ensuring the rights of both biological and adoptive parents. From the vantage of the role perspective, adoptive relationships become familial through their patterns of interaction, which mimic those of biological parent-child relationships. From the sociolegal perspective, however, adoptive relationships are familial by virtue of their legally sanctioned status, which grants to the adoptive parents the same privileges and obligations with respect to caring for children who are afforded biological parents. On this point, it is significant from the sociolegal lens that, with respect to the adoptive process, U.S. laws privilege the rights of the biological parent until those rights are relinquished. This follows the principle that, unless the biological parents are unfit to parent, the needs of children are better served by their biological parents, an implicit recognition of the importance of genetic ties explained by the biogenetic lens, which we describe later.

Common-Law Marriages

Like adoption, common-law marriage has a long history. Around the 12th century, the practice of declaring intent to marry (particularly if consummated by sexual intercourse) was considered sufficient to create a valid marriage under English canonical law (Cretney, 1984). This practice was sustained in most colonial American states, but presently, only 10 U.S. jurisdictions (nine states and the District of Columbia) allow couples to claim the legal status of marriage without being legally married. In this present-day conception of common-law marriage, couples in these jurisdictions can claim at least some of the legal rights and responsibilities of marriage if they have met certain criteria, the majority of which entail behaving as a married couple (e.g., cohabitation, consummation) and representing themselves to others as married (e.g., wearing rings, taking the same name, making reference to one's spouse). As with adoption, then, contemporary common-law marriage is an example of the law sanctioning a relationship that mimics another socially significant familial relationship (marriage).

Same-Sex Relationships

In the United States, the question of whether same-sex romantic partners should be allowed to marry has been socially and politically controversial at least since same-sex couples began filing for marriage licenses in the early 1970s (Zicklin, 1998). Like adoption and common-law marriage, same-sex partnerships are significant from the role perspective because they mimic another significant familial relationship (marriage). Unlike adoption and, to a lesser extent, common-law marriage, however, same-sex relationships have yet to receive legal sanction in the United States. At the federal level, the Defense of Marriage Act, signed into law by President Bill Clinton in 1996, has two major provisions. First, it explicitly specifies that, for purposes of federal law, *marriage* is defined as "a legal union of one man and one woman as husband and wife" and that the term *spouse* can be used only in reference to an opposite-sex marital partner. Second, it authorizes each state to recognize, or fail to recognize, any same-sex relationship considered marital by another state. As of this writing, only the state of Massachusetts formally recognizes same-sex marriages, whereas New Jersey and Vermont offer same-sex partners legal benefits akin to those of spouses. By contrast, 25 states have statutes explicitly limiting marriage to opposite-sex partners, and 17 states have constitutional provisions doing the same. Even common-law marriages, in jurisdictions where they are sanctioned by law, are limited to opposite-sex partners, a limitation affirmed in *De Santo v. Barnsley* (1984).

It should be apparent that all three of these relationships—adoption, common-law marriage, and same-sex partnerships—could qualify as familial under the role lens, which focuses on the presence of patterns of familial interaction (i.e., those characterized by nurturance, interdependence, etc.). By contrast, only common-law marriage would potentially qualify as familial under the biogenetic lens (discussed in the next section), given its potentially reproductive nature. Whether these relationships are deemed familial or not from the sociolegal perspective, however, is a question in flux, whose answer changes according to the jurisdiction being examined and the social and legal climate of the time period in question. This characteristic of the sociolegal lens is both advantageous and problematic for researchers working from this perspective.

Advantages of the Sociolegal Lens

Particularly when considered in comparison to the role lens, one advantage to researchers of adopting the sociolegal lens is that they acquire an external, objective criterion for classifying relationships as familial or nonfamilial. Although the breadth afforded by using internal, subjective criteria (such as those emphasized in the role lens) is appealing to some, it necessarily invites the risk of a conceptual slippery slope ("how much do we have to act like family to be considered family?"). By comparison, the sociolegal lens provides researchers with an objective external criterion, affording greater standardization within and across family research programs. At the same time, however, the standard referenced by the sociolegal lens is one that evolves and develops in response to social changes. Consequently, even though legal sanction is an objective, external criterion for defining families, it is a criterion sustained through social behavior, unlike the criterion of a genetic relationship.

Disadvantages of the Sociolegal Lens

Because laws vary by time and jurisdiction, the primary disadvantage to researchers of adopting the sociolegal lens is that they must be specific about how broadly or narrowly a given relationship is legally sanctioned. As we have noted, this is far less an issue for some relationships (e.g., heterosexual marriage) than for others (e.g., homosexual marriage), but it does require attention to the ways legal sanction of a relationship can vary from area to area or time period to time period (leading, for example, to the conceptual problem that what would qualify as marriage in Massachusetts would not in Texas). A second disadvantage is that the sociolegal lens may not comport as well with native experience of family life as does the role lens. That is, people in relationships such as cohabitation or a stepsibling pair, which generally have no legal sanction, may nonetheless fully experience their relationship as familial, whereas other, legally sanctioned, relationships (such as a child and a "deadbeat dad") may be, for the people involved, familial in name only. These potential disadvantages certainly warrant the attention of researchers working from the sociolegal perspective.

A Biogenetic Lens

A third perspective from which to define familial relationships focuses on their ability to contribute to procreative success. As evolutionary psychology employs the term, procreative (or reproductive) success is served in two ways: by engaging in direct reproduction and by aiding those with whom one shares genetic material (Buss, 2003; Cartwright, 2000). This lens necessarily directs attention, then, at those relationships that have a reproductive or genetic component. Those not sharing a genetic or reproductive link are considered nonfamilial from this perspective, making this perhaps the most conceptually narrow of the three lenses we describe in this chapter.

Relative to the role and sociolegal perspectives, the biogenetic lens directs considerably less attention to behavioral aspects of relationships. Instead, using this approach causes researchers to examine two criteria for determining the familial nature of a relationship. The first is *the extent to which the relationship is directly reproductive, at least potentially.* Because one route to achieving procreative success is directly to procreate, the biogenetic lens gives primacy to relationships that have the potential to support both the reproduction and the rearing of genetic offspring. Several distinctions are relevant on this point. First, mere reproduction is not sufficient for procreative success; required also is the healthy development of the offspring until at least sexual maturity. Thus, from the vantage of the biogenetic lens, reproductive relationships must have the potential both for producing and for successfully rearing offspring to be considered familial. As a result, the biogenetic lens would consider marriages or significant heterosexual romantic attachments to be familial, but not "one-night stands" or other short-term sexually oriented unions.

Second, the biogenetic lens makes the familial/nonfamilial distinction at the global level, not the individual level. In other words, it would treat marriage as a familial relationship, even if spouses in a *specific* marital relationship were unable or unwilling to procreate. Third, the potential to produce genetic progeny disqualifies same-sex romantic relationships from being considered familial under the biogenetic lens. Certainly, individuals in such relationships may have the ability to engage in reproduction, but not with their same-sex partners. Likewise, same-sex pairs who raise children via adoption would similarly be classified as nonfamilial under the biogenetic lens, given that the lack of a genetic relationship with an adopted child prevents adoptive parenting efforts from contributing to reproductive success.

Under the biogenetic lens, the second criterion for determining whether a relationship is familial is *whether or not the relational partners share genetic material.* In a technical sense, genetic relatedness refers to the probability that any particular gene found in one person will be found in another, among the proportion of genes that varies from person to person. Humans typically share approximately 50% genetic relatedness with their parents, children, and full biological siblings, whereas identical twins, triplets, or other monozygotic siblings share 100% of their genetic material. Likewise, we average 25% relatedness with half-siblings, aunts, uncles, grandparents, nieces, and nephews; 12.5% with first cousins; and of course, 0% with step-relatives, adoptive relatives, in-laws, and spouses. As Hamilton (1964) explained in his theory of inclusive fitness, any relationship that involves shared genetic material can contribute to procreative success even if it is not directly reproductive. The reason is that reproductive success depends on replication of the *genes*, not replication of the individual; mathematically, then, having two nieces ($2 \times .25$ relatedness) is equivalent to having one daughter ($1 \times .50$ relatedness) in terms of reproductive success. (Of course, few would consider these situations to be equivalent socially, emotionally, or in terms of individual liability; they are merely equivalent in terms of the proportion of genetic replication.) Hamilton's theory implies that it is adaptive, therefore, for humans to be cognizant of genetic relatedness when allocating resources since resources given to a close genetic relative have the potential to contribute more to the self's reproductive success than resources given to a more distant genetic relative (which are more potentially beneficial than resources given to a nongenetic relative).

Several studies have produced evidence in line with Hamilton's (1964) assertion that humans have an evolved motivation to be cognizant of their levels of genetic relatedness with others. This assertion provides the foundation for the biogenetic lens's focus on shared genetic material as a defining characteristic of familial relationships. Illustrative of this distinction is the body of research examining *discriminative parental solicitude,* or the extent to which people discriminate according to reproductive potential in allocating their resources to offspring. In particular, at least three lines of research indicate that, even if they report doing otherwise, people tend to allocate resources (money, material goods, time, affection) to their progeny in ways that maximize reproductive returns on those investments. Below, we briefly review research on discriminative solicitude with stepchildren, gay children, and grandchildren (each of whom differs in the ability to further the reproductive success of those allocating resources).

Stepchildren

Research has consistently shown that children receive fewer resources from their stepparents than from their biological parents, even when competing explanations for this difference are controlled. For instance, Anderson, Kaplan, and Lancaster (1997) looked at parental investment in their children's college educations and found that, compared to stepchildren, biological children were almost six times as likely to receive money for college from their parents. Moreover, among those children who received money, biological children received an average of $15,000 more than did stepchildren. Similarly, in two studies, Floyd and Morman (2001) found that men received less affection from their stepfathers than from their biological fathers and that this difference could not be accounted for by the closeness or satisfaction levels of the relationships, the fathers' involvement in the relationships, or the ages of the fathers or sons. Additional research has found that children are up to 40 times as likely to be abused by stepparents as by biological parents; this difference also holds even when competing explanations are controlled for (see Daly & Wilson, 1988).

Gay Children

According to the principle of discriminative parental solicitude, gay and lesbian children should also receive less in the way of parental resources than heterosexual children, given their lesser likelihood of reproduction. In line with this prediction, studies by Floyd (2001) and Floyd, Sargent, and Di Corcia (2004) revealed that bisexual and homosexual men received significantly less affection from their biological fathers than did heterosexual men. These differences held true even when the closeness of the father-son relationships was held constant. When fathers were unsure of their sons' sexuality, those sons reported receiving more affection than heterosexual sons but less affection than gay sons.

Grandchildren

The discriminative allocation of resources is also evident beyond the immediate family. DeKay (1995) reported that maternal grandmothers were most likely to report relationship closeness, time spent with grandchildren, and gifts given to grandchildren, followed by maternal grandfathers, paternal grandmothers, and paternal grandfathers. Euler and Weitzel (1996) surveyed 603 adults, asking them which of their four grandparents (all of whom were reported to be alive) cared for them the most. The results demonstrated the same rank ordering. Because grandparents have already successfully achieved reproductive success with their own children, it seems likely that they would continue this favoritism with their children's children, each of whom carries 25% of their genetic material.

Both genetic links and reproductive potential qualify relationships as familial under the biogenetic lens. Enactment of family roles, such as nurturance, caregiving, and emotional support, and legal sanction in the absence of shared genetics or reproductive potential are therefore not considered sufficient under the biogenetic lens to qualify a relationship as familial.

Advantages of the Biogenetic Lens

When it comes to defining relationships as familial or not, perhaps the principal advantage of the biogenetic lens is its simplicity. Like the sociolegal lens, the biogenetic lens offers objective, external criteria for classifying relationships. However, laws are socially created and therefore socially malleable, whereas reproductive potential and shared genetic materials are not, making the biogenetic lens the most objective perspective of the three. Consequently, relative to the role and sociolegal approaches, the biogenetic lens should offer the greatest consistency among researchers and across cultures and time periods with respect to defining relationships as familial. A second advantage is that this perspective explicitly recognizes what may be ingrained motivations for humans to be cognizant of genetic or reproductive ties, as illustrated by the research on discriminative solicitude. That is, even if a given relationship is defined as familial by the role or sociolegal lens, an individual in that relationship may nonetheless be motivated to prefer a genetic relative or a reproductive partner in the allocation of time, attention, or other resources. Of the three perspectives described herein, only the biogenetic lens offers a compelling explanation for such a motivation.

Disadvantages of the Biogenetic Lens

Although the relative concreteness of the biogenetic lens may be appealing in terms of its simplicity and replicability, it offers no real account of those relationships that are not genetic and/or reproductive. That is, significant attachments that may be considered familial from a role perspective (such as intimate friendships or step-grandparental relationships) or a sociolegal perspective (such as adoptive relationships) are not accounted for by the biogenetic approach. To be certain, the biogenetic lens does not discount such relationships or question their importance in people's lives, nor does it lead researchers using the biogenetic lens to do so. Rather, it simply does not consider such relationships to be familial and is therefore silent with respect to their importance or significance in general. To the extent that studying a relationship *as familial* grants social legitimacy to that relationship (as we discussed above), however, the disadvantage of taking the narrower, more concrete approach offered by the biogenetic lens may be to leave certain relationships unstudied.

Because each of these lenses highlights particular aspects of the family relationship and neglects others, none will be sufficient for all purposes. One theme that has characterized our discussion of definitional approaches throughout this chapter focuses on the benefits and risks of taking a broad, inclusive approach to defining the family (such as that advocated by the role lens and by explicit definitions offered in family communication textbooks). To conclude this chapter, we briefly revisit this issue and recommend that family researchers exercise caution to avoid defining familial relationships too broadly.

Balancing Breadth With Responsibility in the Definition of Family

For communication researchers, the appeal of defining the family in a broad, inclusive way is clear. Such an approach focuses attention on attachment and patterns of interaction, allowing that any significant relationships in which people orient emotionally and behaviorally toward each other as family may be considered familial from a scholarly perspective. This is a compelling approach in the service of diversity because it provides that even nontraditional family relationships may fall under the purview of family communication research. In addition, as we noted above, this approach gives primacy to participants' own definitions of their relationships; as such, it may go the furthest of any approach in valuing and legitimizing the very relationships it provides for researchers to study and in insulating the researcher from the pitfalls of academic authority.

We understand and value these advantages, but we also worry that uncritical enthusiasm for this approach can cause researchers to incur some very real liabilities. Thus, to conclude our discussion, we offer two caveats for family scholars to consider when crafting definitions of the family. The first is that unrestrained breadth in the definitional process risks conceptual obfuscation. The broader and more inclusive a definition of family, the less such a definition necessarily excludes—to an important extent, then, the broader the definition of family becomes, the less distinctive the concept of family becomes. If all significant human attachments are *family*, then *family* becomes synonymous with significant attachment and therefore loses its conceptual uniqueness. Taken to an extreme, therefore, excessively broad definitions of the family paradoxically make *family* a less and less important concept.

Second, even though emotional and behavioral aspects of family relationships are clearly important, legal and genetic aspects are influential, too, and family scholars cannot afford to ignore their influence. For example, as we noted above, parents and grandparents allocate both material and communicative resources to their offspring discriminately, based on their offspring's abilities to contribute to their reproductive success, and this occurs even in the absence of parents' and grandparents' conscious awareness and even when differences in emotional closeness are controlled for. To propose that emotional attachment and interaction patterns are all that matter in terms of defining relationships as familial is to risk completely overlooking the ways in which genetic and legal ties also motivate behavior, just as considering only genetic or legal associations risks ignorance of the importance of attachment and behavior (cf. Anderson et al., 1997; DeKay, 1995).

Our appeal to family communication researchers, therefore, is to consider the importance of multiple influences on communicative behavior when studying human relationships and when distinguishing between those that are familial and those that are not. Defining a relationship as nonfamilial need not imply that the relationship is unimportant but simply that it is important as a friendship, a work relationship, an acquaintanceship, or some other form of relational union. Similarly, attending to some characteristics of family relationships at the expense of others will inevitably lead to an incomplete picture of the richness of family life. We opine that the uniqueness of the family as a socially, legally, and genetically oriented relationship warrants particular caution from scholars seeking to understand it.

Note

1. Public Law 104-199, 110 Stat.2419.

References

ABC News. (November 6, 2004). Texas OKs textbooks that define marriage. Story online at http://abcnews.go.com/US/wireStory?id=231412

Anderson, J. G., Kaplan, H. S., & Lancaster, J. B. (1997, June). *Paying for children's college: The paternal investment strategies of Albuquerque men.* Paper presented to the Ninth Annual Conference of the Human Behavior and Evolution Society, Tucson, AZ.

Baumeister, R. F., & Leary, M. R. (1995). The need to belong: Desire for interpersonal attachments as a fundamental human motivation. *Psychological Bulletin, 117*, 497–529.

Baxter, L. A. (2004). Relationships as dialogues. *Personal Relationships, 11*, 1–22.

Burnstein, E., Crandall, C., & Kitayama, S. (1994). Some neo-Darwinian decision rules for altruism: Weighing cues for inclusive fitness as a function of the biological importance of the decision. *Journal of Personality and Social Psychology, 67*, 773–789.

Buss, D. (2003). *Evolutionary psychology: The new science of the mind* (2nd ed.). Boston: Allyn & Bacon.

Cartwright, J. (2000). *Evolution and human behavior.* Cambridge, MA: MIT Press.

Cretney, S. M. (1984). *Principles of family law* (4th ed.). London: Sweet and Maxwell.

Daly, M., & Wilson, M. (1988). *Homicide.* Hawthorne, NY: Aldine.

DeKay, W. T. (1995, July). *Grandparental investment and the uncertainty of kinship.* Paper presented to the Seventh Annual Meeting of the Human Behavior and Evolution Society, Santa Barbara, CA.

De Santo v. Barnsley, 328 Pa.Super 181, 476 A.2d 952 (1984).

Engel, M. (2000). "Do I have an obligation to support my stepchildren?" Retrieved February 2, 2005, from http://www.saafamilies.org

Essock-Vitale, S. M., & McGuire, M. T. (1985). Women's lives viewed from an evolutionary perspective: II. Patterns of helping. *Ethology and Sociobiology, 6*, 155–173.

Euler, H. A., & Weitzel, B. (1996). Discriminative parental solicitude as reproductive strategy. *Human Nature, 7*, 39–59.

Fields, P. (2001). Living arrangements of children 1996. In *Current population reports* (pp. 70–74). Washington, DC: U.S. Census Bureau.

Fingerman, K. L., & Hay, E. L. (2002). Searching under the streetlight? Age biases in the personal and family relationships literature. *Personal Relationships, 9*, 415–433.

Fitzpatrick, M. A., & Caughlin, J. P. (2002). Interpersonal communication in family relationships. In M. L. Knapp & J. A. Daly (Eds.), *Handbook of family relationships* (2nd ed., pp. 726–778). Thousand Oaks, CA: Sage.

Floyd, K. (2001). Human affection exchange: I. Reproductive probability as a predictor of men's affection with their sons. *Journal of Men's Studies, 10*, 39–50.

Floyd, K., & Haynes, M. T. (2005). Applications of the theory of natural selection to the study of family communication. *Journal of Family Communication, 5*, 79–101.

Floyd, K., & Morman, M. T. (2001). Human affection exchange: III. Discriminative parental solicitude in men's affectionate communication with their biological and nonbiological sons. *Communication Quarterly, 49*, 310–327.

Floyd, K., Sargent, J. E., & Di Corcia, M. (2004). Human affection exchange: VI. Further tests of reproductive probability as a predictor of men's affection with their fathers and their sons. *Journal of Social Psychology, 144*, 191–206.

Galvin, K. M. (2006). Joined by hearts and words: Adoptive family relationships. In K. Floyd & M. T. Morman (Eds.), *Widening the family circle: New research on family relationships* (pp. 137–152). Thousand Oaks, CA: Sage.

Galvin, K. M., Bylund, C. L., & Brommel, B. J. (2004). *Family communication: Cohesion and change* (6th ed.). Boston: Pearson/Allyn & Bacon.

General Accounting Office (GAO). (1997). Memo B-275860. Retrieved January 17, 2005, from http://www.gao.gov/archiva/1997/og97016.pdf

Glenn, N. D., & Weaver, C. N. (1981). The contribution of marital happiness to global happiness. *Journal of Marriage and the Family, 42*, 161–168.

Graham, E. E. (1997). Turning points and commitment in post-divorce relationships. *Communication Monographs, 64*, 350–368.

Hamilton, W. D. (1964). The genetical evolution of social behavior: I & II. *Journal of Theoretical Biology, 7,* 1–52.

Irwin, M., Daniels, M., Smith, T. L., Bloom, E., & Weiner, H. (1987). Impaired natural killer cell activity during bereavement. *Brain, Behavior, and Immunity, 1,* 98–104.

Jorgenson, J. (1989). Where is the "family" in family communication? Exploring families' self-definitions. *Journal of Applied Communication Research, 17,* 27–41.

Kiecolt-Glaser, J. K., Kennedy, S., Malkoff, S., Fisher, L., Speicher, C. E., & Glaser, R. (1988). Marital discord and immunity in males. *Psychosomatic Medicine, 50,* 213–229.

Krause, H. D. (2003). *Family law* (2nd ed.). St. Paul, MN: West.

Kurdek, L. A. (2003). Difference between gay and lesbian cohabiting couples. *Journal of Social and Personal Relationships, 20,* 411–436.

Lillard, L. A., & Waite, L. J. (1995). 'Til death do us part: Marital disruption and mortality. *American Journal of Sociology, 100,* 1131–1156.

Madanes, C. (1991). *Strategic family therapy.* San Francisco: Jossey-Bass.

Minuchin, S. (1974). *Families and family therapy.* Cambridge, MA: Harvard University Press.

Minuchin, S. (1981). *Family therapy techniques.* Cambridge, MA: Harvard University Press.

Nichols, M. P., & Schwartz, R. C. (2003). *Family therapy: Concepts and methods* (6th ed.). New York: Allyn & Bacon.

Noller, P., & Fitzpatrick, M. A. (1993). *Communication in family relationships.* Upper Saddle River, NJ: Prentice Hall.

Pearson, J. C. (1993). *Communication in the family: Seeking satisfaction in changing times* (2nd ed.). New York: HarperCollins.

Pinquart, M. (2003). Loneliness in married, widowed, divorced, and never-married older adults. *Journal of Social and Personal Relationships, 20,* 31–54.

Segrin, C., & Flora, J. (2005). *Family communication.* Mahwah, NJ: Lawrence Erlbaum.

Settles, B. H. (1987). A perspective on tomorrow's families. In M. B. Sussman & S. K. Steinmetz (Eds.), *Handbook of marriage and the family* (pp. 307–326). New York: Plenum.

Smith, M. S., Kish, B. J., & Crawford, C. B. (1987). Inheritance of wealth as human kin investment. *Ethology and Sociobiology, 8,* 171–182.

Stafford, L., Kline, S. L., & Ranking, C. T. (2004). Married individuals, cohabiters, and cohabiters who marry: A longitudinal study of relational and individual well-being. *Journal of Social and Personal Relationships, 21,* 231–248.

Taking the sex out of sex ed. (2004, November 18). *San Antonio Current.* Retrieved from http://sacurrent.com/site/news.cfm?newsid=13386177&BRD=2318&PAG=461&dept_id=484045&rfi=6

Trost, J. (1990). Do we mean the same by the concept of family? *Communication Research, 17,* 431–443.

Turner, L. H., & West, R. (2002). *Perspectives on family communication* (2nd ed.). Boston: McGraw-Hill.

Wamboldt, F., & Reiss, D. (1989). Defining a family heritage and a new relationship identity: Two central tasks in the making of a marriage. *Family Process, 2,* 317–335.

Yerby, J., Buerkel-Rothfuss, N. L., & Bochner, A. P. (1998). *Understanding family communication* (2nd ed.). Scottsdale, AZ: Gorsuch Scarisbrick.

Zicklin, G. (1998). Legal trials and tribulations on the road to same-sex marriage. In R. P. Cabaj & D. W. Purcell (Eds.), *On the road to same-sex marriage* (pp. 129–139). San Francisco: Jossey-Bass.

PART II

Theoretical and Methodological Considerations

CHAPTER 3

Theories and Metatheories to Explain Family Communication

An Overview

Teresa C. Sabourin

University of Cincinnati

F amily communication has become an increasingly identifiable field of study within the communication discipline. Still, the roots of family communication are highly interdisciplinary, borrowing and adapting theories from other fields of inquiry (e.g., sociology, psychology). As the study of family communication emerges into an important, systematic area of inquiry with its own unique emphases, four perspectives have remained dominant: symbolic interactionism, systems, dialectics, and developmental approaches. The focus of this chapter is explicating how each of these perspectives serves as a "metatheory," guiding the reflexive processes of research and further theory development to articulate the distinctive discipline of family communication. The chapter also provides specific examples of current research and theoretical developments to illustrate the current state of family communication as a field of study.

Purposes of Theory and Metatheory

In general, theories are abstractions, reducing experience to a set of concepts and relationships between concepts. As such, a given theory portrays only a partial view of experience. Furthermore, theories are social constructions, representing "various ways observers see their environments" (Littlejohn, 2002, p. 19). This means that the partial view of experience is filtered through social and cultural biases, rendering it at least somewhat subjective. A theory is not neutral but a social construction of reality.

All theories share a core set of purposes with respect to a field of study. These purposes generally include explanation, understanding, prediction, and change (Turner & West, 2006). Explanation, which can be causal or practical, allows us to detail how things work together. Understanding is concerned with informing us about why things work. When theory is used for prediction, we are able to take the connections that have been identified through explanation and project them into the future. Although prediction is always based on probability, it provides some ability to chart future courses of action, given a set of circumstances. The change element of theory occurs when the knowledge gained from theory is used to recommend courses of social action.

Theory, in relation to family communication, "would generally involve ideas about the ways family members relate to one another and the factors that affect those relationships" (Noller & Fitzpatrick, 1993, p. 37). This definition points to the fact that when applied to family communication, theories are concerned with explaining, understanding, predicting, and changing the pervasive and dynamic interactions and relationships between and among family members. Since theories are abstract, however, they cannot focus on all aspects of family experience. In order to organize theories and identify their particular levels of abstraction and lenses of focus, it is useful to examine metatheory.

According to Littlejohn (2002), "Metatheory is a body of speculation on the nature of inquiry that is above or over the specific content of given theories, addressing such questions as what should be observed, how observation should take place, and what form theory should take" (p. 26). With respect to family communication, the major metatheoretical perspectives that have guided the study of interaction and relationships agree in some respects on what to observe and how to observe, while they disagree on others. For example, while symbolic interaction, systems, dialectics, and developmental approaches agree that the relationships between and among family members, and not just individual family members, should be studied, their approaches to studying them differ. When examining these metatheories, then, it is instructive to realize that any given perspective is not right or wrong but instead representative of its user's needs and preferences. From each perspective, we gain a way of viewing family interactions and relationships that will answer certain types of questions and produce unique, useful explanations, understandings, predictions, and recommendations for change.

In the following sections of this chapter, I discuss how each metatheory deals with the appropriate unit of analysis for study and elaborate each of the four metatheoretical perspectives, detailing some of the theoretical developments that have taken place under the umbrella of each perspective and highlighting some of the research that has tested and refined these theoretical developments.

Individual and Relational Concerns: The Unit of Analysis

As Galvin, Bylund, and Brommel (2004) state, "There are many ways to make sense out of how a family functions, particularly how communication undergirds every aspect of family life" (p. 52). One of the primary distinctions among the different perspectives discussed here is the relative emphasis they place on either the individual or the relationship as the unit of analysis. Though all agree that social process plays a critical role in the family, each weights relationships and the individual differently.

Symbolic interactionism (McCall & Simmons, 1966; Mead, 1934; Stephen, 1984) is a metatheoretical perspective that pictures the individual as emerging from the social relationship. Accordingly, "the individual achieves selfhood at that point at which he first begins to act toward himself in more or less the same fashion in which he acts toward other people" (McCall & Simmons, 1966, p. 54). The self is differentiated into the components of the "Me" and the "I," each of which reflects a different level of individual-social emphasis. The "Me," for example, contains "all those perspectives on oneself that the individual has learned from others," whereas the "I" is the "'inner forum,' the silent internal conversation that is continually going on inside the human organism" (McCall & Simmons, 1966, p. 55).

In contrast to the stance on the role of self taken by symbolic interactionism, the systems perspective (Kantor & Lehr, 1975; Watzlawick, Beavin, & Jackson, 1967) locates the self entirely within the relationship. In their definition of self and other, Watzlawick et al. (1967) differentiate between the content and relationship dimensions of communication. As such, two people can agree on the content level about a fact (e.g., the family is loud) but disagree on the relationship level, which "amounts to something that is pragmatically far more important than disagreement on the content level" (p. 83). In other words, at the relationship level, people "offer each other definitions of that relationship and, by implication, of themselves" (pp. 83–84). Given that responses to the definition of self can be confirmed, rejected, or disconfirmed, the individual has no meaning outside of the relationship. Hence, in contrast to symbolic interactionism, the systems approach pictures the self with relatively no autonomy separate from the relationship.

The dialectical perspective (Baxter, 1990; Baxter & Montgomery, 1996; Rawlins, 1992; Sabourin, 2003) also centralizes the issue of the individual in the relationship. Baxter and Montgomery (1996) articulate the view that a self exists only in dialectical relationship to another. In other words, self and other can be viewed only as connected polarities, and neither would exist in isolation. Another way of framing the relationship between self and other dialectically is through integration and differentiation (Bopp & Weeks, 1984). Though the distinction may appear to be slight, the process of differentiating allows the individual to develop his or her own uniqueness, while integration of differences allows the family to operate as a whole. The fact that there is a uniqueness to be developed and experienced, though it is in constant tension with the need to connect to the whole, attributes a different meaning to the self than Baxter and Montgomery's interpretation.

A developmental approach (Aldous, 1990; McGoldrick & Carter, 1982) to family communication examines both broad stages through which individuals move through the family (e.g., infancy, adolescence) as well as more specific family transitions (e.g., parenthood, launching). The former emphasis, on individuals moving through the family, represents more of an individual level of analysis, whereas the latter, dealing with issues such as parenting, is more dyadically or relationally focused. Thus, if a researcher's intent was to understand individual-level issues, the developmental approach offers more flexibility than either the systems or the dialectical views. Although the perspectives differ in terms of how they approach the unit of analysis for family communication research, they all share in common the core belief of the centrality of interaction in the family.

With this background in mind, we now examine these perspectives in more detail, as well as some of the specific theories and research emanating from them.

Symbolic Interactionism

Symbolic interactionism was one of the first perspectives to be applied to the study of family communication (McCall & Simmons, 1966). While there are many schools of symbolic interactionism, I rely on the approach outlined in Mead's (1934) *Mind, Self, and Society*. The main unit of analysis in symbolic interaction is the social act, which "involves a three-part relationship: an initial gesture from one individual, a response to that gesture by another, and a result" (Littlejohn, 2002, p. 146). The emphasis on the joint actions of individuals is what makes this theory so relevant to family communication. Society is simply group life that depends on creating and coordinating meanings through symbols. The self is both impulsive and organized and is defined through relations with significant others, allowing identity to emerge and change over time. The mind is a result of being able to think, using symbols, about the self and is a process that allows us to behave socially.

One of the strengths of applying symbolic interaction to the study of family communication is that it allows us to focus on the complexities of mundane reality. From this view, family life is centered on the creation of meanings through symbol use, and the definition of a family member's identity emerges through interactions with significant others. As McCall and Simmons (1966) explain, "Almost from the beginning, he interacts with, rather than merely responds to, his environment, and he exerts influences upon the very forces that influence him so greatly" (p. 204). This mutual influence is one of the things that makes communication a unique field of study from psychology.

Littlejohn (2002) uses the example of an adolescent to illustrate the symbolic interaction process. The self-image of the adolescent, he says, is a result "of their interactions with significant others, such as parents, siblings, and peers," and through this interaction, "teenagers come to view themselves as they think others have viewed them" (p. 147). When they act with this view in mind, the adolescents reinforce the views of others and hence can become constrained to repeat past behaviors. As such, their identity is thought to be a product of the social act.

The symbolic interactionist approach, according to Galvin et al. (2004), is "a meaning-centered theory" and "assumes that (1) humans think about and act according to the meanings they attribute to their actions and context and (2) humans are motivated to create meanings to help them make sense of the world" (p. 68). The focus of this theory, therefore, is on the connection between symbol and interaction and how "interaction fosters the development of self- and group identity" in the social group of the family (p. 68). Accordingly, the discourse of family life is central to understanding how it creates and negotiates meaning. The family is defined through its interaction, therefore, rather than through its biological or legal relations. See the discussion on this point in Galvin (Chapter 1, this volume) and Floyd, Mikkelson, and Judd (Chapter 2, this volume).

Social Construction Theory

Social construction theory is a specific theory fitting under the framework of symbolic interactionism. Social construction has been fruitfully applied to the study of family identity through myths, metaphors, themes, and narratives (Turner & West, 2006; Yerby, 1989; Yerby, Buerkel-Rothfuss, & Bochner, 1995). According to Galvin et al. (2004), "Social constructionism, considered an extension or branch of symbolic interaction, suggests that persons co-construct their social realities through conversation" (p. 69). Stamp (2004) says, "Through socialization, interaction, and language, individuals, within the contexts of social institutions such as the family, collectively construct the realities in which they live" (p. 9).

Social construction theory, therefore, provides a notion of family communication that is emergent and subjective, with the coconstruction of the meaning of what it even means to be a family up for negotiation (Jorgenson, 1989). Whereas the perspective of symbolic interactionism functions as a broad explanation of the centrality of symbol use for human existence, social construction theory more narrowly focuses on the social dimension of meaning making in relationships. Furthermore, since meaning exists through the communicative practices between family members as they live out their mundane realities, social construction can be examined through the symbolic content of family myths, metaphors, themes, and narratives. According to Yerby et al. (1995), "The symbolic content of family communication is a general description of the way that communication can have representational value" (p. 226), which contributes to the sense of collective identity. Turner and West (2006) explain how both verbal and nonverbal symbols are used to develop family identity. These symbols are used, then, in the family's meaning-making processes. The construction of meaning is also situationally determined, reflecting time, place, and culture for any given family.

The collective family identity can be seen in their myths, metaphors, themes, narratives, and rituals. Myths, for example, are beliefs about the family that emerge from a selective, intentional distortion in the representation of family experiences.

As a reflection of collective identity, myths are designed to reflect the family's values. For instance, a cultural myth is "that a 'normal' family is made of two heterosexual parents and one or two children, who are the natural children of their parents" (Yerby et al., 1995, p. 227). A family may remember their particular history in such a way as to support this myth and hence fail to acknowledge divorce among their membership.

The theme is also symbolic and guides family interaction by providing a focus for their energy. Thus, "an analysis of family themes can provide a description of the major issues, goals, concerns, or values of the family" (Yerby et al., 1995, p. 239). If a family values achievement, for example, their guiding theme may be "when the going gets tough, the tough get going." Themes serve the function, then, of helping the family to deal with reality. To the extent that the truth of the theme is taken for granted, the inherent advice may not be open to question. Therefore, themes, like other types of collective symbols, can constrain family interaction in ways that are not entirely functional. The theme "children should be seen and not heard" is an example of how thematic symbols can operate dysfunctionally.

A recent study (White, 2004) examined themes of relational experience in Welsh widows' long-term marriages. White (2004) engaged in this analysis to understand "how participants in relationships make sense of their relational experience" (p. 1). In particular, she examines the "folk-logics that individuals use to understand, and to represent in talk, their relationships" (p. 2). By emphasizing the thematic content of her respondents' accounts of their long-term marriages, White goes beyond understanding of marital success or failure. White identified three themes from her interviews with 25 widows that suggest how they made their marriages work. The first theme is that "imperfection is normal" (p. 6). This suggests to White that long-term marriages endure difficulties, as well as times of ease. The second theme, "strength of the dyad," reflects the couples' emphases on their own relationship, rather than on that with their children or extended family. The final theme, "obligation as an indicator of caring," was accompanied by the notion that "the need to care for a partner is taken for granted" (p. 9). White extends our understanding of long-term marriage by examining themes and concludes that "even happy marriages are likely to have experienced troubles at some point in the relationship" (p. 6).

Metaphor "can help individuals to explain their reality through language without literally having to define the experience" (Pawlowski, Thilborger, & Cieloha-Meekins, 2001, p. 180). This means that metaphor allows us an insider's perspective on the family in a way that literal description cannot. More generally, "a family metaphor is a specific event, object, image, or behavior that represents for family members some aspect of their collective identity" (Yerby et al., 1995, p. 233).

One particular type of metaphor, the representational act, functions as a meaningful symbol for a given concern in the family. For example, sending flowers on a wedding anniversary may signify love for one couple but may be a sign of not caring enough to be creative for another couple. Thus, the meanings of metaphors are very particular to the given family. As linguistic comparisons, metaphors can offer insight as to the collective identity of the family and provide a sense of understanding for both its members and outside observers (Turner & West, 2006).

Rawlins (1989) examined the metaphorical views of interaction in both the family-of-origin and the future family. In his study, he collected 203 student compositions detailing metaphorical descriptions of both the family in which they were raised and the family they wanted to have in the future. He identified seven major themes for the family-of-origin, including "integration/differentiation" and "family as hierarchical preparation for life" as the most frequently cited (p. 56). The first reflects the dominant activity of establishing both autonomy and connection, which is a primary function of family interaction. The second, "hierarchical preparation," is a metaphor where the family is presented "in quite traditional terms with the father in a position of highest authority and responsibility" (p. 58). Interestingly, while the most frequently cited metaphor in the future family was also "integration/differentiation," the second most common metaphor was "shelter and growth." Rawlins concludes that "the distinctions between the two groups of metaphors are provocative" (p. 66). This analysis reveals that while family-of-origin is experienced as hierarchical, with top-down governance, the family sought after for the future is laterally organized and nurtures creativity. Thus, by examining the symbolic content of family metaphors, Rawlins uncovered a new understanding of collective identity.

Pawlowski et al. (2001) also explored students' perceptions of their families through a metaphorical analysis. In particular, they were interested in examining the launching phase of the family life cycle, where young adults leave home and separate from their families-of-origin. One of their findings was that students' metaphors revealed contradictory feelings, while they attempt to separate but also depend on their parents for support, revealing that "the launching stages of families may create a different, or additional, set of family dialectics" (p. 193).

Narratives, often shared through storytelling behavior, also reveal the family's values and collective identity. According to Turner and West (2006), narratives have a number of elements, including the family as a subject, a set sequence of events, a sense of significance, the capacity to teach moral lessons, a purpose of developing individual and family esteem, and a reflection of the family's practices with respect to power and control. Because the subject is so personal, family stories are appealing. They can be linear or circular in their sequencing of events and are important to the family's identity. Yerby et al. (1995) describe two categories of stories: canonical stories and popular stories. According to these authors, "canonical stories express the boundaries of acceptable cultural family practices against which alternative stories or versions are judged" (p. 212). These include stories of courtship, birth, and survival and, while common to all families, have quite different experiential content. It is because they are common, however, that the stories can be compared and judged according to either real or imagined cultural standards.

According to Jorgenson and Bochner (2004), the canonical story, while told in the present, "must justify past actions in such a way as to meet the challenge of going on to a better and more hopeful future" (p. 525). Popular stories are acquired from culture and "transmit our culture's ideals—its taken-for-granted meanings and values" (Yerby et al., 1995, p. 215). Thus, popular stories reflect the influence of mainstream media on family relationships and interactions. A third type of story deals with what Jorgenson and Bochner (2004) call "stories on the margins" (p. 528). These stories express the experiences of marginalized families or talk about socially taboo or uncomfortable topics such as "marital rape, childlessness, unexpected pregnancies" (p. 529), as well as homosexuality, alcoholism, and abuse.

Jorgenson and Bochner (2004) explain the process of "imagining families through stories and rituals" (p. 513). Storytelling is seen as a way to manage the "continuous struggle to create, maintain, and/or restore narrative coherence in the face of unexpected contingencies of lived experiences" (p. 515). For them, then, storytelling is not an isolated family activity but an integral part of a family's daily experience. In another study, Langellier (2002) examined how "family stories participate in the formation of culture as they imagine and reproduce ethnic identity" (p. 56). She specifically focused on the Franco American community and a collection of stories about grandmothers (*memeres*). She observed that these "memere stories narrate the family times that cross households to gather kin, neighbors, and family friends for visits" (p. 65). The stories also were "replete with their protagonists' 'toil and labor'"(p. 66). She concludes that "as cultural performance, memere stories materialize Franco American identity and reproduce the Franco American family" (p. 69). This work is a vivid example of the crucial role that storytelling has in family life.

The contributions of research using social construction theory have been especially profound in providing a qualitative understanding of the meaning-making processes of family life. By examining how families create, sustain, and modify their realities through symbolic manipulation, we are at the heart of the central function of communication in the family. Still, because social construction theory is so heavily focused on the unique meanings achieved through interactions in the family, it tends to allow us to explain and understand phenomena at a very microscopic level. Like any theory, it is limited in its scope. To acquire a more macroscopic vision of family communication, which places less emphasis on the individual, we now turn to the systems perspective.

Systems

Some would argue that systems is the most dominant of all family communication perspectives. The emergence of systems, through the work of Watzlawick et al. (1967) in their book, *Pragmatics of Human Communication,* focuses the attention of family scholars on the actual behaviors among family members, as opposed to their cognitions or intentions. The family fits the basic definition of a system because it is "stable with respect to certain of its variables if these variables tend to remain within defined limits" (Watzlawick et al., 1967, p. 134). The unit of analysis is the relationship, and the individual is in the background. Perhaps the greatest single contribution of systems as a metatheory is that it provides a way to conceptualize family as a whole. To better illustrate this contribution, we will now examine some systems elements and processes as they relate to the study of the family.

In general, a system is defined as "a set of things that affect one another within an environment and form a larger pattern that is different from any of the parts"

(Littlejohn, 2002, p. 37). A noted family therapist, Virginia Satir (1972), explains that "any system consists of several individual parts that are essential and related to one another"; furthermore, "there are actions and reactions and interactions among the parts that keep changing" (p. 112). In particular, the family system, "like all living systems, incorporate[s] two types of characteristics: (1) a set of system elements, and (2) a set of processes that help the system function" (Yerby et al., 1995, p. 58). The elements are the parts of the system and include interdependent components, inputs and outputs, boundaries, rules, goals, and feedback. It is important to recognize that the components are not just the family members themselves but also the roles that are played in the family. Thus, while a particular person can enter and leave a system, the role itself remains. For example, if a family divorces, the biological father may leave the home, but one of the sons may take on the father role. Thus, the person acting the role has changed, but the father role remains in the family.

There are a variety of inputs and outputs with a family system, which indicates that the system is at least somewhat open. The inputs into a family system include survival necessities, such as food, clothing, and shelter, as well as societal influence, through media, school, and church. The family outputs include the paid work of family members, its citizenship (or lack thereof), and the socialization of its children (in a family with children). The boundaries of a family system exist at several levels but most basically differentiate between family and nonfamily membership. Rules emerge from family interaction and also constrain interaction, and family goals provide direction for energy. The final element, feedback, can be both deviation enhancing (positive) or deviation minimizing (negative).

In order for these elements to have meaning, they must work in cooperation with each other. For that to occur, the family system engages in four processes. The processes include nonsummativity, stability, change, and equifinality. Nonsummativity is essential to the systems perspective because it captures how the family is more than the sum of its individual members. It is this relationship between and among members that is of interest to systems theorists and not individuals' behaviors or personalities. The notion of stability is also critical for systems theorists, as they subscribe to the belief that families seek homeostasis, or balance. As a result, stability is seen as a goal of the family, and behaviors are recognized as either discouraging change or promoting stability. The process of change is the third process because any living system must have growth to remain vital. However, the pattern and routine of family life (i.e., its stability) is privileged over change, which is often seen as a necessary evil. The final process, equifinality, focuses on how a family can achieve its goals through a number of ways and means. While families may share similar goals, for example, providing a college education for its children, the ways and means of achieving this goal are various. One family may create a college fund, while another might require children to pay for their own education.

In considering how the elements and processes work together in family systems, the notion of circular causality is central. Circular causality expresses the quality of family systems that is dynamic and emerging, though also repetitive. In other words, as opposed to linear causality, where one behavior might be seen as causing another, the notion of causality in the systems perspective is arbitrary. Any given behavior can be cause or effect. Since interdependence consists of actions, reactions, and interactions, the emergence of patterns is ongoing. In fact, Watzlawick et al. (1967) note that "families of psychiatric patients often demonstrated drastic repercussions . . . when the patient improved" (p. 134). Illness, then, operated as a change-inhibiting factor, "operating to bring the disturbed system back into its delicate balance" (p. 134). Through this example, we can see how circular causality consists of both stability and change but favors stability, even if stability perpetuates family dysfunction.

In addition to examining the family system within its own boundaries, the systems perspective also encourages analysis of how the family interacts with its social environment. Some of the first scholars to observe family systems outside of the clinical arena, Kantor and Lehr (1975), observed that a chief characteristic of social systems "is an almost continuous interchange not only within the system, but across the boundary between the inner environment and the outer environment" (p. 10). Furthermore, family activity itself is seen as "a complex interplay of systemic structures and forces which elaborate and change in response to both internal and external phenomena" (p. 10). The system, then, includes not only family member components but also societal forces and influences.

Jennings and Wartella (2004) used systems to explore the impact of the external environment on family communication. They summarized previous studies examining how digital technology, as an outside influence, affected the spousal, the parental, and the sibling subsystems of the family. They found, for example, "both anecdotal and some evidence from research to indicate that digital media technology and especially networked computers may have a negative impact on marital relations" (p. 599). They also examined how parental regulation of children's media use changes as they adopt new technologies. Thus, the introduction of technology in the home affects family communication.

Relational Theory

One of the most illuminating theories of family communication to come out of the systems tradition is relational theory (Millar & Rogers, 1976, 1987). Millar and Rogers (1987) note that "interaction has been one of the most talked about and least studied phenomena in the social sciences" (p. 117). They go on to say that the relational communication approach remedies this by focusing directly upon interaction. Relational theory used the two dimensions in all interactions, the content dimension and the relational dimension identified by Watzlawick et al. (1967). The content dimension includes the topic of interaction and the relational dimension, which contains implicit direction for how the content is to be understood. Relational theory states that the relational dimension is basically about control and how power is worked out through interaction. The interact (a comment and the response to the comment) is the basic unit of analysis, and it contains both an action and a reaction. The theory further enumerates a coding scheme for examining actual conversation. The patterns that emerge from such coding reveal how the relationship is defined, not simply what the interactants are talking about. Some common patterns to emerge from research using this perspective include symmetry, where both relational partners are exhibiting behavior in the same control direction, or complementarity, where the partners exhibit contrasting control directions.

Sabourin (1995) conducted a relational control analysis of abusive and nonabusive couples' interactions to examine how abusive couples attempt to define their relationships. She recorded couples talking about how they structure their daily routines and then applied relational coding to reveal control patterns inherent in their interactions. What she discovered was that abusive couples tended to have symmetrical patterns, indicating that each partner was vying to control the definition of the relationship, and hence neither agreed with or supported the other. By contrast, the nonabusive couples tended to exhibit a range of control patterns, with support and acceptance of each other's relational definitions in evidence. This pattern partly debunks the myth that women in abusive relationships take a subordinate position while males take a dominant position. According to this research, neither partner was willing to accept the other's bid for dominance. This factor is probably key to understanding the dynamics of an abusive relationship. This study provides one example of how relational theory can be used to unveil deep-lying patterns in interactions, which otherwise go unnoticed.

Dialectical Perspective

The third perspective is dialectics. Turner (2003) explains that this metatheory "maintains that what characterizes relational life is ongoing tensions between contradictory desires" (p. 29). In a family, the desires for both autonomy and connection, for instance, are in contradiction to each other. Importantly, the dialectical perspective does not propose that these contradictions can be resolved; rather, it maintains that the contradictions are managed and negotiated through family interactions. Accordingly, four main assumptions of this approach, according to Turner (2003, p. 29), include the following: (a) Relationships are not linear, (b) relational life is characterized by change, (c) contradiction is a fundamental fact of relational life, and (d) communication is central to negotiating relational contradictions. A dialectical approach focuses on how interactions respond to "the apparently opposing forces that operate in the family" (Yerby et al., 1995, p. 9). These contradictions and competing demands are in constant and dynamic interplay throughout family communication.

The dialectical approach, then, is especially useful for understanding the multiplicity of structures and cultures that characterize the contemporary family (Sabourin, 2003). Currently, the dialectical view is "the road less traveled in family communication" (Sabourin, 2003, p. 2). But as scholars account for the increasing complexity of structural and cultural variations in families, more complex theory is necessary. Because it emphasizes the struggle with integrating polarities, such as autonomy and connection, the dialectical perspective can account for an infinite array of family processes.

The three major concepts of dialectics are change, connection, and contradiction. The view of change adopted by dialectical scholars emphasizes its transformational nature, which is qualitative and not subject to prediction and control. This view of change is a point of departure from the systems notion of change, which posits that families seek balance and homeostasis through communication. The dialectical concept of change produces novel outcomes as opposed to repetitive patterns. Change is also seen as situated in a particular time and space, what Baxter and Montgomery (1996) call the "chronotopical context." Hence, even if an interactional sequence seems repetitive, the fact that it occurs in a different time and place makes it at least, to some degree, novel.

Connection is an indicator of the necessity of opposing forces. In other words, one cannot exist without the other. The need to connect is referred to as the centripetal force, and the need to separate is the centrifugal force. Both of these needs occur simultaneously, meaning that families are not *either* close *or* distant but rather *both* close *and* distant.

The notion of contradiction is central to a dialectical view, making it unique from other metatheories of family communication. Furthermore, family "relationships are shaped and maintained by the ways members manage contradictions" (Galvin et al., 2004, p. 71). Many contradictions permeate family life: the contradiction of autonomy and connection, the need for both stability and change, desires for openness, and self-protection through concealment. Besides these, Rawlins (1992) identified a number of other dialectical tensions, which he classifies as either contextual or interactional. Although he was basing his work on the study of friendships, Sabourin (2003) argues that his categories are equally applicable to family relationships. The contextual dialectics reflect the relationship between the family and the larger cultural environment. Rawlins identified two such tensions: the private and the public, and the ideal and the real. Each of these tensions is negotiated through family interaction with the surrounding culture. Interactional dialectics, on the other hand, are those negotiated within the family system and include dependence/independence, instrumentality/affection, closedness/openness, and expressive/protective. Each of these tensions is managed through family interactions, which constantly evolve and change.

Baxter and Montgomery (1996) have examined some of the praxical patterns that are used to manage dialectical tensions. They stress the improvisational nature of these practices, meaning that while they respond to the givens in a situation, they also have emergent properties. Sabourin (2003) summarizes these patterns as including selection, separation, neutralization, and reformulation. Each of these options stresses the relationship between opposing forces with different emphases. For example, selection as a means of managing contradictory tensions means that one polarity is basically ignored, while the other is held constant. A family may refuse to acknowledge its members' needs for autonomy, for example, while striving for constant closeness. The separation option means that in either time or space, the tension between opposing forces is recognized but held at a distance. A temporal separation may be evident as a family agrees to practice autonomy during the week and to practice closeness on weekends. While simultaneity is present, it is controlled across time. Neutralization is similar to homeostasis and means that a family opts for some kind of balance, or "happy medium," between polarities. They may practice autonomous hobbies while together in the same room. With reformulation, the contradiction is transcended, and for a time, the family opts to see a larger picture, where the autonomy allows for closeness and closeness allows for autonomy.

The dialectical perspective was used in a study by Baxter, Braithwaite, Golish, and Olson (2002) to examine contradictions in the interaction of wives with elderly husbands who suffer adult dementia. These scholars interviewed 21 wives with husbands in nursing homes for the condition of dementia. They found that "as the women described their communication with their husbands, it became evident that the husbands' illness was enormously problematic for their wives, forcing them to redefine what it meant to have a marital relationship with their husbands" (pp. 9–10). They found that the major contradiction that the wives managed was a "tug-of-war between the 'presence' and 'absence' of their partners" (p. 10). These "married widows" had to mourn the loss of their past with their husbands while they tended to the demands of the present. The authors concluded that "although our participants felt a tension between the past and the present, they tended to privilege the past in their verbal communication with their husbands" (p. 19).

Although dialectics has been adopted by a number of scholars in recent studies of family communication (Albada, 2000; Baxter et al., 2002; Baxter, Hirokawa, Lowe, Nathan, & Pearce, 2004; Sabourin & Stamp, 1995; Toller, 2005), no particular theory has been identified as emerging from this metatheory. As one of the most recently adopted perspectives in the study of family communication, dialectics promises to provide theoretical insight in future studies.

The Developmental Perspective

All of the metatheoretical perspectives discussed thus far seek, to varying degrees, to explain and understand the changing and dynamic nature of family communication. The developmental perspective, however, is solely focused on change throughout the lifetime of a family. According to Price, McHenry, and Murphy (2000b), "The developmental approach is the only conceptual framework created specifically for viewing families. In contrast, other frameworks (structural-functional, systems, conflict, symbolic interaction) were developed for other purposes, and their application to families evolved over time" (p. xvii).

A number of terms have been used to describe family development, including *family life cycle, life span, family career,* and *life course* (Price, McHenry, & Murphy, 2000a, p. 2). Sometimes, the developmental metatheory addresses changes across the life span of individuals by focusing on biological growth in stages, such as infancy, toddlerhood, preteen, and adolescence. Concurrently, the life span of the family can be examined according to its individual members' biological development, in which case families are studied as they go through stages of courtship, early parenthood, adolescence, launching, and aging. A limit of looking at family development from a biological viewpoint, however, is that the contemporary family goes through stages in a highly diverse manner (see Chapter 1, this volume). An emphasis on the family life cycle model implies that "families cannot go back; once they experience a stage, phase of development, or change over time, they must move on" (Price et al., 2000a, p. 2). From this view, it is difficult to account for courting couples who are elderly, grandparents who also have newborns of their own, and launching at later adulthood, due to divorce, unemployment, and so forth. Thus, one of the criticisms of a linear approach to development is that it tends to focus on intact, nuclear families (Price et al., 2000a).

It is more fruitful for understanding family communication to look at development holistically, incorporating not only biological stages but also family relationships, interactions, and experiences over time. Whereas some family stages are predictable and common across families, the evolution of relationships, interactions, and experiences will be to a large degree unique. Accordingly, to explain and understand the diversity of family life, it is important to focus on how a family's change over time, through both personal development and facing crisis or major events together, affects the family's operations and the meanings family members create through their interactions.

Life Course Theory

Life course theory "allows us to focus on individuals and families as well as on subsystems and changes in wider society" (Price et al., 2000a, p. 3). This theory is relevant to the study of families today and explains a multitude of influences, including family "members, their life history, and events in the family's social context, culture, and time in history" (Price et al., 2000b, p. xvii). It also illustrates how various notions of time can be emphasized in an examination of family development. Specifically, it looks at individual time, generational time, and historical time. Individual time refers to "the periods of one's life (childhood, adolescence, young adulthood, middle age, old age), or how persons are defined and channeled into positions and roles largely based on chronological age" (Price et al., 2000a, p. 3). Individual time also includes cohort time, which "refers to the age categories or cohorts in which people are grouped, based on when they were born" (Price et al., 2000a, p. 3). Generation X or baby boomers are examples of this type of time. Generational time "refers to the rank order of positions that individuals hold in families (grandparent, parent, child) as well as the roles, expectations, and identities associated with these positions" (Price et al., 2000a, p. 4). Historical time is based on societal conditions, including the economy, war, or technological advancements. Each of these times can be used as an organizational device for examining family development.

A number of recent family communication studies examine individual time. Golish and Caughlin (2002), for example, studied adolescents' use of topic avoidance with their stepfamilies. They selected adolescence as the period of time to study since "the need to establish boundaries and roles may be especially pronounced for adolescents and young adults who are not only adjusting to a new family, but who are also attempting to develop their own identity as adults" (p. 80). Similarly, Saphir and Chaffee (2002) examined adolescents' contributions to family communication patterns, and Sillars, Koerner, and Fitzpatrick (2005) studied communication and understanding in parent-adolescent relationships. Sillars et al. (2005) selected this time in particular because "individually, adolescents undergo profound physical, social and cognitive changes, at the same time that parents navigate significant life stage transitions of their own" (p. 102).

Some family scholars examine the development of structure in nonnuclear families. Braithwaite, Olson, Golish, Soukup, and Tourman (2001), for example, explored the "developmental processes represented in blended family discourse" (p. 221). Specifically, they wanted "to gain a deeper understanding of how (step) blended family members experiencing different developmental pathways discursively represented their processes of becoming a family" (p. 221). They conducted interviews with members from 53 blended families and analyzed their responses to what the first 4 years of blended family experience had been like for them. They identified both positive and negative pathways, as well as turbulent trajectories. They conclude that their results "underscore the utility of looking at the development of blended families not as a unitary model moving always forward but as a process involving different developmental pathways" (p. 240). This type of study should become more common as we examine the contemporary family and try to understand diverse pathways of development.

Conclusion

The metatheories and theories of the future must take into account the enormous diversity and change characterizing the contemporary family. Turner and West (2002) reflect on four conclusions about family communication. Their conclusions provide apt advice for family communication theory in the future. First, they acknowledge that family scholars must recognize the diversity in family communication. They warn against generalizing across families and against using outdated stereotypes. Sabourin (2003) discusses how much research on African American families, for example, has assumed a single-parent structure, with a background of poverty. This perpetuates the stereotype of a homogeneous African American family structure and culture, which is not supported by data. Another charge for the future of family communication theory, as indicated by Turner and West, is a need to recognize the dark and negative elements of family life. As a culture, we tend to prescribe and privilege harmony, yet numerous families experience abuse, alcoholism, and mental illness, creating quite different experiences than those prescribed by mainstream culture. It is important to include what Jorgenson and Bochner (2004) call "stories on the margins" as we illustrate a holistic picture of family life.

Turner and West's (2002) third conclusion is to continue to emphasize and recognize the value of communication in our society. When we look back at the early days of family communication scholarship, when Millar and Rogers (1987) lamented that we talk about studying interaction but never do so, we realize we have come a long way. Sabourin's (1995) study of relational patterns in abusive and nonabusive couples is just one example of a study focusing on interaction. The final plea to family scholars, made by Turner and West, is that we stay current with the changing demographics of families. Internal and external changes are inextricably interwoven in family life, and as scholars and theorists, we must work to keep up with these changes.

Galvin (2004) addresses the family of the future and asks how future changes will affect family communication researchers. She concludes that the family of the future will (a) "reflect an increasing diversity of self-conceptions," (b) live within four and five generations of familial connection, (c) function in a fast-paced world of medical advances, (d) encounter environmental change due to technological advances, and (e) "search for new ways to protect and enhance family life" (p. 676). While the theories and metatheories described in this chapter will play some role in allowing us to understand the family of the future, we must also be open to the need to develop and advance new ways of thinking that can embrace new family realities.

References

Albada, K. F. (2000). The public and private dialogue about the American family on television. *Journal of Communication, 50,* 79–110.

Aldous, J. (1990). Family development and the life course: Two perspectives on family change. *Journal of Marriage and the Family, 52,* 571–583.

Baxter, L. A. (1990). Dialectical contradictions in relationship development. *Journal of Social and Personal Relationships, 7,* 69–88.

Baxter, L. A., Braithwaite, D. O., Golish, T. D., & Olson, L. N. (2002). Contradictions of interactions for wives of elderly husbands with adult dementia. *Journal of Applied Communication Research, 30,* 1–26.

Baxter, L. A., Hirokawa, R., Lowe, J. B., Nathan, P., & Pearce, L. (2004). Dialogic voices in talk about drinking and pregnancy. *Journal of Applied Communication Research, 32,* 224–248.

Baxter, L. A., & Montgomery, B. M. (1996). *Relating: Dialogues and dialectics.* New York: Guilford.

Bopp, M. J., & Weeks, G. R. (1984). Dialectical metatheory in family therapy. *Family Process, 23,* 49–61.

Braithwaite, D. O., Olson, L. N., Golish, T. D., Soukup, C., & Torman, P. (2001). "Becoming a family": Developmental processes represented in blended family discourse. *Journal of Applied Communication Research, 29,* 221–247.

Galvin, K. M. (2004). The family of the future: What do we face? In A. L. Vangelisti (Ed.), *Handbook of family communication* (pp. 675–697). Mahwah, NJ: Lawrence Erlbaum.

Galvin, K. M., Bylund, C. L., & Brommel, B. J. (2004). *Family communication: Cohesion and change.* Boston: Pearson.

Golish, T. D., & Caughlin, J. P. (2002). "I'd rather not talk about it": Adolescents' and young adults' use of topic avoidance in stepfamilies. *Journal of Applied Communication Research, 30,* 78–106.

Jennings, N., & Wartella, E. (2004). Technology and the family. In A. L. Vangelisti (Ed.), *Handbook of family communication* (pp. 593–608). Mahwah, NJ: Lawrence Erlbaum.

Jorgenson, J. (1989). Where is the "family" in family communication? Exploring families' self definitions. *Journal of Applied Communication Research, 17,* 27–41.

Jorgenson, J., & Bochner, A. P. (2004). Imagining families through stories and rituals. In A. L. Vangelisti (Ed.), *Handbook of family communication* (pp. 513–538). Mahwah, NJ: Lawrence Erlbaum.

Kantor, D., & Lehr, W. (1975). *Inside the family.* New York: Harper & Row.

Langellier, K. M. (2002). Performing family stories, forming cultural identity: Franco American memere stories. *Communication Studies, 53,* 56–73.

Littlejohn, S. W. (2002). *Theories of human communication.* Belmont, CA: Wadsworth.

McCall, G. J., & Simmons, J. L. (1966). *Identities and interactions.* New York: Free Press.

McGoldrick, M., & Carter, E. (1982). The family life cycle. In F. Walsh (Ed.), *Normal family processes* (pp. 167–195). New York: Guilford.

Mead, G. H. (1934). *Mind, self, and society.* Chicago: University of Chicago Press.

Millar, F. E., & Rogers, L. E. (1976). A relational approach to interpersonal communication. In G. Miller (Ed.), *Explorations in interpersonal communication* (pp. 87–103). Beverly Hills, CA: Sage.

Millar, F. E., & Rogers, L. E. (1987). Relational dimensions of interpersonal dynamics. In M. E. Roloff & G. R. Miller (Eds.), *Interpersonal processes: New directions in communication research* (pp. 117–138). Newbury Park, CA: Sage.

Noller, P., & Fitzpatrick, M. A. (1993). *Communication in family relationships.* Englewood Cliffs, NJ: Prentice Hall.

Pawlowski, D. R., Thilborger, C., & Cieloha-Meekins, J. (2001). Prisons, old cars, and Christmas trees: A metaphorical analysis of familial communication. *Communication Studies, 52,* 180–196.

Price, S. J., McHenry, P. C., & Murphy, M. J. (2000a). Families across time: A life course perspective. In S. J. Price, P. C. McHenry, & M. J. Murphy (Eds.), *Families across time: A life course perspective* (pp. 2–22). Los Angeles: Roxbury.

Price, S. J., McKenry, P. C., & Murphy, M. J. (2000b). Preface. In S. J. Price, P. C. McHenry, & M. J. Murphy (Eds.), *Families across time: A life course perspective* (pp. xvii–xxi). Los Angeles: Roxbury.

Rawlins, W. (1989). Metaphorical views of interaction in families of origin and future families. *Journal of Applied Communication Research, 17,* 124–154.

Rawlins, W. K. (1992). *Friendship matters.* New York: Aldine de Gruyter.

Sabourin, T. C. (1995). The role of negative reciprocity in spouse abuse: A relational control analysis. *Journal of Applied Communication, 23,* 271–283.

Sabourin, T. C. (2003). *The contemporary American family: A dialectical perspective on communication and relationships.* Thousand Oaks, CA: Sage.

Sabourin, T. C., & Stamp, G. H. (1995). Communication and the experience of dialectical tensions in family life: An examination of abusive and nonabusive families. *Communication Monographs, 62,* 213–242.

Saphir, M. N., & Chaffee, S. H. (2002). Adolescents' contributions to family communication patterns. *Human Communication Research, 28,* 86–108.

Satir, V. (1972). *Peoplemaking.* Palo Alto, CA: Science and Behavior Books.

Sillars, A., Koerner, A., & Fitzpatrick, M. A. (2005). Communication and understanding in parent-adolescent relationships. *Human Communication Research, 31,* 102–128.

Stamp, G. H. (2004). Theories of family relationships and a family relationships theoretical model. In A. L. Vangelisti (Ed.), *Handbook of family communication* (pp. 1–30). Mahwah, NJ: Lawrence Erlbaum.

Stephen, T. (1984). A symbolic exchange framework for the development of intimate relationships. *Human Relations, 37,* 393–408.

Toller, P. W. (2005). Negotiations of dialectical contradictions by parents who have experienced the death of a child. *Journal of Applied Communication Research, 33,* 46–66.

Turner, L. H. (2003). Theories of relational communication. In K. M. Galvin & P. J. Cooper (Eds.), *Making connections: Readings in relational communication* (pp. 20–31). Los Angeles: Roxbury.

Turner, L. H., & West, R. (2002). *Perspectives on family communication* (2nd ed.). New York: McGraw-Hill.

Turner, L.H., & West, R. (2006). *Perspectives on family communication* (3rd ed.). New York: McGraw-Hill.

Watzlawick, P., Beavin, J. H., & Jackson, D. (1967). *Pragmatics of human communication.* New York: Norton.

White, C. H. (2004). Welsh widows' descriptions of their relationships: Themes of relational experience in long term marriages. *Communication Studies, 55,* 1–13.

Yerby, J. (1989). A conceptual framework for analyzing family metaphors. *Journal of Applied Communication Research, 17,* 42–51.

Yerby, J., Buerkel-Rothfuss, N. L., & Bochner, A. P. (1995). *Understanding family communication* (2nd ed.). Scottsdale, AZ: Gorsuch Scarisbrick.

CHAPTER 4

Established and Promising Models for Family Communication Research

Deborah S. Ballard-Reisch

University of Nevada, Reno

Daniel J. Weigel

University of Nevada, Reno

S ignificant research and theory have been directed toward developing models of family functioning that either directly or indirectly address the role of communication behavior. This chapter draws together research on both widely used and promising models of family communication. Toward that end, we first distinguish between theories and models, providing a full definition of models. Second, we review some of the most commonly used models in the family literature. Third, we briefly overview promising but less researched models, including two mathematically based models, an ecological model, and a model grounded in family communication research. Finally, we offer observations on the models reviewed and directions for further model development and research in family communication.

AUTHORS' NOTE: The authors would like to thank Michele Humphreys for her early assistance in the development of this chapter and Jessica Adams for her editing assistance and helpful suggestions.

On Distinguishing Theories and Models

Many diverse and often contradictory definitions of the concepts of "theory" and "model" exist in social science literature. Sometimes, the terms *theory* and *model* seem to be used almost interchangeably. At other times, they seem to represent very distinct sense-making processes. We think it prudent to distinguish between these concepts and offer the following conceptualizations.

Theories

Theories are defined as everything from unsubstantiated assertions (see Littlejohn, 1992) to "complex spatial networks . . . anchored . . . by rules of interpretation" (Hemple, 1952, p. 36) to "abstract and general ideas that are subject to rules of organization" (Klein & White, 1996, p. 6). Doherty, Boss, LaRossa, Schumm, and Steinmetz (1993) define theory as a set of interconnected ideas that emerge from the process of theorizing. Theorizing is the systematic formulization and organization of ideas in order to understand a particular phenomenon. We define *theory* consistent with Kerlinger (1986) as "a set of interrelated concepts, definitions, and propositions that present a systematic view of events or situations by specifying relations among variables in order to explain and predict the events or situations" (p. 9).

Consistent with this view, Klein and White (1996) argue that theories "entail abstract, plausible, and tentative arguments" about the nature of the world that require "empirical evidence" and support (p. 18). They further posit seven functions of theories. They argue that theories (1) "assist in the *accumulation* and organization of research findings" (p. 18), (2) allow researchers to use more *precision* in the clarification of concepts and relationships, (3) provide *guidance* regarding hypothesis development and testing, (4) demonstrate the *connectedness* and coherence of ideas, (5) direct the *interpretation* of phenomena, (6) allow for the *prediction* of future behavior, and (7) provide an *explanation* of "why" and "how" things happen as they do (pp. 18–20).

Models

Models can be seen as "complex empirical generalizations, generally shown in diagrammatic" form, that represent "the relationships among a number of variables" (Doherty et al., 1993, p. 20) or as "scaled down or simplified versions" of complex relationships among phenomena (Klein & White, 1996, p. 6). We define models as representations of the structural or functional properties of theories (Littlejohn, 1990; Smith, 1988) and as "symbolic representation[s]" of things, processes, or ideas (Littlejohn, 1990, p. 5).

Models serve four functions. The first three we draw from Hawes (1975), who viewed models as (1) *descriptive*—able to describe a process with specificity and precision through representation of the underlying structure of the process,

(2) *explorative* of theoretical concepts or relationships, and (3) *simulative* of actual communication processes. Earp and Ennett (1991) add to this conceptualization the potential for models to be (4) *explanative*, drawing on a number of theories to explain specific problems in particular settings or contexts.

In sum, theories provide general, guiding frameworks for understanding family communication behavior, which allow the systematic analysis of concepts and their interconnections to interpret and predict phenomena. Models explicitly concretize a theory, components of a theory, or concept and relationship dynamics particular to a theory or a group of theories. By making the processes within a theory concrete and explicit, models allow for the generation of hypotheses and the systematic testing of theories or components of theories.

Hage (1972) argued that models are composed of three basic elements: "concepts, definitions, and linkages" (Hage, 1972, p. 6). *Concepts* are sets or classes of objects or events bound together by common characteristics (Hage, 1972). For example, viewing the concept of communication as fundamental to family development and family functioning is a hallmark of family communication research. According to Stamp (2004), 28 categories of concepts undergird family research. These include communication, cognition, conflict, context, control, emotion, influence, life course, process, roles, stress, and structure (for a complete description, see Stamp, 2004, pp. 11–16).

Definitions, according to Hage (1972), can be theoretical or operational. Theoretical definitions propose the parameters or limits of a concept; they give a concept its meaning. Operational definitions indicate how a concept can be measured. Definitions within a model delineate what can be considered and what must be omitted from the perspective of that model. Definitional issues relevant to the study of families have included such issues as "what is a family?" and "what structures and types can appropriately be studied as families?" Discussion of these definitions has been compounded by our awareness that the concepts of "family," "normality," and even "communication" are, as Walsh (1993) pointed out, "socially constructed, influenced by our own world view, and by the larger culture" (p. 4) (see also Chapters 1 and 2, this volume).

Linkages, according to Hage (1972), deal with the relationships among concepts. Again, they may be theoretical—telling why concepts are linked, or operational, specifying how concepts are linked. For example, marital commitment is correlated with the use of relational maintenance behaviors (Ballard-Reisch, Weigel, & Zaguidoulline, 1999; Thompson-Hayes & Webb, 2004), and marital communication patterns are associated with marital satisfaction (Cordova, Gee, & Warren, 2005; Weger, 2005).

Commonly Used Models of Family Functioning

Consistent with the above conceptualizations, the five models we discuss are firmly grounded in, operationalize, and expand upon well-developed and articulated theories or metatheories (see Chapter 3, this volume) in the family field. A number of models originate in systems and process approaches to families. Elaborated through academic research, clinical practice, or a combination of both, these models emphasize how families adapt to life events and stressors. Two of the most widely researched and clinically used models are based on the work of Ruben Hill. The circumplex model (Olson, 1986; Olson, Russell, & Sprenkle, 1989) has its foundation in Hill's (1970) work on family development. The double ABCX model (McCubbin & Patterson, 1983) is based on Hill's (1949, 1958) ABCX family crisis model.

The work on general systems theory by Ludwig von Bertalanffy (1968) underlies many of these models, but explicitly, the Beavers systems model (R. Beavers & Hampson, 2000; W. B. Beavers & Hampson, 2000) and the McMaster model of family functioning (Epstein, Bishop, Ryan, Miller, & Keitner, 1993; Miller, Ryan, Keitner, Bishop, & Epstein, 2000), both of which are concerned with the resources and processes families mobilize to function optimally within their environments.

Alternatively, the family communication patterns model (Fitzpatrick & Ritchie, 1994; Koerner & Fitzpatrick, 2002a, 2004; Ritchie & Fitzpatrick, 1990) builds upon Heider's (1946, 1958) balance theory to examine how families strive to create balance in their families through the establishment of patterned interaction behaviors. Each of these models will be discussed in turn.

The Circumplex Model of Marital and Family Systems

Grounded in the work of Ruben Hill (1970), the circumplex model has its foundation in family systems and family development theories. Developed by Olson et al. (1989), the circumplex model is one of the most extensively researched family communication models (see Figure 4.1). Based on the circumplex model, two measurement instruments have been developed, the Family Adaptability and Cohesion Scales (FACES) and the Clinical Rating Scale (CRS), designed to be useful for clinical assessment, treatment planning, and research on effective outcomes of family therapy (Olson, 1990, 1993, 1996). These instruments have been used successfully in more than 250 studies (Olson, 2000). The circumplex model focuses on three dimensions of family systems: cohesion, flexibility, and communication (Olson, 2000).

Family cohesion is defined as emotional bonding between family members (Olson, 2000) and contains concepts including clear boundaries, coalitions, the use of time and space, friends, decision making, interests, and recreation. As Olson (2000) concludes, cohesion emphasizes how separateness and togetherness are balanced within family systems, with the perspective that families balanced between separateness and togetherness are healthier than families who are either too enmeshed or too disengaged.

Flexibility emphasizes how families manage change and stability, including such issues as leadership, control and discipline, negotiation styles, fluidity of role relationships, and relationship rules (Olson, 2000). Similar to cohesion, families who balance stability and change are viewed as being healthier than those who are either too rigid or too chaotic.

Not graphically indicated in their model, communication is considered to play a vital facilitating function along the cohesion and flexibility dimensions. Including issues such as speaking and listening skills, self-disclosure, communication clarity

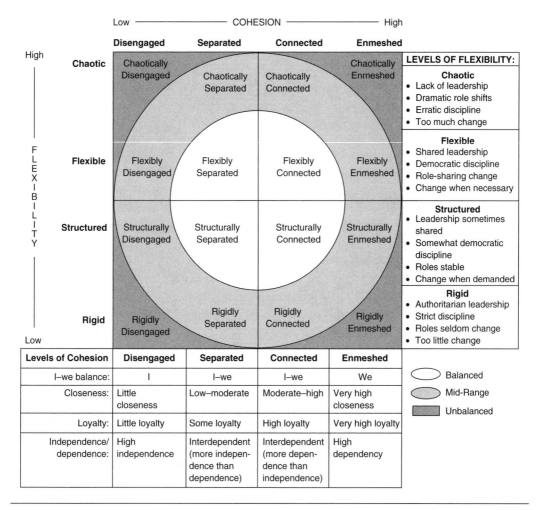

Figure 4.1   Circumplex Model: Couple and Family Map

and continuity, respect, and positive regard, the communication dimension focuses on the family as a unit (Olson, 2000)—again, assuming that families balanced in terms of cohesion and flexibility will have better communication than families at either end of these continua.

Continuously revised and modified, both the circumplex model and the instruments designed to measure various aspects of it are included in the Circumplex Assessment Package (CAP), a group of self-report assessment instruments, and the CRS, designed as clinician assessment of families and couples. Instruments in the CAP package include (1) the Family Adaptability and Cohesion Evaluation Scale (FACES II & III) (Olson, Portner, & Lavee, 1985), (2) the Marital Adaptability and Cohesion Evaluation Scales (MACES III), (3) the Parent-Adolescent Communication Scale (PACS) (Barnes & Olson, 1982), and (4) the PREPARE/ENRICH inventories designed for premarital and marital couples, respectively (Olson, 1997).

These instruments have been used to assess adolescent development as a function of adaptability and cohesion (Gaughan, 1995); functioning in families with children with emotional disorders, with emotional and conduct disorders, and without noted disorders (Drumm, Carr, & Fitzgerald, 2000); battered women's perceptions and expectations regarding expected and ideal marital relationships (Shir, 1999); and adolescent morality (White & Matawie, 2004). The circumplex model is also used to assess family change over time (Olson, 2000).

The Double ABCX Model of Adjustment and Adaptation

A second model of family functioning is the double ABCX model of adjustment and adaptation (McCubbin & Patterson, 1983) (see Figure 4.2). This model is based on Ruben Hill's (1949, 1958) ABCX family crisis model, which was designed to explain how families adapt to stressful events. Specifically, Hill believed that a family's response to a stressor was affected by the family's resources and the perception family members developed of the situation. The interaction of these two factors determined the family's reaction. Resources and perceptions are considered fundamental to a family's ability to adapt to a stressful situation.

The double ABCX model adds the long-term "pileup" of factors that influence families over their life course. The double ABCX model posits that a family's ability to adapt to a long-term stressful situation is affected by a number of factors, including severity of the stressor, additional life stressors on the family (e.g., coping with the chronic illness of a family member), family resources that can be used to manage or counter the stressor (e.g., social support), cognitive processes the family goes through to make sense of the situation, and family coping strategies.

Families are viewed as responding to stress in three ways. The first is through stimulus regulation, or the "family efforts to selectively let, delay, or shut out demands with the intention of minimizing family disruption and exhaustion of resources" (McCubbin, Cauble, & Patterson, 1982, pp. 39–40). The second is through environmental control, "which involves efforts to influence the type and quality of both the demands to which the family may be exposed and the resources needed to facilitate adaptation" (McCubbin et al., 1982, p. 40). Finally, the family responds through balancing, which is "the family's effort to maintain equilibrium or to achieve another more functional level of equilibrium" (McCubbin et al., 1982, p. 41).

Over time, the changing resources available to the family, as well as the family's perception of the situation, continue to affect their ability to successfully adapt to stress. Family adaptation is considered the outcome measure of the model and is measured on a continuum ranging from positive adaptation, which signifies positive outcomes, to maladaptation, which signifies negative outcomes or the emergence of a crisis situation. Coping is understood as the ability of the family to restore balance in the face of the stressful event.

The double ABCX model has supported a variety of measurement and assessment instruments, including (1) the Family Inventory of Life Events (FILE) instrument (McCubbin & Patterson, 1987), designed to measure the pileup of life events affecting

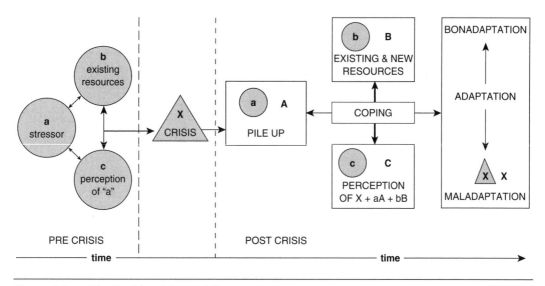

Figure 4.2   The Double ABCX Model

a family due to situational and developmental changes across the life span (Fischer & Corcoran, 1994); (2) the CHIP: Coping Health Inventory for Parents (McCubbin, 1987; McCubbin, Thompson, & McCubbin, 1996), which examines coping patterns of parents with ill children; (3) the Family Inventory of Resources for Management (FIRM), a measure of psychological, social, financial, and community resources a family has to assist their coping efforts (McCubbin, Comeau, & Harkins, 1987); and (4) the Family Crisis Oriented Personal Evaluation Scales (F-Copes) (McCubbin, Olson, & Larsen, 1987), developed to identify problem-solving and behavioral strategies families use to manage stressors. These instruments have been widely used to assess family functioning in the event of a chronic condition or illness, including mental and developmental disabilities (Enns, Reddon, & McDonald, 1999; Saloviita, Itälinna, & Leinonen, 2003; Shin & Crittenden, 2003; Studman, Roberts, Hay, & Kane, 2003), chronic illness (Katz & Krulik, 1999; Pakenham, Sofronoff, & Samios, 2004), childhood cancer (Han, 2003), childhood epilepsy (Mu, 2005), stroke (Clark, 1999), and postdivorce adaptation (Plunkett & Sanchez, 1997).

Beavers Systems Model

Grounded in systems theory (von Bertalanffy, 1968), the Beavers systems model assesses family functioning in terms of strengths and weaknesses within the family system (W. B. Beavers & Hampson, 1990, 1993) on two dimensions: family competence and family style (see Figure 4.3). Family competence reveals the extent to which family structure allows members to be flexible and adaptable (W. B. Beavers & Hampson, 1990). A flexible structure, according to R. Beavers and Hampson

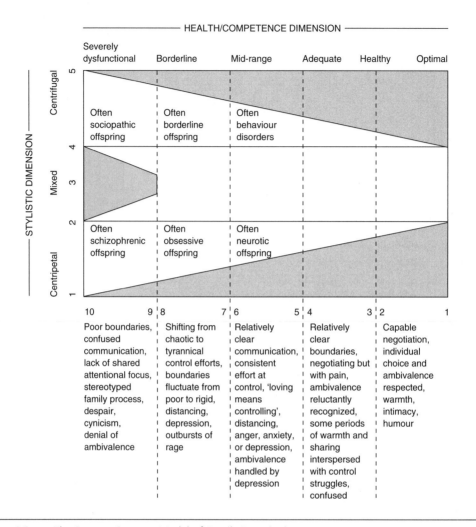

Figure 4.3   The Beavers Systems Model of Family Functioning

(2000), allows families to "negotiate, function and deal effectively with stressful situations" (p. 128). The competence dimensions include such components as (1) family structure (power, coalitions, closeness), (2) family mythology, (3) goal-directed negotiations, (4) autonomy (clarity of expression, responsibility, permeability), and (5) family affect (feelings, mood, tone, conflict, empathy) (R. Beavers & Hampson, 2000). They conclude that "when a family is not bound to rigid behaviour patterns and responses, it has more freedom to evolve and differentiate" (R. Beavers & Hampson, 2000, p. 129).

Family style addresses the stylistic elements of family interaction and is based on the appropriate balance between internal (centripetal) and external (centrifugal) family orientation. Components of style include (1) dependency, (2) conflict, (3) proximity, (4) attitudes toward outsiders, (5) closeness, (6) assertive versus aggressive qualities, (7) positive versus negative feelings, and (8) scapegoating. R. Beavers and Hampson (2000) note that the degree to which a family needs to be centripetal versus centrifugal varies on the basis of life course issues, but that in general, a balance between both is optimal.

Designed for use in training, research, and clinical work, two types of measurement instrument have been developed based on the Beavers systems model. The Self-Report Family Inventory (W. B. Beavers & Hampson, 1993) emphasizes how families see themselves on the competence dimension, and the Beavers Interactional Scales (BIS) are observational rating scales for use by clinicians. The BIS groups families among nine types ranging from optimal to severely dysfunctional (R. Beavers & Hampson, 2000).

These family self-report and clinician assessment instruments are widely used in clinical practice. R. Beavers and Hampson (2000) report the successful use of these instruments in more than 30 published papers and book chapters. The Beavers systems model has been used with families in counseling, families with children with mental retardation, and families in a variety of medical and psychiatric settings (see W. B. Beavers & Hampson, 1993).

The McMaster Model of Family Functioning

Also grounded in systems theory (von Bertalanffy, 1968), the McMaster model of family functioning grew from continuing research with families in clinical settings by scholars affiliated with the Department of Psychiatry and Behavioural Neurosciences at McMaster University, Hamilton, Ontario, Canada. (No graphic representation of the McMaster model was available. For a complete discussion and conceptualization, see Epstein et al., 1993.) The McMaster model assumes the interrelated nature of the parts of a family, the need to view families as a whole as opposed to reducing families to individual members, the need to go beyond the analysis of individuals and subgroups to understand families, and the belief that family structure, organization, and transactional patterns affect the behavior of family members (Miller et al., 2000).

The model emphasizes six dimensions of family functioning: (1) problem solving, (2) communication, (3) roles, (4) affective responsiveness, (5) affective involvement, and (6) behavior control (Epstein et al., 1993). Subdivided into instrumental (finances, living arrangements) and affective (feelings and emotional experience) types, problem solving emphasizes the family's ability to manage issues that have the potential to undermine their integrity and functional capacity (Miller et al., 2000).

Also subdivided into instrumental and affective dimensions, communication deals with how information is verbally exchanged and includes clarity and directness of communication. This model specifically excludes nonverbal behavior as too complex to assess. Roles refer to "the recurrent patterns of behaviour by which individuals fulfil family functions" (Miller et al., 2000, p. 171).

Affective responsiveness addresses the family's ability to respond to situations with the appropriate type, quality, and quantity of emotion. Affective involvement is the extent to which family members are involved in one another's lives, both in terms of what they do together and in terms of their interest and valuing of what is important to one another.

Behavior control addresses how the family manages behavior in physically dangerous situations, situations that involve expressing psychobiological needs (eating, drinking, sleeping, etc.) and situations that involve interpersonal socializing. The extent to which a family has developed appropriate rules and standards of behavior as well as latitude for deviation from these rules and standards determines their behavior control as a family.

Three instruments have been developed for use in clinical practice and research derived from components of the model. Developed to allow for specific, process-based assessment of each dimension of the model, the McMaster Structured Interview for Family Functioning (McSIFF) (Bishop, Epstein, Keitner, Miller, & Zlotnick, 1980) provides a framework for conducting structured interviews with families. The Family Assessment Device (FAD) (Epstein et al., 1993) contains a general scale and subscales designed to measure self-report assessments of family functioning on each of the model's dimensions. The McMaster Clinical Rating Scale (Miller et al., 1994) is designed for use by clinicians, following an in-depth family observation or structured interview. It involves clinical assessment of overall family functioning as well as the six dimensions of the model.

More than 59 publications have resulted from the efforts of the research teams at McMaster University from the mid-1980s to 2000. The model has continued to be used in research on families in a variety of contexts, including families with members with psychiatric diagnoses (Friedmann et al., 1997; Hayden et al., 1998); families coping with chronic medical disorders, including cerebral palsy (Brehaut et al., 2004); recovery from stroke (Clark, Rubenach, & Winsor, 2003); families coping with childhood traumatic brain injury (Barney & Max, 2005); families coping with childhood cancer (Streisand, Kazak, & Tercyak, 2003); and adolescent antisocial behavior (Bergen, Martin, Richardson, Allison, & Roeger, 2004).

Family Communication Patterns

Mary Anne Fitzpatrick and her colleagues (Fitzpatrick & Ritchie, 1994; Koerner & Fitzpatrick, 2002a, 2004; Ritchie & Fitzpatrick, 1990) developed a model called family communication patterns. (No graphic representation of the family communication patterns model was available. For a complete discussion and conceptualization, see Ritchie & Fitzpatrick, 1990.) Family communication patterns describe families' tendencies to develop fairly stable and predictable ways of communicating with one another. These stable "patterns emerge from the process by which families create and share their social realities" (Koerner & Fitzpatrick, 2004, p. 181). The model is based on Heider's (1946, 1958) balance theory, in which people strive for cognitive and behavioral consistency. Families develop regular communication patterns as a way to create consistency.

Two dimensions underlie family communication patterns—conformity orientation and conversation orientation. Conformity orientation refers to "the degree to which family communication stresses a climate of homogeneity of attitudes, values, and beliefs" (Koerner & Fitzpatrick, 2004, p. 184). Conversation orientation refers to "the degree to which families create a climate where all family members are encouraged to participate in unrestrained interaction about a wide array of topics" (Koerner & Fitzpatrick, 2004, p. 184). From these two dimensions, Koerner and Fitzpatrick (2004) identify four types of family communication patterns.

Families high in both conversation and conformity orientation are labeled "consensual." Their communication is characterized by "a tension between pressure to agree and to preserve the existing hierarchy within the family, on the one hand, and an interest in open communication and in exploring new ideas, on the other" (p. 185). Families high in conversation orientation but low in conformity orientation are "pluralistic." Communication in pluralistic families is characterized by open, unconstrained discussions that involve all family members. "Protective" families are low on conversation orientation but high on conformity orientation. Communication in protective families is characterized by "an emphasis on obedience to parental authority and by little concern for . . . open communication within the family" (p. 186). Finally, families low in both conversation orientation and conformity orientation are referred to as "laissez-faire." Their communication is characterized by "few and usually uninvolving interactions among family members that are limited to a small number of topics" (p. 186).

To measure these patterns, Fitzpatrick and her colleagues (Koerner & Fitzpatrick, 2002b; Ritchie & Fitzpatrick, 1990) developed a 26-item self-report instrument, the Revised Family Communication Patterns instrument. The measure yields two scores: conversation orientation and conformity orientation. Studies using the measure have found that conformity and conversation orientations are related to parental power (Ritchie, 1991), empathy in family communication (Koerner & Cvancara, 2002), family role (Ritchie & Fitzpatrick, 1990), age of family member (Ritchie & Fitzpatrick, 1990), and agreement on family type (Ritchie & Fitzpatrick, 1990). Likewise, recent research has linked family communication patterns with family conflict and resolution (Koerner & Fitzpatrick, 1997), children's resiliency (Fitzpatrick & Koerner, 1996), children's communication apprehension (Elwood & Schrader, 1998), the enactment of family rituals (Baxter & Clark, 1996), and effects of parents' work environments on family communication (Ritchie, 1997).

Promising Models of Family Communication

While the models discussed previously are widely used, the following models offer promise for future research. Two of these models, the social relations model (Cook, 2001; Cook & Kenny, 2004; Kashy & Kenny, 1990) and the nonlinear mathematical model of marital interaction (Gottman, Swanson, & Swanson, 2002), are grounded in systems theory (von Bertalanffy, 1968). One, the dynamic contextualism model (Ballard-Reisch & Weigel, 1999; Weigel & Ballard-Reisch, 2004), has its foundation in ecology theory (Bronfenbrenner, 1979, 1989), and the final model, the grounded theory of family life (Stamp, 2004), is based on a thorough content analysis of literature published on family communication between 1990 and 2001.

Social Relations Model

The social relations model is most often associated with William Cook and David Kenny (e.g., Cook, 2001; Cook & Kenny, 2004; Kashy & Kenny, 1990). This model provides a way to conceptually and mathematically examine the complexities of perceptions and interactions within family systems. (As this is a mathematical formula-based model, no effort will be made to replicate diagrams and formulas here. For complete information, see Cook & Kenny, 2004.) The basic perspective of the model is that to understand family communication (and other family characteristics), one needs to consider individual, relationship, and overall family-level influences. To this end, the social relations model provides techniques to isolate the various individual, relationship, and family aspects of communication within a family system.

The formulas in the model were originally presented in Warner, Kenny, and Stoto (1979). Applying complex mathematics to family communication has recently become more manageable due to advances in statistical techniques, such as structural equation modeling and hierarchical linear modeling. Cook and Kenny (2004) have shown how the techniques can be used in assessing a single family. In this way, scholars and practitioners may be able to ascertain if family communication difficulties arise from problems "of one or more individuals (actors or partners), one or more relationships, the family as a whole, or some combination of these components" (Cook & Kenny, 2004, p. 361).

Nonlinear Mathematical Model of Marital Interaction

In another approach applying mathematics to the study of couple (and family) communication, Gottman et al. (2002) developed and Gottman, Ryan, Swanson, and Swanson (2005) further elaborated the nonlinear mathematical model of marital interaction. (As this is a mathematical formula-based model, no effort will be made to replicate diagrams and formulas here. For complete information, see Gottman et al., 2002.) This model includes parameters such as (1) steady states between negative and positive cognition, affect, and physiology (attractors); (2) enduring characteristics such as personality and the past history of the relationship (uninfluenced steady states); (3) communication (influence processes); (4) resistance to change (inertia); and (5) success of each person's repair attempts. This model describes the dynamic, complex nature of family life.

Gottman et al. (2005) have taken the model one step further by attempting to change marriages through model simulation and intervention, what they call "proximal change experiments." They have found that the model makes it possible to simulate a couple's behavior under controlled conditions, then use simulations to help develop intervention strategies to increase the couple's positive verbal and nonverbal communication. Although the nonlinear mathematical model of marital interaction has potential, the complex mathematical formulas may be foreign to many communication scholars.

Dynamic Contextualism Model

Ballard-Reisch and Weigel (1999) and Weigel and Ballard-Reisch (2004) developed the dynamic contextualism model as a means of emphasizing that family communication both shapes and is shaped by the context in which it occurs (see Figure 4.4). Built on earlier work by Bronfenbrenner (1979, 1989) and Lerner (1995), this model focuses on an ecological approach to communication in families. Its foundation premise is that through interaction within multilayered contexts, families continuously define and redefine themselves as they form and re-form their communication patterns. The contexts that affect family communication are nested such that behavior is situated not only within historical, social, and political contexts (macro contexts) but also relational and personal contexts (micro contexts). Thus, within this model, family communication is characterized by change, a continual process in which every experience, every behavior, every relational event is subject to revision and reinterpretation across the family life course.

As a result of the dynamic tension between families and context, communication patterns exhibit periods of stability and change. Stability will be exhibited at times when current communication patterns mesh with current aspects of individual, family, social, and cultural-environmental spheres and when perturbations can be managed by the family. However, as the various contextual spheres exhibit change,

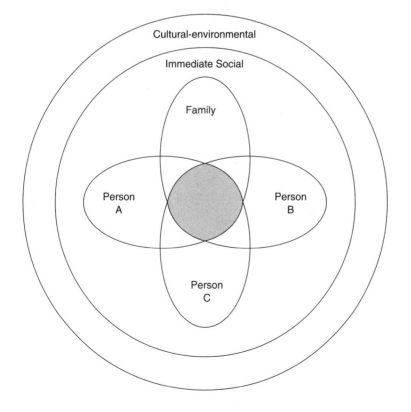

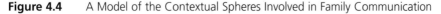

Figure 4.4   A Model of the Contextual Spheres Involved in Family Communication

families need to exhibit change as well to continue to integrate with those changing contexts.

Based on their model, Ballard-Reisch and Weigel (1999) and Weigel and Ballard-Reisch (2004) draw several principles about families: (1) The impact of contextual spheres on families will change over time, (2) family communication may be manifested differently depending on context, (3) families will both shape and be shaped by various contextual spheres, (4) the development of family will be affected by how well the family fits its contextual environment, (5) family communication patterns will be reassessed and often reconstructed at times of normative and nonnormative change, and (6) the impact of previous family/context interactions and events on current communication patterns may be direct or indirect. Thus, the contribution of the dynamic contextualism model is focusing attention on the dynamic aspects of context in the construction and maintenance of family communication patterns.

Grounded Theory of Family Life Model

Taking a different approach to developing a family model, Stamp (2004) constructed a grounded theory model by systematically identifying the most common concepts used in family literature published from 1990 to 2001 and grouping those concepts into related categories (see Figure 4.5).

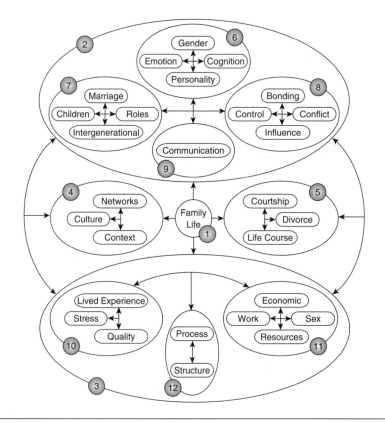

Figure 4.5   A Grounded Theory Model of Family Life

The emergent model consisted of four underlying components: (1) substance, (2) form, (3) space, and (4) time (Stamp, 2004). The first component, substance, represents the essential parts or elements of the family. These essential parts are composed of individual, relationship, and communication characteristics of families. The second component, form, or the configuration or shape of the family, concerns the structure, activities, and interactive patterns of families. Stamp (2004) defines the third component as space, which represents "the area, both literally and figuratively, in which the family resides. . . . This would include the external environment, social conditions, cultural effects, and people external to the family unit" (p. 20). The final component is time, which represents the ongoing change and development of the family.

The grounded theory model has the advantage of being expressively centered in current research and theory on family communication. As such, the model offers both a reflection of current research and a guide for future work.

Observations on Family Models

Concerning the theoretical grounding of the models we have reviewed, we find the following:

1. The majority of models reported here are firmly grounded in theory and research. The most common theoretical perspectives are systems and developmental, with a strong emphasis on the process/dynamic nature of families.

2. The majority of the models considered in this chapter emphasize the family process approach and focus on family management of change and growth, including the management of crisis and chronic events and life span issues.

Concerning the research and measurement issues related to the models in the chapter, we find the following:

1. Of the five models widely used in the family literature, four were developed for use and have been widely tested in clinical settings. This has resulted in well-established research programs within specific universities and research units that systematically promote their use, elaborate and test their efficacy with families facing a variety of issues, refine their measurement instruments, and test their appropriateness for assessing a variety of different types of families.

2. Four of the five widely used models approach measurement from the perspective of both family "insiders," family members who fill out self-report measures of their perceptions of family interaction and dynamics, and family "outsiders," typically clinicians who assess the family based on observation.

3. Model and method development is an evolutionary process, and those models widely in use are constantly refined and clarified, as are their measurement instruments and approaches.

Directions for Future
Model Development and Research

As with theories, family communication models illuminate some issues while obscuring others. There are a number of issues that family communication models could further illuminate.

As it is likely that families in clinical settings may differ in fundamental ways from those not in clinical settings, family communication models should be developed and tested more extensively with nonclinical families. Because most research on family contexts has occurred in clinical settings, it would be useful to supplement this research with that conducted with families in naturalistic settings to assess whether models developed in clinical practice translate well to nonclinical families.

Models designed to stimulate research into the unique dynamics of multiple family types would broaden our understanding of families. Systematic exploration of any unique family communication dynamics in dual-career families, single-parent families, families with lesbian and gay members, blended-culture and blended-race families, multigenerational families, and so on would be useful.

Research is needed to more systematically examine the relational constellations within families and their impacts on one another—specifically how individual, dyadic, triadic, and family-level communication patterns affect and influence one another. Significant steps have been made in a number of these areas, and the process of synthesizing them into an understanding of family dynamics will continue to be illuminating.

Family characteristics typically seen as useful for segmenting families into "types" might be usefully conceptualized as irreducible elements of families, not just as categories for comparison among families. For example, having a family member with a disability is not simply a category that sets some families apart from others. It may conversely be an inherent component of family identity and significantly affect how the family sees and negotiates its place in the world and the communication patterns that result. Communication models designed to examine these family types would be welcome.

If scholars desire that their models be used in family communication research, it is prudent that they develop valid and reliable measures of model components and dynamics. Future family communication models should also incorporate collaborations with other disciplines that will enrich understanding of the dynamics of family communication. These models could include contributions by physiologists who are capable of measuring changes in body indicators, such as temperature, heart rate, and respiration, as family members engage in communication (Floyd, 2004) and energy field researchers who are currently developing technology that allows for the observation of interactions among family members on an energy level (Leigh, 2004). In addition, as researchers have long argued for the prominence of nonverbal factors to meaning in communication, models designed to explain the nonverbal components of family communication need much more thorough investigation

Conclusion

Grounded in well-established theoretical perspectives, the conceptual and mathematical models discussed in this chapter have led to a robust body of research into the study of family communication. The models discussed in this chapter clearly support the definition of models as representations of the structural or functional properties of theories (Littlejohn, 1990; Smith, 1988) used to understand specific problems in particular settings or contexts (Earp & Ennett, 1991). The literature reviewed in this chapter also clearly illustrates that models and research mutually inform one another. The most widely used models are continually refined and revised, along with their measurement instruments and protocols, based on the results of research. Research questions are then modified based on these model refinements, and the process continues.

The majority of the models reviewed in this chapter are also represented in a "diagrammatic form" that illustrates "the relationships among a number of variables" (Doherty et al., 1993, p. 20) and narrows "both research questions and targets of intervention" (Earp & Ennett, 1991, p. 163).

While the models reviewed here were often developed and studied within clinical contexts, a growing body of research also focuses on diverse family forms and families in nonclinical settings. Models need to be developed to explain the unique processes in such families. In addition, a clear need to supplement traditional approaches to family communication that emphasize predominantly verbal patterns is noted, as is the potential for collaboration among disciplines. The development of new models emphasizing these issues or the expansion of existing models to include them will only enhance the comprehensiveness of research inquiries into family communication dynamics.

References

Ballard-Reisch, D. S., & Weigel, D. J. (1999). Communication processes in marital commitment: An integrative approach. In W. H. Jones & J. M. Adams (Eds.), *Handbook of interpersonal commitment and relationship stability* (pp. 377–394). New York: Plenum.

Ballard-Reisch, D. S., Weigel, D. J., & Zaguidoulline, M. G. (1999). Relational maintenance behaviors, marital satisfaction, and commitment in Tatar, Russian, and mixed Russian-Tatar marriages: An exploratory analysis. *Journal of Family Issues, 20,* 677–698.

Barnes, H., & Olson, D. H. (1982). Parent-adolescent *communication* scale. In D. H. Olson, H. I. McCubbin, H. Barnes, A. Larsen, M. Muxen, & M. Wilson (Eds.), *Family inventories* (pp. 33–48). St. Paul: Family Social Science, University of Minnesota.

Barney, M. C. & Max, J. E. (September, 2005). The McMaster family assessment device and clinical rating scale: Questionnaire vs interview in childhood traumatic brain injury. *Brain Injury. 19,* 801–809

Baxter, L. A., & Clark, C. L. (1996). Perceptions of family communication patterns and the enactment of family rituals. *Western Journal of Communication, 60,* 254–286.

Beavers, R., & Hampson, R. B. (2000). The Beavers systems model of family functioning. *Journal of Family Therapy, 22*, 128–143.

Beavers, W. B., & Hampson, R. B. (1990). *Successful families: Assessment and intervention.* New York: Norton.

Beavers, W. B., & Hampson, R. B. (1993). Measuring family competence: The Beavers systems model. In F. Walsh (Ed.), *Normal family processes* (pp. 73–95). New York: Guilford.

Bergen, H. A., Martin, G., Richardson, A. S., Allison, S., & Roeger, L. (2004). Sexual abuse, antisocial behaviour and substance use: Gender differences in young community adolescents. *Australian & New Zealand Journal of Psychiatry, 38*, 34–42.

Bishop, D. S., Epstein, N., Keitner, G., Miller, I., & Zlotnick, C. (1980). *The McMaster structures interview for family functioning.* Providence, RI: Brown University Family Research Program.

Brehaut, J. C., Kohen, D. E., Raina, P., Walter, S. D., Russell, D. J., Swinton, M., O'Donnell, M., & Rosenbaum, P. (2004). The health of primary caregivers of children with cerebral palsy: How does it compare with that of other Canadian caregivers? *Pediatrics, 114*, 182–192.

Bronfenbrenner, U. (1979). *The ecology of human development.* Cambridge, MA: Harvard University Press.

Bronfenbrenner, U. (1989). Ecological systems theory. In R. Vasta (Ed.), *Annals of Child Development* (Vol. 6, pp. 187–249). Greenwich, CT: JAI.

Clark, M. S. (1999). The double ABCX model of family crisis as a representation of family functioning after rehabilitation from stroke. *Psychology, Health & Medicine, 4*, 203–221.

Clark, M. S., Rubenach, S., & Winsor, A. (2003). A randomized controlled trial of an education and counseling intervention for families after stroke. *Clinical Rehabilitation, 17*, 703–713.

Cook, W. L. (2001). Interpersonal influence in family systems: A social relations model analysis. *Child Development, 72*, 1179–1197.

Cook, W. L., & Kenny, D. A. (2004). Application of the social relations model to family assessment. *Journal of Family Psychology, 18*, 361–371.

Cordova, J. V., Gee, C. B., & Warren, L. Z. (2005). Emotional skillfulness in marriage: Intimacy as a mediator of the relationship between emotional skillfulness and marital satisfaction. *Journal of Social & Clinical Psychology, 24*, 218–236.

Doherty, W. J., Boss, P. G., LaRossa, R., Schumm, W. R., & Steinmetz, S. K. (1993). Family theories and methods: A contextual approach. In P. G. Boss, W. J. Doherty, R. LaRossa, W. S. Schumm, & S. Steinmetz (Eds.), *Sourcebook of family theories and methods: A contextual approach* (pp. 3–30). New York: Plenum.

Drumm, M., Carr, A., & Fitzgerald, M. (2000). The Beavers, McMaster and Circumplex clinical rating scales: A study of their sensitivity, specificity and discriminant validity. *Journal of Family Therapy, 22*, 225–239.

Earp, J. A., & Ennett, S. T. (1991). Conceptual models for health education research and practice. *Health Education Research: Theory and Practice, 6*, 163–171.

Elwood, T. D., & Schrader, D. C. (1998). Family communication patterns and communication apprehension. *Journal of Social Behavior and Personality, 13*, 493–502.

Enns, R. A., Reddon, J. R., & McDonald, L. (1999). Indications of resilience among family members of people admitted to a psychiatric facility. *Psychiatric Rehabilitation Journal, 23*, 127–135.

Epstein, N. B., Bishop, D. S., Ryan, C., Miller, I., & Keitner, G. (1993). The McMaster model: View of healthy family functioning. In F. Walsh (Ed.), *Normal family processes* (2nd ed., pp. 138–160). New York: Guilford.

Fischer, J., & Corcoran, K. (1994). *Measures for clinical practice: A sourcebook* (Vol. 1). New York: Free Press.

Fitzpatrick, M. A., & Koerner, A. F. (1996, July). *Family communication schemata and social functions of communication.* Paper presented at the International Research Colloquium on Communication Research, Moscow, Russia.

Fitzpatrick, M. A., & Ritchie, L. D. (1994). Communication schemata within the family: Multiple perspectives on family interaction. *Human Communication Research, 20,* 275–301.

Floyd, K. (2004). An introduction to the uses and potential uses of physiological measurement in the study of family communication. *Journal of Family Communication, 4,* 295–318.

Friedmann, M., McDermot, W., Woloman, D., Ryan, C., Keitner, G., & Miller, I. (1997). A comparison of psychiatric and nonclinical families. *Family Process, 36,* 357–367.

Gaughan, E. (1995). Family assessment in psychoeducational evaluations: Case studies with the Family Adaptability and Cohesion Evaluation Scales. *Journal of School Psychology, 33,* 7–28.

Gottman, J. M., Ryan, K., Swanson, C., & Swanson, K. (2005). Proximal change experiments with couples: A methodology for empirically building a science of effective interventions for changing couples' interaction. *Journal of Family Communication, 5,* 163–189.

Gottman, J. M., Swanson, C., & Swanson, K. (2002). A general systems theory of marriage: Nonlinear difference equation modeling of marital interaction. *Personality and Social Psychology Review, 6,* 326–340.

Hage, J. (1972). *Techniques and problems of theory construction in sociology.* New York: John Wiley.

Han, H. (2003). Issues and innovations in nursing practice: Korean mothers' psychosocial adjustment to their children's cancer. *Journal of Advanced Nursing, 11,* 499–504.

Hawes, L. C. (1975). *Pragmatics of analoguing: Theory and model construction in communication.* Reading, MA: Addison-Wesley.

Hayden, L. S., Schiller, M., Dickstein, S., Seifer, R., Sameroff, A. J., Miller, I., Keitner, G., & Rasmussen, S. (1998). Levels of family assessment: 1. Family, marital, and parent-child interaction. *Journal of Family Psychology, 12,* 7–22.

Heider, F. (1946). Attitudes and cognitive organization. *Journal of Psychology, 21,* 107–112.

Heider, F. (1958). *The psychology of interpersonal relations.* New York: John Wiley.

Hemple, C. G. (1952). *Fundamentals of concept formation in empirical science.* Chicago: University of Chicago Press.

Hill, R. (1949). *Families under stress.* New York: Harper & Row.

Hill, R. (1958). Generic features of families under stress. *Social Case Work, 49,* 139–150.

Hill, R. (1970). *Family development in three generations.* Cambridge, MA: Schenkman.

Kashy, D. A., & Kenny, D. A. (1990). Analysis of family research designs: A model of interdependence. *Communication Research, 17,* 462–482.

Katz, S., & Krulik, T. (1999). Fathers of children with chronic illness: Do they differ from fathers of healthy children? *Journal of Family Nursing, 5,* 292–316.

Kerlinger, F. N. (1986). *Foundations of behavioral research* (3rd ed.). New York: Holt, Rinehart and Winston.

Klein, D. M., & White, J. M. (1996). *Family theories, an introduction.* Thousand Oaks, CA: Sage.

Koerner, A. F., & Cvancara, K. E. (2002). The influence of conformity orientation on communication patterns in family conversations. *Journal of Family Communication, 2,* 132–152.

Koerner, A. F., & Fitzpatrick, M. A. (1997). Family type and conflict: The impact of conversation orientation and conformity orientation on conflict in the family. *Communication Studies, 48,* 59–75.

Koerner, A. F., & Fitzpatrick, M. A. (2002a). Toward a theory of family communication. *Communication Theory, 12,* 70–91.

Koerner, A. F., & Fitzpatrick, M. A. (2002b). You never leave your family in a fight: The impact of families of origin on conflict-behavior in romantic relationships. *Communication Studies, 53*, 234–251.

Koerner, A. F., & Fitzpatrick, M. A. (2004). Communication in intact families. In A. L. Vangelisti (Ed.), *Handbook of family communication* (pp. 177–195). Mahwah, NJ: Lawrence Erlbaum.

Leigh, G. K. (2004). Incorporating human energy fields into studies of family communication. *Journal of Family Communication, 4*, 319–336.

Lerner, R. M. (1995). Developing individuals within changing contexts: Implications of developmental contextualism for human development research, policy, and programs. In T. A. Kindermann & J. Valsiner (Eds.), *Development of person-context relations* (pp. 13–37). Hillsdale, NJ: Lawrence Erlbaum.

Littlejohn, S. W. (1990). *Theories of human communication* (2nd ed.). Belmont, CA: Wadsworth.

Littlejohn, S. W. (1992). *Theories of human communication* (4th ed.). Belmont, CA: Wadsworth.

McCubbin, H. I., Cauble, A. E., & Patterson, J. M. (1982). *Family stress, coping, and social support*. Springfield, IL: Charles C Thomas.

McCubbin, H. I., Comeau, J. K., & Harkins, J. (1987). Family Inventory of Resources for Management (FIRM). In H. I. McCubbin & A. I. Thompson (Eds.), *Family assessment inventories for research and practice* (pp. 159–160). Madison: University of Wisconsin Press.

McCubbin, H. I., Olson, D. H., & Larsen, A. S. (1987). Family Crisis Oriented Personal Scales (F-COPES). In H. I. McCubbin & A. I. Thompson (Eds.), *Family assessment inventories for research and practice* (pp. 206–207). Madison: University of Wisconsin Press.

McCubbin, H. I., & Patterson, J. M. (1983). The family stress process: The double ABCX model of adjustment and adaptation. In H. I. McCubbin, M. B. Sussman, & J. M. Patterson (Eds.), *Social stress and the family: Advances and developments in family stress theory and research* (pp. 7–37). New York: Haworth.

McCubbin, H. I., & Patterson, J. M. (1987). FILE: Family Inventory of Life Events and Changes. In H. I. McCubbin & A. I. Thompson (Eds.), *Family assessment inventories for research and practice* (pp. 79–98). Madison: University of Wisconsin Press.

McCubbin, H. I., Thompson, A. I., & McCubbin, M. A. (1996). CHIP: Coping health inventory for parents. In H. I. McCubbin, A. I. Thompson, & M. A. McCubbin (Eds.), *Family assessment: Resiliency, coping and adaptation: Inventories for research and practice* (pp. 407–447). Madison: University of Wisconsin Press.

McCubbin, M. A. (1987). CHIP: Coping Health Inventory for Parents. In H. I. McCubbin & A. I. Thompson (Eds.), *Family assessment inventories for research and practice* (pp. 173–192). Madison: University of Wisconsin Press.

Miller, I. W., Kabacoff, R. I., Epstein, N. B., Bishop, D. S., Keitner, G. I., Baldwin, L. M., & van der Spuy, H. I. J. (1994). The development of a clinical rating scale for the McMaster model of family functioning. *Family Process, 33*, 53–69.

Miller, I. W., Ryan, C. E., Keitner, G. I., Bishop, D. S., & Epstein, N. B. (2000). The McMaster approach to families: Theory, assessment, treatment and research. *Journal of Family Therapy, 22*, 168–189.

Mu, P. F. (2005). Paternal reactions to a child with epilepsy: Uncertainty, coping strategies, and depression. *Journal of Advanced Nursing, 49*, 367–371.

Olson, D. H. (1986). Circumplex model VII: Validation studies and FACES III. *Family Process, 25*, 337–351.

Olson, D. H. (1990). *Clinical rating scale for circumplex model*. St. Paul, MN: University of Minnesota, Family Social Science.

Olson, D. H. (1993). Circumplex model of marital and family systems: Assessing family functioning. In F. Walsh (Ed.), *Normal family processes* (2nd ed., pp. 104–133). New York: Guilford.

Olson, D. H. (1996). Clinical assessment and treatment interventions using the circumplex model. In F. W. Kaslow (Ed.), *Handbook of relational diagnosis and dysfunctional family patterns* (pp. 59–80). New York: John Wiley.

Olson, D. H. (1997). *PREPARE/ENRICH program: Version 2000.* Minneapolis, MN: Life Innovations.

Olson, D. H. (2000). Circumplex model of marital and family systems. *Journal of Family Therapy, 22,* 144–167.

Olson, D., Portner, J., & Lavee, Y. (1985). *FACES III.* St. Paul: University of Minnesota, Family Social Science.

Olson, D. H., Russell, C. S., & Sprenkle, D. H. (1989). *Circumplex model: Systemic assessment and treatment of families.* New York: Haworth.

Pakenham, K. I., Sofronoff, K., & Samios, C. (2004). Finding meaning in parenting a child with Asperger syndrome: Correlates of sense making and benefit finding. *Research in Developmental Disabilities, 25,* 245–265.

Plunkett, S. W., & Sanchez, M. G. (1997). The double ABCX model and children's post-divorce adaptation. *Journal of Divorce & Remarriage, 27,* 17–38.

Ritchie, L. D. (1991). Family communication patterns: An epistemic analysis and conceptual reinterpretation. *Communication Research, 18,* 548–565.

Ritchie, L. D. (1997). Patients' workplace experiences and family communication patterns. *Communication Research, 24,* 175–187.

Ritchie, L. D., & Fitzpatrick, M. A. (1990). Family communication patterns: Measuring intrapersonal perceptions of interpersonal relationships. *Communication Research, 17,* 523–544.

Saloviita, T., Itälinna, M., & Leinonen, E. (2003). Explaining the parental stress of fathers and mothers caring for a child with intellectual disability: A double ABCX model. *Journal of Intellectual Disability Research, 47,* 300–313.

Shin, J. Y., & Crittenden, K. S. (2003). Well-being of mothers of children with mental retardation: An evaluation of the double ABCX model in a cross-cultural context. *South Asian Journal of Social Psychology, 6,* 171–185.

Shir, J. S. (1999). Battered women's perceptions and expectations of their current and ideal marital relationship. *Journal of Family Violence, 14,* 71–83.

Smith, M. J. (1988). *Contemporary communication research methods.* Belmont, CA: Wadsworth.

Stamp, G. H. (2004). Theories of family relationships and a family relationships theoretical model. In A. L. Vangelisti (Ed.), *Handbook of family communication* (pp. 1–30). Mahwah, NJ: Lawrence Erlbaum.

Streisand, R., Kazak, A. E., & Tercyak, K. P. (2003). Pediatric-specific parenting stress and family functioning in parents of children treated for cancer. *Children's Health Care, 32,* 245–257.

Studman, L. J., Roberts, C. M., Hay, D., & Kane, R. T. (2003). Development and evaluation of a program designed to facilitate family adaptation in families with a child who has a disability. *Australian Journal of Psychology, 55*(Suppl.), 214–216.

Thompson-Hayes, M., & Webb, L. M. (2004). Theory in progress: Commitment under construction: A dyadic and communicative model of marital commitment. *Journal of Family Communication, 4,* 249–261.

von Bertalanffy, L. (1968). *General system theory: Foundations, development, applications.* New York: G. Braziller.

Walsh, F. (1993). Conceptualization of normal family processes. In F. Walsh (Ed.), *Normal family processes* (2nd ed., pp. 3–69). New York: Guilford.

Warner, R. M., Kenny, D. A., & Stoto, M. (1979). A new round-robin analysis of variance for social interaction data. *Journal of Personality and Social Psychology, 37,* 1742–1757.

Weger, H. (2005). Disconfirming communication and self-verification in marriage: Associations among the demand/withdraw interaction pattern, feeling understood, and marital satisfaction. *Journal of Social & Personal Relationships, 22,* 19–32.

Weigel, D. J., & Ballard-Reisch, D. S. (2004, November). *The role of context in relationship development: Contributions of a dynamic contextualism perspective.* Paper presented at Theory Construction and Research Methodology Workshop, National Council on Family Relations, Orlando, FL.

White, F. A., & Matawie, K. M. (2004). Parental morality and family processes as predictors of adolescent morality. *Journal of Child & Family Studies, 13,* 219–234.

CHAPTER 5

Methodological Approaches to the Study of Family Communication

Sandra Metts

Illinois State University

Emily Lamb

University of Nebraska–Lincoln

This chapter provides a profile of methods used to investigate family communication structures, processes, and effects. Given the broad, interdisciplinary interest in family communication, it is not surprising that methods are diverse, including quantitative as well as naturalistic, qualitative designs. We review relevant methods, describing each briefly, illustrating its application in the family domain using research exemplars and reflecting on design issues. Before discussing quantitative methods, however, we address the definitional scope of this chapter.

The question of how "family" should be defined is an important concern in family communication research. Variables of interest, questions or hypotheses advanced, samples used, and the type of data collected are all framed by researchers' notions of what constitutes family. Definitions of family vary a great deal in the scholarly literature and among the ordinary population. For example, some definitions locate family within the constraints of legal (e.g., marriage, remarriage, adoption) or biological (parent/child, grandparents) parameters (Noller & Fitzpatrick, 1993; Chapter 2, this volume). Other approaches suggest that legal and biological constraints are restrictive and endorse the notion that the family unit is a particular type of social system characterized by temporal, physical, and emotional interdependence. For example, Yerby, Buerkel-Rothfuss, and Bochner (1998) define family as

> a *multigenerational* social *system* consisting of at least two *interdependent* people bound together by a common living *space* (at one time or another) and a common *history,* and who share some degree of emotional *attachment to* or *involvement with* one another. (p. 13)

Some scholars privilege personal rather than legal or structural definitions by family members (e.g., Galvin, Bylund, & Brommel, 2004; Chapter 1, this volume). Such approaches focus on the constitutive role of communication in constructing family units. For example, Turner and West (2002) define family as

> a self-defined group of intimates who create and maintain themselves through their own interactions and their interactions with others; a family may include both voluntary and involuntary relationships; it creates both literal and symbolic internal and external boundaries, and it evolves through time. (p. 8)

For our purposes here, it is less important that we align with a particular conceptual definition of family than that we offer an operational definition that focuses our review. We examined any study that specifically addresses family communication, parental communication, or sibling communication. We set no boundaries on the type of family represented. We did, however, exclude studies of marital communication when they focus exclusively on interactions of a couple. While married and unmarried cohabiting couples can be considered a family unit, the methods used to investigate their communication fall beyond the scope of this review (see Noller & Feeney, 2004, for a summary of couple communication).

We turn now to a discussion of quantitative methods. As evident in the relatively greater length of the quantitative section compared to the qualitative, the historical preference in family research has been the use of quantitative methods. As Stamp (2004) reports in his analysis of 1,245 family communication articles published between 1990 and 2001, more than 90% were empirical investigations. As a way to organize the broad scope of quantitative work in family communication, we first review two types of data used, self-report and interactional. We note the advantages and challenges of each and then address common research designs employing both types of data.

Quantitative Methods

As is common in the social sciences in general, quantitative research in family communication tends to rely on self-report data provided by convenience samples of family members. Although national samples are occasionally available, the more common practice is to obtain retrospective accounts of family communication practices from college students, sometimes asking them to distribute questionnaires to other family members. In addition, recent approaches to family communication quantify interactional data, usually from videotaped interactions between parents, between parents and children, and between family members and research interviewers. Once units of conceptual interest are identified, they can be coded and counted to represent frequencies within categories. They can also be rated on message qualities such as intensity, coerciveness, or supportiveness by trained coders or family members. These values can then be used to construct a description of family interaction patterns.

Self-Report Data

The prevailing approach to self-report methods in family communication is to ask respondents to complete a questionnaire that measures various dimensions of their "typical" family communication patterns or practices. Several instruments have been used widely in family communication research and demonstrate strong reliability and validity (Fiese et al., 2002).

One commonly used scale to measure interaction quality between parents and children is the Parent-Adolescent Communication Scale (PACS) (Barnes & Olson, 1982, 1985). The PACS consists of 20 items for mother-child interactions and 20 items for father-child interactions (e.g., "When I ask questions, I get honest answers from my mother/father") followed by Likert scales (*strongly disagree* to *strongly agree*). Ten items assess positive communication practices, and 10 items assess negative communication practices. These two dimensions of communication quality are referred to as *open* and *problem*. The scale has been used successfully by a number of researchers, and its reliability has even been confirmed in a sample of Dutch adolescents (13–15 years old) (Jackson, Bijstra, Oostra, & Bosma, 1998).

Another widely used instrument is the Family Communication Patterns (FCP) scale. As originally constructed by McLeod and Chaffee (1972), the FCP items represent two dimensions characterizing family communication: a *socio-orientation* (directing communication toward other people) and a *concept orientation* (directing communication toward objects and ideas). The socio-orientation dimension reflects absolute or unquestioned parental/adult authority. The concept orientation dimension reflects open discussion of issues and questioning of others' opinions. These two dimensions can be used separately as continuous variables to assign a concept orientation and a socio-orientation score to each respondent. Alternatively, the dimensions can be crossed to form four quadrants, and families can be assigned to a category type based on relatively high or low scores on each dimension. Families that are high on concept orientation and low on socio-orientation are termed *pluralistics*. Families low on concept orientation and high on socio-orientation are termed *protectives*. Families high on both dimensions are considered *consensuals*, and families low on both are considered *laissez-faires*.

Based on concern over the face validity of several items intended to measure the original dimensions, Ritchie and Fitzpatrick (1990) revised the scale and reconceptualized the dimensions as *conformity orientation* and *conversation orientation*. According to Fitzpatrick and Ritchie, *conformity orientation* is a more apt label than *socio-orientation* for parental messages that emphasize parents' use of power or authority to compel a child's conformity. Likewise, they argue that *conversation orientation* is a better label than *concept orientation* for parental messages that emphasize parents' restraint on their own power, encouraging children to express their ideas with interpersonal tact and concern for harmonious relationships.

The validity and reliability of the Revised Family Communication Patterns (RFCP) scale has been established in several studies (Fitzpatrick, Marshall, Leutwiler, & Krçmar, 1996; Fujioka, 2002; Koesten, 2004; Ritchie, 1991), and the instrument has been used successfully in combination with established measures. For example, Fitzpatrick and Ritchie (1994) factor analyzed scores on the FCP and the Relational Dimensions Inventory gathered through telephone interviews with a large sample of families. Three factors emerged (expressiveness, structural traditionalism, and avoidance) and form the basis of the Family Communication Environment Scale.

Advantages

Self-report measures are an efficient, flexible tool for family researchers. They are efficient in that they can be administered to large samples in a variety of contexts, including in classrooms, homes, or labs; conducted over the telephone; sent via regular mail, or sent via electronic mail. Self-report measures are flexible because they can be structured in a variety of formats to provide researchers with the type of information they seek. For example, researcher-generated items can be followed by response formats that assess message frequency (e.g., never to always), message importance (not at all important to extremely important), or message qualities (e.g., confirming, disconfirming, supportive). Such measures provide estimates of the frequency, consistency, or extent to which certain types of targeted messages occur during family interactions, at least as recalled by family members. Furthermore, open-ended questions can be used to solicit respondent-generated descriptions to be coded and counted by researchers.

Perhaps the most important conceptual advantage of self-report measures is that they provide researchers with "insider" information about communication practices that would not typically be available from observations. Some actions (e.g., loss of temper or severe criticism) are not likely to be displayed, and certain topics (e.g., parental messages about sexual conduct) are not likely to be captured on tape but might be reported in confidence by family members. Furthermore, much of the constitutive power of communication resides in family members' perceptions of and emotional reactions to messages. These interpretations are shaped by a long history of interaction practices. The distinction between family rituals and routines, for example, indicates that routines are easily observed because they are repeated and instrumental, whereas rituals are more symbolic, affective, and meaningful only to insiders (Fiese et al., 2002).

Challenges

One challenge inherent in self-reports of family communication patterns is that they necessarily reflect generalized and recollected impressions rather than actual occurrence of behaviors. As a consequence, estimates of message production are likely to be consistent with mental schema such as family scripts, parental role schema, or social desirability bias (e.g., "good" parents would speak this way). In addition, family members engaged in spontaneous, routine, or problematic interactions are not always aware of or willing to report the types of messages they are actually producing. Message awareness is particularly limited when nonverbal elements such as eye gaze, facial expression, vocal tone, volume, rate, and pitch are salient criteria in determining message form, function, and consequence. In sum, if researchers' questions are clearly concerned with perceived or recollected communication patterns, then self-report data are appropriate. However, when researchers offer conclusions about actual communication patterns in the family, these claims are limited by the perceptual nature of self-report data.

A second challenge is that self-reports necessarily present one respondent's perception, even if the items refer to other family members. Thus, parents' or adult children's reports of overall family communication may obscure important differences among family members. For instance, Raffaelli et al. (1999) found that congruence between mothers and their teenage children on whether various topics about sexuality had been discussed showed remarkable diversity, ranging from only 32% agreement on birth control to 84% agreement on dating. Hartos and Power (2000) used canonical correlations to assess the congruence between mothers' and adolescents' (ninth-grade) reports of family communication practices (PACS) and the child's adjustment (Child Behavior Checklist). Results indicated that within-rater correlations were generally higher than cross-rater correlations (i.e., between mother and child), suggesting that quality of communication and amount of aggression reported by mothers and adolescents were largely independent.

A third challenge of self-report measures arises when young children are included in the sample. Although college students and most high school students can complete instruments such as the PACS and the FCP, younger children may require an assessment instrument that is appropriate to their level of comprehension. In some cases, interviewers can ask children questions in simple words and then record their answers on the assessment instrument. Another approach is to use storybook protocols where children can say what a character like himself or herself or like Mom or Dad would do in a situation. For example, Fitzpatrick et al. (1996) created "talking picture books" to help children in Grades 1, 4, 6, and 7 respond to situations based on the revised FCP scale. After hearing audiotapes of dinnertime conversations and seeing the picture book, children responded to questions about their own parents' communication by pointing to boxes on a prompt card—the largest box if the family is "a lot like your family," the middle box if the family is "a little bit like your family," and the smallest box if the family "is not at all like your family."

Interactional Data

In the same way that self-report methods reflect diversity in instrumentation and analysis, quantitative studies of actual interaction reflect a variety of coding instruments and assessment protocols. Various units of analysis, such as nonverbal displays, speech acts, pairs of turns, or conversational episodes, are often coded and counted. In addition, observers and/or family members may be asked to rate actual behavior on some quality (e.g., message clarity or supportiveness) using Likert scales. Data derived from interactional coding can also be used as an antecedent or correlate of other variables such as family satisfaction or children's social adjustment by incorporating self-report data from other family members, teachers, or children's peers.

Several interactional coding systems are available to researchers, each focused in a particular type of conversational behavior. For example, Stiles's (1992) Verbal Response Mode (VRM) is designed for trained observers to code verbal units into one of eight speech act categories: disclosure, edification, advice, confirmation, question, acknowledgment, interpretation, and reflection. The reliability of this instrument for family research has been demonstrated in a number of studies, most recently in a study by Sillars, Koerner, and Fitzpatrick (2005) using 50 parent-child triads who engaged in problem-solving discussions.

Nonverbal behaviors are also coded. Siegel, Friedlander, and Heatherington (1992) adapted the Family Relational Communication Control Coding System (FRCCCS) for use in coding nonverbal control moves in family conversations. The FRCCCS extends symmetrical, complementary, transitory interact control moves of dyadic (marital) interactions to include triadic moves (e.g., coalitionary moves when a speaker goes one-up to one party and one-down to the other). Siegel et al. conducted three studies to (a) generate a nonverbal equivalent of the FRCCCS using relational communication experts, graduate students, and naive adults; (b) confirm reliability and utility of a coding manual using videotape and transcripts of family interactions; and (c) confirm validity by also coding verbal control moves for comparison.

Jacob and Johnson's (2001) revision of the Marital Interaction Coding system for discussions between children and parents uses both verbal and nonverbal cues to sort statements into three broad categories: positivity (agree, approve, assent, humor, smile or laugh, and talk), negativity (criticize, disagree, put down, and negative response), and problem solving (problem description, question, command, and solution). A base rate per minute can be calculated by dividing the number of positive and negative messages by the number of minutes of interaction. Kappa scores can then be used to determine whether positive or negative responses differed from the base rate.

Advantages

The principal advantage of interactional analysis for family researchers is that it allows assessment of actual message behavior embedded in naturally occurring conversation—at least in conversations targeted by the researcher. Behaviors that may not be recognized or recalled in self-report instruments can be coded and counted.

A second advantage is that the analysis of ongoing interaction provides a unique tool for determining both sequential and contingent patterns of message exchange during various types of episodes. These estimates allow researchers to determine, for example, how likely a parent is to produce a certain type of message with a son versus a daughter or how likely a certain parental message is to elicit a particular response from a child. Longitudinal data are particularly useful in determining contingent patterns (Ely, Gleason, & McCabe, 1996). Reese, Haden, and Fivush (1996) collected conversational data from 17 families (with 3- to 5-year-olds) over a 30-month period. Based on conditional probabilities, they concluded that over time, mothers, but not fathers, increased their elaboration responses to their preschool children's descriptions of past events.

A third advantage of quantifying interaction is that it affords researchers the opportunity to link communicative patterns with self-reports of perceptions and affective responses of family members. Using the technique of video-assisted recall, family members can both observe and respond to messages exchanged in an interactional context. Trees (2000, 2002) performed two studies of emotional support episodes between mothers and adult children (college students) as they discussed important relational problems (not associated with the mother). In both studies, participants completed the Quality of Relationships Inventory prior to the discussion. After the discussion, children were shown portions of the videotape and asked to assess the quality of mothers' support using the Recipient Support Perception Scale. Independent coders also rated message qualities within the interaction. In Trees (2000), coders rated cues of nonverbal involvement and interactional synchrony. In Trees (2002), coders rated a broader array of elements, including nonverbal support-seeking behaviors (on semantic differential scales), verbal approach behaviors (1 to 6; almost none to extensive), mother's nonverbal involvement, and mother's verbal support provision behaviors (i.e., extent of nurturant, informational, and tangible support on 5-point scales).

Challenges

Researchers who quantify interaction also face challenges. First, they must decide the appropriate type of interaction to videotape, record, or observe. Researchers interested in questions about routine interactions typifying a family climate might use dinnertime conversations. However, researchers interested in certain types of interaction such as problem solving, social support, or conflict face the challenge of how to induce such episodes without losing ecological validity. One commonly used instrument to elicit problem-solving talk between parents and children is the Area of Change Questionnaire (ACQ) (e.g., Sillars et al., 2005; Slesnick & Waldron, 1997). Typically, parents and/or adolescents are asked to select one topic from a list of items they would like to change or that represent areas of disagreement (e.g., time spent together as a family, chores, criticism and appreciation, allowance, homework, friends). After 10 to 15 minutes of discussion, another family member chooses a new topic.

A second challenge is identifying the unit of analysis. As might be expected given the complexity of language, nonverbal signals, speech acts, conversational turn taking, and coconstructed meaning during interaction episodes, researchers' decisions regarding the observed behavior(s) to isolate are critical steps in the research process. Once the unit of analysis is isolated, researchers must decide how to use these units. Interactional units can be treated as categorical data and counted (e.g., frequency of one-up or one-down statements). Alternatively, interactional units (ranging from single statements to larger exchanges of talk) can be bracketed and then rated by trained coders on Likert scales to assess some type of message quality (e.g., positive/negative communicative behavior). As is true for any methodological decision, a coding decision is appropriate to the extent that it demonstrates reliability in its application, validity in its conceptualization, and utility in meeting the goals of the investigation.

Quantitative Research Designs

In general, quantitative designs used in family communication research reflect traditional methods of the social sciences. Group comparisons are used to determine whether a variable of interest is significantly different between or across groups. Associations among variables or correlational designs are done to determine whether variables of interest are systematically related to each other.

Group Comparisons: Experimental and Quasi-Experimental Designs

Group comparisons are an important research design for family communication researchers, allowing them to address the perennial questions of how communication functions in the family as a cause for or an effect of other circumstances. In true or full experimental designs, the assumption of causality can be tested because control of alternative explanations is high. The sample is randomly selected from the population, the independent variable is systematically manipulated, participants are randomly assigned to groups, and a pretest (or a control group) establishes a baseline to ensure that effects are linked to the manipulation. True experimental designs in family communication research are rare because it is difficult to meet all criteria for a true experimental design (Cummings & Cummings, 1995).

A more common procedure is to incorporate experimental manipulations as part of a larger study. For example, as part of a study on the effects of television violence on children's responses to interpersonal problems, Krçmar (1998) used a convenience sample of children recruited with parental permission from Grades K to 6 but randomly assigned them to view one of three clips from *Walker, Texas Ranger*. All of the clips showed acts of aggression, but the perpetrator's motivation and punishment for the violent act were manipulated. Children were asked by an interviewer if the man was right or wrong in his behavior and how right or wrong. They were then shown a small story booklet with captions and pictures to see if they would be more likely to select an aggressive or nonaggressive solution to an interpersonal problem (e.g., the child's lunch is stolen by the class bully). In addition, they completed a shortened and modified version of the FCP. Regression was used to determine whether the children's responses were predicted by the open or control dimensions in their family's communication.

In two studies of the effects of marital conflict on children, videotapes were constructed displaying either a mother or father initiating conflict and displaying one of 10 types of conflict tactics ranging from highly negative (physical aggression) to neutral (calm discussion) to highly positive (affection) (Cummings, Goeke-Morey, & Papp, 2004; Goeke-Morey, Cummings, Harold, & Shelton, 2003). Children were told to imagine that these couples were their parents and that they were in the room observing the conversation. After viewing each tape (randomly ordered in separate sessions), they were asked by interviewers to respond to a series of questions. These questions were designed to measure their reactions to the observed conflict.

Some researchers employ structural equation modeling (SEM) to establish causal relationships without necessarily using all aspects of a full experimental design. SEM draws from path analysis and allows a researcher to test (and rule out) alternative theoretical models explaining the results. For example, Mann and Gilliom (2002) used SEM and evaluated explanations for adjustment in adult children (college students) as a response to parental conflict during childhood. In a similar vein, Crokenberg and Langrock (2001) used SEM to test several possible explanations for associations among divorced parents' perception of family structure (actual and ideal view of family interaction patterns), parental feelings about the divorce (state vs. trait anger), and parent-child communication about the divorce.

Compared to true experimental designs, quasi-experimental designs, generally involving comparison of groups on some variable of interest, are far more common in the family communication literature. Groups tend to be naturally occurring (e.g., sons or daughters, birth parents or adoptive parents) or researcher constructed from self-report data (e.g., open or problem communication families). Large samples might be drawn from intact or divorced populations, but members of these groups cannot be randomly assigned to their respective conditions. As a result, researchers offer causal claims with caution. Although communication practices might indeed be statistically different between intact and divorced parents, it is impossible to know whether such differences may have caused the divorce or been caused by the divorce.

These reservations aside, quasi-experimental group comparisons provide valuable information about the antecedents and consequences of family communication. In general, two approaches characterize how communication variables are used in quasi-experimental designs: communication as the dependent variable and communication as the independent variable.

In studies using communication as the dependent variable, families are categorized according to a preexisting or exogenous variable that presumably influences family communication patterns. The defining characteristic serves as the independent variable (e.g., family structure), and the categories within it (e.g., intact first marriage, divorced not remarried, divorced remarried) serve as the levels. Dependent variables are self-reports of family communication practices, often augmented by measures of relational satisfaction, or children's attitudes, self-esteem, or social adjustment.

For example, a parental problem such as alcoholism is considered an exogenous variable that affects family communication and children's social adjustment. The Children of Alcoholics Screening Test (CAST) is a 30-item, yes/no response, self-report inventory assessing alcoholism of one's parents. Adult children (college student samples and/or their siblings) often complete this measure and are subsequently assigned to an "alcoholic parent" or "nonalcoholic parent" group.

Dependent measures compared across groups might include children's perceived communication competence (i.e., empathy, self-disclosure, interaction management, behavioral flexibility, and communication anxiety) (Grant, Rosenfeld, & Cissna, 2004) or perceived coping and social skills (i.e., emotional expressivity, emotional sensitivity, social expressivity, and social sensitivity) (Segrin & Menees, 1995).

Perhaps the most common independent variable in this tradition is change in family composition and structure. These studies tend to reflect, implicitly or explicitly, a view of the family as an "ecological system." Thus, events such as adopting a child, divorce, remarriage, and so forth introduce change into the family environment and motivate family members to maintain stability (in both self-identity and relationships) while accommodating to changing structures.

Grinwald (1995) compared three types of family structures: biological families, stepfamilies formed after death of a husband/father, and stepfamilies formed after divorce. As she expected, stepfamilies formed after a divorce exhibited the most problematic communication (measured on the PACS), especially for female adolescents. Lanz, Iafrate, Rosnati, and Scabini (1999) compared three types of family structures in an Italian sample: intact families, separated families, and intercountry adoptive families. Across the three types of family structures, adolescents in separated households experienced more communication difficulties (measured on the PACS) with both parents compared to the other family types, while adoptive adolescents experienced more positive communication with their parents than biological children.

In a study drawing explicitly on theory for its predictions, Afifi and Schrodt (2003) used uncertainty management theory to reason that in postdivorce families, individuals may prefer to maintain their uncertainty by avoiding some discussions. Large samples of both adolescents (12–18 years) and young adult college students (19–22 years) were categorized as members of first-marriage intact families, divorced remarried families, and divorced not remarried families. Dependent variables included perceptions of family members (e.g., emotions, attitudes, and values) and perceived accuracy of predictions about family members, state of the family (e.g., feelings about their parent or stepparent, household rules and expectations), closeness, and satisfaction.

Finally, although less common than comparisons of intact and divorced families, some research addresses the increasingly common change in family structure when parents require in-home care from their adult children. For example, Bethea (2002) found that communication satisfaction of spouses caring for a parent in their home was lower than that of demographically similar couples not caring for a parent in the home.

A second approach in quasi-experimental designs uses family communication patterns as the independent variable. Based on self-reports of communication practices completed by parents and/or children, family communication types are generated and used as levels for the independent variable. Outcomes such as relational satisfaction, children's feelings about themselves and other family members, or children's social adjustment (typically in school) are compared as dependent variables across family communication types.

This approach necessitates a two-step method for assigning participants (or families) to groups. Participants must first complete an instrument that measures communication patterns in their family. Researchers then use an appropriate statistic (typically a median split or standard deviation delimiters) to assign participants (or families) to appropriate categories within the typology.

The PACS and the FCP are frequently employed in categorizing family communication types (Fitzpatrick & Ritchie, 1994; Ritchie & Fitzpatrick, 1990). Fitzpatrick et al. (1996), for example, found differential effects on children's social behavior in school according to the family communication patterns experienced at home. The Family Environment Scale (FES) is also used to identify family types based on levels of conflict in the home. Toomey and Nelson (2001) found that adolescents' attitudes toward intimacy and number of sexual partners differed according to the conflict classification of their family.

Correlational and Regression Designs

Correlational designs are common in family communication research. Although they are not appropriate for testing causal links, they do provide the opportunity to assess variance that might be shared between variables and, when extended to regression analyses, to assess the amount of variance in a criterion variable contributed by predictor variables. Similar to group comparison designs, correlational designs position family communication as either a response to exogenous variables or as an antecedent influence on outcome variables such as children's self-esteem, social adjustment, or behavior outside of the home. Furthermore, correlational designs can be used to provide detailed profiles of message types, sequences, and interpretations that characterize family communication systems. These three formats are illustrated below.

In a study of the possible influence of parents' workplace norms on family communication patterns, Ritchie (1997) measured workplace norms experienced by parents and family communication patterns measured by the revised FCP scale. He found a strong correlation between these two variables.

A more common approach is to position family communication as an antecedent condition influencing children's behavior across a variety of contexts. Clark and Shields (1997) collected data from high school students who completed the PACS and the Self-Report Delinquency Scale. They found that open communication was associated with less frequent and less serious delinquency, especially for male adolescents. Ennett, Bauman, Foshee, Pemberton, and Hicks (2001) used a national sample of adolescent-parent pairs interviewed by telephone at two times a year apart. Unexpectedly, communication about rules and discipline predicted escalation of tobacco and alcohol use. The correlational design allowed the authors to confirm this association by ruling out a curvilinear relationship (i.e., that both high and low amounts of parental communication predicted tobacco and alcohol use).

Investigations using quantitative measures of interactional patterns also explore possible influences on children's behavior outside the home. Two alternative assumptions underlie these investigations. First, to the extent that children model their communication on what they observe at home (social learning theory), family interaction patterns might influence a child's communication with peers and other adults (Davies, Harold, Goeke-Morey, & Cummings, 2002). Second, to the extent that family interaction patterns influence children's self-esteem, self-confidence, attachment style, and social adjustment (Sheehan & Noller, 2002), family interaction patterns should have an indirect effect on their communication outside the home (Valiente, Fabes, Eisenberg, & Spinrad, 2004).

In an investigation of how the emotional climate communicated at home influences children's school adjustment, Boyum and Parke (1995) videotaped dinner conversations of 50 families with kindergarten children. Independent observers coded affect directed by family members to a specific partner using a modified version of Gottman's (1988) affect categories (e.g., humor/tease/laugh, excitement/ joy/surprise, happy/low-level positive/smile, low-level negative/disapproval, anger/mad/hostility, disgust/sarcasm). In addition, parents completed the Family Expressiveness Questionnaire (FEQ). Results indicated that both patterns of observed affect display and self-reported affect intensity and clarity were predictive of sociometric ratings of the children by classmates and teachers. Although studies indicating associations between family communication and outcome variables such as children's adjustment are convincing, scholars caution that findings from cross-sectional correlational designs should be confirmed with longitudinal research (Fincham, Grych, & Osborne, 1994).

Correlational designs are also used to generate profiles of the family system. Both self-report measures and coding of actual conversations (by trained observers and/or family members) can be correlated with measures of relevant constructs (e.g., family satisfaction, responses to conflict, perceptions of social support) to reveal how family members coconstruct their communication practices and family culture.

Researchers can generate family profiles in two general ways. First, they can collect data from family members using multiple measures: self-report data, trained coders' ratings of interactions, and members' evaluations of the same interactions. Sillars et al. (2005) used a sample of 50 parent-adolescent triads. Each person completed the ACQ prior to the interaction indicating what he or she would like to change and what he or she believed others wanted them to change. The triads then engaged in a problem-solving discussion. After the interaction, each family member viewed ten 30-second segments. Thought codes were solicited by asking each person what he or she was thinking and what he or she believed the other two family members were thinking. Family members then completed the revised FCP, a measure of adolescent self-concept, and a five-item relationship satisfaction scale. The conversations were transcribed and coded using the Verbal Response Mode coding system. Results indicated, among other patterns, that perceptions of conformity rather than open communication predicted parental understanding during the interaction.

A second approach to generating a profile of family communication systems is to use the social relations model (SRM) (see Chapter 4, this volume). According to Cook and Kenny (2004), the SRM "articulates the specific components of family relationships: the perceiver (or actor), the target (or partner), the relationship, and the family effects" (p. 361). Thus, it functions to help isolate important features of the family dynamic. A "problem" child, for example, might only be a problem during interactions with a particular parent, or sibling, or with all family members. A round-robin design allows assessment of each family member (as both actor and target), the combination of all possible dyads, and the total score for all combinations within the family. In a study using the SRM, Hsiung and Bagozzi (2003) demonstrated the complex patterns of influence and persuasion among family members in the decision to buy a car.

In sum, quantitative methods enjoy a long history in family communication research. The statistical control they afford researchers allows results to be generalized to families beyond the sample. Cause and effect or associative patterns help researchers articulate the complex structures and functions of communication, both within the family unit and beyond. Quantitative methods are not, however, suitable for all research questions. In some cases, qualitative analyses are more appropriate.

Qualitative Methods

Settled within the interpretative paradigm, qualitative researchers study human behavior as purposive, as a type of action that takes meaning from the different cultures and social groups in which people are socialized (Baxter & Babbie, 2004). Therefore, "the goal of interpretative researchers is to understand what action means to people," which they generally do through the gathering of nonnumerical data, both written and oral (Baxter & Babbie, 2004, p. 59).

To understand how family members make sense and give meaning to their experiences, qualitative family researchers have used such methods as conversation and narrative analysis, ethnography, autoethnography, and qualitative interviewing. The following is a brief description of each qualitative method and how researchers within the discipline have applied them.

Conversation Analysis

Conversation analysis (CA) is a particular form of discourse analysis generally referred to as the study of naturally occurring interaction between and among people (Baxter & Babbie, 2004). In CA research, the verbal and nonverbal elements of conversations, traditionally captured by audiotape and/or videotape, are converted through a transcription notation system developed either by the researcher or a conversation analyst in the field (Baxter & Babbie, 2004). Conversation transcriptions are line-by-line accounts of any given interaction. The notation system uses particular symbols, which allow researchers to account for paralinguistic features within conversation such as vocal pitch, rate, volume, and/or pauses. Thus, CA is an incredibly rigorous and systematic method of qualitative research (Fitch, 1994). Most CA researchers spend considerable time analyzing just one transcription or sequence of talk (Baxter & Babbie, 2004). In a classic example of CA, Abu-Akel (2002) videotaped one dinnertime conversation among an

English-speaking European American family. The analysis identified how family members introduce, sustain, reintroduce, shift, discontinue, and end a topic of conversation. Abu-Akel found that the success and failure of a topic are rooted in the psychological and social rules of conversation.

In terms of research goals, conversation analysts are interested in the wide spectrum of how people construct everyday social order and meaning through talk. Therefore, conversation analysts examine how language works to create interaction structures, serves communicative and relational functions, and intersects with structure to create meaning (Baxter & Babbie, 2004; Fitch, 1994). In essence, then, conversational sequences are the locus of both action and meaning (Pomerantz & Fehr, 1997).

In the family literature, action is often viewed as parental efforts to influence their children. For example, Geer, Tulviste, Mizera, and Tryggvason (2002) analyzed dinnertime conversations among families from Estonia, Finland, and Sweden. The specific conversational action analyzed was parents' use of the "comment" as an explicit or implicit effort to influence their children to behave or speak in a certain way. Similarly, Wilson, Cameron, and Whipple (1997) analyzed the transcripts of five parent-child interactions to assess three aspects of mothers' regulative strategies (e.g., getting her child to help clean up after the conversation). These included patterns in the use of reflection-enhancing and power-assertive regulative strategies, how mothers' strategies vary in response to the child's resistance, and how regulative strategies differ in emotional tone.

The conversational construction of meaning might include identity management, socialization, negotiation of roles within the family, and the interpretation of others' actions (Pomerantz & Fehr, 1997). Pontecorvo, Fasulo, and Sterponi (2001) studied Italian family interaction to understand how parents and children create a sense of meaning and social order. This study highlighted the active role children play in shaping parental socialization talk.

Earlier, Taylor (1995) highlighted the ways in which children react to and interpret (construct the meaning of) their parents' talk. Taylor analyzed the comments of two children (an 8-year-old boy and his 5-year-old sister) who witnessed a disagreement that emerged in their parents' conversation while they were being filmed by the researcher during dinner. Taylor analyzed the use of interpretive phrases and awareness of face threat in comments such as the "film" will see "your FI:GHT" and you were "talking mea::n."

Ethnographic Studies

Similar to CA, ethnographic methods are employed to help researchers understand how people communicate with one another in their everyday lives (Carbaugh, 1995). Conceptualized by Philipsen (1992) as the ethnography of communication, interaction is recognized as a social construction embedded within culture and/or cultural practices. Therefore, an ethnographer of speaking is a "naturalist, who watches listens, and records communicative conduct in its natural setting" (Philipsen, 1992, p. 7). The goal is to observe and describe recognizable patterns within a given speech community. According to Philipsen, a speech community is a "universe of discourse with a finely organized, distinctive pattern of meaning and action" (p. 4). Therefore, it can be any group of people with a discernable social pattern of language used to make meaning in their daily lives. A family can indeed constitute such a community. Philipsen argued that talk is an important phenomenon of study; however, it is a distinctive practice among groups and must be studied in a situated context.

Researchers using ethnographic methods generally study family communication within culturally diverse families. Often, this means studying families from cultures within and outside of the United States to understand more about the cultures in general (Diggs & Socha, 2004). For example, although family communication was not the primary focus, Philipsen's (1992) account of communication in Teamsterville highlighted the communicative practice of disciplining children. In Teamsterville, parents physically punished their children for misbehaving in a comparison to Nacirema community parents, who used supportive speech as a form of disciplining their children. Weider and Pratt (1990) used data collected from Pratt's participant observation of the Osage Indian tribe to describe how Indians make themselves recognizable as real Indians within and outside their culture. It is customary for a community of real Indians to develop and maintain familial-like bonds with nonkin Indians, a practice that is not familiar in Anglo culture. Through naming practices, two Indians may refer to one another as brother or sister. After doing so, that relationship "takes on the same range of rights and obligations that one would have in a relationship with a brother as defined in strict genealogical terms" (Weider & Pratt, 1990, p. 59).

Autoethnographic Method

It is not uncommon for ethnographic qualitative researchers to see their own personal identities and stories mirrored in the personal narratives of those they are observing (Krizek, 2003). The discovered relationship between the researcher's identity and the cultural phenomenon or practice that he or she is observing has generated a new and exciting methodological practice: autoethnography. Autoethnography is a research practice "that connects the personal to the cultural, placing the self within a social context" (Holt, 2003, p. 2). Researchers use the self as a tool to examine the communicative relationship between and among members of a culture (Holt, 2003). According to Ellis and Bochner (2000), autoethnographies are generally written in the first person and are composed of a mixture of dialogue, emotion, and self-consciousness. Autoethnography has gained popularity because it allows researchers to be self-reflexive, asking, "How are they both product and producer of a given cultural phenomenon?" (Wood & Fasset, 2003). In addition, Berger (2001) argued that employing the autoethnographic method enables her to establish and maintain a high level of rapport with the participants she is observing.

Communication scholars have used autoethnography to make sense of family communicative processes and relationships. Ellis and Bochner (2000) argued that autoethnographies are personal narratives affected by history, social structure, and culture; therefore, the focus of many is to give voice to marginalized or silenced individuals. For example, Olson (2004) wrote an autoethnography intertwining her voice as a researcher with her voice as a woman who survived an abusive marital relationship. Olson argued that she wrote her ethnography so that "we can all better understand a battered woman's social, cultural, and political position and how the dominant cultural context influences a battered woman's sense of self" (p. 7). Another example of family-oriented autoethnography is Eicher-Catt's (2004) piece chronicling her struggles as a noncustodial mother. Her account discussed dialectical tensions between competent performance and performative competence of the communicative experience of mothering.

Despite the freedom and insight that autoethnography allows, it has also been criticized for including or privileging the researcher's perspective in a study's focus and findings (Holt, 2003). Therefore, the standards by which we evaluate qualitative research may not be and perhaps should not be the same for the evaluation of autoethnography.

Narrative Analysis

Most often, the narrative approach concerns analysis of interview transcripts in which researchers ask participants to tell a story about an aspect of their lives (Baxter & Babbie, 2004). However, the narrative approach can also refer to the analysis of social texts. In other words, researchers interested in qualitative narrative analysis study the natural occurrence of both written and oral storytelling. Human beings live their lives in narrative by continually telling stories to help them make sense of their experiences (Kellas & Trees, 2005; Turner & West, 2002; see also Chapter 6, this volume). Narrative researchers study these stories and storytelling practices to understand how people live their lives (Baxter & Babbie, 2004).

Narrative analysis is often used to examine the communicative practice of family storytelling from which family members learn to understand both their individual and collective family identity (Kellas & Trees, 2005). According to Turner and West (2002), a family story can "feature a family member or several members; providing lessons, morals, and a sense of connection to the family members who tell and listen to them" (p. 81). Thus, the primary functions of a family story are to build identity, to teach, and to connect family members (Turner & West, 2002). As Langellier (2002) observes, these functions may be especially important, and yet particularly challenging, when families wish to maintain their cultural identities when they are embedded in another culture.

Family researchers working in the narrative tradition tend to focus on the process of storytelling, the structure of the story, and/or the content of the story (Baxter & Babbie, 2004). The most common of these is the performance aspect or process of family storytelling. According to Langellier and Peterson (2004), the performance of family storytelling is "an evolving expression of small group culture rather than a collection of stories" (p. 41). Researchers studying performance first examine how content is ordered—in other words, what content is included in a story, how is it arranged, and how often is the story told with that content (Langellier & Peterson, 2004). Second, performance is evaluated by examining the task ordering of family storytelling. Task ordering refers to how families create structure by showing who tells the stories and who listens to them as well as whether the story is jointly told by several members (Kellas & Trees, 2005; Langellier & Peterson, 2004). Often, task ordering is done according to generation and gender. Although storytelling tasks may be divided equally among the older and younger generations, the first and second generations tend to do most of the telling as well as the female members of the family (Langellier & Peterson, 2004). Storytelling often becomes the women's responsibility in the family. Finally, performance is examined through group ordering, which means family members order group and individual identities by "performing themselves to themselves and others" (Langellier & Peterson, 2004, p. 112).

Interviews

Qualitative interviewing is perhaps the most widely used research method among qualitative communication researchers. According to Baxter and Babbie (2004), it is mainly used for five specific purposes. First, qualitative researchers use interviews to understand a communicative phenomenon that cannot be observed directly. Second, an interview is helpful if a researcher wants to understand the thoughts and feelings of the interviewee on a particular subject or experience. Third, a qualitative researcher may use interviews to examine how a participant uses language in his or her natural environment. Fourth, interviewing can be used as an element of triangulation. In other words, interviews can be used as validation of an already observed behavior or as a supplement to a previous interview. Finally, as mentioned in the previous section, qualitative interviewing can be considered a performance that exemplifies an interviewee's communicative style.

Researchers using interviewing most often conduct individual in-depth interviews. This qualitative interview method has proven especially useful for researchers examining communicative processes within different types of families (i.e., original families, stepfamilies, adopted families). Common topics of study for these qualitative interviewing studies vary; however, the development and maintenance of personal and collective identity remains an important focus. For example, Golden (2002) conducted interviews with 12 married couples, both separately and together. Couples were asked questions concerning how they managed household responsibilities, child care, place of employment, and their perception of their role identity in the marriage. She found that couples tended to collaborate in their perception of their work and family identities. Krusiewicz and Wood (2001) conducted in-depth interviews with adoptive parents using a narrative interview method. Adoptive parents were asked to chronicle and comment on their adoptive children's entrance into the family based on questions from an interview protocol. The researchers found five themes when analyzing the interview narratives: dialectical tensions, destiny, compelling connection, rescue, and legitimacy. Overall, the telling of adoptive entrance stories helped the parents sustain a sense of legitimacy as a real family.

A second area of interest for which interviewing is a useful and appropriate method is the description of dialectical challenges faced by stepfamilies. Baxter and Braithwaite have established a program of research examining the nature of dialectical tensions in stepfamily relationships. For example, Baxter, Braithwaite, and Harper (1998) investigated the dialectical pull (or contradiction) that stepfamily members sometimes feel between loyalty to the family-of-origin and newly developing closeness with the stepfamily. They conducted 53 in-depth interviews with a stepparent or stepchild asking the participant to discuss both successful and unsuccessful rituals within their new stepfamily and how those rituals related to the traditions from their old family. A qualitative analysis of the interviews revealed that the communicative practice of rituals allowed stepfamily members to adapt to their new stepfamily while still valuing the rituals and relationships in their original family. In a subsequent study focused exclusively on stepchildren's perspective, Baxter, Braithwaite, Bryant, and Wagner (2004) interviewed 50 adult children (college student volunteers) who were members of stepfamilies. Semistructured interview protocols were used, and all interviews were transcribed, yielding more than 800 pages of transcripts. Three dialectical contradictions in the stepparent-stepchild relationship emerged from thematic analysis of the transcripts: distance and closeness, stepparent status (authority), and expressive openness and closedness.

Finally, although less frequent, interviews have been used to provide richer understanding of phasic models developed from quantitative research. For example, the family adoption communication (FAC) model was derived from nationwide questionnaire data assessing the dynamics of openness about adoption. In an effort to determine whether the three phases in the model (I: Original Story, II: Adopted Child Questioning, and III: Adopted Child Directed Information Gathering) were fully descriptive of the experiences of adoptive families, Wrobel, Kohler, Grotevant, and McRoy (2003) interviewed 10 families from among 177 families who participated in a second wave of data collection for the Minnesota/Texas Adoption Research Project (Grotevant & McRoy, 1998). The authors used each family as a case study, integrating and comparing the interviews for that family. They found several themes that were not evident in the depiction of the model, for example, adoptive mothers as communication "brokers," communication as emotional as well as informational, and the lingering effects of withholding information.

A common limitation of qualitative interview research has been the lack of group interviews or interviews conducted with multiple members of the same family. A group interview would allow researchers to hear the perspectives of multiple people as well as witness their interaction at the same time (Baxter & Babbie, 2004). Future research in family communication will likely focus more on the multiple-family perspective, although the problem of self-censorship in the presence of other family members will need to be addressed.

Conclusion

This chapter illustrates the broad range of methodological approaches available for studying family communication. Quantitative approaches provide data from large samples that can be used to make claims about communication antecedents and effects. Such claims can be generalized to the larger population from which the sample of families was selected. Qualitative methods provide greater depth and understanding of communication phenomena and interactional nuances that might be lost in quantitative designs. Given the complexity of family communication, both approaches are essential and will no doubt remain complementary tools for future research.

References

Abu-Akel, A. (2002). The psychological and social dynamics of topic performance in family dinnertime conversation. *Journal of Pragmatics, 34,* 1787–1807.

Afifi, T. D., & Schrodt, P. (2003). Uncertainty and the avoidance of the state of one's family in stepfamilies, post divorce single-parent families, and first-marriage families. *Human Communication Research, 29,* 516–532.

Barnes, H. L., & Olson, D. H. (1982). Parent-adolescent communication. In D. H. Olson, H. I. McCubbin, H. L. Barnes, A. Larsen, M. Muxen, & M. Wilson (Eds.), *Family inventories* (pp. 55–70). Minneapolis: University of Minnesota, Family Social Science.

Barnes, H. L., & Olson, D. H. (1985). Parent-adolescent communication and the circumplex model. *Child Development, 56,* 438–447.

Baxter, L. A., & Babbie, E. (2004). *The basics of communication research.* Belmont, CA: Thomson Wadsworth.

Baxter, L. A., Braithwaite, D. O., Bryant, L., & Wagner, A. (2004). Stepchildren's perceptions of the contradictions in communication with stepparents. *Journal of Social and Personal Relationships, 21,* 447–467.

Baxter, L. A., Braithwaite, D. O., & Harper, A. M. (1998). The role of rituals in the management of dialectical tension of "old" and "new" in blended families. *Communication Studies, 49,* 101–120.

Berger, L. (2001). Inside out: Narrative autoethnography as a path toward rapport. *Qualitative Inquiry, 7,* 504–519.

Bethea, L. S. (2002). The impact of an older adult parent on communicative satisfaction and dyadic adjustment in the long-term marital relationship: Adult-children and spouses' retrospective accounts. *Journal of Applied Communication Research, 30,* 107–125.

Boyum, L. A., & Parke, R. D. (1995). The role of family emotional expressiveness in the development of children's social competence. *Journal of Marriage and the Family, 57,* 593–608.

Carbaugh, D. (1995). The ethnographic communication theory of Philipsen and associates. In D. Cushman & B. Koviac (Eds.), *Watershed traditions in communication* (pp. 239–297). Albany: State University of New York Press.

Clark, R. D., & Shields, G. (1997). Family communication and delinquency. *Adolescence, 32,* 125–137.

Cook, W. L., & Kenny, D. A. (2004). Application of the social relations model to family assessment. *Journal of Family Psychology, 18,* 361–371.

Crokenberg, S., & Langrock, A. (2001). The role of specific emotions in children's responses to interparental conflict: A test of the model. *Journal of Family Psychology, 15,* 163–182.

Cummings, E. M., & Cummings, J. S. (1995). The usefulness of experiments for the study of the family. *Journal of Family Psychology, 9,* 175–185.

Cummings, E. M., Goeke-Morey, M. C., & Papp, L. M. (2004). Everyday marital conflict and child aggression. *Journal of Abnormal Child Psychology, 32,* 191–202.

Davies, P. T., Harold, G. T., Goeke-Morey, M. C., & Cummings, E. M. (2002). Introduction and literature review. *Monographs of the Society for Research in Child Development, 67,* 1–26.

Diggs, R. C., & Socha, T. J. (2004). Communication, families, and exploring the boundaries of cultural diversity. In A. L. Vangelisti (Ed.), *Handbook of family communication* (pp. 249–268). Mahwah, NJ: Lawrence Erlbaum.

Eicher-Catt, D. (2004). Noncustodial mothers. *Journal of Contemporary Ethnography, 33,* 72–109.

Ellis, C., & Bochner, A. P. (2000). Autoethnography, personal narrative, reflexivity: Researcher as subject. In N. K. Denzin & Y. S. Lincoln (Eds.), *Handbook of qualitative research* (2nd ed., pp. 733–768). Thousand Oaks, CA: Sage.

Ely, R., Gleason, J. B., & McCabe, A. (1996). "Why didn't you talk to your mommy, Honey?": Parents' and children's talk about talk. *Research on Language and Social Interaction, 29,* 7–25.

Ennett, S. T., Bauman, K. E., Foshee, V. A., Pemberton, M., & Hicks, K. A. (2001). Parent-child communication about adolescent tobacco and alcohol use: What do parents say and does it affect youth behavior? *Journal of Marriage & the Family, 63,* 48–62.

Fiese, B. H., Tomcho, T. J., Douglas, M., Josephs, K., Poltrock, S., & Baker, T. (2002). A review of 50 years of research on naturally occurring family routines and rituals: Cause for celebration? *Journal of Family Psychology, 16,* 381–390.

Fincham, F. D., Grych, J. H., & Osborne, L. N. (1994). Does marital conflict cause child maladjustment? Directions and challenges for longitudinal research. *Journal of Family Psychology, 8,* 128–140.

Fitch, K. L. (1994). Criteria for evidence in qualitative research. *Western Journal of Communication, 58,* 32–39.

Fitzpatrick, M. A., Marshall, L. J., Leutwiler, T. J., & Krçmar, M. (1996). The effect of family communication environments on children's social behavior during middle childhood. *Communication Research, 23,* 379–406.

Fitzpatrick, M. A., & Ritchie, L. D. (1994). Communication schemata within the family: Multiple perspectives on family interaction. *Human Communication Research, 20,* 275–301.

Fujioka, A. (2002). The relationship of family communication patterns to parental mediation styles. *Communication Research, 29,* 642–665.

Galvin, K. M., Bylund, C. L., & Brommel, B. J. (2004). *Family communication: Cohesion and change* (6th ed.). Boston: Allyn & Bacon.

Geer, B. D., Tulviste, T., Mizera, L., & Tryggvason, M. (2002). Socialization in communication: Pragmatic socialization during dinnertime in Estonian, Finnish, and Swedish families. *Journal of Pragmatics, 34,* 1757–1787.

Goeke-Morey, M. C., Cummings, E. M., Harold, G. T., & Shelton, K. H. (2003). Categories and continua of destructive and constructive marital conflict tactics from the perspective of U.S. and Welsh children. *Journal of Family Psychology, 17,* 327–338.

Golden, A. G. (2002). Speaking of work and family: Spousal collaboration on defining role-identities and developing shared meanings. *Southern Communication Journal, 67,* 122–141.

Gottman, J. M. (1988). *Specific affect coding system: Observing emotional communication in marital and family interaction.* Unpublished manuscript, University of Washington, Seattle.

Grant, C. H., Rosenfeld, L. B., & Cissna, K. N. (2004). The effects of family-of-origin alcohol abuse on the self-perceived communication competence of the children. *Communication Research Reports, 21,* 47–69.

Grinwald, S. (1995). Communication-family characteristics: A comparison between stepfamilies (formed after death or divorce) and biological families. *Journal of Divorce & Remarriage, 24,* 183–196.

Grotevant, H. D., & McRoy, R. G. (1998). *Openness in adoption: Exploring family connections.* Thousand Oaks, CA: Sage.

Hartos, J. J., & Power, T. G. (2000). Association between mother and adolescent reports for assessing relations between parent-adolescent communication and adolescent adjustment. *Journal of Youth & Adolescence, 29,* 441–450.

Holt, N. L. (2003). Representation, legitimation, and autoethnography: An autoethnographic writing story. *International Journal of Qualitative Methods, 2,* 1–24.

Hsiung, R. O., & Bagozzi, R. P. (2003). Validating the relationship qualities of influence and persuasion with the family social relations model. *Human Communication Research, 29,* 81–110.

Jackson, S., Bijstra, J., Oostra, L., & Bosma, H. (1998). Adolescents' perceptions of communication with parents relative to specific aspects of relationship with parents and personal development. *Journal of Adolescence, 21,* 305–322.

Jacob, T., & Johnson, S. L. (2001). Sequential interactions in the parent-child communications of depressed fathers and depressed mothers. *Journal of Family Psychology, 15,* 38–52.

Kellas, J. K., & Trees, A. R. (2005). Rating interactional sense-making in the process of joint story-telling. In V. Manusov (Ed.), *The sourcebook of nonverbal measures: Going beyond words* (pp. 281–294). Mahwah, NJ: Lawrence Erlbaum.

Koesten, J. (2004). Family communication patterns, sex of subject, and communication competence. *Communication Monographs, 71,* 226–244.

Krçmar, M. (1998). The contribution of family communication patterns to children's interpretations of television violence. *Journal of Broadcasting & Electronic Media, 42,* 250–264.

Krizek, R. L. (2003). Ethnography as the excavation of personal narrative. In R. P. Clair (Ed.), *Expressions of ethnography: Novel approaches to qualitative methods* (pp. 141–152). Albany: State University of New York Press.

Krusiewicz, E. S., & Wood, J. T. (2001). "He was our child from the moment we walked in that room": Entrance stories of adoptive parents. *Journal of Social and Personal Relationships, 18,* 785–803.

Langellier, K. M. (2002). Performing family stories, forming cultural identity: Franco American mêmêre stories. *Communication Studies, 53,* 56–73.

Langellier, K. M., & Peterson, E. E. (2004). *Storytelling in daily life: Performing narrative.* Philadelphia: Temple University Press.

Lanz, M., Iafrate, R., Rosnati, R., & Scabini, E. (1999). Parent-child communication and adolescent self-esteem in separated, intercountry adoptive and intact non-adoptive families. *Journal of Adolescence, 22,* 785–794.

Mann, B. J., & Gilliom, L. A. (2002). Emotional security and cognitive appraisals mediate the relationship between parents' marital conflict and adjustment in older adolescents. *Journal of Genetic Psychology, 165,* 250–271.

McLeod, J. M., & Chaffee, S. H. (1972). The construction of social reality. In J. Tedeschi (Ed.), *The social influence process* (pp. 50–59). Chicago: Aldine-Etherton.

Noller, P., & Feeney, J. A. (2004). Studying family communication: Multiple methods and multiple sources. In A. L. Vangelisti (Ed.), *Handbook of family communication* (pp. 31–50). Mahwah, NJ: Lawrence Erlbaum.

Noller, P., & Fitzpatrick, M. A. (1993). *Communication in family relationships.* Upper Saddle River, NJ: Prentice Hall.

Olson, L. N. (2004). The role of voice in the (re)construction of a battered woman's identity: An autoethnography of one woman's experiences of abuse. *Women's Studies in Communication, 27,* 1–33.

Philipsen, G. (1992). *Speaking culturally: Explorations in social communication.* Albany: State University of New York Press.

Pomerantz, A., & Fehr, B. J. (1997). Conversation analysis: An approach to the study of social action as sense-making practices. In T. A. Van Dijk (Ed.), *Discourse as social interaction* (pp. 64–91). Thousand Oaks, CA: Sage.

Pontecorvo, C., Fasulo, A., & Sterponi, L. (2001). Mutual apprentices: The making of parenthood and childhood in family dinner conversation. *Human Development, 44,* 340–361.

Raffaelli, M., Smart, L. A., Van Horn, S. C., Hohbein, A. D., Kline, J. E., & Chan, W. (1999). Do mothers and teens disagree about sexual communication? A methodological reappraisal. *Journal of Youth and Adolescence, 28,* 395–402.

Reese, E., Haden, C. A., & Fivush, R. (1996). Mothers, fathers, daughters, sons: Gender differences in autobiographical reminiscing. *Research on Language and Social Interaction, 29,* 27–56.

Ritchie, L. D. (1991). Family communication patterns: An epistemic analysis and conceptual reinterpretation. *Communication Research, 18,* 548–565.

Ritchie, L. D. (1997). Parents' workplace experiences and family communication patterns. *Communication Research, 24,* 175–187.

Ritchie, L. D., & Fitzpatrick, M. A. (1990). Family communication patterns: Measuring intrapersonal perceptions of interpersonal relationships. *Communication Research, 17,* 523–544.

Segrin, C., & Menees, M. M. (1995). The impact of coping styles and family communication on the social skills of children of alcoholics. *Journal of Studies on Alcohol, 57,* 29–33.

Sheehan, G., & Noller, P. (2002). Adolescents' perceptions of differential parenting: Links with attachment style and adolescent adjustment. *Personal Relationships, 9,* 173–190.

Siegel, S. M., Friedlander, M. L., & Heatherington, L. (1992). Nonverbal relational control in family communication. *Journal of Nonverbal Behavior, 15,* 117–139.

Sillars, A., Koerner, A., & Fitzpatrick, M. A. (2005). Communication and understanding in parent-adolescent relationships. *Human Communication Research, 31,* 102–128.

Slesnick, N., & Waldron, H. B. (1997). Interpersonal problem-solving interactions of depressed adolescents and their parents. *Journal of Family Psychology, 11,* 234–245.

Stamp, G. H. (2004). Theories of family relationships and a family relationships theoretical model. In A. L. Vangelisti (Ed.), *Handbook of family communication* (pp. 1–30). Mahwah, NJ: Lawrence Erlbaum.

Stiles, W. B. (1992). *Describing talk: A taxonomy of verbal response modes.* Newbury Park, CA: Sage.

Taylor, C. E. (1995). "You think it was a *fight?*": Co-constructing (the struggle for) meaning, face, and family in everyday narrative activity. *Research on Language and Social Interaction, 28,* 283–317.

Toomey, E. T., & Nelson, E. S. (2001). Family conflict and young adults' attitudes toward intimacy. *Journal of Divorce and Remarriage, 34,* 49–69.

Trees, A. R. (2000). Nonverbal communication and the support process: Interactional sensitivity in interactions between mothers and young adult children. *Communication Monographs, 67,* 239–261.

Trees, A. R. (2002). The influence of relational context on support processes: Points of difference and similarity between young adult sons and daughters in problem talk with mothers. *Journal of Social and Personal Relationships, 19,* 703–722.

Turner, L. H., & West, R. (2002). *Perspectives on family communication* (2nd ed.). New York: McGraw-Hill.

Valiente, C., Fabes, R. A., Eisenberg, N., & Spinrad, T. L. (2004). The relations of parental expressivity and support to children's coping with daily stress. *Journal of Family Psychology, 18,* 97–106.

Weider, D. L., & Pratt, S. (1990). On being a recognizable Indian among Indians. In D. Carbaugh (Ed.), *Cultural communication and intercultural contact* (pp. 45–64). Hillsdale, NJ: Lawrence Erlbaum.

Wilson, S. R., Cameron, K. A., & Whipple, E. E. (1997). Regulative communication strategies within mother-child interactions: Implications for the study of reflection-enhancing parental communication. *Research on Language and Social Interaction, 30,* 73–92.

Wood, A. F., & Fassett, D. L. (2003). Remote control: Identity, power, and technology in the communication classroom. *Communication Education, 52,* 286–296.

Wrobel, G. M., Kohler, J. K., Grotevant, H. D., & McRoy, R. G. (2003). The family adoption communication (FAC) model: Identifying pathways of adoption-related communication. *Adoption Quarterly, 7,* 53–84.

Yerby, J., Buerkel-Rothfuss, N. L., & Bochner, A. P. (1998). *Understanding family communication* (2nd ed.). Scottsdale, AZ: Gorsuch Scarisbrick.

PART III

Internal
Family Dynamics

Storytelling
Conflict
Intimacy
Discipline
Rituals

CHAPTER 6

Family Storytelling as Communication Practice

Kristin M. Langellier

University of Maine

Eric E. Peterson

University of Maine

The communication practice of storytelling is one way, among many others examined in this volume, of "doing family." As surely as we are born into genes, genealogy, and a body of relatives by blood, marriage, and bonds, we are "born into" family stories and histories, family myths and metaphors, family rituals and routines, family language and secrets. Families "take what they tell from experience—their own and that told by others—and, in turn, make it the experience of those who are listening to the tale" (Benjamin, 1969, p. 87). Adapting Walter Benjamin's (1969) analysis of the storyteller to family emphasizes storytelling as communication. As communication practice, storytelling involves how families perform stories of experience and how storytelling forms families. The speech act "let me tell you a story about our family" creates and passes on family events, characters, sensibilities, values, and identities. As much as families are social structures and ties of attachment, they are also small group cultures who perform themselves to themselves and others by doing things with words (Langellier & Peterson, 2004).

How families perform themselves may be most obvious during the special occasions of family celebrations, rituals, and traditions, such as holidays, birthdays, reunions, weddings, anniversaries, and funerals. Certain family members may assume roles as storytellers or keepers of the kin while others are listeners, and a family may develop a canon of stories that are told and retold. Indeed, in the post-modern culture wherein one "gets a life" by telling and consuming stories (Smith & Watson, 1996), one is compelled to narrate family, ritually and often publicly, for friends and communities, to document and display it in photographs and scrap-books, and to perform it on video, the Internet, and the stage.

But equally formative of family culture is storytelling in the interrupted and intertwined conversations and habits of daily life—fragmentary, fleeting, and fluid, embedded among tasks and talk—while playing with children, doing housework and homework, reading the morning paper, preparing food, eating, and traveling to work and school. Family storytellers and listeners are multiple and dispersed, and stories may be contradictory and incoherent or simply bits of memory, speech, image. Such storytelling is so mundane that these stories may be invisible to family outsiders and even to family members themselves. Communication scholars exam-ine family storytelling both in its everyday and its more publicly performative moments, from highly visible to more invisible forms.

A communication approach to families defines family as a small group culture that is created, expressed, and maintained in interaction (Whitchurch & Dickson, 1999). Family is our first group (Socha & Diggs, 1999), and storytelling is called our first language (Stone, 1988) and the family imaginary (Jorgenson & Bochner, 2004). Family emerges from stories, rituals, conversations, and routines of daily life. To invoke Gillis (1996), family is a "world of its own making" as it mediates images of the "family we live with"—actual and empirical—and the "family we live by"—mythic and idealized—in stories. At the intersection of material and imaginary relations, families order information and organize bodies by generation, gender, race, ethnicity, class, and sexuality. Thus, family is both embodied and discursive, both performed and performative. Family stories are not only "under our skin" and "inside" the family but also out in the world, a world of texts and contexts (histor-ical, social, economic, legal, religious, popular, and so on) that order meanings for what family is, what a "good" story is, and how to tell it. Unavoidably intertextual, family storytelling draws on internal and external resources to create habitable stories and models of identity for family and family members. In Stone's (1988) potent formulation, what blood cannot provide, narrative can.

The affirmative feature of small group culture is the creation of generations, and in family, the preceding generations are not merely precursors but ancestors, and the following generations are not merely successors but children. Each generation imag-ines and reimagines family in stories for survival. Family storytelling encompasses the serious work of cultural transmission as well as playful interaction with words and significant others. The formation, maintenance, and survival of culture is a doing and redoing of family within a generation and over generations. The *doing* of family storytelling highlights embodied communication: emotional, dynamic, and creative acts of making meanings and telling stories. The *redoing* of family storytelling highlights its discursive relations: the ritualistic, habitual, and normalizing impulses that repeat the conventions of stories and sediment meanings. In the name of cultural survival, family stories hold on to and let go of familiar, familial meanings and iden-tities as new meanings emerge in changing environments. As communication practice, telling family stories is a multigenerational creation and struggle over meaning: what events and actions are told and passed on, which family values are narrated, who tells stories and how, who listens, and what identities are visible and which muted? In storytelling, families produce themselves as *a family* within, between, and over generations and reproduce *The Family* as a discursive construct.

Family storytelling depends on participation: "active narrative involvement defines what it means to participate in the mainstream American family" (Ochs & Capps, 2001, p. 8). And researchers also participate in that process (Langellier & Peterson, 2006). Jorgenson and Bochner (2004) usefully remind us that we collaborate in making sense of family as we conduct research, and "what we come to say about families involves the indistinguishable provocations of the families we observe, the mediations of language by which we make claims about them, and the images of family we have internalized and project, some of which may be outside our awareness" (p. 516). Their words apply to the research reviewed in the chapter as well as to the chapter itself, which also "thinks about" family storytelling as communication practice.

Taking and making stories from family experience is a practice of ordering, that is, making sense of family sensibilities. We examine the communication practice of family storytelling in three sections: ordering content to make stories, ordering participation to tell and listen, and ordering identities of families and members (McFeat, 1974). Each section examines one level of ordering in more detail, illustrates some of its dynamics, and raises additional questions for thinking about family narrative. While we highlight the range and variety of communication and performance research here, we exclude discussions of family narrative therapy and children's narrative development because of space limitations.

Ordering Content to Make Family Stories

Family storytelling is an evolving cultural performance rather than a fixed canon of stories. Family stories are *made* from the myriad experiences of being family and dispersed in space and time among multiple members. In communication terms, families turn information into communication by ordering content about themselves into meaningful stories; family is the subject, medium, and outcome of storytelling. The content of family stories embraces the range of family experience: past memories, current interactions, and future aspirations. Family stories refer to experience, and they evaluate experiences, characters, and acts from the collective perspective of family or an individual family member. As Stone (1988) noted, "Almost any bit of lore about a family member, living or dead, qualifies as a family story—as long as it's significant, as long as it's worked its way into the family canon to be told and retold" (p. 5). "Working its way" involves communication processes such as remembering and forgetting stories; interpreting, reinterpreting, and emphasizing what has been marginal or muted; sedimenting and innovating meanings; and aestheticizing and dramatizing the "bits" of family experience. Story content is formed in the struggle over meanings for particular events, acts, and identities, and such content is performed as it is told and retold.

task content group

For cultural survival, the meanings and sensibilities of family must not only be made but also stored, retrieved, and transmitted within and over generations. Ordering content to make stories is the most general level of survival because a family that fails to make stories to share and pass along will cease to exist as a culture. Transmission is aided by making memorable stories and memorable storytelling performances. Families may, for example, diffuse content among multiple participants through collective processes of remembering, sediment content into family classics, enlist socially available and visible genres, time the telling so stories are most salient and likely to be passed on, and maintain family secrets through exclusionary practices. Because making family stories is always a cultural, not a natural, process of communication, it varies through history and is marked by differences in race, ethnicity, class, gender, and sexuality.

The communication literature on family stories assumes they are relatively solid texts, typically authored or performed by a single speaker, usually an adult, and often oriented to audiences outside the family in research settings, the classroom, or the public stage. In narrative terms, they are variations on personal narrative, telling about something that happened to us as a family or to me as family member. They enact the referential function by ordering family events in their temporal sequence ("what happened? and then what? what finally happened?") and the evaluative function, which entails the point of view of the narrator and the point of the story ("so what? what does that mean? why does it matter?") and how the events and actions are judged according to family cultural rules.

The turn to family stories by communication scholars is illustrated by Yerby, Buerkel-Rothfuss, and Bochner (1995); Turner and West (2006); and Jorgenson and Bochner (2004). These scholars situate narrative within contemporary life as families face the narrative challenge of keeping themselves alive and coherent, organizing and structuring the inchoate flow of family life into stories (Jorgenson & Bochner, 2004). The approach to family stories as personal narrative tends to evaluate experience from the perspective of an individual family member, noting that it makes a difference who is telling the story, how it is told, and to whom. Family stories recount a version of experience; they are concrete, emotional, dramatic, and evocative. Stories order content sequentially and consequentially: One thing leads to another to represent events that occurred in the past, told from the perspective of the present, in anticipation of the future.

This research tradition emphasizes the ordering of content into a tellable story and the tensions between constructing canonical stories and deconstructing them to be reframed from the margins. As Stone's (1988) definition of a family story suggests, families often develop a canon of stories that are told and retold. Canonical stories, according to Jorgenson and Bochner (2004), "express the boundaries of acceptable relationship and family practices against which alternative forms are judged" (p. 525). Canonical stories privilege normative forms, experiences, and meanings of family—heterosexual love, marriage, and children, in that order—and mute, marginalize, or closet "nontraditional" experience. They draw on familiar and widely circulated genres that order experience into texts. Courtship stories found the genesis of a family, birth stories narrate reproduction, and survival stories inspire the next generation. Canonical family stories draw on other textual resources such as popular culture. The courtship story, for example, may incorporate conventions of the romance plot. Against the forces of canonical stories, narrative scholars offer the power of personal narratives about family to authorize and legitimate marginal, muted, or exceptional experiences, typically focusing on family experiences shrouded in secrecy, such as abortion (Ellis & Bochner, 1992) and mental illness (Ronai, 1996).

Closely aligned with this research tradition is the work of performance scholars who center attention on how storytelling is explicitly embodied by narrators, such as Pollock's (1999) book-length "intimate ethnography" of birth stories told to her. Her analysis of birth stories highlights the intense, visceral, personal, and unique encounters of bodies in space and time—bodies in the stories and bodies in the telling. Other performance scholars, such as Pineau (2000) and Spry (2000), explore the power of embodied storytelling through techniques of performative writing and staged performances to aestheticize and dramatize family stories for audiences outside the family.

Communication researchers have also approached family stories as a way to access "the told" through "the telling." In this research tradition, family stories are assumed to be a particularly rich representation of how people think and feel about their personal relationships (Fiese et al., 1999). Vangelisti, Crumley, and Baker (1999), for example, study family stories as standards that indicate family relationships. Researchers asked participants to write a story about their own family and then to retell it according to an "ideal" family as a standard by which to evaluate their own family experience. Story themes were coded and correlated with measures of individuals' satisfaction with their families. Related research analyzes family stories for gendered themes (Fiese & Skillman, 2000) and ethnic diversity (Bylund, 2003). Content ordering thus refers to the themes of personal narratives about family. Family stories are representations through which researchers examine family relationships and processes.

Ordering content to make family stories raises questions for communication scholars, a few of which we discuss below.

Personal Versus Familial Point of View

The research traditions described above treat family stories as personal narratives about family experience. Ordering content to construct "what happened?" is important, but researchers are typically more interested in evaluation: how the narrator frames and reframes, forms and performs, and judges family relationships and events. Do these communication and performance approaches to family stories privilege the personal? How do personal narratives reflect collective meanings of family culture? How do they reshape, reinterpret, and recontextualize family experience? Studies that clarify, complicate, and challenge the contributions of individual narrators include Delacroix (1995) and Schiffrin (2000).

Remembering Family Stories

Family is a community of memory, recalling people and events of the past. How do aesthetic and dramatic qualities, highlighted by performance scholars in particular, enhance remembering? How is remembering family stories a communicative process (Hirst & Manier, 1996)? To what extent is remembering a cognitive process of the individual or the social process of a family? How is remembering shaped by the forces of history? Andrews (2002), for example, examines how four narrators remember their mothers in counternarratives that challenge myths of mothering. Martin, Hagestad, and Diedrick's (1988) study of family stories investigates who and what was remembered by whom. In these family stories, parents were the main narrators, grandparents were protagonists, and males dominated in numbers and story scenes. Notably, family stories were soon forgotten and virtually lost by the fourth generation.

Constraints on Family Stories

The ease of encoding and telling a family story is heightened by ready-made, well-known, and widely circulated genres and technologies. Jeter (1996), for example, examines "the Great Story" as a cross-national model of heroic family behavior. As we have discussed, experiences outside the canonical, such as family violence (Montalbano-Phelps, 2003), are both harder to tell and harder to hear. Whereas courtship stories abound in family canons, divorce narratives remain muted (Riessman, 1990). Pregnancy and birth stories have recently emerged as culturally tellable (Pollock, 1999; Talbot, Bibace, Bokhour, & Bamberg, 1996), but how does one narrate adoptions, including transracial adoptions (Krusiewicz & Wood, 2001; Patton, 1996)? How are disruptions to the family story such as a perinatal death (Grout & Romanoff, 2000), suicide (Cottle, 2000), or "nonevents" such as infertility (Kirkman, 2003; Riessman, 2000) and failed in vitro fertilization (Bell, 2002; Throsby, 2002) narrated? How do technologies of communication, such as genealogical research, personal and family Web pages, and digital family storytelling, inform and constrain family storytelling? Watson (1996), for example, suggests that family genealogies favor WASP families and frustrate women, African Americans, and adopted children.

Summary

In sum, the personal narrative approach to family stories (ordering content) most often features communication by single narrators to audiences outside the family. Family storytelling is conspicuously informed and constrained by audience and situation. Writing about family and ethnicity, McAdoo (2001) argues that "when one speaks of communication and families, it is important to know whether the dialogue is only within the family or not, whether the family is of color or not of color, the context of the relationship, if one of the persons has a power relationship or not, and if the communication is within or across ethnic groups" (p. 89). For example, Indian families in the United States and India told a researcher personal and family stories only after being incorporated into family as "sister" (Marvin, 2004). In the next section on telling stories, we turn to interactional dynamics of family narrative that render audience, situation, and event more visible than they are in the research traditions described above.

Ordering Participation

Today's families have witnessed change—social, economic, technological—perhaps more profound than at any other time in history. Yet, family storytelling persists, often by way of new communication technologies, through the transformations that have ruptured traditional forms of stability and continuity to form the more fluid, flexible, and virtual postmodern family. If family narrative is an evolving communication practice in which content is ordered to make stories, then someone must retrieve, compose, and perform the stories in such a way that they are memorable: told and told again. And someone must listen and be able to understand and act on what she or he hears for family stories to remain salient. The shift from a concern with making family stories to the work of telling them, what we call task ordering, asks the following: How are stories told, by whom and to whom, under what conditions, and with what consequences for family culture survival? Task ordering is the interactional work that familie do to create and maintain productive internal relationships and external relations with a changing environment.

Task ordering has to do with "the possibility of communication among members in which *some* remain predominantly senders while *others* remain predominantly receivers, and each has or will experience the other's role" (McFeat, 1974, p. 114). Some family members are invited, invoked, demanded, coached, and coaxed to tell stories, while other family members are excluded and listen voluntarily, accidentally, or despite their unwillingness. Family is a unique system of meanings and relationships that are interdependent, strategic, and patterned. Patterns of telling family stories reflect the constraints of gender and generation that regularize and routinize family interaction, but storytelling also forges alliances between spouses or partners, siblings, "sides," "lines," and "outsiders." Family patterns of telling stories reveal rules for the transmission of small group cultures as they are shaped by and shape race, ethnicity, class, gender, generation, and sexual orientation. The hallmark of task ordering is participation, and the interactional research on telling stories frequently highlights varieties of conarration and the group production of stories.

Two studies with contrastive titles suggest gendered and generational patterns of family storytelling. Ochs and Taylor's (1995) study, titled "Father Knows Best," asks how the children's generation comes to understand gender roles through differential modes of telling and hearing stories during dinnertime within middle-class European American families. Narrating a story over family dinner is a collaborative interaction in which participants construct themselves and one another simultaneously as spouse, parent, child, and sibling. In a corpus of 100 storytellings, Ochs and Taylor identify a narrative pattern of children being protagonists in stories introduced by mothers and oriented to fathers as primary recipients. "Father knows best" refers to the collaborative dynamic that sets up the father—through his own and through the mother's and children's recurring narrative practices—to be primary audience, judge, and critic of family members' actions, thoughts, and feelings. The narrative asymmetry of this pattern is both generational (parents over children) and gendered (males over females), and it operates both dyadically (between spouses) and triadically (among mothers and fathers and children). The researchers argue that family storytelling is a window into how gendered hierarchies, enmeshed in social and political institutions, are constituted in daily family interaction. Because narrative roles and gender relations are intertwined, family storytelling reproduces traditional gender roles.

In "Mothers Know Best," Schely-Newman (1999) examines a storytelling round that preceded a family wedding in Israel. Her performance analysis emphasizes family storytelling as a complex narrative event rather than a static text, incorporating the group production of stories among extended family and including her own coproduction as researcher. Gathering at the neighbors', the group was large and multiaged, mixed by sex but predominantly female, and consanguineous except for four nonfamily members, including Schely-Newman. Because marriage requires acceptance of a stranger, it poses a potential threat to the family, and the narratives addressed improper gender and sexual behavior. The phrase "mothers know best" refers to the older Israeli women's group production of a cultural message "beware of the unknown" to the younger generation of women, both inside and outside the immediate family. Schely-Newman argues that family storytelling transmits this traditional message in a changing environment where both the family incorporating a new member through marriage and Israeli family culture undergo transformation.

Researchers who study the telling of family stories as task ordering consider the interacting participants, the communication situation, and the narrative event. Blum-Kulka's (1997) study of dinner talk, for example, distinguishes interaction patterns of Israeli and Jewish American family narrative. In Israeli families, she identifies the proposition to "let *us* (all) tell *your* (singular) story," a pattern of storytelling that emphasized the interpretation of personal experience from a family standpoint. "Let us (all) tell" distributes participation among generations in a group production of family stories. By contrast, Jewish American families enacted the proposition "let *me* tell *our* story," a communication tactic that supports the storytelling rights of the individual narrator. This way of telling stories may have the effect of preserving personal viewpoints and intrafamilial contestation. Moreover, it consolidates storytelling tasks in the hands of one or a few family members: a family storyteller or "keeper of the kin."

Both patterns suggest how participation in telling and listening contributes to collaborative canonization, that is, the production of collective meaning and family hegemony as individual differences may be elided or rendered ambiguous (Georgakopoulou, 1998). Such tactics may have differing effects, however, on the survival of family culture. The wider distribution and greater redundancy of group production may be less efficient in the short run, requiring as it does that each participant become a family, not a personal, narrator, but this narrative knowledge and skill may better serve long-term survival. The greater efficiency in the short run of locating family storytelling in one or a few members may imperil family continuity if the tasks of storytelling are not experienced by others, such as when the death of a family storyteller creates a crisis of memory and cultural transmission.

Gender and generational differences in telling and listening to stories alert us to further interactional variations among families by class, race, ethnicity, and so forth. Blum-Kulka and Snow (1992) identify class differences in the participation patterns of adults and children in American and Israeli family dinnertime narratives. Tafoya (1989) describes a generational structure among Native Americans based on families that are organized in concentric circles of family relations. The senior generation (grandparents) is responsible for storytelling, training, and discipline of the junior generation (all siblings). These elders do not "transmit" information by direct teaching but rather "guide by creating a situation where a youth comes to 're-cognize' what they [the elders] already know" (Tafoya, 1989, p. 40). This pattern differs from a three-generational structure in which the middle generation (parents) transmits and interprets basic information for the younger generation (children), subject to correction by the senior generation (grandparents). Heath (1983) identifies variations in African American families who tell stories cooperatively "with the help of the audience and with two or more participants in an event sharing the recounting" (p. 183). These studies suggest that individuals outside the family's racial, ethnic, or class culture may not understand the interactional dynamics and, consequently, may not even recognize that a story is being told.

Ordering the tasks of telling and listening to family stories raises questions for communication scholars, including the following.

Varieties of Conarration

Participation in family storytelling suggests communication processes whereby family stories are collaboratively created and may assume canonical status. At the same time, participation forms alliances and evokes conflict among family members as they correct, contradict, or complicate a family storyline. How are storytelling roles, rights, and responsibilities distributed? How do marital partners or family "sides" conarrate stories (Thym-Hochrein, 1981; Veroff, Chadiha, Leber, & Sutherland, 1993)? How do generations of motherlines and fatherlines participate in family storytelling (Dills, 1998; Petraki, 2001)? How do siblings interact to tell stories? What patterns of family storytelling emerge in single-parent or blended families?

Storytelling Audiences and Situations

Task ordering in storytelling is constrained by situational and material conditions. Its study requires sensitivity to such conditions of narrative performance. How do researchers attend to differences between family storytelling in situ, storytelling in natural settings with researchers observing, and storytelling in interviews with individuals or groups? How do material differences inform storytelling? To take the example of gender, researchers frequently focus on the sex of the teller, especially women's roles in family storytelling (Baldwin, 1985), identifying a sexual division of labor in storytelling where women bear more responsibility for family maintenance and interaction. The gender of the listener may be equally significant. Reese (1996), for example, found that mothers told birth stories differently to their daughters than to their sons.

Adapting Storytelling to Change

Families adapt their stories and interactional tasks to changes within the family and in relation to the broader social and cultural environment. How do families who undergo internal changes—divorce, remarriage, death of a parent or child, a move, and so on—renegotiate the tasks of storytelling? The three-generational structure of story transmission from parents to children, subject to correction by grandparents, may be favored by contemporary nuclear families in that it requires only intermittent contact with the senior generation. Moreover, in the context of increased geographic mobility, rapidly changing technologies and jobs, and an emphasis on youth culture, does the retrieval of stories from the senior generation lose value while the tasks of innovation and interpretation by younger generations assume greater significance? Do families collapse the tasks of storytelling into two generations? Within immigrant families, information often flows upward from children to older generations as young people quickly adapt to a new language and environment. How might the storytelling patterns of ethnic families be altered by immigration and child-centered family practices that distribute tasks more democratically among generations?

Summary

We reiterate that learning stories and storytelling roles depends on interaction. Family storytelling is enhanced by opportunities to communicate—daily conversations, e-mail and other communication technologies, and special family occasions. Pleck (2000) argues that the labor to plan and prepare "domestic occasions" that celebrate the family are divided by generation and gender. The task of creating occasions for family storytelling is a form of kinwork assumed primarily by women, particularly if they are ethnic women (di Leonardo, 1984). Dixon (2000), for example, describes triennial family reunions of her Oklahoma Cherokee clan inaugurated by Mamaw (grandmother) but, significantly, carried on by the next generations at the "family house" after her death. Family gatherings are a site of storytelling as well as other meaning-making family practices, such as family theme, family myth, and family metaphor (Turner & West, 2006).

A range of storytelling tactics can promote the survival of family culture, but a concern with nonparticipation remains: What if no one tells family stories or if no one listens? Wolin and Bennett (1984) suggest that families with a low level of commitment to ritual are oriented to the present and to "their" family, defined as nuclear rather than extended. Such families may dissolve family rituals that no longer meet their needs. Because task ordering takes place within the context of content ordering, the loss of a storytelling task is more consequential than the loss of particular content, story, storyteller, or ritual. The ways families develop and distribute the tasks of storytelling and story listening feature communication among family members and generate rules for participation, which suggest multiple patterns by generation and gender as well as variations by race, ethnicity, class, and other markers. These patterns adapt as families change and as environments change.

Ordering Identities

We suggested in our introduction that the postmodern family experiences particular urgency to "get a life" through the making and telling of stories about themselves. Narrative is a privileged site of identity construction. A family innovates identities for itself and its members as it successfully adapts to an ever-shifting environment and passes along its culture to a new generation. The ordering of group and personal identities depends on successful content ordering as families make stories and on effective task ordering as families tell and retell them. The outcomes of performing family stories are local models of identity—the external and internal boundaries of "our family" and "their family," of "you" and "me." Storytelling is one way that families become visible and audible to themselves as who "we" are, where "we" came from, and where "we" are going. Simultaneously, family storytelling supports the construction of personal identities as individuals narrate themselves as enfamilied selves. By drawing on and distinguishing social and cultural resources, such as class, race, ethnicity, and sexual orientation embodied in narratives of family relations, family storytelling also constitutes group identities.

A communication approach to family storytelling conceptualizes identity as relational and performative. Understood as relational, identity emerges interactionally in the fluctuating boundaries, internal and external, that define "you" and "me," "our family" and "their family," and "families like ours." Understood as performative, family identities are ongoing cultural formations rather than natural, biological phenomena. Performing family stories forms families in a struggle over identity, which draws upon master narratives of family and upon acceptable models of identity for family members at the same time that it resists those stories and roles. The performative conception of identity multiplies possibilities for family identity, which we discuss below as personal, small group, communal, and cultural identities.

Personal Identities

Family storytelling constructs personal identity in terms of family roles and relations. The uniqueness of family experience—its nonvoluntary nature; the depth, longevity, and complexities of its emotional life; and its orientation to multiple and altruistic goals—distinguishes it from other social systems (Yerby et al., 1995). In phenomenological terms, family is a we-relationship embodied in the intimacy, intensity, and immediacy of family time and space that structures a reciprocity of perspectives. The "I" of the person emerges in relation to the familial "we." For example, individuals tell stories about their fathers as a way to reframe, revise, and revisit canonical family stories and to claim an identity (Jago, 1996; Kiesinger, 2002; Pelias, 2002). Stepmothers (Jones, 2004), lone mothers (May, 2004), and noncustodial mothers (Eicher-Catt, 2004) tell stories that contextualize their identities within normative narratives of motherhood and womanhood. In terms of social class, Winn (2003) examines written family stories of academics from working-class backgrounds who construct what she calls a liminal identity positioned tensively between the worlds of work and home. Narratives of personal identity are embedded in family time and the places called "home."

Small Group Identities

At the same time that family stories produce personal, enfamilied identities, they form small-group cultures. Trujillo's (2004) book-length study of his grandmother Naunny, for example, offers a collage of voices—oral and written family stories of relatives, family letters, Naunny's journals, and the author's memories and insights—that create an "American family" inflected by ethnicity, class, gender, and age. The term *small-group culture* favors a diversity of family identities over the sense of a single normative family. Turner and West (2006) call for inclusive configurations of family, addressing the family-of-origin, nuclear family, lesbian and gay family, extended family, blended family, single-parent family, and cohabitating couples. To suggest some specific challenges and possibilities for ordering small group identity in family storytelling, we focus briefly on lesbian and gay families.

Storytelling places extraordinary constraints on gay, lesbian, bisexual, and transgender family members, and it catalyzes them to extraordinary agency, as evidenced by the historical emergence of the coming-out narrative, including coming out to kin (Plummer, 1995). Social forms and norms that traditionally establish, define, and maintain families are not easily mobilized by gay families; in fact, *gay* and *family* may be constructed as oppositional terms based on the family as a unitary object, paradigmatically heterosexual and procreative (Weston, 1991). Roof (1996) calls the dominant narrative logic—from heterosexual romance to marriage to children—a heteronarrative that not only stabilizes the family but also normalizes and naturalizes sexuality. She argues that both family stories and narrative theory recuperate queer counternarratives and sexualities within the heteronarrative. Against these discursive constraints, lesbian, gay, bisexual, and transgender families narrate their experiences. For example, three different courtship scripts (friendship, romance, and sexually explicit stories) structure lesbian stories in opposition to cultural assumptions that lesbian relationships lack a well-defined courtship stage (Rose, Zand, & Cini, 1993). Taylor's (1998) narrative about her commitment ceremony and family practices draws on notions of love, marriage, and parenting that are performative rather than naturalized: In other words, what we do every day makes us family.

Communal Identities

Families may also form communal identities that extend beyond personal and small group identities. According to Morrow (1999), community identity assumes crucial significance for lesbian, gay, and bisexual (LGB) families. She argues that LGB families are preoccupied with how sexual identity is constructed in narratives because simply sharing stories establishes communities that support other LGB families with children. Circulating family stories forms community by crossing borders between families and blurring the public-private boundary. Telling and retelling "parables of hope" among nonfamily members revises them as two types of stories emerge: family stories adopted by the community and communal stories that become family stories. She observes that LGB families with children incorporate competing explanations of sexual identity in the stories they tell about themselves and their community. In stories about family values and valued families, the performative identities that form LGB families and communities are juxtaposed with the biological determinism that asserts LGB parents' rights to rear children. Morrow emphasizes that the collective life narratives emerge not simply because they are circulated but because LGB family storytelling produces communities.

Cultural Identities

Resources beyond the personal, beyond the small group, and beyond the extended family and community may also be important for families narrating racial and ethnic identities. African American narratives invoke home and homeplace to ground cultural identities, both heterosexual and queer. James (2000), for example, examines how competing family stories from her mother's and father's sides formed her African American identity. Home, domestic space, and family are mined as tropes and transgressive space for Black queer identity by Johnson (2004) and Nero (2000). Other communal definitions of family are suggested by Alexander and LeBlanc (1999), who place their family stories in dialogue to explore identity and difference as "cooking gumbo" in Cajun French traditions. A Black man and White man, respectively, from southern Louisiana, their family narratives suggest that community may include not only extended family or neighbors but also those within a cultural group or region. Langellier and Peterson (2004) offer an analysis of French American identity that embraces personal, nuclear, and communal family identities in Maine, including variations extended by the Internet and other networking strategies that result in large-scale family reunions in northern Maine and Acadian Canada. Identify formation emerges in the relations of their families to each other and to other like families.

The ordering of identities raises questions about family diversity, which we discuss below.

Nonnormative and Neglected Family Formations

The numerous myths and illusions about American families create an idealized identity by which real families must pale or fail in comparison. How do nonnormative, nonintact, and neglected families, such as homeless families, create narrative identities (Turner & West, 2006)? Recently, Boylan (2003) has narrated her transgender transition from male to female within a long-term marriage with two children. How do "intentional families" of partners without children and other "self-defined families" based on friendship or location rather than kinship tell their stories? How do family members and families produce counternarratives of identity that repair and resist normative family narratives?

Family Boundaries

Who is in the family circle of "we" and who, like the black sheep, is not? For example, what family stories are told about the child of a son who is neither married nor in a relationship with the child's mother? How do families-of-origin include or exclude a gay partner (Nero, 2000) in their stories? Is an ex-wife or husband part of the family definition, and how is this narrated? Family identity is formed not just in a miniculture of internal relations but also in interaction across boundaries among families and groups of families. Rich and complex stories are intimated in Leeds-Hurwitz's (2002) study of intercultural weddings and commitment rituals, where *intercultural* may refer to international, interracial, interethnic, interfaith, and interclass alliances that bring together two families and social groups. How do children of intercultural and racially mixed identities narrate their families (Chhuor, 2004; Morris, 2000)?

"American" Families

As families in the United States tell stories about themselves, they also make, unmake, and remake "American" identity. According to Smith and Watson (1996), narrative performance is a "palpable means through which Americans know themselves to be American and not-American in all those complexities and contradictions of that identity" (p. 6). Family storytelling participates in cultural struggle and class competition as families compare themselves to one another and other groups (Rubin, 1994; Stone, 1988) in a hierarchy of "Americanness." Becoming American also involves narratives of immigration, assimilation, and resistance. Immigration is a narrative disruption of roots, language, and social connections that anchor family and cultural identity. How do families and groups of families construct and reconstruct their complex history and positioning in terms of cultural uniqueness and assimilation in a multicultural United States? Hegde (1998), for example, highlights the creative reconstructions of translated enactments of her Asian Indian family, arguing that the ethnic community "provides the cultural repository to fuse narrative disruptions that migrants face in their transplanted lives" (p. 319). Carrillo Rowe (2000) resists forgetting her Mexican identity, writing a postcolonial counternarrative to her mother's assimilation story. This narrative space of remembering and resistance marks and denaturalizes the seeming naturalness of the master narrative of assimilated "American" identity. A multicultural and global world calls for further explorations of migrant, hybrid, and transnational family identities in stories.

Summary

Family storytelling orders personal identities as enfamilied selves narrate their experiences, as small groups of nuclear and extended families construct their self-definitions, and as groups of families form communities and larger networks in narrative reconstructions of themselves across changing landscapes and histories. Family identities are constituted in communication within and across the boundaries of the ever-fluctuating "we" of family. Stories by individual family members, by families, and by family groups draw on master narratives of family identity, but they also resist those discursive forces. For families experiencing the domination of White privilege, the disruptions of immigration, or the duress of heteronormativity, community and network interactions assume particular significance in narrating a "we." Indeed, family stories grounding identity—personal, small group, communal, and cultural—can only be understood within larger social fields that give them meaning.

Conclusion

A narrative approach to family communication argues that one way we "do family" is by telling stories, by performing ourselves to ourselves and others with words. Family storytelling is a communication practice that creates and sustains the diverse small-group cultures called "family." We have described this communication practice as three levels of ordering to make sense of family sensibilities: content ordering to make stories from experience, task ordering to allocate participation in their telling and listening, and group ordering to form family identities of who "we" are. Family storytelling is both creative and ritualist communication; it both produces *a family* we live daily, and it discursively reproduces *The Family* we live by to make its meanings. Hence, it unavoidably engages in a struggle over meanings for what makes a tellable story and what makes a family—indeed, for what makes "good" storytelling and what makes a "good" family.

Our approach to family storytelling as communication practice argues that family is a cultural formation created and sustained in communication rather than a natural, biological phenomenon. In a word, family is performed and performative in its stories. This view decouples the family from nature and restores its historicity as a social institution of Western culture in the past 500 years. Denaturalizing the family simultaneously deconstructs its master narrative. Belsey (2001) notes that a "perfectly and consistently happy family has no story" (p. 295) because such a perfectly and consistently happy family "is silent on both what *goes without saying* and what *cannot be said*" (p. 298). What goes without saying and what goes unsaid in family storytelling and its study? This silence continues to challenge us as members of diverse families and as communication researchers.

References

Alexander, B. K., & LeBlanc III, H. P. (1999). Cooking gumbo—Examining cultural dialogue about family: A Black-White narrativization of lived experience in Southern Louisiana. In T. J. Socha & R. C. Diggs (Eds.), *Communication, race, and family: Exploring communication in Black, White, and biracial families* (pp. 181–208). Mahwah, NJ: Lawrence Erlbaum.

Andrews, M. (2002). Memories of mother: Counter-narratives of early maternal influence. *Narrative Inquiry, 12,* 7–27.

Baldwin, K. (1985). "Woof!" A word on women's roles in family storytelling. In R. A. Jordon and S. J. Kalčik (Eds.), *Women's folklore, women's culture* (pp. 149–162). Philadelphia: University of Pennsylvania Press.

Bell, S. E. (2002). On identifying counter-narratives of failed IVF. *Narrative Inquiry, 12,* 391–395.

Belsey, C. (2001). Denaturalizing the family: History at the level of the signifier. *European Journal of Cultural Studies, 4,* 289–303.

Benjamin, W. (1969). The storyteller. In H. Arendt (Ed.), *Illuminations* (H. Zohn, Trans.) (pp. 83–109). New York: Schocken.

Blum-Kulka, S. (1997). *Dinner talk: Cultural patterns of sociability and socialization in family discourse.* Mahwah, NJ: Lawrence Erlbaum.

Blum-Kulka, S., & Snow, C. E. (1992). Developing autonomy for tellers, tales, and telling in family narrative events. *Journal of Narrative and Life History, 2,* 187–217.

Boylan, J. F. (2003). *She's not there: A life in two genders.* New York: Broadway Books.

Bylund, C. L. (2003). Ethnic diversity and family stories. *Journal of Family Communication, 3,* 215–236.

Carrillo Rowe, A. M. (2000). Women writing borders, borders writing women: Immigration, assimilation, and the politics of speaking. In A. González, M. Houston, & V. Chen (Eds.), *Our voices: Essays in culture, ethnicity, and communication* (pp. 207–219). Los Angeles: Roxbury.

Chhuor, P. (2004). Personal journey: My struggle between Cambodian and Chinese identities. In M. Fong & R. Chuang (Eds.), *Communicating ethnic and cultural identity* (pp. 363–371). Lanham, MD: Rowman & Littlefield.

Cottle, T. J. (2000). Mind shadows: A suicide in the family. *Journal of Contemporary Ethnography, 29,* 222–255.

Delacroix, C. (1995). The cross-telling of life narratives and family stories. *Current Sociology/La Sociologie Contemporarie, 43,* 61–67.

di Leonardo, M. (1984). *The varieties of ethnic experience: Kinship, class, and gender among California Italian Americans.* Ithaca, NY: Cornell University Press.

Dills, V. L. (1998). Transferring and transforming cultural norms: A mother-daughter-son lifestory in process. *Narrative Inquiry, 8,* 213–222.

Dixon, L. D. (2000). A house as symbol, a house as family: Mamaw and her Oklahoma Cherokee family. In A. González, M. Houston, & V. Chen (Eds.), *Our voices: Essays in culture, ethnicity, and communication* (pp. 125–128). Los Angeles: Roxbury.

Eicher-Catt, D. (2004). Non-custodial mothering: A cultural paradox of competent performance-performative competence. *Contemporary Ethnography, 32,* 72–108.

Ellis, C., & Bochner, A. P. (1992). Telling and performing personal stories: The constraints of choice in abortion. In C. Ellis & M. Flaherty (Eds.), *Investigating subjectivity* (pp. 79–101). Newbury Park, CA: Sage.

Fiese, B. H., Sameroff, A. J., Grotevant, H. D., Wambolt, F. S., Dickstein, S., & Fravel, D. L. (1999). *The stories that families tell: Narrative coherence, narrative interaction, and relationship beliefs.* Maldon, MA: Blackwell.

Fiese, B. H., & Skillman, G. (2000). Gender differences in family stories: Moderating influence of parent gender role and child gender. *Sex Roles, 43,* 267–283.

Georgakopoulou, A. (1998). Conversational stories as performances: The case of Greek. *Narrative Inquiry, 8,* 319–350.

Gillis, J. R. (1996). *A world of their own making: Myth, ritual, and the quest for family values.* New York: Basic Books.

Grout, L. A., & Romanoff, B. D. (2000). The myth of the replacement child: Parents' stories and practices after perinatal death. *Death Studies, 24,* 93–113.

Heath, S. B. (1983). *Ways with words: Language, life and work in communities and classroom.* Cambridge, UK: Cambridge University Press.

Hegde, R. S. (1998). Translated enactments: The relational configurations of the Asian Indian immigrant experience. In J. N. Martin, T. K. Nakayama, & L. A. Flores (Eds.), *Readings in cultural contexts* (pp. 315–322). Mountain View, CA: Mayfield.

Hirst, W., & Manier, D. (1996). Remembering as communication: A family recounts its past. In D. C. Rubin (Ed.), *Remembering our past: Studies in autobiographical memory* (pp. 271–290). Cambridge, UK: Cambridge University Press.

Jago, B. (1996). Postcards, ghosts, and fathers: Revising family stories. *Qualitative Inquiry, 2,* 495–516.

James, N. C. (2000). When Miss America was always White. In A. González, M. Houston, & V. Chen (Eds.), *Our voices: Essays in culture, ethnicity, and communication* (pp. 42–46). Los Angeles: Roxbury.

Jeter, K. (1996). Cross-national research on family stories-folktales as archetypical windows to mythological heroic behavior. *Marriage and Family Review, 23,* 745–770.

Johnson, E. P. (2004). Mother knows best: Blackness and transgressive domestic space. In *Appropriating Blackness: Performance and the politics of authenticity.* Durham, NC: Duke University Press.

Jones, A. C. (2004). Transforming the story: Narrative applications to a stepmother support group. *Families in Society, 85,* 129–138.

Jorgenson, J., & Bochner, A. P. (2004). Imagining families through stories and ritual. In A. L. Vangelisti (Ed.), *Handbook of family communication* (pp. 513–538). Mahwah, NJ: Lawrence Erlbaum.

Kiesinger, C. E. (2002). My father's shoes: The therapeutic value of narrative reframing. In A. P. Bochner & C. Ellis (Eds.), *Ethnographically speaking: Autoethnography, literature, and aesthetics* (pp. 95–114). Walnut Creek, CA: AltaMira.

Kirkman, M. (2003). Infertile women and the narrative work of mourning: Barriers to the revision of autobiographical narratives of motherhood. *Narrative Inquiry, 13,* 243–262.

Krusiewicz, E. S., & Wood, J. T. (2001). "He was our child from the moment we walked in that room": Entrance stories of adoptive parents. *Journal of Social and Personal Relationships, 18,* 785–803.

Langellier, K. M., & Peterson, E. E. (2004). *Storytelling in daily life: Performing narrative.* Philadelphia: Temple University Press.

Langellier, K. M., & Peterson, E. E. (2006). Narrative performance theory: Telling stories, doing family. In D. O. Braithwaite & L. A. Baxter (Eds.), *Family communication theories* (pp. 99–114). Thousand Oaks, CA: Sage.

Leeds-Hurwitz, W. (2002). *Wedding as text: Communicating cultural identities through ritual.* Mahwah, NJ: Lawrence Erlbaum.

Martin, P., Hagestad, G. O., & Diedrick, P. (1988). Family stories: Events (temporarily) remembered. *Journal of Marriage and the Family, 50,* 533–541.

Marvin, L. (2004). Why Mamiji cried: Telling stories and defining families. *Storytelling, Self, Society, 1,* 28–43.

May, V. (2004). Narrative identity and the re-conceptualization of lone motherhood. *Narrative Inquiry, 14,* 169–189.

McAdoo, H. P. (2001). Point of view: Ethnicity and family dialogue. *Journal of Family Communication, 1,* 87–90.

McFeat, T. (1974). *Small group cultures.* New York: Pergamon.

Montalbano-Phelps, L. L. (2003). Discourse of survival: Building families free of unhealthy relationships. *Journal of Family Communication, 3,* 149–167.

Morris, R. (2000). Living in/between. In A. González, M. Houston, & V. Chen (Eds.), *Our voices: Essays in culture, ethnicity, and communication* (pp. 195–204). Los Angeles: Roxbury.

Morrow, C. (1999). Family values/valued families: Storytelling and community formation among LGB families with children. *Journal of Gay, Lesbian, and Bisexual Identity, 4,* 345–356.

Nero, C. I. (2000). Black queer identity, imaginative rationality, and the language of home. In A. González, M. Houston, & V. Chen (Eds.), *Our voices: Essays in culture, ethnicity, and communication* (pp. 54–59). Los Angeles: Roxbury.

Ochs, E., & Capps, L. (2001). *Living narrative: Creating lives in everyday storytelling.* Cambridge, MA: Harvard University Press.

Ochs, E., & Taylor, C. (1995). The 'father knows best' dynamic in dinnertime narratives. In K. Hall & M. Bucholtz (Eds.), *Gender articulated: Language and the socially constructed self* (pp. 97–120). New York: Routledge.

Patton, S, (1996). Race/identity/culture/kin: Constructions of African American identity in transracial adoption. In S. Smith & J. Watson (Eds.), *Getting a life: Everyday uses of autobiography* (pp. 271–296). Minneapolis: University of Minnesota Press.

Pelias, R. (2002). For father and son: An ethnodrama with no catharsis. In A. P. Bochner & C. Ellis (Eds.), *Ethnographically speaking: Autoethnography, literature, and aesthetics* (pp. 35–43). Walnut Creek, CA: AltaMira.

Petraki, E. (2001). The play of identities in Cypriot-Australian family storytelling. *Narrative Inquiry, 11,* 335–362.

Pleck, E. H. (2000). *Celebrating the family: Ethnicity, consumer culture, and family rituals.* Cambridge, MA: Harvard University Press.

Pineau, E. (2000). Nursing mother and articulating absence. *Text and Performance Quarterly, 20,* 1–19.

Plummer, K. (1995). *Telling sexual stories: Power, change and social worlds.* New York: Routledge.

Pollock, D. (1999). *Telling bodies, performing birth: Everyday narratives of childbirth.* New York: Columbia University Press.

Reese, E. (1996). Conceptions of self in mother-child birth stories. *Journal of Narrative and Life History, 6,* 23–38.

Riessman, C. K. (1990). *Divorce talk: Women and men make sense of personal relationships.* New Brunswick, NJ: Rutgers University Press.

Riessman, C. K. (2000). Stigma and everyday resistance practices: Childless women in South India. *Gender & Society, 14,* 111–135.

Ronai, C. R. (1996). My mother is mentally retarded. In C. Ellis & A. P. Bochner (Eds.), *Composing ethnography: Alternative forms of qualitative writing* (pp. 109–131). Walnut Creek, CA: AltaMira.

Roof, J. (1996). *Come as you are: Sexuality and narrative.* New York: Columbia University Press.

Rose, S., Zand, D., & Cini, M. A. (1993). Lesbian courtship scripts. In E. D. Rothblum & K. A. Brehony (Eds.), *Boston marriages: Romantic but asexual relationships among contemporary lesbians* (pp. 71–85). Amherst: University of Massachusetts Press.

Rubin, L. (1994). *Families on the faultline: America's working class speaks about the family, the economy, race, and ethnicity.* New York: HarperCollins.

Schely-Newman, E. (1999). Mothers know best: Constructing meaning in a narrative event. *Quarterly Journal of Speech, 85,* 285–302.

Schiffrin, D. (2000). Mother/daughter discourse in a Holocaust oral history: "Because then you admit that you're guilty." *Narrative Inquiry, 10,* 1–44.

Smith, S., & Watson, J. (Eds.). (1996). *Getting a life: Everyday uses of autobiography.* Minneapolis: University of Minnesota Press.

Socha, T. J., & Diggs, R. C. (Eds.). (1999). *Communication, race, and family: Exploring communication in Black, White, and biracial families.* Mahwah, NJ: Lawrence Erlbaum.

Spry, T. (2000). Tattoo stories: A postscript to Skins. *Text and Performance Quarterly, 20,* 84–96.

Stone, E. (1988). *Black sheep and kissing cousins: How our family stories shape us.* New York: Times Books.

Tafoya, T. (1989, August). Coyote's eyes: Native cognition styles. *Journal of American Indian Education* (Special Issue), pp. 29–42. [Reprinted from (1982) *21,* 21–33.]

Talbot, J., Bibace, R., Bokhour, B., & Bamberg, M. (1996). Affirmation and resistance of dominant discourse: The rhetorical construction of pregnancy. *Journal of Narrative and Life History, 6,* 225–251.

Taylor, J. (1998). Performing commitment. In J. N. Martin, T. K. Nakayama, & L. A. Flores (Eds.), *Readings in cultural contexts* (pp. 387–395). Mountain View, CA: Mayfield.

Throsby, K. (2002). Negotiating "normality" when IVF fails. *Narrative Inquiry, 12,* 43–65.

Thym-Hochrein, N. (1981). "Peter left because": A comparative study of oral family histories. *ARV: Scandinavian Journal, 37,* 61–68.

Trujillo, N. (2004). *In search of Naunny's grave: Age, class, gender, and ethnicity in an American family.* Walnut Creek, CA: AltaMira.

Turner, L. H., & West, R. (2006). *Perspectives on family communication* (3rd ed.). New York: McGraw-Hill.

Vangelisti, A. L., Crumley, L. P., & Baker, J. L. (1999). Family portraits: Stories as standards for family relationships. *Journal of Social and Personal Relationships, 16,* 335–368.

Verhoff, J., Chadiha, L., Leber, D., & Sutherland, L. (1993). Affects and interaction in newlyweds' narratives: Black and White couples compared. *Journal of Narrative and Life History, 3,* 361–390.

Watson, J. (1996). Ordering the family: Genealogy as autobiographical pedigree. In S. Smith & J. Watson (Eds.), *Getting a life: Everyday uses of autobiography* (pp. 297–323). Minneapolis: University of Minnesota Press.

Weston, K. (1991). *Families we choose: Lesbians, gays, and kinship.* New York: Columbia University Press.

Whitchurch, G. G., & Dickson, F. C. (1999). Family communication. In M. B. Sussman, S. K. Steinmentz, & G. W. Peterson (Eds.), *Handbook of marriage and the family* (pp. 687–704). New York: Plenum.

Winn, L. L. (2003, November). *Negotiating the liminal identity: Themes of loyalty and loss in the family stories of academics from the working class.* Paper presented at the annual convention of the National Communication Association, Miami Beach, FL.

Wolin, S. J., & Bennett, L. A. (1984). Family rituals. *Family Process, 23,* 401–420.

Yerby, J., Buerkel-Rothfuss, N. L., & Bochner, A. P. (1995). *Understanding family communication* (2nd ed.). Scottsdale, AZ: Gorsuch Scarisbrick.

CHAPTER 7

Cover Stories as Family Communication Practice

Theresa L. Hest

Minnesota State University Moorhead

Judy C. Pearson

North Dakota State University

Jeffrey T. Child

North Dakota State University

I n the last chapter, Langellier and Peterson defined family storytelling as communication practice because it involves performance and representation. Family members use storytelling to create and present family identities. We examine storytelling in this chapter through the vehicle of marital "cover stories," or stories that couples create and co-own. Cover stories are a unique type of family story, constructed for a variety of communicative reasons such as saving face or maintaining privacy. In a cover story, a married couple might agree on an excuse to miss an event or coordinate a narrative about an unwanted gift, making the giver feel appreciated. Married partners learn that working as a team through the use of cover stories could protect their union from outsiders.

Before turning to couples' constructed stories, let us look at storytelling itself, its history, social utility, and its widespread application. Storytelling is omnipresent: Personal narrative is central in the oral tradition (Stahl, 1983). Bruner (1987) states that telling life stories is "ancient and universal. People everywhere can tell you some intelligible account of their lives" (p. 16). Narrative exploration provides an opportunity to understand the process of meaning making (Fiese & Sameroff, 1999) for an individual, a couple, a family, or a culture.

Storytelling is a powerful social means of giving experiences meaning. Over two decades ago, Fisher (1984) argued, "The meaning and significance of life in all of its social dimensions require the recognition of its narrative structure" (p. 3). He defined *narrative* as "words and/or deeds—that have sequence and meaning for those who live, create, or interpret them" (p. 2). Thus, the real and imagined stories of life are important because they create reality for individuals in the past, present, and future. As such, the creation, ownership, and performance of marital cover stories may create a particular reality both within and outside the couple/family unit.

The scholarship on storytelling encompasses many disciplines and many aspects of relationships. Widdershoven (1993), for example, addresses the connections among history, stories, and identity. He argues that people tell stories about their lives, and these stories create a personal identity. Shaw (1997) offers that narrative allows us to talk about ourselves (e.g., impression management) without appearing self-centered. In contrast to the public element of stories, Duck (1998) explores the importance of thinking about and creating stories on an intrapersonal level. Bochner, Ellis, and Tillmann-Healy (2000) relate how storytelling is a coconstructive process that provides a way to define and understand relationships. LaRossa (1995) observes, "Stories and relationships thus are inextricably intertwined, not only in the sense that people exchange information through stories, but also that people come to define themselves and others through the stories they tell" (p. 555). Finally, Jorgenson and Bochner (2004) emphasize the importance of stories by noting, "Our identities hinge largely on the stories we tell about ourselves and the stories we hear and internalize that others tell about us" (p. 515). Thus, research in many contexts continues to highlight the interaction among storytelling, self, and relationships.

Cover Stories

Marital partners create and present a multitude of planned and spontaneous stories concerning their past, present, and future. In some cases, these narratives may have little (or no) semblance to actual fact. Indeed, the concept of a relational story, as McGregor and Holmes (1999) argue, connotes "a certain slippage from the realities of the episode it supposedly portrays, if not wholesale bending of the facts to create a 'good story'" (p. 403). In the case of marital cover stories, a couple may function as "knowing" partners who rely on each other to maintain "a projected definition of the situation" (Goffman, 1959, p. 104).

Cover stories are constructions that are coordinated and then co-owned by a couple. For example, a couple may decide to tell their families that they saved the money to pay for a vacation when, in actuality, they put the trip on credit cards. Couples have co-ownership of this in that there is agreement on the need to create an explanation or a "story." One function of narrative is protection for the couple.

Cover stories may help the couple negotiate daily living, avoid hurting someone's feelings, avoid a conflict situation, or present a positive image to others. This chapter explores these functions for cover stories in a marriage. Specifically, we explore what married couples say are the reasons they cocreate cover stories.

Marital couples tell stories, and even marriage can be viewed as a cocreated story (e.g., a couple may tell "our story"). Couples describe their relationships in "story" terms such as when they first met, turning points or crises in their lives, and the resolution of conflict or serious issues. As with the creation and performance of cover stories, a marriage may be seen as a negotiated coconstruction in which the couple continually structures and gives meaning to experiences (Duck, 1994, 1995). Relational partners "coordinate the enactment of their relationship" through daily joint conversations (Goldsmith & Baxter, 1996, p. 108). Everyday conversation provides the means for coordinating the overall marital story as well as cover stories. A relationship can also be defined as the process of creating a "symbiosis, and ultimately a fusion, of personal meaning systems through communication" (VanderVoort & Duck, 2000, p. 10).

Cover Stories and Deception

Any story that a couple tells may have an element of deception. Putnam, Van Hoeven, and Bullis (1991) reveal, "Stories can develop from actual events or they can be fictional" (p. 87). Deception can be defined as the "intentional misrepresentation of information" (Metts, 1989, p. 160), or "knowingly transmitting a message intended to lead a receiver to a false belief or conclusion" (Burgoon, Buller, White, Afifi, & Buslig, 1999). The use of deception, especially harmless fibs (e.g., I'm late because I had car trouble), is almost an everyday occurrence for many people (Camden, Motley, & Wilson, 1984; DePaulo, Kashy, Kirkendol, Wyer, & Epstein, 1996).

Turner, Edgely, and Olmstead (1975) identify five reasons, directly linked to cover stories, for concealing or distorting information. *Face* is defined by these researchers as "information control to protect . . . identity" of the actor, the other, or a person outside the encounter (p. 77). *Saving face* is also explained as protecting the "positive feelings one has about his (*sic*) identity in a social situation" (p. 78). A couple may share a flattering cover story to hide a less flattering reality. The category of *relationship* involves "information control to maintain, maximize, or terminate the degree of intimacy and/or social distance with the other" (p. 77). *Exploitation* addresses the need to "establish, maintain, or maximize power or influence" (p. 77) or "manipulate others' actions" (p. 80). The reason to *avoid tension/conflict* suggests "information control to preclude conflict or tension" (p. 77). Cover stories may serve to defuse a potential conflict. The final category is *situational control* and represents "information control to maintain, redirect, or terminate" social interactions (p. 77). These researchers conclude that to suggest that "many social problems would be solved if in all social relationships people were one-hundred percent honest" is naive (p. 83). Although potentially deceptive, cover stories may serve many purposes in a couple's interactions with others.

Cover Stories and Privacy Maintenance

Privacy can be viewed as the need to be separate or to keep some information about yourself separate from others. Petronio (2002) explains the connection between privacy and deception. She argues that selective disclosure is not always defined as deceptive and, like Gordon and Miller (2000), suggests that whether deception occurs depends on your perspective. Petronio states that privacy becomes deception based on the rationale for the message. Reasons such as preserving privacy, wanting to spare someone's feelings, or protecting yourself or others may complicate the boundaries between privacy maintenance and deception. This perspective is further enhanced by Rosenfeld (2000): "Given the risks associated with disclosure, people might choose alternatives that include a focus on privacy, secrecy, and even deception" (p. 8).

The theory of communication privacy management (CPM) addresses the everyday communication issues related to privacy (Petronio, 2002). Privacy management is a dialectic of revelation and concealment (Petronio, 2000). Petronio (2002) states, "Privacy has importance for us because it lets us feel separate from others. It gives us a sense that we are the rightful owners of information about us" (p. 1). When partners in a marriage choose to cover for each other by omitting information or even deliberately falsifying information, they highlight information that belongs to them alone. If married partners view certain information as just "theirs," then they may believe that they have the right to reveal or conceal as they choose. Married partners may seek "control over the boundaries" (Petronio, 2002, p. 3).

Cover Stories and Impression Management

Whether deceptive or not, couples create and share cover stories for a variety of reasons. One possible reason is to convey a particular view of the married couple's "self" and to manage the impressions the couple presents to others. The concept of impression management suggests that social life is a series of dramatic performances that people perform for an audience to maintain a stable self-image (Goffman, 1959). Goffman explained this approach as

> the way in which the individual in ordinary work situations presents himself and his activity to others, the ways in which he guides and controls the impression they form of him, and the kinds of things he may and may not do while sustaining his performance before them. (p. xi)[1]

Impression management seeks to maintain the presented sense of self by attempting to control any disruptions or problems presented by the audience that might affect acceptance of the impression (Goffman, 1959).

Because people try to present a certain image when they are performing on the "front stage," they may seek to conceal some features and show only the "finished, polished, and packaged" product (Goffman, 1959, p. 44). This "front stage," for example, is represented by a married couple that hosts a dinner party and assures their guests it was a pleasure. In reality, the couple may have experienced a great deal of tension and conflict in preparing for the party but chose to "cover" this aspect of the event to present a certain image.

Goffman's (1959) basic unit of analysis is the "team," which has application for the study of couples as coconspirators in storytelling. A team is defined as "a set of individuals whose intimate co-operation is required if a given projected definition of the situation is to be maintained" (p. 104). Some of the team characteristics identified by Goffman include the following: Teammates can be trusted to perform properly, teammates are forced to rely on each other's good conduct (not to give the show away), teammates are "in the know" with each other, and teammates should not speak publicly until the position has been selected. These theoretical statements provide the foundation for this investigation of cover stories.

Method

Participants

Data collection for the study involved both in-depth interviews with married couples and open-ended surveys completed by married couples. These data were part of a larger family story project involving 167 married couples.

Face-to-Face Interviews

We interviewed a total of 26 couples (52 individuals), 23 of whom provided cover stories. The age range of interview participants was 28 to 77 years old. The number of years married ranged from 7 years together to 47 years, averaging 18 years of marriage. For 6 of the interview participants, this was a second marriage. The highest education level of interview participants varied, with 5 participants with a high school diploma to 9 interviewees with a Ph.D. degree. All of the interview participants had children, and 20 of the couples still had children living at home. All of the individuals interviewed for the study were White. Participants did not identify income level.

Open-Ended Surveys

Two hundred eight students in five different undergraduate communication courses at a midwestern university received information packets. Of the couples, 141 completed the forms and returned them via U.S. mail, and 13 of these provided cover stories. These participants were anonymous, and no demographic information was collected. The stories were transcribed from the returned forms.

Overall, participants provided a total of 66 cover stories (23 couples from the interviews and 13 from the open-ended survey process). There were a total of 66 stories from 36 couples because many couples submitted more than one story.

Procedures

The Face-to-Face Interview Data Collection Process

The researchers found interview participants through purposeful sampling of married couples who were willing to share their stories. A nonprobability convenience sample obtained through networking was appropriate because the results are not generalizable to other populations (Creswell, 1994; Karney et al., 1995).

The interview setting was informal and the protocol was flexible to reflect the unique dynamic of each interview and to facilitate a level of comfort with the conversation. Both partners were interviewed together. Specifically, 24 of the couples were interviewed in a kitchen or living room setting, 1 couple was interviewed in a coffee shop, and 1 couple was interviewed in an office.

The researchers viewed each interview experience as unique and used different interview approaches throughout the study to maximize the participants' comfort level and facilitate discussion. The most common approach (13 couples, 50%) was the primary researcher interviewing one couple. A second approach was that of the primary researcher and her spouse conversing with one couple (7 couples, 26.9%). The third interview approach (4 couples, 15.4%) was the married interview team questioning two couples at the same time. The final approach was the primary researcher consulting two couples at the same time (2 couples, 7.7%). The approach depended on several factors: the degree to which the participating couple knew the primary researcher and spouse, the logistical issues of availability, and the primary researcher's judgment on the format that would maximize the quality of the interview.

The interview protocol was semistructured with predominantly open-ended questions. With permission of the participants, the researchers audiotaped and transcribed interviews using pseudonyms. Interview participants were orally provided examples of cover stories. Then, during the interview, the primary interviewer introduced the question of cover stories. The probe most commonly used was, "What do you do if you are invited to a social event that you really don't want to attend?" The interviews yielded 914 double-spaced pages of transcription. The shortest interview lasted 45 minutes, and the longest interview lasted 3½ hours. The average interview length was 1½ to 2 hours.

The Open-Ended Survey Data Collection Process

Students from the undergraduate communication courses participating in the survey collection process were provided with an open-ended survey information packet. Each packet contained an information sheet for the student, a letter explaining the project to the married couple, a written story form, and an addressed, postage-paid envelope. The students were provided with instructions to give the form to any married couple (including parents, relatives, or themselves). Each couple was instructed to complete the open-ended survey together, reflecting a similar data collection process as was employed with the face-to-face interviews. Similar to the couples who were interviewed face-to-face, couples who submitted stories through the open-ended survey received examples of cover stories in the survey information packet.

Data Analysis

To discover the functions of marital cover stories, the researchers employed a qualitative approach to the data. Each cover story served as the unit of analysis. The analysis began with the method suggested by Bulmer (1979) of sorting a subset of categories and then applying the rest of the data to this set, creating additional categories as needed. The primary researcher first isolated each of the identified purposes of cover stories (e.g., "to save face"). The next step was to organize these purposes into similar categories based on code words (key or common words). The themes were derived from the interviews, with the survey data serving to further illustrate these themes. After the primary researcher identified the categories, two other researchers independently coded 10 of the cover stories (15% of the sample) to test intercoder reliability.

Results

The data suggested a variety of reasons that couples coconstructed cover stories. The interviewed couples provided six reasons for cover stories, which were divided into two main categories: *For Couples* and *For Others*. Under the *For Couples* category were the following subcategories: *The Couple Team, Reciprocity,* and *Privacy Maintenance.* The category of *For Others* includes subcategories of *Saving Face, Keeping the Peace,* and *Image Management.* These categories are not mutually exclusive in that a cover story can serve more than one function. For example, married partners may agree to not disclose the actual price they paid for their home (*Privacy Maintenance*), but they may tell others a created low price in order to not look like they paid too much (*Image Management*).

Neuendorf (2002) recommends kappa values greater than .75 for excellent agreement among coders, between .75 and .40 for fair to good agreement, and below .40 for poor agreement. Cohen's kappa intercoder reliabilities for the categories were as follows: couple team ($\alpha = 1.00$), reciprocity ($\alpha = 1.00$), privacy maintenance ($\alpha = 1.00$), keeping the peace ($\alpha = 1.00$), image management ($\alpha = 1.00$), and saving face ($\alpha = .80$).

The Couple Team

This subcategory establishes married couples as the basic relationship unit in that the partners share more with each other than they do with others (including parents and children). Eight cover stories (12% of the sample) alluded to this function. In this category, couples share more information with each other than they do with others, they establish more trust, and they are protective of each other. One participant commented that spouses cover for each other because "we love them; it is so simple. You want to protect them" (21:43).[2] Key words included *bond, trust,* and *connection.* Anna offered, "That is like one more thing that just Dave and I have that I don't have with other people. . . . So that is one more thing that is just ours"

(9:29–30). James suggested, "I think it helps our relationship to let each other know that we may tell white lies to other people, but we are not going to lie to each other" (14:18). Kim commented, "And I think we realize that basically we can count on each other more than we can count on anybody else" (5:32). Couples cover for each other because they are part of a knowing, sharing, and trusting team.

Reciprocity

This function was offered by four cover stories (6% of the sample) and involves the notion of exchange. Couples believe that they can count on their partner to return the favor of covering for them. There is an "economic" motive for the couples. As Dave stated,

> It is probably just one good turn. You know, you scratch my back, and I'll scratch yours. You know, you get me out of this, and I'll get you out of one of the next ones that you don't want to go to. I think that is how it works. (9:29)

Kelly commented to her husband, "You get me out of some jams. I suppose I owe you" (25:21). Other participants mentioned, "we know they will do that for us" and "she can never leave because I have so much stuff on her." Ilsa indicated that "it makes us coconspirators" in "a joint lie" (17:19). This category represents the notion of "tit for tat," with couples returning the favor for each other.

Privacy Maintenance

Two cover stories (3% of the sample) reflected this function of cover stories. One participant shared that cover stories are "like a secret" (10:32). Ilsa offered, "I think today a big part of it is maintaining some privacy" and "to keep some things personal" (17:12). One couple provided the example of when the wife missed work to have some medical tests conducted; they agreed to tell coworkers that she just had the flu. They stated, "it just wasn't their business" (17:12). Cover stories may serve a privacy maintenance function for couples.

The functions of saving face, keeping the peace, and image management serve relational maintenance purposes for the couple with others. Couples use cover stories as a means of facilitating interactions and maintaining harmony with others.

Saving Face

This function comprised the largest overall category, with 11 cover stories (17% of the sample) highlighting the face-saving aspect of cover stories. This function addresses the need to not hurt, embarrass, or humiliate others or ourselves. As Ilsa mentioned, "Nobody wants to hear, 'I don't want to go to your party because I don't like you'" (17:18). Participants frequently mentioned, "It doesn't hurt feelings," "to be courteous," "to save face," and "to save other people's feelings." One participant stated that he and his spouse cover "to get ourselves out of a situation in a socially acceptable fashion" (13:21). Mark and Susan shared this story to avoid hurting her mother's feelings:

Susan: So I looked in the fridge and I am like, "Oh, what are these?" She [mother] says, "Oh, those are these really good chocolate bars. Take them home for Mark. He will really like them," and I said, "Oh, they are kind of dry." And she said, "Oh no, they are really good. They are really good." So, I took them and . . . immediately put them in the garbage, and I said to him, "By the way, if she asks you, the bars were really good."

Interviewer: And you knew if she asked him . . .

Mark: I would say, "Yum, my those were good." (13:20)

    Another couple offered this story of an unsuccessful attempt at covering that involves them wanting to save face.

> My husband and I were arguing one night when we were supposed to meet some friends at their apartment. Our argument went long, and we just decided not to go over to their place. The next day I stopped by and told my girlfriend that my mom had called and we talked too long. In the meantime, my husband called his buddy and told him we had to go to the grocery store and just couldn't make it over there! (W43b)[3]

    A final representative story is one that a couple uses to save face every time they visit his mother:

> As we plan our visits to my mother-in-law's, my husband and I plan to be too busy to have a meal with her, or we say that we already ate. This is because of all the cooking. She has different tastes and, also, because she uses no salt or sugar, which makes her meals not very good. (W89b)

Keeping the Peace

    Six cover stories (9% of the sample) reflected the theme of telling cover stories to maintain harmony, avoid conflict, and keep everyone happy. Joy said she covers because "you don't want to come out and have open warfare with someone" (24:6). One participant offered the following example of agreeing on a story with his wife before a holiday visit:

When Sandy and I went home for Thanksgiving, we made an agreement that, if anyone asks, we had both gotten flu shots already. Mostly because her mom is a nurse and has been hounding us to get them for the last month and a half. (W23b)

Several couples identified keeping the peace in the relationship and avoiding conflict as a reason for telling cover stories.

Image Management

The final function of storytelling identified by the interviewed couples was that, sometimes, they cover for each other for strategic reasons. Four cover stories (6% of the sample) mentioned this function. One participant indicated, "The lie is to be political, I guess. . . . So that people will think of you in a certain way" (1:14). This participant's spouse also stated, "One of the reasons . . . [is] to maintain a social status either with the family or with neighbors or the community" (1:16). Another woman keeps her smoking habit secret and has her husband cover for her when they are out in public by pretending they are his cigarettes. She commented, "I know what people are thinking, and they would just label me . . . I don't want to deal with that. I just don't want to deal with the repercussions" (9:13). Another participant said that he and his spouse will create stories about schedules and activities in order "to keep upstanding in the community" (17:12).

Discussion

As partners in a relationship, the couples in this study understand the process of "covering," and most acknowledged that they do it, but rarely do they openly discuss cover stories. In general, the deceptive nature of cover stories is open for debate, but some couples in the present study clearly identified that many of their cover stories are deceptive. Some couples stated, "we lied," "we tell whoppers," and we shared a "joint lie." The couples indicated an awareness of the deception but felt it was justified. DePaulo and colleagues (1996) extend the link to impression management by suggesting that "lying is a commonplace strategy for managing impressions and social interactions. . . . It is a more extreme form of impression management that involves the deliberate fostering of a false impression rather than the judicious editing of a true one" (p. 980). People tell more lies to benefit themselves than to benefit others (DePaulo et al., 1996; Hample, 1980).

For Couples

Cover stories enhance *The Couple Team* as they suggest the primacy of the marital relationship over all other relationships. In this sense, couples cover for each other to increase "trust," increase "the bond," and affirm that they can count on each other more than they can count on anyone else. The process of covering for each other, more than the specific content (or product) of the stories, has become a routine part of their marital communication. For many couples, cover stories are a regular interaction pattern (e.g., "If she calls in the evening, tell her I'm busy."). As such, cover stories are a way for a relationship to be enacted in everyday encounters (VanderVoort & Duck, 2000).

Couples who cover for each other on a regular basis are constantly affirming their "we-ness." The couples in this study count on each other to cover, establishing a pattern of communication in the relationship that often does not need to be articulated. They are at the point where they "just know" to cover for each other and covering becomes automatic in the relationship. The suggested irony is that, through a potentially deceptive act (covering for each other), a relationship can be affirmed. For the couples in this study, covering for each other enhances their connection with each other.

In some cases, couples cover for each other to keep some information private. Certain information belongs to just the married partners and is "theirs." The category of *Privacy Maintenance,* in this case, is interconnected to the category of *The Couple Team.* Within a marriage, negotiation can occur about privacy boundaries. A couple may develop the amount and types of information that are kept within the boundaries of the marriage and what is to be shared with others. Petronio (2002) articulates that "couples link through transforming personal information into dyadically held private information" (p. 142).

The theme of *Reciprocity* can be understood through interdependence or social exchange theory (Thibaut & Kelley, 1959). The participants in this study indicated that, when they cover for their partner, they hold the expectation that the favor will be returned. The connection between *Reciprocity* and social exchange is further supported by Canary and Zelley's (2000) argument that social exchange is at the heart of relational maintenance. An economic view of covering for each other suggests a level of reciprocity in the relationship (e.g., Gouldner, 1960). Participants in the present study spoke of "owing" each other, being bound to each other because of what they know, and getting each other out of things.

For Others

The function of *Saving Face* reflects a couple's need to avoid hurting, humiliating, or embarrassing anyone. Turner et al. (1975) focus on the deceptive element by identifying face saving as a reason for lying. Other scholars, however, emphasize the more altruistic element of consideration for others and their feelings (Cupach & Metts, 1994; Petronio, 2002). The interviewed couples in this study acknowledged both elements. They admitted that cover stories were often deceptive but that they had good intentions for using them. We often save face by keeping some information private in difficult situations (Metts, Cupach, & Imahori, 1992).

Many of the interview respondents specifically indicated that they cover to "protect" each other, family members, and others. DePaulo et al. (1996) address the issue of protection, stating, "Participants . . . claimed that both they and the targets . . . would have felt a bit worse if the truth had been told" (p. 989). Protecting others connotes a positive motivation for covering. As such, identification of protection is also a facet of impression management.

Couples concerned with *Keeping the Peace* often tell cover stories to maintain harmony. Couples stated that they did not want conflict and that it was sometimes better to just keep everybody happy. The need to avoid tensions and conflict and the need to make social interactions run smoothly are reasons for deception. Individuals may tell "white lies" to avoid conflict and disruption (Camden et al., 1984).

The stories involved in *Image Management* address couples' needs to gain power or guide social interactions. These strategic needs are reasons for deception (Turner et al., 1975). Kashy and DePaulo (1996) suggest that social interaction goals, such as influencing others, are involved with deception. The couples in this study told stories to improve their standing in the neighborhood and to be "political," suggesting elements of impression management. In telling strategic stories, a couple may be attempting to manipulate others. As LaRossa (1995) offers, "All stories suggest some degree of manipulation" (p. 553).

Overall, the implications of our study suggest that couples get both relational and image benefits from coconstructing cover stories. Relational benefits come from "living the story" or enacting the story together. The image functions, outside the relationship, result from adjusting the story to save face. Specifically, cover stories serve to increase the bond between the partners through privacy, reciprocity, and protection. For the most part, cover stories are employed to save the feelings of others. These stories can also be used for manipulative and self-serving purposes. Cover stories may be deceptive, but for the couples in this study, covering for each other was a routine part of everyday interactions. Because covering is routine, any deceptive elements were not identified as problematic. Furthermore, our analysis suggests that cover stories operate as Langellier and Peterson (Chapter 6, this volume) say all family stories do. They illustrate the ways couples make (or fabricate) stories from experience, participate in their performance, and form family identities through them.

Notes

1. The male-linked terms here occur in the original writing. Rather than insert *sic* each time, we provide this explanation.

2. As the interview stories are presented, the citation refers to their couple number and the page number(s) in the individual transcripts.

3. The stories from the surveys are cited with a "W" (for written story) followed by the couple number. A letter after the couple number indicates that more than one cover story was submitted by that couple. The majority of the written stories were only one typed page in length, so a page number is not indicated.

References

Bochner, A. P., Ellis, C., & Tillmann-Healy, L. M. (2000). Relationships as stories: Accounts, storied lives, evocative narratives. In K. Dindia & S. Duck (Eds.), *Communication and personal relationships* (pp. 13–29). New York: John Wiley.

Bruner, J. S. (1987). Life as narrative. *Social Research, 54,* 11–32.

Bulmer, M. (1979). Concepts in the analysis of qualitative data. *Sociological Review, 27,* 651–677.

Burgoon, J. K., Buller, D. B., White, C. H., Afifi, W., & Buslig, A. L. S. (1999). The role of conversational involvement in deceptive interpersonal interactions. *Personality and Social Psychology Bulletin, 25,* 669–685.

Camden, C., Motley, M. T., & Wilson, A. (1984). White lies in interpersonal communication: A taxonomy and preliminary investigation of social motivations. *The Western Journal of Speech Communication, 48,* 309–325.

Canary, D. J., & Zelley, E. D. (2000). Current research programs on relational maintenance behaviors. In M. E. Roloff (Ed.), *Communication yearbook 23* (pp. 304–339). Thousand Oaks, CA: Sage.

Creswell, J. W. (1994). *Research design: Qualitative and quantitative approaches.* Thousand Oaks, CA: Sage.

Cupach, W. R., & Metts, S. (1994). *Facework.* Thousand Oaks, CA: Sage.

DePaulo, B. M., Kashy, D. A., Kirkendol, S. E., Wyer, M. M., & Epstein, J. A. (1996). Lying in everyday life. *Journal of Personality and Social Psychology, 70,* 979–995.

Duck, S. W. (1994). *Meaningful relationships: Talking, sense, and relating.* Thousand Oaks, CA: Sage.

Duck, S. W. (1995). Talking relationships into being. *Journal of Social and Personal Relationships, 12,* 535–540.

Duck, S. W. (1998). *Human relationships.* Thousand Oaks, CA: Sage.

Fiese, B. H., & Sameroff, A. J. (1999). The family narrative consortium: A multidimensional approach to narratives. In B. Fiese, A. Sameroff, H. Grotevant, F. Wamboldt, S. Dickstein, & D. Lewis Fravel (Eds.), *The stories that families tell: Narrative coherence, narrative interaction, and relationship beliefs* (pp. 1–36). Malden, MA: Blackwell.

Fisher, W. R. (1984). Narration as a human communication paradigm: The case of public moral argument. *Communication Monographs, 51,* 1–22.

Goffman, E. (1959). *The presentation of self in everyday life.* Garden City, NY: Doubleday.

Goldsmith, D. J., & Baxter, L. A. (1996). Constituting relationships in talk: A taxonomy of speech events in social and personal relationships. *Human Communication Research, 23,* 87–114.

Gordon, A. K., & Miller, A. G. (2000). Perspective differences in the construal of lies: Is deception in the eye of the beholder? *Personality and Social Psychology Bulletin, 26,* 46–56.

Gouldner, A. W. (1960). The norm of reciprocity: A preliminary statement. *American Sociological Review, 25,* 161–178.

Hample, D. (1980). Purposes and effects of lying. *The Southern Speech Communication Journal, 46,* 33–47.

Jorgenson, J., & Bochner, A. P. (2004). Imagining families through stories and rituals. In A. L. Vangelisti (Ed.), *Handbook of family communication* (pp. 513–540). Mahwah, NJ: Lawrence Erlbaum.

Karney, B. R., Davila, J., Cohan, C. L., Sullivan, K. T., Johnson, M. D., & Bradbury, T. N. (1995). An empirical investigation of sampling strategies in marital research. *Journal of Marriage and the Family, 57,* 909–920.

Kashy, D. A., & DePaulo, B. M. (1996). Who lies? *Journal of Personality and Social Psychology, 70,* 1037–1051.

LaRossa, R. (1995). Stories and relationships. *Journal of Social and Personal Relationships, 12,* 553–558.

McGregor, I., & Holmes, J. G. (1999). How storytelling shapes memory and impressions of relationship events over time. *Journal of Personality and Social Psychology, 76,* 403–419.

Metts, S. (1989). An exploratory investigation of deception in close relationships. *Journal of Social and Personal Relationships, 6,* 159–179.

Metts, S., Cupach, W. R., & Imahori, T. T. (1992). Perceptions of sexual compliance-resisting messages in three types of cross-sex relationships. *Western Journal of Communication 56,* 1–17.

Neuendorf, K. A. (2002). *The content analysis guidebook.* Thousand Oaks, CA: Sage.

Petronio, S. (2000). The embarrassment of private disclosures: A case study of newly married couples. In D. O. Braithwaite & J. T. Wood (Eds.), *Case studies in interpersonal communication: Processes and problems* (pp. 131–144). Belmont, CA: Wadsworth.

Petronio, S. (2002). *Boundaries of privacy: Dialectics of disclosure.* New York: State University of New York Press.

Putnam, L. L., Van Hoeven, S. A., & Bullis, C. A. (1991). The role of rituals and fantasy themes in teachers' bargaining. *Western Journal of Speech Communication, 55,* 85–103.

Rosenfeld, L. B. (2000). Overview of the ways privacy, secrecy, and disclosure are balanced in today's society. In S. Petronio (Ed.), *Balancing the secrets of private disclosures* (pp. 3–17). Mahwah, NJ: Lawrence Erlbaum.

Shaw, C. L. M. (1997). Personal narrative: Revealing self and reflecting other. *Human Communication Research, 24,* 302–319.

Stahl, S. K. D. (1983). Personal experience stories. In R. M. Dorson (Ed.), *Handbook of American folklore* (pp. 268–275). Bloomington: Indiana University Press.

Thibaut, J. W., & Kelley, H. K. (1959). *The social psychology of groups.* New York: John Wiley.

Turner, R. E., Edgely, C., & Olmstead, G. (1975). Information control in conversation: Honesty is not always the best policy. *Kansas Journal of Sociology, 11,* 69–89.

VanderVoort, L., & Duck, S. W. (2000). Talking about "relationships": Variations on a theme. In K. Dindia & S. Duck (Eds.), *Communication and personal relationships* (pp. 1–12). New York: John Wiley.

Widdershoven, G. A. M. (1993). The story of life: Hermeneutic perspectives on the relationship between narrative and life history. In R. Josselson & A. Lieblich (Eds.), *The narrative study of lives* (pp. 1–20). Newbury Park, CA: Sage.

CHAPTER 8

Mulling About Family Conflict and Communication

What We Know and What We Need to Know

Michael E. Roloff

Northwestern University

Courtney Waite Miller

Elmhurst College

Jetse Sprey (1969) noted that family can be viewed as a system in conflict consisting of "ongoing confrontation between its members, a confrontation between individuals with conflicting interests in their common situation" (p. 702). There is evidence in support of this observation. Relative to other types of relationships, adults report that they experience the greatest degree of criticism and emotional conflict in their marriage, followed closely by their relationships with siblings, adolescent children, and parents (Argyle & Furnham, 1983). Although diary research indicates that disagreement is most frequent among unhappily married couples, even those in happy marriages are not immune from everyday arguing (e.g., Birchler, Weiss, & Vincent, 1975; Kirchler, Rodler, Holzl, & Meier, 2001). Although the frequency of family conflict declines with a child's age (Laursen, Coy, & Collins, 1998; Steinmetz, 1977), adolescents report that about 40% of their daily conflicts occur with a sibling or a parent (Jensen-Campbell & Graziano, 2000).

Some former spouses continue arguing even after they are divorced (e.g., Masheter, 1991), especially about their children (Schaeffer, 1989). Certainly, most family interactions are not disagreements (e.g., Kirchler et al., 2001), but the evidence suggests that conflict is a feature of family life.

The potential for negative consequences arising from conflict is equally well documented. Growing evidence shows marital arguments to be stressful for spouses (see Kiecolt-Glaser & Newton, 2001) and for children who observe them (see Davies & Cummings, 1998). Parents and children may say hurtful things that can change their self-perceptions and feelings toward one another (Mills, Nazar, & Farrell, 2002). In some cases, family arguments can escalate into physically abusive episodes (see Roloff, 1996). The frequency of marital disagreements and their negativity increases the likelihood of divorce (McGonagle, Kessler, & Gotlib, 1993). Conflicts between parents can aversely affect their children's social and behavioral adjustment (see Cummings, Goeke-Morey, & Papp, 2001).

Given the aforementioned evidence, it is not surprising that the study of family conflict has grown dramatically in the past three decades. Indeed, some scholars have noted that more published research has focused on marriage and conflict than on marriage and love, communication, or social support (Bradbury, Rogge, & Lawrence, 2001). In this chapter, we examine research on family conflict and communication. Because the study of family conflict and communication is multi-disciplinary and interdisciplinary, we have included research conducted by scholars from fields and disciplines allied with communication. We found that the research base is too voluminous to cover in a single chapter, and we chose to limit the scope of our analysis. In doing so, we have excluded research that does not have a strong focus on conflict and communication or that does not seem related to a prominent theory and/or program of research. However, we believe the excluded scholarship is valuable, and we encourage readers to consult additional sources for broader exposure (e.g., Gottman & Notarius, 2000; Sillars, Canary, & Tafoya, 2004).

Our chapter is divided into three main areas. First, we discuss the nature of family conflict and communication. Second, we examine the topics being addressed by researchers. Finally, we highlight future directions for those researching in this area.

Nature of Family Conflict and Communication

Defining family is, in and of itself, an issue of conflict (see Chapters 1–2, this volume). In part because the term has political, moral, and identity implications, it is difficult to reach consensus about the definition of a family. Not surprisingly, different definitions abound (see Fitzpatrick & Caughlin, 2002). Rather than privilege one definition over another, we do not define family per se but focus on "family-like" relationships that have captured the attention of family conflict researchers. Families can be decomposed into a variety of specific relationships, and although the conflict processes occurring within each are correlated (e.g., Noller, Feeney, Sheehan, & Peterson, 2000), their individual effects on the family can vary (e.g., Shagle & Barber, 1993). Consequently, it is useful to investigate conflict in a particular type of relationship as well as the impact it may have on other family relationships.

Conflict is the existence of incompatible activity (Deutsch, 1973). Although conflict can be manifested in a variety of ways, the one drawing greatest attention among family researchers is verbalized conflict, which is also referred to as expressed disagreement or arguing. It is useful to think of verbalized conflict as a type of confrontational episode during which one party challenges the behavior of another (Newell & Stutman, 1991). In doing so, one can investigate how the episode begins and proceeds until it is terminated. Family researchers have looked at specific episodes as well as processes that occur across episodes.

Specific Conflict Episodes

Some family conflict researchers have been interested in the structure of a conflict episode. In his research on family quarrels at the supper table, Vuchinich (1984, 1986, 1987, 1990) observed that verbal conflict begins with a provocative action by a family member that is challenged by another. If the challenge is met with compliance or agreement, then the individuals avoid having conflict. However, if the provocateur resists the challenge, then a disagreement takes place. Vuchinich's observational method has yielded useful insights. In about two thirds of the instances in his study (1990), the challenge was met with resistance and an argument ensued. Hence, not all provocative behaviors or challenges produce conflicts. Vuchinich hypothesized that an attenuation factor keeps arguments brief. Indeed, most expressed disagreements ended after two to three speaking turns. These disagreements typically ended with a standoff rather than a resolution.

Other researchers have been interested in the precise communication behaviors enacted during an episode. A variety of coding schemes have been developed that assess verbal (e.g., disclosure, insults) and nonverbal behaviors (e.g., vocal tone, facial affect) during a marital argument (e.g., Gottman & Krokoff, 1989; Krokoff, Gottman, & Hass, 1989). Although not without critics (e.g., King, 2001), these approaches have proved useful in identifying episodic processes that predict the likelihood that couples will eventually divorce (e.g., Gottman, Swanson, & Murray, 1999). In a similar vein, coding schemes have been developed for parent-child arguments that have proved useful for understanding how conflicts are perceived (e.g., Beaumont & Wagner, 2004).

Finally, researchers have been interested in the cognitive processes that occur during an argumentative episode. In some studies, participants watch a recording of an argument in which they participated and describe what they were thinking at various points (e.g., Sillars, Roberts, Leonard, & Dun, 2000). Alternatively, participants are sometimes asked to imagine they engaged in an argument and to record their thoughts at various points (e.g., O'Brien, Margolin, John, & Krueger, 1991). Other researchers try to assess cognition during an argument by having participants record their intended meaning for a given statement. After hearing the statement, their partners record how they perceive its intended meaning (Notarius, Benson, Sloane, Vanzetti, & Hornyak, 1989). Although each method has disadvantages, they all have provided useful insights into individuals' perceptions of disagreements.

Cross-Episodic Patterns

Although identifying the processes that occur during a given disagreement is useful, it is also important to determine whether there are consistencies across argumentative episodes. Accordingly, some researchers have been interested in behaviors typically enacted across conflicts. For example, Kurdek (1994b) created an ineffective-arguing scale that measures the degree to which individuals feel their typical arguments are predictable, repetitive, unsatisfying, and unresolved. Kurdek also created a conflict-style scale that asks individuals to indicate how frequently they use conflict engagement, positive problem solving, compliance, and withdrawal to deal with their disagreements. He found that gay/lesbian and heterosexual parent/nonparent couples did not differ significantly in their responses to either scale. In general, ineffective arguing, conflict engagement, and withdrawal reduced relational satisfaction over time and increased the likelihood of relational dissolution. On the other hand, positive problem solving was associated with increased satisfaction and lower rates of relational dissolution. Compliance was unrelated to either relational outcome.

Another commonly used instrument is the Conflict Tactics Scale (Straus, 1979). This instrument asks individuals to indicate how many times they engaged in a variety of conflict behaviors during the past year. The measure is commonly used to assess the degree of physical and psychological abuse occurring within a wide variety of family relationships (e.g., Straus & Gelles, 1990) and has been translated in several languages (Straus, 2004).

Other researchers have been interested in behavioral patterns or interaction sequences that are repeated across argumentative episodes (e.g., Sullaway & Christensen, 1983). One of the most common means of assessment is the Communication Patterns Questionnaire (Christensen & Sullaway, 1984). This self-report measure focuses on whether couples discuss a problem or avoid it, how they communicate during the episode, and what happens after the episode. Two inter-action patterns are assessed within the questionnaire: (a) the degree to which one partner demands the other change and the other responds by withdrawing and (b) the degree to which there is mutual constructive communication. The self-report measure discriminates among couples who differ in marital distress (Noller & White, 1990) and is positively related to similar coded behaviors enacted during an actual argument (Hahlweg, Kaiser, Christensen, Fehm-Wolfsdorf, & Groth, 2000). It has proved useful for studying parent-child conflict and its impact on issues such as self-esteem, substance abuse, and relational satisfaction (Caughlin & Malis, 2004a, 2004b).

Questions Addressed by Family Conflict Researchers

In discussing these questions, we will look at research focused on conflict within three types of family relationships: marital, parent-child, and sibling.

Marriage

Although marital researchers are interested in many issues, we believe their research is directed toward two primary questions, each of which reflects an "effects orientation." First, how is conflict related to marital distress? And second, what is the impact of marital conflict on children? We will consider each in turn.

Marital Distress

A large body of research has examined how marital distress is related to the way spouses act during argumentative episodes. Researchers have generally used a social learning perspective that assumes global marital evaluations are affected by the types of actions that occur within marriage. In particular, when attempting to resolve disagreements, distressed couples rely on negative rather than positive techniques (Jacobson & Margolin, 1979). Using a variety of methods and measures, research suggests that marital distress is positively associated with personal complaints (Alberts, 1988), negative problem-solving behavior (Vincent, Weiss, & Birchler, 1975), criticism (Koren, Carlton, & Shaw, 1980), and mind-reading statements (Gottman, 1979). Marital distress is negatively related to positive problem-solving actions (Vincent et al., 1975), behavioral complaints (Alberts, 1988), positive nonverbal behaviors (Alberts, 1988; Margolin & Wampold, 1981), agreement statements (Alberts, 1988), and responsiveness (Koren et al., 1980).

Beyond the behavioral frequencies, research also suggests that marital distress is related to interaction sequences. Marital distress increases the likelihood of countercomplaining loops (Alberts, 1988; Gottman, 1979), reciprocity of negative affect (Gottman, 1979; Margolin & Wampold, 1981), reciprocity of negative conflict behavior (Revenstorf, Vogel, Wegener, Hahlweg, & Schindler, 1980), confrontation-complaint-defense cycles (Ting-Toomey, 1983), and demand-withdraw interaction patterns (Gottman & Levinson, 2000; Heavey, Christensen, & Malamuth, 1995; Heavey, Layne, & Christensen, 1993; Kurdek, 1995). Marital distress decreases the frequency of reciprocity of positive nonverbal affect (Gottman, 1979; Margolin & Wampald, 1981), reciprocity of positive conflict behavior (Revenstorf et al., 1980), and validation loops (Gottman, 1979).

Gottman and Krokoff (1989) focused on the effect of interaction patterns over time. They found that although anger and disagreement reduce current marital satisfaction, they improve relational satisfaction over time. They identified three interaction patterns that predicted the long-term erosion of marital satisfaction: defensiveness, stubbornness, and withdrawal. However, it is important to note that some research has not confirmed this (e.g., Gill, Christensen, & Fincham, 1999).

Gottman, Coan, Carrere, and Swanson (1998) investigated the degree to which seven different processes evident in newlywed interactions predict marital satisfaction and divorce 2 years into the future. Their data indicated that the most satisfied and stable marriages were those in which the wife reduced the intensity with which she initiated confrontation and used humor during the argument to soothe her husband's arousal. Her husband was willing to be influenced by her and acted to de-escalate low-intensity affect and to reduce his own arousal. Anger, active listening, and reciprocity of negative affect were not related to marital satisfaction and divorce.

Although research on marital distress and communication is deeper and more nuanced than we can discuss here, the general pattern suggests that marital distress arises from behaviors that are unlikely to resolve problems and could make them worse. Indeed, marital distress is positively related to the number of unresolved problems in a relationship (Birchler & Webb, 1977). Not surprisingly, this observation has prompted some researchers to create instruments that assess a couple's conflict management skills (e.g., Arellano & Markman, 1995).

However, some couples may be able to survive the negativity that accompanies marital conflict. Gottman (1993, 1994) proposed a theory of marital dissolution that posits that the impact of negativity on a marriage depends on the spouses' ability to offset it with positive affect. In his research, couples in stable relationships maintain a ratio of five positive conflict behaviors for every one negative action. However, couples vary in how they maintain this ratio. During an argument, volatile couples are highly confrontational and negative but mix such behavior with a great deal of positive behaviors. Validating couples maintain the ratio by mixing moderate amounts of both positive and negative behavior, and avoidant couples engage in low levels of both positive and negative behaviors. Although their ways of dealing with conflict differ, each couple is stable and satisfied. Only when couples are unable to maintain the five-to-one ratio—such as in the case of hostile and hostile/detached couples—does relational quality suffer.

Research clearly demonstrates a link between arguing and marital distress. Some scholars have moved beyond this base to demonstrate that marital arguing may be related to other forms of distress. Negative behaviors enacted during arguments increase stress hormones, especially among wives (e.g., Kiecolt-Glaser et al., 1993; Kiecolt-Glaser et al., 1996). Furthermore, wives who experience stress during arguments are at greater risk for health problems (Kimmel et al., 2000), and their marriages are at greater risk of divorce (Kiecolt-Glaser, Bane, Glaser, & Malarkey, 2003). Wives who have greater power or who share power with their husbands show greater stress reduction after an argument than those in a less powerful role (Loving, Heffner, Kiecolt-Glaser, Glaser, & Malarkey, 2004). Interestingly, husbands who have greater power or less power than their wives experience greater reductions in stress than those who share power with their wives (Loving et al., 2004).

Research also suggests that depression is related to marital conflict. In particular, depression increases the likelihood that a spouse will enact destructive conflict behaviors and decreases the likelihood that he or she will enact constructive conflict behaviors (e.g., Coyne, Thompson, & Palmer, 2002; Schudlich, Papp, & Cummings, 2004). A husband's depression can reduce the likelihood that his nondepressed wife will respond positively to his positive problem-solving behaviors (Johnson & Jacob, 2000).

Impact on Children

Research suggests that the effect of marital conflict extends beyond parents to their children. Marital discord is positively related to a variety of adjustment problems in children (Grych & Fincham, 2001). Researchers have identified a number of different ways that marital conflict produces these effects. We examine three.

First, the effect of marital conflict on children may result from the link between marital conflict and parenting styles. A recent meta-analysis indicates that inter-parental conflict is positively related to harsh parenting styles and negatively related to parental support and acceptance (Krishnakumar & Buehler, 2000). In part, this link could result from negative moods experienced by parents after a marital dis-agreement. This may produce ambiguous or threatening actions toward children (Jouriles & Farris, 1992). These negative parental styles increase the likelihood of child maladjustment (e.g., Buehler & Gerard, 2002) and decrease a child's sense of well-being (Vandewater & Lansford, 1998). Furthermore, they increase a child's negative understanding of family relationships (Shamir, Schudlich, & Cummings, 2001) and may be passed on from one generation to the next (Simons, Whitbeck, Conger, & Chy-In, 1991).

Second, marital conflict may directly affect a child. Although many marital disagreements take place without the child being present, the child may directly observe them in some cases. Research suggests that the arguments children witness are often the most hostile and most emotionally negative (Papp, Cummings, & Goeke-Morey, 2002). Negative effects occur when children appraise a conflict as threatening (Davies & Cummings, 1994; Grych & Fincham, 1990). Indeed, exposure to such conflicts can adversely affect a young child's emotional state (Crockenberg & Langrock, 2001; Cummings, Goeke-Morey, Papp, & Dukewich, 2002; Jenkins, 2000) as well as those of adult children (Hall & Cummings, 1997). Moreover, expo-sure to marital conflict negatively influences the manner in which a child interprets and acts in conflicts with other people (Buehler et al., 1998; El-Sheikh, 1997; Jenkins, 2000; Kinsfogel & Grych, 2004; Marcus, Lindahl, & Malik, 2001; Stocker & Youngblade, 1999). However, it should be noted that although destructive marital conflict behaviors and negative emotion adversely affect a child, the child's exposure to marital conflict that is handled constructively does not appear to be as harmful (Cummings et al., 2002).

Third, Jenkins, Simpson, Dunn, Rasbash, and O'Connor (2005) found an unfold-ing pattern among marital conflict and children's problems. Marital conflict about a child's behavior was positively related to a child's subsequent behavioral problems. This, in turn, stimulated more marital arguing, especially in stepfamilies. This implies that marital conflict and a child's behavioral problems influence each other.

Thus, marital disagreement can have far-reaching effects on the family unit. If disagreements are dealt with inappropriately, the marriage may be in danger and children may be harmed.

Parent-Child Conflict

The introduction of children into a family can create disagreement. In the prior section, we noted that marital conflict could affect a child. In this section, we review evidence that parent-child conflict can influence a marriage, including the likeli-hood of marital disagreement.

Socialization

When raising children, parents have the responsibility of teaching skills and controlling behavior so as to ensure the safety and well-being of the child and others. In doing so, the child may resist, and a struggle for control may emerge. Hence, most research is conducted from a power or control perspective (e.g., Steinmetz, 1977).

Research focused on younger children has focused on the degree to which children are compliant with the control techniques of their parents as well as how parents exert control. For example, some research suggests that among children ages 15 to 24 months, mothers are most effective at gaining compliance when they engage in behaviors that first draw the attention of the child and then move to stimulating action (Schaffer & Crook, 1980). Other research indicates that compliance among 1½-year-olds is greater when parents use directives rather than suggestions but that the pattern reverses itself when children reach the age of 3 (McLaughlin, 1983). This implies that parents are most successful when they adapt their strategies to the age of the child. Indeed, Kuczynski, Kochanska, Radke-Yarrow, and Girnius-Brown (1987) found that mothers of 3½-year-olds were more likely to use explanations, bargaining, and reprimands to gain compliance and were less likely to use distraction than were mothers of 1½-year-olds. Furthermore, 3½-year-olds were more likely to resist through negotiation and less likely to be defiant or passive than were 1½-year-olds. When mothers reasoned with their child, the child often attempted to negotiate. Maternal attempts to control the child directly often were met with defiance. However, not all research suggests that reasoning is effective at creating compliance. Several studies have found that reasoning is effective only if combined with consistent but mild punishment (e.g., Larzelere & Merenda, 1994; Larzelere, Sather, Schneider, Larson, & Pike, 1998). Although controversial, a recent meta-analysis suggests that conditional spanking (i.e., used in a controlled manner as a backup for reasoning with a defiant child) increases compliance and reduces antisocial behavior relative to other forms of parental discipline (Larzelere & Kuhn, 2005).

In some cases, parent-child conflict may extend for quite some time. Ritchie (1999) distinguished between single acts of noncompliance and power bouts (extended disagreements). In a sample of mothers with 3-year-olds, Ritchie found that 70% of the conflicts were power bouts. Most often, the bouts were about eating or bedtime. Furthermore, mothers became more coercive as power bouts continued and had increasingly negative thoughts about their child.

Adolescence is thought to be a time of increased parent-child conflict. This development phase is often recalled by parents and children as being rife with conflict (Fingerman, 1997; Riesch, Jackson, & Chanchong, 2003). During this time, parents and adolescents often have different interpretations of the conflict, with parents seeing the disagreements arising from morality, personal safety, and conformity concerns and adolescents viewing them as issues of personal choice (Smetana, 1989). However, some research suggests parent-child conflict depends on the issue. Galambos and Almeda (1992) found that conflicts over chores, appearance, and politeness decreased and disagreements over substance abuse remained the same as adolescents progressed from sixth to eighth grades. Only conflicts over finances increased. Also, certain topics seem to be especially consequential. Barber and Delfabbro (2000) found that adolescent adjustment was negatively related to the frequency of parent-conflict over domestic issues (e.g., chores) and a child's friends. However, Adams and Laursen (2001) reported that relative to conflicts with friends, parental conflict with adolescents involved more daily hassles, negative affect afterwards, power-assertive actions, and win/lose resolutions. Moreover, adolescents who had developed a dismissive attachment style with their parents report that many of their conflicts end unresolved (Ducharme, Doyle, & Markiewicz, 2002).

Yet, not all conflicts during adolescence are resolved in a negative way. Conflicts with boys are more difficult to resolve than those with girls, and conflicts about chores and interpersonal relationships were more difficult to resolve than those about personal style (Smetana, Yau, & Hanson, 1991). There is some evidence that parent-child conflicts during adolescence are worse when negative emotions are expressed (Beaumont & Wagner, 2004). Similarly, Reuter and Conger (1995) found that if most family interactions were warm and supportive prior to adolescence, then parent-child conflict during adolescence was lessened and parent-child relations improved. However, among families who had a hostile, coercive climate, conflict increased and relational quality decayed during adolescence. Finally, an authoritarian parental style is positively related to the frequency and intensity of parent-adolescent conflict, but parents who granted adolescents control over some areas of personal style experienced less conflict (Smetana, 1995).

Parent-child conflict does not end at adolescence. Research indicates that adults have conflicts with their parents. Clarke, Preston, Raskin, and Bengston (1999) found that intergenerational conflicts can occur about communication/interaction style, habits/lifestyle choices, child-rearing practices/values, politics/religion/ideology, work habits/orientation, and household standards/maintenance. Fisher, Reid, and Melendez (1989) found that elderly parents reported conflict with their adult children focused on the unwillingness of the child to adhere to family rules, the child's inability to accept parental control, and the child's failure to live up to role expectations. Adult children reported that most conflicts with their elderly parents resulted from the parent's unwillingness to provide assistance and accept the child's autonomy. Women have more conflict with their parents about family matters, whereas men have more conflict with their parents about social and political issues (Hagestad, 1987). In addition, greater conflict is reported between daughters and mothers and fathers and sons than between daughters and fathers and sons and mothers (Suitor, Pillemer, Keeton, & Robinson, 1995; Umberson, 1992).

There is evidence that adult children who perceive they cannot control their conflicts with their parents act in a verbally aggressive manner toward them, whereas adult children who feel they are in control are more argumentative (Copstead, Lanzetta, & Avtgis, 2001). But there is also evidence that most conflicts between adult daughters and their mothers typically are handled in a constructive fashion (Fingerman, 1998). Adult children who live with their parents have increased conflict when they are financially dependent and unemployed (Aquilino & Supple, 1991). Thus, parent-child conflict can occur throughout life.

Marital Effects

The manner in which parents deal with conflict between themselves and their children is related to marital satisfaction (Crohan, 1996). Destructive conflict behaviors (e.g., insults) and active avoidance (e.g., leaving for a while) reduce marital satisfaction for both mothers and fathers. Unexpectedly, engaging in constructive communication (e.g., calmly discussing things) is negatively but not significantly related to marital satisfaction. Only engaging in passive avoidance (e.g., becoming quiet and pulling away) is positively related to marital satisfaction. This suggests that finding ways to temporarily disengage on an emotional level may be functional.

However, increased marital conflict may also be a result of a child's behavioral problems. Two longitudinal studies have found that a child's behavioral problems increase the level of marital conflict (Jenkins et al., 2005; O'Connor & Insabella, 1999).

In some cases, intergenerational problems affect an adult child's marriage. Topham, Larson, and Holman (2005) found that having a history of harsh parent-child conflicts predicts marital conflict at the newlywed stage, especially among women. Moreover, Beaton, Norris, and Pratt (2003) found that adult children often discuss with their spouses problems that involve their parents, including handling holidays, involving grandparents with grandchildren, accepting money from parents, having a parent coming to live with them, and intervening about a parent's health. Most decide to try to solve the problems without involving the parent. Some couples simply decide to avoid discussing the issue with the parent or try to deal with it indirectly. However, in some cases, the problem is serious enough that the husband and wife feel it is necessary to confront the parent.

Siblings

Among children, sibling conflict is frequent. Some research finds that sibling conflict among preschoolers on average occurs seven times an hour (Dunn & Munn, 1986; Ross, Filyer, Lollis, Perlman, & Martin, 1994). On a daily basis, adolescents report more disagreements with siblings than with their mothers or fathers (Montemayor & Hanson, 1985). Some adults report that they still quarrel with their siblings (Bedford, 1998; Stewart, Verbrugge, & Beilfuss, 1998). Moreover, adolescent sibling conflict is related to increased risk of anxiety, depression, and delinquent behavior (Stocker, Burwell, & Briggs, 2002). Research indicates that sibling abuse is the most common form of family abuse (Gelles & Straus, 1988). Given its prevalence and consequences, researchers have investigated sibling conflict to understand both its characteristics and ways parents might respond to it. We will examine each issue in turn.

Characteristics

Researchers have investigated the causes of sibling conflict and the processes that occur once it has started. Although early research focused on sibling rivalry as a cause of sibling conflict, recent research suggests that causes may simply reflect interdependency. Generally, research has uncovered three causes of sibling conflict (Felson, 1983; Montemayor & Hanson, 1985; Raffaelli, 1992; Steinmetz, 1977): ownership issues, division of labor, and objectionable behaviors. First, many sibling disputes result from disagreements about the use or ownership of possessions (e.g., toys, clothes). Although they are most common at younger ages, sibling disagreements over possessions may also occur later in life (Taylor & Norris, 2000). Among older children, sibling conflict emerges from disagreements over the division of labor or family duties (e.g., chores) and from annoying, objectionable behavior (e.g., touching, habits, aggression, teasing). Conflict appears to be most frequent when siblings are similar in age (Felson, 1983) or the same gender (Felson, 1983; Montemayor & Hanson, 1985). Although most sibling conflicts appear to be one-time events, some conflicts—especially those about possessions and among girls—are recurring (Raffaelli, 1992).

A few researchers have studied the processes that unfold during sibling conflicts. Raffaelli (1992) found that most preadolescent or young adolescent sibling conflicts ended within 5 minutes. Those involving older adolescents lasted longer. About half of the disagreements escalated into verbal or physical aggression, and most siblings report feeling angry or unhappy during the interaction. Most of the disputes ended without resolution when one or both parties withdrew psychologically or physically. In most cases, neither sibling attempted to repair any damage done during the argument.

About one quarter of the siblings reported feeling so angry at the end of the dispute that it caused them to think about the disagreement afterwards. About one third of the siblings felt better after the disagreement largely because the fight had ended or, in some cases, because they felt they had won the argument.

Other researchers have been interested in long-term effects of sibling disagreements. Graham-Bermann, Cutler, Litzenberger, and Schwartz (1994) found that young adults—and especially young women who experienced emotional abuse from a sibling as a child—showed lower levels of emotional adjustment than those who did not experience it. Although this finding suggests that serious forms of sibling conflict can have a lasting negative impact, Bedford (1998) found that individuals may find ways to cope with it so as to reduce the negative consequences. Specifically, in a sample of middle-aged adults, those who could see the benefits arising from sibling conflicts in their childhood had a somewhat stronger sense of well-being than those who could not. However, the benefits seen in current sibling conflicts were unrelated to well-being. Thus, although the ability to reframe conflicts from the past seems an effective coping device, it does not work as well with regard to current disagreements.

Parental Response

In some cases, a sibling conflict may occur in the presence of one or both parents, and they may decide whether to become involved. Interestingly, not all parents choose to do so. In an observational study, Ross et al. (1994) found that parents became involved in 59% of the sibling conflicts between their 2- to 4-year-olds that took place in their presence. Raffaelli (1992) found that parents of adolescents became involved in only 54% of the sibling conflicts. The decision to become involved is negatively related to the parents' orientation toward autonomy and positively related to the degree to which they value conformity (McHale, Updegraff, Tucker, & Crouter, 2000). Not surprisingly, parents are most likely to become involved when the conflict is intense and evokes an emotional reaction from the children (Perlman & Ross, 1997b; Ross et al., 1994).

When parents become involved, they typically state rules and seek information about the dispute. In addition, they often side with the sibling who seems to have been victimized (Ross et al., 1994) or who has property rights (Raffaelli, 1992). However, there is some evidence that parental involvement may not always be effective and, under some conditions, could be counterproductive. For example, Felson and Russo (1988) found that parents often side with the weaker sibling. In the long term, such an alliance results in greater sibling conflict and aggression. Indeed, other research suggests that unequal treatment of siblings is correlated with increased sibling conflict (Brody, Stoneman, McCoy, & Forehand, 1992). Furthermore, McHale et al. (2000) found that parental intervention into sibling conflicts (e.g., punishment) was positively correlated with negativity between the siblings. Coaching (e.g., providing advice, explaining feelings) was unrelated.

Part of the problem with parental involvement may stem from the parents' desire to dictate a solution rather than to help mediate the dispute (Perozynski & Kramer, 1999). In some cases, less controlling parental intervention may not immediately resolve the problem, but the children are able to do so at a later point (Perlman & Ross, 1997a). This mediation approach may empower siblings to solve their future problems more effectively on their own (Siddiqui & Ross, 1999, 2004).

Thus, sibling disputes are a common form of family conflict. In some cases, they can have a lasting impact on siblings. Not surprisingly, parents can be drawn into sibling disputes, and that involvement is not always positive. However, current research suggests that parents might be able to mediate such disputes and produce long-term benefits.

Future Directions

The literature on family conflict and communication has grown substantially over the past few decades. The issues being researched are important, and the methods used to study them are rigorous. In particular, we endorse the continued use of diverse samples. Although a great deal of research continues to study U.S. samples, there is a growing body of research that includes non-U.S. samples (e.g., Yau & Smetana, 1996) or analyzes specific ethnic-racial groups within the United States (e.g., Farver, Narang, & Bhadha, 2002; Flores, Tschann, Marin, & Pantoja, 2004; Smetana & Gaines, 1999; Tschann, Flores, Pasch, & Marin, 1999; Vuchinich & De Baryshe, 1997). Furthermore, with a growing number of blended families, scholars have focused on stepfamily conflict (Coleman, Fine, Ganong, Downs, & Pauk, 2001; Hanson, McLanahan, & Thomson, 1996; MacDonald & DeMaris, 1995).

However, as we wrote this chapter, we identified some key questions that thus far have received insufficient attention. These questions flow from our observation that many family conflicts go unresolved. Unfortunately, few researchers have investigated how argumentative episodes end. But when arguments do end, researchers find that most of them end without resolution. Typically, individuals simply stop talking or leave the scene physically or psychologically. This implies that families may experience longstanding, irresolvable disputes. Indeed, Gottman (1999) reports that 69% of couples involved in his research have perpetual problems— longstanding disputes that defy resolution. These disputes are likely to be consequential for family functioning. Cramer (2002) found that unresolved conflicts were especially unsatisfying and had a stronger correlation with relational satisfaction than did the processes used to try to resolve them. Unfortunately, there is no clear evidence as to how individuals best can deal with these problems. To help focus attention on this critical issue, we offer four related questions that we believe are worthy of research.

First, what does it mean to say that a conflict has been resolved? We doubt that the cessation of arguing means the conflict has been resolved. Individuals often mull over conflict after an argumentative episode has ended, and such cognitive activity may prolong the experience of being in a disagreement (Johnson & Roloff, 1998). If so, it is important that we identify the factors that indicate people have reached a sense of resolution. One possibility is forgiveness. Individuals who are prone to forgive their spouse's transgressions are more likely to end their arguments, feeling that the issue has been resolved effectively (Fincham, Beach, & Davila, 2004).

Second, what makes some conflicts difficult to resolve? A great deal of the research has focused on skills deficit. In other words, researchers assume that training individuals in conflict management would facilitate conflict resolution. Although there is some evidence that poor conflict management skills make couples vulnerable to marital distress (e.g., Pasch & Bradbury, 1998), there is little evidence that these skills can be used to solve perpetual problems. It is possible that irresolvable conflicts stem from the issues themselves. Perpetual problems often occur as a result of fundamental personality, cultural or religious differences, or as a result of essential needs of each spouse (Driver, Tabares, Shapiro, Nahm, & Gottman, 2003). These issues are central to the individuals and perhaps beyond their control. Therefore, it is difficult to find common ground. Furthermore, some issues are difficult to discuss and may retard a couple's general ability to deal with all problems in their relationship (Sanford, 2003).

Third, does it matter if some conflicts are irresolvable? Some families may be able to live with irresolvable disputes without damaging their relationships. For example, some research suggests that the effect of conflict depends on the issue. Conflicts about issues such as intimacy and power seem to have greater impact on relational satisfaction than those about social issues, personal habits, or personal distance (Kurdek, 1994a). Certainly, it is possible that unresolved disputes concerning minor issues may accumulate to the point that they become a major problem. It also may be the case that relatively minor annoyances may never diminish relational quality.

It also is possible that some families develop norms that protect members against the harmful aspects of unresolved conflicts (Koerner & Fizpatrick, 1997).

Fourth, if some irresolvable conflicts do matter, how might individuals cope with these conflicts? Conflicts typically involve a relational problem. Hence, there may be ways to deal with these problems besides arguing. For example, Bowman (1990) found that in addition to arguing, individuals respond to their chronic marital problems through avoidance, introspective self-blame, looking for rewards outside of marriage, and focusing on positive aspects of the marriage. Focusing on the positive was the only coping device that was positively associated with marital satisfaction. Similarly, Menaghan (1982) found that spouses reported they coped with relational problems through negotiation, optimistic comparisons, selective ignoring, or resignation. Over time, negotiation was negatively related to ongoing problems, but, importantly, it was not correlated with reductions in marital distress. Only optimistic comparisons reduced relational problems and marital distress. Menaghan (1983) focused on parents' use of similar techniques to cope with problems they experienced with their children. Only optimistic comparisons reduced parents' anxiety over time. None of the coping techniques was significantly related to future problems with children. These results suggest that maintaining a positive outlook may be a more effective way of reducing stress arising from relational problems than confronting each other. Certainly, it may not be possible or desirable to maintain a positive view during all conflicts, but it also seems that there are some conflicts that cannot be managed through communication. We are not suggesting that researchers abandon the search for effective methods of resolving ongoing disagreements. However, conflict management involves more than resolution, and for some problems, we suspect that thinking optimistically is an effective option.

We began our chapter with Sprey's (1969) observation that families can be viewed as a system in conflict. Although the assertion is almost four decades old, research indicates that it remains an accurate assessment of family life. Furthermore, conflict is likely to remain a feature of family interaction. Rather than decreasing with time, there is evidence that marital conflict occurs regardless of the age of the spouses or the duration of their marriage (Hatch & Bulcroft, 2004) and that spouses in recent cohorts are reporting greater marital disagreement than are those in earlier cohorts (Rogers & Amato, 2000). This implies that researchers should continue to investigate this common and consequential phenomenon.

References

Adams, R., & Laursen, B. (2001). The organization and dynamics of adolescent conflict with parents and friends. *Journal of Marriage and the Family, 63,* 97–110.

Alberts, J. K. (1988). An analysis of couples' conversational complaints. *Communication Monographs, 55,* 184–196.

Aquilino, W. S., & Supple, K. R. (1991). Parent-child relations and parent's satisfaction with living arrangements when adult children live at home. *Journal of Marriage and the Family, 53,* 13–27.

Arellano, C. M., & Markman, H. J. (1995). The Managing Affect and Difference Scale (MADS): A self-report measure assessing conflict management in couples. *Journal of Family Psychology, 9,* 319–334.

Argyle, M., & Furnham, A. (1983). Sources of satisfaction and conflict in long-term relationships. *Journal of Marriage and the Family, 45,* 481–493.

Barber, J. G., & Delfabbro, P. (2000). Predictors of adolescent adjustment: Parent-peer relationships and parent-child conflict. *Child and Adolescent Social Work Journal, 17,* 278–288.

Beaton, J. M., Norris, J. E., & Pratt, M. W. (2003). Unresolved issues in adult children's marital relationships involving intergenerational problems. *Family Relations, 52,* 143–153.

Beaumont, S. L., & Wagner, S. L. (2004). Adolescent-parent verbal conflict: The roles of conversational styles and disgust emotions. *Journal of Language and Social Psychology, 23,* 338–368.

Bedford, V. H. (1998). Sibling relationship troubles and well-being in middle and old age. *Family Relations, 47,* 369–376.

Birchler, G. R., & Webb, L. J. (1977). Discriminating interaction behaviors in happy and unhappy marriages. *Journal of Consulting and Clinical Psychology, 45,* 341–343.

Birchler, G. R., Weiss, R. L., & Vincent, J. P. (1975). Multimethod analysis of social reinforcement exchange between maritally distressed and nondistressed spouse and stranger dyads. *Journal of Personality and Social Psychology, 31,* 349–360.

Bowman, M. L. (1990). Coping efforts and marital satisfaction: Measuring marital coping and its correlates. *Journal of Marriage and the Family, 52,* 463–474.

Bradbury, T., Rogge, R., & Lawrence, E. (2001). Reconsidering the role of conflict in marriage. In A. Booth, A. C. Crouter, & M. Clements (Eds.), *Couples in conflict* (pp. 59–82). Mahwah, NJ: Lawrence Erlbaum.

Brody, G. H., Stoneman, Z., McCoy, J. K., & Forehand, R. (1992). Contemporaneous and longitudinal associations of sibling conflict with family relationship assessments and family discussion about sibling problems. *Child Development, 63,* 391–400.

Buehler, C., & Gerard, J. M. (2002). Marital conflict, ineffective parenting, and children's and adolescents' maladjustment. *Journal of Marriage and the Family, 64,* 78–92.

Buehler, C., Krishnakumar, A., Stone, G., Anthony, C., Pemberton, S., Gerard, J., et al. (1998). Interparental conflict styles and youth problem behaviors: A two-sample replication study. *Journal of Marriage and the Family, 60,* 119–132.

Caughlin, J. P., & Malis, R. S. (2004a). Demand/withdraw communication between parents and adolescents: Connections with self-esteem and substance use. *Journal of Social and Personal Relationships, 21,* 125–148.

Caughlin, J. P., & Malis, R. S. (2004b). Demand/withdraw communication between parents and adolescents as a correlate of relational satisfaction. *Communication Reports, 17,* 59–71.

Christensen, A., & Sullaway, M. (1984). *Communication patterns questionnaire.* Los Angeles: University of California, Los Angeles.

Clarke, E. J., Preston, M., Raskin, J., & Bengtson, V. L. (1999). Types of conflicts and tensions between older parents and adult child. *The Gerontologist, 39,* 261–270.

Coleman, M., Fine, M. A., Ganong, L. H., Downs, K. J. M., & Pauk, N. (2001). When you're not the Brady Bunch: Identifying perceived conflicts and resolution strategies in stepfamilies. *Personal Relationships, 8,* 55–73.

Copstead, G. J., Lanzetta, C. N., & Avtgis, T. A. (2001). Adult children conflict control expectancies: Effects on aggressive communication toward parents. *Communication Research Reports, 18,* 75–83.

Coyne, J. C., Thompson, R., & Palmer, S. C. (2002). Marital quality, coping with conflict, marital complaints, and affection in couples with a depressed wife. *Journal of Family Psychology, 16,* 26–37.

Cramer, D. (2002). Linking conflict management behaviours and relational satisfaction: The inventing role of conflict outcome satisfaction. *Journal of Social and Personal Relationships, 19,* 425–432.

Crockenberg, S., & Langrock, A. (2001). The role of specific emotions in children's response to interparental conflict: A test of the model. *Journal of Family Psychology, 15,* 163–182.

Crohan, S. E. (1996). Marital quality and conflict across the transition to parenthood in African American and White couples. *Journal of Marriage and the Family, 58,* 933–944.

Cummings, E. M., Goeke-Morey, M. C., & Papp, L. M. (2001). Couple conflict, children, and families: It's not just you and me, babe. In A. Booth, A. C. Crouter, & M. Clements (Eds.), *Couples in conflict* (pp. 117–148). Mahwah, NJ: Lawrence Erlbaum.

Cummings, E. M., Goeke-Morey, M. C., Papp, L. M., & Dukewich, T. L. (2002). Children's response to mothers' and fathers' emotionality and tactics in marital conflict in the home. *Journal of Family Psychology, 16,* 478–492.

Davies, P. T., & Cummings, E. M. (1994). Marital conflict and child adjustment: An emotional security hypothesis. *Psychological Bulletin, 116,* 387–411.

Davies, P. T., & Cummings, E. M. (1998). Exploring children's emotional security as a mediator of the link between marital relations and child adjustment. *Child Development, 69,* 124–139.

Deutsch, M. (1973). *The resolution of conflict: Constructive and destructive processes.* New Haven, CT: Yale University Press.

Driver, J., Tabares, A., Shapiro, A., Nahm, E. Y., & Gottman, J. M. (2003). Interactional patterns in marital success or failure: Gottman laboratory studies. In F. Walsh (Ed.), *Normal family processes: Growing diversity and complexity* (pp. 493–513). New York: Guilford.

Ducharme, J., Doyle, A. B., & Markiewicz, D. (2002). Attachment security with mother and father: Associations with adolescents' reports of interpersonal behavior with parents and peers. *Journal of Social and Personal Relationships, 19,* 203–231.

Dunn, J., & Munn, P. (1986). Sibling quarrels and maternal intervention: Individual differences in understanding and aggression. *Journal of Child Psychology and Psychiatry, 27,* 791–798.

El-Sheikh, M. (1997). Children's responses to adult-adult and mother-child arguments: The role of parental marital conflict and distress. *Journal of Family Psychology, 11,* 165–175.

Farver, J. A. M., Narang, S. K., & Bhadha, B. R. (2002). East meets West: Ethnic identity, acculturation, and conflict in Asian Indian families. *Journal of Family Psychology, 16,* 338–350.

Felson, R. B. (1983). Aggression and violence between siblings. *Social Psychology Quarterly, 46,* 271–285.

Felson, R. B., & Russo, N. (1988). Parental punishment and sibling aggression. *Social Psychology Quarterly, 51,* 11–18.

Fincham, F. D., Beach, S. R. H., & Davila, J. (2004). Forgiveness and conflict resolution in marriage. *Journal of Family Psychology, 18,* 72–81.

Fingerman, K. L. (1997). Aging mothers' and adult daughters' retrospective rating of conflict in their past relationships. *Current Psychology: Developmental, Learning, Personality, and Social, 16,* 131–154.

Fingerman, K. L. (1998). Tight lips? Aging mothers' and adult daughters' response to interpersonal tensions in their relationships. *Personal Relationships, 5,* 121–138.

Fisher, C. B., Reid, J. D., & Melendez, M. (1989). Conflict in families and friendships of later life. *Family Relations, 38,* 83–89.

Fitzpatrick, M. A., & Caughlin, J. P. (2002). Interpersonal conflict: A review. In M. L. Knapp & J. A. Daly (Eds.), *Handbook of interpersonal communication* (3rd ed., pp. 726–778). Thousand Oaks, CA: Sage.

Flores, E., Tschann, J. M., Marin, B. V., & Pantoja, P. (2004). Marital conflict and acculturation among Mexican American husbands and wives. *Cultural Diversity and Ethnic Minority Psychology, 10,* 39–52.

Galambos, N. L., & Almeda, D. M. (1992). Does parent-adolescent conflict increase in early adolescence? *Journal of Marriage and the Family, 4,* 737–747.

Gelles, R. J., & Straus, M. A. (1988). *Intimate violence.* New York: Simon & Schuster.

Gill, D. S., Christensen, A., & Fincham, F. D. (1999). Predicting marital satisfaction from behavior: Do all roads really lead to Rome? *Personal Relationships, 6,* 369–387.

Gottman, J. M. (1979). *Marital interaction: Experimental investigations.* New York: Academic Press.

Gottman, J. M. (1993). The roles of conflict engagement, escalation, and avoidance in marital interaction: A longitudinal view of five types of couples. *Journal of Consulting and Clinical Psychology, 61,* 6–15.

Gottman, J. M. (1994). *What predicts divorce? The relationships between marital processes and marital outcomes.* Hillsdale, NJ: Lawrence Erlbaum.

Gottman, J. M. (1999). *The marriage clinic: A scientifically-based marital therapy.* New York: Norton.

Gottman, J. M., Coan, J., Carrere, S., & Swanson, C. (1998). Predicting marital happiness and stability from newlywed interactions. *Journal of Marriage and the Family, 60,* 5–22.

Gottman, J. M., & Krokoff, L. J. (1989). Marital interaction and satisfaction: A longitudinal view. *Journal of Counseling and Clinical Psychology, 57,* 47–52.

Gottman, J. M., & Levinson, R. W. (2000). The timing of divorce: Predicting when a couple will divorce over a 14-year period. *Journal of Marriage and the Family, 62,* 737–745.

Gottman, J. M., & Notarius, C. I. (2000). Decade review: Observing marital interaction. *Journal of Marriage and the Family, 62,* 927–947.

Gottman, J. M., Swanson, C., & Murray, J. (1999). The mathematics of marital conflict: Dynamic mathematical nonlinear modeling of newlywed marital interaction. *Journal of Family Psychology, 13,* 3–19.

Graham-Bermann, S. A., Cutler, S. E., Litzenberger, B. W., & Schwartz, W. E. (1994). Perceived conflict and violence in childhood sibling relationships and later emotional adjustment. *Journal of Family Psychology, 8,* 85–97.

Grych, J. H., & Fincham, F. D. (1990). Marital conflict and children's adjustment: A cognitive-contextual framework. *Psychological Bulletin, 108,* 267–290.

Grych, J. H., & Fincham, F. D. (2001). *Interparental conflict and child development: Theory, research, and application.* New York: Cambridge University Press.

Hagestad, G. O. (1987). Parent-child relations in later life: Trends and gaps in past research. In J. Lancaster, J. Altmann, A. Rossi, & L. Sherrod (Eds.), *Parenting across the life span: Biosocial dimensions* (pp. 405–435). New York: Aldine de Gruter.

Hahlweg, K., Kaiser, A., Christensen, A., Fehm-Wolfsdorf, G., & Groth, T. (2000). Self-report and observational assessment of couples' conflict: The concordance between the communication patterns questionnaires and the KPI observation system. *Journal of Marriage and the Family, 62,* 61–67.

Hall, E. J., & Cummings, E. M. (1997). The effects of marital and parent-child conflicts on other family members: Grandmothers and grown children. *Family Relations, 46,* 135–143.

Hanson, T. L., McLanahan, S. S., & Thomson, E. (1996). Double jeopardy: Parental conflict and stepfamily outcomes for children. *Journal of Marriage and the Family, 58,* 141–154.

Hatch, L. R., & Bulcroft, K. (2004). Does long-term marriage bring less frequent disagreements? Five explanatory frameworks. *Journal of Family Issues, 25,* 465–495.

Heavey, C. L., Christensen, A., & Malamuth, N. M. (1995). The longitudinal impact of demand and withdrawal during marital conflict. *Journal of Consulting and Clinical Psychology, 63,* 797–801.

Heavey, C. L., Layne, C., & Christensen, A. (1993). Gender and conflict structure in marital interactions: A replication and extension. *Journal of Consulting and Clinical Psychology, 61,* 16–27.

Jacobson, N. S., & Margolin, G. (1979). *Marital therapy: Strategies based on social learning and behavior exchange principles.* New York: Brunner/Mazel.

Jenkins, J. M. (2000). Marital conflict and children's emotions: The development of an anger organization. *Journal of Marriage and the Family, 62,* 723–736.

Jenkins, J. M., Simpson, A., Dunn, J., Rasbash, J., & O'Connor, T. G. (2005). Mutual influence of marital conflict and children's behavior problems: Shared and nonshared family risks. *Child Development, 76,* 24–39.

Jensen-Campbell, L. A., & Graziano, W. G. (2000). Beyond the schoolyard: Relationships as moderators of daily interpersonal conflict. *Personality and Social Psychology Bulletin, 26,* 925–935.

Johnson, K. L., & Roloff, M. E. (1998). Serial arguing and relational quality: Determinants and consequences of perceived resolvability. *Communication Research, 25,* 327–343.

Johnson, S. L., & Jacob, T. (2000). Sequential interactions in the marital communication of depressed men and women. *Journal of Consulting and Clinical Psychology, 68,* 4–12.

Jouriles, E. N., & Farris, A. M. (1992). Effects of marital conflict on subsequent parent-son interactions. *Behavior Therapy, 23,* 355–374.

Kiecolt-Glaser, J. K., Bane, C., Glaser, R., & Malarkey, W. B. (2003). Love, marriage, and divorce: Newlyweds' stress hormones foreshadow relationship changes. *Journal of Consulting and Clinical Psychology, 71,* 176–188.

Kiecolt-Glaser, J. K., Malarkey, W. B., Chee, M. A., Newton, T., Cacioppo, J. T., Mao, H., et al. (1993). Negative behavior during marital conflict is associated with immunological down-regulation. *Psychosomatic Medicine, 55,* 395–409.

Kiecolt-Glaser, J. K., & Newton, T. L. (2001). Marriage and health: His and hers. *Psychological Bulletin, 127,* 472–501.

Kiecolt-Glaser, J. K., Newton, T. L., Cacioppo, J. T., MacCallum, R. C., Glaser, R., & Malarkey, W. B. (1996). Marital conflict and endocrine function: Are men really more physiologically affected than women? *Journal of Consulting and Clinical Psychology, 64,* 324–332.

Kimmel, P. L., Peterson, R. A., Weihs, K. L., Shidler, N., Simmens, S. J., Alleyne, S., et al. (2000). Dyadic relationship conflict, gender, and mortality in urban hemodialysis patients. *Journal of the American Society of Nephrology, 11,* 1518–1525.

King, K. (2001). A critique of behavioral observational coding system of couples' interaction: CISS and RCISS. *Journal of Social and Clinical Psychology, 20,* 1–23.

Kinsfogel, K. M., & Grych, J. H. (2004). Interparental conflict and adolescent dating relationships: Integrating cognitive, emotional and peer influence. *Journal of Family Psychology, 18,* 505–515.

Kirchler, E., Rodler, C., Holzl, E., & Meier, K. (2001). *Conflict and decision-making in close relationships: Love, money, and daily routines.* Philadelphia: Psychology Press.

Koerner, A. F., & Fitzpatrick, M. A. (1997). Family type and conflict: The impact of conversation orientation and conformity orientation on conflict in the family. *Communication Monographs, 48,* 59–75.

Koren, P., Carlton, K., & Shaw, D. (1980). Marital conflict: Relations among behaviors, outcomes, and distress. *Journal of Consulting and Clinical Psychology, 48,* 460–468.

Krishnakumar, A., & Buehler, C. (2000). Interparental conflict and parenting behaviors: A meta-analytic review. *Family Relations, 49,* 25–44.

Krokoff, L. J., Gottman, J. M., & Hass, S. D. (1989). Validation of a global rapid couples interaction scoring system. *Behavioral Assessment, 11,* 65–80.

Kuczynski, L., Kochanska, G., Radke-Yarrow, M., & Girnius-Brown, O. (1987). A developmental interpretation of young children's noncompliance. *Developmental Psychology, 23,* 799–806.

Kurdek, L. A. (1994a). Areas of conflict for gay, lesbian, and heterosexual couples: What couples argue about influences relationship satisfaction. *Journal of Marriage and the Family, 56,* 923–934.

Kurdek, L. A. (1994b). Conflict resolution styles in gay, lesbian, heterosexual nonparent, and heterosexual parent couples. *Journal of Marriage and the Family, 56,* 705–722.

Kurdek, L. A. (1995). Predicting change in marital satisfaction from husbands' and wives' conflict resolution strategies. *Journal of Marriage and the Family, 57,* 153–164.

Larzelere, R. E., & Kuhn, B. R. (2005). Comparing child outcomes of physical punishment and alternative disciplinary tactics: A meta-analysis. *Clinical Child and Family Psychology Review, 8,* 1–37.

Larzelere, R. E., & Merenda, J. A. (1994). The effectiveness of parental discipline for toddler misbehavior at different levels of child distress. *Family Relations, 43,* 480–488.

Larzelere, R. E., Sather, P. R., Schneider, W. N., Larson, D. B., & Pike, P. L. (1998). Punishment enhances reasoning's effectiveness as a disciplinary response to toddlers. *Journal of Marriage and the Family, 60,* 388–403.

Laursen, B., Coy, K. C., & Collins, W. A. (1998). Reconsidering changes in parent-child conflict across adolescence: A meta-analysis. *Child Development, 69,* 817–832.

Loving, T. J., Heffner, K. L., Kiecolt-Glaser, J. K., Glaser, R., & Malarkey, W. B. (2004). Stress hormone changes and marital conflict: Spouses' relative power makes a difference. *Journal of Marriage and the Family, 66,* 595–612.

MacDonald, W. L., & DeMaris, A. (1995). Remarriage, stepchildren, and marital conflict: Challenges to the incomplete institutionalization hypothesis. *Journal of Marriage and the Family, 57,* 387–398.

Marcus, N. E., Lindahl, K. M., & Malik, N. M. (2001). Interparental conflict, children's social cognitions, and child aggression: A test of a mediational model. *Journal of Family Psychology, 15,* 315–333.

Margolin, G., & Wampold, B. E. (1981). Sequential analysis of conflict and accord in distressed and nondistressed marital partners. *Journal of Consulting and Clinical Psychology, 49,* 554–567.

Masheter, C. (1991). Postdivorce relationships between ex-spouses: The roles of attachment and interpersonal conflict. *Journal of Marriage and the Family, 53,* 103–111.

McGonagle, K. A., Kessler, R. C., & Gotlib, I. H. (1993). The effects of marital disagreement style, frequency, and outcome on marital disruption. *Journal of Social and Personal Relationships, 10,* 385–404.

McHale, S. M., Updegraff, K. A., Tucker, C. J., & Crouter, A. C. (2000). Step in or stay out? Parents' roles in adolescent siblings' relationships. *Journal of Marriage and the Family, 62,* 746–760.

McLaughlin, B. (1983). Child compliance to parental control techniques. *Developmental Psychology, 19,* 667–673.

Menaghan, E. G. (1982). Measuring coping effectiveness: A panel analysis of marital problems and coping efforts. *Journal of Health and Social Behavior, 23,* 220–234.

Menaghan, E. G. (1983). Coping with parental problems: Panel assessments of effectiveness. *Journal of Family Issues, 4,* 483–506.

Mills, R. S. L., Nazar, J., & Farrell, H. M. (2002). Child and parent perceptions of hurtful messages. *Journal of Social and Personal Relationships, 19,* 731–754.

Montemayor, R., & Hanson, E. (1985). A naturalistic view of conflict between adolescents and their parents and siblings. *Journal of Early Adolescence, 5,* 23–30.

Newell, S. E., & Stutman, R. K. (1991). The episodic nature of social confrontation. In K. Anderson (Ed.), *Communication yearbook 14* (pp. 359–392). Thousand Oaks, CA: Sage.

Noller, P., Feeney, J. A., Sheehan, G., & Peterson, C. (2000). Marital conflict patterns: Links with family conflict and family members' perceptions of one another. *Personal Relationships, 7,* 79–94.

Noller, P., & White, A. (1990). The validity of the communication patterns questionnaire. *Psychological Assessment: A Journal of Consulting and Clinical Psychology, 2,* 478–482.

Notarius, C. I., Benson, P. R., Sloane, D., Vanzetti, N. A., & Hornyak, L. M. (1989). Exploring the interface between perception and behavior: An analysis of marital interaction in distressed and nondistressed couples. *Behavioral Assessment, 11,* 39–64.

O'Brien, M., Margolin, G., John, R. S., & Krueger, L. (1991). Mothers' and sons' cognitive and emotional reactions to simulated marital and family conflict. *Journal of Consulting and Clinical Psychology, 59,* 692–703.

O'Connor, T. G., & Insabella, G. (1999). Marital satisfaction, relationships and roles. *Monographs of the Society for Research in Child Development, 64*(4, Serial No. 259).

Papp, L. M., Cummings, E. M., & Goeke-Morey, M. C. (2002). Marital conflicts in the home when children are present versus absent. *Developmental Psychology, 38,* 774–783.

Pasch, L. A., & Bradbury, T. N. (1998). Social support, conflict and the development of marital dysfunction. *Journal of Consulting and Clinical Psychology, 66,* 219–230.

Perlman, M., & Ross, H. S. (1997a). The benefits of parental intervention in children's disputes: An examination of concurrent changes in children's fighting styles. *Child Development, 64,* 690–700.

Perlman, M., & Ross, H. S. (1997b). Who's the boss? Parents' failed attempts to influence the outcomes of conflicts between their children. *Journal of Social and Personal Relationships, 14,* 463–480.

Perozynski, L., & Kramer, L. (1999). Parental beliefs about managing sibling conflict. *Developmental Psychology, 35,* 489–499.

Raffaelli, M. (1992). Sibling conflict in early adolescence. *Journal of Marriage and the Family, 54,* 652–663.

Reuter, M. A., & Conger, R. D. (1995). Antecedents of parent-adolescent disagreements. *Journal of Marriage and the Family, 57,* 435–448.

Revenstorf, D., Vogel, B., Wegener, C., Hahlweg, K., & Schindler, L. (1980). Escalation phenomena in interaction sequences: An empirical comparison of distressed and non-distressed couples. *Behaviour Analysis and Modification, 4,* 97–115.

Riesch, S. K., Jackson, M. M., & Chanchong, W. (2003). Communication approaches to parent-child conflict: Young adolescence to young adult. *Journal of Pediatric Nursing, 18,* 244–256.

Ritchie, K. L. (1999). Maternal behaviors and cognitions during discipline episodes: A comparison between power bouts and single acts of noncompliance. *Developmental Psychology, 35,* 580–589.

Rogers, S. J., & Amato, P. R. (2000). Have changes in gender relations affected marital quality? *Social Forces, 79,* 731–753.

Roloff, M. E. (1996). The catalyst hypothesis: Conditions under which coercive communication leads to physical aggression. In D. D. Cahn & S. A. Lloyd (Eds.), *Family violence from a communication perspective* (pp. 20–36). Thousand Oaks, CA: Sage.

Ross, H. S., Filyer, R. E., Lollis, S. P., Perlman, M., & Martin, J. L. (1994). Administering justice in the family. *Journal of Family Psychology, 8,* 254–273.

Sanford, K. (2003). Problem-solving conversation in marriage: Does it matter what topics couples discuss? *Personal Relationships, 10,* 97–112.

Schaeffer, N. C. (1989). The frequency and intensity of parental conflict: Choosing response dimensions. *Journal of Marriage and the Family, 51,* 759–776.

Schaffer, H. R., & Crook, C. K. (1980). Child compliance and maternal control techniques. *Developmental Psychology, 16,* 54–61.

Schudlich, D. D. R., Papp, L. M., & Cummings, E. M. (2004). Relations of husbands' and wives' dysphoria to marital conflict resolution strategies. *Journal of Family Psychology, 18,* 171–183.

Shagle, S. C., & Barber, B. K. (1993). Effects of family, marital, and parent-child conflict on adolescent self-derogation and suicidal ideation. *Journal of Marriage and the Family, 55,* 964–974.

Shamir, H., Schudlich, T. D. R., & Cummings, E. M. (2001). Marital conflict, parenting styles, and children's representation of family relationships. *Parenting: Science and Practice, 1,* 123–151.

Siddiqui, A., & Ross, H. (1999). How do sibling conflicts end? *Early Education and Development, 10,* 315–332.

Siddiqui, A., & Ross, H. (2004). Mediation as a method of parent intervention in children's disputes. *Journal of Family Psychology, 18,* 147–159.

Sillars, A., Canary, D. J., & Tafoya, M. (2004). Communication, conflict, and the quality of family relationships. In A. L. Vangelisti (Ed.), *Handbook of family communication* (pp. 379–412). Mahwah, NJ: Lawrence Erlbaum.

Sillars, A., Roberts, L. J., Leonard, K. E., & Dun, T. (2000). Cognition during marital conflict: The relationship of thought and talk. *Journal of Social and Personal Relationships, 17,* 479–502.

Simons, R. L., Whitbeck, L. B., Conger, R. D., & Chy-In, W. (1991). Intergenerational transmission of harsh parenting. *Developmental Psychology, 27,* 159–171.

Smetana, J. G. (1989). Adolescents' and parents' reasoning about actual family conflict. *Child Development, 60,* 1052–1067.

Smetana, J. G. (1995). Parenting styles and conceptions of parental authority during adolescence. *Child Development, 66,* 299–316.

Smetana, J. G., & Gaines, C. (1999). Adolescent-parent conflict in middle-class African American families. *Child Development, 70,* 1447–1463.

Smetana, J. G., Yau, J., & Hanson, S. (1991). Conflict resolution in families with adolescents. *Journal of Research on Adolescence, 1,* 189–206.

Sprey, J. (1969). The family as a system in conflict. *Journal of Marriage and the Family, 31,* 699–706.

Steinmetz, S. K. (1977). *The cycle of violence: Assertive, aggressive and abusive family interaction.* New York: Praeger.

Stewart, R. B., Verbrugge, K. M., & Beilfuss, M. C. (1998). Sibling relationships in early adulthood: A typology. *Personal Relationships, 5,* 59–74.

Stocker, C., Burwell, R., & Briggs, M. (2002). Sibling conflict in middle childhood predicts children's adjustment in early adolescence. *Journal of Family Psychology, 16,* 50–57.

Stocker, C. M., & Youngblade, L. (1999). Marital conflict and parental hostility: Links with children's sibling and peer relationships. *Journal of Family Psychology, 13,* 598–609.

Straus, M. A. (1979). Measuring intrafamily conflict and violence: The conflict tactics (CT) scales. *Journal of Marriage and the Family, 41,* 75–88.

Straus, M. A. (2004). Cross-cultural reliability and validity of the revised conflict tactics scales: A study of university student dating couples in 17 nations. *Cross-Cultural Research, 38,* 407–432.

Straus, M. A., & Gelles, R. J. (1990). *Physical violence in American families: Risk factors and adaptations to violence in 8,145 families.* New Brunswick, NJ: Transaction.

Suitor, J. J., Pillemer, K., Keeton, S., & Robinson, J. (1995). Aged parents and aging children: Determinants of relationship quality. In R. Blieswzner & V. H. Bedford (Eds.), *Handbook of aging and the family* (pp. 223–242). Westport, CT: Greenwood.

Sullaway, M., & Christensen, A. (1983). Assessment of dysfunctional interaction patterns in couples. *Journal of Marriage and the Family, 45,* 653–660.

Taylor, J. E., & Norris, J. E. (2000). Sibling relationships, fairness, and conflict over transfer of the farm. *Journal of Marriage and the Family, 49,* 277–283.

Ting-Toomey, S. (1983). An analysis of verbal communication patterns in high and low marital adjustment groups. *Human Communication Research, 9,* 306–319.

Topham, G. L., Larson, J. H., & Holman, T. B. (2005). Family-of-origin predictors of hostile conflict in early marriage. *Contemporary Family Therapy, 27,* 101–121.

Tschann, J. M., Flores, E., Pasch, L. A., & Marin, B. V. (1999). Assessing interparental conflict: Reports of parents and adolescents in European American and Mexican American families. *Journal of Marriage and the Family, 61,* 169–283.

Umberson, D. (1992). Relationships between adult children and their parents: Psychological consequences for both generations. *Journal of Marriage and the Family, 54,* 664–674.

Vandewater, E. A., & Lansford, J. E. (1998). Influences of family structure and parental conflict on children's well-being. *Family Relations, 47,* 323–330.

Vincent, J. P., Weiss, R. L., & Birchler, G. R. (1975). A behavioral analysis of problem solving in distressed and nondistressed married and stranger dyads. *Behavior Therapy, 6,* 475–487.

Vuchinich, S. (1984). Sequencing and social structure in family conflict. *Social Psychology Quarterly, 47,* 217–234.

Vuchinich, S. (1986). On attenuation in verbal family conflict. *Social Psychology Quarterly, 49,* 281–293.

Vuchinich, S. (1987). Starting and stopping spontaneous family conflicts. *Journal of Marriage and the Family, 49,* 591–601.

Vuchinich, S. (1990). The sequential organization of closing in verbal family conflict. In A. D. Grimshaw (Ed.), *Conflict talk: Sociolinguistic investigations of arguments in conversations* (pp. 118–138). New York: Cambridge University Press.

Vuchinich, S., & De Baryshe, B. (1997). Factor structure and predictive validity of questionnaire reports on family problem solving. *Journal of Marriage and the Family, 59,* 915–927.

Yau, J., & Smetana, J. G. (1996). Adolescent-parent conflict among Chinese adolescents in Hong Kong. *Child Development, 67,* 1262–1275.

CHAPTER 9

Family Conflict and Adolescents

Patricia Noller

University of Queensland, Australia

Sharon Atkin

University of Queensland, Australia

Judith A. Feeney

University of Queensland, Australia

Candida Peterson

University of Queensland, Australia

As Roloff and Miller discussed in the previous chapter, there is no doubt conflict is a pervasive feature of family life that can have beneficial or harmful effects depending on how it is expressed and how (or if) it is resolved (Noller & Fitzpatrick, 1993). This is especially the case in adolescence. Evidence suggests that conflict with parents tends to increase at that stage of child development (Steinberg, 1991), at least partly because adolescents come to see their parents' rules and demands as less legitimate and more arbitrary (Smetana, 1988) than they did when they were younger. In addition, family conflict has been found to predict depression and distress in adolescents, particularly where family cohesion is low (Meyerson, Long, Miranda, & Marx, 2002).

In the two studies reported here, we explored normative reactions to marital and parent-adolescent conflict of both parents and adolescents. Our aim was to shed light on what adolescents and parents perceive as typical in conflict and the effects of different conflict styles. The establishment of normative reactions to family conflict will help with understanding clinically significant conflict (Foster, 1994) and with identification of adolescents who are at high risk for associated problems (O'Brien, Margolin, John, & Krueger, 1991). For example, fewer problem-solving skills have been observed in adolescents who have mothers who are avoidant during conflict (McCombs, Forehand, & Smith, 1988).

To explore this issue, we used an analog paradigm where adolescents and their parents listened to a series of specially prepared tapes depicting conflicts between parents, as well as between parents and adolescents, and then responded to questions about those tapes and their reactions. All of the conflict discussions involved conflicts about household tasks (untidy adolescent room, sharing tasks between husband and wife, and bringing in washing).

Cummings and his colleagues have frequently conducted this type of study (e.g., Cummings, Ianotti, & Zahn-Waxler, 1985; Cummings, Pellegrini, Notarius, & Cummings, 1989; Cummings, Zahn-Waxler, & Radke-Yarrow, 1981). They showed that children responded with distress and/or aggressive behavior when they were exposed to an angry interaction between adults. In addition, children became even more distressed when these angry interactions between adults were experienced frequently or involved physical violence. They also tended to become distressed when the conflict was not resolved. Our goal was to conduct this type of analog study with adolescents and their parents, to see how family members would respond in such situations.

Grych and Fincham (1990, 1993) note that there are important issues about effects of conflict on children that require further research. For example, it is important to understand whether children respond differently to marital conflicts that are child related from those that are not because such an understanding may enable better responses to the impact of marital conflict on children. Is the major impact of marital conflict on children in the family related to conflict that involves the young person, or does all marital conflict have a similar effect?

We also were interested in whether adolescents and their parents would respond differently to conflicts dealt with constructively and those dealt with destructively, or whether all conflict has the same perceived impact. Given the large body of research indicating gender differences in responses to conflict in close relationships, we also investigated whether responses would vary with the sex of parent and sex of adolescent involved in the conflict.

In this chapter, we first describe and report the results for the study involving parents' and adolescents' responses to tapes of marital conflict. Second, we describe and report the results involving parents' and adolescents' responses to parent-adolescent conflict. These studies should increase our understanding of adolescents' responses to family conflict and aid those who work with families with adolescents in helping them find more constructive ways of dealing with the inevitable conflicts that arise in families.

Study 1: Perceptions of Marital Conflict

Two parents and one adolescent from each of 55 intact families with at least two adolescent children between the ages of 12 and 16 participated in the study. There were 29 adolescent males and 26 females, with an average age of 13½ years. The families were recruited through public and private schools, as well as through newspaper advertisements. It is important to note that the respondents are Australian, in contrast to much of the research on families that tends to be based on U.S. samples (see Chapter 8, this volume).

A set of eight audiotapes, all pretested to ensure that they reflected the intended styles, were used in this study. All of the tapes involved an argument between the parents, and half involved a child-related issue (the adolescent's untidy room), and the other half involved a non-child-related marital issue (husband and wife sharing the housework).

Four different styles of conflict were represented on the tapes. These styles were selected based on the literature on marital conflict (Christensen, 1988; Christensen & Heavey, 1990; Noller & White, 1990). The four styles were (a) a coercive style where partners verbally attacked one another (blaming the other and defending their own position), (b) a wife demands/husband withdraws style (where the wife demands more help from the husband but he does not want to discuss the issue), (c) a husband demands/wife withdraws style (where the husband demands change and his wife does not want to discuss the issue), and (d) a mutual style (where the spouses listen to each other's point of view and respond with understanding). To ensure that family members were responding to the style of the conflict, rather than to how the issue was resolved, the conflict discussions were standardized so that they all ended at a similar point, with no resolution of the issue.

Family members completed the Conflict Resolution Styles Questionnaire (CRS; Rands, Levinger, & Mellinger, 1981) as modified by Peterson (1990). The inclusion of this measure enabled us to assess the validity of the taped discussions and the extent to which ratings of the tapes correlated with family members' reports of typical family conflict. The CRS includes three four-item factors: (a) fight (attack or act aggressively or coercively), (b) avoid (refuse to discuss the issue or deny that there is an issue), and (c) mutual (listen and try to understand each other's point of view). Rather than reporting on their own behavior, participants report on the behavior of the other person in the conflict (e.g., spouse for parents, parents for adolescents). This technique is based on the belief that individuals are likely to be able to report more objectively on the other person's behavior than on their own (Rands et al., 1981).

After listening to each tape, all three family members rated that discussion in terms of its typicality (how similar it was to interactions in their own families), stressfulness, the likelihood that the conflict would be resolved, and the positive and negative emotions family members experienced in listening to the argument between the adults. All ratings were made on 6-point scales. Ratings of three scales (happy, satisfied, and comfortable) were summed to give a possible score of 18 for positive emotion, and five scales (angry, sad, worried, ashamed, and helpless) were summed to give a possible score out of 30 for negative emotion. For the CRS, participants received scores for each of the three scales, as described earlier.

Results

Ratings of typicality, stressfulness, likelihood of resolution, and positive and negative emotions were analyzed to explore the question of whether such factors as the type of conflict (child related or not), which family member was reporting (mother, father, or adolescent), and the style of conflict being presented on the tape (coercive, wife demands, husband demands, and mutual) had an impact on these ratings.

Typicality

All three family members indicated that the mutual style was the most typical style in their own families and that the wife demands/husband withdraws style was more typical than the other negative styles (see Table 9.1). In addition, adolescents saw the mutual style as less typical of interactions between their parents than parents did.

Given that the mutual style was seen as more typical than the negative styles, it seems likely that these families were generally not highly conflicted. The finding that adolescents reported more negative views of family interactions than other family members is in line with other studies showing that adolescents tend to *express* more negative views of their families than their parents do (Noller & Callan, 1988). The high typicality ratings for the wife demands/husband withdraws style in comparison with the other negative styles fits with work on sex differences in the demand/withdraw pattern in marriage (e.g., Christensen, 1988; Christensen & Heavey, 1990), with women seen as more likely to be the demanders in this type of interaction and men more likely to be the withdrawers.

Stressfulness

The levels of stress experienced when listening to the tapes depended on the conflict style and which family member was doing the rating. Coercive tapes were experienced as more stressful than other styles, and mutual tapes were experienced as less stressful, indicating that family members were able to distinguish among different styles. Fathers tended to rate mutual interactions as more stressful than did other family members. This finding fits with work by Gottman and Levenson (1988), suggesting that men find family conflict highly stressful (see Table 9.2). Given that mean ratings of stressfulness were generally lower than the midpoint of 3, it seems likely

Table 9.1   Means and Standard Deviations for Typicality Ratings by Type of Conflict, Reporter, and Conflict Style for Marital Conflict Study (Study 1)

Reporter	Child Related	Non–Child Related
Adolescent		
Coercion	2.02 (1.41)	1.93 (1.50)
Father demands	2.0 (1.30)	1.62 (1.16)
Mother demands	2.32 (1.57)	2.25 (1.47)
Mutual	3.13 (1.43)	2.79 (1.38)
Mother		
Coercion	2.04 (1.52)	1.79 (1.34)
Father demands	1.74 (1.23)	1.55 (1.28)
Mother demands	2.45 (1.73)	2.62 (1.63)
Mutual	3.4 (1.52)	3.21 (1.47)
Father		
Coercion	2.02 (1.35)	1.89 (1.41)
Father demands	1.76 (1.24)	1.72 (1.29)
Mother demands	2.32 (1.45)	2.49 (1.61)
Mutual	3.66 (1.57)	3.4 (1.49)

Note: Ratings are on a single 6-point scale. Standard deviations are in parentheses.

that listening to these tapes was not highly stressful. Of course, if the interactions were occurring in their own homes and had direct consequences for them, family members would probably experience more stress. The low stressfulness ratings point to possible limitations for fully understanding the impact of conflict on families, based on this type of research.

Likelihood of Resolution

Ratings of likelihood of resolution also depended on conflict style and family member. Mutual conflicts were seen as more likely to be resolved than other conflicts, suggesting that family members distinguished clearly between mutual interactions on the tapes and the interactions involving negative styles. In addition, it seems clear that family members were again able to discriminate constructive from destructive conflicts.

Adolescents were generally more optimistic about the likelihood of conflicts being resolved than were their parents (see Table 9.3). Perhaps these young people are more naive and less experienced than other family members, or they may just be expressing the hope that the conflict would be resolved. It is also possible, however, that they are basing their judgments on their experience of conflict in the family where they may have seen conflicts resolved. Alternatively, it may be easier for them as "outsiders" not actually involved in the conflict to see the possibility of resolution.

Table 9.2   Means and Standard Deviations for Ratings of Stressfulness by Type of Conflict, Reporter, and Conflict Style for Marital Conflict Study (Study 1)

Reporter	Child Related	Non–Child Related
Adolescent		
Coercion	2.27 (1.62)	2.56 (1.78)
Father demands	2.31 (1.69)	2.35 (1.64)
Mother demands	2.04 (1.31)	1.92 (1.34)
Mutual	1.4 (0.80)	1.39 (0.95)
Mother		
Coercion	2.96 (1.6)	3.12 (1.87)
Father demands	2.5 (1.49)	2.46 (1.49)
Mother demands	2.65 (1.84)	2.37 (1.56)
Mutual	1.64 (0.93)	1.44 (0.73)
Father		
Coercion	2.96 (1.6)	2.71 (1.61)
Father demands	2.79 (1.66)	2.75 (1.52)
Mother demands	2.87 (1.59)	2.48 (1.45)
Mutual	2.02 (1.23)	1.9 (1.11)

Note: Ratings are on a single 6-point scale. Standard deviations are in parentheses.

Table 9.3   Means and Standard Deviations for Ratings of the Likelihood of Resolution, by Type of Conflict, Reporter, and Conflict Style for Marital Conflict Study (Study 1)

Reporter	Child Related	Non–Child Related
Adolescent		
Coercion	5.42 (2.46)	5.06 (2.32)
Father demands	5.31 (2.35)	5.04 (2.38)
Mother demands	5.16 (2.43)	5.75 (2.7)
Mutual	10.14 (2.02)	10.31 (2.19)
Mother		
Coercion	3.61 (2.02)	3.18 (1.65)
Father demands	4.0 (2.43)	3.69 (1.82)
Mother demands	4.24 (2.21)	3.69 (1.82)
Mutual	9.75 (2.12)	10.2 (1.93)
Father		
Coercion	4.31 (2.24)	4.08 (2.51)
Father demands	4.55 (2.6)	4.2 (1.92)
Mother demands	4.73 (2.32)	4.2 (1.92)
Mutual	9.47 (2.02)	9.71 (2.25)

Note: These scores are summed from two 6-point scales: "How likely is the conflict to be resolved?" and "How likely is the conflict to get worse?" Thus, ratings are on a 12-point scale. Standard deviations are in parentheses.

The wife demands/husband withdraws style may be seen as more likely to be resolved than the other negative styles because family members are more accustomed to this type of conflict and therefore more optimistic about parents moving to a resolution. It is important to note, however, that adolescents again were more optimistic about the likelihood of a resolution than parents, regardless of conflict style.

Emotional Reactions

As would be expected, mutual tapes induced the most positive emotion, and coercive tapes induced the least. Adolescents tended to report lower levels of positive emotion for mutual child-related tapes than did their parents, whereas there were no differences among reporters for non-child-related conflicts. Perhaps child-related conflicts are particularly unpleasant for adolescents. It is important to note, however, that this is the only effect for the child-related versus non-child-related variable.

The mutual style also induced less negative emotion than other styles, although fathers reported more negative emotion in response to mutual conflicts than other family members. Means were 9.28, 9.57, and 10.87, respectively, for adolescents, mothers, and fathers for child-related conflicts and 7.66, 8.34, and 9.70, respectively, for adolescents, mothers, and fathers for non-child-related conflicts, providing further support for the claims of Gottman and Levenson (1988) discussed earlier.

Coercive tapes induced more negative emotion than demand/withdraw tapes. Having the members of the couple attacking each other verbally would seem to be more stressful for family members than having one member attacking and the other withdrawing. Whether the conflict was child related or not did not seem to affect the level of negative emotion reported by family members.

Correlations With the Conflict Resolution Style Questionnaire

Correlations between family members' ratings of typicality and their scores on the CRS provide further evidence for the validity of the tapes. For example, adolescents' ratings of the typicality of the coercive child-related interaction were negatively related to the level of mutuality reported in interactions with mothers. They were also positively related to reports of their extent of fighting with mothers. How typical the adolescents rated the mother demands tape was positively associated with their reports of the fathers' avoidance in conflict interactions, as well as the extent to which they fought with both mothers and fathers. In addition, those adolescents who reported high levels of mutuality with mothers rated mother demands as less typical.

Discussion

The findings from this study support the validity of the analog method for studying responses to marital conflict. There were strong style effects, mainly for differences between the mutual and more negative styles, with the mutual style seen as more typical, less stressful, more likely to be resolved, and as inducing more positive and less negative emotion. The coercive style, on the other hand, was seen as more stressful to listen to and as inducing more negative emotion than all the other styles.

It was also interesting to see that ratings of typicality were correlated with adolescents' reports of how conflicts between parents and children were dealt with in their families. For example, ratings of typicality correlated negatively with reports of mutual conflict interactions with mothers and positively with fighting with mothers, in line with what would be expected.

Ratings of typicality showed that the mutual style was seen as the most typical across the families. It is also interesting to note, however, that adolescents regarded mutual constructive conflict resolution as less typical than did their parents. As noted earlier, this finding fits with previous work on differences between parents and adolescents in their views of family processes. It is possible that the adolescents use a different standard in evaluating these processes, but it is also possible that parents overestimate their use of mutual strategies, as would be suggested by the self-serving bias.

Fathers found listening to the conflict tapes more stressful overall, in line with evidence that men generally find conflict in family relationships more stressful than do other family members. Gottman and Levenson (1988) argue that men have stronger physiological reactions to stress and conflict and that this is why they often avoid conflict or try to withdraw from it.

Although adolescents did not report finding the tapes more stressful, they did report lower levels of positive emotion in response to the mutual tapes than did their parents, particularly for the child-related conflicts. There were no differences among family members for conflicts that were not child related, with reports of positive emotion being moderate to high. These findings suggest that listening to child-related marital conflict is, at least in some ways, more difficult for adolescents than for their parents. Perhaps being the source of conflict is stressful for adolescents, causing feelings of guilt and insecurity.

In our second study, we used parent-adolescent conflicts as the stimuli. We were again interested in whether family members would be able to discriminate among different conflict styles in terms of their typicality, stressfulness, likelihood of resolution, and emotional reactions in this different context of parent-adolescent conflict, a situation that is likely to be even more salient for adolescents. Because conflicts between parents and adolescents are child related by definition, that variable was not included in this study, but we were able to compare reactions to father-adolescent conflicts with those to mother-adolescent conflicts.

Study 2: Perceptions of Parent-Adolescent Conflict

The participants for this study were a separate group of 58 families with adolescents. A set of eight tapes was prepared similarly to the marital tapes, except that these tapes involved parent-adolescent conflicts. Half of the tapes involved a mother-adolescent conflict, and the other half involved a father-adolescent conflict. Each of the four styles used in the earlier study was included for both the mother-adolescent and father-adolescent conflicts. Family members listened to tapes involving an adolescent of the same gender as the adolescent participating from their family. The conflict issue in the taped discussions was about bringing in washing from an outdoor clothesline, seen as an everyday task for families in Australia.

Results

We discuss the results in the following categories: typicality, stressfulness, likelihood of resolution, emotional reactions, and correlations with the CRS, consistent with our results for Study 1.

Typicality

Analysis of participant ratings of typicality of the tapes showed effects of the parent engaged in the conflict (mother vs. father) and discussion style (see Table 9.4). The participants rated mother-adolescent discussions, as opposed to father-adolescent discussions, as more typical, irrespective of style ($M = 3.07$ and 2.71, respectively). This finding fits with evidence that adolescents spend more time talking with their mothers than with their fathers and that they talk with their mothers across a broader range of topics (Noller & Bagi, 1985).

In addition, mothers tend to enforce family rules more than fathers, are more likely to reprimand their children for inappropriate interpersonal behavior (Montemayor & Hanson, 1985), and are usually more involved in monitoring their children's lives (Larson & Richards, 1994). Given this situation, mothers are more likely than fathers to be involved in conflict with their adolescents. Adolescents may use communication with their mothers rather than fathers to negotiate greater autonomy. With increasing age, adolescents gain in power relative to their mothers, whereas in adolescent-father interactions, fathers tend to remain dominant (Larson & Richards, 1994; Montemayor, 1983).

Pairwise comparisons of style ratings showed that participants rated the mutual style as more typical of their own conflicts with parents than any other style. These families also reported that the parent demands/adolescent withdraws style was more typical of their families than the adolescent demands/parent withdraws style. It is acknowledged that conflict resolution may be learned through family relationships (Noller, Feeney, Peterson, & Sheehan, 1995) and that having avoidant parents, particularly an avoidant mother, is associated with low problem-solving abilities in adolescents (McCombs et al., 1988).

In general, mothers differentiated between styles more than did fathers or adolescents. Mothers rated the mutual style as more typical of their own family discussions, followed by the parent demands/adolescent withdraws style; the coercive and adolescent demands/parent withdraws styles were rated as least typical. Fathers' ratings reflected a similar pattern, but fathers did not differentiate between the coercive and parent demands/adolescent withdraws styles. Adolescents differentiated the least among the styles, with ratings showing mutual discussions as more typical of their families than adolescent demands/parent withdraws but no other significant differences.

Table 9.4 Means and Standard Deviations for Parent and Adolescent Ratings of Typicality of Parent-Adolescent Conflict (Study 2)

Reporter	Mother-Adolescent	Father-Adolescent
Adolescent		
Coercion	3.26 (1.77)	2.79 (1.7)
Parent demands	2.98 (1.49)	2.71 (1.44)
Parent withdraws	2.60 (1.64)	2.24 (1.37)
Mutual	3.29 (1.51)	3.59 (1.39)
Mother		
Coercion	2.78 (1.79)	2.10 (1.54)
Parent demands	3.52 (1.69)	2.79 (1.67)
Parent withdraws	2.47 (1.54)	2.24 (1.37)
Mutual	4.02 (1.54)	3.62 (1.61)
Father		
Coercion	2.91 (1.61)	2.5 (1.47)
Parent demands	3.05 (1.61)	2.48 (1.34)
Parent withdraws	2.41 (1.63)	2.16 (1.21)
Mutual	3.59 (1.39)	3.41 (1.46)

Note: Ratings are on a single 6-point scale. Standard deviations are in parentheses.

Fathers' reports were not significantly different from either mothers' or adolescents' reports for any of the styles. Adolescents, however, perceived the mutual style as less typical than did mothers and the coercive style as more typical than did mothers, again suggesting a negative bias in how adolescents perceive communication in their families.

Stressfulness

All reporters rated the mutual style as less stressful to listen to than the other styles and the coercive tapes as more stressful. In general, adolescents found listening to the tapes less stressful than did mothers or fathers, who did not differ significantly from each other ($M = 1.84$, 2.32, and 2.16, respectively), although ratings were generally low. Mothers in particular rated the parent demands/adolescent withdraws style as more stressful than did either fathers or adolescents, and unlike fathers, mothers rated that style as more stressful than listening to the adolescent demands/parent withdraws style. Mothers' reactions to the demand/withdraw tapes suggest that mothers dislike having to be demanding with their adolescents, even more than they dislike adolescents being demanding with them (see Table 9.5).

Likelihood of Resolution

The mutual style was seen as most likely to reach resolution, and the coercive style was seen as least likely. Discussions involving mothers were rated as more likely to be

Table 9.5 Means and Standard Deviations for Parent and Adolescent Ratings of How Stressful They Felt Listening to the Parent-Adolescent Conflict Discussions (Study 2)

Reporter	Mother-Adolescent	Father-Adolescent
Adolescent		
Coercion	1.86 (1.19)	2.07 (1.32)
Parent demands	1.79 (1.16)	1.89 (1.25)
Parent withdraws	1.61 (0.92)	1.95 (1.34)
Mutual	1.61 (0.92)	1.63 (0.99)
Mother		
Coercion	2.79 (1.75)	2.96 (1.88)
Parent demands	2.77 (1.56)	2.33 (1.42)
Parent withdraws	2.19 (1.37)	2.37 (1.52)
Mutual	1.65 (1.09)	1.53 (0.87)
Father		
Coercion	2.67 (1.75)	2.65 (1.55)
Parent demands	2.12 (1.3)	2.25 (1.54)
Parent withdraws	2.23 (1.54)	2.07 (1.33)
Mutual	1.58 (0.80)	1.67 (0.97)

Note: Ratings are on a single 6-point scale. Standard deviations are in parentheses.

resolved than discussions involving fathers ($M = 2.91$ and 2.76, respectively). This finding fits with research showing that adolescents find their mothers more open and supportive than their fathers (Ellis-Schwabe & Thornburg, 1986; Noller & Callan, 1990; Youniss & Smoller, 1985).

Adolescents rated the coercive and the demand/withdraw styles as more likely to be resolved than did mothers or fathers, and mothers rated the mutual style as more likely to be resolved than did fathers or adolescents. Mother and father ratings did not distinguish between the demand/withdraw styles; however, adolescents rated the parent demands/adolescent withdraws style as more likely to be resolved than the adolescent demands/parent withdraws style. Adolescent ratings did not distinguish between the coercive and adolescent demands/parent withdraws styles, suggesting that adolescents understand the need for their parents' involvement in discussions in order to reach resolution (see Table 9.6).

Emotional Reactions

Overall, adolescents, mothers, and fathers reported the highest levels of positive emotion when listening to the mutual discussions ($M = 2.39$, 3.14, and 3.24, respectively) and the lowest levels when listening to the coercive discussions ($M = 1.83$, 1.20, and 1.32, respectively). Adolescents reported more positive emotion when listening to the coercive discussions than did either mothers or fathers and less positive emotion when listening to the mutual discussions than did fathers or mothers, whose reports did not differ. The participants in this study were, in general,

Table 9.6   Means and Standard Deviations of Parent and Adolescent Ratings of Likelihood That the Conflict in the Tapes Would Be Resolved (Study 2)

Reporter	Mother-Adolescent	Father-Adolescent
Adolescent		
Coercion	2.68 (1.36)	2.58 (1.39)
Parent demands	3.05 (1.32)	2.82 (1.48)
Parent withdraws	2.68 (1.42)	2.56 (1.35)
Mutual	3.98 (1.48)	4.12 (1.32)
Mother		
Coercion	1.88 (1.51)	1.86 (1.61)
Parent demands	2.51 (1.57)	2.39 (1.42)
Parent withdraws	2.37 (1.64)	2.23 (1.40)
Mutual	4.91 (1.37)	4.74 (1.28)
Father		
Coercion	1.72 (1.00)	1.61 (0.96)
Parent demands	2.21 (1.18)	2.23 (1.23)
Parent withdraws	2.23 (1.40)	1.93 (1.32)
Mutual	4.46 (1.43)	4.0 (1.45)

Note: Ratings are on a single 6-point scale. Standard deviations are in parentheses.

not from highly conflicted families, and this finding suggests that parents were emotionally invested in positive communication with their adolescents.

Adolescents also reported significantly less positive emotion when listening to the adolescent demands/parent withdraws style ($M = 1.46$) than the parent demands/adolescent withdraws style ($M = 1.89$). This finding again indicates that adolescents prefer that parents are involved, and they recognize that problems cannot be resolved without their cooperation.

Sex differences in levels of positive emotional response to the parent-adolescent discussions were found for both sex of parent and sex of adolescent. Fathers reported significantly more positive emotion for the adolescent demands/parent withdraws style than did adolescents or mothers, whose reports did not differ ($M = 1.75, 1.46$, and 1.52, respectively). Fathers may adapt less effectively to adolescents' perspectives, be less likely than mothers to seek agreement to resolve conflict, and engage in less discussion with their adolescents in general (Larson & Richards, 1994). This finding suggests a tendency for fathers to report a higher degree of comfort with withdrawal as a parental response to conflict. Perhaps fathers use this approach to lessen the tension between them and their adolescents and avoid escalating arguments.

Fathers also reported more positive emotion for mother-daughter than for father-daughter coercive discussions ($M = 1.54$ and 1.17, respectively). This difference may be related to fathers' discomfort with conflict, as well as to their expectation that mothers will take primary responsibility for monitoring adolescents' lives.

Mothers reported more positive emotion for the father demands/son withdraws style ($M = 1.62$) as opposed to the mother demands/son withdraws style

($M = 1.22$). Perhaps mothers prefer their husbands to be in the demanding role with their sons, rather than having to be in that role themselves. Mothers of adolescent boys may feel a certain impotence in trying to get behavior change in their sons and believe that fathers may be more successful.

Mothers also reported more positive emotion for the son demands/mother withdraws style ($M = 1.68$) as opposed to the son demands/father withdraws style ($M = 1.37$). While mothers seem happy to withdraw from a conflict with their sons, they seem less happy when their husbands withdraw. This finding would lend support to the possibility that mothers want fathers to be involved in conflicts with their sons. There were no reported differences for such discussions involving daughters.

Boys reported more positive emotion for mutual discussions with fathers than for those with mothers ($M = 3.06$ and 2.68, respectively). Mutual discussions with fathers as opposed to mothers may be more salient for boys. Fathers have been found to lag behind mothers in terms of their perceptions of the personal characteristics of their sons (Collins & Russell, 1991); in addition, relationships between fathers and their adolescent sons tend to involve more sarcasm and mixed messages than is true for other parent-adolescent dyads (Flannery, Montemayor, Eberly, & Torquati, 1993). This situation may make positive discussions between fathers and sons particularly rewarding for adolescent boys.

Adolescents reported less negative emotion in general than did either mothers or fathers, whose reports did not significantly differ from each other ($M = 2.50$, 2.88, and 3.05, respectively). Adolescents also reported significantly less negative emotion for the coercive styles, regardless of parent, than did mothers or fathers, who did not differ in their reports ($M = 2.64$, 3.86, and 4.00, respectively). The same pattern was found for mother demands/adolescent withdraws discussions ($M = 2.26$, 2.96, and 3.22, respectively). Again, this finding is suggestive that in this sample, the parents were invested in positive communication and resolving issues with their adolescents.

In line with the findings for positive emotion, mothers reported significantly more negative emotion for the mother demands/adolescent withdraws style ($M = 3.09$) than for the father demands/adolescent withdraws style ($M = 2.82$); conversely, adolescents and fathers reported more negative emotion for the father demands/adolescent withdraws style ($M = 2.36$ and 3.38, respectively) than for the mother demands/adolescent withdraws style ($M = 2.16$ and 3.04, respectively). For the discussions involving the father demands/adolescent withdraws style, fathers reported experiencing significantly more negative emotion than either adolescents or mothers. This finding again may be indicative of fathers' discomfort with family conflict in general and mothers not liking to be demanding with adolescents. Also, adolescents may be more accustomed to demands from their mothers.

Correlations With the Conflict Resolution Style Questionnaire

Correlations between family members' ratings of typicality and their scores on the CRS again supported the validity of this set of tapes. For example, adolescents' ratings of the typicality of the coercive parent-adolescent interactions were positively related to reports of their extent of fighting with their own parents; in addition, coercive mother-adolescent interactions were negatively related to the level of mutuality reported in interactions with mothers. For the parent demands/adolescent withdraws interactions, family members' reports of typicality were positively related to their reports of fighting within their relationships. Also, mothers' reports of the typicality of mother demands/adolescent withdraws discussions were positively related to adolescents' reports of the degree to which they avoided their mothers in conflict situations.

Discussion

Family members were generally able to discriminate among the different types of conflict in terms of the variables in this study. The discrimination between the mutual style and the negative styles was most consistent. Mutual conflicts were rated as more typical, less stressful, more likely to be resolved, and as engendering more positive and less negative emotion than the negative styles. In addition, participants rated the mutual style as more typical of the parent-adolescent conflict discussions in which they were involved, perhaps suggesting a self-serving bias by family members.

The coercive conflict discussions, on the other hand, tended to be rated quite differently from the mutual style. The coercive style was rated as least typical, along with the adolescent demands/parent withdraws style, suggesting both that the families were not highly conflicted but also that parents tended to be in charge, not succumbing too easily to adolescents' inappropriate demands. Adolescents saw the coercive style as more typical than did mothers, confirming once again that adolescents tend to have a more negative perception of their families than their parents. Coercive discussions were also rated as more stressful to listen to than other styles, although adolescents found them less stressful than did their parents. The coercive and parent demands/adolescent withdraws styles were rated as less likely to be resolved than the mutual style. The lowest levels of positive emotion and the highest levels of negative emotion followed from listening to the coercive discussions.

Family members differed in their emotional reactions to the conflict styles. For example, adolescents responded with more positive emotion than their parents when listening to the coercive discussion and with less positive emotion than their parents when listening to the mutual discussion. In addition, adolescents responded with less negative emotion than their parents in response to the more destructive styles of conflict. Thus, adolescents seemed to discriminate less among the conflict styles than their parents in terms of emotional reactions. It is interesting that adolescents' more negative perceptions of the conflict did not seem to engender more negative emotional reactions to it. In fact, it seems that adolescents were not particularly upset by hearing these conflicts and certainly not as upset as their parents were. Perhaps adolescents see arguments with parents as just part of the process of gaining more autonomy and more control over their own lives.

There were also some effects for gender of parent and gender of adolescent. Mothers differentiated more among conflict styles than did fathers and adolescents for typicality. Conflicts with mothers were seen as more typical than conflicts with fathers, and conflicts with mothers were seen as more likely to be resolved than those with fathers. In general, parents tended to report more positive reactions when listening to conflicts involving the opposite-sex parent than for conflicts involving the same-sex parent. In addition, boys reported more positive emotional reactions for mutual discussions with fathers than with mothers, and adolescents tended to report more negative reactions than mothers to father-adolescent discussions.

Our finding that conflicts with mothers were more typical and likely to be resolved than those with fathers fits with earlier research showing greater openness in communication between mothers and adolescents than between fathers and adolescents (Barnes & Olson, 1985; Noller & Callan, 1990) but also more conflict (Ellis-Schwabe & Thornburg, 1986). Adolescents also see their mothers as more understanding and accepting, more willing than fathers to listen to their attitudes and opinions, and less judgmental and more willing to be involved in discussions of feelings than fathers (Youniss & Smoller, 1985).

Discussion

There were both similarities and differences between the two studies in terms of family members' reactions to conflict between family members. In both studies, family members responded differently to mutual discussions than they did to the more destructive ways of dealing with conflict, but adolescents in both studies tended to see mutual discussions as less typical of their families than did their parents. In addition, although mutual discussions were seen as more likely to be resolved than the other styles in both studies, adolescents were only more optimistic than their parents about the likelihood that the conflicts would be resolved, regardless of style, for marital discussions. For the parent-adolescent conflicts, they did see the parent demands/adolescent withdraws style as more likely to be resolved than the adolescent demands/parent withdraws style. This finding suggests that adolescents realize that a conflict is not resolved when the parent withdraws and that resolution requires involvement from parents to achieve a constructive solution.

Whereas fathers tended to experience listening to the mutual tapes of marital discussions as more stressful than did other family members, both parents rated both the mutual and the coercive parent-adolescent tapes as more stress inducing than did adolescents. In addition, mothers found the parent demands style as more stressful than did other family members and more stressful than the adolescent demands style. It seems that mothers find demanding a change in behavior from adolescents more difficult than do fathers and such a conflict more difficult to listen to than do the adolescents themselves. Of course, adolescents are likely to be somewhat habituated to parents' angry demands, given that adolescence is about renegotiating relations with parents and testing boundaries. Yet, angry conflicts may be more salient for those adolescents who experience such demands on a regular basis.

As for the marital tapes, family members experienced more positive emotion in response to the mutual parent-adolescent discussions than the other styles and less positive emotion in response to the coercive discussions. Although fathers found the mutual marital conflict discussions more stressful than other family members, fathers did not find the mutual parent-adolescent conflict discussions more stressful. Fathers did, however, report experiencing more negative emotion in response to the coercive father-adolescent conflict than did mothers or adolescents. This finding suggests that males find family conflict in which they themselves are involved particularly uncomfortable. Adolescents, on the other hand, tended to report less negative responses to the coercive conflicts than their parents, irrespective of which parent was involved. It is possible, of course, that adolescents may be downplaying their negative reactions to the taped conflicts or be more adept at distancing themselves from the parent-adolescent conflicts in particular because of their increased needs for autonomy and distance from the family.

Limitations

The limitations of the studies include the relatively small sample, although studies where each family is seen separately tend to involve smaller samples. Another possible problem is that the reports of typicality are likely to be affected by social desirability bias or, as we have already suggested, by self-serving bias. These biases are ubiquitous in self-report studies, yet it is important not to lose sight of the fact that self-report can provide valuable information about participants' perceptions of situations. In addition, it is clear that the participants in this study responded differently to the different conflict styles and were clearly able to distinguish among them.

The conflicts presented on the audiotapes may not be as salient for family members as conflicts actually occurring in their own homes. The ratings of stressfulness tended to be low but with a reasonable range, and negative emotional reactions were fairly high, with quite a large range. These ratings suggest that some family members responded quite negatively to at least some of the tapes.

We were able to show in these studies that a range of variables affects family members' responses to marital conflict, including which family member is reporting his or her reactions, the style of the conflict, and whether the conflict is child related or not (although this latter variable had less impact than we would have anticipated). For parent-adolescent conflict, style was important, but there were also effects for reporter, sex of parent, and sex of adolescent. More research is needed on marital conflict to explore such issues as adolescents' responses to conflict that is actually resolved versus conflict that is not resolved, as well as the links between reactions to marital conflict and general psychological adjustment.

Further research is needed on parent-adolescent conflict as well. For example, we need to understand the reactions of adolescents in single-parent families to conflict with their resident parent, as well as the associations between their reactions to such conflict and their general psychological adjustment.

In conclusion, these studies have shown the usefulness of an analog methodology for exploring family members' reactions to marital and parent-adolescent conflict. We were able to show that family members, including adolescents, seem able to distinguish between constructive and destructive family conflict and respond differently to different styles. Our findings suggest that it is not family conflict per se that is problematic for adolescents but how that conflict is handled. More resources need to be devoted to teaching family members appropriate ways of dealing with conflict so that issues can be resolved without unduly increasing the stress levels of family members and undermining their psychological well-being.

References

Barnes, H. L., & Olson, D. H. (1985). Parent-adolescent communication and the circumplex model. *Child Development, 56,* 437–447.

Christensen, A. (1988). Dysfunctional interaction patterns in couples. In P. Noller & M. A. Fitzpatrick (Eds.), *Perspectives on marital interaction* (pp. 31–52). Avon, UK: Multilingual Matters.

Christensen, A., & Heavey, C. L. (1990). Gender, power and marital conflict. *Journal of Personality and Social Psychology, 59,* 73–85.

Collins, W. A., & Russell, G. (1991). Mother-child and father-child relationships in middle childhood and adolescence: A developmental analysis. *Developmental Review, 11,* 99–136.

Cummings, E. M., Ianotti, R. J., & Zahn-Waxler, C. (1985). The influence of conflict between adults on the emotion and aggression of young children. *Developmental Psychology, 21,* 495–507.

Cummings, E. M., Zahn-Waxler, C., & Radke-Yarrow, M. (1981). Young children's responses to expressions of anger and affection by others in the family. *Child Development, 52,* 1274–1282.

Cummings, J. S., Pellegrini, D. S., Notarius, C. I., & Cummings, E. M. (1989). Children's responses to angry adult behaviour as a function of marital distress and history of interparent hostility. *Child Development, 60,* 1035–1043.

Ellis-Schwabe, M., & Thornburg, H. D. (1986). Conflict areas between parents and their adolescents. *Journal of Psychology, 120,* 59–68.

Flannery, D. J., Montemayor, R., Eberly, M., & Torquati, J. (1993). Unravelling the ties that bind: Affective expression and perceived conflict in parent-adolescent interactions. *Journal of Social and Personal Relationships, 10,* 495–509.

Foster, S. L. (1994). Assessing and treating parent-adolescent conflict. *Progress in Behaviour Modification, 29,* 53–72.

Gottman, J. M., & Levenson, R. L. (1988). The social psychophysiology of marriage. In P. Noller & M. A. Fitzpatrick (Eds.), *Perspectives on marital interaction* (pp. 182–200). Avon, UK: Multilingual Matters.

Grych, J. H., & Fincham, F. D. (1990). Marital conflict and children's adjustment: A cognitive-contextual framework. *Psychological Bulletin, 108,* 267–290.

Grych, J. H., & Fincham, F. D. (1993). Children's appraisals of marital conflict: Initial investigation of the cognitive-contextual framework. *Child Development, 64,* 215–230.

Larson, R., & Richards, M. H. (1994). *Divergent realities: The emotional lives of mothers, fathers and adolescents.* New York: Basic Books.

McCombs, A., Forehand, R., & Smith, K. (1988). The relationship between maternal problem-solving style and adolescent social adjustment. *Journal of Family Psychology, 2,* 57–66.

Meyerson, L. A., Long, P. L., Miranda, R. J., & Marx, B. P. (2002). The influence of childhood sexual abuse, physical abuse, family environment and gender on the psychological adjustment of adolescents. *Child Abuse and Neglect, 26,* 387–405.

Montemayor, R. (1983). Parents and adolescents in conflict: All families some of the time and some families most of the time. *Journal of Early Adolescence, 3,* 83–102.

Montemayor, R., & Hanson, E. (1985). A naturalistic view of conflict between adolescents and their parents and siblings. *Journal of Early Adolescence, 5,* 23–30.

Noller, P., & Bagi, S. (1985). Parent-adolescent communication. *Journal of Adolescence, 8,* 125–144.

Noller, P., & Callan, V. J. (1988). Understanding parent-adolescent interactions: Perceptions of family and outsiders. *Developmental Psychology, 24,* 707–714.

Noller, P., & Callan, V. J. (1990). Adolescents' perceptions of the nature of their communication with parents. *Journal of Youth and Adolescence, 19,* 349–362.

Noller, P., Feeney, J., Peterson, C., & Sheehan, G. (1995) Learning conflict patterns in the family: Links between marital, parental and sibling relationships. In T. J. Socha & G. Stamp (Eds.), *Parents, children and communication: Frontiers of theory and research* (pp. 273–298). Hillsdale, NJ: Lawrence Elbaum.

Noller, P., & Fitzpatrick, M. A. (1993). *Communication in family relationships.* New York: Prentice Hall.

Noller, P., & White, A. (1990). The validity of the Communication Patterns Questionnaire. *Psychological Assessment: A Journal of Consulting and Clinical Psychology, 2,* 478–482.

O'Brien, M., Margolin, G., John, R. S., & Krueger, L. (1991). Mothers' and sons' cognitive and emotional reactions to simulated marital and family conflict. *Journal of Consulting and Clinical Psychology, 59,* 692–703.

Peterson, C. C. (1990). Disagreement, negotiation and conflict resolution in families with adolescents. In P. Heaven & V. J. Callan (Eds.), *Adolescence: An Australian perspective* (pp. 66–79). Sydney, Australia: Harcourt Brace Jovanovich.

Rands, M., Levinger, G., & Mellinger, G. (1981). Patterns of conflict resolution and marital satisfaction. *Journal of Family Issues, 2,* 297–321.

Smetana, J. (1988). Adolescents' and parents' conceptions of parental authority. *Child Development, 59,* 321–335.

Steinberg, L. (1991). Autonomy, conflict and harmony in the family relationship. In S. S. Feldman & G. R. Elliott (Eds.), *At the threshold: The developing adolescent* (pp. 255–276). Cambridge, MA: Harvard University Press.

Youniss, J., & Smoller, J. (1985). *Adolescents' relations with mothers, fathers and friends.* Chicago: University of Chicago Press.

CHAPTER 10

"That Dear Octopus"

A Family-Based Model of Intimacy

Megan K. Foley

University of Iowa

Steve Duck

University of Iowa

> *To the family—that dear octopus from whose tentacles we never quite escape nor, in our inmost hearts, ever quite wish to.*
>
> —Dodie Smith, 1948

Like the octopus in the epigram above, the family is one head with many hands that embrace and ensnare us. The octopus serves equally well as a metaphor for the slippery but enveloping tentacles of intimacy since this concept also has many unruly, uncoordinated, but grasping elements. Our goal here is to first clarify the slippery definition of intimacy in general and as it applies to the family. This discussion focuses on intimacy primarily in dyadic terms because research up to this point has focused on the many tentacles of the octopus and how they reach out or connect to others. Next, we explore an alternative definition of family intimacy that foregrounds the octopus's head—a focus on the family as a whole as the locus of intimacy, distinct from relationships between its individual members. Finally, we seek to integrate the perspective of the family as a system of dyadic relationships with the discursive construction of the family as a single social unit. Through synthesizing these two, we hope to provide a more complete understanding of family intimacy.

Defining Dyadic Intimacy: A Slippery Concept

Dyadic intimacy has long been a knotty problem for researchers. Hirschberger, Florian, and Mikulincer (2003) explain, "Intimacy is a term that, despite its widespread use, remains relatively ambiguous" (p. 676). Although broadly correct in their implicit despair, they are of course wrong in a crucial way: *Intimacy* is a term that is *both* ambiguous in semantic meaning *and also* uncertain in operational denotation, such that our chances of defining it to everyone's satisfaction are flatly nil, and our operationalizations are excitingly variegated.

Intimacy, as erudite scholars point out at this juncture, refers originally to the interior or inmost aspects of anything (from the Latin *intimus,* meaning inside). By extension, the term comes to refer to those things that are beneath the surface and hard to reach. It is only a small leap to extend the meaning again to things private or secret and thence to things personal and reserved, even if not particularly inaccessible or far below the surface.

Already one can see that the metaphorical extensions of intimacy take us from the physically deep to the psychologically deep, hidden, or private elements of a person and hence ultimately come to concern those things that are regarded by social convention and practice as simply personal or reserved from common access. This, in turn, moves us to grounds for legitimate discussion about what is theoretically "intimate." Reasonable minds may differ about things that are or should be held back and reserved from common access. The metaphor implicit in the famous onion skin model of intimacy (Altman & Taylor, 1973) suggests that there is a single center surrounded by successive layers of concentric protection, layers of privacy, or layers of intimacy. Different people could reasonably dispute whether a given fact about another person is part of this center. There is great room for argument about the "intimacy" that is represented by a person's declaration of dislike for a parent, for example, especially if such dislike is openly and frequently expressed. Since *intimacy* in the metaphorical sense is essentially undefined by shifting social and personal attitudes and conventions, the latitudes of convention can be disputed, ranges of behaviors around those latitudes can be discussed, and before long, it is evident that one person's private and intimate thought or feeling is another person's unremarkable commonplace.

The simple failure of language and usage to stand and deliver uncontestable truths about "intimacy" has rendered it almost impossible for researchers to indicate behaviors that no one would dispute as such. Even physical closeness is not a paradigm case. For example, a stroke on the shoulder blades by someone we know to be a lover is "intimate" in a sensual, erotic, and relational way when the circumstances are previously defined as "intimate," itself a neat begging of the question, but the same stroke by a masseuse is—if intimate at all—intimate in a completely different sense. In one case, the touch is seen as private and erotic, but in the other, it is merely personal and distantly professional. In short, it is circumstances and understandings between the people involved that make behaviors either intimate or nonintimate. Behavior itself cannot be simply defined as intimate or not. One meaning is based on knowledge that a personal relationship exists, and the other is based on the knowledge that it does not. Nor can intimacy be surely inferred from observation of behavioral acts. Many court cases begin with agreement that behavioral acts occurred but diverge in the two sides' interpretation of these acts. As usual in legal cases, the issue of intent behind behavior becomes as crucial in disputes about "intimacy" as it does in differentiating murder from manslaughter.

It would be patently uncomplicated to argue that there are no words or behaviors that are in and of themselves intimate. Clearly, the words "I love you" and a caress are intimately loaded for the sender on most occasions, though both can be unwanted by the recipient. Thus, for at least one of the participants, they are not necessarily "intimate" (see Chapter 11, this volume, for a specific case of "undesired intimacy"). Also grunts, "mmmmm," and a wink can be intimate in the right circumstances, which we will leave you to imagine, but are not sounds or behaviors normally associated with intimacy. Their intimacy on a particular occasion is circumscribed and even demonstrated by the context in which they occur rather than by their inherent qualities. Some argue for a process approach to intimacy, as something that is evident in the doing or—not their term—the *praxis* of relationships (Reis & Shaver, 1988), while other scholars have clearly identified levels of intimacy that may be found in types of speech (for example, Davis & Sloan, 1974, developed a scale to measure the intimacy of self-disclosive statements). Some of the better models have wrestled with the characterization and definition of intimacy in terms of processes or foundational characteristics and argue in essence that it is found between people rather than in individual behavior (Prager, 1995).

Intimacy cannot therefore be readily and certainly associated with specific activities or words. In that respect, intimacy does not differ substantially from other key words used freely by relationship scholars, such as *love* or *dating*. Exactly the same complaint about variety of usage as well as operationalizations in different studies can be, and has been, leveled with various degrees of frustration and desperation at countless other terms (e.g., Wright, 1985, on *exchange;* Spitzberg, 1993, on *competence;* Sprecher & Duck, 1993, on *dating;* Dainton, 2000, on *maintenance;* and Wood, 2001, on *sex* as distinct from *gender*). One issue, noted by Hirschberger et al. (2003), therefore is that even at the dyadic level, intimacy is difficult for scholars to operationalize acceptably and consistently.

One reason for this is that different scholars use different definitions of intimacy and do not note these differences when comparing results across studies, a failure of semantic meta-analysis as it were (Duck, 1984). Others looking at *dyadic* intimacy therefore have pronounced intimacy to be the proverbial elephant (Acitelli & Duck, 1987), whose various bits are felt in separation from one another, with no one having the full picture. More important, these scholars are unable to make useful comparisons of the bits they can feel with those they have not felt, and so such scholars can argue for hours about whether the parts are indeed the same, before even reaching the question of whether they belong to the same animal.

Given that researchers cannot identify it, do not concur about what it is, and cannot agree whether it is an individual performance of an inherently intimate act or something that prerequires conjoint activity and agreement by the partners, it is nevertheless apparent that, like obscenity, we all know intimacy when we see it even if we cannot articulate what it is. It becomes necessary, then, to attempt a clarification of the ways in which the term *intimacy* has been used in the relationships literature. While use of the term *intimacy* is rarely fixed or consistent, a constellation of dimensions does nevertheless emerge from the literature.

In his "Triangular Theory of Love," Sternberg (1986) describes intimacy as "close, connected, and bonded feelings in a loving relationship" (p. 120). Indeed, the metaphor of closeness recurs in the intimacy literature. While Parks and Floyd (1996) caution that qualitative differences may exist in the lay use of the terms *closeness* and *intimacy,* the theme of "closeness" is realized in three overarching dimensions in the intimacy literature: presence (closeness as proximity), interdependence (closeness as imbrication), and positivity (closeness as desire).

Presence

Largely, intimacy is understood as presence, "being there" for another. In some cases, intimacy is expressed through bodily presence—that is, making physical contact with the other (Monsour, 1992; Register & Henley, 1992). Presence can also mean spatial and temporal presence—that is, spending time together (Register & Henley, 1992; Wood & Inman, 1993). Physical presence is presence in its most literal sense, creating intimacy through material closeness.

In addition to *physical presence,* the theme of *emotional presence* recurs throughout figurations of intimacy. Emotional presence is partners' affective involvement in the relationship (Monsour, 1992; Parks & Floyd, 1996). Often, this affective involvement is achieved through empathy, a shared internal state achieved through caring interaction (Kerem, Fishman, & Josselson, 2001). Here, presence means not only proximity to another but symbolic fusion with the other, taking the other's perspective. Emotional presence promotes intimacy by "getting inside" the experiences of another.

Finally, in *cognitive presence,* relaters come to know each other through self-disclosure, the most common intimate behavior cited (Monsour, 1992; Parks & Floyd, 1996; Prager & Buhrmester, 1998; Sanderson & Cantor, 1995). Prager and Buhrmester (1998) underscore the importance of cognitive presence by adding that the partner must listen and understand the other on the basis of his or her disclosures. Relaters can also achieve cognitive presence by being similar to the other (e.g., shared interests, Parks & Floyd, 1996) or becoming similar to the other (e.g., transformation, Register & Henley, 1992). Whether physical, emotional, or cognitive, presence is significant in several conceptualizations of intimacy.

Interdependence

Another recurring theme throughout the intimacy literature is *interdependence*, processes of mutual influence in which interaction partners affect one another's relational outcomes, behaviors, and motivations (Kelley & Thibaut, 1978; Thibaut & Kelley, 1959). While Sanderson and Cantor (1995) mention interdependence by name, other scholars include social support and trust, key components of interdependence, in their conceptualizations of intimacy. Intimate interdependence is regularly discussed in terms of social support, in which intimates help each other fulfill their material and emotional needs (Monsour, 1992; Parks & Floyd, 1996). Burleson, Delia, and Applegate's (1995) link between social support and person-centered communication (open, empathic communication reflecting the thoughts and feelings of others) suggests an analogous link between interdependence-based and presence-based intimacy, respectively. Hobfoll, Nadler, and Leiberman (1986) suggest that relational intimacy is a primary determinant of satisfaction with social support. While social support provision is primarily behavioral, interdependence also surfaces in the intimacy literature at an emotiocognitive level as trust (Monsour, 1992; Sanderson & Cantor, 1995). Interdependence is a regularly cited way that relaters enact intimacy.

Positivity

Intimacy is almost always described as positive. Most explicitly, value of relationship (Parks & Floyd, 1996) and positive affective tone (Prager & Buhrmester, 1998) are dimensions that demonstrate the positive characterization of intimacy. While those dimensions solely address the positivity of intimacy, the characterization of presence and interdependence is also positively valenced (i.e., trust, unconditional support, emotional expressiveness, shared interests). For this reason, the theme of positivity operates on a different level of analysis than presence and interdependence: It represents a meta-theme that characterizes both interdependence and presence.

Overall, definitions of dyadic intimacy are characterized by presence, interdependence, and positivity. Here, presence and interdependence are mutually supporting: Interdependence renders interlocutors present to one another, and presence makes interlocutors interdependent. Largely, this mutual relation of presence and interdependence is positively valenced. In short, from a dyadic perspective, intimacy has been defined as the *positive presence and interdependence of interlocutors*.

The Octopus's Many Hands: Intimacy in Familial Dyads

How, if at all, can this general definition of intimacy inform a conceptualization of family intimacy in particular? McLain and Weigert (1979) claim that the family is "characterized by a unique intimacy and intensity as well as a unique mutual knowing" (p. 175). Indeed, family relationships differ from nonfamilial relationships in that they are less often voluntary, tend to last longer, and exist within denser social networks—all of which would appear to affect intimacy. However, Duck and Sants (1983) warn that specific cases of human behavior are only unwisely separated conceptually from the broader principles underlying general behavior.

Our review of dyadic intimacy above suggests that differences in the practice of family relationships do not constitute a different kind of intimacy but instead modify family members' opportunities for achieving intimacy. For example, the less voluntary nature of family relationships may make them less positive, the longer length of familial relationships may increase relaters' emotional presence, and denser social networks may increase family members' interdependence. While the differences between family and nonfamily relationships certainly do not determine how intimate a relationship will become, they represent different fields of possibility in which intimacy can be practiced. Overall, the literature suggests that presence, interdependence, and positivity are also important for the intimacy of family relationships.

Presence in Family Relationships

Like intimacy in other dyads, intimacy in family relationships is largely based on presence. For example, Harwood and Lin (2000) found that grandparents' intimacy with grandchildren was enhanced when grandchildren initiated contact with them or disclosed private information—in other words, when grandchildren chose to become physically and emotionally present. The importance of presence is similarly evident in Rollie's (2005) study of the multiple relational continuity strategies that nonresidential parents use to maintain intimacy with their children. Empathetic (read emotionally present) stepparents report more intimate and positive relationships with stepchildren (Ganong, Coleman, Fine, & Martin, 1999). Caughlin and Petronio (2004) demonstrate that both positive and negative self-disclosure between spouses, a type of cognitive presence, enhance spouses' "sense of solidarity and liking" (p. 394). The literature on family intimacy is rife with descriptions of physical, emotional, and cognitive presence.

Interdependence in Family Relationships

Interdependence is a significant factor in the intimacy of familial dyads. For example, Gardner and Cutrona (2004) discuss how marital support acts as a buffer that protects against decreases in closeness when stressful events occur. Laursen and Collins (2004) explain that renegotiations of interdependence change the degree of intimacy between parents and their adolescent children. A significant line of work on familial emotion suggests that family members' emotional reactions to each other are based on behavioral interdependencies; familial emotion is produced through family members' attempts to coordinate their actions with one another

(Berscheid, 1983; Berscheid & Ammazzalorzo, 2001). Interdependence is clearly important in promoting intimacy in family relationships.

Positivity in Family Relationships

Although presence and interdependence are generally characterized as positive in dyadic intimacy literature, understanding the literature on dyadic family intimacy requires a dialectical approach to valence. According to Baxter and Montgomery (1997), relationship dialectics are characterized by two key principles: unity and negation. That is, while dialectical relationship forces coexist, they coexist in dynamic tension. Relational dialectics exist between centrifugal and centripetal forces: Relational partners struggle between moving together and moving apart. These opposing forces are not an antagonism between the partners but rather are located within the relationship itself. Intimacy, as commonly defined, is based on closeness, a centrifugal "moving together."

However, because both centrifugal and centripetal forces constitute family relationships, family members often experience intimacy as both positive and negative—often simultaneously. For example, as blended families develop and adapt, they create rituals in an attempt to manage the tension between the old and new family (Braithwaite, Baxter, & Harper, 1998). The new blended family cannot become present and interdependent (i.e., intimate) unproblematically—they experience a centripetal pull to honor old family relationships. Baxter and Braithwaite's research program has provided strong continued support for dialectical contradictions in family dyads, including relationships between stepchildren and stepparents (Baxter, Braithwaite, Bryant, & Wagner, 2004) and between children and their nonresidential parents (Baxter & Braithwaite, 2006). While the centrifugal force of presence and interdependence can be experienced as positive, it may also be experienced as stifling or interfering if not balanced by some relational distance.

Strengths and Limitations of the Dyadic Approach to Family Intimacy

Above, we have demonstrated that the same dimensions of intimacy—plus some important supplementations—emerge from the literature on both family and nonfamily relationships. Is family intimacy, then, indistinguishable from other forms of intimacy? Do presence, interdependence, and positivity represent general, acontextual principles of human intimacy? As evidenced by the discussion above, current literature focuses on intimacy in particular family dyads—marital pairs, parent-child relationships, and so on. This dyad-focused work is undoubtedly important as family interaction is increasingly accomplished not at family dinner or other gatherings where all can be present and interdependently coordinating their behavior but in the temporal interstices between other activities (Tyler, 2005). While "family time" becomes increasingly rare, we argue that it is still crucial to take the family, not only the dyads within it, as an object of study. When family interaction is increasingly a matter of bridging absence, focus on the construction of family as a cohesive unit becomes even more poignant as families work to remain "close" when they are not together (Rollie, 2005).

Because of the prevalence of this focus, it is easy to forget the contextual framing of these findings. In light of the overwhelming dyadic focus of current intimacy research reviewed above, we revisit McLain and Weigert's (1979) claim that family intimacy is unique not only in degree but in character. Emphasis on the dyad positions family not as the figure but as the ground, or context, of intimacy. Thus, the quantitative difference between the family dyad and the family system has qualitative theoretical significance for the way in which the three primary dimensions of intimacy we have identified can be conceptualized.

The Octopus's Head: Intimacy With the Family Unit

Rather than being defined as the positive presence and interdependence of specific interlocutors, this conceptualization of family intimacy focuses on the relation between the family member and the family unit. That is, instead of intimacy with a *particular other,* this is intimacy with a *generalized other.* For Mead (1934), particular others are specific others whose roles we internalize. For example, a child might learn to take the perspective of his or her mother by playing house. The generalized other, to the contrary, is an amalgamation of social expectations that arises from taking the perspective of a group (Mead, 1934). For example, to play as a shortstop, a player must also understand the roles of all other players on the baseball field, not only his or her own. Most research currently focuses on how we become positively present to and interdependent with particular family members. However, family members also become intimate with their families as a generalized other that is not reducible to dyadic relationships.

Being present to and interdependent with an individual family member is commonly discussed as a matter of intersubjectivity—that is, it depends on the dyads' access to one another's thoughts and feelings. For example, Gardner and Cutrona (2004) state that individuals provide more effective social support to their spouses when they are aware of their partner's problems. Ganong et al. (1999) found that stepparents who take the perspective of their stepchildren (e.g., participating in activities of interest to stepchildren) had more cohesive relationships with them. Although these are only two examples, they illustrate the significance attributed to intersubjectivity in achieving intimacy through interdependence (in the first example) and presence (in the second example). As we pointed out previously, the Latin root of the word *intimacy* points us to the interior.

The family does not have this interior—there is no literal head to the family octopus. Thus, the construction of presence to and interdependence with the family as a whole differs from dyadic forms of intimacy in that it cannot depend on intersubjectivity. Intimacy with the family unit cannot rely on access to the thoughts and feelings of the other because the other in this case is not a particular individual but rather a generalized amalgam. How can an individual be intimate with the family as a unit if it is not a subject? Family members discursively produce their families as subjects through practices of interdependence and become intersubjective with the family-subject through practices of presence.

Interdependence With the Family as Subject

To achieve intimate intersubjectivity with the family as a unit, the family must first be produced as a subject, an entity that can act (i.e., be the subject of a sentence) and be acted upon (i.e., be subjected to something) (Foucault, 1991). Treating the family as a unit with which one can become interdependent does exactly this—recall the definition of interdependence as mutual influence. For example, this occurs when family members pool financial or material resources, such as sharing bank accounts and living quarters. Indeed, Koerner and Fitzpatrick (2004) explain that joint psychosocial tasks such as household maintenance are a primary way researchers define family. While family members may contribute unequally to the accrual of shared material resources, those resources nevertheless are understood under the joint name of the family. In this way, complex dynamics of exchange among family members can be elided in favor of the family unit as a single source of material support.

This same dynamic is also at work with emotional support. Bengtson and Roberts (1991) explain that family solidarity, an overall sense of cohesion, is based on particular interactive dynamics of both instrumental and affective support. Here, too, the actions of specific agents are understood to represent the agency of the family. Individuals treat the family as a whole as a subject with whom they are interdependent. In so doing, they produce the family as a subject with whom they can become intersubjective.

Presence to the Family as Subject

With interdependence, we create an interior for the head of the octopus; with presence, we get inside it. For a dyad, shared understanding can be understood as inclusion of self in the other, the degree to which the conception of self overlaps the conception of the other (Aron & McLaughlin-Volpe, 2001). Before family members can include themselves in the generalized other of the family, they must first create an identity—a self—for the family. Family members create the family as an other through ritual and storytelling. Family ritual and storytelling, commonplace practices of family identity (see Chapters 6, 7, 14, and 15, this volume), are especially suited to constitute family intimacy because they unite family members not on an individual basis but to an image of the family as a whole. Laing (1971) explains that storytelling is a primary way in which the image of family is internalized and made meaningful. By creating a liminal space apart from mundane practices, rituals also engender deep feelings of mutual understanding (Turner, 1982).

The particular tellers of stories or performers of rituals become agents that act in the name of the family itself. Family rituals are "enacted systematically and repeatedly over time and . . . hold special meaning for family members" (Wolin & Bennett, 1984). Similarly, Jorgenson and Bochner (2004) explain that "these stories are told and retold until they sink in" (p. 524). Here, the specific source of the story is irrelevant; the particular actions of individuals are understood as the agency of the family. Family members use rituals and stories to craft family identity, rendering their family more present to themselves.

Positivity of the Family as Subject

At the level of the family unit, intimacy is certainly considered positive, although it operates differently than it does in dyadic family relationships. Family intimacy is a cultural ideal (Jorgenson & Bochner, 2004). Positive intimacy is central in the canonical stories, legitimated narratives of meaningful social practices (Jorgenson & Bochner) that are told about families in American culture. In families, it is presumed normal, natural, and positive for families to be intimate. Intimacy is a significant predictor for marital satisfaction (e.g., Johnson, Hobfoll, & Zalcberg-Linetzy, 1993). In fact, intimacy is often considered synonymous with family satisfaction—if a family is happy, it is intimate; if a family is intimate, it is happy. However, as in dyadic family intimacy, family unit intimacy is perhaps most positive when balanced with reasonable family distance. For example, an authoritative parenting style, which implies a moderate level of presence and interdependence, is generally more successful than authoritarian (high-level presence and interdependence) or permissive (low-level presence and interdependence) parenting styles (Baumrind, 1996). Similarly, sibling relationships often become more positive and satisfying in adulthood, when the siblings' presence and interdependence are balanced with distance (Sillars, Canary, & Tafoya, 2004). These findings suggest that although family unit intimacy is a cultural ideal, intimacy and distance are equally important in building positive family experiences.

Because family unit intimacy is promoted as a cultural ideal despite the equal importance of family unit distance, family intimacy only attains significance when it is partial or missing; at other times, it is simply accepted as background to the very idea of "family." For example, stepfamilies often unrealistically expect that they will achieve instant intimacy when they form and are often disappointed when they find that intimacy is difficult to cultivate (Braithwaite, Olson, Golish, Soukup, & Turman, 2001). Furthermore, this example demonstrates that producing the family as a unit, a single subject, makes this ideal difficult to reach. Individuals produce their families as subjects and create intersubjectivity with them on the basis of interdependence and presence, dimensions of dyadic intimacy. Using the intersubjective dyad as a model sets up family intimacy as an unachievable goal. Goffman's (1961) concept of role distancing suggests that while performing a particular kind of self can realize that self, the artifice of the performance can make the individual detach from that identity. For example, if a stepchild adopts the role of child with a stepparent, his or her performance may only serve to remind the stepchild that the role does not quite fit. Similarly, individuals' treatment of their families as selves with whom they are intimately intersubjective may actually emphasize the artificiality of treating the family as a subject and hence the difficulty of achieving family intimacy. In this way, treating the family as a subject with whom its members become intimate makes family intimacy a state that is highly desirable, yet ultimately impossible.

Reassembling the Octopus

While an understanding of family intimacy only in terms of the dyadic relationships between its members fails to account for the irreducible significance of the family system, conceptualizing intimacy on the basis of the family unit fails to account for actual practices of family intimacy. While neither the hands nor the head of the octopus alone provide a satisfying model, they can both inform an understanding of the unique performance of family intimacy. These two texts—the intimacy of the family unit and the intimacy of family dyads—become meaningful in relation to one another. First, we recognize that intimacy is constituted differently for the head and the hands of the family octopus. While both are characterized by presence, interdependence, and positivity, we have argued that these dimensions operate differently in dyadic and unitary family intimacy. In family dyads, the conceptualization of these three dimensions is predicated on an implicit premise of intersubjectivity; in family units, the possibility of intersubjectivity cannot be presumed but instead must be *performed*. While these differently constituted forms of intimacy clearly differ, they operate simultaneously. That is, we do intimacy with family members while we do intimacy with the family as a unit. How are these different formulations of family intimacy articulated together?

Presence to Significant Absence

How do we articulate our presence to particular family members while articulating our presence to the family as a whole? The subjective presence of particular family members to one another, for example, through self-disclosure and shared relational history, when taken as an object, can construct the family unity as a subject with whom relaters can become present. While dyadic and unitary family intimacy both rely on an understanding of presence to an other, taken together, they highlight how the absence of a subject can enable intimacy.

As discussed above, one of the key ways in which interlocutors become present to each other is self-disclosure. The complex dynamics of individual disclosures can contribute to the construction of a family identity. Yet, in taking the family unit itself as a constructed other with whom individuals seek intimacy, those individuals must find other means of coming to know the family—a family cannot self-disclose because it has no self as such. Instead, individuals learn about the family-subject through two other methods of uncertainty reduction: observation and third-party information seeking (Berger & Calabrese, 1975). That is, through discussion with other family members and observation of family life, family members come to know and thus become present to the family as a generalized other.

This is not only a difference in strategy. Self-disclosure privileges the intentionality of the encoder: A statement's degree of self-disclosure depends on how private the discloser considers it to be (Altman & Taylor, 1973). On the other hand, observation and third-party information seeking are strategies that privilege the interpretive ability of the decoder, regardless of (and in some dyadic situations, in spite of) the intentions of the object. While family (and other) dyads come to know one another as both subject and object, the generalized other of the family unit can be known only as an object. Indeed, it becomes a subject only insofar as it is taken as an object by social actors.

However, this contingency of the family unit's subjectivity does not necessarily limit the possibility for intimate presence—it seems to enable it. Relational dyads, including those in families, create their relationships by building a shared history (Duck, 2002). Shared history is the linking of emotional/cognitive and physical presence. That is, relaters come to know one another through their shared past. While family dyads build intimacy based on their shared history together, *unitary family intimacy can be achieved even with absent others.* Family members participate in collective remembering of significant family events and figures, even if they did not personally participate in the events themselves or know the figures. Halbwachs (1992), who first conceptualized collective memory, explained that "a remembrance is in very large measure a reconstruction of the past achieved with data borrowed from the present, a reconstruction prepared, furthermore, by reconstructions of earlier periods wherein past images had already been altered" (p. 69). Turner (1982) similarly states that remembering is literally re-membering, or putting pieces of experience back together into a new coherent whole. Halbwachs compared memory work to retouching a portrait, a process in which "new images overlay the old" (p. 72). What is crucial here is not that family members accurately access the selves of the characters in family stories but that these stories help construct a character for the family as a whole in terms of their own experience.

In each of the cases above, the comparison of dyadic and unitary family intimacy highlights the absence that undergirds intimate presence. The different formulations of the other on which dyadic and unitary family intimacy rely imply different relationships between self and other. In dyadic family intimacy, the other is present, but we can never become fully present to that other. Because we understand family members as subjects in their own right, they must always be different from ourselves. Regardless of how much time we spend with them, how much they disclose, or how emotionally expressive they are, all we can do is take their perspective, a perspective that is always marked as other. Ironically, to become present to someone else, we must first acknowledge the necessary difference between that person and ourselves.

On the other hand, in unitary family intimacy, the other is necessarily absent, but we can identify with that other completely. We cannot presume the existence of the family as subject; while we may treat the family unit as a subject, this very treatment belies its impossibility of being taken as such. Yet because the subject status of the family unit is contingent on a particular family member's constructions, family members can create the family-subject in their own image. Because the family as a unit is not an other, it is not other. Again ironically, the very absence of the self of the family unit enables us to construct it as fully present on the basis of our own selves.

Interdependence to Displaced Dependence

Often, positively valenced interdependence is not easy to maintain with both particular family members and with the family as a whole. Many studies (see Huston & Holmes, 2004, for a review) show that marital satisfaction drops when couples have children; however, satisfaction with the family as a whole is established in its place. Later, "empty-nest" spouses are prone to divorce because they sometimes have trouble reestablishing intimacy as a couple (Arp & Arp, 1996). Although it may seem that intimate individual family relationships should lead to intimacy with the family as a whole (and vice versa), these two formulations of intimacy seem to be, at least to some degree, mutually exclusive. In other words, dependence on either the family unit or its particular members displaces the other.

While dyadic intimacy (in families and elsewhere) is based on mutual acknowledgment and mutual acceptance, the introduction of a triad (or more) implies that family members will be differentially intimate. Rather than understanding the degree of intimacy in terms of abstract criteria, family members understand intimacy as relative to others in the family group. Take, for instance, the classic example of sibling rivalry, in which siblings vie for the emotional and material resources of parents (R. Smith, 1991). Of course, sibling relationships are not always contentious and can themselves be supportive (Floyd & Parks, 1995), particularly in the absence of parental support (Cummings & Smith, 1989). Here, rather than comparing the relationship with a parent to a sibling's relationship with that parent, children compare their own relationship with a sibling to their relationship with a parent. The exception proves the rule: Intimate support is still understood in hierarchical comparative terms. Increased intimacy with one family member throws into relief a relative lack of intimacy with others. Thus, it is difficult for supportive relationships with individual family members to contribute to attributions of family-wide support.

While individual family members' coalition formation interrupts holistic understandings of familial support, attributing support to the family can conversely problematize support-based expressions of intimacy between particular family members. To attribute support to the family rather than its members, a person must understand the individual performing the supportive act as an agent of the family—that is, in terms of his or her family role. For example, a daughter may dismiss her father's compliments: "You have to say that because you're my dad." Acting supportively in one's capacity as a family member, it is never entirely clear whether the supportive act expresses genuine care for the other or merely an obligation to help. In dyads, including family dyads, an assumption of choice underlies intimate interdependence: The individual-level expression of support depends on voluntariness. Because it is assumed that families should be supportive (Gardner & Cutrona, 2004), family-level support is constructed as involuntary. When family members support one another, it can be hard to tease apart voluntary care from compulsory duty.

Both coalition formation in family dyads and the involuntariness of family support make maintaining intimate interdependence at both dyadic and unitary levels a challenge. Relatively higher levels of intimacy in some family dyads can cover over the intimacy felt for the family as a whole; the norm of family support can cover over the sincere care for family members in their individuality. While this may appear to paint a bleak picture, far from the typically positive valence of intimate presence, it is important to note that dyadic and unitary family intimacy both cover over and draw on one another. As is evident in the discussion above, the notion of family-wide interdependence emerges from the specific supportive acts of particular family members. Thus, the formulation that appears to nullify dyadic family interdependence could not exist without it. Similarly, to compare the support provided in different family dyads, family members must understand support in terms of the whole family rather than on a purely individual basis. Dyadic and unitary family intimacy are constructed in necessary opposition to each other; it is by pushing against the other that both remain intact.

Conclusion

To grab hold of the slippery octopus of family intimacy, we have distilled from current research on intimacy three primary dimensions: presence, interdependence, and positivity. As they are currently being conceptualized, these dimensions best describe the relationships among the multiple interacting family members that compose family life—that is, the tentacles of the family intimacy octopus. However, we argue that family members also understand themselves as close to or distant from the family as a whole, constructing the family as a generalized other with whom they are more or less intimate, imagining a head for the family octopus. The construction of the family as subject both depends on and conflicts with the dyadic formulation of family intimacy. The unitary conception of family intimacy relies on the subject-based dyadic model of family intimacy, against which it necessarily appears lacking. However, while it is unlikely that the family unit can achieve the same subject status accorded to its individual members, it may actually be easier for family members to take this generalized, nonsubject other as themselves. A complete understanding of family intimacy requires acknowledging that the head and members of the family octopus are themselves present and interdependent: Although they may conflict, they are always coexistent and contingent on one another.

References

Acitelli, L. K., & Duck, S. W. (1987). Intimacy as the proverbial elephant. In D. Perlman & S. Duck (Eds.), *Intimate relationships: Development, dynamics, and deterioration* (pp. 297–308). Newbury Park, CA: Sage.

Altman, I., & Taylor, D. (1973). *Social penetration: The development of interpersonal relationships.* New York: Holt, Rinehart, & Winston.

Aron, A., & McLaughlin-Volpe, T. (2001). Including others in the self: Extensions to own and partner's group memberships. In M. Brewer & C. Sedikides (Eds.), *Individual self, relational self, and collective self: Partners, opponents, or strangers* (pp. 89–108). Mahwah, NJ: Lawrence Erlbaum.

Arp, D., & Arp, C. (1996). *The second half of marriage.* New York: Zondervan.

Baumrind, D. (1996). The discipline controversy revisited. *Family Relations, 45,* 405–411.

Baxter, L. A., & Braithwaite, D. O. (2006). "You're my parent but you're not": Dialectical tensions in stepchildren's perceptions about communicating with the nonresidential parent. *Journal of Applied Communication Research, 34,* 30–48.

Baxter, L. A., Braithwaite, D. O., Bryant, L., & Wagner, A. (2004). Stepchildren's perceptions of the contradictions of communication with stepparents. *Journal of Social and Personal Relationships, 21,* 447–467.

Baxter, L. A., & Montgomery, B. M. (1997). Rethinking communication in personal relationships from a dialectical perspective. In S. Duck (Ed.), *Handbook of personal relationships* (2nd ed., pp. 325–349). London: Wiley.

Bengtson, V. L., & Roberts, R. E. L. (1991). Intergenerational solidarity in aging families: An example of formal theory construction. *Journal of Marriage and the Family, 53,* 856–870.

Berger, C. R., & Calabrese, R. J. (1975). Some explorations in initial interaction and beyond: Toward a developmental theory of interpersonal communication. *Human Communication Research, 1,* 99–112.

Berscheid, E. (1983). Emotion. In H. H. Kelley, E. Berscheid, A. Christensen, J. H. Harvey, T. L. Huston, G. Levinger, et al. (Eds.), *Close relationships* (pp. 110–168). New York: Freeman.

Berscheid, E., & Ammazzalorzo, H. (2001). Emotional experience in close relationships. In G. J. O. Fletcher & M. S. Clark (Eds.), *Blackwell handbook of social psychology: Interpersonal processes* (pp. 308–330). Malden, MA: Blackwell.

Braithwaite, D. O., Baxter, L. A., & Harper, A. M. (1998). The role of rituals in the management of the dialectical tension of "old" and "new" in blended families. *Communication Studies, 49,* 101–120.

Braithwaite, D. O., Olson, L. N., Golish, T. D., Soukup, C., & Turman, P. (2001). "Becoming a family": Developmental processes represented in blended family discourse. *Journal of Applied Communication Research, 29,* 221–247.

Burleson, B. R., Delia, J. G., & Applegate, J. L. (1995). The socialization of person-centered communication: Parents' contributions to their children's social-cognitive and communication skills. In M. A. Fitzpatrick & A. L. Vangelisti (Eds.), *Explaining family interactions* (pp. 34–76). Thousand Oaks, CA: Sage.

Caughlin, J. P., & Petronio, S. (2004). Privacy in families. In A. L. Vangelisti (Ed.), *Handbook of family communication* (pp. 379–412). Mahwah, NJ: Lawrence Erlbaum.

Cummings, E. M., & Smith, D. (1989). The impact of anger between adults on siblings' emotions and social behavior. *Journal of Child Psychology and Psychiatry, 25,* 63–74.

Dainton, M. (2000). Maintenance behaviors, expectations for maintenance, and satisfaction: Linking comparison levels to relational maintenance strategies. *Journal of Social and Personal Relationships, 17,* 827–842.

Davis, J. D., & Sloan, M. (1974). The basis of interviewee matching of interviewer self disclosure. *British Journal of Social and Clinical Psychology, 13,* 359–367.

Duck, S. W. (1984). A rose is a rose (is a tadpole is a freeway is a film) is a rose. *Journal of Social and Personal Relationships, 1,* 507–510.

Duck, S. W. (2002). Hypertext in the key of G: Three types of "history" as influences on conversational structure and flow. *Communication Theory, 12,* 41–62.

Duck, S. W., & Sants, H. K. A. (1983). On the origin of the specious: Are interpersonal relationships really interpersonal states? *Journal of Social and Clinical Psychology, 1,* 27–41.

Floyd, K., & Parks, M. R. (1995). Manifesting closeness in the interactions of peers: A look at siblings and friends. *Communication Reports, 8,* 69–77.

Foucault, M. (1991). The subject and power. In J. Fabian (Ed.), *Michel Foucault: Power* (Vol. 3, pp. 326–348). New York: The New Press.

Ganong, L. H., Coleman, M., Fine, M., & Martin, P. (1999). Stepparents' affinity-seeking and affinity-maintaining strategies in stepfamilies. *Journal of Family Issues, 20,* 299–327.

Gardner, K. A., & Cutrona, C. E. (2004). Social support communication in families. In A. L. Vangelisti (Ed.), *Handbook of family communication* (pp. 495–512). Mahwah, NJ: Lawrence Erlbaum.

Goffman, E. (1961). *Encounters: Two studies in the sociology of interaction.* Indianapolis, IN: Bobbs-Merrill.

Halbwachs, M. (1992). *On collective memory.* Chicago: University of Chicago Press.

Harwood, J., & Lin, M. (2000). Affiliation, pride, exchange, and distance in grandparents' accounts of relationships with their college-aged grandchildren. *Journal of Communication, 50,* 31–47.

Hirschberger, G., Florian, V., & Mikulincer, M. (2003). Strivings for romantic intimacy following partner complaint or partner criticism: A terror management perspective. *Journal of Social and Personal Relationships, 20,* 675–687.

Hobfoll, S. E., Nadler, A., & Leiberman, J. (1986). Satisfaction with social support during crisis: Intimacy and self-esteem as critical determinants. *Journal of Personality and Social Psychology, 51,* 296–304.

Huston, T. L., & Holmes, E. K. (2004). Becoming parents. In A. L. Vangelisti (Ed.), *Handbook of family communication* (pp. 105–134). Mahwah, NJ: Lawrence Erlbaum.

Johnson, R., Hobfoll, S. E., & Zalcberg-Linetzy, A. (1993). Social support knowledge and behavior and relational intimacy: A dyadic study. *Journal of Family Psychology, 6,* 266–277.

Jorgenson, J., & Bochner, A. P. (2004). Imagining families through stories and rituals. In A. L. Vangelisti (Ed.), *Handbook of family communication* (pp. 513–538). Mahwah, NJ: Lawrence Erlbaum.

Kelley, H., & Thibaut, J. (1978). *Interpersonal relations: A theory of interdependence.* New York: John Wiley.

Kerem, E., Fishman, N., & Josselson, R. (2001). The experience of empathy in everyday relationships: Cognitive and affective elements. *Journal of Social and Personal Relationships, 18,* 709–729.

Koerner, A. F., & Fitzpatrick, M. A. (2004). Communication in intact families. In A. L. Vangelisti (Ed.), *Handbook of family communication* (pp. 177–195). Mahwah, NJ: Lawrence Erlbaum.

Laing, R. D. (1971). *The politics of the family and other essays.* New York: Vintage.

Laursen, B., & Collins, W. A. (2004). Parent-child communication during adolescence. In A. L. Vangelisti (Ed.), *Handbook of family communication* (pp. 333–349). Mahwah, NJ: Lawrence Erlbaum.

McLain, R., & Weigert, A. (1979). Toward a phenomenological sociology of the family: A programmatic essay. In W. R. Burr, R. Hill, F. I. Nye, & I. Reiss (Eds.), *Contemporary theories about the family* (Vol. 2, pp. 160–205). New York: Free Press.

Mead, G. H. (1934). *Mind, self and society.* Chicago: University of Chicago Press.

Monsour, M. (1992). Meanings of intimacy in cross- and same-sex friendships. *Journal of Social and Personal Relationships, 9,* 277–295.

Parks, M. R., & Floyd, K. (1996). Meanings for closeness and intimacy in friendship. *Journal of Social and Personal Relationships, 13,* 85–107.

Prager, K. J. (1995). *The psychology of intimacy.* New York: Guilford.

Prager, K. J., & Buhrmester, D. (1998). Intimacy and need fulfillment in couple relationships. *Journal of Social and Personal Relationships, 15,* 435–469.

Register, L. M., & Henley, T. B. (1992). The phenomenology of intimacy. *Journal of Social and Personal Relationships, 9,* 467–481.

Reis, H. T., & Shaver, P. R. (1988). Intimacy as an interpersonal process. In S. W. Duck (Ed.), *Handbook of personal relationships: Theory, research, and interventions* (pp. 367–390). New York: John Wiley.

Rollie, S. S. (2005). *MIA (maintenance in absence): Maintaining the nonresidential parent-child relationship.* Unpublished doctoral dissertation, University of Iowa, Iowa City.

Sanderson, C. A., & Cantor, N. (1995). Social dating goals in late adolescence: Implications for safer sexual activity. *Journal of Personality and Social Psychology, 68,* 1121–1134.

Sillars, A., Canary, D. J., & Tafoya, M. (2004). Communication, conflict, and the quality of family relationships. In A. L. Vangelisti (Ed.), *Handbook of family communication* (pp. 413–446). Mahwah, NJ: Lawrence Erlbaum.

Smith, D. (1948). *I capture the castle.* New York: St. Martin's Griffin.

Smith, R. (1991). Envy and the sense of injustice. In P. Salovey (Ed.), *The psychology of jealousy and envy* (pp. 79–102). New York: Guilford.

Spitzberg, B. H. (1993). The dialectics of (in)competence. *Journal of Social and Personal Relationships, 10,* 137–158.

Sprecher, S., & Duck, S. W. (1993). Sweet talk: The role of communication in consolidating relationships. *Personality and Social Psychology Bulletin, 20,* 391–400.

Sternberg, R. J. (1986). A triangular theory of love. *Psychological Review, 93,* 119–135.

Thibaut, J., & Kelley, H. (1959). *The social psychology of groups.* New York: John Wiley.

Turner, V. (1982). *From ritual to theatre: The human seriousness of play.* New York: PAJ Publications.

Tyler, J. (2005, November). *Family communication and the negotiation of boundaries between home, work, and community.* Paper presented at the annual convention of the National Communication Association, Boston.

Wolin, S. J., & Bennett, L. A. (1984). Family rituals. *Family Process, 23,* 401–420.

Wood, J. T. (2001). The normalization of violence in heterosexual romantic relationships: Women's narratives of love and violence. *Journal of Social and Personal Relationships, 18,* 239–262.

Wood, J. T., & Inman, C. C. (1993). In a different mode: Masculine styles of communicating closeness. *Journal of Applied Communication Research, 21,* 279–295.

Wright, P. H. (1985). Self referent motivation and the intrinsic quality of friendship. *Journal of Social and Personal Relationships, 1,* 114–130.

CHAPTER 11

When "Friendly Advice" Becomes a Privacy Dilemma for Pregnant Couples

Applying Communication Privacy Management Theory

Sandra Petronio

Indiana University–Purdue University, Indianapolis

Susanne M. Jones

University of Minnesota, Twin Cities

Pregnancy is a transformative event filled with excitement and joy, as well as anxiety and emotional distress. It is particularly stressful for first-time parents, who cope with fears ranging from worries about the health of mother and newborn to the trials and tribulations of parenthood (Cutrona, 1984;

AUTHORS' NOTE: Portions of this chapter were presented at the 1995 National Communication Association Conference, San Antonio, TX. The authors would like to thank Samantha Kovach for her contributions to an earlier version of this project.

Cutrona & Russell, 1990; Dunkel-Schetter, 1998). To manage the immense physiological and social challenges of pregnancy, expecting couples rely on the support of friends and family (Collins, Dunkel-Schetter, Lobel, & Scrimshaw, 1993/2004; Dunkel-Schetter, Sagrestano, & Killingsworth, 1996; Stern & Bitsko, 2003). Numerous studies examine health outcomes and strategic influences of social support during pregnancy (for a review, see Stern & Bitsko, 2003). In fact, Cutrona and Russell (1990) state that more experimental investigations are concerned with examining the dynamics of the transition to parenthood than with *any other single life event.*

Expecting couples count on support from friends and family in various ways, including receiving advice, tangible aid, and emotional care (Collins et al., 1993/2004). It is also noteworthy that, even though significant others are the most important supporters, family, members, friends, nurses, and doctors are also important sources offering support during pregnancy. Indeed, women with large social support networks containing various sources of assistance have been found to be best prepared for the stresses associated with pregnancy (Collins et al., 1993/2004). Although provisions of social support take on various forms, opinions and advice usually come in particular abundance (Cutrona, 1984; Cutrona & Russell, 1990). Collins et al. (1993/2004) report that instrumental support (i.e., advice) is more predictive of psychological well-being than emotional support.

Privacy Dilemmas for Pregnant Couples

Advice may be viewed as comforting (Knapp, Stohl, & Reardon, 1981), but there are times when recipients may not want advice, particularly if the nature of the advice is disclosive. Getting unrequested disclosure-advice from family and friends may contribute to privacy dilemmas for pregnant couples. If pregnant couples do not want to hurt the discloser's feelings but also do not want to cope with the information revealed, they are in a "damned if you do, damned if you don't" situation.

Communication privacy management (CPM) theory provides a useful theoretical framework to understand this problem (Petronio, 2000a, 2000b, 2002). CPM theory offers a valuable method of understanding the ways people manage the dialectical tensions of disclosing and protecting privacy. Using the concept of privacy rules, CPM helps us see how people depend on rules to guide them in making decisions about when to disclose, thereby opening their privacy boundaries, and when to remain private, thus keeping them closed (Petronio, 2002). For CPM theory, the recipient is featured as an integral and dominant part of the privacy-disclosure process. Consequently, the theory is well equipped to provide insights into times, as we see with pregnant couples, when receiving disclosure feels more like a violation of the recipient's privacy than a privilege.

Because pregnancy is a crucial event for a couple involving a reasonable exchange of personal information with others, the application of CPM is useful. Specific to the two studies we present here, CPM helps us examine how couples interpret well-meant advice from others. A dilemma often arises because unsolicited advice often creates a contrived and factitious sense of intimacy between the person offering the advice and the pregnant couple. As Foley and Duck (Chapter 10, this volume) observe, when information sounds intimate but is undesired by the receiver, the very definition of intimacy is compromised. This may be especially true when the advice is in the form of a disclosed experience that is highly personal, sensitive, potentially stress provoking, and at times difficult. Given that receiving unsolicited disclosure-advice in general often results in privacy dilemmas (Petronio, Jones, & Morr, 2003), it seems clear that the way disclosure-advice occurs during pregnancies can result in privacy dilemmas for couples, adding a tremendous amount of psychological and physiological stress to their lives.

The nature of a privacy dilemma may become exacerbated because of the type of advice communicated to pregnant couples. Several studies examined the face-threatening aspects of advice in the context of social support and found that advice is a common yet not always a beneficial form of support (Goldsmith & MacGeorge, 2000; MacGeorge, Lichtman, & Pressey, 2002). MacGeorge, Feng, Butler, and Budarz (2004) went beyond examining the relational consequences of advice (i.e., face threats) and analyzed the *kinds* of advice that are more and less beneficial when offering help to others. Based on stock issues commonly used in argumentation and debate, MacGeorge et al. (2004) found that comprehensibility, relevance, feasibility, and absence of limitations (i.e., the drawbacks of the advice should not be too severe and numerous) are four important factors of more and less beneficial advice.

This chapter adds to research on advice in social support encounters because it focuses particularly on advice that is unsolicited. Advice becomes *unsolicited* when the recipient—in this case, the expecting couple—has not requested it (or any other form of support). Furthermore, we argue that disclosing about a personal experience expressed as advice leads to a privacy dilemma for the recipient. Because friends, family members, and even strangers often feel compelled to share personal experiences and assume that personal disclosures about pregnancy prepare expecting parents for upcoming challenges, these disclosures result in consequences for the pregnant couple (Peterson, 1987). Even if advice is meant to be helpful, receiving unsolicited disclosures about personal experiences may be stressful because the content of advice may contain troubling and upsetting details (Petronio, 2002; Petronio et al., 2003). When advice contains personal experience, the advice-donor may be perceived as offering information that has significant import, making it more difficult to reject. Consequently, this kind of advice may have greater potency than advice that does not contain personal experience, and in high-stress life events such as pregnancy, the impact may be more acute. Thus, advice associated with personal experience can be potentially stress provoking for the expecting couple precisely because such advice contains real personal experiences. Unsolicited disclosure-advice that includes painful personal incidents reinforces the uncontrollability and uncertainty associated with childbirth and thus increases the emotional distress level of the expecting couple.

Expecting couples frequently are involuntarily exposed to advice that is laced with potentially anxiety-provoking personal stories (Peterson, 1987). For instance, an advice-donor might recommend against an epidural during the birth to avoid potential harm to the baby by drawing on graphic and painful personal events during her child's birth. The consequences of such potentially agitating incidents have been documented in numerous studies (Collins et al., 1993/2004; Glazier, Elgar,

Goel, & Holzapfel, 2004; Thompson, Parahoo, McCurry, O'Doherty, & Doherty, 2004; Zacharia, 2004; for a review, see also Stern & Bitsko, 2003). For example, such advice can lead to outcomes such as postpartum depression and possibly heightened anxiety experienced by the mother (Glazier et al., 2004). In addition, birth weight for the baby (Collins et al., 1993/2004) as well as lower Apgar scores (i.e., Activity, Pulse, Grimace, Appearance, Respiration scores) may result from receiving fewer support messages and more messages that increase anxiety and apprehension about the impending birth of the child. Mothers who experience adverse support might also develop a weaker attachment to their babies (Zacharia, 2004). Although advice-donors may have the best intentions, the impact on the recipient—in this case, pregnant couples—may be counterproductive.

Communication Privacy Management and Unsolicited Disclosure-Advice

CPM theory proposes that when people, such as expecting couples, receive unsolicited advice in the form of personal disclosures, they often initiate actions that are necessary to protect or repair their privacy boundaries (Petronio, 2002). Research suggests that once a perceived invasion occurs, people use various strategies to restore their privacy (Burgoon et al., 1989). For example, hearing unwanted information, especially the kind that increases stress, may result in developing coping strategies to lessen the impact of the information on the recipient (Petronio, 2002). In cases where privacy invasions occur on a regular basis, successful repair strategies may evolve into rules people use frequently to ward off boundary-violating behaviors. People are able to successfully repair a privacy boundary once they have determined why the violation occurred in the first place. Making sense of the unsolicited nature of the revelation may help put the information into a manageable perspective for the expecting couple. To this end, attributional searches are one way for the recipient to assess intended meanings for disclosures (Petronio, 1991, 2000a, 2000b).

The Nature of Unsolicited Disclosure-Advice

As Peterson (1987) notes, expecting mothers are frequently exposed to personal stories from friends, relatives, and sometimes strangers because they function as a "rite of passage." Peterson argues that pregnant women receive at least three types of stories. The first story type organizes *content* and *information* and illustrates change or crisis. Friends and family alike may define pregnancy as a possible crisis or a catalyst for change. They may make comments such as advising against taking medications, caffeine, or alcohol because they learned in their pregnancy that doing so is bad for the unborn child (see also Thompson et al., 2004). The second story type organizes *interpreted information* about birth. These stories center on childbirth as a positive *event* and involve advice that prepares the expecting mother for birth. Similar to athletic training preparations, the expecting couple is coached in breathing exercises, relaxation techniques, and other exercises that mimic actual childbirth. The third story type organizes innovated information and circles around *relational information*. These stories allow the couple to reorganize and reinvent their *identity* from a couple to a family and revolve around advice and information about the meaning, role, and life of "mom" and "dad."

Peterson's (1987) phenomenological analysis of the narrative structure of personal stories illustrates that expecting couples may receive different types of unsolicited advice that fulfill various functions. For example, content information functions to establish the new status of expecting couples. Advice-donors share similar experiences (e.g., "I know how you feel; the same thing happened to me"). Event information functions to prepare the expecting couple for the big event, whereas relational advice serves to help the expecting couple cope with their new identity.

Although well-intended advice that is disclosive may come easily to those who want to share their experiences, it may, in fact, have at least two stress-causing consequences for the expecting couple. First, unsolicited disclosure-advice might be perceived as stressful to expecting couples because they might feel pressured to accept the recommendations contained in it. Goldsmith and Fitch (1997) identify the predicament of "making one's own decision vs. showing respect and gratitude" (p. 468) toward receiving advice. If advice is not accepted, expecting couples might appear ungrateful.

The second and more deleterious consequence of unsolicited disclosure-advice is that it might enhance the fears of an expecting couple anxiously awaiting a healthy baby. For example, an expecting couple that knows of past complications experienced by other family members might be especially sensitive to content stories about complications at birth. Expecting mothers in particular, who have to cope with the anticipation of labor pain, might experience increased emotional distress when listening to the birth ordeals of other mothers. Hearing about problems may lead to feelings of increased helplessness and depression about the pregnancy (Norbeck & Tilden, 1983). This may account for why research on distress disclosure shows that recipients tend to make more negative than positive attributions about the discloser (Coates & Winston, 1987; Peters-Golden, 1982; Winer, Bonner, Blaney, & Murray, 1981). Interestingly, many experimental studies use the technique of unsolicited disclosure to investigate a wide array of issues such as attraction (Rosenfeld, Civikly, & Herron, 1979), style (Norton & Montgomery, 1982), eliciting disclosure (Miller, Berg, & Archer, 1983), reciprocity (Derlega, Winstead, Wong, & Greenspan, 1987), and personality issues (Jourard, 1970). Unfortunately, since the unsolicited nature of information has not been a controlled variable, we do not really know much about this practice.

Coping With the Consequences of Unsolicited Disclosure-Advice

Coping efforts often consist of appraisals of and responses to external stressors, such as illness, divorce, or, in our case, unsolicited disclosure-advice. In general, two different types of coping have been consistently identified: emotion-focused coping and problem-focused coping (Folkman & Lazarus, 1988). *Emotion-focused coping* encompasses the vast arsenal of cognitive process directed at lessening emotional distresses. Strategies might include minimization, avoidance, selective attention, or positive comparisons. *Problem-focused coping* includes strategies directed at defining the problem, generating alternative solutions, and choosing among them (Lazarus & Folkman, 1984). Both types facilitate the coping process and are often used simultaneously. Thus, a pregnant couple might cope by putting a positive "twist" on the reasons for receiving the information, seek to define the context of the advice, and find alternative solutions.

Attributions About the Disclosure Advice-Donor

As is suggested by CPM theory, people whose privacy boundaries have been violated will engage in an attributional search to assess the causes of and potential coping strategies (or repair mechanisms) for the privacy invasion (Petronio, 1991, 2002). Expecting couples might engage in an attributional search to assess the causes for the unsolicited disclosure-advice, as well as to determine the expertise of the advice donor. Expecting couples can better cope with emotionally distressing information once they know *why* the advice-donor disclosed the particular story. Eckenrode and Wethington (1990) maintain that attributions made by recipients may be instrumental in determining whether advice will result in positive outcomes. Not only might this knowledge help decrease emotional distress, but it might also reduce relational tensions between the expecting couple and the advice-donor. These assumptions reflect causal attribution theory's primary postulate that people act as naive scientists determined to find out "why" others *act* in specific ways (Heider, 1958). Given that the expecting couple is concerned with causes for the unsolicited disclosure from the advice-donor, they might engage in an attributional search for behavioral causes rather than personality qualities of the advice-donor.

Barbee, Rowatt, and Cunningham (1998) suggest an interactive process between the advice-donor and the recipient. Specifically, they point out that the value and importance of advice is interactively negotiated between provider and recipient. This interactive process is influenced by various important variables, such as credibility of the advice-donor and importance of the relationship.

Given that expecting couples face several dilemmas when dealing with unsolicited disclosure-advice, it is even more crucial that they make behavioral attributions about the causes of unsolicited disclosures. For instance, the advice-donor might rely solely on personal experience when forewarning an expecting couple about potential dangers of childbirth (e.g., "You will have a lot of pain in the last three weeks of the pregnancy, because it happened to me"). In this instance, the couple might decide to ignore the forewarning because they attribute low levels of credibility to the advice-donor, as the unsolicited disclosure-advice was solely based on anecdotal evidence. Consider, however, an example where the discloser reveals information about breathing exercises she learned in her Lamaze course. In this instance, the expecting couple might consider the advice because it reflects some expertise on behalf of the advice-donor. Thus, coping strategies are dependent on the causal attributions that expecting couples make about the advice-donor.

Study 1

In this study, we mapped the conceptual domain of unsolicited disclosure-advice in the context of pregnancy. Specifically, we posed the following research questions:

RQ1:   What types of unsolicited disclosure-advice do expecting couples receive?

RQ2:   What types of emotion-focused and problem-focused coping strategies do expecting couples use to maintain their privacy boundaries after having received unsolicited disclosure-advice?

RQ3:   What attributions do expecting couples make about the person providing the unsolicited disclosure-advice?

Method

Participants

A total of 10 expecting participants from birthing classes were recruited by requesting volunteers willing to keep a diary for Study 1. All 10 participants were in their second or third trimester of pregnancy. Data were collected in a large metropolitan area. All participants were White, and the average age was 30 years. All except 2 of the participants were married. A total of 7 participants were female, whereas 3 participants were male partners of pregnant women.[1] While female and male partners certainly experience pregnancy differently, we assumed that expecting fathers and mothers are equally stressed by unsolicited advice. Seven participants were having their first child, 2 participants were expecting their second, and 1 participant was expecting her third child.

Procedures

Participants were asked to keep diaries for 1 week. They were specifically instructed to record all unsolicited disclosure-advice about childbirth and pregnancy that they received in the week. Typically, the diary entries did not indicate whether the disclosure was directed toward the partner or pregnant woman but was recorded only if the content was about the pregnancy. Participants were also asked to record how they reacted to these disclosures (the coping strategies employed to maintain privacy boundaries) and why they thought people disclosed that particular kind of information (attributions made about the intent of the discloser). Second, face-to-face recorded interviews were conducted as a follow-up to data generated in the diaries. Participants were asked to elaborate on the information they recorded and comment on additional disclosures they encountered regarding perceptions of the unsolicited disclosure-advice, their own responses to the disclosures, and participants' attributions for the unsolicited disclosure-advice.

Results

For the analysis of the interview and diary data, we engaged in a thematic analysis to determine the types of stories disclosed to pregnant couples, kinds of coping mechanisms used, and reasons why pregnant couples believed they received this unsolicited information.

Types of Disclosure-Advice

From the analysis, 15 themes emerged as describing the stories disclosed to pregnant couples: family pressure to select a name, deformities, miscarriages, parent's birthing experience, having a cesarean section procedure, waiting period before the birth, breastfeeding, the way husbands act during pregnancy, fetal movement, caring for the baby, financial issues, long delivery, weight gain for the pregnant woman, having a boy or girl, and changes in lifestyle. Interestingly, the most common theme expecting couples reported concerned the name of the baby. Undoubtedly, this issue is of primary importance to expecting parents, who are acutely aware that names shape people's perceptions of the child. This point has been supported by Mehrabian's (1992) research suggesting that names are identity markers. For example, people associate femininity and sensitivity with names such as Rachel and Susie, whereas Conan is perceived as masculine and strong. A brief glance at the popular literature with its numerous examples of books investigating the meanings as well as the cultural trends of names reflects the tremendous importance of this topic. Thus, it is not a surprise that couples receive a lot of suggestions about potential names for their baby.

Other themes found primarily mirrored Peterson's (1987) content and information categories. Advice of this nature is much more sensitive and disturbing than those about baby names. Content and information kinds of advice are also often more disclosive because they reference situations that are private and disturbing in nature. For example, one woman wrote about long deliveries:

> A teacher I work with was telling me about how her second child had to be induced. She had to suck on 17 pills before she went into labor. And then it went so hard and fast that the baby just flew out and the doctor could hardly catch him. I was appalled that they had to give her so much of that drug in a 2-hour span of time. I hope that if I need to be induced, the doctors will be more patient. I told my husband about this. (Participant 1)

This next statement illustrates the stories about deformities, which was another recurring theme found in the data. The participant stated,

My mother-in-law told me about a baby in her family that was born 2 months prematurely. The baby had "Hyland Lung??" and a blood clot in the foot. The doctors could treat only one condition—the Hyland lung—so they wrapped the baby's foot and eventually all the toes of that foot dropped off. The baby survived, and they say it will be able to walk all right. This is one of those stories I don't care to hear about just because of my own fears about the health of my own baby. Haven't told anyone about this yet. (Participant 2)

An entry from a male participant also demonstrates the theme of long delivery:

One woman told me that we should be practicing our breathing exercises more so we really know how to do them in the hospital and can have some "control" like she did (and not have a long delivery). She is a colleague at work and a school nurse. She made me feel guilty, like we haven't practiced enough (which we probably haven't). I told my wife about it when I got home. (Participant 5)

The same participant also noted the following:

A friend shared her labor story—not too bad but she was constipated and the nurse told her she couldn't go or she'd have the baby in the toilet! (Participant 5)

Another participant's story illustrates the theme of miscarriages:

One thing I did not expect to hear from people is the topic of miscarriages. Some of my wife's coworkers have recently had miscarriages. One woman would not even talk to me or my wife because she wanted a baby so much. I was getting scared that my wife might have a miscarriage or deformed baby. We had an ultrasound to determine the due date and the little baby looked beautiful. My wife was hospitalized with a kidney infection during the first 5 months. We were both very worried for her health [and our] baby's health. (Participant 4)

As these examples illustrate, disclosure-advice can range from less to more stress-producing outcomes for pregnant couples.

Coping Strategies

We found six themes that focused on how the pregnant couples coped with receiving the disclosed advice. The themes included (a) telling others about the disclosure, (b) ignoring the information received, (c) asking oneself why the person is telling the information, (d) verifying the information with an authority, (e) worrying about the disclosed information, and (f) waiting to see if the information received seems important. Several coping strategies are emotion focused in nature (e.g., worrying about the disclosed information), whereas other strategies are more problem focused in nature (e.g., telling others about the disclosure, asking oneself why the person is telling the information, verifying the information with an authority, waiting to see if the information received seems important).

Attributions About the Advice-Donor

The themes concerning attributions about why people disclose private information about pregnancy included the following: (a) helping (people disclose to help others by revealing information), (b) reliving (people disclose to relive the experience), (c) sharing (people disclose to communicate the way pregnancy was for them), (d) educating (people disclose to educate others about the problems associated with pregnancy and childbirth), (e) creating a common bond (people disclose to create a common bond or identity), and (f) ameliorating (people disclose to get others through a crisis).

Study 2

The themes found in Study 1 were suggestive of needing a more in-depth study. Consequently, we extended examination of these themes in Study 2, exploring the relationship between types of disclosure-advice, coping mechanisms, and attributions made about the discloser. Study 2 was guided specifically by the following research questions:

RQ1:   Is there a relationship between certain types of unsolicited disclosure-advice and the coping strategies used by expecting couples to maintain their privacy boundaries?

RQ2:   Is there a relationship between unsolicited disclosure-advice and the attributions that pregnant couples make about the intent of the advice-donor?

In addition, it is important to determine whether attributions for the discloser actually predict the coping strategies used by expecting couples. We suggest that attributions subsequently influence the coping behaviors of help recipients. This assertion is reflected in our last research question:

RQ3:   Do types of attributions of expecting couples predict types of coping strategies they use to deal with the unsolicited disclosure-advice?

Method

A self-report questionnaire format was used to examine the research questions. A total of 92 participants were recruited from birthing classes held in the midwestern region of the United States. Ten birthing classes were randomly selected, using a stratified procedure from 100 possible time slots across the week during the winter and spring months. Of the 92 respondents ($n = 40$ men, 52 women), 51% resided in a rural area and 49% lived in an urban area in the Midwest. The majority of the respondents (86%) had never experienced pregnancy before, whereas 9% reported experiencing their second or third pregnancy. All respondents were in their second (26%) and third (74%) trimesters of pregnancy.

Instrumentation

Disclosure-Advice Scale

This scale measured the extent to which participants reported receiving certain kinds of unsolicited disclosure-advice. The 15 unsolicited disclosure-advice types, developed from themes in Study 1, were used to construct the survey items. Respondents were asked to respond on a 5-point Likert-type scale that ranged from 1 (*not at all*) to 5 (*very often*) how frequently they received each of the 15 types of unsolicited disclosure-advice (Cronbach's $\alpha = .83$).[2]

Disclosure-Advice Coping Scale

This scale measured the extent to which participants reported using coping strategies to deal with the unsolicited disclosure-advice. Participants were asked to evaluate the extent to which the six coping strategies derived from Study 1 were useful in coping with the unsolicited disclosure-advice. Again, participants indicated on a 5-point Likert-type scale that ranged from 1 (*not useful at all*) to 5 (*very useful*) the extent to which the following coping mechanisms were useful: (a) ignoring, (b) asking oneself why the person is telling the information, (c) verifying with authority, (d) worrying about it, (e) waiting to see if important, and (f) telling others (Cronbach's $\alpha = .95$).

Disclosure-Advice Attribution Scale

Finally, respondents were asked to evaluate attributions for the unsolicited disclosure-advice. Using 6-point Likert-type scales that ranged from 1 (*very unlikely*) to 6 (*very likely*), participants were asked how likely it is that people provide unsolicited advice to (a) relive the experience, (b) help others through a crisis, (c) share the experience, (d) communicate the way pregnancy really is, (e) educate others, and (f) create a common identity (Cronbach's $\alpha = .84$).

Results

To assess the relationship between unsolicited disclosure-advice and the coping strategies used by pregnant couples to maintain their privacy boundaries (RQ1), a canonical correlation was conducted between the set of variables comprising the unsolicited disclosures and the set of variables comprising the coping strategies. No significant results emerged from the analysis.

To assess the relationship between unsolicited disclosure-advice and the attributions that pregnant couples make about the intent of the discloser (RQ2), a second canonical correlation was conducted between the set of variables comprising the unsolicited disclosure and the set of variables comprising the attributions that pregnant couples make about the intent of the discloser. Again, no significant results emerged from the analyses.

To assess whether the attributions pregnant couples make about the intent of the discloser predict the types of coping strategies that are employed (RQ3), six stepwise multiple regressions were conducted, with each of the coping strategies as the criterion and the six attributions as the predictors.

The first stepwise multiple regression analysis regressed the six attributions on the coping strategy of "telling others about the disclosure." The attribution of "sharing the experience" predicted a significant amount of variance in "telling others about the disclosure," $F(1, 75) = 16.66$, $p < .001$, $\beta = .43$, $R^2 = .18$. The second stepwise multiple regression analysis regressed the six attributions on the second coping strategy of "simply ignoring the advice." The attribution that the discloser wants to "relive the experience" predicted a significant amount of variance in the second coping strategy, "ignoring it," $F(1, 73) = 7.07$, $p < .05$, $\beta = -.30$, $R^2 = .08$. In cases where expecting couples assumed that the advice-donor wanted to relive his or her pregnancy experience, expecting couples were not able to simply ignore the advice. Indeed, this might suggest that expecting couples now found themselves in the role of support provider (which itself can be interpreted as a coping strategy). The third stepwise multiple regression analysis regressed the six attributions on the third coping strategy, "asking why the discloser is giving the advice," and did not detect any significant differences. The fourth stepwise multiple regression analysis regressed the six attributions on the fourth coping strategy, "verifying information with authorities," and was significant, $F(1, 74) = 13.22$, $p < .001$, $\beta = .39$, $R^2 = .15$. The fifth stepwise multiple regression analysis regressed the six attributions on the fifth coping strategy, "worrying about advice," and did not detect any significant results. The final stepwise multiple regression analysis regressed the six attributions on the coping strategy of "waiting to see if the advice is important." The attribution that the discloser "wants to educate" predicted a significant amount of variance in the coping strategy of "waiting to see if the advice is important," $F(1, 73) = 6.00$, $p < .05$, $\beta = .28$, $R^2 = .06$. Table 11.1 presents a summary of the regression results.

Supplemental Analysis

While research indicates that couples generally have similar fears, worries, and uncertainties about having a child, our nonsignificant findings called for a post hoc examination of sex with respect to unsolicited disclosure-advice. Such a decision was warranted because the data were collected independently. Indeed, some research indicates that men's and women's responses to pregnancy may differ (Goldberg, Michaels, & Lamb, 1985; Harriman, 1983). Thus, to alleviate any possibility that sex influenced the outcome of our analyses, we conducted a multivariate analysis of variance to assess sex differences between the frequencies of received unsolicited disclosure-advice, coping strategies, and attributions. Results suggest

Table 11.1   Stepwise Regression Analysis: Predicting Coping Styles From Attributions

	β	t	p
1. *telling others* sharing the experience	.43	4.01	.00
2. *ignoring information* reliving the experience	−.30	−2.66	.01
3. *asking self why discloser tells*	—	—	—
4. *verifying information with authority* educating others	.39	3.63	.01
5. *worrying about it*	—	—	—
6. *waiting to see if information is important* educating others	.28	2.45	.05

Note: *t* value probabilities are two-tailed. Only significant results are reported.

only one significant effect for sex with respect to these three variables, $F(27, 43) = .46$, $p < .05$, Wilks's $\ddot{E} = .45$. Interestingly, while expecting women and men did not differ significantly from each other with respect to coping strategies and attributions, the univariate analyses revealed a significant effect for sex differences concerning the types of unsolicited disclosure-advice that was received by male and female participants. Specifically, women heard more disclosure-advice about long delivery ($M = 4.17$), weight gain ($M = 4.02$), waiting period before birth ($M = 2.78$), breastfeeding ($M = 2.83$), and deformities ($M = 2.27$) than did men ($M = 2.90, 2.63, 2.33, 2.03$, and 1.56, respectively).

Discussion

Expecting parents of both sexes experience the stresses and difficulties of pregnancy. Strangers and family members alike want to participate in recognizing this life cycle event (Imber-Black & Roberts, 1992). Perhaps because pregnancy is often ritualized, most people feel they know something about the experience. However, this often creates a dilemma for the pregnant couple because the unsolicited advice they receive invades their privacy boundaries and is often counterproductive for them. Advice-donors tend to feel that it is appropriate to offer unsolicited disclosure-advice to the couple. Although pregnant couples may not always find this breach of privacy particularly offensive, they still find themselves hearing information they did not request. Thus, being pregnant is a condition where we discover the necessity of repairing a privacy boundary that is often compromised by the good intentions of others.

As has been suggested earlier, coping strategies may be emotion focused and/or problem focused. Indeed, our study corroborates previous findings and suggests that pregnant couples rely on emotion-focused coping as well as problem-focused coping (for a review, see Lazarus & Folkman, 1984). As this study shows, there are a number of ways to repair privacy boundaries that have been breached by hearing unsolicited disclosure-advice. Consequently, we know that when these pregnant couples received information that they did not ask for, they coped by telling others, ignoring the information, asking why that person told them in the first place, verifying the information with an authority, worrying about what they were told, and waiting to see if the information turned out to be important. As reluctant recipients, pregnant couples manage their privacy boundaries by using these strategies to calm the turbulence of receiving uninvited advice that may heighten their anxieties rather than soothe their fears. For example, one of the stories reported in the diary data from Study 1 serves to illustrate this need for coping. A pregnant woman and her husband were standing at the checkout counter in a grocery store. A woman behind them was staring at the pregnant woman's stomach, sizing her up. At last, she spoke to the couple. They turned to listen in a polite way. The woman said, "You know, when I was pregnant with my daughter, I carried like that in my last trimester. I just want you to know that I think you should see the doctor immediately, because the umbilical cord could be wrapped around your baby's neck, just like mine was. I wouldn't wait too long."

As our data suggest, there is no apparent relationship between receiving a particular type of story and the strategies people use to cope with these stories. This may be due to a multitude of factors that enter the judgment of how to repair a privacy boundary once invaded by others. This is true, although these data indicate that pregnant women and their male partners hear different kinds of stories. Nevertheless, there are a number of possible ways to repair privacy boundaries that, for these data, are independent of different kinds of advice.

Our study also demonstrates that the kind of attributions pregnant couples made about the reason for receiving unsolicited disclosure-advice affects the coping strategies used to repair the privacy boundary. For instance, if the pregnant couple believed that they were receiving the unsolicited disclosure-advice because it helped educate them, they were more likely to wait and see if the information turned out to be important. The desire to educate others also predicted that the couple would verify the information with an authority. When the couples believed that advice-donors were trying to relive their own experience, they were more likely to ignore the information. Finally, when the couple believed that the advice was given because the person wanted to share in the experience, they generally told others what they heard. Consequently, attributions that pregnant couples made about the reasons for the information played a more significant role than type of advice in determining ways to cope with privacy invasion.

Although Rawlins (1983) argues that disclosers have a responsibility to protect themselves and be mindful of the way disclosure may affect others, not all advice-donors acknowledge that responsibility. The reasons may be varied. For example, individuals may miscalculate the impact of the disclosive message, have a great need to tell private information, or have personality characteristics such as being egocentric that disallow sensitivity to the recipient.

At the most fundamental level, the person disclosing in an unsolicited manner may not recognize that the information is unwelcome. Because communication is irreversible, recipients then must take into account information that they would rather not know. Reluctant recipients receiving advice must find ways to incorporate unwanted and often stress-inducing new information into their lives (Petronio, 2002). As Derlega and Chaikin (1977) note, "Another person's self-disclosure input, by creating an obligation to reciprocate, may threaten one's freedom of choice to regulate interacts with others" (p. 107). CPM theory suggests that the use of coping strategies, such as those found in this study for pregnant couples, affords the recipient a way to repair the boundary lines that have been invaded and guard against additional vulnerability.

In conclusion, the two studies presented here address the issue of unsolicited disclosure-advice and its influence on recipients' coping strategies to restore privacy. Too little is known about the impact that precarious messages have on a recipient (Petronio, 2002). The literature on reciprocity is one attempt to acknowledge the importance of the receiver. However, as Dindia (1982) points out, reactions to disclosure reciprocity are mixed at best. There are many contexts in which people receive unrequested disclosures that result in privacy invasion for recipients. This is particularly true when the disclosure comes in the form of advice. For example, parents often tell children how they should behave. From the parents' point of view, this is an important part of socializing their children. From the children's vantage point, the information may not be viewed as positively (Petronio, 1994). Unsolicited advice occurs and has consequences in all kinds of communication contexts: the workplace, the classroom, the home, and so forth. Researchers have thoroughly investigated why people disclose (for a review, see Petronio, 2002), but much less is known about those who receive disclosive information, particularly when they do not ask for it.

Our studies highlight the need to consider different ways in which disclosive information is communicated. Revealing private information may be communicated upon request or in an unrequested fashion. Although preliminary, the research presented here suggests a need to continue examining the way receivers mend privacy boundaries that have been invaded by unwanted disclosures from others. Pregnant couples who are experiencing the tensions of high stress and great joy may benefit from understanding that coping depends on their attributions for the disclosures. Timing plays a part in readiness to hear information that might cause stress and alarm (Dindia, 1982; Pennebaker, 1990). Consequently, help providers should be mindful of possible ramifications for the pregnant couple when offering unsolicited disclosure-advice.

Notes

1. Not all male partners were married to the pregnant women, although they were typically the fathers.

2. Because each scale item is unique, the scale alphas might not be meaningful indicators for the overall reliability of the scale.

References

Barbee, A. P., Rowatt, T. L., & Cunningham, M. R. (1998). When a friend is in need: Feelings about seeking, giving, and receiving social support. In P. A. Andersen & L. K. Guerrero (Eds.), *Handbook of communication and emotion* (pp. 282–298). San Diego: Academic Press.

Burgoon, J. K., Parrott, R., Le Poire, B. A., Kelley, D. L., Walther, J. B., & Perry, D. (1989). Maintaining and restoring privacy through communication in different types of relationships. *Journal of Social and Personal Relationships, 6,* 131–158.

Coates, D., & Winston, T. (1987). The dilemma of distress disclosure. In V. J. Derlega & J. H. Berg (Eds.), *Self-disclosure: Theory, research, and therapy* (pp. 229–255). New York: Plenum.

Collins, N., Dunkel-Schetter, C., Lobel, M., & Scrimshaw, S. (2004). Social support in pregnancy: Psychosocial correlates of birth outcomes and postpartum depression. In H. T. Reis & C. E. Rusbult (Eds.), *Close relationships: Key readings* (pp. 35–55). Philadelphia: Taylor & Francis. (Original work published 1993)

Cutrona, C. E. (1984). Social support and stress in the transition to parenthood. *Journal of Abnormal Psychology, 93,* 378–390.

Cutrona, C. E., & Russell, D. W. (1990). Type of social support and specific stress: Toward a theory of optimal matching. In B. R. Sarason, I. G. Sarason, & G. R. Pierce (Eds.), *Social support: An interactionist view* (pp. 9–25). New York: John Wiley.

Derlega, V. J., & Chaikin, A. L. (1977). Privacy and self-disclosure in social relationships. *Journal of Social Issues, 33,* 102–115.

Derlega, V. J., Winstead, B. A., Wong, P. T., & Greenspan, P. (1987). Self-disclosure and relational development: An attributional analysis. In M. E. Roloff & G. R. Miller (Eds.), *Interpersonal processes: New directions in communication research* (pp. 172–187). Newbury Park, CA: Sage.

Dindia, K. (1982). Reciprocity of self-disclosure: A sequential analysis. In M. Burgoon (Ed.), *Communication yearbook 6* (pp. 206–249). Beverly Hills, CA: Sage.

Dunkel-Schetter, C. (1998). Maternal stress and preterm delivery. *Prenatal and Neonatal Medicine, 3,* 39–42.

Dunkel-Schetter, C., Sagrestano, P. F, & Killingsworth, C. (1996). Social support and pregnancy. In G. R. Pierce, B. R. Sarason, & I. G. Sarason (Eds.), *Handbook of social support and the family* (pp. 375–412). New York: Plenum.

Eckenrode, J., & Wethington, E. (1990). The process and outcome of mobilizing social support. In S. Duck (Ed.) (with R. Silver), *Personal relationships and social support* (pp. 83–103). London: Sage.

Folkman, S., & Lazarus, R. S. (1988). Coping as a mediator of emotion. *Journal of Personality and Social Psychology, 54,* 466–475.

Glazier, R. H., Elgar, F. J., Goel, V., & Holzapfel, S. (2004). Stress, social support, and emotional distress in a community sample of pregnant women. *Journal of Psychosomatic Obstetrics & Gynecology, 25,* 247–255.

Goldberg, W., Michaels, G., & Lamb, M. (1985). Husbands' and wives' adjustment to pregnancy and first parenthood. *Journal of Family Issues, 6,* 483–503.

Goldsmith, D. J., & Fitch, K. (1997). The normative context of advice as social support. *Human Communication Research, 23,* 454–476.

Goldsmith, D. J., & MacGeorge, E. L. (2000). The impact of politeness and relationship on perceived quality of advice about a problem. *Human Communication Research, 26,* 234–263.

Harriman, L. (1983). Personal and marital changes accompanying parenthood. *Family Relations, 32,* 387–394.

Heider, F. (1958). *The psychology of interpersonal relations.* New York: John Wiley.

Imber-Black, E., & Roberts, J. (1992). *Rituals for our times: Celebrating, healing, and changing our lives and our relationships.* New York: Harper Perennial.

Jourard, S. (1970). *The transparent self.* New York: VanNostrand.

Knapp, M., Stohl, C., & Reardon, K. (1981). "Memorable" messages. *Journal of Communication, 31,* 27–41.

Lazarus, R. S., & Folkman, S. (1984). *Stress, appraisal, and coping.* New York: Springer.

MacGeorge, E., Feng, B., Butler, G., & Budarz, S. K. (2004). Understanding advice in supportive interactions: Beyond the facework and message evaluation paradigm. *Human Communication Research, 30,* 42–70.

MacGeorge, E. L., Lichtman, R. M., & Pressey, L. C. (2002). The evaluation of advice in supportive interactions: Facework and contextual factors. *Human Communication Research, 28,* 451–463.

Mehrabian, A. (1992). Interrelationships among name desirability, name uniqueness, emotion characteristics connoted by names, and temperament. *Journal of Applied Social Psychology, 22,* 1797–1808.

Miller, L. C., Berg, J. H., & Archer, R. L. (1983). Openers: Individuals who elicit intimate self-disclosures. *Journal of Personality and Social Psychology, 44,* 1234–1244.

Norbeck, J. S., & Tilden, V. P. (1983). Life stress, social support, and emotional disequilibrium in complications of pregnancy: A prospective, multivariate study. *Journal of Health and Social Behavior, 24,* 30–46.

Norton, R., & Montgomery, B. M. (1982). Style, content, and target components of openness. *Communication Research, 9,* 399–431.

Pennebaker, J. W. (1990). *Opening up: The healing power of confiding in others.* New York: Avon.

Peters-Golden, H. (1982). Breast cancer: Varied perceptions of social support in the illness experience. *Social Science and Medicine, 16,* 483–491.

Peterson, E. E. (1987). The stories of pregnancy: On interpretation of small group cultures. *Communication Quarterly, 35,* 39–47.

Petronio, S. (1991). Communication boundary management: A theoretical model of managing disclosure of private information between marital couples. *Communication Theory, 1,* 311–335.

Petronio, S. (1994). Privacy binds in family interactions: The case of parental privacy invasion. In W. R. Cupach & B. H. Spitzberg (Eds.), *The dark side of interpersonal relationships* (pp. 241–258). Mahwah, NJ: Lawrence Erlbaum.

Petronio, S. (2000a). The boundaries of privacy: Praxis of everyday life. In S. Petronio (Ed.), *Balancing the secrets of private disclosures* (pp. 37–49). Mahwah, NJ: Lawrence Erlbaum.

Petronio, S. (2000b). A disclosure confidant: Being reluctant to listen. In A. C. Richards & T. Schumrum (Eds.), *Invitations to dialogue: The legacy of Sidney Jourard* (pp. 113–132). Dubuque, IA: Kendall/Hunt.

Petronio, S. (2002). *Boundaries of privacy: Dialectics of disclosure.* New York: SUNY Press.

Petronio, S., Jones, S., & Morr, M. C. (2003). Family privacy dilemmas: Managing communication boundaries within family groups. In L. Frey (Ed.), *Group communication in contexts: Studies of bona fide groups* (pp. 23–56). Mahwah, NJ: Lawrence Erlbaum.

Rawlins, W. K. (1983). Openness as problematic in ongoing friendships: Two conversational dilemmas. *Communication Monographs, 50,* 1–13.

Rosenfeld, L. B., Civikly, J. M., & Herron, J. R. (1979). Anatomical and psychological sex differences. In G. J. Chelune (Ed.), *Self-disclosure: Origins, patterns, and implementations of openness in interpersonal relationships* (pp. 80–109). San Francisco: Jossey-Bass.

Stern, M., & Bitsko, M. J. (2003). Pregnancy, childbirth, and postpartum outcomes: Selected issues and implications for counseling interventions. In M. Kopala & M. A. Keitel (Eds.), *Handbook of counseling women* (pp. 256–265). Thousand Oaks, CA: Sage.

Thompson, K. A., Parahoo, K. P., McCurry, N., O'Doherty, E., & Doherty, A. M. (2004). Women's perceptions of support from partners, family members, and close friends for smoking cessation during pregnancy: Combining quantitative and qualitative findings. *Health Education Research, 19,* 29–39.

Winer, D. L., Bonner, T. O., Blaney, P. H., & Murray, E. J. (1981). Depression and social attraction. *Motivation and Emotion, 5,* 153–166.

Zacharia, R. (2004). Attachment, social support, life stress, and psychological well-being in pregnant low-income women: A pilot study. *Clinical Excellence for Nurse Practitioners, 8,* 60–62.

CHAPTER 12

Orchestrating and Directing Domestic Potential Through Communication

Toward a Positive Reframing of "Discipline"

Thomas J. Socha

Old Dominion University

E ach generation develops its own meanings for concepts such as "children," "caregivers," and "caring relationships." These meanings are informed by traditions, personal memories and experiences, and societal discourse encountered in relationships and exposure to media. Developmental psychology and education continue to figure large in societal discourse about childhood and child care practices (James, Jenks, & Prout, 1998). But scholars, recognizing the need for more comprehensive images and broader understandings of childhood (Lamb & Hwang, 1996), are now opening doors to other fields, not only to better understand today's children but also to develop child care practices that best fit contemporary circumstances. As research lenses on childhood widen, communication comes into focus as an essential factor in developing theories concerning children and child care practices (Socha & Yingling, 2005), including theories about the enduring topic of discipline.

In this chapter, I review inherited understandings of discipline in U.S. families, from the vantage point of the communication field. Then, based on this analysis and a brief look at contemporary scholarship, I propose alternative conceptual ground in which to replant communication theorizing and research about discipline. Specifically, I draw on Safilios-Rothschild's (1970, 1975) theory of family power, the recent positive psychology movement (e.g., McDermott & Hastings, 2000; Snyder, 2000), and communication scholarship, including relational communication (e.g., Rogers, 2001, 2004), regulative communication (e.g., Wilson, Cameron, & Whipple, 1997; Wilson & Morgan, 2004; see also Chapter 13, this volume), constructivist theory (e.g., Applegate, Burke, Burleson, Delia, & Kline, 1985), applied family communication (e.g., Socha, in press), and developmental communication (e.g., Haslett & Samter, 1997; Socha & Yingling, 2005; Yingling, 2004). Using these sources and others, I propose that family communication studies move away from the previously narrow and negative conceptual framing of discipline (e.g., a process of getting children to do what adults want them to do) toward a broader, more positive framing of how communication *orchestrates and directs children's potential*. The chapter concludes by considering some implications of this alternative framing not only for the study of family communication but also for communication across the life span.

Inherited Understandings

Discipline and Domestic Authority

Historically, in U.S. families, the concept of discipline typically refers to a social process taking place between family members of unequal strength or power (e.g., Sennett, 1980, pp. 17–18)—between adult family members (parents or parent-designates) and child family members (family participants who have yet to reach adulthood) and, less so today, between husbands and wives (Morgan, 1952). Relationships of unequal strength provide a sociocultural context that encourages discipline enactments. The strong discipline the weak: Parents are expected to discipline children, and superiors discipline subordinates, but not the other way around. Relationships of equal strength and power inhibit discipline's enactment. Equals do not use discipline; they persuade, rely on self-discipline, and so on.

Past research on discipline traditions in families tends to focus on the qualities and messages of strong family participants, or those in authority, and far less on those of weaker family participants or their interactions (e.g., for reviews in communication, see Prusank, 1995; Wilson & Morgan, 2004; Wilson & Whipple, 1995; in sociology, see Cromwell & Olson, 1975; Scanzoni & Szinovacz, 1980; and for a study of children's perceptions of family power, see Kahn & Meyer, 2001). This situation is changing, however, due in part to evolving conceptualizations of children, caregivers, and caregiving authority, as well as concern about abuse of domestic authority that results in physical and psychological injury to children (e.g., see Wilson, 2002; Wilson & Whipple, 1995, 2001).

According to Sennett (1980), an "authority" is someone "who has strength and uses it to guide others through disciplining them . . . [that is], changing how they act by reference to a higher standard" (p. 17). Authorities' interpretations of what a higher standard means hold sway with those of lesser power. Sennett reminds us that the concepts of "authority" and "strength" do not mean the same thing— authorities can vary in strength—and there is an important duality concerning authority. "In English the root of authority is 'author'; the connotation is that authority involves something productive. Yet the word 'authoritarian' is used to describe a person or system which is repressive" (p. 18). Referring to family, Sennett cautions that "the integrity of the parent who inspires fear and awe in its children . . . is very much open to question. For the strength which gives these figures authority may not be used in service of a higher ideal or of nurturing the subjects, but simply of dominating them" (p. 19).

Historically, society plays a significant role in granting domestic authority and shaping domestic authorities' interpretations and practices. This includes granting legitimacy to child care agents and child care practices (in accordance with societal norms and customs). Traditionally, until the late 20th century, U.S. society granted primary domestic authority to adult married males (heads of household) and ultimately held them responsible for the character of the family (Sennett, 1980). Should a head of household somehow fail, domestic authority was then claimed, in loco parentis, by other societal institutions (jails, orphanages, etc.). According to Sennett (1980), in loco parentis (in the place of parents) is a key conceptual mechanism though which society extended child care authority outside the home and also allowed societal input into domestic child care practices. Sennett states,

> The "reforming" character [of institutions outside the family] was thought necessary because the original formation of the family had failed [some citizens]; it was for this reason that in the 19th Century asylums, workhouses, and prisons claimed for themselves the formal rights in loco parentis. This concept . . . is based on the . . . assumptions [that] there are certain moral diseases which the normal family is too weak to cope with: insanity, sexual perversion, and the like. There are other diseases which the normal family, especially the normal poor family, causes: indolence, despairing alcoholism, prostitution. (p. 58)

Heads of U.S. households were at liberty to extend domestic authority to their wives. And traditionally, most heads of household chose to do so in domains related to child care (e.g., children's socialization, education, and health care). Although this afforded women greater domestic authority, the final say still resided with the head of household (e.g., see Therborn, 2004, for a discussion of this in a global context).

Historically, relying on the doctrine of in loco parentis, society widened child care authority sharing far beyond the boundaries of home (e.g., to schools, day cares, summer camps, child welfare/protection agencies, churches, etc.) and granted institutions, including churches (e.g., see Greven, 1991) and the academy (e.g., see Sclafani, 2004), prominent roles in child care guidance and regulation. This practice is reflected in contemporary societal debates about the boundaries of parental authority, children's rights, and an expanding web of input into child care from day care workers, teachers, counselors, coaches, social workers, clergy, physicians, law enforcement officers, governmental agencies, and more. Of course, increased involvement from many participants increases potential for conflicts regarding meanings and practices that constitute "optimal" child care. The Web site of a children's hospital in Australia, for example, points out that expectations of parents, teachers, and health care providers thought to be shared, may differ:

> "Loco Parentis," meaning "in place of parents," describes the temporary guardianship that each undertakes whilst a child is at school. Nowadays the phrase "Duty of Care" has taken its place, however, the basic premise is the same and the definition of what constitutes "enough care" still remains somewhat grey especially when it involves children with a medical condition. Inevitably, an imbalance develops between the expectations of parents and teachers. (Royal Children's Hospital–Melbourne, 2004)

Included among these differing, sometimes conflicting, viewpoints are historical differences between men's and women's understandings of children and approaches to child care.

Paternal Authority

Although there are many ways historical domestic power differences between men and women might be understood, Safilios-Rothschild (1970, 1975) interpreted the distinction in terms of two domains of power. Specifically, she argued that traditional husbands wielded "orchestration power"—they created the terms or conditions of authority and granted wives "implementation power"—the power to act on directives within authority conditions set by them. Socha (1989) supported this theory when he found, for example, that some husbands orchestrated family decision making by reserving the right to pick and choose the decisions in which they would participate. Socha found significant differences between wives' and husbands' relative degrees of interest in participating in family decision making across 50 topic areas. Wives wanted a say in almost all domestic decisions, whereas husbands were relatively less interested, only wanting a greater relative say than wives in a few selected decision topics. Specifically, and consistent with the historical notion of head of household, husbands in this sample expressed a relatively greater desire than wives to have a say in the disciplining of children (Socha, 1989).

Histories of fatherhood shed additional light on inherited understandings and practices of discipline (e.g., see Miller, 2003; Nelson, 1995; Sardoff, 1982, for historical discussions). Sennett's (1980) discussion of "patriarchy," "partrimonialism," and "paternalism" offers a framework of how male authority has been understood in society and at home. First, "a patriarchy is a society in which all people are *consciously* related by blood ties . . . [where] males are the linchpins. They decide who marries whom, property passes through male lines, and so on" (p. 52). Second, in "a patrimonial society . . . property passes from generation to generation through male relatives [such as] from eldest male of one generation to the next" (p. 52). Although referring to Japanese families (past and present), Sennett noted that "even when males of different generations were in fact not related by blood, they acted as though they were" (p. 53). Finally, according to Sennett,

> Paternalism differs from patrimonialism in the most basic way: the patrimony itself does not exist. Property no longer passes legally from father to son ... nor does society guarantee that the position held by a person of one generation will be held by a person from the next. . . . In a paternalistic society, males continue to dominate. The domination is based on their roles as fathers: protectors, stern judges, the strong. But the basis is symbolic rather than material as in a patrimonial order. (pp. 53–54)

Sennett (1980) also offered a developmental framing of authority that illustrated how male children take what they learn about authority from their fathers into society as adult workers and later as fathers (e.g., see DeMeo, 2003, for a memoir of a mafia boss's son). Although Sennett points out that what is learned about authority from a father is not the same as what is learned from an employer, "as every human passes out of the family into which he or she was born, that human sees these [authority] relationships reflected in work or politics as in a distorting mirror" (p. 54). Thus, although learning about what authority means is a developmental process, distinctions need to be drawn between sources of learning and how individuals' conceptions of authority and models of authority change via interaction and individual development.

Maternal Authority

Each generation of women also develops understandings of child care, child care practices, and domestic authority (e.g., see Daly & Reddy, 1991; Hrdy, 1999), albeit in the context of patriarchy. Gilligan (e.g., Gilligan, 1982; Gilligan, Ward, Taylor, & Bardige, 1988), Ong (1981), and others have written about women's societal understandings and practices that stand in contrast to men's. For example, according to Gilligan (1982), women's ethic of care, or responsibility orientation, contrasts with men's ethic of equal rights, or justice orientation. Both of these points of view can potentially shape attitudes toward child care and interaction with children. For example, holding an ethic of care may inhibit mothers' tendencies to engage in discipline that could result in physical harm to a child but rather may promote strategies that feature dialogue, care, and support. Ong echoed this notion when he contrasted females' and males' traditional notions of contest. Specifically, Ong pointed out that males of all animal species engage in episodes of ceremonial combat typically using brute force to establish dominance, whereas women's understandings of contest are qualitatively different (e.g., more subtle, avoiding use of brute force, favoring interaction-based, cooperative strategies).

Daniel and Daniel (1999), however, remind us that maternal and paternal domestic authority practices are cultural constructions and often differ across cultures. For example, African American caregivers, particularly African American mothers, discipline by relying on what Daniel and Daniel label the "imperative mode" (pp. 30–35) and enact behaviors that seem harsh to Whites. This does not mean that they do not care, but rather they find themselves and their children in "extremely dangerous environments, [where] effective parents are likely to be stricter but remain warm and caring" (Masten & Coatsworth, 1998, p. 215). African American culture also leans toward collectivistic values that privilege advancement of the group over the individual as well as communal structures for child care as shared family activity (e.g., see Socha & Diggs, 1999).

Authority Messages

Parallels can be seen in histories of paternal and maternal authority and in research on messages that parents use to "discipline" children. Baumrind (1971, 1980, 1996) wrote about authoritarian (low responsiveness), authoritative (high responsiveness and high demandingness), and permissive (low demandingness) parental patterns. Hoffman (1980) described three forms of discipline that include power assertion, induction, and love withdrawal. Bernstein (1974) focused on restricted codes (used by authoritarian parents) and elaborated codes (used by authoritative parents). And Applegate and colleagues (Applegate, Burleson, & Delia, 1992; Applegate et al., 1985; Burleson, Delia, & Applegate, 1992) developed a six-level message hierarchy ranging from strategies that discourage children's reflection to those that encourage detailed reflection about the potential effects of their behavior, as well as how to handle problematic situations. Wilson and Morgan (2004) insightfully noted that although there seem to be two camps when it comes to conceptualizing discipline (i.e., power assertive parents [paralleling paternal traditions] and parents who discuss and reason with their children [paralleling maternal traditions]), the reality is that mothers and fathers use a mixture of styles and sequencing that can vary depending on circumstances. Furthermore, Wilson (2002) and Wilson and Morgan (2004) suggest that researchers interested in studying influence in families, including discipline, consider politeness theory (Brown & Levinson, 1987). Although families are often far from "polite" as they interact (e.g., for a review, see Fitzpatrick & Winke, 1979; Miller, 2003), Wilson argues that positive face (esteem needs) and negative face (autonomy needs) are important dimensions shaping interaction in general as well as interaction that seeks to bring about and resist change.

Summary

Although admittedly selective and abbreviated, this review highlights a few threads of inherited tradition in the complex tapestry of contemporary domestic discipline. Specifically, the historical threads include males as heads-of-households, males as orchestrators of family authority, males distancing themselves from child care by delegating it to wives, males relying on brute force, family governance by paternalism, and women left alone to shoulder child caregiving authority and its burden. These historical threads are interwoven with contemporary threads of changing models of women's and men's domestic authority, evolving familial roles, and societal discourse about child care that is informed by research and disseminated by mass media.

Among contemporary threads are individuals' personal experiences of parental "authority," including positive models as well as negative ones that feature the abuse of parental authority (see Chapter 13, this volume). Among these negative experiences is the use of physical force that results not only in injury (physical, psychological, relational, etc.) but also sometimes in death (National Clearinghouse on Abuse and Neglect Information, 2004). Furthermore, physical child abuse may precipitate long-term developmental impairment realized later on in adult parenthood (e.g., Duncan, 2004; Kendall-Tackett, 2003).

Prusank (1995) pointed out and Wilson (2002) affirmed that communication scholars are newcomers to the topic of discipline. However, communication holds great promise in bringing a fresh understanding to contemporary caregiving. In particular, communication studies can shed light on how parents and children manage mismatches between contemporary understandings and practices of child care, on one hand, and the varied and often negative threads of inherited traditions, on the other. Thus, before communication research about discipline in domestic contexts continues, it is worth reflecting on the utility that the concept of discipline holds for communication theorizing.

A Turn Onto a Positive and Wider Road

Wilson and Morgan (2004) advanced the study of discipline by widening the concept to persuasion. I see at least six theoretical advantages to such a move. First, "family realities" are created through daily interaction, and contemporary families—who favor democratic models of domestic governance—must rely on persuasion. Second, no matter what their model of family governance, all family participants, adults and children alike, engage in persuasion. Third, persuasion is a developmental communication activity that is first learned and practiced in the context of home and family and later employed in other contexts. Fourth, children are active participants in family processes and not simply passive receivers; there is mutual and reciprocal influence between and among adults and children in family systems. Fifth, the term *persuading* has a more positive connotation than the term *disciplining*. And sixth, existing theories of persuasion might profitably be extended to explain persuasion in the context of homes and families.

Wilson and Morgan (2004) also posed three questions for future communication studies, all of which also widen "discipline's" historically narrow frame:

What attributes do husbands and wives, mothers and fathers, sons and daughters, stepparents and stepchildren, grandmothers and grandfathers, and so forth desire to be seen as possessing in the eyes of other family members? What rights and obligations do these roles entail in various cultures? How do family members negotiate levels of power and distance in their family and in what ways do persuasive appeals both reflect and reinforce/challenge existing levels? (pp. 465–466)

However, conceptualizing discipline as persuasion might not quite capture the many and varied levels and kinds of influence taking place within families. That is, as broad as the concept of persuasion is, it, too, is one communication process among many (e.g., informing, comforting, disclosing) that comprises how families enact discipline. What is needed is a conceptual framework that also takes into account that families use various kinds of communication processes in service of family governance, including structural elements (e.g., family roles and rules) as well as functional ones (e.g., persuading, informing, comforting). Also, family groups and their members seek to accomplish many kinds of goals (e.g., socialization of the young, companionship, economic support) and use communication in many ways to shape behaviors (theirs and others) to reach these goals. They sometimes act alone, sometimes as dyads, and sometimes as a group or network. To move toward a better understanding of how family participants blend and shape the varied and sometimes dissonant voices of family participants into desired patterns, I borrow a metaphor from music performance.

Domestic Orchestration

Metaphorically, running a family is like running a symphony orchestra. For example, those who run families and orchestras plan some of their primary activities. Those running orchestras plan the season's performance events, while those who run families plan the year's family events (holidays, vacations, etc.). Second, they both create policies that govern their participants' choices and actions. Orchestras typically use a policy of blind auditioning to determine who will occupy a particular instrumental chair. Families create policies based on individual qualities and traditions to determine who will sit where at a family meal. In my family-of-origin, for example, as a matter of policy, our senior matriarch (my maternal grandmother, Mae) brings a gelatin mold to a family gathering or, at her discretion, passes the honor to a younger female (my mother, Mary). And third, those who run orchestras oversee rehearsals or practices designed to improve the orchestra's performance. And although we might not immediately think that families "practice" (or rehearse) their typical activities, families do hold wedding rehearsals and wedding rehearsal dinners. And for children, in theory every family event is in part a rehearsal for future events— as parents engage in parenting, they are teaching parenting by example.

Safilios-Rothschild's (1970, 1975) notion of orchestration power—that is, power at the level of planning, policy making, oversight of practicing, and so on— illustrates family governance taking place at a structural level; that is, domestic orchestrators shape and assist in the realization of domestic family life by means of structures such as plans, policies, and practices. Poole, Seibold, and McPhee's (1986) structuration theory, for example, is useful here, as it explains how and why group behaviors become structured or how group participants use rules and resources to order their activities. Structures enable participants to perform certain behaviors, inhibit them from performing others, and assist them as they make decisions about how to behave in a group.

Domestic orchestration is a complex activity. Extending Powers's (1995) tier model of the field of communication to family systems, we find that domestic orchestration involves at least four layers requiring management: (a) family messages, (b) family factors (participants, social and cultural factors), (c) family levels (family relationships, family group, family network), and (d) family episodes (e.g., decision making, entertaining). For example, orchestrating a "family dinner" means, first, thinking about the kinds of topics for dinner discussion, permissible language choices, and so on. Second, it involves managing individual communication differences among participants (e.g., young children's temperaments, social factors such as varied communication goals) and cultural communication factors (e.g., whether children participate with adults or sit at a separate children's table). Third, dinner orchestration also means keeping in mind the dynamics of family relationships, as well as the family "ensemble" or group. For example, are the sister and her husband, who do not drink alcohol, offended by an uncle's detailed lesson to the family about how to mix the perfect adult beverage? Is the unmarried aunt, who dislikes children, going to say something offensive when the youngest child—who takes forever to tell a story—relays how he got his latest boo-boo? And fourth, is the family accomplishing its many chosen activities during the meal in ways that meet their standards? Are they learning about family members' activities, hearing good news, sharing laughter, and so on?

Some family activities are *consciously orchestrated,* like the command performances of the world's greatest orchestras. However, based on my experiences and observations, more often typical family activities occur with little or no conscious orchestration—running instead on family autopilot (e.g., see Langer, 1997) as families repeat previously orchestrated and long-practiced routines. Conscious orchestration (planning, policy making, practicing, etc.) may precede some episodes, such as expressing enduring love in early married life, but as time passes, it seems that whatever practice "works" is kept, repeated, and continued. In this sense, domestic orchestration interactions would seem likely to occur at points when family participants become aware that something no longer "works," is no longer desired, or is perceived to be in need of reorchestration for whatever reason. Of course, differences in domestic orchestration among family participants may also result in conflict, particularly in situations that require a unified orchestral vision (e.g., a wedding) and/or where family participants might be vying for family orchestral authority.

In sum, running a family, like running an orchestra, involves structural work (macro level) such as planning, policy making, and practicing. However, after the music is chosen and rehearsals begin, participants require direction, or in terms of Safilios-Rothschild's theory, implementation power needs to be awarded to participants who will do the ground-level work necessary to realize the group's larger goals. This turns our attention toward orchestration's companion process: *direction.*

Domestic Direction

Orchestral directors, much like athletic coaches, teachers, and parents, wear multiple hats. They not only orchestrate (plan, make policy, and practice) but also provide *direction* to realize their vision (i.e., they conduct). "Direction" implies understanding of a goal(s) and having a sense of the various ways to go about managing factors that facilitate or inhibit moving toward the goal(s). Again using Safilios-Rothschild (1970, 1975), I interpret many of the previously mentioned lists of what has been labeled parental discipline messages or styles (e.g., Applegate et al., 1985) as forms of "direction" (or conducting). Adler (1984) used a related term *coaching* to describe complex directorial activities meant to increase participants' understandings, as well as motivate participants to execute a behavior or sequence of behaviors in a desired fashion. Coaching is "hands-on" as well as informational. For example, during orchestra rehearsal, conductors, like coaches, seek to bring out the best in their players by motivating and modifying performances; in short, they "direct" the behavior of their charges. Similarly, those overseeing families seek to bring out the best from family participants as they direct their behaviors.

The parallels between the literature about "parenting" and the literature about "leading" (or directing) groups are striking. For example, comparing Lewin, Lippitt, and White's (1939) study of young boys' experiences of autocratic, democratic, and laissez-faire "leading" styles with Baumrind's (1971) study of authoritarian, authoritative, and laissez-faire "parenting" styles reveals obvious similarities. Both democratic leaders and authoritative parents rely on information, discussion, negotiation, and so forth. Socha (2003) further pointed out similarities between "parenting," "teaching," and "leading," particularly when these processes are thought about along a developmental continuum—"parenting" creates a scaffold for later formal school "teaching," upon which "leading" in business and industry is later built. Furthermore, a focus of leadership studies since the early 1970s has been on the "locus of leadership" (Shaw, 1981) or the dynamic interplay of leaders, followers, and situations or, in the context of families, the intersection of parents, children, and family life.

Summary

Studying communication in service of domestic orchestration and direction, rather than discipline, not only sets a positive tone for future inquiry but also suggests additional avenues for theorizing. For example, Rogers's (e.g., Rogers, 2001, 2004) work on relational control and support messages (one-up, one-down, one-across moves) represents a useful way of thinking about "directing" (as leading-following) across many family communication functions across the life span. Wilson and Morgan (2004) remind us of the importance of face management in domestic governance (i.e., the orchestration and direction of family life). That is, as family participants orchestrate and direct domestic life, all family participants, especially children, desire to be prized, loved, and valued (e.g., see Satir, 1972). The uses of direction-messages that demean, hurt, or threaten positive face are not only unlikely to be effective but can damage relationships and undermine family orchestrations. Adult caregivers are supposed to assist and support their charges to, paraphrasing Sennett (1980), aspire to and achieve higher standards or, in musical parlance, to create beautiful music together.

Families Orchestrate and Direct Potential

If parents are asked why they "discipline" children, they may respond as follows: "To teach them how to behave and follow the rules," "So that they grow up to be good citizens," "So that they learn to listen and do what they are told," or "So that I don't have to bail them out of jail later on." These outcomes are desirable, but they are also framed negatively—discipline is something that is necessary to prevent "bad" things from happening. Alternatively, a more positive way to frame these goals would be to say that parents are seeking to facilitate children's *potential.* Writings in the emerging paradigm of positive psychology (e.g., McDermott & Hastings, 2000) draw our attention to the vital role of parental communication in facilitating positive outcomes, not just preventing bad ones. According to Socha (in press), in previous studies of families, researchers

neglected to add a positive endpoint to the "functional/dysfunctional" dichotomy, making it *optimal*/functional/dysfunctional, or *nurturing*/non-abusive/abusive, *peaceful*/non-violent/violent, and so on. Adding positive endpoints leads applied family communication researchers away from the "solving problems" towards, for instance, identifying family communication strengths and studying the role of family communication in augmenting *changeable* family inputs, such as individuals' capacities for positive emotions such as compassion, forgiveness, empathy, altruism, spirituality, self-esteem, and hope, as well as moving communication processes beyond "competent/incompetent" to, for instance, expert/competent/developing, elegant/polite/ crude, and stunning/typical/unremarkable.

The omission of a positive framing neglects a key concept that lies at the heart of family life. Specifically, "family" is a societal agency charged with facilitating the potential of its members (potentials that include economic, educational, emotional, psychological, relational, etc.). And adult caregivers (family members and outsiders) orchestrate and direct children's potential using communication. Let's consider a hypothetical example to illustrate the promise of reframing discipline as the orchestration and direction of children's potential.

The Joneses, a family of four—Mom, Dad, Alice (age 9), and Freddy (age 4)—sit down to an evening meal that Dad prepared. Dad wanted to surprise Mom with an elegant meal using their best china, crystal glasses, and candles. The meal features squab, vegetable medley, risotto, and crème brûlée for dessert, accompanied by an Oregon pinot noir for the adults and sparkling cider for the children. Earlier, Dad said to Freddy, "Son, we are using the good dishes tonight for dinner, and I expect you to be on your best behavior during dinner." Turning to Alice, he said, "And the same goes for you," to which she rolled her eyes. Mom arrives home. They sit down to eat, and Freddy gestures to his sister, waving his arms. Dad glares at Freddy as a way to remind him to "behave." Two minutes into the meal, Freddy again gestures wildly toward his sister but this time he knocks over the remaining half bottle of pinot noir onto the table, turning the white tablecloth, risotto, and squab, red. The family is silent.

How might this situation be understood from the different vantage points of the family participants? What should be said and done next? How should the Joneses manage this situation? What are their message options? What are the implications of their potential messages? Many will say that Freddy should be "punished" or disciplined by his parents. Some will add that the punishment should be somewhat severe, maybe include spanking, possibly accompanied by intense, threatening language. Others may recommend punishing Freddy by taking away something that Freddy likes to do for a period of time. Still others may say that the parents should say, "Accidents happen, kids will be kids," while cleaning up the mess after excusing the children from the table. There are endless possibilities and combinations of possibilities.

From the point of view of *orchestrating and directing potential,* how might this situation be managed? First, orchestration would have started *prior to embarking on meal preparation;* Dad should ask himself, "How best might I orchestrate a 'nice' dinner for my wife?" What are the goals of this "nice" meal? What should be accomplished by this "nice" meal? Should this include the children? Or, should a romantic late-night snack for two be orchestrated instead? If the children are included in dinner, Dad should wonder how best to envision this. As tempting as china and crystal might be, some rehearsal might be needed with a 4-year-old in using fine dishware as well as practicing fine-dining behaviors. How should Freddy act? What do people participating in polite, fine dining look like? Will big sister participate and help Freddy in reaching his potential as a fine diner? Or will she inhibit their fine-dining potential? How should Freddy and his sister, as well as Dad, dress for dinner? Will Freddy really eat squab? What if Freddy, Alice, Dad, and/or Mom arrive at the meal after experiencing a poor day? How might this unexpected situation be managed so as to realize the goals of the meal? What might help Freddy and his sister meet the challenges of fine dining at home? Is Dad asking too much?

In my experience as a parent and observer of children, optimal domestic outcomes can be orchestrated with children of varied ages, but thought is necessary about the specific needs, understandings, and developmental levels of children participants. For example, orchestrating a "quick stop" with hungry children into a local grocery store during the dinner hour can turn out favorably if the children are given a snack prior to heading out, accompanied by an explanation as to why the trip is needed. Orchestrating episodes from "quick trips" to the grocery store to elegant dinners and so on can increase the chances that family aims will be accomplished, and children will require fewer messages to re-redirect their behavior: Good orchestration and some practice will help to show them optimal ways to conduct themselves.

To further show the benefits of a positive ontology of family governance, let's apply one of the emerging positive psychology theories, Snyder's (2000) hope theory, to the spilled wine example. According to Snyder, cultivating high hope involves supporting two kinds of thinking: agentic thinking (i.e., I am a good and capable person, worthy of reaching my goals) and pathways thinking (i.e., I can envision ways to manage the inevitable obstacles inhibiting goal attainment). In this example, to cultivate high hope, messages directed to Freddy and the family should be designed to enhance self-images and show how to manage obstacles. Thus, similar to positive face in politeness theory (Brown & Levinson, 1987), in hope theory, messages that remind and acknowledge that Freddy is a "good person," explain that everyone makes mistakes, and teach Freddy ways to manage mistakes will have a better chance of creating "hope." Messages that damage Freddy's self-image, link his mistakes to "bad" personality qualities, and/or fail to coach Freddy in ways to fix his mistakes may diminish agentic and pathways thinking and reduce Freddy's hopefulness. A positive, hopeful message in the spilled wine situation might be something like the following: "Freddy, I know you are capable of more controlled behavior at the dinner table. It is unfortunate that your gesture spilled the wine and damaged dinner. We will help you figure out what needs to be done to make things right: We need to clean things up, think about how to get the family fed, and make the family feel better about things, and then we will coach you to help make this situation less likely to happen during our next dinner." Some will undoubtedly say that this message is unrealistic, "unnatural," and, of course, easy to write when not in the heat of the moment. I agree but also add that if "Dad," "Mom," or any parent has these kinds of messages rehearsed and handy, he or she might be less likely to overreact but rather use rehearsed messages to orchestrate and direct the children's potential, even in stressful circumstances. There is potential for learning even when things "look bad."

Among the important upsides of *orchestrating and directing potential* is that it reinforces a conscious, prosocial model of interaction that children can take forward into future episodes during childhood and later as parents. Many can remember their parents' discipline messages vividly, and some can provide Oscar-caliber performances of what their parents might say and do in a spilled wine scene.

Second, facilitation of potential is a theme that applies to all interaction and can help redirect thoughts and energies into positive avenues. What kinds of potentialities are enhanced or diminished by any given message? In the spilled wine example, a parent who yells insults at the child and cleans up the mess alone at the very least misses an opportunity to further the development of the child's agentic and pathways thinking and, worse, may diminish a child's interaction potential (in the short term and possibly long term). Socha (in press) framed families as agencies of potential and caregivers as society's agents of potential.

Although the idea of orchestrating and directing interaction within the theme of facilitating potential is new, an example of what such an endeavor might look like can be found in Nancy Cecil's (1995) book, *Raising Peaceful Children in a Violent World.* Cecil systematically orchestrates the theme of "peace" into communication, entertainment, and relationships by informing and coaching. In her chapter on "peace-compatible discipline," Cecil wrote, "Discipline is probably the most challenging facet of non-violent child-rearing. As parents we have all felt the frustration of trying to balance affirmation and correction, freedom and structure, and the uncertainty of wondering if we have made the mixture effective for our children" (p. 93). Cecil's approach to discipline is "preventative . . . whole family . . . and problem-solving [oriented]" (p. 97). She orchestrates and directs peace comprehensively into conversation, literature, film, and TV, including how to confront violence using peaceful strategies. A similar approach can be taken to integrate "potential" into family interactions.

Conclusion

The idea of orchestrating and directing domestic potential of course requires a great deal of further thought and study but does have advantages. First, a turn toward a positive ontology highlights the need to study how communication facilitates the bright sides (as opposed to the dark sides) of family relationships. Focusing on preventing problems, augmenting family resources (knowledge, skills, etc.), empowering family participants by advancing their skills (communication, money, health care, etc.), and working toward positive outcomes (e.g., laughing more) create hope and can increase a family's resiliency as family members manage their inevitable problems.

Second, a positive turn reminds us that all messages, especially those shared at home, have developmental implications. By consciously focusing on the concept of "potential" in messages, we are adding what could be a useful element to family communication theorizing. That is, if a primary job of families is to facilitate the potential of its members (e.g., help children become economically successful as adults), then the role of messages in facilitating and diminishing potential requires study (e.g., How does a family's messages about money facilitate or inhibit children's economic potential?).

Third, orchestration and direction of potential occur across the life span but also may occur in unique ways at various stages of development as well as in various contexts. Studies are needed of the continuities and discontinuities in orchestrating and directing potential across the life span from early childhood through later adulthood. When we think of potential, we tend to think about children, but potential exists across the life span—there is always something to be learned (and it is never too late to learn it).

Fourth, a turn toward orchestration focuses the communication field's attention toward message planning. Outside the context of public speaking (which features conscious message orchestration), we do not know much about people's everyday message orchestration habits, especially in contexts such as homes and families where routines seem to dominate. For example, parents who may find that talking about sex with their children is uncomfortable may spend lots of time orchestrating "the talk," whereas those who feel more at ease with the topic may spend less time planning a single event and instead weave the topic more seamlessly into regular interaction. Providing parents with conversation starters (e.g., I was reading in the paper that teen pregnancy rates are declining. What you do you think about that?), for example, may prove effective for parents as they attempt to orchestrate uncomfortable interactions.

Fifth, the idea of practicing and rehearsing messages at home is also brought out by this positive turn, as well as the idea of learning from communication mistakes. We need to accept that communication learners make mistakes; they get things wrong; they mess up. However, by becoming conscious of communication mistakes and learning how to handle them, we can facilitate learning. My first band director, Mr. Golden, used to tell us that during rehearsals, he did not want us to hide our mistakes but instead to make them, loud and proud. Why? During rehearsals, Mr. Golden could help us to play better by directing us through our mistakes. In my home, we provide a way to acknowledge and correct communication mistakes using what I call "take-2." Similar to movie "takes," we welcome communication takes and offer "do overs" (many golfers call "do overs" mulligans). For example, if someone forgets and speaks a hurtful message, the receiver can say "take-2," meaning that he or she thinks a communication mistake was made and is giving a chance to try the message again. Most of the time, the communicator becomes conscious of the interaction, thinks about the message, and is given the gift of a chance to correct it (or not) and replay the scene. Instead of "punishing" for communication mistakes using a "discipline" approach, my wife and I try to prompt orchestration thinking and self-monitoring that might lead to more effective interactions. To my way of thinking, if "mulligans" are a staple of golf duffers (including me), why not allow for communicative mulligans at home? I think the idea has potential and is worth developing further.

In short, widening our thinking about discipline and adopting *orchestration and direction of potential* framing has potential. It may open new paths for theorizing and researching how people use communication in family life to facilitate development, warts and all.

References

Adler, M. J. (1984). *The paideia program: An educational syllabus.* New York: Macmillan.

Applegate, J. L., Burke, J. A., Burleson, B. R., Delia, J. G., & Kline, S. L. (1985). Reflection-enhancing parental communication. In I. E. Sigel (Ed.), *Parental belief systems: The psychological consequences for children* (pp. 107–142). Mahwah, NJ: Lawrence Erlbaum.

Applegate, J. L., Burleson, B. R., & Delia, J. G. (1992). Reflection-enhancing parental communication. In I. E. Sigel (Ed.), *Parental belief systems: The psychological consequences for children* (Vol. 2, pp. 3–39). Mahwah, NJ: Lawrence Erlbaum.

Baumrind, D. (1971). Current patterns of parental authority. *Developmental Psychology Monographs, 4*(1), 1–103.

Baumrind, D. (1980). New directions in socialization research. *American Psychologist, 35,* 639–652.

Baumrind, D. (1996). The discipline controversy revisited. *Family Relations, 45,* 405–411.

Bernstein, B. (1974). *Class, codes, and control* (2nd ed.). New York: Schocken.

Brown, P., & Levinson, S. C. (1987). *Politeness: Some universals in language use.* Cambridge, UK: Cambridge University Press.

Burleson, B. R., Delia, J. G., & Applegate, J. L. (1992). Effects of maternal communication and children's social-cognitive and communication skills on children's acceptance by the peer group. *Family Relations, 41,* 264–272.

Cecil, N. L. (1995). *Raising peaceful children in a violent world.* San Diego: LuraMedia.

Cromwell, R. E., & Olson, D. H. (Eds.). (1975). *Power in families.* Beverly Hills, CA: Sage.

Daly, B. O., & Reddy, M. T. (Eds.). (1991). *Narrating mothers: Theorizing maternal subjectivities.* Knoxville: University of Tennessee Press.

Daniel, J. L., & Daniel, J. E. (1999). African-American childrearing: The context of a hot stove. In T. J. Socha & R. C. Diggs (Eds.), *Communication, race, and family: Exploring communication in Black, White, and biracial families* (pp. 25–43). Mahwah, NJ: Lawrence Erlbaum.

DeMeo, A. (2003). *For the sins of my father: A mafia killer, his son, and the legacy of a mob life.* New York: Broadway.

Duncan, K. A. (2004). *Healing from childhood sexual abuse: The journey for women.* Westport, CT: Praeger.

Fitzpatrick, M. A., & Winke, J. (1979). You always hurt the one you love: Strategies and tactics in interpersonal conflict. *Communication Quarterly, 27,* 3–11.

Gilligan, C. (1982). *In a different voice: Psychological theory and women's development.* Cambridge, MA: Harvard University Press.

Gilligan, C., Ward, J. V., Taylor, J. M., & Bardige, B. (Eds.). (1988). *Mapping the moral domain: A contribution of women's thinking to psychological and educational theory.* Cambridge, MA: Harvard University Press.

Greven, P. J. (1991). *Spare the child: The religious roots of punishment and the psychological impact of physical abuse.* New York: Knopf.

Haslett, B., & Samter, W. (1997). *Children communicating: The first five years.* Mahwah, NJ: Lawrence Erlbaum.

Hoffman, M. L. (1980). Moral development in adolescence. In J. Adleson (Ed.), *Handbook of adolescent psychology* (pp. 295–343). New York: John Wiley.

Hrdy, S. B. (1999). *Mother nature: A history of mothers, infants, and natural selection.* New York: Pantheon.

James, A., Jenks, C., & Prout, A. (1998). *Theorizing childhood.* New York: Teachers College Press, Columbia University.

Kahn, J. S., & Meyer, J. T. (2001). Children's definitions of family power and cohesion affect scores on the family system test. *American Journal of Family Therapy, 29,* 141–154.

Kendall-Tackett, K. A. (2003). *Treating the lifetime health effects of childhood victimization.* Kingston, NJ: Civic Research Institute.

Lamb, M. E., & Hwang, C. P. (1996). Images of childhood: An introduction. In C. P. Hwang, M. Lamb, & I. E. Siegel (Eds.), *Images of childhood* (pp. 3–12). Mahwah, NJ: Lawrence Erlbaum.

Langer, E. (1997). *The power of mindful learning.* Reading, MA: Addison-Wesley.

Lewin, K., Lippitt, R., & White, R. K. (1939). Patterns of aggressive behavior in experimentally created "social climates." *Journal of Social Psychology, 10,* 271–299.

Masten, A. S., & Coatsworth, J. D. (1998). The development of competence in favorable and unfavorable environments: Lessons from research on successful children. *American Psychologist, 53,* 205–220.

McDermott, D., & Hastings, S. (2000). Children: Raising future hopes. In C. R. Snyder (Ed.), *Handbook of hope: Theory, measures, and applications* (pp. 185–199). San Diego: Academic Press.

Miller, D. L. (2003). *Dreams of the burning child: Sacrificial sons and the father's witness.* Ithaca, NY: Cornell University Press.

Morgan, E. S. (1952). *Virginians at home: Family life in the eighteenth century.* Williamsburg, VA: The Colonial Williamsburg Foundation.

National Clearinghouse on Abuse and Neglect Information. (2004). *Child abuse and neglect fatalities: Statistics and interventions.* Retrieved on December 20, 2004, from http://nccanch.acf.hhs.gov/pubs/factsheets/fatality.cfm

Nelson, C. (1995). *Invisible men: Fatherhood in Victorian periodicals 1850–1910.* Athens: University of Georgia Press.

Ong, W. (1981). *Fighting for life: Contest, sexuality, and consciousness.* Ithaca, NY: Cornell University Press.

Poole, M. S., Seibold, D. R., & McPhee, R. D. (1986). A structurational approach to theory building in group decision-making research. In R Y. Hirokawa & M. S. Poole (Eds.), *Communication and group decision-making* (pp. 237–264). Beverly Hills, CA: Sage.

Powers, J. H. (1995). On the intellectual structure of the human communication discipline. *Communication Education, 44,* 191–222.

Prusank, D. T. (1995). Studying parent-child discipline from a communication perspective. In T. J. Socha & G. H. Stamp (Eds.), *Parents, children and communication: Frontiers of theory and research* (pp. 249–271). Mahwah, NJ: Lawrence Erlbaum.

Rogers, L. E. (2001). Relational communication in the context of the family. *Journal of Family Communication, 1,* 25–35.

Rogers, L. E. (2004). The development of relational communication: A personal narrative. *Journal of Family Communication, 3/4,* 157–165.

Royal Children's Hospital–Melbourne. (2004). *Loco parentis: Managing diabetes at school.* Retrieved December 20, 2004, from http://www.rch.org.au/erc/video/index.cfm?doc_id=7431

Safilios-Rothschild, C. (1970). The study of family power structure 1960–1969. *Journal of Marriage and the Family, 32,* 539–552.

Safilios-Rothschild, C. (1975). A macro- and micro- examination of family power and love: An exchange model. *Journal of Marriage and the Family, 37,* 335–362.

Sardoff, D. F. (1982). *Monsters of affection: Dickens, Elliot, and Bronte on fatherhood.* Baltimore: Johns Hopkins University Press.

Satir, V. (1972). *Peoplemaking.* Palo Alto, CA: Science & Behavior Books.

Scanzoni, J. H., & Szinovacz, M. (1980). *Family decision making: A developmental sex roles model.* Beverly Hills, CA: Sage.

Sclafani, J. D. (2004). *The educated parent: Recent trends in raising children.* Westport, CT: Praeger.

Sennett, R. (1980). *Authority.* New York: Vintage.

Shaw, M. E. (1981). *Group dynamics: The psychology of small group behavior.* New York: McGraw-Hill.

Snyder, C. R. (Ed.). (2000). *Handbook of hope: Theory, measures, and applications.* San Diego: Academic Press.

Socha, T. J. (1989). Marital decision conversation: An investigation of decision topics and relational communication control and support structures. *Dissertation Abstracts International, 50*(4), 829A.

Socha, T. J. (2003, July). *How has the field of communication treated children?* A keynote address presented at the National Communication Association's Summer Faculty Development Institute, Luther College, Decorah, IA.

Socha, T. J. (in press). Family as agency of potential: Toward a positive, integrative model of applied family communication theory and research. In L. Frey & K. Cissna (Eds.), *Handbook of applied communication.* Mahwah, NJ: Lawrence Erlbaum.

Socha, T. J., & Diggs, R. (Eds.). (1999). *Communication, race, and family: Exploring communication in Black, White, and biracial families.* Mahwah, NJ: Lawrence Erlbaum.

Socha, T. J., & Yingling, J. A. (2005). *Children are communicators too: Towards a comprehensive, developmental view of communication.* Manuscript submitted for publication.

Therborn, G. (2004). *Between sex and power: Family in the world 1900–2000.* London: Routledge.

Wilson, S. R. (2002). *Seeking and resisting compliance: Why people say what they do when trying to influence others.* Thousand Oaks, CA: Sage.

Wilson, S. R., Cameron, K. A., & Whipple, E. E. (1997). Regulative communication strategies within mother-child interactions: Implications for the study of reflection-enhancing parental communication. *Research in Language and Social Interaction, 30,* 73–92.

Wilson, S. R., & Morgan, W. M. (2004). Persuasion and families. In A. Vangelisiti (Ed.), *Handbook of family communication* (pp. 447–471). Mahwah, NJ: Lawrence Erlbaum.

Wilson, S. R., & Whipple, E. E. (1995). Communication, discipline, and physical child abuse. In T. J. Socha & G. H. Stamp (Eds.), *Parents, children, and communication: Frontiers of theory and research* (pp. 299–317). Mahwah, NJ: Lawrence Erlbaum.

Wilson, S. R., & Whipple, E. E. (2001). Attributions and regulative communication by parents participating in a child abuse prevention program. In V. Manusov & J. H. Harvey (Eds.), *Attributions, communication behavior, and close relationships* (pp. 227–247). New York: Cambridge University Press.

Yingling, J. A. (2004). A *lifetime of communication: Transformations through relational dialogues.* Mahwah, NJ: Lawrence Erlbaum.

CHAPTER 13

Parental Physical Negative Touch and Child Noncompliance in Abusive, Neglectful, and Comparison Families

A Meta-Analysis of Observational Studies

Steven R. Wilson

Purdue University

Xiaowei Shi

Purdue University

Lisa Tirmenstein

Purdue University

Alda Norris

Purdue University

Jessica J. Rack

Purdue University

C hild abuse and neglect are serious, persistent social problems. In its most recent 50-state survey of Child Protective Services (CPS) agencies, Prevent Child Abuse America concluded that more than 1 million cases of child abuse and neglect were officially documented in the United States in 1999 (Peddle & Wang, 2001). These represent only officially documented cases, and nationally representative surveys of parents indicate that the actual prevalence of child physical abuse is much higher (e.g., Straus, Hamby, Finkelhor, Moore, & Runyan, 1998). An estimated 1,356 children died as a result of abuse or neglect in 2000, or nearly 4 children per day (Peddle, Wang, Diaz, & Reid, 2002). Aside from immediate risk of injury or death, abused and neglected children suffer from a host of psychological and behavioral problems, including low self-esteem and academic performance, poor interpersonal relationships, externalizing and/ or internalizing behavior, and juvenile delinquency (Hildyard & Wolfe, 2002; Kolko, 1996).

The etiology of child abuse and neglect is complex, with maltreatment arising from the interplay of individual-, family-, community-, and cultural-level factors (Belsky, 1993). Within this complex of factors, research on parent-child communication is critical for understanding and responding to child abuse and neglect. Child physical abuse is an interactional event. Parents do not strike their children at random but rather at predictable moments that arise out of larger interactions usually involving discipline (Crittenden, 1998; Reid, 1986; Wilson, 1999). Indeed, Reid (1986) asserts that "there is a growing body of evidence indicating that most child-abusive episodes represent direct escalations of discipline confrontations" (p. 240).

Child neglect pertains to deficits in providing for a child's basic needs, such as failing to provide adequate supervision. Neglect involves chronic situations that are less easily identified as specific episodes. Despite this, what Hildyard and Wolfe (2002) describe as the "hallmarks of neglect"—a "lack of parental care and nurturance"—clearly manifest through parent-child interaction. Hence, it is not surprising that a growing body of observational studies document patterns of parent-child interaction in abusive and, to a lesser extent, neglectful families (for narrative reviews, see Cerezo, 1997; Wilson, 1999; Wilson & Morgan, 2004).

This chapter presents a meta-analysis of observational studies that code for parental physical negative touch (PNT) and/or child noncompliance in abusive, neglectful, and comparison families. Parental PNT and child noncompliance are important behaviors for describing how disciplinary episodes can escalate to dangerous levels, and they also may be diagnostic of the overall quality of parent-child relationships. Our goals are to clarify the degree to which abusive, neglectful, and comparison families are distinguished by these two behaviors and to identify child, parent, or study characteristics that may qualify general conclusions. We review Reid's (1986) social-interactional view of child physical abuse to justify our predictions about parental PNT and child noncompliance in abusive families, explain why a meta-analysis of observational studies coding these behaviors is useful, and clarify our expectations regarding interaction in neglectful families.

A Social-Interactional View
of Child Physical Abuse

Reid (1986) offers a social-interactional explanation for the occurrence of child physical abuse. The basic premise is that instances of child physical abuse typically arise out of interactions in which parents are responding to what they perceive as child misbehavior. Physically abusive parents are thought to engage in inconsistent and ineffective attempts to gain their children's compliance and hence escalate their use and intensity of physical discipline more quickly than nonmaltreating parents. From this view, the

> probability of abuse is assumed to be a function of (1) the rate or number of discipline confrontations, and (2) the degree to which any discipline confrontation can be resolved quickly, without resort to physical aggression by the parent. (Reid, 1986, p. 239)

To assess this view, Reid and colleagues (e.g., Reid, 1986; Reid, Taplin, & Lorber, 1981) compare home interactions involving parents and children in families with a documented history of child physical abuse and sociodemographically matched nonmaltreating families. Using the Family Interaction Coding System (FICS), these researchers code all behaviors enacted by each family member at 6-second intervals into 29 behavior categories. Categories are then grouped into three larger clusters: positive behaviors (e.g., approval, laughter), neutral behaviors (e.g., nonthreatening commands), and aversive behaviors (e.g., disapproval, noncompliance). Within the 13 aversive categories, 4 are labeled "abusive" because of their negative intensity: physical negative touch, threatening commands, humiliation, and yelling.

Although the vast majority of parental and child behaviors in both abusive and nonmaltreating families are either positive or neutral, Reid (1986; Reid et al., 1981) shows that aversive behaviors occur more frequently in physically abusive as opposed to comparison families and that a larger percentage of the aversive behaviors enacted by physically abusive parents are intense. In addition, parents and children in abusive families are more likely to reciprocate each other's aversive behaviors and do so for longer periods and with quicker increases in behavioral intensity as compared to nonmaltreating families. As noted above, these findings are based on the FICS, which, like many other coding schemes, analyzes a large number of specific behaviors but then lumps them into three global clusters based on valence (positive, neutral, aversive). Findings from these studies offer a picture of the overall "tone" of interactions in abusive and comparison families but do not reveal how these families differ in terms of concrete things that might be said or done.

In this meta-analysis, we focus on two concrete behaviors that clearly have significance within the social-interactional view of child abuse: parental physical negative touch and child noncompliance. Parental PNT has been defined as "any physical touch that is intended to be antagonistic, aversive, hurtful, or restrictive of the . . . child's activity" (Borrego, Timmer, Urquiza, & Follette, 2004, p. 899). Examples of parental PNT include hitting, grabbing, slapping, spanking, or taking an object roughly from a child (Bousha & Twentyman, 1984; Koenig, Cicchetti, & Rogosch, 2000). Reid (1986) views escalation to physical aggression as an important turning point in any discipline interaction; hence, it is important to know to what degree and under what conditions physically abusive and comparison parents differ in their use of PNT during family interactions. Based on the social-interactional view, we expect that *physically abusive parents will enact PNT more frequently than nonmaltreating parents* (Hypothesis 1).

Child noncompliance typically is defined as a child's failure to obey, or begin obeying, a parent's command within a short time frame (e.g., 5 seconds; Borrego et al., 2004; Bousha & Twentyman, 1984). Children who are frequently noncompliant present their parents with a larger number of discipline episodes to manage. Sustained child noncompliance also extends the length of discipline episodes, making them more challenging for parents to resolve quickly. Based on the social-interactional view, we predict that *physically abused children will display higher rates of noncompliance in comparison to nonmaltreated children* (Hypothesis 2). Having explained our predictions regarding parental PNT and child noncompliance, we turn to our rationale.

Rationale for Meta-Analysis

Although the social-interactional view suggests that rates of parental PNT and child noncompliance should be higher in physically abusive than comparison families, empirical findings for both behaviors are mixed. Some observational studies report that physically abusive parents engage in PNT significantly more frequently than comparison parents (e.g., Bousha & Twentyman, 1984; Oldershaw, Walters, & Hall, 1986, 1989), but other studies do not detect significant differences in PNT (e.g., Koenig et al., 2000; Whipple & Webster-Stratton, 1991). Similarly, some observational studies report significantly higher rates of noncompliance by abused as compared to nonmaltreated children (e.g., Borrego et al., 2004; Oldershaw et al., 1986), but other studies do not (e.g., Schindler & Arkowitz, 1986; Webster-Stratton, 1985).

Statistical power and moderating factors offer two possible explanations for these inconsistent findings, and both possibilities can be evaluated via meta-analysis. With regard to statistical power, observational studies of parent-child interaction are labor intensive; hence sample sizes in these studies often are small. For example, Oldershaw et al. (1986) observed parent-child interactions in 10 abusive and 10 comparison families, Bousha and Twentyman (1984) in 12 abusive and 12 comparison families, and Schindler and Arkowitz (1986) in 11 abusive and 12 comparison families. If one assumes that the actual differences in parental PNT or child noncompliance between the populations of abusive and comparison families are what Cohen (1988) would describe as "medium" in effect size ($d = .50$ or $r = .24$), then these studies had a statistical power to detect significant differences of only .21 (assuming $n = 24$, $p < .05$, and a two-tailed test). Even if the actual differences in parental PNT and child noncompliance are assumed to be what Cohen would classify as "large" ($d = .80$ or $r = .37$), statistical power to detect significant differences in these studies would be only .42. Put simply, fewer than half of the studies with this sample size would be expected to detect a significant difference even if the actual mean differences between the two populations were large. By accumulating findings across studies and capitalizing on much larger combined sample sizes, meta-analysis should help clarify the actual magnitude of differences that exist between abusive and comparison families in terms of parental PNT and child noncompliance.

A second possible explanation for inconsistent findings is that study, parental, or child characteristics may qualify the general conclusions. Regarding study characteristics, some researchers have observed interactions in the home (e.g., Bousha & Twentyman, 1984; Whipple & Webster-Stratton, 1991), whereas others have brought families to a research lab (e.g., Koenig et al., 2000; Oldershaw et al., 1986, 1989). Length of interaction observed also has varied dramatically, from 15 minutes or less (e.g., Borrego et al., 2004; Koenig et al., 2000) to more than 2 hours (e.g., Bousha & Twentyman, 1984; Reid, 1986). One might expect to see more frequent PNT and noncompliance, as well as potentially larger differences between abusive and comparison families, in studies that observe families at home for longer time periods. In terms of parental characteristics, most studies have only gathered data with mothers, but a few also include fathers (e.g., Reid, 1986; Whipple & Webster-Stratton, 1991). Regarding child characteristics, most studies in our meta-analysis involve samples of children whose mean age is 3 or 4 years, but a few include samples where the mean child age is younger (e.g., Crittenden, 1992) or older (e.g., Reid et al., 1981). Likewise, studies vary in terms of whether child gender is balanced versus whether most children are boys. By testing whether effect sizes across studies are homogeneous and, if not, whether moderating factors are correlated with obtained effect sizes, meta-analysis offers an empirical test of whether general conclusions about PNT and noncompliance are warranted (Hunter & Schmidt, 1990; Rosenthal, 1991). This issue leads to our first research question: *Do child, parental, or study characteristics moderate differences between parental PNT and child noncompliance in abusive versus comparison families* (RQ1)?

What About Child Neglect?

Neglect is the most common form of child maltreatment; indeed, nearly half (46%) of the cases of maltreatment substantiated by CPS agencies nationwide in 1999 involved children who were victims of neglect (Peddle & Wang, 2001). Despite this, surprisingly few observational studies of parent-child interaction include data from families with a history of neglect. This mirrors a larger pattern in which child neglect has received less research attention than physical or sexual abuse: "The 'neglect of neglect' has been acknowledged for over two decades . . . yet child neglect remains the poor cousin of child maltreatment research" (Hildyard & Wolfe, 2002, p. 680). Fortunately, a few studies (e.g., Bousha & Twentyman, 1984; Crittenden, 1992; Egeland, Sroufe, & Erickson, 1983; Koenig et al., 2000) have compared parent-child interactions in neglectful with those in both abusive and non-maltreating families, and hence it is important to consider how parental PNT and child noncompliance would be associated with neglect.

Neglectful parents, almost by definition, should display low levels of attentiveness and responsiveness to their children during family interactions (Crittenden, 1981). PNT, though unpleasant and potentially dangerous in terms of possible escalation to severe violence, is a form of contact that signals attentiveness to the child's behavior. For this reason, neglectful parents might be expected to display lower levels of PNT, at least in comparison to physically abusive parents. Neglected children display a host of cognitive, social, and emotional problems from infancy onward, but these tend to involve internalizing as opposed to externalizing problems (Hildyard & Wolfe, 2002). In a factor analysis of maltreated children's behavior, refusing (overt noncompliance) and ignoring (passive noncompliance) both loaded with other externalizing behaviors (e.g., teasing, hitting) as opposed to solitary (internalizing) behaviors (DiLalla & Crittenden, 1988). Hence, neglected children also might be expected to display lower levels of noncompliance, at least in comparison to physically abused children. Our second research question asks the following: *How do rates of parental PNT and child noncompliance in neglectful families compare to those in abusive and comparison families* (RQ2)?

Method

This section describes three phases of our meta-analysis: (a) searching the literature based on inclusion criteria, (b) deriving effect size estimates and coding characteristics from included studies, and (c) calculating cumulative measures of effect size and testing for moderating factors.

Inclusion Criteria and Literature Search

Given our hypotheses and research questions, we developed four criteria for including studies in this meta-analysis. Specifically, studies were analyzed only if they included the following:

1. A sample of parents with a documented history of child physical abuse and/or child neglect. [1] Typically this meant recorded involvement with local or state CPS agencies. Studies relying on parents' self-reported child abuse potential (e.g., Dolz, Cerezo, & Milner, 1997; Wilson, Morgan, Hayes, Bylund, & Herman, 2004) were not included.

2. A comparison sample of parents with no history of child maltreatment, matched with the abusive or neglectful parents on sociodemographic characteristics (e.g., parental age, ethnicity, and education; family size and income). Thus, studies that coded parent-child interaction in abusive families before and after treatment but with no comparison group (e.g., Wolfe & Sandler, 1981) were not included. [2]

3. Observational data on parent-child interaction. For example, studies that gathered data on child noncompliance via parental diaries (e.g., Trickett & Kuczynski, 1986) or telephone reports (e.g., Whipple & Wilson, 1996) were not included, in part because abusive parents tend to overestimate their children's behavioral problems in comparison to ratings of those same children by other observers (Reid, Kavanagh, & Baldwin, 1987). Studies gathering self-reported data on parental PNT via the Conflict Tactics Scale (Straus et al., 1998) or diaries (e.g., Trickett & Kuczynski, 1986) also were not included.

4. Information needed to derive estimates of effect size for parental PNT and/or child noncompliance. For example, studies that coded parental PNT but then grouped it with other categories into a cluster of aversive behaviors (e.g., Reid, 1986) were not included unless we found separate findings for PNT from the author (see below).

Several search strategies were employed to identify studies meeting these inclusion criteria. First, online databases (Communication Abstracts, Dissertation Abstracts, Family & Society Studies Worldwide, Linguistics and Language Behavior Abstracts, PsycINFO, Social Sciences Abstracts, Women's Studies International) were searched using the keywords *child abuse, child physical abuse,* or *child neglect* in combination with *communication, interaction,* or *parenting.* Potentially relevant unpublished dissertations were ordered from UMI. Second, when studies meeting our inclusion criteria were identified, their reference lists were checked for citations to earlier studies. Reference lists from narrative reviews (e.g., Cerezo, 1997) also were checked. Third, a complementary "search-forward" strategy was employed by using the Social Science Citation Index to identify every subsequent citation to two early studies that met our criteria (Bousha & Twentyman, 1984; Oldershaw et al., 1986). Fourth, we searched the table of contents and abstracts for the journal *Child Abuse & Neglect* from 1994–2004 to ensure we had not missed relevant studies. Finally, we contacted scholars who had published extensively on child maltreatment and family interaction, sent them our list of studies, and asked them to identify possibly relevant studies that we might have overlooked.

Deriving Effect Size Estimates and Coding Study Characteristics

The correlation coefficient (r) was used as the measure of effect size due to its simplicity of interpretation (for arguments favoring r as an effect size metric, see Hunter & Schmidt, 1990; Rosenthal, 1991). For each study with data on parental PNT and/or child noncompliance, an effect size was calculated in one of two ways. When a study reported the value of an inferential statistic (e.g., a t test or F test with 1 degree of freedom in the numerator) from a test for differences in PNT frequencies between abusive or neglectful versus comparison parents, that statistic was converted to r using formulas provided by Hunter and Schmidt (1990) or Rosenthal (1991). For example, the conversion formula from t to r is (Rosenthal, 1991, p. 25):

$$r = \sqrt{\frac{t^2}{t^2 + df}}$$

(1)

The same was done for studies reporting the value of an inferential statistic testing for differences between rates of noncompliance for abused or neglected versus comparison children.

Many studies failed to report the value of an inferential test if that test was not statistically significant. As noted earlier, a study may fail to detect a statistically significant difference even when an actual difference exists in the larger population. Hence, when a study reported descriptive statistics (means, standard deviations, and sample sizes) separately for abusive (or neglectful) and comparison parents' use of PNT, these data were used to calculate an independent-groups t test using the following formula (a = abuse, c = comparison; Sprinthal, 1990, p. 175):

$$t = \frac{M_a - M_c}{\sqrt{\left[\frac{(n_a - 1)SD_a^2 + (n_c - 1)SD_c^2}{n_a + n_c - 2}\right]\left(\frac{1}{n_a} + \frac{1}{n_c}\right)}},$$

(2)

and this t-test in turn was converted to r using formula (1). Given this ordering, a positive r reflects higher frequencies of PNT by abusive relative to comparison parents. The same was done with studies reporting descriptive statistics separately for abused (or neglected) versus nonmaltreated children's rates of noncompliance.

Studies with nonsignificant findings in some cases also did not provide a complete report of descriptive statistics (e.g., presenting means but not standard deviations, or reporting them across groups but not separately for abusive/neglectful vs. comparison families). We contacted the authors in such cases to see if they could provide us with the missing descriptive statistics. We also checked whether the study reported results from a dissertation and, if so, whether the missing descriptive statistics could be obtained from the unpublished dissertation. In cases where we could not derive an estimate of effect size for a study using any of these methods, that study was excluded from the meta-analysis.[3]

In most cases, "the study" was treated as our unit of analysis. For example, several studies (e.g., Borrego et al., 2004; Schindler & Arkowitz, 1986) coded the frequency of compliant and the frequency of noncompliant acts by children per minute. For each study that did this, we first calculated separate effect size estimates for abused (or neglected) versus nonmaltreated children in terms of differences in compliant and in noncompliant acts, then reversed the sign of the effect size for compliant acts (so that positive correlations always meant more noncompliance by abused children), and finally averaged the two *r*s to get a single noncompliance effect size for that study.[4]

Having said this, there were two instances where we allowed a single study to provide two effect size estimates. When a single study included data from abusive, neglectful, and comparison families, we derived two effect size estimates from that study: one comparing abusive versus comparison families and a second comparing neglectful versus the same comparison families. In addition, when a study reported data on fathers as well as mothers, we derived separate effect size estimates for abusive versus comparison fathers and for abusive versus comparison mothers in terms of their use of PNT. Following these procedures, we ended up with a total of 12 effect sizes from eight different studies (total $N = 751$ parents) in the analysis of PNT and 13 effect sizes from nine different studies (total $N = 743$ children) in the analysis of noncompliance.

Aside from calculating effect sizes, we also recorded the following characteristics for each study meeting the inclusion criteria: maltreatment status (abusive, neglectful, comparison), parent gender (mother or father), mean child age, percentage of children in the sample who were male, whether observations took place in the family's home or a research lab, and the time that families were observed (in minutes).

Statistical Analyses of Effect Sizes

Our analyses of PNT and noncompliance took place in three steps. First, we computed the mean effect size (weighted by sample size) and variance from all studies. The weighted mean effect size is used because it gives greater weight to studies with larger sample sizes; this is done because the effect size estimates from small sample studies contain greater sampling error and hence are more likely to depart from the true population parameter (Hunter & Schmidt, 1990, pp. 100–101). Second, the amount of observed variability in effect size estimates across studies is compared to the amount of variability that would be expected by chance. Even if all the effect sizes come from the same population (i.e., there are no moderating factors), one would not expect effect sizes from all studies to be identical due to sampling error. An estimate of the variance in effect sizes due to sampling error is calculated using the following formula:

$$\sigma_e^2 = \frac{(1 - \bar{r}^2)^2\, K}{N}, \qquad (3)$$

where *K* is number of studies and *N* is total number of participants across studies (Hunter & Schmidt, 1990, p. 107). If the observed variance in effect sizes is greater than the variance expected due to sampling error, then a moderator variable may be present.

When warranted, categorical (nominal-level) and continuous (interval-level) moderators can be tested. Testing for a categorical moderator involves subdividing the effect size estimates based on a meaningful moderator (e.g., studies conducted in the home vs. in the lab); calculating the category means, variances, and sampling errors; and determining if all the unexplained variance is accounted for. If there are differences in mean effect sizes between the categories and if the variance within categories is reduced to within sampling error, then a moderating factor is said to account for the residual variance (Hunter & Schmidt, 1990). If not, the search continues for other moderators. Testing for a continuous moderator (e.g., length of observation) involves correlating effect sizes from studies with corresponding scores on the continuous variable, where n = the number of effect sizes.

Results

Parental PNT

Table 13.1 reports 12 effect sizes from eight studies comparing maltreating (abusive or neglectful) versus nonmaltreating parents in terms of their use of PNT. All 12 effect sizes are positive, indicating more frequent use of PNT by maltreating parents. The mean weighted r across the 12 effect sizes is .25, which Cohen (1988) would label a medium-sized effect. The CI_{95} for this mean weighted effect size has the lower and upper bounds of r = .15 to .35, a range that does not include zero. Using a formula provided by Hunter and Schmidt (1990, p. 273), the corresponding Cohen's d is .52; that is, maltreating parents on average are approximately half a standard deviation higher than nonmaltreating parents in terms of use of PNT. In a normal distribution where nonmaltreating parents' average use of PNT fell at the median, maltreating parents' average use would fall at the 70th percentile.

The observed variance across these 12 effect sizes (weighted by sample size) is .029 (SD = .17). The amount of variance that would be expected due to sampling error, calculated using formula (3), was .014. Thus, sampling error accounts for slightly less than half (48%) of the observed variance in effect sizes, suggesting the presence of moderating factors. Rosenthal (1991, p. 74) presents a significance test for heterogeneity of effect sizes distributed as χ^2 with $K - 1$ degrees of freedom:

$$\chi^2 = \sum (N_j - 3)(z_{rj} - \bar{z}_r)^2, \qquad (4)$$

where K is the number of effect sizes, z_{rj} is the Fisher z_r corresponding to the r from any study j, and $\bar{z}_r$ is the weighted mean z_r. Performing this test on the 12 effect sizes resulted in χ^2 (11) = 34.46, p < .01, which confirms the high probability of moderating variables. General conclusions about parental maltreatment status and use of PNT may be qualified by other factors.

Categorical Moderators

Initially, we assessed whether heterogeneity of effect sizes in PNT might be attributable to maltreatment type—that is, whether studies comparing abusive

Table 13.1   Effect Size Estimates for Physical Negative Touch

Study	Groups		n	Home/Lab	Observation Length (min)	Mean Child (years)	% Boys	Effect Size (r)
Bousha and Twentyman (1984)		A vs. C	24	H	270.00	4.45	NA	.80
		N vs. C	24	H	270.00	4.25	NA	.27
Koenig, Cicchetti, and Rogosch (2000)		A vs. C	63	L	2.59	3.65	52	.21
		N vs. C	69	L	2.59	3.50	52	.09
Lahey, Conger, Atkeson, and Treiber (1984)		A vs. C	16	H	270.00	5.67	63	.52
Oldershaw, Walters, and Hall (1986)		A vs. C	20	L	40.00	3.00	50	.64
Oldershaw, Walters, and Hall (1989)		A vs. C	116	L	40.00	3.78	50	.21
Reid, Taplin, and Lorber (1981)	(moms)	A vs. C	87	H	213.00	8.80	91	.43
	(dads)	A vs. C	62	H	213.00	8.80	91	.23
Webster-Stratton (1985)		A vs. C	40	H	60.00	4.79	73	.35
Whipple and Webster-Stratton (1991)	(moms)	A vs. C	121	H	60.00	4.88	69	.08
	(dads)	A vs. C	109	H	60.00	4.88	69	.17

Note: A = physically abusive; C = comparison (nonmaltreating); N = neglectful parents; H = home; L = research lab; NA = not available. Mean weighted effect size is $r = .25$; observed variance = .029, based on 12 effect sizes from eight studies (total $N = 751$ parents). Positive r indicates more frequent physical negative touch by abusive or neglectful versus comparison parents.

versus nonmaltreating parents might obtain larger effect sizes than those comparing neglectful versus nonmaltreating families (RQ2). The mean weighted effect size for the 10 effects comparing physically abusive versus comparison parents is $r_a = .26$ ($\sigma_a = .03$). These findings are consistent with Hypothesis 1, which predicted that physically abusive parents would enact PNT more frequently than comparison parents. The mean weighted effect size for the two studies comparing neglectful and nonmaltreating ($r_n = .14$, $\sigma_n = .006$) parents is slightly smaller. The observed variance in the two effect sizes from studies with data on neglectful families does fall within what would be expected due to sampling error, though one must be cautious given that this conclusion is based on only two studies. In contrast, sampling error accounts for only 43% of the observed variance in the 10 effect sizes from studies of abusive parents, suggesting that additional systematic variance remains to be explained.

There also is a small difference in effect sizes for studies conducted in the home ($r_h = .27$, $\sigma_h = .034$) as opposed to in a research lab ($r_l = .21$, $\sigma_l = .018$). Sampling error accounted for 41% of the variance in the eight effect sizes from home studies and 76% of the variance in the four effect sizes from lab studies, suggesting that additional systematic variance remains to be explained (especially for the home studies). Because home studies on average involved longer periods of observation ($M_h = 134.6$ minutes) than lab studies ($M_l = 27.53$ minutes; see Table 13.1), any conclusion about research site also must take into account observation length (see below).

Finally, studies comparing abusive versus nonmaltreating mothers ($r_m = .29$, $\sigma_m = .038$) obtained slightly larger effect sizes than studies comparing abusive versus nonmaltreating fathers ($r_f = .19$, $\sigma_f = .001$). Observed variance in the two effect sizes for fathers were within what would be expected due to sampling error, though again this conclusion is based on data from only two studies, both of which involve fathers with a history of abuse (but not neglect). In contrast, sampling error accounts for only 36% of the variance in effect sizes for mothers, suggesting that additional systematic variance remains to be explained.

Continuous Moderators

Table 13.2 displays correlations between effect sizes and three interval-level variables: length of observation, mean child age, and percentage of children in the sample who were male.[5] Length of observation shares a strong positive association with effect size ($r = .52$). When only the 10 effect sizes from studies comparing abusive versus nonmaltreating parents are considered, the correlation between observation length and effect size is slightly larger ($r = .56$). These findings indicate that studies that observed longer periods of interaction tended to obtain large effect sizes in terms of differences in maltreating versus comparison parents' use of PNT, whereas studies that observed short periods of interaction obtained small effect sizes (see Table 13.1). In contrast, neither mean age of children nor percentage of male children in the sample is associated with effect size magnitude across the 12 effect sizes.

As noted earlier, studies conducted at home on average observed longer periods of interaction compared to lab studies. To disentangle these two moderators, we conducted a multiple regression analysis in which effect size served as the criterion variable. Length of observation and research site (dummy coded 0 = lab, 1 = home) were entered simultaneously as predictors. The effect for observation length ($\beta = .78$, $p = .067$) remains strong and approaches conventional levels of statistical significance, even with only $n = 12$ effect sizes, whereas the effect for research site ($\beta = -.38$, ns) is smaller and actually becomes negative (indicating larger effects for lab as opposed to home studies once length of interaction has been controlled).

Our first RQ asked what study, parent, and child characteristics might moderate differences in physically abusive versus nonmaltreating parents' use of PNT, whereas RQ2 asked whether smaller effects would occur when comparing neglectful versus nonmaltreating parents. Among all of the factors for which we coded, observation length is the most powerful moderator of the effects of parental maltreatment status on the frequency of enacting PNT. Slightly larger effects also were obtained for studies of abusive as opposed to neglectful parents as well as for mothers as opposed to fathers, though both conclusions should be viewed

Table 13.2   Correlations Between Continuous Moderator Variables and Effect Sizes for Parental Physical Negative Behavior (PNT) and Child Noncompliance

	Effect Sizes	
Moderator	Parental PNT	Child Noncompliance
Length of observation	.52	.37 (.80)[a]
Mean child age	−.01	.29
% male children	.01	.03

Note: For PNT, $n = 12$ effect sizes except for percent male children, where $n = 10$ effect sizes (Bousha & Twentyman, 1984, did not report what percentages of their children were male or female). For child noncompliance, $n = 11$ effect sizes except for percent male children, where $n = 6$ effect sizes (Bousha & Twentyman, 1984; Egeland, Sroufe, and Erickson, 1983; and Schindler & Arkowitz, 1986, did not report what percentages of their children were male or female).

a. Correlation between observation length and effect sizes from only those studies that compared abused versus nonmaltreated children.

cautiously given the limited studies with fathers or neglectful mothers. Small and somewhat inconsistent differences were obtained for research site (home vs. lab).

Child Noncompliance

Table 13.3 reports 13 effect sizes from nine studies comparing maltreated (abused or neglected) versus nonmaltreated children in terms of their rates of noncompliance. Eleven of the 13 effect sizes are positive, indicating more frequent noncompliance by maltreated children. The mean weighted r across the 13 effect sizes is .13, which Cohen (1988) would label a small-sized effect. The observed variance across these 13 effect sizes (weighted by sample size) is .065 ($SD = .25$). The amount of variance that would be expected due to sampling error was .017; thus, sampling error accounts for only about a quarter (26%) of the observed variance in effect sizes.

Crittenden (1992) is the only study that reports more noncompliance by non-maltreated children than either abused or neglected children (see Table 13.3). Her study coded parent-child interactions for the degree to which children displayed "compulsive compliance," which is described as "wariness and hyper-vigilance towards adults, over-compliance with adult's wishes, and a general inhibition of playful activity" (Crittenden & DiLalla, 1988, p. 586).[6] Ratings of compulsive compliance were based on the child's facial expression, vocal expression, position and body contact, pacing of turns, and choice of activities. Thus, the two negative correlations in Table 13.3 reflect that nonmaltreated children in Crittenden displayed less compulsive compliance relative to abused or neglected children. Being rated as compulsively compliant did not ensure that a child would display pleasant or cooperative behavior; indeed, the same abused and neglected children who were more

Table 13.3   Effect Size Estimates of Child Noncompliance

Study	Groups	n	Home/Lab	Observation Length (min)	Mean Child (years)	% Boys	Effect Size (r)
Borrego, Timmer,Urquiza, and Follette (2004)	A vs. C	30	L	15.00	4.15	60	.11
Bousha and Twentyman (1984)	A vs. C	24	H	270.00	4.45	NA	.77
	N vs. C	24	H	270.00	4.25	NA	.07
Crittenden (1992)	A vs. C	64	H	3.00	2.00	49	−.48
	N vs. C	64	H	3.00	2.00	49	−.16
Egeland, Sroufe, and Erickson (1983)	A vs. C	109	L	37.50	3.50	NA	.25
	N vs. C	97	L	37.50	3.50	NA	.20
Koenig, Cicchetti, and Rogosch (2000)	A vs. C	63	L	2.59	3.62	52	.15
	N vs. C	69	L	2.59	3.50	52	.08
Oldershaw, Walters, and Hall (1986)	A vs. C	20	L	40.00	3.00	50	.53
Oldershaw, Walters, and Hall (1989)	A vs. C	116	L	40.00	3.78	50	.14
Schindler and Arkowitz (1986)	A vs. C	23	L	35.00	4.79	NA	.46
Webster-Stratton (1985)	A vs. C	40	H	60.00	4.79	73	.29

Note: A = abuse; C = control; N = neglect; NA = not available. Mean weighted effect size is $r = .13$ (.22 without Crittenden, 1992), observed variance = .065 (.023 without Crittenden, 1992), based on 13 effect sizes from nine studies ($N = 743$ children). Positive r indicates more frequent noncompliance by abused or neglected versus comparison children.

compulsively compliant also were rated as being more difficult and less pleasant relative to nonmaltreated children (see Crittenden, 1992, p. 335). Because Crittenden appears to be coding something qualitatively different from other studies (perhaps something akin to situational as opposed to committed compliance; see note 4), we excluded her study as an outlier in all subsequent analyses.

After excluding Crittenden (1992), the mean weighted r across the 11 remaining effect sizes jumped to .22, which Cohen (1988) would label as a medium effect. The CI_{95} for this mean weighted effect size has the lower and upper bounds of $r = .13$ and .31. The corresponding Cohen's d is .45; thus, in a normal distribution where nonmaltreated children's rate of noncompliance fell at the median, maltreated children's average noncompliance rate would fall at the 67th percentile. The observed variance also dropped to .023 ($SD = .15$) after excluding Crittenden. Although this is nearly three times smaller than before, it is still greater than the amount of variance expected due to sampling error (.016). Rosenthal's (1991) test for heterogeneity of effect sizes is statistically significant even without Crittenden, χ^2 (10) = 20.74, $p < .05$, which confirms the high probability of moderating variables.

Categorical Moderators

Once again, we initially assessed whether heterogeneity of effect sizes in noncompliance might be attributable to maltreatment type—that is, whether studies comparing abused versus nonmaltreated children obtained larger effect sizes than those comparing neglected versus nonmaltreated families (RQ2). The effect size for the eight studies comparing abused and neglected children is $r_a = .25$ ($\sigma_a = .028$). Consistent with Hypothesis 2, abused children displayed higher rates of noncompliance than comparison children. The mean weighted effect size for the three studies comparing neglected and nonmaltreated children is slightly smaller ($r_n = .14$, $\sigma_n = .020$). Sampling error accounts for 81% of the observed variance in effect sizes from the three studies with data on neglectful families but only 61% of the variance in effect sizes from the eight studies of abused children, suggesting that additional systematic variance remains to be explained.

There also is a moderate difference in effect sizes for studies conducted in the home ($r_h = .36$, $\sigma_h = .071$) as opposed to a research lab ($r_l = .19$, $\sigma_l = .011$). The observed variance in effect sizes from the eight lab studies falls within what would be expected due to sampling error. In contrast, sampling error accounted for only 37% of the variance in the three effect sizes from home studies, suggesting that additional systematic variance remains to be explained. Because home studies on average involved longer observation periods ($M_h = 165$ minutes) than did lab studies ($M_l = 28.35$ minutes; see Table 13.3), any conclusion about research site must take into account observation length (see below). Finally, none of the studies coded rates of child noncompliance during interactions with fathers; hence, parent gender could not be explored as a moderator.

Continuous Moderators

Table 13.2 displays correlations between effect sizes and three interval-level variables: length of observation, mean child age, and percentage of children in the sample who were male. Length of observation shares a strong positive association with effect size ($r = .37$). When only the eight effect sizes from studies comparing abusive versus nonmaltreating parents are considered, the correlation between observation length and effect size leaps to $r = .80$ and is statistically significant ($p < .01$) even with $n = 8$ effects. These findings indicate that studies that observed longer periods of interaction tended to obtain large effect sizes in terms of differences in maltreated (especially physically abused) versus comparison children's noncompliance, whereas studies observing short periods of interaction obtained small effects (see Table 13.3). In addition, larger effects were obtained in studies that employed older as opposed to younger children ($r = .21$); however, this finding should be viewed tentatively because studies with older children also employed longer periods of observation ($r = .39$ between mean observation length and child age across studies). Finally, percentage of male children is not associated with effect size magnitude across the 11 effect sizes (see Table 13.2).

As noted earlier, studies conducted at home on average observed longer periods of interaction compared to lab studies. To disentangle the effects of observation length, research site, and child age, we conducted a regression analysis in which effect size served as the criterion variable. Length of observation, child age, and research site (dummy coded 0 = lab, 1 = home) all were entered simultaneously as predictors. The effect for observation length ($\beta = .47$) remained strong, whereas effects for child age ($\beta = .14$) and research site ($\beta = -.18$) were much smaller. The beta coefficient for research site actually became negative, indicating larger effects for lab as opposed to home studies in terms of child noncompliance once length of interaction and child age were controlled. In sum, observation length is a strong moderator of the effects of maltreatment status on child noncompliance (RQ1). Slightly larger effects also were obtained for studies of abused as opposed to neglected children (RQ2). Larger effects were obtained in studies with older children, though the role of child age as a moderator was diminished once length of observation was controlled. Inconsistent differences were obtained for research site.

Discussion

Researchers, family therapists, and child welfare advocates alike are interested in patterns of parent-child interaction distinguishing families with a history of child physical abuse or child neglect from sociodemographically similar nonmaltreating families. This chapter provides a meta-analysis of observational studies comparing abusive and neglectful versus nonmaltreating parents' use of PNT as well as abused and neglected versus nonmaltreated children's rates of noncompliance with parental request or commands. According to Reid's (1986) social-interactional perspective, parental PNT and child noncompliance are behaviors that mark potentially dangerous patterns of interaction during which children are at risk for physical abuse.

Consistent with Reid's (1986) account, rates of parental PNT and child noncompliance are higher in maltreating than nonmaltreating families. With the exception of one study on child noncompliance, the direction of effect was consistent across all studies in the meta-analysis. The mean weighted effect size was "medium" for both parental PNT and child noncompliance, and the CI_{95} did not include zero for either behavior. In both cases, slightly larger effects were obtained from comparisons of physically abusive and nonmaltreating as opposed to neglectful and nonmaltreating families, perhaps reflecting that Reid's account of "discipline episodes gone awry" is especially relevant for explaining the physical abuse of children.

Reid (1986) argues that the probability of child physical abuse is a function of the number of discipline confrontations that occur day to day and the percentage of these confrontations that can be resolved quickly without parental physical aggression. This suggests that interventions with families need to focus on reducing rates of child noncompliance as well as parents' use of PNT. Regarding noncompliance, physically abused children present their parents with a larger number of challenging interactions to manage each day. Abused children obviously should not be blamed for their plight; indeed, physically abusive parents often interact with their children in ways that unintentionally reinforce child noncompliance (see Borrego et al., 2004; Oldershaw et al., 1986). But given that physically abused children tend to form lower quality relationships with peers (Howe & Park, 2001) and teachers (Cicchetti & Toth, 1995), interventions need to teach abused children communicative skills that enhance relationships with adults and peers, especially during the transition to school (Ladd, Buhs, & Troop, 2002).

Interventions also need to teach physically abusive parents alternatives to PNT for responding to perceived child misbehavior, such as time-out or choices-and-consequences (see Chapter 12, this volume). The focus needs to be on the skillful use of disciplinary techniques, teaching parents to (a) respond to the same type of child misbehavior consistently over time, (b) respond to different types of child behavior with relevant mixes of inductive and power-assertive techniques, (c) avoid using verbal aggression, (d) refrain from reciprocating child aversive behaviors unconnected to the issue at hand, and (e) reinforce child compliance each time it occurs (Wilson & Morgan, 2004). Equally important, interventions need to work on altering spontaneous parental thoughts and feelings (e.g., making internal and overly global attributions for child misbehavior, feeling powerlessness relative to one's child) that often precipitate abusive parents' use of PNT (see Azar, 1997; Milner, 2000; Wilson & Whipple, 2001). Interventions also must take account of how the larger ecological context (e.g., inadequate child care, unemployment) creates parental stress and depression, which in turn magnify spontaneous negative thoughts and use of PNT (Belsky, 1993; Wilson & Whipple, 2001).

Reducing parents' use of PNT would be beneficial for several reasons. In addition to short-circuiting reciprocated aversive behaviors between parent and child before the child is physically injured, reducing parental PNT itself might improve the parent-child relationship and the child's self esteem. Parental behaviors such as hitting, grabbing, slapping, spanking, or taking an object roughly from a child are worrisome not just because they may escalate to more intense physical aggression; rather, frequent parental PNT itself may send messages that undermine children's self-esteem and perceived competence (see Morgan & Wilson, 2005).

Although maltreating and nonmaltreating families differ in terms of frequencies of parental PNT and child noncompliance, the magnitude of difference varies depending on other factors. In particular, length of observation emerged as a strong moderator of effect size magnitude (see Table 13.2). Studies that observed longer periods of parent-child interaction (e.g., 2 or more hours) tended to obtain larger effect sizes; those that observed short time periods (e.g., 10 minutes or less) tended to obtain small effect sizes. This finding held up regardless of whether observation took place in the family's home or a research lab, in that the effects of research site on both parental PNT and child noncompliance were small once length of observation had been controlled.

The role of observational length as a moderator has implications for researchers and practitioners. Researchers who wish to test explanations for why physically abusive parents use more PNT or why physically abused children are more frequently noncompliant need to observe longer periods of interaction, or else the phenomena they are trying to explain are unlikely to be observed. Clinicians and child welfare advocates also need to observe longer periods of interaction if they are relying on parental PNT or child noncompliance as indicators of whether a family is in need of services or whether program interventions have made a difference.

Future meta-analyses also need to explore whether observational length is an important moderator for positive parental behaviors (e.g., praise, positive physical touch) or, alternatively, whether maltreating and nonmaltreating families are clearly distinguished by positive behaviors even during short periods of interaction. Several studies with small sample sizes have detected statistically significant differences between physically abusive (or high-risk) and nonmaltreating (or low-risk) parents' use of positive behaviors even when observing families for short time intervals (e.g., Kavanagh, Youngblade, Reid, & Fagot, 1988; Wilson et al., 2004), which suggests that observation length might not matter so much for positively valenced behaviors.

We close by acknowledging several limitations of this meta-analysis. Inspection of Tables 13.1 and 13.3 reveals that few of our studies gathered data from families with a history of child neglect or from fathers in general, and this limits how much confidence can be placed in our analysis of maltreatment type or parent gender as moderators. Our findings tentatively indicate that parental PNT and child noncompliance are less useful in distinguishing families with a history of child neglect (as opposed to physical abuse) from nonmaltreating families, and hence future research might explore whether variables indicative of conversational or relational involvement (e.g., talk time, question asking) are more useful in distinguishing neglectful and nonmaltreating families. In addition, the vast majority of studies included in our meta-analysis involved samples of children whose average age ranged from 3 to 5 years old; hence, our meta-analysis offers limited insight about which behaviors best distinguish maltreated versus nonmaltreated infants or adolescents.

One final limitation is that the number of studies meeting all four criteria for inclusion is fairly small. Summary statistics from Tables 13.1 and 13.3 are based on data from more than 700 parents and children, and this certainly advances knowledge beyond what is gained from any single observational study based on a small sample. Having said this, the total number of studies examined is small compared to many meta-analyses.

We see two options for expanding the number of studies included in future meta-analyses on this topic. First, a future meta-analysis could remain focused on observational studies but analyze a broader range of aversive behaviors. We identified a number of observational studies that met our first three inclusion criteria but that either (a) did not code parental PNT or child noncompliance or (b) coded one or both behaviors but grouped them along with other behaviors (e.g., threats, verbal aggression, yelling, harsh vocal tone, facial expressions signaling anger or disgust) into a more abstract cluster of aversive behavior without presenting descriptive statistics for PNT or noncompliance. Drawing on Reid's (1986) conceptual definition of "aversive behavior," a future meta-analysis could include any observational study that coded one or more categories falling into this general behavioral cluster. Such an approach would likely more than double the number of studies included in the meta-analysis, providing even more accurate estimates of population parameters and more effect sizes from which to test potential moderating factors. The downside of this first approach is that it offers researchers and practitioners less information about the precise behaviors that distinguish maltreating and nonmaltreating families. Parenting programs, for example, can work on alternatives to PNT when seeking a child's compliance, but alternatives to "aversive behavior" in general are a more abstract and potentially less useful concept. This first approach would thus complement but not replace the need for the present meta-analysis.

A second approach to expanding the number of studies would be to remain focused on parental PNT and child noncompliance but include studies using self- and other-report procedures as well. Parental PNT, for example, might be analyzed based on data about mild physical aggression from the revised Parent-Child Conflict Tactics Scales (Straus et al., 1998), just as child noncompliance might be analyzed from studies gathering parental diaries (Trickett & Kuczynski, 1986) or telephone reports (Whipple & Wilson, 1996). Measurement type (observational coding, self-report, third-party report) could be explored as a potential moderating factor. We chose to focus initially on observational studies because of concerns about perceptual biases in how maltreating parents view their own children (Milner, 2000; Reid et al., 1987), but this second approach also would offer a valuable extension to our current understanding of parent-child interaction, discipline, and child maltreatment.

Notes

1. Crittenden (1992) and Egeland et al. (1983) compared children who were abused, neglected, or abused and neglected (had experienced both forms of maltreatment) with children who had not been maltreated. Because these were the only two studies that explicitly included a group of children with a history of both abuse *and* neglect, we included data from their "abuse" and "neglect" groups but not their "abuse/neglect" group in our meta-analysis.

2. Lahey, Conger, Atkeson, and Treiber (1984) included data from both a matched (low socioeconomic status) and a middle-class comparison group; here, only data from the matched comparison group were used. Similarly, Reid et al. (1981) included data from distressed-abusive families as well as distressed/nonmaltreating and nondistressed/nonmaltreating families; here, only data from distressed/nonmaltreating families were used for the "comparison" group.

3. One study (Egeland et al., 1983) did not report an exact value for an inferential statistic and also did not report complete descriptive statistics; however, the authors do report that comparisons between abused and comparison children as well as between neglected (but not abused) and comparison children were statistically significant (the former at $p < .01$, the latter at $p < .05$; see Table 2 in their article). In this case, we determined that the smallest value for a t test that would have been statistically significant given the sample size (i.e., from a table of critical values for the independent-groups t test) and then converted that value to Pearson r to obtain an effect size estimate. This procedure is conservative as it likely underestimates the true size of the t tests. The Egeland et al. (1983) study also assessed a subset of children at a second point in time, approximately 18 months after the first assessment. Because the authors did not report how many children from each subgroup (abused, neglected, comparison) were assessed at Time 2, we did not include those data in our meta-analysis.

4. One study (Koenig et al., 2000) drew even finer-grain conceptual distinctions in terms of types of noncompliance and compliance. Drawing on Kochanska and Aksan (1995), the authors distinguish between "committed" compliance (which involves a child's full endorsement of a parental command) and "situational" compliance (which involves a child complying

only as long as the parent is observing the child's action). Koenig et al. (2000, p. 1021) predicted that maltreated children would display less committed compliance and greater situational compliance as well as two forms of noncompliance (passive and overt) compared to nonmaltreated children. The authors also found that rates of committed compliance were inversely associated with rates of both situational compliance and two forms of noncompliance. Given that committed and situational compliance were inversely associated both conceptually and empirically, it did not make sense to treat them equivalently. To derive a single effect size estimate for this study, we first computed four separate effect sizes in terms of how abused versus comparison children differed on committed compliance, situational compliance, passive noncompliance, and overt noncompliance. Then we reversed the sign of the latter three effect sizes and averaged all four. A positive r indicates that abused children displayed more committed compliance as well as less situational compliance, passive noncompliance, and overt noncompliance relative to comparison children. We followed the same procedure to compute a single noncompliance effect size for neglected versus comparison children.

5. Studies did not report whether differences between maltreating versus nonmaltreating parents' use of PNT varied depending on whether they were interacting with male or female children, and in some home studies, parents were interacting with multiple children, including both boys and girls. Hence, the only way of exploring potential effects of child gender was to analyze whether studies that contained a larger percentage of male (as opposed to female) children obtained larger effect sizes.

6. Findings reported in Crittenden (1992) are based on reanalysis of multiple data sets from several earlier published studies (e.g., Crittenden & DiLalla, 1988); however, none of the earlier reports provided sufficient descriptive statistics on compulsive compliance to be included in this meta-analysis, and hence our analysis is limited to data reported in Crittenden (1992).

References

Azar, S. T. (1997). A cognitive behavioral approach to understanding and treating parents who physically abuse their children. In D. Wolfe, R. J. McHahon, & R. D. Peters (Eds.), *Child abuse: New directions in prevention and treatment across the lifespan* (pp. 79–101). Thousand Oaks, CA: Sage.

Belsky, J. (1993). Etiology of child maltreatment: A developmental-ecological analysis. *Psychological Bulletin, 114,* 413–434.

*Borrego, J., Timmer, S. G., Urquiza, A. J., & Follette, W. C. (2004). Physically abusive mothers' responses following episodes of child noncompliance and compliance. *Journal of Consulting and Clinical Psychology, 72,* 897–903.

*Bousha, D. M., & Twentyman, C. T. (1984). Mother-child interactional style in abuse, neglect, and control groups: Observations in the home. *Journal of Abnormal Psychology, 93,* 106–114.

Cerezo, M. A. (1997). Abusive family interaction: A review. *Aggression and Violent Behavior, 2,* 215–240.

Cicchetti, D., & Toth, S. L. (1995). Child maltreatment and attachment organization: Implications for intervention. In S. Goldberg & R. Muir (Eds.), *Attachment theory: Social, developmental, and clinical perspectives* (pp. 279–308). Hillsdale, NJ: Analytic Press.

NOTE: References marked with an asterisk indicate studies included in the meta-analysis.

Cohen, J. (1988). *Statistical power analysis for the behavioral sciences* (2nd ed.). Mahwah, NJ: Lawrence Erlbaum.

Crittenden, P. M. (1981). Abusing, neglecting, problematic, and adequate dyads: Differentiating by patterns of interaction. *Merrill-Palmer Quarterly, 27,* 201–218.

*Crittenden, P. M. (1992). Children's strategies for coping with adverse home environments: An interpretation using attachment theory. *Child Abuse & Neglect, 16,* 329–343.

Crittenden, P. M. (1998). Dangerous behavior and dangerous contexts: A 35-year perspective on research on the developmental effects of child physical abuse. In P. K. Trickett & C. J. Shellenbach (Eds.), *Violence against children in the family and the community* (pp. 11–38). Washington, DC: American Psychological Association.

Crittenden, P. M., & DiLalla, D. L. (1988). Compulsive compliance: The development of an inhibitory coping strategy in infancy. *Journal of Abnormal Child Psychology, 16,* 585–599.

DiLalla, D. L., & Crittenden, P. M. (1988). Dimensions of maltreated children's home behavior: A factor-analytic approach. *Infant Behavior and Development, 13,* 439–460.

Dolz, L., Cerezo, M. A., & Milner, J. S. (1997). Mother-child interactional patterns in abusive families versus nonabusive families: An observational study. *Child Abuse & Neglect, 21,* 1149–1158.

*Egeland, B., Sroufe, A., & Erickson, M. (1983). The developmental consequences of different patterns of maltreatment. *Child Abuse & Neglect, 7,* 459–469.

Hildyard, K. L., & Wolfe, D. A. (2002). Child neglect: Development issues and outcomes. *Child Abuse & Neglect, 26,* 679–695.

Howe, T. R., & Park, R. D. (2001). Friendship quality and sociometric status: Between-group differences and links to loneliness in severely abused and nonabused children. *Child Abuse & Neglect, 25,* 585–606.

Hunter, J. E., & Schmidt, F. L. (1990). *Methods of meta-analysis: Correcting error and bias in research findings.* Newbury Park, CA: Sage.

Kavanagh, K. A., Youngblade, L., Reid, R. J., & Fagot, B. I. (1988). Interactions between children and abusive versus control parents. *Journal of Clinical Child Psychology, 17,* 137–142.

Kochanska, G., & Askan, N. (1995). Mother-child mutuality, positive affect, the quality of child compliance to requests and prohibitions, and maternal control as correlates of early internalization. *Child Development, 66,* 236–254.

*Koenig, A. L., Cicchetti, D., & Rogosch, F. A. (2000). Child compliance/noncompliance and maternal contributions to internalization in maltreating and nonmaltreating dyads. *Child Development, 71,* 1018–1032.

Kolko, D. J. (1996). Child physical abuse. In J. Briere & L. Berliner (Eds.), *The APSAC handbook on child maltreatment* (pp. 21–50). Thousand Oaks, CA: Sage.

Ladd, G. W., Buhs, E., & Troop, W. (2002). Children's interpersonal skills and relationships in school settings: Adaptive significance and implications for school-based prevention and intervention programs. In P. K. Smith & C. H. Hart (Eds.), *Blackwell's handbook of childhood social development* (pp. 394–415). London: Blackwell.

*Lahey, B. B., Conger, R. D., Atkeson, B. M., & Treiber, F. A. (1984). Parenting behavior and emotional status of physically abusive mothers. *Journal of Consulting and Clinical Psychology, 52,* 1062–1071.

Milner, J. S. (2000). Social information processing and child physical abuse: Theory and research. In D. J. Hersen (Ed.), *Nebraska symposium on motivation: Vol. 45. Motivation and child maltreatment* (pp. 39–84). Lincoln: University of Nebraska Press.

Morgan, W. M., & Wilson, S. R. (2005). Nonphysical child abuse: A review of literature and challenge to communication scholars. In P. Kalbfleisch (Ed.), *Communication yearbook 29* (pp. 1–33). Mahwah, NJ: Lawrence Erlbaum.

*Oldershaw, L., Walters, G. C., & Hall, D. K. (1986). Control strategies and noncompliance in abusive mother-child dyads: An observational study. *Child Development, 1986,* 722–732.

*Oldershaw, L., Walters, G. C., & Hall, D. K. (1989). A behavioral approach to the classification of different types of physically abusive mothers. *Merrill-Palmer Quarterly, 35,* 255–279.

Peddle, N., & Wang, C.-T. (2001). *Current trends in child abuse prevention, reporting, and fatalities: The 1999 Annual Fifty State Survey.* Retrieved on March 15, 2005, from http://www.preventchildabuse.org/learn_more/research_docs/1999_50_survey.pdf

Peddle, N., Wang, C.-T., Diaz, J., & Reid, R. (2002). *Current trends in child abuse prevention and fatalities: The 2000 fifty state survey.* Retrieved on March 15, 2005, from http://www.preventchildabuse.org/learn_more/research_docs/2000_50_survey.pdf

Reid, J. S. (1986). Social interactional patterns in families of abused and non-abused children. In C. Zahn-Waxler, E. M. Cummings, & R. Iannotti (Eds.), *Altruism and aggression: Biological and social origins* (pp. 238–257). Cambridge, UK: Cambridge University Press.

Reid, J. S., Kavanagh, K., & Baldwin, D. V. (1987). Abusive parents' perceptions of child problem behaviors: An example of parental bias. *Journal of Abnormal Child Psychology, 15,* 457–466.

*Reid, J. S., Taplin, P. S., & Lorber, R. (1981). A social interactional approach to the treatment of abusive families. In R. B. Stuart (Ed.), *Violent behavior: Social learning approaches to prediction, management, and treatment* (pp. 83–101). New York: Brunner/Mazel.

Rosenthal, R. (1991). *Meta-analytic procedures for social research* (Rev. ed.). Newbury Park, CA: Sage.

*Schindler, F., & Arkowitz, H. (1986). The assessment of mother-child interactions in physically abusive and nonabusive families. *Journal of Family Violence, 1,* 247–257.

Sprinthal, R. C. (1990). *Basic statistical analysis* (3rd ed.). Englewood Cliffs, NJ: Prentice Hall.

Straus, M. A., Hamby, S. L., Finkelhor, D., Moore, D. W., & Runyan, D. (1998). Identification of child maltreatment with the Parent-Child Conflict Tactics Scales: Development and psychometric data from a national sample of American parents. *Child Abuse & Neglect, 22,* 249–270.

Trickett, P. K., & Kuczynski, L. (1986). Children's misbehaviors and parental discipline strategies in abusive and non-abusive families. *Developmental Psychology, 22,* 115–123.

*Webster-Stratton, C. (1985). Comparison of abusive and nonabusive families with conduct-disordered children. *American Journal of Orthopsychiatry, 55,* 59–69.

*Whipple, E. E., & Webster-Stratton, C. (1991). The role of parental stress in physically abusive families. *Child Abuse & Neglect, 15,* 279–291.

Whipple, E. E., & Wilson, S. R. (1996). Evaluation of a parent education and support program for families at risk for physical child abuse. *Families in Society, 77,* 227–239.

Wilson, S. R. (1999). Child physical abuse: The relevance of language and social interaction research. *Research on Language and Social Interaction, 32,* 173–184.

Wilson, S. R., & Morgan, W. M. (2004). Persuasion and families. In A. L. Vangelisti (Ed.), *Handbook of family communication* (pp. 447–471). Mahwah, NJ: Lawrence Erlbaum.

Wilson, S. R., Morgan, W. M., Hayes, J., Bylund, C. L., & Herman, A. (2004). Mothers' child abuse potential as a predictor of maternal and child behaviors during play-time interactions. *Communication Monographs, 71,* 395–421.

Wilson, S. R., & Whipple, E. E. (2001). Attributions and regulative communication by parents participating in a child physical abuse prevention program. In V. Manusov & J. H. Harvey (Eds.), *Attribution, communication behavior, and close relationships* (pp. 227–247). Cambridge, UK: Cambridge University Press.

Wolfe, D. A., & Sandler, J. (1981). Training abusive parents in effective child management. *Behavior Modification, 5,* 320–335.

CHAPTER 14

Family Rituals

Leslie A. Baxter

University of Iowa

Dawn O. Braithwaite

University of Nebraska–Lincoln

My "Gotcha Day" is just before school is out. My birthday is in the summer when school's out, but I get to have a school party anyway—that's my adoption party! It's just like a birthday party! My mom brings treats, and everybody sings "Happy Adoption Day to You," like the "Happy Birthday" song. What's different is that since kindergarten, my mom and I get to explain to my class what adoption day means. When I was young, my mom read books to my class about it. Now that I'm a big kid, I get to talk to everybody and answer questions about what it means to be adopted. And when I get home, I get "Gotcha" presents, just like I do on my birthday. And then I hear the stories about the trip to China to get me.

—Emma, age 9

Whe begin this chapter about rituals with the description provided by the elementary-aged daughter of the first author. Her daughter described an important ritual in her family—an annual celebration of the day she was adopted as a baby. Like Emma, family members can recount their own rituals that matter as they reflect on communication in their families. Families celebrate holidays, birthdays, anniversaries, weddings, and other special times. They celebrate family identity in both large and small ways, from formal events such as religious confirmations and weddings to less formal, mundane practices such as "family game night" or the use of nicknames for family members. They celebrate family members, both living and dead, and what it means to be a member of the family. Although family rituals come in different forms, they are important recurring communication practices that pay homage to, or honor, some aspect of family life. Rituals are a communication genre of significance to family well-being and merit serious scholarly attention (for an examination of research examining this wellness aspect in stepfamilies, see Chapter 15, this volume).

The purpose of this chapter is to bring together research and theory from the interdisciplinary fields of ritual studies and family studies, as well as from family communication, to address five basic questions: How can we conceptualize "ritual" in the family context? What theoretical approaches do scholars use to understand rituals? How have researchers studied rituals? How do families ritualize? What are possible directions for future research by family communication scholars who study rituals? These and other topics will be explored as we try to unravel the richness and complexity pertaining to family rituals.

Conceptualizing "Ritual" in Families

Scholars use the "ritual" concept differently. First, some communication scholars, most notably Carey (1975, 1988), argue that all communication is ritual. According to this view, communication-as-ritual serves as an alternative root metaphor for the more dominant root metaphor of communication-as-transmission. Communication-as-transmission emphasizes the rational or goal-directed transmission of information to produce some desired effect, whether understanding or attitude change. The ritual metaphor, by contrast, emphasizes communication as a performance jointly enacted by people, to be appreciated for its "magical, reality-constituting, symbolic-effectivity" (Rothenbuhler, 1998, p. 126).

From the communication-as-ritual viewpoint, any time we study communication in families, we would be studying ritual. Carey's (1975, 1988) view is similar to Goffman's (1967) focus on interaction ritual. Goffman regarded all interaction as part of the ceremonial order, ritualized in its orientation toward the sacred object of the self; through demeanor and deference, interactants sustain their own and others' face. Although we see value in these all-encompassing efforts to equate communication and ritual, we join the majority of ritual scholars who take more narrowly focused approaches to ritual.

In taking this more narrow approach to ritual, we view *ritual as a genre of communication events*. Scholars have studied ritual in a variety of academic disciplines, and Eric Rothenbuhler (1998, pp. 7–27) summarized much of the work on ritual studies, arguing that 12 characteristics of ritual are common across various definitions. We briefly summarize each of these characteristics because they are useful in helping us understand what ritual is and is not. Rituals are the following:

- *Performance based.* Ritual is performed, which means that it is action according to preexisting conceptions that guide its enactment and provide criteria for its evaluation. A family may import these guidelines from the society at large (e.g., holding a barbeque on the 4th of July), or guidelines might emerge from the traces of prior ritual performances (e.g., a family may begin an annual visit to the gravesite of a departed relative on the anniversary of her birthday).

- *Social.* Implicit in the fact that rituals are performances is their social nature. Rituals take a minimum of two people to be enacted; they are not solitary undertakings. All performances require the coparticipation of at least one other person, even if that coparticipation appears to be a passive enactment of the "audience" role.

- *Voluntary.* Rituals are matters of choice, both whether to participate and how to participate. Some families might hold rigid expectations of mandatory participation in prescribed ways, but family members can choose to violate these expectations. For example, we may be expected to attend family holiday celebrations or Sunday dinners, and although we might not even recognize it, in the end we choose to be there. Rituals are also subject to change across time, as participants choose to reproduce or change a ritual through its enactment on an ongoing basis.

- *Noninstrumental yet serious.* Rituals are rarely organized by a rational means-ends logic in which participants are using communication to accomplish some instrumental or technical goal. Rituals do perform important social functions, but they are not intentionally deployed for strategic purpose. We may feel closer as a family after participating in a birthday dinner ritual, but ask family members, and they will not say that they hold that dinner in order to feel closer. Some scholars use the noninstrumental nature of rituals to view them as trivial communication practices. However, the nonrational nature of rituals should not be confused with their social importance. Even the most frivolous, playful, and fun rituals have serious social functions. In the context of families, rituals do important work for families, most importantly establishing and sustaining family identities and bonds of affection.

- *Expressive of social relations.* Rituals have as their referents the social relations of the performers. In the context of the family, rituals depict the patterns of control and affection that characterize the relationships among family members. For example, when children are seated at a card table at a holiday dinner, this indexes their status as nonadults in the family hierarchy. For older children, moving to the "adult table" is indicative of their changed status in the family.

- *Evaluative.* Rituals do not merely reflect social relations in a neutral way; they are performed in a key of reflection, or evaluation. Rituals are moral commentaries about what is valued, or an expressive hope for what could be. The performance of this commentary or evaluation often requires a liminal time and space, when a "time-out" of some kind is taken from the enactment of everyday life. Families may stop and reflect on their rituals and the status of their family. A family that has taken a yearly trip to Disneyland may reflect on the changes in their family as they talk about whether the "kids will be too old for this trip next year."

- *Powerful.* The symbols invoked in rituals are effective, not in a rational means-ends way, but rather in their power to affect: Ritual symbolizing gets things done. When a couple exchanges vows at their wedding, symbolic expressions such as "I do" bring into being the state of marriage. When family members have dinner together nightly, they accomplish the construction of their family identity as cohesive. Rituals thus construct social life; they do not merely reflect it or evaluate it.

- *Condensed.* The symbols invoked in rituals have multiple, simultaneous referents. Thus, multiple meanings are condensed, or packed into, a limited number of symbols and symbolic actions. A single birthday celebration can symbolize ongoing relationships, individual and family changes, anticipation of the future, and regrets over the past.

- *Aesthetic.* Rituals have an element of stylization to them. *How* a ritual is performed is thus an important quality in constituting its meaning and the success of its enactment. We often become aware of this characteristic of rituals when we experience how other families enact similar rituals.

- *Regularly recurring.* Rituals are repeated behavior, whether the repetition was done this way before by others or by a given family at a prior point in time. The temporal rhythms of repetition can vary—from the regular cycle of the annual, monthly, weekly, or daily calendar to the more erratic repetitions that are situation specific. To say that rituals are repetitive, however, is not to say that they are mere habits or routines. Each of our families routinely takes the garbage to the curbside on garbage day, but this recurring behavior lacks the other elements that transform ordinary habits and routines into rituals.

- *Emphasizing form.* Some scholars criticize rituals as "empty" enactments of form over substance in which participants say and do predictable things in predictable ways in predictable sequences. However, this criticism misses an important feature of ritual: Its "substance" is the predictable forms of its performance. Part of what is meaningful about a Christmas or Hanukkah celebration is doing or performing the ritual in a similar way each year.

- *Emphasizing the sacred.* Rituals deal in the realm of sacred objects, however *sacred* might be defined by the participants. In the context of the family, rituals pay homage to that which is valued by family members—whether individual family members, family memories, valued family possessions, family processes, or family identity.

Our own definition of family ritual is informed by Rothenbuhler's (1998) characteristics of a ritual discussed above. For our purposes, we define a family ritual broadly as *a voluntary, recurring, patterned communication event whose jointly enacted performance by family members pays homage to what they regard as sacred, thereby producing and reproducing a family's identity and its web of social relations.*

This definition also grows out the work of earlier family studies scholars. In their classic work on family living, Bossard and Boll (1950) defined a family ritual as interaction that is localized around family living and characterized by prescription, recurrence, and a "sense of rightness which emerges from the past history of the process" (p. 16). Wolin and Bennett (1984) advanced a second classic conception of family ritual: a symbolic form of communication that is enacted systematically and repeatedly over time and that holds special meaning for family members. Cheal (1988) defined a family ritual as a repetitive, stylized act that is directed toward people or things that are highly valued by the family. All of these definitions share elements of communication, repetition, prescribed form, and homage. Central to us as family communication scholars is viewing ritual as a communication event.

Theoretical Approaches to Inform the Study of Family Rituals

Theories that inform our understanding of family ritual are located in three fields: (a) the interdisciplinary field of ritual studies (made up largely of anthropologists and religious scholars), (b) the interdisciplinary field of family studies (made up largely by psychologists and sociologists), and (c) the field of communication (to which family communication scholars contribute). We will discuss the theoretical approaches taken in these three fields.

Theoretical Approaches Found in Ritual Studies

Ritual studies offer several theoretical approaches relevant to the study of family rituals, and these scholars tend to focus their studies on religious ceremonies and the formal rites and rituals of various cultural groups. Scholarship in ritual studies is informed by three theoretical approaches: functional, semiotic/cultural, and performative (Bell, 1997).

Functional Approaches

Functional approaches to rituals are guided by the general question, "What are the functions of ritual for the individual and the social group?" Because our space here is limited, we can only point to the major theorists identified with this tradition. The functional perspective can be traced to the work of sociologist Emile Durkheim (1965), whose focus on religious rites emphasized the social function of ritual to express collective representations in the form of religious beliefs. He argued that rites and rituals produced religious beliefs in individual participants, thereby producing feelings of solidarity in a society's members. Anthropologists

Malinowski and Radcliffe-Brown further developed the functional approach begun by Durkheim. While Radcliffe-Brown (1964) continued Durkheim's focus on the functions of ritual for the social group, Malinowski (1948) placed more emphasis on the individual experience in the enactment of rituals, for example, the role of rituals in alleviating a person's anxiety, fears, or doubts.

These early functionalists were followed by various neo-functionalists who viewed ritual as a way to regulate and stabilize an individual system or a social system, restoring it to a state of harmony after disruption and thereby maintaining equilibrium. Rappaport (1968), for example, emphasized how rituals function to maintain an environmental balance between a social group and its natural resources. Ethologists such as Huxley (1966) and Lorenz (1966) argued that the ritualized behaviors of animals functioned to maintain their social groups, thereby contributing to survival of the species. In his focus on life crisis rituals or rites of passage, Van Gennep (1960) argued that ritual's three-stage sequential order (separation from one identity, transition into a state of liminality, and incorporation into a new identity) helped to provide a social group, as well as the individual participants, with order during times of chaotic social change. In an effort to complicate Durkheim's focus on ritualized expressions of unity, Gluckman (1962) viewed social life as rife with conflict, divisions, and struggles, rather than an experience of unitary solidarity and cohesion. According to his view, rituals expressed these tensions, struggles, and conflicts and then affirmed unity despite such social divisiveness. Turner's (1957, 1969, 1974) conception of ritual as social drama echoed Gluckman's work; Turner argued that when a social system experienced disruption and conflict, ritual was a mechanism of renewal, returning the system to harmonious equilibrium.

Despite their theoretical differences, the theorists identified with the functional approach to understanding ritual seek to identify how rituals facilitate individual psychic coherence or coherence of the social group. Some functionalists emphasize the individual more so than the social group, and others reverse this emphasis. Functionalists see rituals as expressing preexisting order (whether psychological or social) or producing and sustaining social order in a process of dynamic equilibrium. However, some overlap exists between theorists identified with the functionalist approach and the second approach we will discuss, especially for Turner.

Semiotic/Cultural Approaches

Semiotic/cultural approaches are the second theoretical tradition to emerge in the interdisciplinary field of ritual studies. This theoretical tradition centers on the question, "What are the meanings expressed in rituals?" Bell (1997) summarized how this approach differs from the functional approach:

> Culturalists interpret the symbols and symbolic action so important to ritual less in terms of their connection to the structures of social organization and more in terms of an independent system organized like a language for the primary purpose of communication. . . . This new focus . . . illuminates something other than the social organization of human groups; it illuminates "culture" as a more primary level of meanings, values, and attitudes. (p. 61)

Some functional theorists also emphasized the symbolic nature of rituals. In addition to viewing ritual as social drama, Turner (1969, 1974) also took a hermeneutic turn in studying ritual symbols, which he regarded as the fundamental units of ritual activity. Ritual symbols, Turner argued, are multivocal: They exist at many layers of meaning, often oppositional. Such semantic density produces complex systems of meaning, at once contradictory yet complementary. For example, the wedding ceremony contains symbols of separation (from families-of-origin) and unity (the formation of a marital unit connected to a larger network of extended families).

Various structuralists are also aligned with the semiotic/cultural approach. Levi-Strauss (1963), Douglas (1982), and Leach (1976) viewed ritual as a symbolic system of communication, expressing deep binary structures of human thought and manifested in social structure—for example, binaries such as good/evil, nature/nurture, high/low, cooked/raw. Because culture, in the form of beliefs and values, was a product of human mind, a ritual's symbols illuminated a culture's system of meanings. A religious rite of making a sacrifice to a god figure, for example, might gain its meaning in the underlying binary of good and evil: The god figure is aligned with all that is good, whereas humans are viewed as inherently evil beings who become good through sacrifice.

Another theorist identified with the semiotic/cultural approach, Geertz (1973), viewed a ritual's symbols as expressions of cultural ideals, providing a model of how things were and ought to be. His famous analysis of a Balinese cockfight, for example, provides a rich understanding of how the Balinese culture conceptualizes, orders, and attributes meaning to social life. Geertz argued that rituals are to be interpreted as if they were texts that illuminate a culture's code, or system, of meanings.

Other semiotic/cultural theorists, such as Bloch (1989), argue that meaning is communicated not only in the content of a ritual's symbols but additionally through form. Stylized form is a benchmark of ritual, according to Bloch, because of its centrality to a ritual's meaning. Staal's (1989) theory of ritual echoes this focus on form. What makes an ordinary action into a meaning-laden ritual, according to Staal, is its stylization. For example, family dinnertime might be highly stylized for a family with a particular table setting, seating arrangement, and expected topics of talk among family members. These stylizations transform a nightly routine into a ritual, according to these theorists.

Theorists who are identified with the semiotic/cultural theoretical approach are focused on the meanings of rituals. In attending to ritual content (its symbols) and to ritual form (stylized or formalized features of ritual structure and organization), the question is less how rituals function to sustain the individual psyche or the social group and more what they reveal about cultural values and beliefs.

Performance Approaches

Performance approaches are the third theoretical orientation in the interdisciplinary field of ritual studies. In a performative approach, the key shift is to view rituals not as mere expressions of culture but as activities that *construct* meanings and values. This is a shift from a representational view of communication to a constitutive view (Craig, 1999). Thus, the key question from a performative perspective is, "How is social reality constituted in the enactment of rituals?"

The performative approach positions participants in the ritual as active, creative creatures. As Bell (1997) noted, "Ritual does not mold people; people fashion rituals that mold their world" (p. 73). The physical and sensual aspects of ritual activity are important to performative approaches, for example, in Grimes's (1985, 1990) work on contemporary U.S. rituals. Reflexivity is also an important element in much performative work, meaning that ritual performances give participants the opportunity of "standing back and apart" from everyday life, thereby allowing reflection on it. Turner (1969) referred to this quality as the liminality of ritual, which refers to bracketing life-as-usual for purposes of ritual enactment.

Performance theorists have opened up a variety of social activities for their ritual quality, arguing that artificial conceptual boundaries have been made between ritual and such genres as play, festivals, drama, rock concerts, and so forth. Some performative theorists take a critical turn in their focus on how ritual enactments construct (and resist) relations of domination and subordination (e.g., Bourdieu, 1977; Sahlins, 1976, 1981).

What we see from the discussion above is that the interdisciplinary field of ritual studies has three well-established theoretical traditions from which to study rituals of all sorts, and we can identify traces of several of these approaches in the scholarship more narrowly focused on family rituals, which we will discuss next.

Theoretical Approaches to Family Rituals Found in Family Studies and in Communication

Although Bossard and Boll (1950) are usually credited as the first scholars in family studies to investigate family rituals, much contemporary work also draws on the classic essays by Reiss (1981) and Wolin and Bennett (1984), who were associated with the Center for Family Research at George Washington University during the 1980s. Reiss initially proposed that family rituals facilitate relational coherence and group integration; in addition, rituals situate a family in time and place. He argued that families could be distinguished by how they enacted rituals and maintained them across generations.

Wolin and Bennett (1984) elaborated on these issues in their theory of family ritualizing. Central to their theory is a typology of three ritual forms that has been very influential to researchers: celebrations, traditions, and patterned family interactions. *Celebrations* are rituals widely practiced throughout the culture, for example, holidays such as Thanksgiving or the Fourth of July, or rites of passage such as weddings or funerals. Although these events are culturally standardized, families uniquely adapt them to their own needs and desires. Having a Christmas tree is a standard element of celebrating Christmas in the U.S. culture, but families vary in when they put up their tree, how they decorate it, when gifts are placed under it, and how long the tree is left standing. *Traditions* are more idiosyncratic for each family and include events such as family vacations, reunions with extended family members, anniversaries, and birthdays. The "Gotcha Day" ritual described in the epigraph at the beginning of the chapter exemplifies a tradition. *Patterned family interactions* are mundane rituals, probably enacted most frequently of all ritual forms but with the least deliberate planning. Events such as family dinnertime, bedtime routines, and greetings are classified as this third ritual form.

These three ritual forms do different work, according to Wolin and Bennett (1984). Celebrations construct and sustain a family's membership in a larger culture, whereas traditions revolve around a family's temporal identity with its past. Patterned family interactions are commonplace activities that construct and sustain a family's identity in the here-and-now.

Wolin and Bennett's (1984) classic essay also drew attention to the process of ritualizing, drawing heavily from Turner's (1957, 1969, 1974) work, discussed above. Ritual enactments involve three important properties: transformation, communication, and stabilization. Transformation begins when a family's everyday life is suspended and they enter a period of liminality. At Easter, for example, the family might ready the house, buy the food, make up beds in the guest rooms, and plan and prepare the feast. The process of transformation produces the experience of *communitas* for the participants, as they emphasize their common family identity. The second property, communication, is related to the ritual's enactment. As a performance, the enactment of a ritual evokes a strong affective reaction from participants; all the senses are engaged in "a hyperaffective state" (Wolin & Bennett, 1984, p. 410). Through its symbol use, a ritual's performance is endowed with meaning for family members, whatever that might be. The third property, stabilization, renders life within a family steady. As a ritual is repeated, family members buttress themselves against chaotic and unpredictable change, thereby constructing and sustaining continuity between past, present, and future. Thus, a ritual such as Easter dinner gives family members the opportunity to step back and reflect on their family, evokes strong emotional meaning, and is repeated year after year as the family undergoes the large and small changes of life.

Wolin and Bennett (1984) also argued that families vary in their ritual practices. In particular, they identified two important dimensions of family ritualization: commitment to rituals and the ability to adapt rituals. First, families will differ in terms of their commitment to rituals. Families with a high commitment to rituals value ritual events. They value, as well, a historical perspective and ties to the past—whether prior generations or events from the immediate family's own past. They tend to exhibit a strong ethnic, religious, or community identity. In addition, argued Wolin and Bennett, high-commitment families tend to value their family intergenerational structure, with a hierarchy of positions between parents and children. By contrast, low-commitment families downplay the importance of rituals. Low-commitment families are oriented to the present and do not use rituals as occasions to celebrate their cultural/ethnic/religious identity. Low-commitment families have less clear-cut generational roles and structures.

Second, families need to establish flexibility and adaptability and modify their rituals in response to changing family needs. Families need flexibility and adaptability to prevent their rituals from becoming hollow and empty. An annual birthday celebration at a pizza house oriented toward children works well for young children but will not be appreciated once the child outgrows the experience. Rituals need to adapt to changes in individual family members and in family circumstances more generally.

Wolin and Bennett's (1984) family rituals theory combined functional, semiotic, and performative elements. However, its articulation of ritual functions has probably received the most attention by subsequent scholars, as well as in Wolin and Bennett's own program of research on the function of rituals in alcoholic families.

Dialectical theorists have also focused on family rituals. In their transactional-dialectical theory, Altman and his colleagues (e.g., Altman & Ginat, 1996; Brown, Werner, & Altman, 1998; Werner, Altman, Brown, & Ginat, 1993) emphasized the functional view that rituals are key sites where parties explore, develop, and celebrate their unique and their collective identities simultaneously. In other words, rituals are opportunities for parties to negotiate the individual-collective dialectic. For example, their research on the celebration of Christmas demonstrates how this ritual allows a family to negotiate its membership in a broader community through decorating the home's exterior. At the same time, the family might establish its link to prior generations through its use of heirloom family ornaments. Individual identities are also sustained as family members give gifts that are responsive to the wants and desires of individual family members. From the perspective of Altman et al., the "Gotcha" ritual at the opening of this chapter evidences the ability to sustain individual and communal identities at once. The focus on the individual child celebrates her unique identity with her own special day. In addition, however, the ritual's enactment in her classroom makes it a communal celebration in which everyone participates in experiencing "adoption" as a "normal" way to have a family, similar to an event common to all—the birthday event.

A second dialectical theory that more recently has emerged in communication studies to understand family rituals is Baxter and Montgomery's (1996) relational dialectics theory. Grounding their theory in the dialogism work of Russian social theorist Mikhail Bakhtin (1981, 1984, 1986), Baxter and Montgomery argued that all interpersonal communication is the discursive interplay of different, often contradictory, voices (perspectives, discourse systems, ideologies), or what Bakhtin referred to as dialogue. Relational dialectics is a theory about interpersonal communication in general, but rituals are highlighted as an important communication genre in exemplifying the concept of the aesthetic moment. Bakhtin (1981) viewed social life as a fragmented, disorderly, and messy interweave of opposing discourses. In such a social world, order is not given; it is a task to be accomplished. Occasionally, parties create fleeting moments of wholeness or order in which fragments and disorder are temporarily united. These are conceptualized as *aesthetic moments* (Bakhtin, 1990, p. 67). This momentary sense of unity is accomplished through a profound respect for the disparate voices in dialogue. The focus on ongoing opposition in play with unity bears some resemblance to the conflict-based approaches of Gluckman (1962) and Turner (1957, 1969, 1974) that we discussed above.

Baxter and Montgomery (1996; Baxter, 2004) conceptualized rituals as aesthetic moments. Rituals are meaningful because they are simultaneously responsive to contradictory discourses. In jointly performing a ritual, parties construct a fleeting moment of wholeness or unity in which homage is paid in some way through the interplay of multiple, competing voices. For example, Baxter and Braithwaite

(2002) argued that couples who participate in the ritual of renewing their marriage vows simultaneously give voice to two competing discourses of marriage in U.S. society: marriage as a traditional institution replete with responsibilities and obligations and marriage as a site of individual choice making and fulfillment.

Conceptualizing ritual as an aesthetic moment encourages us to think of ritual as more than means-end instrumentality; ritual is an emotion-laden and aesthetic event, as well (Baxter & DeGooyer, 2001). Communicative moments that parties experience as deeply meaningful are aesthetic, resulting from a powerful feeling of completion or consummation, a dynamic sense of unity in which "every successive part flows freely without seam and without unfilled blanks, into what ensures" (Dewey, 1934, p. 36). An aesthetic moment captures participants in the flow of the moment, evoking a feeling that extends beyond mere judgments of means-end utility or efficiency to include a deeply felt appreciation or realization of wholeness or completion. Feelings are intense in aesthetic moments—a combination of passion, vitality, and awe at the beauty of the experience. When a family ritualistically watches the sunrise together the first morning at their summer cabin, its members feel one with nature and one another.

Scholars committed to a relational dialectics approach to ritual ask what are the competing voices, or perspectives, that are at play in a ritual's performance and how ritual performances produce and reproduce a sense of social reality as coherent and orderly. With respect to the "Gotcha Day" account with which the chapter opened, a relational dialectics perspective asks, "What are the competing discourses, or perspectives, at play in the event's enactment?" and "How are these discourses interwoven into an aesthetic whole?" For example, "Gotcha Day" is distinguished from the day of birth, perhaps marking the rupture of the child's biological family and her social rebirth into an adopted family. These two different senses of "birth" are at play in the event. But it is their interweave that results in an aesthetic moment of wholeness for the child in which she is honored. "Gotcha Day" is modeled after the child's birthday celebration, but it is also marked as different from that celebration. In socializing the child's classmates about adoption, the ritual's enactment normalizes adoption, constructing a social reality in which adoptive families can be seen as a normal kind of family. A relational dialectics perspective displays traces of the semiotic/cultural tradition in its emphases on the content of rituals (the competing discourses) and the form of ritual (the aesthetics of wholeness). In addition, the theoretical perspective evidences a performance orientation in its focus on the construction of social reality as orderly.

Methodological Approaches to the Study of Family Rituals

In turning to the issue of methods, we can appreciate how scholars have produced a wealth of knowledge about family rituals. Researchers interested in family rituals have employed ethnographic, interview, text analysis, and survey methods, often in combination. The ethnographic approach, with its focus on participant observation in natural settings, is well established among cultural anthropologists in the interdisciplinary field of ritual studies. An example of participant-observation research in the study of family rituals is Braithwaite's (1995) study of ritualized wedding and baby showers. Braithwaite observed several shower events that included both women and men in wedding and baby shower rituals, videotaping several and taking descriptive field notes on her observations. In addition, Braithwaite interviewed shower participants about their expectations for, and experiences of, the shower event. Researchers using participant-observation usually combine it with informal and formal interviews with participants to gain further insights into the social practices being studied and their meanings. Braithwaite found that these wedding and shower events were occasions in which women socialized men in the meanings of husband and father roles, playing off of the gendered opposition of men versus women in producing occasions of intimacy and group solidarity.

Scholars often use interviews as a stand-alone method to study family rituals. The interview method has a long history in family ritual research, serving as the primary method by Wolin and Bennett (1984) in their research program on the role of rituals in families with alcohol abuse. These researchers interviewed family members from more than 100 alcohol abusive families on the rituals that were enacted in their families. In general, their findings suggested that when parental alcohol abuse disrupted family rituals, children were more likely to become alcoholic when they grew up, thereby resulting in the intergenerational transmission of alcoholism. In our research, we have relied on interviews quite extensively, whether to understand ceremonies in which longtime married partners renew their marriage vows (Baxter & Braithwaite, 2002; Braithwaite & Baxter, 1995) or to understand the role of rituals in stepfamily development (Braithwaite, Baxter, & Harper, 1998).

Researchers who use text analysis view a ritual enactment as a "text" whose symbols and forms are studied for their underlying meanings. Leeds-Hurwitz's (2002) work on intercultural weddings illustrates this analytic method. Leeds-Hurwitz grounded her data collection in ethnographic and interview methods. However, her analysis of these data illustrates text analysis. Among other things, she examined the symbolic artifacts of weddings—bridal bouquets, clothing, and religious symbols— as a way to "read" the underlying cultural meanings and identities at play in weddings between persons of different cultural backgrounds.

A fourth methodological approach is the use of surveys or questionnaires. Researchers distributing surveys to study rituals gather participants' self-report on the rituals in their families. Surveys can be relatively unstructured, as exemplified in the classic research by Bossard and Boll (1950) in which university students were asked to write descriptions of the ritual enactments in their families-of-origin. Survey research can also take a more structured approach, as exemplified in Fiese's (1992, 1993; Fiese & Kline, 1993) development of the Family Rituals Questionnaire (FRQ).

The FRQ is a 56-item forced-choice questionnaire, grounded in the theoretical work of Wolin and Bennett (1984), that solicits the perceptions of family members with respect to a variety of family rituals, including informal patterned interactions surrounding dinnertime and weekend activities, traditions related to family vacations and annual events such as birthdays, and celebrations such as religious holidays. Perceptions are elicited for each type of ritual with respect to eight underlying characteristics of ritualizing: the frequency of the ritual's occurrence, the assignment of regular roles and duties during the ritual's enactment, regularity in how the ritual is conducted, expectations for mandatory attendance, family members' emotional investment in the ritual activity, family members' attachment of meaning to the activity, the perseverance of the ritual across family generations, and the deliberateness of the ritual with respect to advance planning and preparation.

Based on factor analyses of the FRQ items, Fiese (1992) has identified two underlying dimensions of ritualization that correspond quite closely to Wolin and Bennett's (1984) posited dimensions of ritualizing. First, the characteristics of emotional involvement, symbolic significance, frequency of occurrence, mandatory attendance, and deliberateness load on a factor that captures the family's commitment to ritualizing. The second factor, consisting of role assignment and regularity, captures routinization or adaptability. The FRQ has been used by several family researchers. For example, Baxter and Clark (1996) employed the FRQ in examining differences in ritual enactment among families of varying family communication patterns.

Research on Family Rituals: An Overview

Our intent in this section is to summarize major themes in existing research on family rituals. We begin with a discussion of research on ritualizing in general and then turn to research on each of the three ritual forms identified by Wolin and Bennett (1984)—celebrations, traditions, and patterned interactions.

Research on Ritualizing

A number of scholars have focused on ritualizing in families rather than on the enactment of specific ritual forms. However, one limitation of this body of research is that routines often have not been clearly differentiated from rituals (Fiese et al., 2002). Nonetheless, important findings can be identified.

Ritualizing appears to be linked to health and well-being for individual family members. Wolin, Bennett, and their colleagues identified how rituals function to protect offspring from the damaging effects of parental alcoholism (Bennett, Wolin, & McAvity, 1988; Bennett, Wolin, Reiss, & Teitlebaum, 1987; Steinglass, Bennett, Wolin, & Reiss, 1987; Wolin & Bennett, 1984; Wolin, Bennett, Noonan, & Teitlebaum, 1980). Maintaining family rituals appears to facilitate better adaptation among children during times of family disruption, for example, following divorce and remarriage (Braithwaite et al., 1998; Brody & Flor, 1997; Guidabaldi, Cleminshaw, Perry, Nastasi, & Lightel, 1986; Henry & Lovelace, 1995).

Family ritualizing is related to positive adolescent identity (Fiese, 1992) and to adolescent well-being more generally (Compan, Moreno, Ruiz, & Pascual, 2002; Deinham, 2003). Family ritualizing also appears to correlate positively with a number of relational outcomes. Partner satisfaction and commitment, for example, are related to ritualizing among committed partners and married couples (e.g., Baxter, 1992; Bruess & Pearson, 1993, 1997, 2002; Fiese, Hooker, Kotary, &

Schwagler, 1993). For example, Berg-Cross, Daniels, and Carr (1992) found that married couples reported more frequent ritualizing activity than comparable divorced pairs.

Why and how does ritualizing correlate with positive individual and relational outcomes? Function-oriented research suggests that rituals provide certainty and stability for family members, functioning to buffer them against times of stress or transition (Baxter, 1987; Fiese et al., 2002; Oring, 1984; Wolin et al., 1980). To some extent, this certainty comes from the construction of continuity with the family's own past history (e.g., Baxter, 1987; Baxter & Pittman, 2001), for example, the continuity that comes from repeating the same family origin story at the Thanksgiving table from one year to the next. Certainty also can result from cross-generational ritualizing that functions to sustain continuity with prior family generations (Meredith, 1985; Rosenthal & Marshall, 1988; Schvaneveldt & Lee, 1983). Other function-oriented research suggests that rituals are sources of stimulation, fun, and entertainment for family members (e.g., Baxter, 1987, 1992) and that rituals have positive outcomes for individuals and for families. Still other function-oriented research suggests that when a family enacts rituals together, such joint activity builds and sustains communion, cohesion, and intimacy (e.g., Baxter, 1987; Bruess & Pearson, 1997, 2002; Meske, Sanders, Meredith, & Abbott, 1994), which in turn enhance individual and relational well-being.

Scholars from a semiotic/cultural perspective argue that family rituals are linked with positive outcomes because they create and sustain webs of meaning that bring coherence to family life. Although the meaning of family rituals may be incomprehensible to an outsider, to "insider" family members, rituals contain deep symbolism about family identity and individual identity as a family member (e.g., Bruess & Pearson, 1993, 2002; Olson & Haynes, 1993). For example, rituals contain symbols that mark the family as unique from other families (e.g., Baxter, 1987), thereby creating a sense that there is no other family quite like one's own.

From a dialectical perspective, rituals are important because they capture the interplay of competing, or opposing, discourses. As Roberts (1988) has cogently observed,

> Rituals can hold both sides of a contradiction at the same time. We all live with the ultimate paradoxes of life/death, connection/distance, ideal/real, good/evil. Ritual can incorporate both sides of contradictions so that they can be managed simultaneously. For instance, a wedding ceremony has within it both loss and mourning and joy and celebration. (p. 16)

For example, Braithwaite and her colleagues (1998) interviewed stepfamily members and heard them framing the "old family" (the family-of-origin) as oppositional to the "new family" (the stepfamily). Rituals perceived to be successful by stepfamily members where those in which the "old" and "new" families were mutually celebrated at once. For example, one stepfamily displayed some Christmas decorations brought from both of the "old" families," and then each year the stepfamily members made some Christmas decorations together to celebrate the stepfamily as well. By contrast, failed rituals were those in which either the "old family" was celebrated to the neglect of the "new family," or vice versa.

Ritualizing varies by family characteristic. Baxter and Clark (1996), for example, found that commitment to ritualizing was greater among families high in conversation-orientation, a communication pattern characterized by open discussion among family members with no necessary expectation of consensus. Among European Americans (but not Asian Americans), the commitment to ritualizing was also greater for families with high conformity-orientation, a communication pattern characterized by a hierarchical model of family rights and obligations in which difference of opinion is discouraged. Among European Americans (but not Asian Americans), routinization in the enactment of family rituals was greater among families high in conformity-orientation. Parental attachment styles also appear related to family ritualizing (Leon & Jacobvitz, 2003). In particular, when two parents have different attachment styles, families tend to ritualize less. Furthermore, insecure parental attachment appears related to overly rigid ritualization in families, with inadequate adaptability and change.

Ritualizing appears to vary across the life cycle. For example, Berg-Cross and her colleagues (1992) found that the number and range of rituals was greater for longer married couples (more than 10 years) as opposed to couples in shorter marriages (less than 3 years). Ritualizing also appears to increase as children move from infancy to older childhood, as does the meaningfulness of those rituals (Fiese et al., 1993).

Ritualizing is experienced differently depending on one's family position or role. In general, parents find ritualizing more meaningful than do their college-aged offspring (Fiese, 1992; Meredith, Abbott, Lamanna, & Sanders, 1989). Ritualizing appears to become important for offspring only when they become parents themselves (Fiese et al., 2002). Leach and Braithwaite (1996) found that the responsibility for family "kin-keeping" activity, including family ritualizing, appears to fall on middle-generation female family members.

Ritualizing—a family's commitment to its rituals and its capacity to adapt rituals to changing needs—appears to vary by several family characteristics, including family communication patterns, family life cycle, individual family role, and dispositional features of individual family members. Across various families, ritualizing is powerfully related to family and individual well-being. Instead of focusing on ritualizing per se, a number of scholars have concentrated on particular types of rituals.

Research on Particular Ritual Forms

In this section, we summarize briefly what has been done in studying particular types of rituals—celebrations, traditions, and patterned interactions.

Celebrations

The most frequently reported ritual celebrations among family members include the cultural and religious events of New Year's Eve, Christmas, Thanksgiving, Easter, and Passover (Berg-Cross et al., 1992; Meske et al., 1994; Rosenthal & Marshall, 1988). However, research attention has focused almost exclusively on Christmas celebrations. Altman and Ginat's (1996) dialectical study of Christmas celebrations among Mormon polygynist families, for example, portrayed a complex interweaving of symbolic efforts to pay homage both to the family as a whole (headed by the husband-father) as well as the individual families of which the larger whole is comprised (the separate families that are associated with each wife). Oxley, Haggard, Werner, and Altman (1986) provided a dialectical analysis of Christmas Street, a cul-de-sac neighborhood whose annual Christmas decorations and partying paid homage both to individual family identities and to the larger community identity as coresidents of the neighborhood.

Celebrations surrounding rites of passage have also received scholarly attention. The rituals that surround the formal bonding of a couple are complicated sites of ritualizing, and scholars have used functional, semiotic/cultural, and performance-based theoretical approaches. Wedding showers (Braithwaite, 1995), weddings (Altman & Ginat, 1996; Leeds-Hurwitz, 2002; Oswald, 2000), and renewal of marriage vows (Baxter & Braithwaite, 2002; Braithwaite & Baxter, 1995) are significant communal events in which a variety of identities are circulating, sometimes seamlessly and sometimes with struggle: individual, family, gender, sexual orientation, cultural, and religious. For example, Oswald (2000) studied challenges homosexual family members faced when attending heterosexual family weddings. Communally centered rituals surrounding birth (e.g., Braithwaite, 1995) and death (e.g., McIlwain, 2002) similarly suggest that complicated symbolic work is enacted surrounding individual, family, and cultural identities.

A common finding that emerges in the research on celebrations is that families are embedded in larger group identification processes in the enactment of rituals. Although these celebrations have a standardized component to them, in that they are similarly enacted across families that share an identity, they simultaneously allow families to "poach" and adapt the standardized ritual scripts in ways that symbolize each family's own uniqueness.

Traditions

Traditions, rituals that are unique to the individual family's autobiography and calendar, have received surprisingly little scholarly attention. Birthdays, wedding anniversaries, and family reunions have been frequently reported by family members (Altman & Ginat, 1996; Berg-Cross et al., 1992; Meske et al., 1994; Rosenthal & Marshall, 1988), yet we know very little about these and other family traditions. Altman and Ginat's (1996) study of Mormon polygynist families provides a rare insight into the complexities that surround the homage events of birthdays and wedding anniversaries. In polygynist families, wedding anniversaries for the husband and a given wife are generally dyadic celebrations only, rather than communal events that involve all of a husband's family units associated with his multiple wives. Similarly, a wife's birthday and the birthdays of her children are celebrated within the family structure of the child's mother and her children, joined by the husband-father. By contrast, the birthday of the husband-father tends to be a full communal event, in which all of the wives and their children join in paying birthday homage. However, exceptions to this general pattern are evident; for example, if co-wives become friends, they may join in one another's birthday celebration or those of each other's children or offer to perform babysitting services so that a co-wife and the husband can enjoy private time together during their anniversary.

Patterned Interactions

Interestingly, the majority of work on family rituals has been done surrounding the third of Wolin and Bennett's (1984) ritual types. Patterned interactions tend to be informal routines with symbolic significance for family members. The most frequently reported patterned-interaction rituals include dinnertime (e.g., Blum-Kulka, 1997; Feiring & Lewis, 1987; Ramey & Juliusson, 1998), children's bedtime (e.g., Nucci & Smetana, 1996), ritualized storytelling (e.g., Baxter & Pittman, 2001; Blum-Kulka, 1997; Langellier & Peterson, 2004), mundane behavioral events such as listening to music together (e.g., Baxter, 1987, 1992; Berg-Cross et al., 1992; Bruess & Pearson, 1997, 2002), ritualized play (e.g., Baxter, 1992; Bruess & Pearson, 1997, 2002), and episodes organized around idiomatic expressions (e.g., Bruess & Pearson, 1993).

Considered as a set, patterned interactions are most likely to be confused with routines because they appear on their surface to be merely mundane activities (e.g., bedtime) or activities with instrumental purpose (e.g., feeding at dinnertime). However, patterned interactions are rituals in that they hold symbolic import in which homage of some kind is at stake. If dinnertime is important because it symbolizes a family's togetherness, it steps beyond the boundaries of everyday instrumental routines to take on ritualistic significance. Similarly, an idiomatic expression (e.g., nicknames) shared by family members to pay homage in some way to their identity moves from the domain of the mundane to function as an important family ritual.

Conclusion

Family rituals are an important communicative activity that positions us to study family communication as a whole cloth, rather than segmented into a series of dyad-based communication patterns such as husband-wife or parent-child interaction. Rituals are important to the well-being of families and of individual family members.

Although scholarship on family rituals is vast, several avenues for future research are fruitful. First, research on family rituals tends to be dominated by a functional approach. Ritual studies provides a long intellectual tradition rich in potential theoretical insight into family rituals, and future research on family rituals should draw more broadly from the full theoretical range—functional, semiotic/cultural, and performance theoretical perspectives.

Second, future research on family rituals should examine specific rituals and ritual forms, especially the neglected type of family traditions. With some exceptions, existing research is also biased in the direction of traditional family structures, and the rituals of nontraditional families also merit greater attention—for example, adoption rituals, commitment ceremonies among cohabiting heterosexual and homosexual couples, Kwanza celebrations, and so forth.

Third, taken as a whole, research on family rituals tends to lack a process perspective in its reliance on static and cross-sectional research designs. As a result, we currently have limited insight into how rituals change over time in families, and thus we have little understanding of how some rituals become "empty" as the years pass, while others are adapted to sustain meaningfulness. A focus on ritualizing is incomplete in the absence of longitudinal work.

Fourth, family rituals have been studied with a "positivity bias." We have tended to ignore the "dark side" of rituals and ritualizing. For example, we have little critical insight into how power dynamics are enacted in rituals and how disenfranchised family members resist dominant family meanings associated with rituals. In addition, we have no understanding of how rituals themselves can be sources of stress for family members, for example, the stress associated with the decision as to where children in postdivorce families will celebrate important events such as Christmas and birthdays.

References

Altman, I., & Ginat, J. (1996). *Polygamous families in contemporary society.* New York: Cambridge University Press.

Bakhtin, M. M. (1981). *The dialogic imagination: Four essays by M. M. Bakhtin* (M. Holquist, Ed.; C. Emerson & M. Holquist, Trans.). Austin: University of Texas Press.

Bakhtin, M. M. (1984). *Problems of Dostoyevsky's poetics* (C. Emerson, Ed. and Trans.). Minneapolis: University of Minnesota Press.

Bakhtin, M. M. (1986). *Speech genres and other late essays* (C. Emerson & M. Holquist, Eds.; V. McGee, Trans.). Austin: University of Texas Press.

Bakhtin, M. M. (1990). *Art and answerability: Early philosophical essays by M. M. Bakhtin* (M. Holquist & V. Liapunov, Eds.; V. Liapunov & K. Brostrom, Trans.). Austin: University of Texas Press.

Baxter, L. A. (1987). Symbols of relationship identity in relationship cultures. *Journal of Social and Personal Relationships, 4,* 261–280.

Baxter, L. A. (1992). Forms and functions of intimate play in personal relationships. *Human Communication Research, 18,* 336–363.

Baxter, L. A. (2004). Distinguished Scholar Article: Relationships as dialogues. *Personal Relationships, 11,* 1–22.

Baxter, L. A., & Braithwaite, D. O. (2002). Performing marriage: The marriage renewal ritual as cultural performance. *Southern Communication Journal, 67,* 94–109.

Baxter, L. A., & Clark, C. (1996). Perceptions of family communication patterns and the enactment of family rituals. *Western Journal of Communication, 60,* 254–268.

Baxter, L. A., & DeGooyer, D. (2001). Perceived aesthetic characteristics of interpersonal conversations. *Southern Communication Journal, 67,* 1–18.

Baxter, L. A., & Montgomery, B. M. (1996). *Relating: Dialogues and dialectics.* New York: Guilford.

Baxter, L. A., & Pittman, G. (2001). Communicatively remembering turning points of relationship development. *Communication Reports, 14,* 1–18.

Bell, C. (1997). *Ritual: Perspectives and dimensions.* New York: Oxford University Press.

Bennett, L. A., Wolin, S. J., & McAvity, K. J. (1988). Family identity, ritual, and myth: A cultural perspective on life cycle transition. In C. J. Falicov (Ed.), *Family transitions: Continuity and change over the life cycle* (pp. 211–234). New York: Guilford.

Bennett, L. A., Wolin, S. J., Reiss, D., & Teitelbaum, M. A. (1987). Couples at risk for transmission of alcoholism: Protective influences. *Family Process, 26,* 11–129.

Berg-Cross, L., Daniels, C., & Carr, P. (1992). Marital rituals among divorced and married couples. *Journal of Divorce & Remarriage, 18,* 1–30.

Bloch, M. (1989). *Ritual, history, and power: Selected papers in anthropology.* London: Athlone.

Blum-Kulka, S. (1997). *Dinner talk.* Mahwah, NJ: Lawrence Erlbaum.

Bossard, J. H. S., & Boll, E. S. (1950). *Ritual in family living: A contemporary study.* Philadelphia: University of Pennsylvania Press.

Bourdieu, P. (1977). *Outline of a theory of practice* (R. Nice, Trans.). Cambridge, UK: Cambridge University Press.

Braithwaite, D. O. (1995). Ritualized embarrassment at "coed" wedding and baby showers. *Communication Reports, 8,* 145–157.

Braithwaite, D. O., & Baxter, L. A. (1995). "I do" again: The relational dialectics of renewing marriage vows. *Journal of Social and Personal Relationships, 12,* 177–198.

Braithwaite, D. O., Baxter, L. A., & Harper, A. M. (1998). The role of rituals in the management of the dialectical tension of "old" and "new" in blended families. *Communication Studies, 48,* 101–120.

Brody, G. H., & Flor, D. L. (1997). Maternal psychological functioning, family processes, and child adjustment in rural, single-parent, African-American families. *Developmental Psychology, 33,* 1000–1011.

Brown, B., Werner, C., & Altman, I. (1998). Choice points for dialecticians: A dialectical-transactional perspective on close relationships. In B. M. Montgomery & L. A. Baxter (Eds.), *Dialectical approaches to studying personal relationships* (pp. 137–154). Mahwah, NJ: Lawrence Erlbaum.

Bruess, C., & Pearson, J. C. (1993). "Sweet pea" and "pussy cat"? An examination of idiom use and marital satisfaction over the life cycle. *Journal of Social and Personal Relationships, 10,* 609–615.

Bruess, C., & Pearson, J. C. (1997). Interpersonal rituals in marriage and adult friendship. *Communication Monographs, 64,* 25–46.

Bruess, C., & Pearson, J. C. (2002). The function of mundane ritualizing in adult friendship and marriage. *Communication Research Reports, 19,* 314–326.

Carey, J. (1975). A cultural approach to communication. *Communication, 2,* 1–22.

Carey, J. (1988). *Communication as culture: Essays on media and society.* Boston: Unwin Hyman.

Cheal, D. J. (1988). Relationships in time: Ritual, social structure, and the life course. *Studies in Symbolic Interaction, 9,* 83–109.

Compan, E., Moreno, J., Ruiz, M., & Pascual, E. (2002). Doing things together: Adolescent health and family rituals. *Journal of Epidemiology & Community Health, 56,* 89–95.

Craig, R. T. (1999). Communication theory as a field. *Communication Theory, 9,* 119–161.

Deinham, S. (2003). Relationships between family rituals, family routines, and health. *Journal of Family Nursing, 9,* 305–330.

Dewey, J. (1934). *Art as experience.* New York: Perigree.

Douglas, M. (1982). *Natural symbols: Explorations in cosmology.* New York: Pantheon. (Original work published 1970)

Durkheim, E. (1965). *The elementary forms of the religious life* (J. W. Swain, Trans.). New York: Free Press. (Original work published 1912)

Feiring, C., & Lewis, M. (1987). The ecology of some middle class families at dinner. *International Journal of Behavioral Development, 10,* 377–390.

Fiese, B. H. (1992). Dimensions of family rituals across two generations: Relations to adolescent identity. *Family Process, 31,* 151–162.

Fiese, B. H. (1993). Family rituals in alcoholic and nonalcoholic households. *Family Relations, 42,* 187–192.

Fiese, B. H., Hooker, K. A., Kotary, L., & Schwagler, J. (1993). Family rituals in the early stages of parenthood. *Journal of Marriage and the Family, 57,* 633–642.

Fiese, B. H., & Kline, C. A. (1993). Development of the Family Ritual Questionnaire (FRQ): Initial reliability and validation studies. *Journal of Family Psychology, 6,* 290–299.

Fiese, B. H., Tomcho, T., Douglas, M., Josephs, K., Poltrock, S., & Baker, T. (2002). A review of 50 years of research on naturally occurring family routines and rituals: Cause for celebration? *Journal of Family Psychology, 16,* 381–390.

Geertz, C. (1973). *The interpretation of culture.* New York: Basic Books.

Gluckman, M. (1962). Les rites de passage. In M. Gluckman (Ed.), *Essays on the ritual of social relations* (pp. 1–52). Manchester, UK: Manchester University Press.

Goffman, E. (1967). *Interaction ritual: Essays on face-to-face behavior.* New York: Anchor.

Grimes, R. (1985). *Research in ritual studies.* Metuchen, NJ: Scarecrow.

Grimes, R. (1990). *Ritual criticism: Case studies in its practice, essays on its theory.* Columbia: University of South Carolina Press.

Guidabaldi, J., Cleminshaw, H. K., Perry, J. D., Nastasi, B. K., & Lightel, J. (1986). The role of selected family environment factors in children's post-divorce adjustment. *Family Relations, 35,* 141–151.

Henry, C. S., & Lovelace, S. G. (1995). Family resources and adolescent family life satisfaction in remarried family households. *Journal of Family Issues, 16,* 765–786.

Huxley, J. (Ed.). (1966). A discussion of ritualization of behaviour in animals and man [Special issue]. *Philosophical Transactions of the Royal Society of London, 251*(Series B: Biological Sciences), 247–526.

Langellier, K. M., & Peterson, E. E. (2004). *Storytelling in daily life.* Philadelphia: Temple University Press.

Leach, E. R. (1976). *Culture and communication: The logic by which symbols are connected.* Cambridge, UK: Cambridge University Press.

Leach, M. S., & Braithwaite, D. O. (1996). A binding tie: Supportive communication of family kinkeepers. *Journal of Applied Communication Research, 24,* 200–216.

Leeds-Hurwitz, W. (2002). *Wedding as text: Communicating cultural identities through ritual.* Mahwah, NJ: Lawrence Erlbaum.

Leon, K., & Jacobvitz, D. B. (2003). Relationships between adult attachment representations and family ritual quality: A prospective, longitudinal study. *Family Process, 42,* 419–432.

Levi-Strauss, C. (1963). *Structural anthropology* (C. Jacobson & B. G. Schoepf, Trans.). New York: Basic Books. (Original work published 1958)

Lorenz, K. Z. (1966). Evolution of ritualization in the biological and cultural spheres. *Philosophical Transactions of the Royal Society of London, 251*(Series B: Biological Sciences), 273–284.

Malinowski, B. (1948). *Magic, science, and religion, and other essays.* Boston: Beacon. (Original work published 1925)

McIlwain, C. D. (2002). Death in black and white: A study of family differences in the performance of death rituals. *Qualitative Research Reports in Communication, 3,* 1–6.

Meredith, W. (1985). The importance of family traditions. *Wellness Perspectives, 2,* 17–19.

Meredith, W. H., Abbott, D. A., Lamanna, M. A., & Sanders, G. (1989). Rituals and family strengths: A three-generation study. *Family Perspective, 23,* 75–83.

Meske, C., Sanders, G. F., Meredith, W. H., & Abbott, D. A. (1994). Perceptions of rituals and traditions among elderly persons. *Activities, Adaptation and Aging: The Journal of Activities Management, 18,* 13–26.

Nucci, L., & Smetana, J. G. (1996). Mothers' concepts of young children's areas of personal freedom. *Child Development, 67,* 1870–1886.

Olson, M. R., & Haynes, J. A. (1993). Successful single parents. *Families in Society, 74,* 259–267.

Oring, E. (1984). Dyadic traditions. *Journal of Folklore Research, 21,* 19–28.

Oswald, R. F. (2000). A member of the wedding? Heterosexism and family ritual. *Journal of Social and Personal Relationships, 17,* 349–368.

Oxley, D., Haggard, J. M., Werner, C. M., & Altman, I. (1986). Transactional qualities of neighborhood social networks: A case study of "Christmas Street." *Environment and Behavior, 18,* 640–677.

Radcliffe-Brown, A. R. (1964). *The Andaman Islanders.* New York: Free Press. (Original work published 1922)

Ramey, S. L., & Juliusson, H. K. (1998). Family dynamics at dinner: A natural context for revealing basic family processes. In M. Lewis & C. Feiring (Eds.), *Families, risk, and competence* (pp. 31–52). Mahwah, NJ: Lawrence Erlbaum.

Rappaport, R. A. (1968). *Pigs for the ancestors: Ritual in the ecology of a New Guinea people.* New Haven, CT: Yale University Press.

Reiss, D. (1981). *The family's construction of reality.* Cambridge, MA: Harvard University Press.

Roberts, J. (1988). Setting the frame: Definition, functions, and typology of rituals. In E. Imber-Black, J. Roberts, & R. A. Whiting (Eds.), *Rituals in families and family therapy* (pp. 3–46). New York: Norton.

Rosenthal, C. J., & Marshall, V. W. (1988). Generational transmission of family ritual. *American Behavioral Scientist, 31,* 669–684.

Rothenbuhler, E. W. (1998). *Ritual communication: From everyday conversation to mediated ceremony.* Thousand Oaks, CA: Sage.

Sahlins, M. (1976). *Culture and practical reason.* Chicago: University of Chicago Press.

Sahlins, M. (1981). *Historical metaphors and mythical realities.* Ann Arbor: University of Michigan Press.

Schvaneveldt, J., & Lee, R. (1983). The emergence and practice of ritual in the American family. *Family Perspective, 17,* 137–143.

Staal, F. (1989). *Rules without meaning: Ritual, mantras and the human sciences.* Bern, Switzerland: Peter Lang.

Steinglass, P., Bennett, L. A., Wolin, S. J., & Reiss, D. (1987). *The alcoholic family.* New York: Basic Books.

Turner, V. (1957). *Schism and continuity in an African society: A study of Ndembu village life.* Manchester, UK: Manchester University Press.

Turner, V. (1969). *The ritual process: Structure and anti-structure.* Ithaca, NY: Cornell University Press.

Turner, V. (1974). *Dramas, fields, and metaphors: Symbolic action in human society.* Ithaca, NY: Cornell University Press.

Van Gennep, A. (1960). *The rites of passage* (M. B. Vizedom & G. L. Caffee, Trans.). Chicago: University of Chicago Press.

Werner, C. M., Altman, I., Brown, B., & Ginat, J. (1993). Celebrations in personal relationships: A transactional/dialectical perspective. In S. Duck (Ed.), *Social context and relationships* (pp. 109–139). Newbury Park, CA: Sage.

Wolin, S. J., & Bennett, L. A. (1984). Family rituals. *Family Process, 23,* 401–420.

Wolin, S. J., Bennett, L. A., Noonan, D. L., & Teitlebaum, M. A. (1980). Disrupted family rituals: A factor in generational transmission of alcoholism. *Journal of Studies on Alcohol, 41,* 199–214.

CHAPTER 15

Ritual (In)Activity in Postbereaved Stepfamilies

Leah E. Bryant

DePaul University

F amily rituals function to define family identity. As stepfamilies are formed and maintained, they create a sense of who they are through rituals. Family meanings and affect are expressed through stylized interaction that rituals provide to help individuals interpret and explain experiences (Fiese, 1992; Jorgenson & Bochner, 2004). Essentially, rituals are vital for creating and maintaining family cohesion (Wolin & Bennett, 1984). Wolin and Bennett (1984) define rituals as a "symbolic form of communication that . . . through its repetition, is acted out in a systematic fashion over time" (p. 401). The special and repetitive nature of rituals that are developed cooperatively helps to stimulate group participation and aids in establishing family identity (Bossard & Boll, 1949; Wolin & Bennett, 1984) (for a further detailed examination of the interdisciplinary nature of family rituals, see Chapter 14, this volume).

Previous researchers of stepfamily rituals identified a dialectical tension between the "old family" and the "new family" (Braithwaite, Baxter, & Harper, 1998). It was found that for successful ritual enactment to occur, stepfamilies needed to develop and participate in rituals that celebrated both the new family while simultaneously valuing the old family. Essentially, successful rituals were those that could pay homage to both the current as well as the old family.

Postbereaved stepfamily (stepfamilies formed following the death of a parent) members often find it difficult to develop and enact rituals in their new family. This may be due to loyalty conflicts. Children have to invest energy in the new stepparent relationship, but this new relationship can conflict with the need to maintain an attachment to the deceased parent (Baker, Sedney, & Gross, 1992). Replacing an old ritual, one enacted in the previous family structure, with a new one may also be perceived as betraying the deceased parent. This may be because the members of the previous family structure may interpret the new ritual as an attempt to forget the deceased parent and the old family structure.

Family rituals are of import to help children adjust to parental death. Clinicians suggest that the family follow regular routines because changes are unsettling to children (Tellerman, Chernoff, Grossman, & Adams, 1998). Grieving family members are likely to experience anniversary reactions, which are recurrences of sad feelings that are often triggered by an anniversary or ritual, such as the deceased parent's birthday or day of death (Baker et al., 1992; Plotkin, 1983).

Rituals are created through communication among family members. However, communication about the previous family and the deceased parent is often stifled or nonexistent among surviving family members. This pattern of not communicating about the deceased parent or previous family structure may continue into the stepfamily (Bryant, 2003). There is a tendency for the surviving parent to withhold information about parental death to protect children from the pain associated with loss. Yet, this cyclical nature of constrained communication between the parent and children is not conducive to open communication about the deceased parent. And due to societal taboos against talking about the deceased, children may not feel they can be open with stepparents about their previous family, and stepparents may feel they cannot ask about the previous family. Golish and Caughlin (2002) found that stepchildren avoided talking about the other parent/family with their stepparent to avoid conflict.

It is important to communicate about the deceased parent, though it may not happen in the stepfamily (Baker et al., 1992). Christ (2000) interviewed children and found that before the age of 12, children want to talk about and be surrounded by artifacts of the deceased parent. However, after the age of 12, it becomes increasingly difficult for the children to communicate about the deceased parent. Yet, openness and general communication with the surviving parent about parental death have been associated with better psychological outcomes in children (Christ, 2000; Hurd, 1999; Worden, 1996). Involvement in activities such as attending funeral-related events, keeping mementos of the deceased parent, hearing stories about the deceased parent, and visiting the grave was associated with less risk for subsequent depression (Saler & Skolnick, 1992).

Although many children did not feel that they could be open with their family about their deceased parent or previous family (Bryant, 2003; Golish & Caughlin, 2002), the children worried about not being able to remember their deceased parent (Tellerman et al., 1998). Many of the children often made an effort to stay connected with their deceased parent in some way, often by visiting their parent's grave and keeping things that had belonged to him or her (Silverman & Worden, 1992).

The concept of a "social ghost" captures children's sense of their parent's continuing presence even many years after the parent's death (Riches & Dawson, 1998; Stroebe, Gergen, Gergen, & Stroebe, 1992). When the surviving parent remarries, stepfamily members are faced with communicatively negotiating the presence of the deceased parent. This creates a conversational dilemma where talking about the deceased parent evokes difficult responses. Not talking about the deceased parent produces feelings of denial of that person's existence (Riches & Dawson, 1998). Furthermore, it may be difficult for the stepparent to discuss the deceased parent, especially if he or she did not know the deceased. This sends the implicit message that the stepparent is not accepting of the previous family.

The need to publicly discuss the deceased parent partially compensates for the inability of the parent to actually respond, thus providing bereaved children with additional material to construct internal images of their parent (Riches & Dawson, 1998). Talking about memories (the happy times, the funny times, and the sad times) helps to fix them in the child's mind and may help children preserve their memories and come to terms with their grief (Tellerman et al., 1998). To continue a dialogue about the deceased parent, families may need to develop a norm of talking about the deceased to maintain a memory of him or her, which then can continue on into the stepfamily. Therefore, issues surrounding communicating about the deceased parent must be addressed for the stepfamily to establish its own identity and for children to adjust to the new family.

In a pilot study of postbereaved stepfamily communication, adult stepchildren described the difficulty of discussing the deceased parent because of socially constructed taboos against communicating about someone who was deceased (Bryant, 2001). Many of the participants explained they did not ever discuss the deceased parent, and these participants could not recall communication in their family before their parent died (Bryant, 2001, 2003). Conversely, the participants who actively engaged in remembering often used pictures of the deceased parent to facilitate communication about that person, and these individuals had vivid memories of their relationship with the deceased parent (Bryant, 2001, 2003). These findings suggest the critical dimension of communicating about the deceased parent to manage a relationship postbereavement.

The similarities and differences in the enactment of rituals between stepfamilies formed after the death of a parent versus those that form after parental divorce warrant scholarly attention. The goal of this study is to better understand how family rituals play out in postbereaved stepfamilies. The research question guiding the present study is the following:

RQ: How do members of stepfamilies formed after the death of a parent experience family rituals?

Method

Participants

A purposive sample, those who met the criteria for this study (Miles & Huberman, 1994), of 21 participants (11 females and 10 males) volunteered for participation in this study. The mean age of the participants was 34.28 years ($SD = 14.91$). The mean age of the participants when their parents died was 6.76 years ($SD = 3.34$), and the mean age at the time of parental remarriage was

10.38 years ($SD = 4.00$). The sample was 94% Caucasian and 6% African American. Seven of the participants were members of simple stepfamilies (where one of the remarried parents brings children into the stepfamily), and 14 participants came from a complex stepfamily structure (where both remarried parents bring children into the stepfamily).

To participate in the study, participants had to meet five criteria. First, the child's parents must have been married or cohabiting at the time when one of the parents died. Second, the participant must have been at least 2 years old when the parent died. Third, the child must have been living at home when the stepfamily began. The fourth criterion for participation in the present study was that the surviving parent's current partner must be the same individual from the original stepfamily following parental death. The fifth and final criterion was that the participant be at least 19 years of age.

The interviews followed a semistructured focused format (Kvale, 1996; McCracken, 1988; Stewart & Cash, 2000). Semistructured interviews contain all the major questions and also provide freedom to change the phrasing in the interview guide, adapt to each participant, and probe into answers for further clarification. Participants were asked to provide retrospective self-reports of family rituals in their stepfamily. Retrospective self-reports allow researchers to explore the complex multifaceted nature of relationship constructs and the multidimensional nature of the phenomena (Metts, Sprecher, & Cupach, 1991).

The retrospective self-report interviewing technique was ideal for the purposes of the study. Open-ended questions, which were broad and did not restrict the participants' answers, were used to elicit a narrative response (Stewart & Cash, 2000). Hypothetical-interaction questions were used to get at the nature of the relationships in the family by having the participants imagine a situation that was based on plausible relationships (e.g., what would ideal communication in your stepfamily be like?) (Lindlof, 1995). Probing or follow-up questions were also used when the participants' answers appeared to be incomplete or vague (Stewart & Cash, 2000). Probing questions were used to elicit further information and to have participants elaborate on their experience (Lindlof, 1995).

The interviews for this study occurred both face to face and over the telephone. Each interview was audio-recorded. The interviews lasted between 45 minutes and 6 hours, with an average length of approximately 2 hours. After each interview was completed, the recorded data were transcribed, yielding 864 pages of text. After approximately 15 interviews, theoretical saturation was reached, when no new or relevant data were revealed in each category, the category development was comprehensive, and the relationships within categories were well substantiated (Morse, 1994; Strauss & Corbin, 1990).

Data Analysis

The goal of data analysis is to describe recurring patterns and meaning of the participants' experience (Creswell, 1998; Strauss & Corbin, 1990). The data were approached with an open mind but with the knowledge and frame of family rituals to explain the findings (e.g., Braithwaite et al., 1998). To gain a holistic understanding of the data, the data were read in their entirety before coding.

The actual coding process used in the present study was an adaptation of Glaser and Strauss's (1967) grounded theory (Strauss & Corbin, 1990). The constant comparative method was used to identify how family rituals were, or were not, enacted in the stepfamily (Strauss & Corbin, 1990). Through open and axial coding, semantic relationships were identified (Spradley, 1979; Strauss & Corbin, 1990). Open coding is an iterative process where data are compared for similarity and difference (Strauss & Corbin, 1990). Axial coding involves making connections between the data that were open coded (Strauss & Corbin, 1990). This is a process of searching for commonalities to find more general themes that make the analysis coherent. This is a more refined process of using categories to generate broader conceptual frameworks by going beyond a summary approach to expand on the data (Coffey & Atkinson, 1996; Strauss & Corbin, 1990).

After the entire data set was coded, a negative case analysis technique was used to ensure that categories were not forced on the data where they did not exist (Erlandson, Harris, Skipper, & Allen, 1993). A negative case analysis is an interpretive method where data are examined to search for alternative explanations that would render the findings invalid. Throughout data analysis, rival explanations were continually considered (Miles & Huberman, 1994). To further ensure the accuracy of the findings, two outside coders were used to validate the interpretation of the results (Strauss & Corbin, 1990).

Results

A family typology was created by identifying how the families managed dialectical tensions (Baxter & Montgomery, 1996). A dialectical perspective presumes that relating is an ongoing challenge for individuals who must communicatively negotiate the dynamic interplay of oppositional forces (Baxter & Montgomery, 1996). Central to a dialectical perspective is the notion of contradiction, "the dynamic interplay between unified opposites" (p. 326), which is the basic driver of change in relationships (Baxter & Montgomery, 1997). Relational characteristics are considered to be opposites when they are incompatible and mutually negate one another (Baxter & Montgomery, 1997). Rather than either/or contradictions in relationships, in a dialectical perspective, contradictions have a both/and quality. This means that both contradictions must be present simultaneously in relationships; the presence of one does not preclude the presence of the other. It is through relating and interacting that contradictions are managed.

The dialectic of presence-absence occurs through the use, or nonuse, of rituals related to the deceased parent. The three types of families identified were integrated, denial, and segmented families (Bryant, 2003). *Integrated families* use the strategy of integration (Baxter & Montgomery, 1996), which addresses the needs of both tensions simultaneously to manage the dialectical tension of presence-absence of the deceased parent. *Denial families* use the strategy of denial (Baxter & Montgomery, 1996), denying the presence of a competing tension. And *segmented families* use the strategy of segmentation (Baxter & Montgomery, 1996), vacillating between each dialectical tension of presence-absence.

All of the stepfamilies managed the presence-absence dialectical contradiction through the use, or nonuse, of rituals. Through the use or lack of rituals, stepfamilies either provided a place for the deceased parent in the family's lives (in the case of integrated families) or kept the deceased parent absent by not enacting rituals that celebrated the deceased parent (in the case of denial and segmented families).

Integrated Families

Integrated families addressed the need for the deceased parent to be present in the children's lives even though they were physically absent. The families created rituals to memorialize and celebrate the deceased parent's life. This allowed the stepfamily to acknowledge both the old family and new stepfamily. The rituals allowed the stepparents to be a part of the new stepfamily while they simultaneously preserved a part of the old family.

In integrated families, the stepparents did not change any family rituals; rather, they created rituals that celebrated the deceased parent. The most common family ritual or tradition was celebrating the deceased parent's birthday. This ritual provided a way for the stepparent to acknowledge the deceased parent, without imposing the threat of replacing him or her. The willingness of the stepparents to initiate the ritual indicated their comfort with the child and the family's history.

It was most common for the stepparent to initiate rituals or family traditions that celebrated the life of the deceased parent. A 24-year-old female participant who was 2 when her mother died and 3 when her father remarried explained,

> She [stepmom] would take me to the cemetery and we would go visit her [deceased parent] grave on Mother's Day and my [step]mom now, we would take balloons every Mother's Day and every birthday and every anniversary, just her and I and go visit her grave. (17: 139–144)[1]

The same participant went on to explain,

> We would always go visit her grave on the day that she died, on Memorial Day and on Mother's Day. And I never took flowers. Me and my [step]mom started the ritual of helium-filled balloons like with pictures on them and stuff. Like everyone knew that Joan [participant] and Debbie [stepmom] were already here because the balloons are here. But that was our thing. Like nobody else brought balloons. My mom would take me and pick them out and buy them and we would go. And she would always ask me like when we were sitting there, you know, "Is there anything you want to talk about?" or "Any questions that you want to ask?" (17: 1050–1057)

The unique rituals shared with the stepparent and participant provided ways for the family to celebrate the old and new family by providing a presence for the deceased parent. This provided an opportunity for the stepparent to initiate communication about the deceased parent, which further helps to provide a presence for the absent parent.

Following remarriage, the stepparent's involvement with the deceased parent's extended family was another way integrated families kept the deceased parent a part of the children's lives. The stepparents in integrated families were willing to be involved in family rituals, especially those that had once involved the deceased parent, which helped promote family unity.

A 51-year-old female participant who was 11 when her father died and 16 when her mother remarried explained the following:

E: My grandmother passed away, but my grandfather lived to be 94. So you know, that's a lot of what kept our family together cause he was in the same town we were in, so he'd come eat Sunday dinner with us or whatever and . . .

I: Your family, your mom and her husband, [yeah]. How neat.

E: Yeah and my stepdad, he would make soup and take it to my grandpa, you know [your dad's side] Uh huh. (7: 351–358)[2]

The stepparent's willingness to join in the everyday events that included the deceased parent's extended family members provided a way for the deceased parent to still have a place in the stepfamily.

Denial Families

For denial families, the death of a parent and remarriage of the surviving parent often meant an end to the family rituals that had been enacted in the family when the parent was still alive. Denial families are characterized by a lack of rituals that acknowledged the deceased parent or old family. In contrast, for integrated families, family rituals were created following remarriage and served as a benchmark for family unity and an acknowledgment of the deceased parent. In the denial families, when the stepparent entered the family, the unity that once existed in the denial families that was reflected in rituals disappeared, as well as any reference to the deceased parent. When asked which rituals the family discontinued following the death of her parent, a 40-year-old participant who was 14 when her mother died and 17 when her father remarried revealed,

Sunday night, popcorn, and the Disney movie, that [having popcorn and watching movies] quit. *Wonderful World of Disney*—that is what it was called. There would be like a Peter Pan movie or something, *Lassie,* shows like that. And we did quit doing that on Sunday night. (19: 1673–1677)

The introduction of the stepparent meant an end to the Sunday ritual of watching movies together.

For another participant, the family's ritual of playing cards together with other families ended when the stepparent entered into the family. The 45-year-old participant who was 6 when his father died and 13 when his mother remarried explained,

> I guess one of the things that probably stopped was we didn't go . . . we didn't do card playing like we used to, 'cause usually once a month, we'd either go to the Abbott's or to the Smith's [friends of the family] and play cards, and after mom got married, 'cause Oliver [stepfather] didn't play cards and didn't like cards, that did not happen anymore. So the card playing with other families ended. We still as a family ourselves played, but we didn't go like we used to once a month on a Saturday or Sunday. (11: 830–835)

The stepparent was cited as the reason for the disappearance of the family rituals that existed in the family prior to remarriage.

The stepparent's lack of participation in a family ritual from the previous family communicated a lack of acceptance of the old family—specifically, the deceased parent. Rituals function to celebrate the family, and because the participants in denial families reported a lack of closeness toward their stepparent, old rituals were not enacted and new rituals were not developed for the stepfamily. This is in clear contrast to the integrated family type, where both the old and new families were celebrated through the acknowledgment of the deceased parent in the new family.

The adult children from denial families voiced a desire for a place in their lives for the deceased parent, and that desire was met with resistance from their surviving parent as well as the stepparent. For example, a 40-year-old participant who was 14 when her mother died and 17 when her father remarried depicted how she desired a ritual that involved the deceased parent:

> When I was in high school, on Mother's Day—wanted to put flowers on the grave. Dad didn't like that. I couldn't tell Cora [stepmother] I wanted to. But I would tell Dad, and he's like, "Well you need to do something for Cora." And I am like, "No, my mom is THIS person." (19: 1635–1638)

This example is indicative of denial families, where the deceased parent was not allowed any kind of presence in the new family's life, through rituals.

Segmented Families

Segmented families are characterized by the lack of consistency with which the family negotiated the tensions of presence-absence of the deceased parent. The stepparents in some of the segmented families developed rituals that the children resisted because they did not provide a presence for the deceased parent.

Many of the stepparents in segmented families tried to develop rituals for the family, but they did not provide a presence for the deceased parent and were subsequently met with resistance by stepchildren. A 19-year-old female whose father died when she was 8 and whose mother remarried when she was 10 illustrated how her stepfather demanded that she and her siblings eat breakfast together:

Eating breakfast. . . . we had never been made to eat breakfast. If we wanted to eat breakfast, we would go eat breakfast. If we didn't want to eat breakfast, we wouldn't get up . . . it was like this huge argument because we were supposed to get up because my mom had cooked breakfast and . . . no, that's not the way it was before. If we wanted to eat, if we were hungry, we got up. If we weren't, then we didn't. So . . . just a lot of stuff, everyday stuff that was causing questions after that. (1: 398–403)

The participant never had to eat breakfast in her previous family and resented her stepparent for trying to impose the new ritual.

For another participant, the tradition of going to church together continued when his mother remarried. A 33-year-old male who was 10 when his father died and 11 when his mother remarried explained,

We always managed to go to church together, so in some ways, I think attending Mass kind of replaced other communication. You know, I think we kind of stopped [communicating] since we did this . . . families that went to Mass together stayed together. . . . We didn't have to deal with a lot of things directly. (9: 739–742)

Rather than developing a ritual that addressed the deceased parent, the family used the ritual of church attendance as a way of not communicating about the deceased parent. The lack of communication about the deceased parent was replaced with the ritual that carried over from the previous family.

In segmented families, when the stepparent initiated rituals that did not acknowledge the old family or the deceased parent, it was not meaningful to the children. Consequently, the children resisted the ritual as well as the stepparent for imposing it.

Discussion

In all the interviews, it was clear that all of the stepchild participants in the present study wanted their deceased parent to have some kind of presence in their lives. This finding is aligned with previous researchers who found that children want a sense of openness with their stepparents (Baxter, Braithwaite, Bryant, & Wagner, 2004). More specifically, children who lose a parent frequently make an effort to stay connected with their deceased parent in some way, such as talking about that person or keeping some of his or her artifacts to serve as mementos (Silverman & Worden, 1992).

Rituals allow for an acknowledgment of the old family, giving it a presence much like how pictures and artifacts serve as more than just records of memory but also as a substitute presence (Braithwaite et al., 1998; Radley, 1990; Riches & Dawson, 1998). Because the deceased parent was physically absent from the family and the children desired that person's presence, it was often difficult for the stepfamilies to find a way for the deceased parent to have some kind of place that was comfortable and meaningful for them.

The contradiction of presence-absence was handled differently according to each family type. Integrated families addressed the need for the deceased parent to have a presence in the children's lives by creating rituals to memorialize and celebrate the deceased parent's life. They developed family traditions, usually around birthdays, and anniversary customs that were specific for each family (Wolin & Bennett, 1984). The creation of family rituals was successful because it showed respect for the original family—specifically, the deceased parent—by highlighting the "interplay of both the old and new families" (Braithwaite et al., 1998, p. 112).

Extending Baxter, Braithwaite, and Nicholson's (1999) work on turning points in stepfamilies, the creation of the family tradition ritual served as a turning point in the integrated families. The "celebration of holidays and special events" turning point provided an opportunity for stepfamily members to create emotional closeness, which subsequently functioned to increase the stepfamily's perception of feeling like a family (Baxter et al., 1999). Not only do family tradition rituals provide a presence for the deceased parent, but they also provide a place for the stepparent in the new family because, according to Whiteside (1989), "just being part of the group one is included in its membership and its evolving history" (p. 35). Integrated families were able to enact productive rituals, which is characteristic of successful stepfamilies (Visher & Visher, 1990).

Denial families were characterized by their tendency to keep the deceased parent absent by discontinuing rituals that had involved the deceased parent and not developing rituals that allowed the deceased parent to have a presence in their lives. Successful rituals from the old family were perceived as inappropriate to enact in the new family, such as visiting family friends, because the stepparent remained an outsider. Braithwaite et al. (1998) found similar results in their study of stepfamily rituals. In times of catastrophe, such as the death of a parent, families are forced to reevaluate who they are as a family, and it is through rituals that they make sense of their experience (Jorgenson & Bochner, 2004). But as Whiteside (1989) explains, "The more dysfunctional families have more difficulty both developing and preserving family rituals" (p. 38), which seems characteristic of denial families.

For segmented families, there was no consistency with which the family negotiated the tensions of presence-absence. In some of the segmented families, the stepparent attempted to develop rituals, but those were not successful because they did not provide a presence for the deceased parent. For example, the stepparent who wanted the family to eat breakfast together was trying to create patterned family interactions. These types of rituals involve daily routines that occur in the family, such as mealtime and bedtime regularities (Wolin & Bennett, 1984). These regular patterns of interaction were not enacted in the previous family, and the children resented the imposition of them by the stepparent.

Ultimately, family rituals, or the lack of them, play an important role in the stepfamilies formed postbereavement. The enactment of rituals in integrated families extends Braithwaite et al.'s (1998) research finding that successful stepfamily rituals address both the old and new families. Successful rituals occurred in integrated families, where a presence was provided for the deceased parent as well as room for the development of new family rituals. However, in denial families, rituals were discontinued in the stepfamilies, and in segmented families, the rituals that were imposed did not address the old family and were met with resistance from the stepchildren. Just as in Braithwaite et al.'s study, the successful rituals were the ones that were able to pay homage to both the old family, by providing a presence for the deceased parent, and the new family, by enacting the ritual in the stepfamily.

Much more research is needed to study the dialectical tension of presence-absence in stepfamilies. In fact, even in stepfamilies that do not experience the death of a parent, this contradiction may have utility. Certainly, the loss of the old family and the place of that old family in the stepfamily is one application of the presence-absence dialectic. In remarried families, vestiges of the previous family form bear some kind of presence in the new family form.

The role of the dialectical tension, presence-absence, as it relates to acknowledging the deceased parent in the stepfamily is a vital one. Through the performance of rituals, a family can alter its definition (Whiteside, 1989). This has great import for postbereaved stepfamilies because through rituals, they can include both the deceased parent as well as the stepparent in the formation of the new family identity.

Notes

1. The interview transcripts are cited by the interview number and line numbers. So the example, 16: 386–389, refers to Interviewee 16 and line numbers 386–389.

2. "I" represents the interviewer and "E" represents the interviewee.

References

Baker, J. E., Sedney, M. A., & Gross, E. G. (1992). Psychological tasks for bereaved children. *American Journal of Orthopsychiatry, 62,* 105–117.

Baxter, L. A., Braithwaite, D. O., Bryant, L. E., & Wagner, A. (2004). Stepchildren's perceptions of the contradictions of blended family communication. *Journal of Social and Personal Relationships, 21,* 447–467.

Baxter, L., Braithwaite, D. O., & Nicholson, J. (1999). Turning points in the development of blended families. *Journal of Social and Personal Relationships, 16,* 291–313.

Baxter, L. A., & Montgomery, B. M. (1996). *Relating: Dialogues and dialectics.* New York: Guilford.

Baxter, L. A., & Montgomery, B. M. (1997). Rethinking communication in personal relationships from a dialectic perspective. In S. Duck (Ed.), *Handbook of personal relationships* (pp. 328–349). New York: John Wiley.

Bossard, J. H. S., & Boll, E. S. (1949). Ritual in family living. *American Sociological Review, 14,* 463–469.

Braithwaite, D. O., Baxter, L. A., & Harper, A. (1998). The role of rituals in the management of the dialectical tension of "old" and "new" in blended families. *Communication Studies, 49,* 101–120.

Bryant, L. E. (2001, November). *Stepchildren's perceptions of dialectical tensions in a blended family formed after the death of a parent.* Paper presented to the annual meeting of the National Communication Association, Atlanta, GA.

Bryant, L. E. (2003). Stepchildren's perceptions of the contradictions in communication with stepfamilies formed post bereavement (Doctoral dissertation, University of Nebraska–Lincoln, 2003). *Dissertation Abstracts International, 64,* 1463.

Christ, G. H. (2000). Impact of development on children's mourning. *Cancer Practice: A Multidisciplinary Journal of Cancer Care, 8,* 72–81.

Coffey, A., & Atkinson, P. (1996). *Making sense of qualitative data: Complementary research strategies.* Thousand Oaks, CA: Sage.

Creswell, J. W. (1998). *Qualitative inquiry and research design: Choosing among five traditions.* Thousand Oaks, CA: Sage.

Erlandson, D. A., Harris, E. L., Skipper, B. L., & Allen, S. D. (1993). *Doing naturalistic inquiry: A guide to methods.* Newbury Park, CA: Sage.

Fiese, B. H. (1992). Dimensions of family rituals across two generations: Relation to adolescent identity. *Family Process, 31,* 151–162.

Glaser, B. G., & Strauss, A. L. (1967). *The discovery of grounded theory: Strategies for qualitative research.* New York: Aldine de Gruyter.

Golish, T. D., & Caughlin, J. (2002). I'd rather not talk about it: Adolescents' and young adults' use of topic avoidance in stepfamilies. *Journal of Applied Communication Research, 30,* 78–106.

Hurd, R. (1999). Adults view their childhood bereavement experiences. *Death Studies, 23,* 17–41.

Jorgenson, J., & Bochner, A. P. (2004). Imagining families through stories and rituals. In A. L. Vangelisti (Ed.), *Handbook of family communication* (pp. 513–538). Mahwah, NJ: Lawrence Erlbaum.

Kvale, S. (1996). *InterViews: An introduction to qualitative research interviewing.* Thousand Oaks, CA: Sage.

Lindlof, T. R. (1995). *Qualitative communication research methods.* Thousand Oaks, CA: Sage.

McCracken, D. (1988). *The long interview.* Newbury Park, CA: Sage.

Metts, S., Sprecher, S., & Cupach, W. R. (1991). Retrospective self-reports. In B. M. Montgomery & S. Duck (Eds.), *Studying interpersonal interaction* (pp. 162–178). New York: Guilford.

Miles, M. B., & Huberman, A. M. (1994). *Qualitative data analysis* (2nd ed.). Thousand Oaks, CA: Sage.

Morse, J. M. (1994). Designing funded qualitative research. In N. K. Denzin & Y. S. Lincoln (Eds.), *Handbook of qualitative research* (pp. 220–235). Thousand Oaks, CA: Sage.

Plotkin, D. R. (1983, June). Children's anniversary reactions following the death of a family member. *Canada's Mental Health,* pp. 13–15.

Radley, A. (1990). Artifacts, memory and a sense of the past. In D. Middleton & D. Edwards (Eds.), *Collective remembering* (pp. 46–59). London: Sage.

Riches, G., & Dawson, P. (1998). Lost children, living memories: The role of photographs in processes of grief and adjustment among bereaved parents. *Death Studies, 22,* 121–40.

Saler, L., & Skolnick, N. (1992). Childhood parental death and depression in adulthood: Roles of surviving parent and family environment. *American Journal of Orthopsychiatry, 62,* 504–516.

Silverman, P. R., & Worden, J. W. (1992). Children's reactions in the early months after the death of a parent. *American Journal of Orthopsychiatry, 62,* 93–104.

Spradley, J. P. (1979). *The ethnographic interview.* New York: Holt, Rinehart and Winston.

Stewart, C. J., & Cash, W. B. (2000). *Interviewing: Principles and practices* (9th ed.). Boston: McGraw-Hill.

Strauss, A., & Corbin, J. (1990). *Basics of qualitative research: Grounded theory procedures and techniques.* Newbury Park, CA: Sage.

Stroebe, M., Gergen, M., Gergen, G., & Stroebe, W. (1992). Broken hearts or broken bonds? *American Psychologist, 47,* 1205–1212.

Tellerman, K., Chernoff, R., Grossman, L., & Adams, P. (1998). When a parent dies. *Contemporary Pediatrics, 15,* 145–150.

Visher, E. B., & Visher, J. S. (1990). Dynamics of successful stepfamilies. *Journal of Divorce and Remarriage, 14,* 3–12.

Whiteside, M. F. (1989). Family rituals as a key to kinship connections in remarried families. *Family Relations, 38,* 34–39.

Wolin, S. J., & Bennett, L. A. (1984). Family rituals. *Family Process, 23,* 401–420.

Worden, J. W. (1996). *Children and grief: When a parent dies.* New York: Guilford.

PART IV

External Structural Frameworks

Media-Family Interface
Work-Family Interface
Religion-Family Interface
School-Family Interface
Health Care–Family Interface

CHAPTER 16

Implications of Living in a Wired Family

New Directions in Family and Media Research

J. Alison Bryant

Indiana University

Jennings Bryant

University of Alabama

I f that proverbial scouting party from outer space were to land on Planet Earth today, bringing no preconceived notions about family units, their observations might well lead them to conclude that media are part and parcel of the contemporary family. After all, myriad and manifold media are integrated into the modern household to such an extent that we often interact with media more than we do with other family members. Therefore, as Goodman (1983) observed more than two decades ago, media should be examined as part of the family system when studying family communication.

In this chapter, we attempt to paint a word portrait of the rapidly evolving family-media matrix, first examining changes in family, then in media, and finally in their interfaces. Two major thrusts of this discussion are on psychologically "healthy" families and how being a modern "wired" family affects social interactions within the family (for additional insight into how children and parents react to being a "wired family," see Chapter 17, this volume). We conclude by considering how our theories and methods of family communication research need to change if we are to veridically describe, explain, and predict family communication behaviors in the contemporary environment, and we offer some suggestions about potentially fruitful approaches in this regard. In particular, we highlight the need to move toward a multitheoretical, multilevel model of the family system and incorporate social and communication network theories analysis into our research agendas.

Two Institutions in Flux: Family and Media

Family

The more cynical of our social critics might proclaim that the prototypical nuclear American family of Mom, Dad, Sis, and Junior is on the verge of extinction. Two major research projects conducted by the National Opinion Research Center (NORC) at the cusp of the 21st century—"The Emerging 21st Century Family" (Welna, 1999) and "American Sexual Behavior" (Smith, 2003)—indicated that the form of the American family that most people probably envision truly has become rather rare. For example, unlike two decades ago, when most households in the United States included children, only 38% of today's households do so (Welna, 1999; cf. J. Bryant & J. A. Bryant, 2001). The "normal" American family of two married parents with children can now be found in only one in four households, and the most typical household today is that of an unmarried individual with no children. In addition, not only are people marrying 4 to 5 years later than they did four decades ago, but only slightly more than half of U.S. adults are married today, compared with a generation ago. Moreover, single-parent homes have become much more prevalent as the number of unmarried women giving birth has increased dramatically over the past generation to nearly one third of all births, and the portion of children living with a single parent has increased to one out of five children.

The NORC survey (Smith, 2003), which focused on various aspects of American sexual behavior rather than on the nature of families per se, updated, extended, and often amplified the earlier findings of Welna (1999). For example, Smith (2003) reported that increases in levels of premarital sexual intercourse, coupled with the rising age of first marriage, have resulted in men and women spending longer and longer periods of their sexual life outside of marriage and a dramatic increase in the number of sexual partners for both genders. Consequently, the number of cohabiting couples between 1970 and the present has increased sixfold. Finally, at the turn of the century, the connection between marriage and procreation had also weakened, to the point where fewer than 25% of women who conceived children before marriage got married before their child's birth.

Lest we think that this phenomenon is uniquely American, it should be noted that many other countries are also undergoing foundational shifts in family structure. For example, in the United States, 49% of all marriages end in divorce. Even higher divorce rates occur in Belarus (68%), Russia (65%), Sweden (64%), the Czech Republic (61%), Belgium (56%), and the United Kingdom (53%), for example ("Percentage of Divorces," 2004). Clearly, marked changes in families are occurring around the world.

Media

Changes in media are at least as dramatic as changes in the family. Digitalization has produced convergence to such an extent that we now routinely receive video on computers and cell phones and play it back in settings as diverse as airplanes and farm tractors; we get and send text messages on our watches, wireless phones, and Blackberries; we retrieve news reports via online sources as diverse as blogs, desktop tickers, and specialized e-mail services, as well as via satirical television programs (e.g., *The Daily Show With Jon Stewart*); and we currently spend more of our discretionary income on video games, DVD rentals, and premium television channel royalties than on motion picture tickets (e.g., "Statistics in Entertainment Industry," 2004; Vorderer, Bryant, Pieper, & Weber, 2006). In other words, in general, modern technological innovations have shaken up the entire entertainment and information industries of the previous millennium.

Perhaps equally important are the attendant changes in media ownership patterns, which are shifting dramatically and sometimes ruthlessly toward consolidation of ownership in ways that tend to disregard the entertainment, educational, informational, and political needs of consumers and families (e.g., Bryant & Miron, 2004) and that ignore the benefits of diverse and local voices. Moreover, some of these changes in the nature of media systems and institutions can potentially cause major problems for their host societies, including the public good and other social institutions, including the family (e.g., McChesney, 2004).

From a consumer perspective, the changes of the early 21st century have been truly dramatic. For example, the so-called Sovereign Consumer was the archetype of the innocent 20th-century portion of the information age. Ready access to vast amounts of information and entertainment was perceived to be desirable because information was power, and consumption of it was perceived to be wholly satisfying. However, as this optimistic earlier era has evolved into the more realistic, if not cynical and pessimistic, 21st century, the new archetype may well be the Overwhelmed Consumer, as the explosion in modern media offers an excess of abundance of every conceivable type of message system (e.g., Bryant & Davies, 2006). For example, trying to choose among wireless service providers, or the best type of mobile phone hardware, or the right long-distance carrier, or the best specialized Internet portal has become an increasingly difficult decision-making process. Penetrating the intentionally muddled messages that characterize such ulterior communication is difficult at best. And with television having achieved its 500-channel, enhanced-TV digital promise (albeit still with "nothing on"), the incredible lags in development of functional on-screen "guides" have viewers spending more time searching for something to watch and less time in pleasurable, informative, or educational viewing. These information management challenges truly are the veritable tip of the iceberg for today's constantly challenged critical consumer.

Media-Family Interfaces

Among the most challenging developments—theoretically and practically—are those at the interface of changes in media and families. For example, compared with the more authoritative, obedience-oriented family structures of previous eras, today's family tends to rely more on negotiated, equalitarian models of decision making (Torrance, 1998). This affects families' media adoption patterns and media consumption behaviors by increasing the influence of children, who are often much more techno-savvy than their parents. New media and technologies are often introduced through the younger generations, whose swift adoption of these technologies and wholesale reliance on them in their daily communication behaviors forces older family members to adopt the technologies to maintain communication ties. Intergenerational communication within families, particularly grandparent-grandchild communication, may become increasingly difficult to negotiate as the younger generations become accustomed to newer forms of mediated communication, such as e-mail and instant messaging (IM), whereas older generations prefer traditional communication technologies, such as the telephone or letters.

A concomitant development that may well cause problems in the future is the creation within many contemporary families of what has essentially become independent media rooms for each child, in what previously were the children's bedrooms (e.g., Rideout, Foehr, Roberts, & Brodie, 1999). Parents rarely coview with their children when the media reside in these rooms. Add to this trend the following emerging profile of children's media use (Rideout et al., 1999), and what may be emerging is a recipe for chaos and anarchy within the family. Succinctly put, the trend is for parents to not monitor their children's media use and for media to dominate children's leisure time (see Chapter 17, this volume). Moreover, there seems to be a socioeconomic disparity in media use, with Black and Hispanic children spending significantly more time using media than White children and children in single-parent homes watching more television than do those in two-parent homes.

This complex evolution of the interface of media and family may well be one reason why one of the most popular mass communication research venues of the 21st century has been media intervention strategies and media education programs (e.g., Bryant & Miron, 2004). Unfortunately, no one has as yet found an effective means of getting families to take seriously the need for critical media education in homes or schools or appropriate motivational strategies that lead to the adoption of such mediation programs in a widespread manner. These may well be some of the fundamental challenges of the next phase of the information age, if the family is to remain psychologically healthy and sociologically viable.

Engaging the New Family-Media Environment

During the past quarter century, a perennially popular topic in family-study circles has been what makes for psychologically healthy or strong families. As Butner (2003) noted,

Much of the impetus of this body of research has been in response to some disturbing sociological and familial trends that have become prominent. Among these problems are: escalating rates of divorce, proliferation of illegal drug use, increasing reports of domestic violence, the diminishing presence and influence of supportive fathers, and a declining sense of communally shared moral values. (pp. 30–31)

Whether the research on determinants of family well-being has been conducted in departments of psychiatry, psychology, human development, social work, or communication, one factor seems to make all of the lists: communication. In fact, communication often enters into the very definition of family. For example, Galvin and Brommel (2000) define the family, in part, as "a system constituted, defined, and managed through its communication" (p. 47). Their emphasis on the importance of communication has been mirrored on the academic front in marriage and family textbooks, which devote entire chapters to the importance of family communication and make claims such as, "strong families are characterized by good communication patterns" (Stinnett, Walters, & Stinnett, 1991, p. 133). Moreover, research in human development has identified six factors that strong families had in common, one of which is "good communication" (Stinnett, Sanders, DeFrain, & Parkhurst, 1982).

In addition, practitioners in family-related fields have realized the importance of communication. Lewis (1989), a psychiatrist, lists "how the family communicates" as one of the most important of the nine determinants of healthy families. Carl Rogers (1961) similarly emphasized the importance of understanding the role of communication in family therapy by stating, "The whole task of psychotherapy is the task of dealing with a failure in communication" (p. 330). Likewise, Curran (1983) surveyed 561 family counselors and found that "communicating and listening was chosen as the number one trait found in healthy families" (p. 31). These academic and practitioner statements about family communication illustrate how extremely communication-centric normative conceptualizations of strong families have become. Healthy families and effective communication within the family system seem to go hand in hand.

Assessing Media Use in Healthy (and Dysfunctional) Families

Given the communication-centric nature of traditional healthy families, an appropriate information-age question might be, What is the place of communication in strong, healthy *wired* families? Or, more generally, what is the place of mediated communication in healthy "information-age" families? What about the place and role of mediated communication in less healthy, even dysfunctional, postmodern families? Where does causality—or reciprocal causality—lie in any unhealthy media-family interaction? Or, more specifically, does online communication displace traditional communication or supplement it in today's wired families? What media literacy or other mediation strategies or programs are most effective in facilitating judicious media usage in wired families? The heuristic potential of considering the place and role of mediated communication in today's wired families—healthy or unhealthy—would appear to be incredibly rich. Unfortunately, empirical research designed to address such pressing questions is largely lacking.

To the best of our knowledge, only one investigation has systematically examined the interface between media usage and healthy families. Butner (2003) conducted dissertation research on *The Relationship Between Family Television Use and Family Strength.* Using the McMaster Family Assessment Device (e.g., Bray, 1995; Epstein, Baldwin, & Bishop, 1983) and the Family Strengths Inventory (e.g., Stinnett, Lynn, Kimmons, Fennings, & DeFrain, 1981; Stinnett, Stinnett, Beam, & Beam, 1999) to assess the strength of families and a specially developed inventory to assess family television use, Butner examined how families at various levels of well-being interacted with television, with television interaction parsed into four different styles of family-television interaction—laissez faire, simple coviewing, restrictive mediation, and engaged evaluation (e.g., Austin, 2001; Buerkel-Rothfuss & Buerkel, 2001; Valkenburg, Krçmar, Peeters, & Marseille, 1999). Results revealed that the engaged evaluation family-television interaction style was most closely related to measured overall family strength, but none of the other family-television interaction styles correlated significantly with family strength, either positively or negatively.

Such findings hint at the rich potential of systematically assessing the relationships between the clinical well-being of families, various structural and process elements of families, and any number of family media use, regulation, and other mediation variables in the modern media-rich environment. The rapid evolution in family forms in the late 20th and early 21st centuries, coupled with the remarkable changes occurring in media messages and institutions, practically cries out for theoretical, empirical, and critical attention to be paid to the interaction of these complex variables, processes, and social institutions.

One of the major adaptations of more traditional family-media interactions that must be made when including new media is the interactive function or prospects of most of these technologies. Unlike previous research on media as part of the family system, which focused primarily on relatively noninteractive technology (television), current and future theory and research needs to incorporate this notion of mediated interactivity.

Interacting in the Wired Family

New forms of communication via technology are, for families, a double-edged sword—they allow for more opportunities for family members to stay in contact but also have the potential to displace time spent with family members with other online relationships or pursuits. Both of these arguments have found support in recent research. On one hand, Internet use has been shown to decrease face-to-face interactions with family and friends (Nie, 2001), promote underdeveloped or shallow relationships with online communication partners (Parks & Roberts, 1998), and promote lower quality, online conversations instead of "richer" face-to-face and telephone ones (Cummings, Butler, & Kraut, 2002). Conversely, research has shown that Internet use can supplement other forms of communication to increase opportunities for family social interaction (Cole & Robinson, 2002; Katz & Rice, 2002) and increase total communication time between family members (Robinson, Kestnbaum, Neustadtl, & Alvarez, 2000).

In addition, parents seem to perennially fear that the outside contacts that their children make may be threatening. Part of this fear comes with differences in technology use between the generations. With regard to general Internet usage, 78% of American teens (12–17) go online, compared with 63% of all adult Americans (Lenhart, 2003). In fact, many parents have begun using the Internet specifically because they want to know what their kids are up to and/or they feel that knowledge of computers and the Internet is necessary for their children to succeed (Lenhart, 2003) (for more information on research on children's use of the Internet, see Chapter 17, this volume). Unlike many aspects of "growing up," it is usually the kids who teach the parents how to use the Internet (Lenhart, 2003). This can be seen in the trend of parents going online more than nonparent adults (70% vs. 53%; Lenhart, 2003).

Both kids and parents have conflicts about the role of interactive media in family life. Of those teens online, 64% report that the use of the Internet takes away from the time youth spend with their families, whereas only 20% indicate that it helped family communication a lot (Lenhart, Rainie, & Lewis, 2001). On the other hand, some families actually use the Internet and its social applications to help coordinate time spent together (Lenhart, 2003). Seventy-nine percent of U.S. Internet users who say they communicate with friends and family use the Internet for such communication, and 21% of those users *only* communicate online (Fallows, 2004). More than half of online teens IM with their siblings, and one quarter of parents report that using these technologies has improved the way they spend time with their children (Lenhart et al., 2001). Although this research gives us a preliminary understanding of how families may be using IM, it does not extend to look at how this use is then affecting the family communication network. Moreover, research on text messaging within the family context has yet to be addressed (Jennings & Wartella, 2004).

Another interesting intergenerational movement can be seen between the youngest and oldest Internet users. Among Internet users 65 and older, 89% think the Internet is a good communication arena, with 87% communicating to family and friends online, versus 85% of younger users who think it is a good place to communicate, 79% of whom communicate to family and friends (Fallows, 2004). In other words, age per se is not the critical determinant in intergenerational Internet effects.

In addition to generational differences, gender differences within families exist as to how new media are used for interpersonal communication. Women tend to be more likely to use the Internet for maintaining interpersonal relationships with family members, with 64% of women communicating with friends and family online at least several times a week, compared to 59% of men (Fallows, 2004). In addition, although men are heavier users of the World Wide Web, women are heavier users of e-mail, presumably because of its interpersonal communication function (Kraut, Mukhopadhyay, Szczypula, Kiesler, & Scherlis, 1999). In the instant messaging realm, girls have been the heaviest adopters of IM, with their numbers continuing to grow rapidly. From October 2003 to October 2004, girls ages 2 to 11 increased their use of MSN Messenger by 381% and AOL Instant Messenger by 177% (Nielson//NetRatings, 2004).

Many of the differences in experiences with online activity between families seem to stem from demographic and economic factors. Only 44% of those households with an income less than $30,000 have Internet access, compared to 89% of those households making more than $75,000 (Pew Internet, 2004). For example, although single parents are less likely to be online than married parents, they are more likely to use the Internet for communication instead of for information (Lenhart, 2003). In addition, similar to the statistics regarding Internet access and use, youth from wealthier families use instant messaging more than those from lower-income families (Lenhart et al., 2001).

The changing structure of families and family communication networks also affects how communication technology is used. As previously delineated, families—and our understanding of them—has changed dramatically during the past few decades. In particular, the United States has seen fertility rates decline as life expectancy rates have increased (Schmeeckle & Sprecher, 2004). This has created a situation in which we have smaller nuclear families, but we often find extended families living in the same home. In addition, the increase in divorce rates and remarriages has complicated the definition of who "fits" under the term *family*.

Technology use has also aided in this redefinition of family. Sprecher, Felmlee, Orbuch, and Willetts (2002), looking at technologies and families from a historical perspective, found that the use of airplane travel and telephones increased interactions between geographically dispersed, extended family members. More recently, research on computer-assisted communication, such as e-mail, found that these newer technologies are also prevailing over place-based communication issues (Schmeeckle & Sprecher, 2004). Moreover, new "richer" online technologies, such as videoconferencing using Webcams, have the potential to increase communication within dispersed families, especially as the quality of these services has increased dramatically while the price has decreased to become competitive with voice phone rates. Videoconferencing is even being used to "create" families, with adoption agencies using the technology to let prospective adopters know about and meet children who are waiting for families (Lumpe, 2004). Finally, the recent proliferation of online social network facilitation sites, especially those related to genealogy, have also assisted families in (re)creating and maintaining more extended family networks (Andrews, 2000).

Another form of media that has begun to play a greater role in the family system is electronic (video and computer) gaming. In the United States in 2003, electronic game software sales grew 8% to $7 billion, more than double the sales since 1996; moreover, almost two games were sold for every household (Entertainment Software Association, 2004). In Europe, the average daily use of computer games by 9- to 16-year-olds varies greatly among European countries, with Belgian youth playing for 20 minutes, Germans for 34 minutes, British for 44 minutes, and Danish for 57 minutes in 1998 (Drotner, 2001). Online gaming has also become a large global phenomenon, with use in Europe, for example, doubling between 2002 and 2003 (Greenspan, 2003). In Japan and South Korea, electronic game use has been a hot topic in both the press and research, and much of the innovation in wireless gaming, as well as many of the players, especially of massive multiplayer online games, is coming from this region.

For children, especially for boys, electronic games have become one of the most popular forms of entertainment (Funk, 2002). But it is important to note that gaming is no longer exclusively a "younger male" pastime. Approximately 50% of Americans play video games (Entertainment Software Association, 2004). For all electronic gaming, 39% of game players are women (Entertainment Software Association, 2004), but for online gaming only, according to the Nielsen// NetRatings, almost half of the players are women (Greenspan, 2004). Looking at the demographics of gamers, 34% are younger than age 18, 46% are 18 to 50, and 17% are older than 50 (with the average age of a computer or video game player being 29) (Entertainment Software Association, 2004). This means that, within the family, it is as likely (or even more likely) for a parent than for a child to be playing electronic games.

Like other forms of media, electronic games can both bring together and isolate family members. With regard to family fusion, often family members play electronic games together, similar to the way in which family members have coviewed television. In the United States, for example, 55% of parents play electronic games with their child once a month (Entertainment Software Association, 2004). Moreover, research by the Digiplay Initiative found that 41.5% of young people start playing electronic games with their parents (Digiplay Initiative, 2004).

Heavy game use can also be problematic for the family system. Alienation from other family members is also a factor in electronic game use, especially in teens (Slater, 2003). Addiction to electronic games may also alter interactions within the household by transferring time that would normally be spent with family members to time spent with games. A survey of 387 adolescents, for example, found that 20% were "dependent" on video games (Griffiths & Hunt, 1998). This type of dependence on electronic games may alter communication patterns and social support within the family.

Electronic games, socially interactive technologies, and the Internet have all affected the way families communicate, relate, and develop. These newer technologies affect families by creating both spheres for interaction and places of isolation. Most current research focuses on media adoption patterns and usage (Meszaros, 2004), but what we need to focus on is how these newer technologies affect the family as a whole over time and how the family structures and processes affect the uses and effects of gaming. The next section provides a starting point for rethinking and revising our approach to research on wired families.

Reconfiguring the Theoretical and Methodological Toolbox

Research on families and media to this point, as highlighted in the sections above, has tended to implicitly assume that the family-media relationship is relatively static. Most of the research has looked at media usage or interactions at a single point in time and has often delineated between "parts" of the family (e.g., parents vs. kids, women vs. men). We contend that these perspectives of family-media interactions are only partial views of the whole picture. To improve research in this arena, we need to make several adjustments in our approach. Succinctly put, we need to focus on family systems as the unit of analysis, incorporating new technologies into our understanding of the evolution of those systems; incorporate social network analysis into our research; and generate multitheoretical, multilevel (MTML) models (Monge & Contractor, 2003) of the family system.

Using Family as the Unit of Analysis

It is not unusual for family communication scholars to call for or declare benefits from using families rather than individuals as the primary unit of analysis for empirical research. Pioneering family researcher Goodman (1983) staked such a claim more than two decades ago. More recent scholarly volumes on family media research have frequently stressed the importance of such perspectives. For example, F. H. Hooper and J. O. Hooper (1990) clearly delineated the differences in these methodological approaches:

> It is easy to see that both the general orientation and the specifics of any of the present research programs depend upon whether you begin with families and derive your questions regarding individual development secondarily, or if you begin with individuals . . . and treat the new family collective as a type of outcome event. . . . This becomes immediately clear if one changes the question to—Which is fundamentally more important, sociology or psychology? (p. 295)

Hooper and Hooper also indicate that the individual approach to family research results in what is essentially an organismic perspective, whereas the family approach typically results in a systems perspective.

The cybernetics and general systems movements (e.g., von Bertalanffy, 1968; Weiner, 1948) had a powerful influence on those who were studying the family, although it took until the mid-1960s for the lessons of those movements to take hold in family therapy and until the early 1970s for the more academic side of the discipline to catch on (Broderick, 1993). No longer were dyadic or interpersonal relationships the only focus of study; instead, it was the entire family system. There is, however, no one theory of the family system and no specified canon (Merkel & Searight, 1992). Different systems metaphors have yielded different interpretations of "family systems theory," although for the most part, common threads seem to run through all of the interpretations: (a) Family interactions are not just a collection of dyadic relationships but are a complex system of individuals, dyads, and triads that interacts with other systems, and (b) interactions that occur within each of these smaller units affect the workings of the larger system (Rosenblatt, 1994).

Goodman (1983) called for using families as the primary unit of analysis in family-media research and advocated changes in the ways in which we view the role of media in the family. Two principles within family systems research were presented as being of great importance to the study of television as a part of the family system. The first was the use of the family as a unit of analysis. The second was to study family processes, "an intricate phenomenon, involving family boundaries, rules, decision making, independence, control, roles, and communication, among other components" (p. 409), as part of the family systems approach. Referring to the work by Minuchin (1974) on family systems, Goodman elaborated on how the television fit perfectly within the three components of the family system: the structure of the family, by being included in the interaction patterns; the development of the family, by changing its role within the family (e.g., from a babysitter for the infant to a social and cultural teacher for the teenager), as well as the way in which the human members of the family system negotiate their relationships around the set; and the adaptation of the family system.

Although Goodman (1983) was referring to television in her work, reflecting the media landscape at that time, it is clear that the elaborations made on the family systems model are relevant in today's media environment, perhaps even more than they were two decades ago, when Goodman's article was published. Newer media and applications, such as computers, the Internet, e-mail, mobile phones, instant messaging, portable video game players, and so on, all have become part of the way in which our households interact, develop, and adapt.

Jordan (2002) adopted this broadening of the family system framework by focusing on how all media, particularly the Internet, are major factors in family structure and social dimensions:

> Families make available certain kinds of media within the home but also provide notions about *how* and *when* to use the media . . . and how to interpret media content. . . . The interactions of family members subtly create patterned ways of thinking about and using the media. These patterns become habits, and the habits become the stuff of everyday experience. (p. 231)

By using a family systems perspective that includes the media, we move from linear models of causality, in which families simply use the media as an end, to a complex, nonlinear, interdependent model, in which families use the media *and* the media have an active role within the social and communication functioning of the family. Very few attempts to integrate family systems theories into research on technology and the family have been undertaken, however (Jennings & Wartella, 2004).

Incorporating Social Network Analysis

Although the notion of family systems has been around for decades, researchers have not approached data collection and analysis using a systems approach. Specifically, examining family systems from the perspective of social network analysis allows us to capture the dynamic evolution of the family system and include media as a part of that system. Network analysis is fundamentally concerned with relationships between a set of entities. More specifically, Wasserman and Faust (1994) identify four relational concepts important to social network analysis

Table 16.1 Integrating Social Network Analysis Concepts With Family Systems Theory

Social Network Analysis Concept (from Wasserman & Faust, 1994, p. 4)	Family Systems Theory Adaptation
Actors and their actions are viewed as interdependent rather than independent, autonomous units.	Family members and their interactions are interdependent.
Relational ties (linkages) between actors are channels for transfer or "flow" of resources (either material or nonmaterial).	Relationships between family members, either interpersonal or mediated, are important for family "resources" (e.g., social support, socialization, cultural transference).
Network models focusing on individuals view the network structural environment as providing opportunities for or constraints on individual action.	The ecology of the household and extrafamilial relationships (i.e., the network structural environment) influences family relationships.
Network models conceptualize structure (social, economic, political, etc.) as lasting patterns of relations among actors.	The relational structure of the family, specifically the social and technological structure, is a lasting pattern of relations among family members.

that can be transcribed to the basic tenets of family systems theory. Table 16.1 outlines those concepts. In addition, network analysis provides measures and statistical tools for the quantitative analysis of these family system networks (Faber & Wasserman, 2001).

By using network measures, we can gather information about where support ties exist within the family system, what type and how strong those ties are, and the extent to which those ties are mediated (or interpersonal). For example, we can collect network data from families that focus on who talks to whom, via what form of communication, how often, and about what. In addition, we can create a set of attributes for each family member (node in the network) that describes their media use, communication skills, role(s) in the family, and so forth. Using both of these types of data, we can then analyze the family system to understand how all of these variables affect the family system as a whole.

By examining the positional propositions offered by social network analysis, we can garner a better idea of how individual interaction choices create relational patterns within the network (Wasserman & Faust, 1994). For example, a family system in which the mother has very high centrality or prestige within the network may illuminate several different support issues: (a) The mother offers the most support within the subsystem relationship in that network (which would fit with Wellman and Wortley's [1990] findings that women are more likely than men to provide emotional support), (b) the mother is overbearing and smothering through her excessive social support; or (c) there are support problems in the subsystem that do not include the mother, so that the mother is bearing the brunt of the social support needed to keep the family functioning. Moreover, if the strongest ties within a family tend to be mediated ties, then we can presume that the role of mediated communication within the family has become primary in the family's communication network. Finally, we may see different interaction, support, and influence patterns when we compare a family's mediated communication networks with their face-to-face interpersonal communication network. For example, when family decisions are made via the interpersonal communication network, parents may have more influence on decision making. When decisions are made via the mediated communication network, however, teenage children (the tech "gurus" in the family) may have more influence because they are better able to express themselves in an efficient manner via these mediums.

Multitheoretical, Multilevel (MTML) Models for Family-Media Use

A network approach to studying the family system also supports a more multitheoretical, multilevel (MTML) approach to studying family communication. The MTML model, advanced by Monge and Contractor (2003), suggests that communication research—specifically, communication network research—can benefit from moving away from single-theory explanations of network properties and evolution and from single-level understandings of network phenomena. Instead, there is a need to integrate multiple theories of communication and social relationships to explain the complexity of communication networks and to "increase the amount of variance accounted for by these theoretical mechanisms" and "collect and collate data at various levels of analysis (person, dyad, triad, group, organizational, and interorganizational)" (p. 46). From a family systems perspective, this means that as we study families as communication and social networks, we must (a) look to multiple theoretical explanations to understand the complex familial relationships and (b) understand the family as a complete system (a group), as an aggregate of its many parts (person, dyads [Mom and Dad], and triads [Sally, Junior, and Mom]), and as part of a larger network (organizational [the larger nonnuclear family] and interorganizational [community and society]).

Thus far, from a theoretical perspective, most of network analysis conducted on families has been to model theories of social support (Faber & Wasserman, 2001), specifically focusing on emotional aid, material aid, information, and companionship (Barrera & Ainlay, 1983; Cutrona & Russell, 1990; Wellman & Wortley, 1989, 1990). Although to date, theories of social support tend to be the most comprehensive in explaining family functioning and interaction, other network theories also hold explanatory power for individual aspects of family functioning. For example, contagion theories, which assume that members of the same social and communication networks will develop similar attitudes, beliefs, and assumptions (Burt, 1980, 1987; Carely, 1991; Carely & Kaufer, 1993; Contractor & Eisenberg, 1990), can help us understand the family functioning concepts of role performance, values and norms, and control. Cognitive constructs, such as semantic networks (Monge & Eisenberg, 1987), which focus on shared meaning created through organizational narratives and metanarratives, and cognitive consistency (Heider, 1958), which focuses on individuals' desire and drive for consistency, are also useful in understanding how families create norms, perpetuate values, and may have shared interpretations of events or mediated messages. Moreover, uncertainty reduction theory, which highlights the need for people to communicate to make their environment more predictable (Weick, 1979), helps explain the communication function within the family system and why communication within a family system may increase as external events or relationships become uncertain or strained (e.g., the dramatic increase in family communication post-9/11). Diffusion theory addresses whether the adoption of media and technology depends on the adoption habits of particular members of the family, such as older siblings (E. M. Rogers, 1995). Finally, ecological theories look at whether media and communication technologies simply re-create the same family communication networks that already existed or substitute, enlarge, diminish, or reconfigure these networks (Monge & Contractor, 2003).

The common trait of each of the above theories and questions is that they are inherently based in communication networks and can therefore be studied using network analysis techniques (Monge & Contractor, 2003). Taking a multilevel network perspective on the family system, we see that looking at the same family network at different levels may compel us to offer multiple theoretical explanations. For example, at the individual level, a family member with high centrality may highlight the importance of that particular family member in fostering communication within the family. In other words, if that family member is absent from the network, communication between other family members may dramatically decrease. At the dyadic level, it may be more likely that two family members will have frequent communication if they are both active e-mail users. At the triadic level, if one family member has strong positive relationships with two other members, then those two members are more likely to have a strong positive relationship. For example, if a father has an equally positive relationship with both his son and his daughter, it is likely that the siblings also have a positive relationship. Finally, from a global (system) perspective, families that have very dense, decentralized ties (e.g., frequent communication with no domineering family member, either mediated or nonmediated) may be hypothesized to be more psychologically healthy. These are just a few of the many levels at which we can study the family system. Using a network approach to data collection and analysis, we can more easily elucidate these multilevel relationships and explain them through multiple theoretical lenses, incorporating media as additional *nodes in the family system.*

Conclusion

The media undoubtedly serve the social systems functions that have been long touted by communication scholars—information, education, entertainment, and surveillance—but as older and newer technologies become more important members of the family system, they assume other functions: facilitator, companion, mediator, reward/punishment, scapegoat, boundary marker, and so on (Goodman, 1983). The media, therefore, are not just appliances but also integral parts of the family functioning and interaction patterns (J. A. Bryant & J. Bryant, 2001).

Up to now, research on families and media has focused primarily on who is using the technology and why (often relying on established media theories such as uses and gratifications) and has employed primarily survey and ethnographic data (Meszaros, 2004). Although this type of research is vital to preliminary understandings of how media are integrated into daily family life, it does not address the dynamic, multilevel process of family-media system evolution. In addition, traditional research perspectives do not delve into the heart of some of the more interesting questions, such as the following: What are the group dynamics that press family members to adopt particular technologies or to use them in a particular manner, and how does using these technologies actually affect how kids communicate with one another or with their family members over time? According to Goodman (1983), the use of the family as the unit of analysis creates the need for a multilevel, multitheoretical, and multimethod approach to the research on family systems. By using network analysis and its corresponding theories and methodologies, we can more veridically "capture" the motivations, processes, and effects of mediated and nonmediated communication as the wired family continues to evolve with our constantly changing information society.

References

Andrews, W. (2000, March 1). It's more than sticky. It's more than viral. It's magnetic: How the next generation of Web sites is pulling customers into its force field. *Internet World.* Retrieved December 5, 2004, from http://www.myfamilyinc.com/pressroom/archive/magnetic.pdf.

Austin, E. W. (2001). Effects of family communication on children's interpretation of television. In J. Bryant & J. A. Bryant (Eds.), *Television and the American family* (2nd ed., pp. 377–395). Mahwah, NJ: Lawrence Erlbaum.

Barrera, M. J., & Ainlay, S. L. (1983). The structure of social support: A conceptual and empirical analysis. *Journal of Community Psychology, 11,* 133–143.

Bray, J. H. (1995). Family assessment: Current issues in evaluating families. *Family Relations, 4,* 469–483.

Broderick, C. B. (1993). *Understanding family process: Basics of family systems theory.* Newbury Park, CA: Sage.

Bryant, J., & Bryant, J. A. (2001). *Television and the American family* (2nd ed.). Mahwah, NJ: Lawrence Erlbaum.

Bryant, J., & Davies, J. (2006). Selective exposure processes. In J. Bryant & P. Vorderer (Eds.), *Psychology of entertainment* (pp. 19–33). Mahwah, NJ: Lawrence Erlbaum.

Bryant, J., & Miron, D. (2004). Theory and research in mass communication. *Journal of Communication, 54,* 662–704.

Bryant, J. A., & Bryant, J. (2001). Living with an invisible family medium. *Journal of Mundane Behavior, 2,* 26–41. Retrieved December 3, 2004, from http://www.mundanebehavior.org/issues/v2n1/bryants.htm

Buerkel-Rothfuss, N. L., & Buerkel, R. A. (2001). Family mediation. In J. Bryant & J. A. Bryant (Eds.), *Television and the American family* (2nd ed., pp. 355–376). Mahwah, NJ: Lawrence Erlbaum.

Burt, R. S. (1980). Models of network structure. *Annual Review of Sociology, 6,* 79–141.

Burt, R. S. (1987). Social contagion and innovation: Cohesion versus structural equivalence. *American Journal of Sociology, 9,* 1287–1335.

Butner, R. D. (2003). *The relationship between family television use and family strength.* Unpublished doctoral dissertation, University of Alabama.

Carely, K. (1991). A theory of group stability. *American Sociological Review, 56,* 331–354.

Carely, K., & Kaufer, D. S. (1993). Semantic connectivity: An approach for analyzing symbols in semantic networks. *Communication Theory, 3,* 183–213.

Cole, J. I., & Robinson, J. P. (2002). Internet use and sociability in the UCLA data: A simplified MCA analysis. *IT & Society, 1,* 202–218.

Contractor, N. S., & Eisenberg, E. M. (1990). Communication networks and the new media in organizations. In J. Fulk & C. Steinfeld (Eds.), *Organizations and communication technology* (pp. 143–172). Newbury Park, CA: Sage.

Cummings, J., Butler, B., & Kraut, R. (2002). The quality of online social relationships. *Communications of the ACM, 45,* 103–108.

Curran, D. (1983). *Traits of a healthy family: Fifteen traits commonly found in healthy families by those who work with them.* Minneapolis, MN: Winston.

Cutrona, C. E., & Russell, D. W. (1990). Type of social support and specific stress: Toward a theory of optimal matching. In B. R. Sarason, I. G. Sarason, & G. R. Pierce (Eds.), *Social support: An interactional view* (pp. 319–366). New York: John Wiley.

Digiplay Initiative. (2004). *Some key gaming facts.* Retrieved December 2, 2004, from http://www.digiplay.org.uk/facts.php

Drotner, K. (2001). *Medier for Fremtiden.* Copenhagen: Høst og Søn.

Entertainment Software Association. (2004). *Essential facts about the video and computer game industry.* Washington, DC. Retrieved December 2, 2004, from http://www.theesa.com/ EFBrochure.pdf

Epstein, N. B., Baldwin, L. M., & Bishop, D. S. (1983). The McMaster family assessment device. *Journal of Marital and Family Therapy, 9,* 171–180.

Faber, A., & Wasserman, S. (2001). Social support and social networks: Synthesis and review. In J. Levy & B. Pescosolido (Eds.), *Social networks and health: Advances in medical sociology* (pp. 29–72). Stamford, CT: JAI.

Fallows, D. (2004). *The Internet and daily life.* Washington, DC: Pew Internet & American Life Project.

Funk, J. B. (2002). Electronic games. In V. C. Strasburger & B. J. Wilson (Eds.), *Children, adolescents, & the media* (pp. 117–144). Thousand Oaks, CA: Sage.

Galvin, K. M., & Brommel, B. J. (2000). *Family communication: Cohesion and change* (5th ed.). New York: Longman.

Goodman, I. F. (1983). Television's role in family interaction: A family systems perspective. *Journal of Family Issues, 4,* 405–424.

Greenspan, R. (2003, February 20). *Online gaming doubles in Europe.* ClickZ Network. Retrieved December 2, 2004, from http://www.clickz.com/stats/sectors/entertainment/article.php/1588291

Greenspan, R. (2004, September 7). *Online gaming revenue to quadruple.* ClickZ Network. Retrieved December 2, 2004, from http://www.clickz.com/stats/sectors/entertainment/article.php/3403931

Griffiths, M. D., & Hunt, N. (1998). Computer game playing in adolescence: Prevalence and demographic indicators. *Journal of Community and Applied Social Psychology, 5,* 189–193.

Heider, F. (1958). *The psychology of interpersonal relationships.* New York: John Wiley.

Hooper, F. H., & Hooper, J. O. (1990). The family as a system of reciprocal relations: Searching for a developmental lifespan perspective. In I. E. Siegel & G. H. Brody (Eds.),

Methods of family research: Biographies of research projects: Vol. 1. Normal families (pp. 289–316). Hillsdale, NJ: Lawrence Erlbaum.

Jennings, N., & Wartella, E. (2004). Technology and the family. In A. L. Vangelisti (Ed.), *Handbook of family communication* (pp. 593–608). Mahwah, NJ: Lawrence Erlbaum.

Jordan, A. (2002). A family systems approach to examining the role of the Internet in the home. In S. Calvert, A. Jordan, & R. Cocking (Eds.), *Children in the digital age: Influences of electronic media on development* (pp. 231–247). Westport, CT: Praeger.

Katz, J. E., & Rice, R. E. (2002). *Social consequences of Internet use: Access, involvement, and interaction.* Cambridge: MIT Press.

Kraut, R., Mukhopadhyay, T., Szczypula, J., Kiesler, S., & Scherlis, B. (1999). Information and communication: Alternative uses of the Internet in households. *Information Systems Research, 10,* 287–303.

Lenhart, A. (2003). *Teens, parents and technology: Highlights from the Pew Internet & American Life Project.* Presentation to the Lawlor Group, Long Beach, CA. Retrieved July 10, 2004, from http://www.pewinternet.org/ppt/Teens,ParentsandTechnology-Lawlor10.03.03a.nn.ppt

Lenhart, A., Rainie, L., & Lewis, O. (2001). *Teenage life online: The rise of the instant-message generation and the Internet's impact on friendships and family relationships.* Report of the Pew Internet & American Life Project, Washington, DC.

Lewis, J. M. (1989). *How's your family? A guide to identifying your family's strengths and weaknesses* (Rev. ed.). New York: Brunner/Mazel.

Lumpe, L. (2004). *Creating families through videoconferencing.* St. Paul, MN: North American Council on Adoptable Children. Retrieved November 25, 2004, from http://www.nacac .org/newsletters/videoconferencing/videoconf.html

McChesney, R. W. (2004). *The problem of the media: U.S. communication politics in the 21st century.* New York: Monthly Review Press.

Merkel, W. T., & Searight, H. R. (1992). Why families are not like swamps, solar systems, or thermostats: Some limits of systems theory as applied to family therapy. *Contemporary Family Therapy, 14,* 33–50.

Meszaros, P. S. (2004). The wired family: Living digitally in the Postinformation Age. *American Behavioral Scientist, 48,* 377–390.

Minuchin, S. (1974). *Families and family therapy.* Cambridge, MA: Harvard University Press.

Monge, P. R., & Contractor, N. S. (2003). *Theories of communication networks.* New York: Oxford University Press.

Monge, P. R., & Eisenberg, E. M. (1987). Emergent communication networks. In F. M. Jablin, L. L. Putnam, K. H. Roberts, & L. W. Porter (Eds.), *Handbook of organizational communication: An interdisciplinary perspective* (pp. 304–342). Newbury Park, CA: Sage.

Nie, N. H. (2001). Sociability, interpersonal relations and the Internet: Reconciling conflicting findings. *American Behavioral Scientist, 45,* 420–435.

Nielson//NetRatings. (2004). *Kids ages 2–11 lead growth in Web page consumption according to Nielsen//NetRatings.* Retrieved December 2, 2004, from http://www.nielsen-netratings.com/pr/pr_041118.pdf

Parks, M. R., & Roberts, L. D. (1998). 'Making MOOsic': The development of personal relationships on line and a comparison to their off-line counterparts. *Journal of Social and Personal Relationships, 15,* 517–537.

Percentage of divorces in selected countries. (2004). Retrieved November 26, 2004, from http://www.infoplease.com/ipa/A0200806.html

Pew Internet & American Life Project. (2004). *Latest trends: Online activities.* Washington, DC: Author. Retrieved July 10, 2004, from http://www.pewinternet.org/trends.asp

Rideout, V. J., Foehr, U. G., Roberts, D. F., & Brodie, M. (1999). *Kids & media @ the new millennium.* Menlo Park, CA: Kaiser Family Foundation.

Robinson, J. P., Kestnbaum, M., Neustadtl, A., & Alvarez, A. (2000). Mass media use and social life among Internet users. *Social Science Computer Review, 18,* 490–501.

Rogers, C. (1961). *On becoming a person: A therapist's view of psychotherapy.* Boston: Houghton Mifflin.

Rogers, E. M. (1995). *Diffusion of innovations* (4th ed.). New York: Free Press.

Rosenblatt, P. (1994). *Metaphors of family systems: Toward new constructions.* New York: Guilford.

Schmeeckle, M., & Sprecher, S. (2004). Extended family and social networks. In A. L. Vangelisti (Ed.), *Handbook of family communication* (pp. 349–375). Mahwah, NJ: Lawrence Erlbaum.

Slater, M. D. (2003). Alienation, aggression, and sensation seeking as predictors of adolescent use of violent film, computer, and website content. *Journal of Communication, 53,* 105–121.

Smith, T. W. (2003). *American sexual behavior: Trends, socio-demographic differences, and risk behavior.* Chicago: University of Chicago National Opinion Research Center.

Sprecher, S., Felmlee, D., Orbuch, D. L., & Willetts, M. C. (2002). Social networks and change in personal relationships. In A. L. Vangelisti, H. Reis, & M. A. Fitzpatrick (Eds.), *Stability and change in relationships* (pp. 257–284). Cambridge, UK: Cambridge University Press.

Statistics in entertainment industry. (2004). Retrieved November 27, 2004, from http://www.plunkettresearch.com/entertainment/entertainment_statistics_1.htm

Stinnett, N., Lynn, D., Kimmons, L., Fenning, S., & DeFrain, J. (1981). Family strengths and personal wellness. *Wellness Perspectives, 1,* 25–31.

Stinnett, N., Sanders, G., DeFrain, J., & Parkhurst, A. (1982). A nationwide study of families who perceive themselves as strong. *Family Perspective, 16,* 15–22.

Stinnett, N., Stinnett, N., Beam, J., & Beam, A. (1999). *Fantastic families: 6 proven steps to building a strong family.* West Monroe, LA: Howard.

Stinnett, N., Walters, J., & Stinnett, N. (1991). *Relationships in marriage and the family* (3rd ed.). New York: Macmillan.

Torrance, K. (1998). *Contemporary childhood: Parent-child relationships and child culture.* Leiden, The Netherlands: DSWO Press.

Valkenburg, P. M., Krçmar, M., Peeters, A. L., & Marseille, N. M. (1999). Developing a scale to assess three styles of television mediation: "Instructive mediation," "restrictive mediation," and "social coviewing." *Journal of Broadcasting & Electronic Media, 43,* 52–67.

von Bertalanffy, L. (1968). *General system theory: Foundations, development, applications.* New York: George Braziller.

Vorderer, P., Bryant, J., Pieper, K. M., & Weber, R. (2006). Playing video games as entertainment. In P. Vorderer & J. Bryant (Eds.), *Playing video games: Motives, responses, and consequences* (pp. 1–7). Mahwah, NJ: Lawrence Erlbaum.

Wasserman, S., & Faust, K. (1994). *Social network analysis: Methods and applications.* New York: Cambridge University Press.

Weick, K. E. (1979). *The social psychology of organizing* (2nd ed.). Reading, MA: Addison-Wesley.

Weiner, N. (1948). *Cybernetics: or, control and communication in the animal and the machine.* New York: John Wiley.

Wellman, B., & Wortley, S. (1989). Brother's keepers: Situating kinship relations in broader networks of social support. *Sociological Perspectives, 32,* 273–306.

Wellman, B., & Wortley, S. (1990). Different strokes from different folks: Community ties and social support. *American Journal of Sociology, 96,* 558–588.

Welna, D. (1999, November 24). University of Chicago survey on the changing American family. *All things considered* [Radio broadcast]. Washington, DC: National Public Radio.

CHAPTER 17

Cyberkids

*The Influence of Mediation
and Motivation on Children's Use of
and Attitudes Toward the Internet*

Alison Alexander

University of Georgia

Seok Kang

Arkansas Tech

Yeora Kim

Choong-Ang University, Seoul

C hildren who grow up with computers and use them daily are familiar with the offerings on the Internet. The number of child Internet users is increasing daily. The Internet is now in 75% of U.S. homes, and 65% of American children use the Internet from home, school, or other locations.

The rapid increase of children's Internet access raises many concerns. Although aware of its educational and informational potential, parents are justifiably concerned about their children's use of the Internet. They worry about access to inappropriate content, the long hours in front of the screen, and the potential for isolation from friends and family members. A study by the Annenberg Public Policy Center found that 78% of U.S. parents worried specifically about access to pornography or that their children might give out personal information over the Internet (Turrow, 1999). Park and Floyd (1996) reported parental concern about cyber relationships their children might form with strangers on the Internet. Nonetheless, 75% of the parents surveyed believe that the Internet makes a positive impact on children as a learning tool (Turrow, 1999).

Altogether, increased access to the Internet has highlighted the importance of parental mediation of children's use of and attitudes toward the Internet. Previous research has established that parents can play an important role in mediating the potential negative effects of media (cf. Austin, 2001). Parents' behaviors, concerns, attitudes, and communication styles can be crucial in directly or indirectly shaping the experiences of the "netgeneration" on the Web.

Little academic work has addressed how parents are mediating the Internet or how that may affect children's use of the Internet for both positive and negative outcomes. Clearly, there are varying routes by which family influences children's response to media messages. Restrictive mediation through direct controls and rulemaking comprise one method; another is the active conversational approach consisting of critical discussions with the child. Although several critics have suggested parental Internet guidelines (Aftab, 1997, 2000; Hughes & Campbell, 1998), there has been no attempt to measure how these guides work in mediating children's Internet use.

An old cliché suggests that the message sent does not equal the message received. How a child receives and interprets parental messages must be considered. Several studies report weak correlations between children's and parents' perceptions of television mediation (Austin, 1993; Nathanson, 2001). How this finding may hold in the Internet domain is presently unknown.

Thus, this study examines Internet mediation from the perspective of both parent and child. We respond to Bryant and Bryant's (Chapter 16, this volume) call for studies at the interface of media and family, and we agree with their assessment that this approach tackles "some of the fundamental challenges of the next phase of the information age, if the family is to remain psychologically healthy and socio-logically viable" (p. 300). We posit that children's Internet use, concerns, and attitudes toward the Internet differ depending on parents' mediation patterns, children's perceptions of parental mediation, the media environment of the home, child motivations, and demographics. The study is unique in examining data from both child and parent.

Shaping the Use of the Internet: Parental Mediation in the New Media Environment

New media and their relationship with family interaction have been mainly discussed in connection with previous media use patterns. For example, studies on parental intervention for children's VCR use found few differences between broadcast and VCR viewing groups (Kim, Baran, & Massey, 1988; Greenberg & Heeter, 1987). Lin and Atkin (1989) contended that there are similar underlying predictor sets for broadcast and VCR mediation. It seems probable that parental mediation is similar across media. Therefore, any study of parental mediation of children's Internet use must first consider mediation patterns of preexisting media such as television and VCRs.

The literature suggests that for television, intentional mediation is sparse, despite parents' agreement on its importance (Abelman, 1990; Bower, 1973; Comstock, 1975; McLeod & Chaffee, 1972). Although parents agree that active mediation, including coviewing and parental monitoring, is crucial, they report little engagement in either activity (Thompson & Slater, 1983). Nor is restrictive mediation consistent. For example, Greenberg, Ericson, and Vlahos (1972) found that the most common form was rules about how late to watch, but even that mediation was neither common nor consistent.

Recently, some studies are beginning to examine what rules parents have when children use the media, including television, the Internet, and video games (Turrow & Nir, 2000; Woodard & Gridina, 2000). Woodard and Gridina (2000) found that about 7 in 10 children could not use any of the three media until they were finished with schoolwork and that about half of the children were restricted in their use of some media: Parents allowed children to watch television and play video games for as long as they wished, but most of the parents placed restrictions on the amount of time on the Internet (Woodard & Gridina, 2000). Restrictions included not giving the children passwords, using blocking software, and instituting age restrictions on chat room use. Parents' concerns about children's media use increase with age for the Internet, which is in contrast to television, for which those concerns diminish with age (Schmitt, 2000).

Parental mediation is also reduced when media systems leave the family viewing area. In addition, as the number of media increases, less mediation has been found due to the difficulty of controlling children's exposure. For example, with a greater number of child-owned media, parental supervision is reduced (Lin & Atkin, 1989). Therefore, not only the addition of more media outlets but also the possible isolation of the "computer room" would lead us to predict reduced supervision.

Shaping the Use of the Internet: Children's Internet Use in the Home Environment

The Internet is being quickly adopted. It only took 5 years to reach 50 million users compared to 10 years for cable (Morgan Stanley Technology Research, 1999). Because the Internet is a relatively new medium, much of the research so far has described its acquisition and initial usage patterns (Katz & Aspden, 1997; Korgaonkar & Wolin, 1999).

Surveys found that high income, younger age, and high education levels were associated with early adoption and heavy use of the Internet (Graphics, Visualization, & Userbilities Center, 1995; Katz & Aspden, 1997; Korgaonkar & Wolin, 1999). Cost and difficulties in understanding how to use the Internet were the significant barriers to adoption. In the home, family members use the Internet for e-mail, chatting, and information search (Roberts, Foehr, Rideout, & Brodie, 1999).

Of course, Internet use presupposes computer use, about which more is known. According to a Kaiser Family Foundation report (Roberts et al., 1999), a larger proportion of kids from more advantaged backgrounds report using a computer both in and out of school, with boys reporting slightly more computer use than girls. Parent education level is positively related to children's time spent with computers.

Like the displacement studies of early television viewers, research has demonstrated what the Internet replaces. The Stanford Institute for the Quantitative Study of Society found a negative relationship between times spent using the Internet and social activities such as interpersonal contact (Nie & Erbring, 2000). Critics have pointed out that children's use of the Internet results in less time with family members, friends, and in after-school activities (Kaiser Family Foundation, 1999).

Shaping the Use of the Internet: User Motivations

Given that different motivations for television viewing exist, in what ways might motives differ in the Internet environment? Uses and gratifications research has traditionally focused on audience motivation and its relationship to consumption. Fundamental to this perspective is the assumption that individuals make active choices from available media content to satisfy their needs and wants. From this perspective, one can explore not only what users are looking for but also what they are finding in their ongoing use of a particular medium, in this case the Internet. This psychological understanding provides a snapshot of the user: What needs and wants does the Internet satisfy? Analogizing from traditional television motives, one could predict that social utility (companionship, enhancing relationships with friends), information seeking (acquiring news and information), and diversion (escape, relaxation, to pass time, enjoyment) factors might emerge. Rubin's (1981) description of media use as primarily ritualized (diversionary) or instrumental (utilitarian) in nature provides a useful dichotomy. Diversion motives, for example, tend to relate to greater exposure to the medium itself and to more ritual uses. Alternatively, instrumental or information-seeking motives are usually more related to exposure to news and other informational content. Exposure is less, but involvement and selectivity are high.

Nonetheless, the Internet is a different medium, and we cannot simply presume that the same motivation structure will apply. The Internet creates new levels of interactivity. While it is clear that the Internet can be used for entertainment purposes such as game playing, the diversion motives of relaxation may not apply in such an active environment.

Research Questions

This study examines the factors in the home shaping the "netgeneration": the mediation environment created by the parent(s), as perceived by the child; the child's motivations, which shape their uses of and attitudes toward the Internet; the access within the home; and the demographics of the family, which provide a context for use and attitude. Specifically, the present study explores four interrelated research questions:

RQ1:   Do parents and children perceive the mediation environment differently?

RQ2:   How does mediation predict children's use of the Internet as well as concerns and attitudes toward the Internet?

RQ3:   How do children's motivations predict usage, concerns, and attitudes? Do parental motivations influence the child's motivations or use, concerns, and attitudes?

RQ4:   How do parents' demographic factors predict children's Internet use, concerns, and attitudes toward the Internet?

In sum, this study explores children's Internet use, concerns, and attitudes toward the Internet as related to children's motivations, parental mediation styles, children's perceptions of mediation, and demographic factors.

Method

Independent variables include parents' mediation styles for children's Internet use, child's perception of parental mediation, parents' and child's motivations for Internet use, parents' and child's demographic characteristics such as age and gender, family size, educational level, income, the number of computers in the home, and media usage, including amount of computer use and television viewing. Dependent variables are children's amount of Internet use, levels of concerns about the Internet, and positive and negative attitudes toward the Internet.

We surveyed sixth-, seventh-, and eighth-grade children at three private schools located in Athens, Georgia, from September 2000 to May 2001, using a convenience sampling method. Once permission from the school was obtained, all parents received written explanations about the study. Only parents and children who had written signed consent forms were surveyed. The families who agreed to participate received a packet that included a cover letter, a consent form, two questionnaires, and a postage-paid envelope for return of the questionnaires. A pretest was conducted to assess the readability of the survey, to solicit and test Internet motivational and mediation items, and to refine the procedure for involving parents.

Of 600 packets sent to homes, a total of 141 families completed both questionnaires, representing a 23.5% response rate and a total sample of 282 individuals. Both questionnaires for parents and children were composed of seven sections regarding demographic characteristics (i.e., age, gender, number of family members, parents' education, income), media environment (i.e., number of computers, ability to access the Internet, amount of computer use, amount of Internet use), television uses and gratifications, Internet uses and gratifications, parental mediations of television and Internet, concerns about the Internet, and attitudes toward the Internet.

Independent Measures

Demographic Profile of the Sample

Sixty-six percent of parents were between 41 and 50 years of age (as indicated from $1 = less\ than\ 30$ to $5 = over\ 60$, $SD = .64$). Completed educational level of parents sampled ranged from less than 12th grade to graduate degree. Those with graduate degrees made up the largest group (45.7%) followed by college graduates, 37.1%. Parents whose annual income is more than $60,000 were 77.1%, confirming the relative affluence of this sample. As previous research has shown, children's amount of computer and Internet use was significantly higher in high-income homes (computer: $t = 6.899$, $p = .01$; Internet: $t = 5.615$, $p = .019$). Forty-four percent of the families sampled lived with four family members, followed by five and three (24.3%). The mean age of children was 11.77 years ($SD = 1.32$).

Children in this study spend each day about 2 hours (1:53) watching television, 28 minutes watching VCR recordings, 24 minutes playing video games, 43 minutes with books and newspapers, and nearly 1.5 hours with their computer at home (1:22) and 46 minutes in using the computer at school. The national sample from the study by Roberts (2000) showed a similar picture. Children in Roberts's study watched television 3 hours and 16 minutes per day but spent much less time using their computer. Thus, the caveat must be made that this is a more computer-active sample and a wealthier sample than the national average. Thus, generalizability to the population is limited, but generalizability to the most computer-active homes is possible.

Media Environment

Media within the home and at school/work were operationalized as the number of electronic media devices, including television and computer; amounts of television viewing, computer use, and Internet use; the presence or absence of a parent when using the Internet; and the place of the computer within the home. For each day of the week, parents watched television over an hour (minutes per day: $M = 87.28$, $SD = 68.31$). They spent more time with the computer and the Internet at work (minutes per day for computer: $M = 167.55$, $SD = 165.18$; minutes per day for Internet use: $M = 57.85$, $SD = 93.43$) than at home (minutes per day for computer: $M = 71.78$, $SD = 74.17$; minutes per day for Internet use: $M = 37.97$, $SD = 43.34$). Their technological ability to access the Internet was surprisingly well shaped. More than half of families had more than two computers in their homes (62.8%), and 40% of them had DSL or cable modem. In the home, children use the Internet for e-mail or instant messaging, music, surfing, and schoolwork. Parents use the Internet for e-mail, business, news, and travel information. Children use the Internet mostly in their home (61.4%). In general, when children use the Internet, they "often" or "very often" use it alone (69.6%). They only rarely use it with friends (17.0%), with parents (11.1%), and with siblings (7.2%). There were no significant gender differences in the amount of time on the Internet. Boys, however, spend significantly more time on the computer ($t = 6.568$, $p = .01$), playing computer games. More than half of the children sampled (60%) answered that they never or rarely use the Internet in a room where they can watch TV while on the Internet. Of the children, 56.5% own their own computer with online access. These data suggest that these children use the Internet mostly at home alone, using a computer that they can control.

Parents, however, perceived children's Internet use differently. Only 27.4% of parents reported that their child uses the Internet alone. They reported that children used the Internet mostly with the parent (40.1%). This is one of the many discrepancies between parent and child reports.

The media environment of the sample reflects the fact that the computer and the Internet have become as much a part of family life as television.

Media Motives

Both parents and children were asked about their motives for using the Internet. They were asked the same questions in both questionnaires and indicated one of five answers (strongly disagree, disagree, neutral, agree, and strongly agree). Questions were adapted from previous studies of television uses and gratifications (Rubin, 1981). This study grouped 10 items[1] found in traditional uses and gratification studies of television into three factors: personal/social utility (i.e., it shows me how to get along with others), information seeking (i.e., I can learn from it), and relaxation (i.e., I can relax).

Then Internet items were added: "I can make friends online," "The Internet gives quick, easy access to a lot of information," "It gives me a sense of power and control," and "It is interactive." These items were adapted from previous studies about the Internet and new media (Katz & Aspden, 1997; Korgaonkar & Wolin, 1999; Schmitt, 2000). Although several items were newly included in the measure, the projected factor structure was predicted to be the same as the factors of television uses and gratifications. In other words, personal utility, information-seeking, and relaxation factors were expected.

Internet motives were factor analyzed using a principal axis factoring solution with oblique rotation. At the first step, we conducted exploratory factor analysis with two separate files, children and parents. However, the factors created from the respective file produced low reliability coefficients among items measured by Cronbach's alphas. Low correlations among items in a factor can eventually lead to low Cronbach's alphas on the basis of conceptual formula (Bollen, 1989, p. 216). Since larger sample size can yield improved correlations, which can lead to high Cronbach's alphas, the two data sets (children and parents) were merged to produce much clearer factor structures. Items from each factor derived through exploratory factor analysis were summated and divided by the number of items based on the premise that any measurement error could mask relationships between independent and dependent variables if factor loading coefficients were used that contained interrelated values among factors (Hair, Anderson, & Tatham, 1998).[2] Table 17.1

Table 17.1 Means, Standard Deviations, and Reliabilities of Independent Variables

Variables	n		Mean (SD)		Range	t	p
	Parents	Child	Parents	Child			
Index: Personal utility motivation	139	138	1.59 (0.67)	2.16 (0.84)		−6.439	.000
I use the Internet because							
It stirs me up	139	138	1.67 (0.88)	2.00 (1.03)	1–5		
I can forget about worries	139	138	1.59 (0.77)	2.20 (1.08)	1–5		
It makes me feel less lonely	139	138	1.58 (0.78)	2.22 (1.13)	1–5		
I can make friends online	139	138	1.37 (0.67)	2.38 (1.28)	1–5		
It takes me into another world	139	138	1.73 (0.97)	2.01 (1.02)	1–5		
Cronbach's alpha (index)			.86	.83			
Index: Information-seeking motivation	139	139	3.97 (0.83)	3.52 (0.95)		4.522	.000
I use the Internet because							
It gives quick easy access to a lot of information	139	139	4.37 (0.82)	3.83 (1.03)	1–5		
I learn a lot from using the Web	139	139	3.73 (0.99)	3.44 (1.18)	1–5		
I learn about things happening in the world	139	139	3.81 (1.01)	3.29 (1.0)	1–5		
Cronbach's alpha (index)			.86	.83			
Index: Relaxation motivation	139	138	2.59 (0.86)	3.63 (0.86)		10.317	.000
I use the Internet because							
I can pass time	139	138	1.99 (1.10)	3.38 (1.22)	1–5		
I can relax	139	138	2.42 (1.11)	3.38 (1.13)	1–5		
I enjoy it	139	138	3.37 (1.00)	4.12 (0.90)	1–5		
Cronbach's alpha (index)			.72	.70			
Index: Active mediation	133	134	3.27 (0.78)	2.54 (0.83)		7.984	.000
How often parents say							
Explain why should not visit certain sites	133	134	4.04 (1.09)	3.28 (1.11)	1–5		
Point out good things about sites	133	134	3.48 (1.06)	2.83 (1.07)	1–5		

| | n | | Mean (SD) | | | | |
Variables	Parents	Child	Parents	Child	Range	t	p
Discuss certain sites	133	134	2.44 (1.26)	2.41 (1.13)	1–5		
Explain about Web ads	133	134	2.55 (1.26)	2.07 (1.11)	1–5		
Stay with child while on the Internet	133	134	3.05 (1.15)	2.09 (1.21)	1–5		
Cronbach's alpha (index)			.73	.79			
Index: Restrictive mediation	133	133	4.45 (0.69)	3.41 (1.08)		10.636	.000
How often parents say							
Spend as much time as child wants to[a]	133	133	4.09 (1.06)	3.35 (1.27)	1–5		
Have rules about information child can give out	133	133	4.65 (.80)	3.38 (1.40)	1–5		
Have rules about sites or places child can visit	133	133	4.62 (0.81)	3.51 (1.40)	1–5		
Cronbach's alpha (index)			.66	.71			
Index: Endorsement mediation	129	134	2.43 (0.80)	2.70 (0.80)		−3.550	.001
How often parents say							
Allow child to go on the Internet without any restrictions	129	134	1.95 (1.33)	2.75 (1.50)	1–5		
Spend as much time as child wants to	129	134	1.91 (1.05)	2.66 (1.26)	1–5		
Encourage child to go on the Internet	129	134	2.94 (1.17)	2.58 (0.94)	1–5		
Prefer child to spend time on the Internet instead of watching TV	129	134	2.92 (1.07)	2.80 (.94)	1–5		
Cronbach's alpha (index)			.63	.60			

Note: High score indicates an answer of more frequent behavior.

a. Indicates a reverse-coded item.

shows the items that loaded on each factor of the motivation scales and the Cronbach's alpha of the resulting scale. As expected, three factors emerged that were titled personal utility ($R^2 = .42$), information seeking ($R^2 = .17$), and relaxation ($R^2 = .08$). Because of the low R^2 value and Cronbach's alpha, the relaxation motivation should be interpreted cautiously.

Parental Mediation

Both parents and children were asked about parental mediation of the Internet. This study measured parental mediation with a parental guidance scale developed and refined by previous studies about media mediation: active, restrictive, and coviewing. Active mediation refers to critical discussions with the child. Restrictive mediation refers to rules that restrict a child's use of the medium. Coviewing refers to viewing with the child, which Nathanson (2001) found could be interpreted as endorsement. Since there is no parallel to coviewing in the Internet area, we attempted to measure explicit endorsement of Internet usage (Austin, 1993; van der Voort, Nikken, & van Lil, 1992). From parental mediation of the children's television viewing measure, eight items[3] were adapted to represent the three different mediation styles: active, restrictive, and endorsement. To measure parental mediation styles concerning the Internet, four items were added[4] in consideration of Internet characteristics (1 = *never* to 5 = *very often*). These items were based on previous studies about parental Internet guidelines (Aftab, 1997, 2000; Hughes & Campbell, 1998; Turrow & Nir, 2000).

These items were combined and adapted from previous studies for the purpose of creating factors conceptualizing different mediation styles: active, restrictive, and endorsement. These items were summed and a reliability test was performed. Table 17.1 reports the items and the reliability of the resulting scales for measures of active, restrictive, and endorsement mediation as reported by parents and by children. Although these three factors did emerge, low Cronbach's alphas suggest that endorsement should be interpreted cautiously.

Dependent Measures

Children's Media Use

The primary dependent variable was the amount of Internet use by the child. This was a single-item measure in which the child was asked to indicate the amount of time spent using the Internet per day. Other measures of child media use are reported below.

Children in the sample of this study watched television over an hour (minutes per day: $M = 113.15$, $SD = 103.09$). Given the amounts of computer (minutes per day: $M = 82.48$, $SD = 65.20$) and Internet use (minutes per day: $M = 52.54$, $SD = 59.25$) in the homes, television is still the dominant medium. However, it is worth noticing that they are spending about an hour every day on the computer and Internet. They co-use the Internet for an insignificant amount of time with family (minutes per day: $M = 8.68$, $SD = 17.21$).

Concerns and Attitudes About the Internet

Five items were combined and adapted from Schmitt (2000) and Turrow and Nir (2000) about Internet concerns and privacy.[5] Since the first item was adapted from Turrow and Nir's study (2000), we followed response options used in the original study (1 = *strongly disagree* to 5 = *strongly agree*). For the other four items, we used four answers (1 = *big problem* to 4 = *don't know*). These items were used as dependent variables to examine how parents' media motives, media mediation, and media environment could influence children's levels of concerns about the Internet. See Table 17.2 for the means, standard deviations, and reliabilities of these dependent variables.

Based on studies by Bybee, Robinson, and Turrow (1982) and van der Voort et al. (1992), 12 items about positive or negative attitudes toward the Internet were selected. As found in the pretest survey, both parents and children had negative attitudes as well as positive attitudes toward the Internet.

Results

Tables 17.1 and 17.2 display mean scores for all the indices used in this analysis. The first research question asked if children would perceive the mediation styles of the parents differently from the parents' reporting of those styles. In all cases, the answer is yes. Parents report more evaluative mediation than do children (parental mean = 3.27, child mean = 2.54, $t = 7.984$, $p = .000$). Parents also report more restrictions than do children (parents = 4.45, children = 3.41, $t = 10.636$, $p = .000$). Alternatively, parents report less endorsement mediation than do children (parents = 2.43, child = 2.7, $t = -3.550$, $p = .001$). In short, parents report more discussion with children than do the children themselves, and parents report more restrictions and less endorsement of the use of the Internet than do children.

Tables 17.3 and 17.4 report the results of the regression tests, which examined the best predictors of a child's use of the Internet, as well as their attitudes and concerns about the Internet. This analysis also allowed us to explore the research question of whether child or parent perceptions would provide the best predictors of Internet attitudes and behavior.

A stepwise multivariate regression analysis was performed to assess the relative influences of children's versus parents' mediation perceptions, media motives, and demographics on amount of child Internet use and the children's concerns and attitudes toward the Internet. We entered the independent variables block by block in a stepwise method that entered demographic data as control variables in the first step. The second block contained the mediation measures to gauge their role as a key criterion in the development of children's usage, attitudes, and concerns. The third block contained the motivation measures to gauge individual differences in motivation as a factor in Internet choices.

In a very strong model that accounted in total for 33.6% of the variance, the best predictors among the child report variables for the child's *amount* of Internet use were child's age ($\beta = .193$, $p = .005$), the child's relaxation motive ($\beta = .277$,

Table 17.2 Means, Standard Deviations, and Reliabilities of Dependent Variables

Variables	n		Mean (SD)		Range	t	p
	Parents	Child	Parents	Child			
Index: Internet concern	140	137	1.61 (0.57)	2.05 (0.64)		−6.860	.000
I am concerned about							
Security of personal info[a]	140	137	1.97 (0.82)	2.92 (1.04)	1–5		
Violent games	140	137	1.86 (1.06)	2.26 (0.96)	1–4[b]		
Dangerous strangers	140	137	1.39 (0.77)	1.53 (0.91)	1–4[b]		
Pornography	140	137	1.21 (0.63)	1.53 (1.02)	1–4[b]		
Loss of privacy	140	137	1.61 (0.75)	2.01 (1.01)	1–4[b]		
Cronbach's alpha (index)			.74	.66			
Index: Positive attitude toward the Internet	139	138	3.91 (0.52)	3.42 (0.71)		6.892	.000
Internet increases							
Support education	139	138	3.83 (0.72)	3.31 (0.85)	1–5		
Knowledge of news events	139	138	3.91 (0.66)	2.59 (0.88)	1–5		
Awareness of the world	139	138	3.96 (0.62)	3.42 (0.99)	1–5		
Curiosity	139	138	3.90 (0.66)	3.34 (1.00)	1–5		
Cronbach's alpha (index)			.79	.77			

Variables	n		Mean (SD)		Range	t	p
	Parents	Child	Parents	Child			
Index: Negative attitude toward the Internet	139	134	2.92 (0.62)	2.54 (0.60)		5.745	.000
Internet							
Increases buying behavior	139	134	2.98 (0.97)	2.74 (1.03)	1–5		
Increases anxiety	139	134	2.60 (0.82)	2.39 (0.99)	1–5		
Increases aggressive behavior	139	134	2.42 (0.01)	2.22 (0.95)	1–5		
Decreases physical activity	139	134	3.91 (1.00)	3.16 (1.17)	1–5		
Increases alienation	139	134	3.19 (0.92)	2.50 (1.05)	1–5		
Decreases creativity	139	134	2.79 (0.95)	2.34 (1.08)	1–5		
Decreases reading	139	134	2.82 (1.06)	2.61 (1.18)	1–5		
Breaks down social values	139	134	2.66 (0.91)	2.40 (1.00)	1–5		
Cronbach's alpha (index)			.82	.70			

Note: High score indicates an answer of more frequent behavior.

a. Indicates a reverse-coded item.

b. Low score indicates big concern.

Table 17.3   Results of Stepwise Regression: Regression of Child Variables

Dependent Variables Independent Variables	R^2 Change	β	df	F	p
Child's amount of Internet use					
Child's age	.062	.193*	(1, 122)	8.109	.005
Child's relaxation motivation	.124	.277**	(1, 121)	13.824	.000
Child's information-seeking motivation	.049	−.195*	(1, 120)	12.298	.000
Endorsement mediation style (child)	.101	.357***	(1, 119)	15.070	.000
Child's Internet concern					
Child's gender	.084	−.256**	(1, 124)	11.438	.001
Restrictive mediation style (child)	.069	−.265**	(1, 123)	11.131	.000
Child's positive attitude toward the Internet					
Child's information-seeking motivation	.195	.352***	(1, 124)	30.069	.000
Endorsement mediation style (child)	.078	.320***	(1, 123)	23.064	.000
Active mediation style (child)	.070	.276***	(1, 122)	21.249	.000
Child's negative attitude toward the Internet					
Restrictive mediation style (child)	.041	.203*	(1, 120)	5.147	.025

Note: Child indicates child's reports. Gender (male = 0, female = 1).

*$p \leq .05$. **$p \leq .01$. ***$p \leq .001$.

Table 17.4   Results of Stepwise Regression Tests: Parental Variables on Child Dependent Measures

Dependent Variables Independent Variables	R^2 Change	β	df	F	p
Child's amount of Internet use					
Parent's age	.109	.331***	(1, 112)	13.767	.000
Child's Internet concern					
Active mediation style (parent)	.044	−.210*	(1, 112)	5.148	.025
Child's positive attitude toward the Internet					
Parent's gender	.035	−.189*	(1, 111)	4.250	.017
Child's negative attitude toward the Internet					
Family income (parent)	.037	−.192*	(1, 108)	4.125	.045

Note: Parent indicates parent's reports. Gender (male = 0, female = 1).

*$p \leq .05$. ***$p \leq .001$.

$p = .000$) and information-seeking motive ($\beta = -.195$, $p = .000$), and the child's perception of an endorsement ($\beta = .357$, $p = .000$). See Table 17.3, which shows the significant findings. For amount of use, the significant mediation variable was endorsement. Two motivational variables were significant in opposite directions, with relaxation motives correlating with more Internet use and informational motives correlating with less use. The only demographic variable was age, showing that older children used the Internet more. The results indicate that older children who seek relaxation, not information, and who perceive that their parents endorse the Internet will use the Internet more. A separate regression equation that used parental data was less successful in that only parent age predicted the child's amount of Internet use ($\beta = .331$, $p = .000$). These results indicate that older parents had children who used the Internet more (see Table 17.4).

Not only do motivation and mediation predict amount of use, but they should also predict attitudes toward this emerging medium. Tables 17.3 and 17.4 also show the best predictors of a child's *attitudes* and *concerns*. With 15.3% of the total variance accounted for, the child's gender ($\beta = -.256$, $p = .001$) and the perception of restrictive mediation ($\beta = -.265$, $p = .000$) predicted a child's agreement with the Internet concern items. Similarly, negative attitudes were best explained by restrictive mediation perceptions ($\beta = .203$, $p = .025$). Positive attitudes toward the Internet were best explained by the child's information-seeking motivation ($\beta = .352$, $p = .000$) and by the perception of endorsement ($\beta = .320$, $p = .000$) and active mediation styles ($\beta = .276$, $p = .000$). Positive attitudes were predicted by information seeking, endorsement, and active mediation. Negative attitudes and concerns were predicted by gender and restrictive mediation.

Again, parent variables were disappointing in terms of their ability to predict child use and attitudes. Only one variable was significant for each equation, and in no case was the variance accounted for above 11%.

To account for the total variability across the sample, the child and parent data were entered together into a stepwise regression. In all cases, this failed to significantly change the solution. For *amount,* for example, children's age was not a significant factor. Evaluative mediation style as reported by parents did enter the equation. For *concerns,* only the parental variable did not make it into the equation. Similarly for *positive attitude* toward the Internet, only the parent's gender did not appear in the solution, and for *negative attitude,* the family income variable did not appear. This reinforces the finding that child variables are better predictors than are parental variables. Thus, active and endorsement mediation predicted positive attitudes while restrictive mediation predicted greater concerns and negative attitudes. Information-seeking motivations predicted positive attitudes.

In trying to explain the constellation of variables that make up a child's use of the Internet, we selected amount of use and attitude as dependent measures. One unanswered question is whether there are significant differences in the type of content, which are not apparent when examining only amount of use. Factor analysis failed to yield an interpretable solution of the different types of Internet use (i.e., e-mail, games, surfing, shopping, checking weather, etc.). However, motivations, which describe the reasons why people use the Internet, give us some insight into the use. Therefore, we regressed demographics and mediation on motivations. Table 17.5 shows a very clear picture.

Endorsement mediation is a powerful predictor of the motives of personal utility ($\beta = .401$, $p = .000$) and relaxation ($\beta = .422$, $p = .000$) (what might be called the ritual uses of the Internet). This was true whether it was the child's perception of parental mediation or the parents' report of their own mediation style (personal

Table 17.5   Results of Stepwise Regression Tests: Regression of Child and Parent Demographic and Mediation Variables on Child Motivation

Dependent Variables Independent Variables	R^2 Change	β	df	F	p
Child demographic and mediation **variables on child motivation**					
Child's personal utility motivation					
Endorsement mediation (child)	.161	.401***	(1, 127)	24.340	.000
Child's information-seeking motivation					
Active mediation (child)	.058	.240**	(1, 127)	7.752	.006
Child's relaxation motivation					
Endorsement mediation (child)	.178	.422***	(1, 126)	27.346	.000
Parent demographic and mediation **variables on child motivation**					
Child's personal utility motivation					
Family income	.060	.226*	(1, 114)	7.291	.008
Endorsement mediation (parent)	.060	.245**	(1, 113)	7.684	.001
Child's relaxation motivation					
Parent's age	.085	.225*	(1, 114)	10.601	.001
Endorsement mediation (parent)	.038	.206*	(1, 113)	7.931	.001

Note: Child indicates child's reports. Parent indicates parent's reports.

*$p \leq .05$. **$p \leq .01$. ***$p \leq .001$.

utility: $\beta = .245$, $p = .001$; relaxation: $\beta = .206$, $p = .001$). Alternatively, the single predictor of information-seeking motivation was a child's perception of an active mediation style by parents ($\beta = .240$, $p = .006$).

Discussion

This study investigated mediation, motivation, and home environment to better understand children's Internet use and attitudes. Several strong findings emerged from this analysis.

First, we asked if children and parents would perceive the mediation environment differently. According to our results, parents see themselves as engaging in more active mediation than do children. Generalized evaluative discussions of the Internet (good and bad things about sites, discussion of Web ads, staying with the child while using the Internet), often viewed as the heart of mediation, may be overestimated by parents because they are seen as socially desirable. Similarly, these generalized discussions may not register with the child, if they are handled in a casual and positive manner. Nonetheless, there could be a danger that children are perceiving much less evaluative communication than parents would wish. A similar pattern emerged for restrictions. Parents report more restrictive mediation than did children. Children report having the freedom to spend as much time as they wish online and not having rules about information to be given out or sites to visit. Restrictions are where one might expect most agreement between parent and child. But in both of these cases, the children see themselves as more free and unconstrained agents than do the parents.

Endorsement mediation (encourage the child to go online, prefer Internet to TV, no restrictions of time or place) showed the opposite pattern. Children perceived more parental endorsement of the Internet than did the parents. Overall, these discrepancies paint a clear picture: Parents and children see mediation differently. Children feel they are free agents in the Internet world, with the endorsement of their parents. Parents disagree.

Given the above discrepancies, our question becomes even more intriguing. What better predicts child use and attitude? This study provided strong evidence, agreeing with Fujioka and Austin (2003), that a child's perspective provides better prediction than parents' perspectives. In all cases, the dependent variables of amount, concerns, and positive or negative attitude toward the Internet were better predicted by child variables than by parental ones. In some ways, it is self-evident that an individual would be a better predictor of his or her own behavior than someone else. However, much of our research in parental mediation relies on parental report measures even with middle school–age children. Even more important, from a theoretical perspective, is to understand the interpretive process that intervenes between parental behavior and child interpretation.

A family interaction anomaly emerges as we find that what *does* predict a child's amount of Internet use are age, relaxation motivation, and a perception of endorsement. Despite reports of restrictions, endorsement emerges powerfully. Parents might be seen to be "leaking" endorsement cues, which overwhelm their cautionary statements. This potential anomaly, which may not be revealed in parents' reports of how they talk about the Internet with their children, suggests that intensive in-home observation is required to understand this process. Information seeking factored in as negative in the prediction of the amount of use. The prediction of concerns and attitude is more complex and seems to be predicted more often by mediation than by motivation. Restrictive mediation negatively predicted a child's level of concern about the Internet and positively predicted negative attitudes toward the Internet. Positive attitudes are predicted by information-seeking motivation and by perceptions of endorsement and evaluative mediation styles. The primary motive for amount of Internet use is relaxation. Positive attitudes are predicted by an information-seeking motivation and by perceptions of parental endorsement and discussion of the Internet. The perception of parental reinforcement has important implications for the child. Also clearly, that endorsement may result in increased amount of usage with the child motivated to seek entertainment and relaxation. With a child motivated to seek information, the result of this interaction is a positive attitude toward the Internet. Thus, motivations of relaxation and information seeking predict amount of Internet use, but only information seeking predicts attitudes. All forms of mediation (active, restrictive, and endorsement) predict various attitudes; only endorsement predicts amount of Internet use.

Demographic variables were unimpressive in this analysis. A child's age and gender each appeared once in the child regressions. Parents' age, gender, and family income also each appeared once. No patterns of effects could be judged from these findings. The variable, introduced in this study, of endorsement of Internet usage warrants further study. It emerged as a powerful predictor, despite its low Cronbach's alpha. This was conceptualized as a functional communicative parallel of coviewing, using Nathanson's (2001) description of coviewing as endorsement. Results suggest that a construct validity study separating positive and negative active mediation and endorsement would yield stronger factors.

In an ad hoc attempt to explore the different types of Internet use as measured by motivations, some interesting findings emerged. Endorsement mediation was a powerful predictor of the motives of personal utility and relaxation (what might be called the ritual uses of the Internet). This was true whether it was the child's perception of parental mediation or the parents' report of their own mediation style. Paired with the earlier findings that endorsement was linked with increased amount of usage for the child motivated to seek entertainment and relaxation, a picture emerges of one important type of user: one with a high amount of Internet use, parental endorsement, and relaxation and personal utility motives. Alternatively, the single predictor of information-seeking motivation was a child's perception of an active mediation style by parents. Hence, a second user type appears: low amount of Internet use, positive attitudes toward the Internet, high information-seeking motivation, and active parental discussion about the Internet. Although the research questions did not posit an ordering of influence variables, the ad hoc analysis suggests strong direct and indirect effects of the family communication patterns within the home, with mediation styles strongly influencing the dependent variables of amount and attitudes about the Internet but also indirectly and strongly influencing the development of motivation for the use of the Internet as well.

Meaningful differences exist between parent and child reports of mediation. The results further indicate that the child's report predicts uses and attitudes better than does the parental report. The results suggest that a combination of relaxation motivation and the perception of parental endorsement best predicts the amount of Internet use. Two different child Internet types emerged. One is the entertainment cluster, where high amount of use is paired with the perception of parental endorsement, as well as with relaxation and social utility motives. The second is the information-seeking user, where positive attitudes and perceptions of active parental mediations are paired with information-seeking motives and lower overall Internet use. These two very different types demonstrate the importance of understanding the powerful interactions between individual motivation and family mediation.

Notes

1. Ten items include the following: I watch television because (1) it stirs me up, (2) I can forget about worries, (3) it makes me feel less lonely, (4) it shows me how to get along with others, (5) I can pass time, (6) it takes me into another world, (7) I can learn from it, (8) I can relax, (9) I can get information, and (10) I enjoy it.

2. The oblique rotational method is more flexible because the factor axes need not be orthogonal. It is also more realistic because the theoretically important underlying dimensions are not assumed to be uncorrelated with each other. It is notable that the oblique factor rotation represents the clustering of variables more accurately (Hair et al., 1998, p. 109). The oblique Promax method assumes the possible relations among factors (oblique) with sequential weight on the order of factors (Promax). Meanwhile, Kaiser normalization of the orthogonal method represents that all possible variables are considered to be analyzed for factor construction.

3. Eight items are as follows: (1) I (my parents) encourage my child (me) to watch television, (2) I (my parents) set limits on the amount of television my child (me) watches, (3) I (my parents) limit the kinds of shows my child (me) watches, (4) I (my parents) limit viewing until after homework/chores are done, (5) I (my parents) discuss the television shows we view together, (6) I (my parents) point out bad things about some shows, (7) I (my parents) point out that some things on TV are good, and (8) I (my parents) watch television with my child (me).

4. Added items are the following: (1) I (my parents) allow my child (me) to go on the Internet without any restrictions, (2) I (my parents) allow my child (me) to spend as much time on the Internet as he/she wants to, (3) I (my parents) prefer that my child (I) spends time going on the Internet instead of watching television, and (4) I (my parents) explain about Web ads to my child (me).

5. Internet concerns are itemized as follows: (1) I am concerned over the security of personal information on the Web, (2) I see violent games as a problem, (3) I see dangerous strangers making contact with kids on the Web as a problem, (4) I see pornography that kids can see as a problem, and (5) I see loss of privacy as a problem.

References

Abelman, R. (1990). Determinants of parental mediation of children's television viewing. In J. Bryant (Ed.), *Television and the American family* (pp. 311–326). Hillsdale, NJ: Lawrence Erlbaum.

Aftab, P. (1997). *A parents' guide to the Internet . . . And how to protect your children in cyberspace.* New York: SC Press.

Aftab, P. (2000). *The parent's guide to protecting your children in cyberspace.* New York: McGraw-Hill.

Austin, E. W. (1993). Exploring the effects of active parental mediation of television content. *Journal of Broadcasting & Electronic Media, 37,* 147–158.

Austin, E. W. (2001). The role of parental mediation in the political socialization process. *Journal of Broadcasting & Electronic Media, 45,* 221–240.

Bollen, K. A. (1989). *Structural equations with latent variables.* New York: John Wiley.

Bower, R. T. (1973). *Television and the public.* New York: Holt, Rinehart and Winston.

Bybee, C., Robinson, D., & Turrow, J. (1982). Determinants of parental guidance of children's television viewing for a special subgroup: Mass media scholars. *Journal of Broadcasting, 26,* 697–710.

Comstock, G. (1975). The evidence so far. *Journal of Communication, 25,* 25–34.

Fujioka, Y., & Austin, E. W. (2003). The implication of vantage point in parental mediation of television and children's attitudes toward drinking alcohol. *Journal of Broadcasting & Electronic Media, 47,* 418–434.

Graphics, Visualization, & Userbilities Center. (1995). *GVU's 10th user survey* [Online report]. Retrieved from http://www.gvu.gatech.edu/user_surveys/survey-1998–10/

Greenberg, B. S., Ericson, P., & Vlahos, M. (1972). A comparison of parental mediation behaviors for mothers and their children. *Journal of Broadcasting, 13,* 1331–1334.

Greenberg, B. S., & Heeter, C. (1987). VCRs and young people. *American Behavioral Scientist, 30,* 486–494.

Hair, J. F., Anderson, R. E., & Tatham, R. L. (1998). *Multivariate data analysis* (5th ed.). Upper Saddle River, NJ: Prentice Hall.

Hughes, D. R., & Campbell, P. (1998). *Kids online: Protecting your children in cyberspace.* Grand Rapids, MI: Revell.

Katz, J., & Aspden, P. (1997). Motivations for and barriers to Internet usage: Results of a national public-opinion survey. *Internet Research-Electronic Networking Applications and Policy, 7,* 170.

Kim, W. Y., Baran, S., & Massey, K. K. (1988). Impact of the VCR on control of television viewing. *Journal of Broadcasting & Electronic Media, 32,* 351–358.

Korgaonkar, P., & Wolin, L. (1999). A multivariate analysis of Web usage. *Journal of Advertising Research, 39,* 53–68.

Lin, C. A., & Atkin, D. J. (1989). Parental mediation and rulemaking for adolescent use of television and VCRs. *Journal of Broadcasting and Electronic Media, 33,* 53-67.

McLeod, J. M., & Chaffee, S. H. (1972). The construction of social reality. In J. T. Tedschi (Ed.), *The social influence processes* (pp. 50–99). Chicago: Aldine-Atherton.

Morgan Stanley Technology Research. (1999). *The Internet data service reports.* New York: Author.

Nathanson, A. (2001). Parent and child perspectives on the presence and meaning of parental television mediation. *Journal of Broadcasting & Electronic Media, 45,* 201–220.

Nie, N. H., & Erbring, L. (2000). *Internet and society: A preliminary report.* Stanford, CA: Stanford Institute for the Quantitative Study of Society.

Park, M. R., & Floyd, K. (1996). Making friends in cyberspace. *Journal of Communication, 46,* 80–95.

Roberts, D. F. (2000). Media and youth: Access, exposure, and privatization. *Journal of Adolescent Health, 27,* 8–14.

Roberts, D. F., Foehr, U. G., Rideout, V. J., & Brodie, M. (1999). *Kids & media @ the new millennium.* Menlo Park, CA: Kaiser Family Foundation.

Rubin, A. M. (1981). An examination of television viewing motivations. *Communication Research, 8,* 141–166.

Schmitt, K. L. (2000). *Public policy, family rules and children's media use in the home* (Reports Series No. 35). Philadelphia: The Annenberg Public Policy Center of the University of Pennsylvania.

Thompson, T. L., & Slater, D. (1983, November). *Parent-child co-viewing and parental monitoring of television: Their impacts and interaction.* Paper presented at the annual convention of the Speech Communication Association, Washington, DC.

Turrow, J. (1999). *The Internet and the family: The view from parents, the view from the press.* Philadelphia: The Annenburg Public Policy Center of the University of Pennsylvania.

Turrow, J., & Nir, L. (2000). *The Internet and the family 2000: The view from parents: The view from kids.* Philadelphia: Annenberg Public Policy Center of the University of Pennsylvania.

van der Voort, T. H. A., Nikken, P., & van Lil, J. E. (1992). Determinants of parental guidance of children's television viewing: A Dutch replication study. *Journal of Broadcasting & Electronic Media, 36,* 61–75.

Woodard, E. H., & Gridina, N. (2000). *Media in the home 2000: The Fifth Annual Survey of Parents and Children.* Philadelphia: The Annenberg Public Policy Center of the University of Pennsylvania.

CHAPTER 18

Employees "Without" Families

Discourses of Family as an
External Constraint to Work-Life Balance

Kristen Lucas

University of Nebraska–Lincoln

Patrice M. Buzzanell

Purdue University

F or most people, work is an essential ingredient of daily life (Ciulla, 2000). In the United States, the proportion of people engaged in paid employment and the amount of time they invest in work have been on the rise for decades. According to Mishel, Bernstein, and Boushey (2003), economists from the U.S. Economic Policy Institute and authors of *The State of Working America* (a biennial compilation of statistics and analyses regarding the U.S. labor market), the employment rate for those older than age 16 years increased by 10% between 1973 and 2001. Notably, working women contributed substantially to this upsurge, with the employment rate of women older than age 20 increasing by 38%, including a 6% jump since 1999.

Not only are more people working, but people are working more. Mishel et al. (2003; see also Schor, 1991) report that, on average, people are working 10% more hours per year than they did in 1979. Among married couples with children, men are working 4% and women are working 44% more hours per year than couples did in 1979. People do not appreciate this change (see Bookman, 2004; Saltzman, 1991). Of those who work full-time, 37% feel overworked, and 44% of all employed people indicate that they work more hours than they prefer (Mishel et al., 2003). Furthermore, today's employees are less likely to receive paid time off for vacation and holidays than they were three decades ago (Mishel et al.).

It is no wonder that people are concerned with work-life balance issues. Finding time to fulfill "nonwork" responsibilities such as cooking and cleaning, relationship nurturing, and civic commitments (e.g., PTA, faith-based organizations, volunteer work) is an increasingly difficult task. Somewhere between the competing demands of work and home, millions of overworked employees are trying to find "balance" or at least some reprieve from the daunting demands on their time.[1] When a problem affects so many people—and Americans certainly are not alone in this struggle (see Joplin, Shaffer, Francesco, & Lau, 2003; Wharton & Blair-Loy, 2002)—it is essential for practitioners and scholars to turn their attention to finding solutions.

Accordingly, there is a growing corpus of literature on work-life balance, from both organizational and family communication perspectives. Organizational scholars focus on the impact that lack of balance has on outcomes such as job satisfaction, burnout, productivity, and turnover (e.g., Greenblatt, 2002; Westman, Etzion, & Gortler, 2004), whereas family scholars examine processes and outcomes such as negotiation of "second shift" duties and relationship stress due to spillover effects (e.g., Perry-Jenkins, Pierce, & Goldberg, 2004; Zimmerman, Haddock, Current, & Ziemba, 2003). These scholars largely have focused on either work or family, positioning these matters as separate anchors in a dichotomy. Even when family communication is the focus, researchers have backgrounded the term *family* and its assumptions (Kirby, 2004).

In this chapter, we position work and life as two facets of the same phenomenon. Rather than viewing each as an impediment to the other (i.e., work gets in the way of having a fulfilling life and vice versa), we foreground family within the work context. Granted, there are many external constraints to achieving work-life balance, such as the gendered nature of work and career, "work devotion schema," skyrocketing health care costs, and job insecurities (e.g., Blair-Loy, 2003; Buzzanell, 2000). However, we believe that one issue stands out from the rest. This issue or problem, we argue, is the definition of family itself. In other words, the very discourses and language we use to talk about family—whether in office hallways, living rooms, or Congress—serve to hide our assumptions, entrench our ideologies, and mute alternative views. Consequently, policy making at both governmental and local organizational levels honors a particular social construction of family and devalues, dismisses, or demonizes all others. Simply put, the lack of sufficient and representative family definitions serves as a constraint to individuals' work-life balancing abilities and to society's construction of policies that meet members' needs.

Following a brief overview of work-life balance, we problematize "family" by detailing both explicit and implicit family discourses in the scholarly literature. Next, we address the changing demographics and family trends that demonstrate the out-of-date nature of the dominant family discourses and explain how particular groups of people are disadvantaged disproportionately by the current definitions. Finally, we suggest how a middle-range definition can be used to overcome some work-life obstacles and to develop more innovative and meaningful employer-sponsored programs.

Problematizing "Family" in Work-Life Issues

The advent of work-life programs can be traced to the 1970s, a period marked by the beginning of a steady and substantial rise in the number of women in the U.S. labor force (Barnett, 1999; Young, 1999). This increase in women workers brought not only economic change but also significant social change. Gone was the nostalgic image of the 1950s family with its breadwinner father and stay-at-home mother (see Coontz, 1992). In its place was a mixture of "traditional" nuclear families (i.e., father, mother, and children), dual-earner couples, and single working mothers. By the 1980s, the workplace adapted to this demographic shift by implementing "family-friendly" policies. While touted as programs to meet "workers' needs," they actually were designed to assist *women* in meeting workplace and child-rearing demands (Barnett, 1999). Strict gender role expectations presumably are disappearing; yet, the three primary categories of today's work-life benefits remain firmly focused on management of familial responsibility: flexible work options, family leave policies, and dependent care benefits (see Kirby & Krone, 2002).

By the 1990s, particularly in light of the strong economy, organizations realized that they could recruit and retain valuable employees who did not have dependent children by broadening their work-family policies to include more all-encompassing "work-life" initiatives, such as health club memberships or on-site workout facilities, adoption assistance, domestic partner benefits coverage, concierge services, transit benefits, and flextime/telework programs (Charas & Kushner, 2002; Young, 1999). However, despite the shift in terminology from work-family to work-life, "family friendly" remains synonymous with work-life programs, and a traditional construction of "family" remains the core of these programs.

Past research has demonstrated the vital role that communication plays with regard to work-life and/or family-friendly workplace policies. For example, interpersonal discourses greatly influence the use of family-friendly benefits. Coworkers' perceptions of who uses or abuses benefits, such as child care or parental leave, have a significant effect on who takes advantage of benefits for which they are eligible (Kirby & Krone, 2002). Similarly, women's perceived abilities to negotiate maternity leaves can involve complex and contradictory discourses of justice and care ethics as well as of organizational and personal imperatives that are evident in organizational members' talk (Liu & Buzzanell, 2004). And bosses' mixed messages about benefits policies and utilization appropriateness can hinder employees' likelihood of using family-friendly programs (Kirby, 2000).

However, we maintain that communication plays an even more fundamental role than is demonstrated in this research. We argue that the discourses of family in informal workplace and formal policy-setting discussions operate as external constraints to work-life balance achievement. In other words, the very messages of what constitutes and does not constitute family both enable and constrain material choices and affect individuals' negotiation or adoption of benefits, workplace practices, organizational policies, and government legislation. To initiate meaningful change, it is necessary to step back from and question the definitions of family that are so deeply ingrained in our ideology.

In their call for new theorizing in the arena of work-life issues, MacDermid, Roy, and Zvonkovic (2005) explain that one promising way to advance new theory is to problematize core concepts through (a) surfacing the concept, "bringing to awareness assumptions that can then be evaluated for their accuracy and utility in the contemporary context" (p. 500), and (b) taking "a value stance on unfairness in the concept" (p. 503). We problematize "family" to examine the pervasiveness of current definitions and expose their unfairness and inadequacy for building meaningful and diverse work-life policies and practices. (See Chapters 1 and 2, this volume.)

Surfacing the Concept

Surfacing a concept focuses attention on the way that it is defined and used in current literature. One example of surfacing in work-family research is evidenced in the concerted effort to differentiate between wage work and nonpaid work (e.g., Williams, 2000). This move was inspired by the need to validate the work that was done—primarily by women—but did not earn a paycheck. While "work" has been surfaced, "family" remains a backgrounded concept in contemporary research. Perhaps the societal notion of family is so taken for granted that it appears to need no explanation. However, the little research that does define family indicates that further explanation and exploration of this important term are absolutely vital.

Popenoe (1993), codirector of the National Marriage Project, offers one of the boldest definitions of family. Although he is a strong advocate of a husband-wife-biological/adopted children family unit and bemoans its decline, he does offer a somewhat broader definition of family:

> A relatively small domestic group of kin (or people in kin-like relationship) consisting of at least one adult and one dependent person. [Family refers] particularly to an intergenerational unit that includes (or once included) children, but handicapped and infirm adults, the elderly, and other dependents also qualify. (p. 529)

Popenoe includes in his definition single-parent families, stepfamilies, and non-married and homosexual couples *with* dependents. Married couples with grown children also are considered families. However, he specifically excludes committed couples without children from the definition, explaining that relationships, regardless of permanence, formed from "sexually bonded or sexually based primary relationships" (p. 529) are not families unless there is a dependent child or dependent adult present. In addition to the growing number of adults who choose to remain childfree, committed couples who long for but who are unable to conceive and/or adopt dependent children are not considered to constitute a family. Interestingly, however, their prior presence in their family-of-origin allows their parents (presumably now "empty nesters") to remain classified as a family.

Granted, one definition written by one person should not cause alarm. However, Popenoe's influence reaches far beyond scholarly publications and audiences. He frequently is interviewed and quoted in national media outlets, including newspapers, television, and radio (National Marriage Project, n.d.). Therefore, his views are gaining widespread attention and credence in current popular culture. In addition, Popenoe's colleague Whitehead (who shares the codirectorship of the National Marriage Project) has testified to the U.S. Senate regarding family issues (National Marriage Project, 2004). Thus, the definition of family Popenoe advocates also influences federal policy making.

Furthermore, Smith (1993) explains that family units similar to those detailed by Popenoe are the foundation of what she calls the standard North American family (SNAF). Rather than a simple definition, she explains, SNAF acts as an ideological code that governs how we talk about and interpret messages about family. Furthermore, SNAF assigns roles to family members: male as breadwinner, female as primary caregiver. SNAF carries political force insofar as it informs such things as research on the family, public debate, and policy making (for a discussion of the family definition informing welfare policy, see Gring-Pemble, 2003).

As one example of practices stemming from particular definitions, Bould (1993) shows that the U.S. census relies on a two-component definition of family similar to the definition advocated by Popenoe (1993) and critiqued by Smith (1993). First, there is an assumption of coresidence. That is, family members are those people who live together. The second component is that there must be a relationship of blood, marriage, or adoption. In fact, the only categories on the census form for relationships are spouse, child, parent, and sibling. All other family members in residence are categorized as *boarders* (Smith, 1993). Perhaps this operationalization is necessary for census data collection; however, it renders invisible other viable and important kin relationships.

Emery and Lloyd (2001) offer hope that restrictive definitions of family are changing. They note that past conceptualizations, such as Popenoe's (1993) definition, emphasize "marriage plus progeny" (Christensen, 1946, as cited by Emery & Lloyd, 2001). However, Emery and Lloyd claim that current definitions embrace more diversity and emphasize the importance of emotional bonds. They cite Allen, Fine, and Demo's (2000) definition of family as "two or more persons related by birth, marriage, adoption, or *choice*" (p. 1, emphasis added). As further evidence that recent family conceptualizations incorporate bonds of different types, Edwards and Rothbard (2000) label as family any "persons related by biological ties, marriage, *social custom*, or adoption" (p. 179, emphasis added) and further refine this definition by addressing family members' functions (i.e., ways individual members contribute toward family maintenance and well-being).

Even less restrictive are conceptualizations of family grounded in communication and individual needs. Whitchurch and Dickson (1999) assert that, from a communicative approach (as compared to a structural approach), "a family is defined through its communication—both verbal and nonverbal—rather than solely through biological or legal kinship" (p. 687). They further explain that "a family unit constitutes itself through a process in which people differentiate themselves from nonfamily members by interacting together as a family" (p. 687). An interaction-based definition allows for the inclusion of fictive kin, such as unmarried couples or longtime friends, who otherwise would be excluded by structural definitions.[2]

Notably, although Whitchurch and Dickson (1999) state that a communication approach to families has at its core a belief that families are constructed through *both* interaction and structure, there still exists a reliance on structural labels to describe families (e.g., husband, mother, sister, stepson). They emphasize that although communication scholars may use these structural labels to describe family, they are not defining the family by its structure. Rather, labels are simply that—labels. Unfortunately, in practice, the use of structural labels falls short of validating diversity in family forms.

The tendency to revert to structural and traditional conceptualizations of family occurs despite the best intentions of researchers and policy makers. For example, Haas (1999) initially defines "family" in a broad, inclusive way: "an emotional unit, based on love and affection, that provides psychological security and nurturance to its members" (p. 571). Yet, her ensuing review of research focuses exclusively on marriage, divorce, and childbirth. Perhaps this is a result of insufficient literature being available that operationalizes family in a way that includes relationships beyond marriage and/or children. Likewise, in workplace matters, it appears that, at minimum, a person has to be either married *or* have dependent children to be considered to have a family. The Family and Medical Leave Act (FMLA) of 1993 outlines rights of employees to take leave for family needs (e.g., birth of children, family member illness, and funerals). Yet, despite its gender-neutral language, the policy dictates that family members include only spouses, children, and parents.

Taking a Value Stance

It is nothing new to say that the above definitions of family are out of touch with today's family structures. In this section, first we document contemporary family trends. Then, we link these trends to the unfairness that outdated or insufficient family definitions have on work-life policies and practices as well as on quality of life.

Family Trends

MacDermid et al. (2005) explain that past theorizing based on historic demographic realities leaves current theorizing incomplete. Teachman, Tedrow, and Crowder (2000) state that the limitations of the legal definitions of family dismiss not only family relationships that extend across households but also cohabitating couples. In addition, DeFrain and Olson (1999) maintain that the Parsonian definition of the "classical nuclear family" simply is not sufficient to describe U.S. relationship trends. They call for new, more positive terminology to describe current family forms.

Some of the demographic trends that have affected U.S. family forms are decreases in the rates of marriage, increases in the number of divorces, increases in the number of cohabitating couples, and decreases in the number of women having children. First, marriages are being delayed and are decreasing. Teachman et al.

(2000) identify trends from the 1960s through the late 1990s that demonstrate that the number of early marriages (i.e., marriages before 24 years of age) has declined steadily in the past 30 years. Whereas in 1975, approximately 65% of women between the ages of 20 and 24 had been married, by 2003, that number dropped to 25% (Teachman et al., 2000; U.S. Census Bureau, 2003). This decline could be accounted for by the fact that remaining single increasingly is being regarded as an acceptable alternative to marriage (DeFrain & Olson, 1999). Also, as people are marrying later in life, more people also are remaining unmarried their entire lives (Haas, 1999). Currently, 40% of women and 43% of men older than age 18 are unmarried (U.S. Census Bureau, 2003). Second, accompanying the drop in marriage rates is an increase in the number of divorces and trends indicating that people are less likely to remarry after divorce (Haas, 1999; Teachman et al., 2000).

Third, the number of women having children is decreasing. Gold and Wilson (2002) explain that in family life cycle research, it is presumed that the presence of children is what transforms a "couple" into a "family." Consequently, children are an essential ingredient in families. However, adults increasingly are *choosing* not to have children. These couples are called "childfree" families, as compared to "childless" couples who experience the absence of a desired member, often through involuntary conditions such as infertility (Gold & Wilson, 2002). Whether by choice or circumstance, the U.S. Census Bureau reports that 22% of women born between 1956 and 1972 will never have children (Gold & Wilson, 2002, p. 70) and predicts that the most common household in 2005 will be a single person or a married couple without children (Young, 1999, p. 33).

Unfair Consequences

As these demographic trends attest, many people simply do not fit within the traditional definition of family. As such, the current conception is not only out of touch with reality but also has unfair, material consequences. That is, although virtually all employees have responsibilities that strain their work-life balance efforts, many do not have access to programs and policies to assist them, as work-life initiatives typically are designed to assist those people whose family meets select criteria. In short, when only a certain form of family is privileged via daily discourses, all other forms are marginalized.

Discourses of family can have serious implications for work-life balance. Specifically, discourses strengthen current beliefs and shape policies and day-to-day practices in the workplace. Although a complete list is impossible to create, some of the marginalized employees include childfree singles (including people dating, not dating, widowed, and never been married), divorced people (including those who lost custody of [step]children in a divorce), cohabiting couples (including opposite-sex and same-sex couples), infertile childless couples (including opposite-sex, same-sex, married, and unmarried couples), unmarried noncustodial coparents (including those who live alone, maintain ties with coparents, and remain involved in children's lives but do not bear primary financial responsibility), people providing primary care for young children without having legal custody, and kin and fictive kin not living in the household.

People in each of these groups face unique challenges with regard to work-life balance. Rather than cover all groups, we focus our attention on one particular group: those people who have neither a spouse nor a dependent. According to many scholarly definitions, U.S. census operationalizations, and FMLA regulations, these people do not have families. Furthermore, this group can include people with or without a committed partner and people who are either heterosexual or homosexual. To explore the resulting unfairness, we describe some of the unique challenges faced by this group of people "without" families, including (a) workplace burdens, (b) unequal access to benefits, and (c) long-term consequences of work-life imbalance, in hopes of effecting positive change in the work-life balance efforts of all employees.

With regard to *workplace burdens,* Kirby and Krone (2002) and Young (1999) found that employees perceived that there was preferential treatment, particularly for workers with children and especially *women* workers with children. Employees without children perceived that parents received preferential treatment for using leave policies, that the benefits as a whole were targeted to parents, and that childfree employees had to travel for work more than employees with children. In addition, childfree employees felt that their workdays were burdened by the responsibility of picking up the slack for other employees who were using family-friendly policies. Gold and Wilson (2002) explained the situation this way:

> In the workplace, [childfree employees] are seen as ready replacements for peers who attend to family crises and report being asked to work longer hours than their peers, to sacrifice personal time for work more often, and to accept family-related concerns as the only legitimate reason for absence from work. (p. 71)

There is a growing resentment among single employees with regard to work-family policies at their workplaces. Flynn (1996) reported survey results indicating the depth of these feelings: 80% of employees believe that single employees without children are being left out of work-family programs, 81% believe that single employees without children carry additional workload burden, and 80% believe that the needs of workers with children receive more attention than the needs of childfree employees.

In addition to workplace burdens, employees also perceive *unequal access to benefits.* Despite two thirds of U.S. employees not having children younger than age 18 living at home, most family-friendly workplace policies are geared toward people with children (Flynn, 1996). As such, single/childfree employees do not reap the benefits associated with dependent health care, insurance, and subsidized child care (Young, 1999). Furthermore, childfree employees perceive themselves as having less access to flexible work arrangements or unpaid leaves. Single/childfree employees also are less likely than married/parent employees to ask supervisors and peers for informal accommodations "when their personal lives conflict with the demands of work, for fear that they will be viewed negatively" (Young, 1999, p. 36).

Another example of unequal access to benefits is access to infertility treatment. New Jersey is one of several states that have passed a law requiring that insurance companies cover costs associated with infertility treatment (Infertility Health Insurance Coverage, 2001). However, New Jersey's definition of infertility presupposes a traditional notion of family, specifically outlining a criterion of "the female partner" being unable to conceive during a given timeframe. As a result, this type of policy benefits only heterosexual partners, even though half of gay men in committed relationships desire parenthood (Patterson, 2000).

Finally, there are *long-term consequences* of inadequate family conceptualizations. For instance, when childfree employees take on extra work responsibilities, there are trade-offs. Hewlett (2002; see also Sheehy, 1995) writes about family-based costs that women bear to advance their careers. While putting in extra hours at work, relocating, and traveling for business purposes, today's women increasingly are staying single longer and are delaying childbirth. Ultimately, these delays make it more difficult to find a partner and have a baby, as many career-focused women (33% overall; 42% in corporate America) are childless, despite their desires otherwise. Instead of choosing to be childfree, Hewlett explains, their situation becomes a "creeping nonchoice" (p. 66). Hewlett suggests that women work for companies that provide policies that allow for better work-life balance and choose a career that gives the "gift of time" to remedy this situation.[3] However, when work-life programs are designed to assist employees who already have children, this may be easier said than done.

As evidenced by the above examples, work-life programs tend to privilege people with spouses and children. There also is an assumption that family caregiving is the greatest non(paid)work priority. As a result, organizational practices and governmental legislation perpetuate thinking that has direct and indirect effects on people's abilities to achieve some sort of balance in their lives. However, when envisioned as ways of enhancing individuals' enactment of more fulfilling, identity-affirming activities in multiple domains (Thompson & Bunderson, 2001), the notions of work-life balance in general and of family in particular can be broadened meaningfully. These changes require recognition that the ways people talk about family have material consequences for everyone's ability to achieve some sort of work-life balance.

A Communicative Solution

Just because discourses of family have contributed to biased work-life programs, it does not mean that these discourses are set in stone. Gubrium and Holstein (1990, cited in Emery & Lloyd, 2001) maintain that family is socially constructed through individual and societal discourses. In addition, MacDermid et al. (2005) explain that the "hallmarks of problematizing a concept would be the illumination that the concept is not determined by biology, by society, or by law, but is instead socially constructed and thus, able to be negotiated and changed" (p. 503). We hope that new discourses can modify social constructions to be more representative of contemporary families. And consequently, organizational policies and governmental legislation can be designed to better meet the changing needs of the U.S. workforce. To this end, we propose what Bould (1993) would call a "middle-range definition" of family specific to the context of work-life balance. Although a middle-range definition may not replace the deeply entrenched mainstream definitions of family, it can be consciously and carefully called upon when determining organizational and legislative policy.

Bould (1993) explains that the effects of the traditional definition of family can be devastating, as it not only evaluates family forms not meeting the standard (i.e., husband, wife, and children living together) as deficient but also judges what structures are familial or not familial at all. She says, "Instead of arriving at a position of 'no families,' definitions of family might best be developed in the 'middle range,' putting aside the search for the grand theoretical conceptualization and developing definitions that are appropriate to specific contexts" (p. 134).

However, Bould (1993) disagrees with the move to an all-inclusive definition of family. She cites Zinn and Eitzen (1987), who define family as any relationship based on bonds of affection. This type of definition, Bould explains, is too amorphous and presents researchers with an insurmountable task both empirically and theoretically. Instead, she suggests that we use middle-range, context-specific definitions. For instance, in the context of caregiving, she defines family as "the informal unit where those who cannot take care of themselves can find care in time of need" (p. 138). For example, in the case of a terminally ill individual, especially when the individual has severed ties with biological kin, family can be constituted via an ongoing commitment to provide acts of care (e.g., providing a home, arranging for medical care, administering prescriptions, cooking meals, offering companionship), regardless of biological or legal relationships. A key element of this example is the ongoing commitment aspect. That is, someone without sustained commitment to the particular individual (e.g., a home health care nurse who is hired to provide many of the services described above) is not family. Instead, the person or people who take responsibility for caregiving—whether they personally perform the duties or make arrangements for others to do so—are. Bould explains that this middle-range definition has pragmatic significance, particularly in cases of deciding state versus family intervention (e.g., foster care for children, nursing homes for aging adults, and institutionalization for severely handicapped persons).

Likewise, we believe that to achieve (or come near achieving) work-life balance, it is necessary to develop a context-specific, middle-range definition of family for the workplace. We offer one such definition—not with the assumption that we have it right but instead with the hope that initiating an ongoing dialogue can help scholars and practitioners arrive at an acceptable answer for a particular place and time. In the work-family context, a middle-range definition must include employment and career issues. That is, within a work context, family should be defined as those people who are (inter)dependent with regard to the paid employment of another individual. This includes but is not limited to (inter)dependence of resources generated by employment, the negotiation of employment-related decision making, and the sacrifices and consequences related to career, such as promotions, relocations, and job loss.

First, (inter)dependence is a key element of this definition. Family members include individuals who are dependent on another member (e.g., a child is dependent on the financial resources of a parent), individuals who are depended upon by other members (e.g., person is depended upon by a spouse for employer-provided medical insurance), or interdependence between members (e.g., a couple depends on each other's income to pay the mortgage). Interdependence can also include family forms that typically are not recognized by traditional definitions: aging parents who depend on the financial support of an adult child, same-sex domestic partners who receive medical insurance through one partner's employer, or a young child who is being raised by an adult sibling without being legally adopted.

The second issue is negotiation of career decisions. For example, in a work-life context, family members would be considered to be the people with whom career decisions are negotiated. More than just a listening ear, family members would be those people without whose input employees would not consider important career moves, including relocations and resignations. This means that the employee depends on the input of certain individuals and contemplates the consequences for them when making career decisions. More than whether to work overtime on a given day, family is constituted by the people with whom employees discuss and make decisions regarding significant career changes, organizational moves, and geographic relocations.

Third, family members share sacrifices and consequences related to career issues. These costs and benefits involve members' willingness to compromise. For example, a couple who makes career concessions (e.g., one partner declining a "dream job" offer that would require relocation, one partner taking the role of breadwinner while the other returns to school) constitutes family, regardless of their martial status or presence of dependents.

A benefit of this middle-range definition is that it acknowledges and validates fictive kin (e.g., nonbiological and nonlegally bound "aunts" and "uncles"), "projected kin" (e.g., planned children), and other kinds of family members who do not fit so easily into cookie-cutter definitions. For example, unmarried young adults can have close ties to their families-of-origin, despite living thousands of miles away. Many of these young adults also have aspirations toward (non)traditional families of their own and make career decisions accordingly. In other words, although people may not have a spouse or children, it does not mean that they do not have familial relationships. Therefore, organizational policies must take into consideration identity-affirming programs for all kinds of people.

Middle-Range Definitions in Practice

Young (1999) details two faulty assumptions guiding work-life practice and scholarship. First, there is an assumption that the prototypical family unit consisting of one or more parents living with one or more children is the most common household unit for members of the U.S. workforce. We have shown that this is not the case. Second, many existing work-life programs are based on the standpoint that dependent care is the primary work-life issue with which employees grapple. Young reports that employees with and without dependents identify as top work-life priorities programs that meet personal needs such as fitness, education, and commuting (see Hays, 1999). When these assumptions are eliminated and the proposed middle-range definition is used, a variety of well-targeted, innovative work-life policies and practices are possible. These policies and practices would acknowledge and celebrate a variety of family forms and meet a broader range of employee needs.

Perhaps one of the first steps to developing organizational work-life policies is to look beyond the balance metaphor. Thompson and Bunderson (2001) provide an interesting alternative: the container. They highlight the problems with the notion of work-nonwork balance. The container metaphor recognizes a finite amount of time and external constraints to time. But rather than quantifying time and work or family activities, they "measure" the *meaning* of the use of the time within the container. In short, they say that if people engage in identity-affirming activities, regardless of whether those activities are in the work or nonwork realms, these people will experience less tension and conflict in their lives. However, if the activities are seen as identity discrepant, then people will have negative effects. Specifically, we can use the concept of anchor points to realize that with or without family per se, employees are individually anchored in work and nonwork realms. This means, for some people, that identity affirmation comes through traditional career development (e.g., additional training and education, fast-track careers, recognition programs). Yet, others are anchored in nonwork arenas (e.g., child care programs, leave opportunities to pursue personally significant life opportunities, physical fitness programs). Therefore, work-life programs should include activities and benefits that target both realms.

At the outset, it should be noted that work-life programs do come at an expense to employers. Especially during tight economic times, costs associated with innovative work-life initiatives may seem to be extravagant and prohibitive. However, organizations should look at the long-term benefits of work-life programs that focus on a variety of family forms and individual needs. Juggling work schedules to allow for days away from the office or offering unpaid leaves is not very expensive at all. The benefits that these programs could bring, such as employee loyalty, improved morale, increased productivity, and savings from not having to hire and retrain new employees, make them well worth the initial expense. Innovative work-life programs also can help recruit new employees, regardless of their family status. Tsui, Pearce, Porter, and Tripoli (1997) have demonstrated that even single and childfree employees perceive family-friendly companies to be better employers than their competitors.

Below, we describe a few examples of work-life programs for employees "without" families. One way that organizations could validate employees' families is through a voluntary extension of the protections provided by the FMLA to all employees' family members, regardless of biological or legal kinship. A company could extend the same amount of leave to an employee who is grieving the death of a domestic partner as it would to a married employee grieving the death of a spouse. It could provide the same child care benefits to an employee who temporarily is providing care for a young niece or nephew as it would to an employee with a biological or adopted child. It could offer the same eldercare accommodations to an employee caring for an elderly aunt, uncle, or grandparent as it would to an employee caring for a parent. Moreover, this type of protection also would have the added benefit of better serving diverse workforce members who may hold expanded conceptions of family and concomitant responsibilities for caregiving (e.g., immigrant employees, Ebaugh & Curry, 2000; African American employees, Gerstel & McGonagle, 1999).

Also, many young adults are making long-distance geographic moves after college to pursue their careers. The fact that they live independently and do not have a family based on coresidence does not mean that they do not have a family. Another relatively low-cost benefit that could be provided is family travel time. In exchange for single employees' flexibility with regard to working overtime and taking on additional business travel burdens, companies could juggle schedules to offer a 3- or 4-day weekend (in addition to regular paid vacation days) and, possibly, plane tickets for a weekend visit with out-of-town family. The cost of juggling work schedules and of plane tickets to allow for 3-day weekends would be relatively minimal for organizations, particularly when compared with benefits reaped through improvements in employee morale and decreases in turnover of valued workers (see Lambert, 2000; Roehling, Roehling, & Moen, 2001). In addition, such flexibility and bonuses could be an excellent perk for recruiting talented employees.

Another issue that is important for unmarried employees is that many do want to pursue meaningful personal relationships. However, they have difficulty finding time to do so, especially since they tend to be saddled with a disproportionate amount of overtime, business travel, and work over holidays. These work demands make it difficult to start new relationships. Establishing new friendships and/or romantic relationships becomes nearly impossible if employees cannot count on being in town for the weekend or home at a predictable hour. Therefore, one way that companies could compensate for long and irregular work hours is by hosting—or at least accommodating employee involvement in—social events (e.g., soccer teams, social mixers). These social opportunities could allow employees to meet new people who share similar interests and professional backgrounds.

Yet another way of providing meaningful work-life balance programs is to allow unpaid leave for unique personal experiences (see Flynn, 1996). Perhaps a recent college graduate could take leave to backpack through Europe the summer after a younger friend or sibling graduates. Another employee could volunteer with the Peace Corps to fulfill a lifelong dream. Still others could engage in full-time study at a university that is located out of state. Whatever the reason for the leave, it would be a big boon to business to offer such a unique benefit to employees, as the knowledge and insights gained from those experiences could benefit the organization. Employees could improve their fluency in a foreign language by traveling or studying abroad; others could learn valuable leadership and team-building skills by doing mission work; still others could gain credentials and skills from additional formal education.

Two caveats are needed here. First, we are not saying that the gains that have been made for traditional families should be revoked. These advances in work-life programs are absolutely essential. We only call for policies and programs to be constructed for additional people and varied family forms. Second, it is important to note that we are not proposing further legislation. The key to effective work-life programs is flexibility and individuality, not government mandates. Federal legislation cannot be context specific. It typically only applies to organizations that meet certain conditions (e.g., size, number of employees). Therefore, our hope is that companies will develop their own policies and programs for the unique needs of their employees.

From a practical standpoint, these benefits can be developed through a well-informed and well-targeted cafeteria-style list of benefits. For example, Scully and Creed (1999) provide a case study of one organization that sent out a widescale anonymous survey asking for employee input on the benefits program. The vast majority of employees did not fit into the married-with-two-children structure for whom the existing benefits program had been designed. Instead, employees were reporting that their health benefits concerns were for nonmarried partners, aging parents, disabled siblings, special aunts and uncles who had played important roles in their lives, nieces, nephews, and godchildren. These responses caused the company to adopt a benefits structure that allotted a flat amount to each employee to allocate as he or she desired.

Conclusion

By adhering to strict definitions of family, by not making assumptions explicit, and by not admitting the socially constructed (and changeable) nature of both work and family, scholars and practitioners are neglecting many viable family forms as well as the needs of individuals struggling on a day-to-day basis to maintain some semblance of balance between the work and nonwork realms of their lives. In short, the policies that come into play based on traditional definitions of family have serious implications for individuals. To a certain extent, these policies dictate for whom employees can and cannot provide care, as well as who they can and cannot grieve. They prioritize relationships that should be prioritized by the heart and by individual action.

If we are to make a true and meaningful impact on work-life practice, it is essential to foreground deeply embedded assumptions and common discourses that guide policy making. Inherent in the middle-range definition, analysis, and implementation processes we propose is a call for more nuanced research, theory, and practice in work-life balance from a communicative perspective. One of the steps we can take is making our assumptions explicit in work-life scholarship. For instance, in Teachman et al.'s (2000) analysis of demographic trends, they are explicit in pointing out that they are "forced" to "assume a legal definition of marriage and family" (p. 1234) but state that the limitations of the legal definitions dismiss family relationships that extend across households or do not conform in other ways. Scholars also should be encouraged to at least identify how the findings of their research could be applied to and/or affect other types of family forms (e.g., single parent–child, husband–wife–foster child, and same-sex partners). More important, it is essential for practitioners to adopt more inclusive definitions of family as they develop policies and programs to help employees negotiate the competing demands for their time.

Notes

1. Admittedly, the notion of "balance" is fraught with difficulties. Scholars have been calling for a rethinking of the work-life balance metaphor (e.g., Clark, 2000; MacDermid et al., 2005), and the popular press calls balance "bunk" (Hammonds, 2004) with regard to the improbability of achieving it. On many levels, we agree. First, "balance" is a problematic metaphor for work-life. For instance, there is an inherent fallacy to the work-life balance metaphor. That is, work is *part* of an individual's *whole* life, and a part cannot be balanced against a whole. Second, taking the metaphor less literally by examining the balance between work and nonwork activities, it is clear that the balance metaphor is based on a faulty assumption that the ideal state is equal time for both domains. Although equal time may be ideal for some people, it is not true for everyone. Finally, focusing on balance has meant that its relationship to and differences from other related constructs, such as "fit," have not been explored sufficiently (Clarke, Koch, & Hill, 2004). As Clarke et al. (2004) found, balance refers to perceived integration of and satisfaction with family activities. In contrast, fit aligns with structural issues, such as work hours, family income, and household division of labor. Thus, while we agree with criticisms and believe that alternative metaphors may better represent the realities and goals of finding fulfillment in both work and nonwork activities, we use the popular term *work-life balance* throughout this chapter.

2. Process-based definitions of family date back to Burgess (1926), who was the first to define family by its interaction: A family is "a unity of interacting persons" rather than "a mere collection of individuals" (p. 5, cited in Whitchurch & Dickson, 1999).

3. Unfortunately, selection of occupations and careers that provide the "gift of time" has been aligned with female-intensive, lower paying, and/or individualized work, such as that done by artists or novelists, as well as fewer advancement-oriented and more "mommy track" careers (see Buzzanell & Goldzwig, 1991; Schwartz, 1992). Indeed, Glass (2004) uncovered wage penalties for women who used policies such as flexible scheduling, reduced hours, and telework. Smithson, Lewis, Cooper, and Dyer (2004) also found wage and career penalties for women but not for men.

To encourage greater occupational and career flexibility, Bailyn (2004) notes that many occupations and successful careers are clock driven or bounded (i.e., controlled). She challenges us to move toward more performance- and/or enjoyment-driven conceptualizations of career that take human life cycles and rhythms into consideration.

References

Allen, K. R., Fine, M. A., & Demo, D. H. (2000). An overview of family diversity: Controversies, questions, and values. In D. H. Demo, K. R. Allen, & M. A. Fine (Eds.), *Handbook of family diversity* (pp. 1–14). New York: Oxford University Press.

Bailyn, L. (2004). Time in careers—careers in time. *Human Relations, 57,* 1507–1521.

Barnett, R. C. (1999). A new work-life model for the twenty-first century. *Annals of the American Academy of Political and Social Science, 562,* 143–158.

Blair-Loy, M. (2003). *Competing devotions: Career and family among women executives.* Cambridge, MA: Harvard University Press.

Bookman, A. (2004). *Starting in our own backyards: How working families can build community and survive the new economy.* New York: Routledge.

Bould, S. (1993). Familial caretaking: A middle-range definition of family in the context of social policy. *Journal of Family Issues, 14,* 133–151.

Burgess, E. W. (1926). The family as a unity of interacting personalities. *The Family, 7*, 3–9.

Buzzanell, P. M. (2000). The promise and practice of the new career and social contract: Illusions exposed and suggestions for reform. In P. M. Buzzanell (Ed.), *Rethinking organizational and managerial communication from feminist perspectives* (pp. 209–235). Thousand Oaks, CA: Sage.

Buzzanell, P. M., & Goldzwig, S. (1991). Linear and nonlinear career models: Metaphors, paradigms, and ideologies. *Management Communication Quarterly, 4*, 466–505.

Charas, S., & Kushner, I. (2002). Family-friendly benefit legislation: What's next? *Compensation and Benefits Review, 34*, 79–84.

Christensen, H. T. (1946). The development of the family field of study. In H. T. Christensen (Ed.), *Handbook of marriage and the family* (pp. 3–32). Chicago: Rand McNally.

Ciulla, J. (2000). *The working life: The promise and betrayal of modern work.* New York: Crown.

Clark, S. C. (2000). Work/family border theory: A new theory of work/family balance. *Human Relations, 53*, 747–770.

Clarke, M. C., Koch, L. C., & Hill, E. J. (2004). The work-family interface: Differentiating balance and fit. *Family and Consumer Sciences Research Journal, 33*, 121–140.

Coontz, S. (1992). *The way we never were: American families and the nostalgia trap.* New York: Basic Books.

DeFrain, J., & Olson, D. H. (1999). Contemporary family patterns and relationships. In M. B. Sussman, S. K. Steinmetz, & G. W. Peterson (Eds.), *Handbook of marriage and the family* (2nd ed., pp. 309–326). New York: Plenum.

Ebaugh, H. R., & Curry, M. (2000). Fictive kin as social capital in new immigrant communities. *Sociological Perspectives, 43*, 189–209.

Edwards, J. R., & Rothbard, N. P. (2000). Mechanisms linking work and family: Clarifying the relationship between work and family constructs. *Academy of Management Review, 25*, 178–199.

Emery, B. C., & Lloyd, S. A. (2001). The evolution of family studies research. *Family and Consumer Sciences Research Journal, 30*, 197–222.

Family and Medical Leave Act, 5 U.S.C. § 630 (1993).

Flynn, G. (1996). Backlash: Why single employees are angry. *Personnel Journal, 75*, 59–69.

Gerstel, N., & McGonagle, K. (1999). Job leaves and the limits of the Family and Medical Leave Act. *Work and Occupations, 26*, 510–534.

Glass, J. (2004). Blessing or curse? Work-family policies and mother's wage growth over time. *Work and Occupations, 31*, 367–394.

Gold, J. M., & Wilson, J. S. (2002). Legitimizing the child-free family: The role of the family counselor. *The Family Journal: Counseling and Therapy for Couples and Families, 10*, 70–74.

Greenblatt, E. (2002). Work/life balance: Wisdom or whining? *Organizational Dynamics, 31*, 177–193.

Gring-Pemble, L. M. (2003). Legislating a "normal, classic family": The rhetorical construction of families in American welfare policy. *Political Communication, 20*, 473–498.

Gubrium, J. F., & Holstein, J. A. (1990). *Where is family?* Mountain View, CA: Mayfield.

Haas, L. (1999). Families and work. In M. B. Sussman, S. K. Steinmetz, & G. W. Peterson (Eds.), *Handbook of marriage and the family* (2nd ed., pp. 571–612). New York: Plenum.

Hammonds, K. H. (2004, October). Balance is bunk. *Fast Company, 87*, 68–76.

Hays, S. (1999). Generation X and the art of the reward. *Workforce, 78*, 45–48.

Hewlett, S. A. (2002). Executive women and the myth of having it all. *Harvard Business Review, 80*, 66–73.

Infertility Health Insurance Coverage, New Jersey P.L.2001, c.236 (2001).

Joplin, J., Shaffer, M., Francesco, A., & Lau, T. (2003). The macro-environment and work-family conflict: Development of a cross cultural comparative framework. *International Journal of Cross Cultural Management, 3,* 305–328.

Kirby, E. L. (2004, November). *Moving family forward in work-family research.* Paper presented at the annual conference of the National Communication Association, Chicago.

Kirby, E. L. (2000). Should I do as you say, or do as you do? Mixed messages about work and family. *Electronic Journal of Communication, 10*(3–4). Retrieved from http://www.cios.org/www/ejcrec2.htm

Kirby, E. L., & Krone, K. J. (2002). "The policy exists but you can't really use it": Communication and the structuration of work-family policies. *Journal of Applied Communication Research, 30,* 50–77.

Lambert, S. J. (2000). Added benefits: The link between work-life benefits and organizational citizenship behavior. *Academy of Management Journal, 43,* 801–815.

Liu, M., & Buzzanell, P. M. (2004). Negotiating maternity leave expectations: Perceived tensions between ethics of justice and care. *Journal of Business Communication, 41,* 323–349.

MacDermid, S. M., Roy, K., & Zvonkovic, A. M. (2005). Don't stop at the borders: Theorizing beyond dichotomies of work and family. In V. L. Bengston, A. C. Acock, K. R. Allen, P. Dilworth-Anderson, & D. M. Klein (Eds.), *Sourcebook of family theory and research* (pp. 493–516). Thousand Oaks, CA: Sage.

Mishel, L., Bernstein, J., & Boushey, H. (2003). *The state of working America 2002/2003.* Ithaca, NY: ILR Press.

National Marriage Project. (2004). *Whitehead Senate testimony Apr 04.* Retrieved March 5, 2005, from http://marriage.rutgers.edu/Publications/Pub%20Whitehead%20Testimony%20Apr%2004.htm

National Marriage Project. (n.d.). *CoDirectors.* Retrieved March 5, 2005, from http://marriage.rutgers.edu/codirectors.htm

Patterson, C. J. (2000). Family relationships of lesbians and gay men. *Journal of Marriage and the Family, 62,* 1052–1069.

Perry-Jenkins, M., Pierce, C. P., & Goldberg, A. E. (2004). Discourse on diapers and dirty laundry: Family communication about child care and housework. In A. L. Vangelisti (Ed.), *Handbook of family communication* (pp. 541–561). Mahwah, NJ: Lawrence Erlbaum.

Popenoe, D. (1993). American family decline, 1960–1990: A review and appraisal. *Journal of Marriage and the Family, 55,* 527–555.

Roehling, P. V., Roehling, M. V., & Moen, P. (2001). The relationship between work-life policies and practices and employee loyalty: A life course perspective. *Journal of Family & Economic Issues, 22,* 141–170.

Saltzman, A. (1991). *Downshifting: Reinventing success on a slower track.* New York: HarperCollins.

Schor, J. B. (1991). *The overworked American: The unexpected decline of leisure.* New York: Basic Books.

Schwartz, F. N. (1992). Women as a business imperative. *Harvard Business Review, 70,* 105–113.

Scully, M., & Creed, W. E. D. (1999). Restructured families: Issues of equality and need. Annals of the American Academy of Political and Social Science, 562, 47–65.

Sheehy, G. (1995). *New passages: Mapping your life across time.* New York: Ballantine.

Smith, D. E. (1993). The standard North American family: SNAF as an ideological code. *Journal of Family Issues, 14,* 50–65.

Smithson, J., Lewis, S., Cooper, C., & Dyer, J. (2004). Flexible working and the gender pay gap in the accountancy profession. *Work, Employment and Society, 18,* 115–135.

Teachman, J. D., Tedrow, L. M., & Crowder, K. D. (2000). The changing demography of America's families. *Journal of Marriage and the Family, 62,* 1234–1246.

Thompson, J. A., & Bunderson, J. S. (2001). Work-nonwork conflict and the phenomenology of time. *Work and Occupations, 28,* 17–39.

Tsui, A. S., Pearce, J. L., Porter, L. W., & Tripoli, A. M. (1997). Alternative approaches to the employee-organization relationship: Does investment in employees pay off? *Academy of Management Journal, 40,* 1089–1121.

U.S. Census Bureau. (2003). *Marital status of people 15 years and over, by age, sex, personal earnings, race, and Hispanic origin.* Retrieved January 24, 2005, from http://www .census.gov/population/socdemo/hh-fam/cps2003/tabA1-all.pdf

Westman, M., Etzion, D., & Gortler, E. (2004). The work-family interface and burnout. *International Journal of Stress Management, 11,* 413–428.

Wharton, A. S., & Blair-Loy, M. (2002). The "overtime culture" in a global corporation: A cross-national study of finance professionals' interest in working part-time. *Work and Occupations, 29,* 32–63.

Whitchurch, G. G., & Dickson, F. C. (1999). Family communication. In M. B. Sussman, S. K. Steinmetz, & G. W. Peterson (Eds.), *Handbook of marriage and the family* (2nd ed., pp. 687–704). New York: Plenum.

Williams, J. (2000). *Unbending gender: Why work and family conflict and what to do about it.* New York: Oxford University Press.

Young, M. B. (1999). Work-family backlash: Begging the question, what's fair? *Annals of the American Academy of Political and Social Science, 562,* 32–46.

Zimmerman, T. S., Haddock, S. A., Current, L. R., & Ziemba, S. (2003). Intimate partnership: Foundation to the successful balance of family and work. *American Journal of Family Therapy, 31,* 107–124.

Zinn, M. B., & Eitzen, D. S. (1987). *Diversity in American families.* New York: Harper & Row.

CHAPTER 19

Communicating Contradictions

(Re)Producing Dialectical Tensions Through Work, Family, and Balance Socialization Messages

Caryn E. Medved

Ohio University

Elizabeth E. Graham

Ohio University

In the United States today, we are surrounded by conflicting expectations about how we "should" enact our work and family lives. Women are told they can balance or "have it all" but simultaneously are encircled by the biting judgments of media figures such as Dr. Laura Schlessinger (2001), who suggests, "*Don't have kids if you won't raise them.*" Men are told to be "active fathers" yet cautioned by coworkers about taking paternity leave; colleagues might advise, "Just take your vacation time, it will look better in the long run." Other popular press offerings tout ways to balance work and family in a "three ring circus" (Jefferson & Welch, 2004) by "sequencing"—not combining—activities such as childrearing and workforce participation (Cardozo, 1986/2000) and by writing an individual career/family balance plan (Lee & Lee, 1997). Women and men construct themselves, as well as their vision for career success and family relationships, in the midst of voluminous competing and contradictory discourses (Douglas & Michaels, 2004) (additional information on the discourses of family can be gleaned by examining Chapter 18, this volume). This process starts early as we hear messages and develop ways of understanding and talking about the boundaries between our public and private lives and, inescapably, our gendered selves and choices (Galinsky, 1999; Risman, 1998).

In this chapter, we present a study that explores dialectical tensions that are constructed in everyday family communication. Through an exploration of parental socialization messages about work, family, and balance, we see how oppositional discourses such as public-private, masculinity-femininity, and emotionality-rationality are perpetuated, blurred, and, at times, challenged. As identities are formed at the intersection of competing discourses (Ashcraft & Mumby, 2003), knowing more about the nature and production of such tensions offers a uniquely communicative contribution to work and family communication scholarship.

This research is not without precedent. Communication scholars Kirby, Golden, Medved, Jorgenson, and Buzzanell (2003) published the first review of work-family scholarship in the field of communication and set an agenda for future research. In particular, Medved and colleagues' research laid the groundwork for the present study through the investigation of communicative practices that reproduce the boundaries between work and family lives (Medved, 2004; Medved, Brogan, McClanahan, Morris, & Shepherd, 2004; Medved & Heisler, 2002; Medved & Kirby, 2005; Medved et al., 1999). By exploring communicative practices embedded in the daily work and family routines, Medved (2004) demonstrated that communication is not viewed only as a "tool" to facilitate balance but also as a routine element of work and family management itself. That is, interactions such as connecting ("checking in" with day care providers), requesting assistance (asking family members to help during child care emergencies), evading (lying to supervisors or spouses), negotiating (perceiving incompatible goals regarding division of labor), and deliberating (weighing alternatives or considering various options for child care) were all perceived as constitutive of daily routines and/or a part of handling work-family conflict on both short- and long-term bases. Finally, as a result of Medved's research, we also know that women and men are provided different messages from family members about how to balance their personal and organizational lives (Medved et al., 2004). Their inductive analysis of more than 1,500 memorable messages (i.e., a verbal message that appears to be remembered for a long period of time and perceived to have a significant influence on people's lives; see Knapp, Stohl, & Reardon, 1981) resulted in 21 content categories describing work, family, and balance messages.

This current study is an extension of the prior work of Knapp et al. (1981). Socializing messages are rarely independent or able to be encapsulated in a finite fashion because this is not how messages are shared in interaction. Because we are exposed to multiple messages, both interpersonal and mediated, we will explore *pairs* of work, family, and balance messages shared with young adults by parental figures. To illustrate: When Allison graduated from high school, she remembers her tearful mother saying, "Children grow up so fast. I'm so glad I stayed home with you all these years!" A few years later, as college graduation was looming, Allison recalls discussing possible career options with her father. She hears her father's voice, "Allison, always be able to support yourself financially. You never know what will happen." Today, a young mother of two, Allison hears the following advice from her mother-in-law: "You'll be ready to go back to work in a few months. I just couldn't handle the isolation of staying at home." Over time, Allison must make sense of contradictory messages. Thus, the present investigation focuses on pairs of work, family, and balance messages.

Messages present various options, constraints, or consequences for combining or balancing work and family responsibilities—options that may be interpreted as consistent or, at times, contradictory. We believe that parental messages do not determine particular choices or attitudes of young adults but contribute both to individual and societal stocks of knowledge about how we should or could participate in both (or only one) of these two life spheres. Furthermore, we do not view the "meaning" of the messages as static. Over time and across contexts, young adults may assign different meaning to key messages they recall about the role that work and family should play in life. We do know that parents are a main source of information about family and work roles for their children (Galinsky, 1999; Piotrkowski, 1979; Piotrkowski & Katz, 1982; Piotrokowski & Stark, 1987). As a new generation of young adults enters the workforce and begins family life, they take part in the historical communicative construction of the public and private spheres. While research indicates that younger participants in the workforce today are less "work centric" than their baby boomer parents (Families and Work Institute, 2004), we know little about what shapes their knowledge and attitudes toward work and family.

For these reasons, we pose the first research question:

RQ1:   What work, family, and balance message pairs do young adults report receiving from parental figures?

Prior research revealed that college-age women received different socialization messages from men (Heisler, 2000) as well as advice regarding how to balance work and family (Medved et al., 2004). Specifically, Medved and colleagues (2004) found that women more often than men were encouraged to select a career that would allow them to handle family responsibilities. Women were also advised to rationally plan the order of key life events. Finally, women received messages about stopping work when raising young children. In a study of 40 adult women, Freeman (1997) found that messages from mothers were influential on women's career decision making. She reported that mothers of study participants who had followed traditional "homemaker" life paths consciously attempted to influence their daughters' career decision making by trying to persuade them to take a different path from their own. Freeman explains, "Recognizing the limitations imposed upon them by economic dependence, they encouraged their daughters to increase the possibilities for their own lives" (p. 34). Fathers, on the other hand, often provided expertise about the world of work. While these few studies have begun to tease out some connections between gender and work-family socialization messages, much uncertainty remains.

Therefore, the second research question is the following:

RQ2:   Do men and women report receiving different work, family, and balance message pairs from parental figures?

Dialectics in Work and Family Scholarship

Thinking dialectically about human communication privileges the inconsistencies, interrelatedness, and complexities of relationships (Baxter & Montgomery, 1996; Rawlins, 1992). As relational dialectics are guiding our inquiry, three principal contradictions in work and family scholarship will be the focus of this research: public-private, masculinity-femininity, and emotionality-rationality. These contradictions were chosen because of their prevalence in current work-family scholarship (see Kirby et al., 2003; Lopata, 1993; Williams, 2000) and because they best capture the complexities of looking across these life spheres. We acknowledge that the separation of these tensions is rather artificial yet analytically useful.

The Public-Private Dialectic

Scholarly representations of our public (work) and our private (family) lives in the United States have varied both historically and ontologically. Key points on this continuum can be marked from (a) dualistic or "separate-spheres"[1] approaches in which work and family are seen as discrete and separate temporal-spatial or physical entities (see Lopata, 1993; Williams, 2000, for historical accounts of this approach) to (b) subjectivist or interpretive approaches that view this boundary as an historical, permeable, and negotiable system of behaviors or interactions and, even further, (c) to scholarship that views this "boundary" as primarily a set of interrelated discursive and, occasionally, dialogic practices.

To illustrate, some communication scholarship tends to treat the connection between public and private spheres as a dualism—that is, foregrounding meaning construction or interaction in one sphere while backgrounding symbolic connections to the opposite sphere. For example, Miller, Jablin, Casey, Lamphear-Van Horn, and Ethington (1996) present a model of maternity leave as a role negotiation process, although little attention is given to the private sphere. Relationships and interactions within a leavetaker's private role set (spouses/partners, day care providers, friends) may interlock with organizational processes. However, antecedents, negotiation tactics, and outcomes studied in absence of these influences will only tell part of the story and may inaccurately represent such influences. Other references to work-family boundaries presuppose clear distinctions between public and private domains, not only in terms of physical locations and tasks but also in value and psychological orientations (Hochschild, 1997; Kanter, 1977; Nippert-Eng, 1996).

Yet another representation of the public-private boundaries favors social constructionist approaches to the tension between the public and private spheres. Golden (2002) investigates how dual-career couples' accounts of work and family arrangements evidence collaborative sensemaking and role-identity construction. She argues that knowing how couples ascribe meaning to ways of managing work and family is essential to fully understanding these arrangements. Management scholar Sue Clark's (2000, 2002) "border theory" also adopts a similar social constructivist perspective in its use of organizational sensemaking (Weick, 1979) and systems theory. She explains that her work "is about the social construction of work/family experience through conversation. It is about how individuals attempt to integrate, separate, and ultimately balance . . . by communicating with work associates and family members" (Clark, 2002, p. 25). Clark explores factors that influence the amount and effect of communication on work-family balance by recognizing interaction's role in constructing boundaries.

Finally, even more fluid representations of the tension between public and private spheres can be seen in Buzzanell's (2003) maternity leave research. Notably different from Miller and colleagues, Buzzanell states that an "examination of a specific woman's maternity leave discourse can provide opportunities to uncover how public-private boundaries shift and dissolve" (p. 5). This work conceptualizes the public-private boundary not only as socially constructed but also as dialectic. To illustrate, in her feminist standpoint analysis of a disabled woman's experiences of pregnancy, maternity leave, and returning to work, Buzzanell demonstrates how her private life becomes visibly public for the first time with her predominantly male colleagues through her pregnancy. She is normalized as a human being, contrary to the previous treatment she experienced from her work colleagues. This status change occurs in the organization, paradoxically, through an alteration of her private self. Unfortunately, this positive change, as Julianna views it, is not sustained after her return to work, which marks a parallel return to collegial perceptions of her as the "other" or a disembodied self. Thus, we see a distinctly fluid and contradictory sense of the public and private; this contradiction exists in discursive and behavioral practices that are continuous and discontinuous, empowering and disempowering, joyful and hurtful.

The Femininity-Masculinity Dialectic

Another foundational dialectic underlying the study of work and family is masculinity-femininity (Kirby et al., 2003). It is impossible to untangle discussions of public-private from masculinity-femininity. Extensive historical treatment of what has become known as the "separate-spheres" ideology notes that this gendered two-sphere division of labor emerged in relation to early U.S. industrialization with men in the public (paid occupational) sphere and women in the private (familial/domestic) sphere (Crittenden, 2001; Ferree, 1995; Mumby, 2000). Feminist scholars have challenged both the existence of (Kanter, 1977) and the explanations for the separate-spheres orientations (Fletcher, 1999). Representations of masculinity-femininity in work and family communication scholarship can be aligned on a continuum starting with (a) dualistic or binary approaches focusing on sex differences between men and women, proceeding to (b) views of gender as a socially constructed process, to (c) critically positioning masculinity and femininity as a power-laden process of social construction.

Dualistic research operationalizes masculinity and femininity as sex differences. While assumptions about what is masculine or feminine are often implicit in underlying justifications or research questions, neither pole is meaningfully or critically problematized, nor is the intent to do so (see Krueger, 1986; Medved & Heisler, 2002; Miller et al., 1996; Rosenfeld, Bowen, & Richman, 1995). Another way that masculinity and femininity are represented focuses on gender as a process of meaning negotiation. In Golden's (2002) work on identity and dual-career couples, she finds that both gender convergence and schematicity are evidenced in dual-career couples' talk about their work and family arrangements. Through "mirror talk" (symmetrical positioning), spouses demonstrate similarities in meanings, while "complement talk" (relying on role specialization) ascribes different tasks and meanings for the boundaries of work and family by sex. Women were found also to negotiate the gendered contradictions between men's work and women's work by maintaining strict separation between the public and private spheres and masking family commitments to create socially approved, professional identities (Jorgenson, 2000; Jorgenson, Gregory, & Goodier, 1997).

Finally, some organizational communication studies have foregrounded issues of power in relation to gender through the use of critical and feminist theories. Kirby et al. (2003) define gender as a hierarchical and inequitable structure. One illustration of this representation of masculinity-femininity was offered by Farley-Lucas (2000). She concluded that gendered practices of parenting and career contribute to women's subordination and discriminatory organizational practices. Feminist critical conceptions of power and gender have also been used to explore gender in women's use of communication technologies. While making women's lives easier, technology paradoxically further colonizes women's lives through increased expectations of availability and work hours (Edley, 2001). Indeed, Edley (2001) concluded that "the organizations' needs outweigh the family's needs and important decisions are based on what is best for the employer" (p. 33). Thus, the masculine or public sphere often takes precedence over the feminine or private sphere when work and family collide.

What is less often apparent in these studies is how work and family messages, interactions, and structures serve to coconstruct, enable, and constrain possibilities for femininity and masculinity. As Mumby (1998) noted, men must also be central to our discussions of "gender." Until private-sphere expectations, including hegemonic structures of masculinity, are concomitantly reshaped, men are constrained in their abilities to take advantage of paternity leave policies and other family-friendly incentives, as well as gain social approval for being stay-at-home fathers. Doing so requires constant attention to shifting notions of power in gender relations. Mumby comments, "By continuing to study and define work-family as only a woman's issue, we not only devalue or ignore men's experiences of conflict, stress and challenge of managing work and family issues, we also continue to constrain the possibilities of change for women as we conflate 'women' and 'gender'" (p. 164).

The Emotionality-Rationality Dialectic

The last dialectical contradiction, emotionality-rationality, is perhaps less prominent in the literature than the public-private and masculine-feminine dialectics yet inherently interrelated. Emotion has often been associated with historical constructions of caregiving in the private or family sphere and assigned to women. With the rise of the organization as the primary site for "productive" and paid labor, care labor is constructed as nonessential or inactive (Marshall, 1989). Even emotion or relational work carried out in the organization and mainly accomplished by women has been devalued (Fletcher, 1999). Rationality (technical or expert) is often defined as "intentional, reasoned, goal-directed behavior" (Mumby & Putnam, 1992) and associated with masculine-identified organizational processes and structures (Buzzanell, 1995; Buzzanell & Goldzwig, 1991). Emotion and emotionality (even emotional labor or emotion work; see Buzzanell, 1997) are feminized concepts often associated with intuition or practical experience. These tensions have been portrayed as (a) a dualism that favors the rational (public or masculine), (b) a dichotomy constructed through communication, and (c) an explanatory mechanism or key dialectic that shapes knowledge about work and family.

The privileging of public, masculine meanings in the organization and, at times, in the family reflects the power of rationality in shaping work and family lives (Medved & Kirby, 2005). Catchphrases such as "face time," "bottom-line impact" of family-friendly policies, and "24/7 availability" through technology all represent the pervasiveness of rational assumptions in work and family discourse. In constructing this tension, rational decision-making processes are often foregrounded with limited attention to emotional issues. For example, while Miller et al. (1996) depict maternity leave as an overwhelmingly rational process, they also casually note that women must face the dilemma to "convince others that they will return following the leave. . . . This is particularly true for women who will soon be mothers for the first time," who may have "greater uncertainty about their physiological and emotional states" (Miller et al., 1996, p. 287). Emotion in this study is relegated to the unpredictability of women's behavior and negative biases of others.

The privileging of rationality is also evidenced in how technology and work-family issues collide (Hymlö, 2004). Shifting from a dualist rendering of emotionality-rationality to a social constructivist stance, Hymlö (2004) explores how this dichotomy is constructed in employee talk about telecommuting. She finds that "billability" and "productivity" override family-oriented explanations for the benefits of telecommuting. Identifying billable hours allows employees to measure their productivity (rationality). The ostensibly emotional or private-sphere benefits of telecommuting often disappeared in employee discourse (ironically, more often in women's than men's talk).

Finally, Buzzanell (1997) explored the potential for fundamental change inherent in a feminist emotion-centered perspective on dual-career couples. Gender is a fundamentally constitutive element of emotion and inherently shaped by feminist critiques of marital power. Buzzanell sees emotionality as heuristic and emancipatory in its ability to reveal understudied aspects of work and family relations. Furthermore, emotionality's traditional association with the feminine private sphere relegates care labor to secondary status. Emotional work performed both inside and outside the home has historically been devalued (see Fletcher, 1999; Hochschild, 1983, 2003; Wood, 1994). The consequences of ignoring care work or emotion-laden work performed in the private sphere are tragically recounted and analyzed by Mattson, Clair, Chapman Sanger, and Kunkel (2000). They tell the story of a woman named Rose, who called a radio program in New York, threatening to jump off a bridge because of the stress associated with being the mother of five children younger than age 3. Their deconstruction of this narrative reveals that prevalent distinctions between carework (emotional, feminine, private) and "real work" (rational, masculine, public) prevented Rose's experience from being seen as "work-related" stress. Yet Rose's "story is an articulation of the gender structuring of society. . . . [Her] stress spawned not only from her work as the mother, wife, and caretaker of the home and family but also from her position as a politically marginalized and isolated woman in society because of her work" (Mattson et al., 2000, pp. 171–172). Thus, emotion is an emerging topic of research intimately connected to public-private and masculine-feminine tensions.

To summarize, three key tensions are embedded in work family-life discourse, but they are rarely treated as dialectical. Furthermore, we know little about how dialectical frameworks begin to develop through socialization messages (for exceptions, see Mains & Hardesty, 1987; Medved et al., 2004), particularly for young men in the United States today. Thus, this study explores the dialectic tensions reflected in multiple messages about work, family, and balance provided to young adults primarily by their parents. That is, in this study, contradictions are located at the nexus of competing messages or message pairs. This dialectical perspective frames our third research question:

RQ3: Which dialectical tensions (public-private, femininity-masculinity, and emotionality-rationality) are embedded in work, family, and balance message pairs?

Method

Participants

A total of 384 participants from a midsized midwestern university were solicited for participation in this study.[2] Sampling criteria for this study were as follows: 25 years of age or younger, single, and without children. The gender composition of the sample was 64% female ($n = 243$) and 36% male ($n = 139$), with 4 nonresponses to this question. Participants' average age was 20 years old ($M = 19.97$, $SD = 1.21$). Ethnically, this sample was fairly homogeneous, with 92.2% Caucasian, 3.1% African American, 0.5% Asian, and 2.1% of participants reporting being of other ethnic backgrounds, while 1.6% did not respond to this question.

Soliciting Socialization Messages

The survey used for this study was modeled after Heisler's (2000) gender and memorable messages work. Participants were asked to provide three separate messages they recalled about work, family, and balance received from parental figures. Each participant provided messages about (a) the role that work should play in life,

(b) the role that family should play in life, and (c) the best way to balance work and family. After reporting each message, participants indicated who said the message (parents or other "parental figures" such as aunt, uncle, grandmother, grandfather, or other). All responses were handwritten on blank sheets of paper provided by the researcher.

Message Coding

All message coding was conducted from the written responses provided by the participants. The initial coding scheme was developed inductively by a team of researchers in which 21 categories emerged from a total of 1,541 messages (528 work, 524 family, and 489 balance). Coding was completed by two members of the research team, and Cohen's kappas were calculated on 25% of the sample data and resulted in interrater agreements of .86, .83, and .79, respectively. The present study used a subset of this larger data set and resulted in the analysis of 1,076 work, family, and balance messages. For clarity and manageability, the original 21 categories were collapsed to 13 categories (see Table 19.1 for definitions and example message categories).[3]

Next, combinations of "message pairs" were determined through cross-tabular procedures (RQ1). Seventy-eight memorable message pairs emerged from this analysis. Data were further reduced by selecting only message pairs reported by at least 5% of participants. The 5% criterion was employed for manageability purposes and to focus our attention on more (as determined by frequency) meaningful message pairs. This procedure resulted in 19 message pairs (see Table 19.2 for a listing of message pairs). An example of a message pair is stopping work and enjoying work. This message pair represents an instance when a participant reported receiving both a message to leave the paid workforce while his or her children are young (e.g., "Take time off of work; kids grow up so quickly.") and to find his or her work enjoyable or personally fulfilling (e.g., "If you don't enjoy it, it's not worth doing."). The second research question concerned the possibility of gender differences in the frequency of message pairs received. Finally, significant message pairs were examined for underlying dialectical tensions (RQ3).

Results

The first research question concerned the frequency of work, family, and balance message pairs received by young adults by parental figures (see Table 19.2 for results). Although a total of 19 message pairs meeting the 5% criterion emerged from the cross-tabulation procedure, the following message pairs were most frequently reported: family importance and career enjoyment ($n = 83$), family permanence and career enjoyment ($n = 76$), prioritizing family and career enjoyment ($n = 75$), work choice and career enjoyment ($n = 43$), prioritize family and family importance ($n = 33$), family importance and financial support ($n = 32$), and life planning and career enjoyment ($n = 30$). These seven message combinations

Table 19.1 Definition and Example of Message Categories

Message Category	Category Definition	Example Message
Career general	General messages about the role of work in life or types of career choices	"Go into engineering."
Career enjoyment	Messages that link career choices to the importance of liking, enjoying, or being fulfilled by the work	"Be sure to choose a career you love."
Work ethic	Messages about the importance of hard work or perseverance in being successful	"Hard work pays off."
Financial support	Messages about making money to support yourself or a family	"You've got to work to live."
Prioritize work	Messages that advocate work must come first over other things in life	"Work must come first."
Permanency	Messages that stress dependability permanence of family relations	"Family will always be with you!"
Importance	Messages that describe the emotional importance or centrality of family relations	"Most families aren't as close-knit as ours."
Prioritize family	Messages that advocate family must come before work or other things in life	"Family first!"
Life planning	Messages that argue for a particular plan, rationale, or order to life events	"Be successful at work first, then think about having children."
Combining	Messages that encourage having both work and family interests in life	"Find time for both family and enjoying your work."
Segmenting	Messages arguing for the separation of work and family duties	"Work should stay at work, home is for family!"
Stopping work	Messages that encourage stopping participation in paid labor while children are young	"Stay home when your kids are young."
Work choice	Messages that advocate selecting a particular career because it will allow you to balance work and family responsibilities	"Don't take a job where you travel a lot; you'll never see your family."

Table 19.2   Message Pair Frequency and Pair by Sex Frequency

Message Pair	n	n Male	n Female	Chi-Square
Family permanency/career general	22	5	17	1.88
Family permanency/career enjoy	76	28	48	0.08
Family permanency/financial support	24	7	17	0.57
Family importance/career general	27	11	16	0.24
Family importance/career enjoyment	83	31	52	0.04
Family importance/financial support	32	12	20	0.02
Prioritize family/career enjoyment	75	27`	48	0.01
Prioritize family/family importance	33	13	20	0.14
Life planning/career enjoyment	30	9	21	0.57
Life planning/family permanency	22	4	18	3.34*
Life planning/family importance	26	11	15	0.42
Combining/career enjoyment	28	10	18	0.01
Combining/family permanency	20	8	12	0.12
Combining/family importance	24	10	14	0.31
Work choice/career enjoyment	43	11	32	2.44
Work choice/family permanency	25	7	18	0.81
Work choice/prioritize family	25	4	21	4.80*
Work choice/career general	23	7	16	0.37
Stop work/career enjoyment	19	0	19	11.44**

Note: Pair frequency ≥ 5% of total messages for inclusion.

$*p < .05. **p < .001.$

are interesting and informative, independent from each other as well as collectively. The most often reported message shared with young adults is that family is very important and so is enjoying your work. Indeed, career fulfillment is a consistent message across these data, paired with other suggestions to prioritize family and choose work that will accommodate a pleasing and balanced family work life. These results are consistent with prior research that also found that young adults were counseled by parental figures that their families should be important and central to their lives and their work should be enjoyable and fulfilling (Medved et al., 2004).

Analyzing the message pairs as a collective reveals a set of themes that capture the essence of the messages that are shared with young adults by parental figures. Through thematic analysis, the authors sifted through the 19 pairs of messages and inductively derived three themes. The first theme, *career fulfillment*, captures the dictate to young adults to enjoy their work and find meaning in their chosen careers. The second theme, *family centrality*, is a message steeped in the reminder that family comes first and is at the center of one's life. The third theme, *rational career planning*, is, in essence, an appeal to young adults to organize their lives so that they are better positioned to enjoy their career and prioritize their family, with the underlying assumption being that without planning, work and family life will be difficult to balance.

The second research question examined the association between message pairs received by young men and women. Out of a total of 19 message pairs, 3 were significantly different for young men and women: *life planning and family permanency* (e.g., " . . . don't have kids until you feel you are ready" and "No matter what you do, good or bad, your family is always going to be there") (χ^2 [1, $N = 382$] = 3.34, $p < .05$), *work choice and prioritize family* (e.g., "Don't pick a job that will take all of your time from your family" and "Family first") (χ^2 [1, $N = 382$] = 4.80, $p < .05$), and *stopping work and career enjoyment* (e.g., "It is important for mothers to stay home with their children" and "Choose a career that [you] will be happy with") (χ^2 [1, $N = 382$] = 11.44, $p < .001$). Each of these pairs enjoins a message about ways to privilege or accommodate family responsibilities with advice about finding work that is pleasurable and fulfilling. Women were the recipients of these messages significantly more often than men.

Finally, the last research question posed in this study asks us to revisit the above findings from a dialectical perspective. To answer the third research question, the message pairs reported to have a significant association with recipient sex will be explored in relation to the dialectics of public-private, femininity-masculinity, and emotionality-rationality. The three message pairs women received more often than men were as follows: life planning and family permanency, work choice and prioritize family, and stopping work and career enjoyment. Life planning and family permanency can be interpreted in relation to elements of the rationality and emotionality dialectic. One woman, for example, was told, "Don't start a family until you have enough money and time to devote to them" and "Friends will come and go but in the end, family will always be there for you." The need for women to strategically plan out the order of life events portrays life as a rational or logical process. On the other hand, family permanency messages were often seen as emotion laden, almost fearful messages warning against the "loss" of family relationships ("make time for your family; they are the only one you get"). To offer a contrasting example: Messages *not* reportedly received by women were, "Let life take its course; as things happen, you'll make do" and "Friends are essential; you don't know how long family will be around." The juxtaposing of these messages can also be seen as directives for women to privilege relationships and activities in the private sphere because the private sphere is enduring. This construction reifies the importance of the interconnection between the private and the feminine for female participants of this study.

The reification of women's roles in the private sphere, however, is evidenced even further in our second message pair: work choice and prioritize family. For example, one participant was cautioned by the words of her parents, who lamented that "I didn't spend enough time with my family" and "Do not work a job that will make you work too many hours." Both of these messages offer a consistent framework for young women's socialization into work and family roles: Family comes first. Choose a career that will accommodate eventual childrearing, and always place family responsibilities at the forefront of life. As noted above, our separation of these three key dialectics is useful to simplify our analysis but artificial. In this message pair, we see women being advised also to pay attention and privilege the private-feminine-emotional aspects of life.

Finally, stopping work and enjoyment of work, the third message pair, can be interpreted to pit the private sphere against the public sphere or the feminine against the masculine. One participant's mother reflected that "she wished she didn't work full-time when we were younger because those are precious years and you can never get them back." Women are placed in a paradoxical position through these messages. Find work that is enjoyable and personally fulfilling, yet stop doing that work to attend to family, particularly when children are young. Interestingly, both of these messages focus on the emotional dialectic. Work is of value when it is enjoyable and satisfying. Conversely, family relationships are the most important and should be the priority.

Three additional message pairs also can be interpreted in a similar paradoxical manner: family importance and career enjoyment, family permanency and career enjoyment, and prioritize family and career enjoyment. Each of these message pairs advises that work should be the site of personal enjoyment while reminding us, however, that family is our stable source of emotional support. These three pairs also illustrate the consistent assumption that work should be enjoyable. Messages such as, "If it's not fun, it's not worth doing" or "If work is fun, you'll never work a day in your life" set high expectations for the role that work should play in life. While paid labor does often provide a source of fulfillment, work can also be one of our main sources of stress and frustration in life.

Emergent Tensions

In addition to the three dialectics just discussed, two additional and related tensions emerged from the analysis of the message pairs. These are (a) the tension between self and other and (b) choice and constraint. Across these message pairs, we see the construction of tensions between responsibility and/or honoring of self versus service to others, particularly family members. Perhaps not surprisingly, two of the three message pairs more often reported to be received by women (work choice and prioritize family and stopping work and career enjoyment) can be viewed as attempts to construct understandings that women should value service to family over recognition of personal needs. That is, when choosing a career, keep future family (i.e., "other") obligations in mind, and when "family" in the form of children comes along, cease doing work that may (and should) be personally enjoyable. The tension between self and other is also related to a second emergent binary: choice and constraint. As noted from the outset of this chapter, dialectical tensions are richly understood as interrelated ideas; thus, as women are encouraged to privilege the "other," we see how a sense of freedom to choose, for example, an occupation is reduced. While men participating in this study were similarly told that work should be enjoyable, they were less frequently given boundaries or parameters around the choice of work. For example, one woman was told, "I'm glad you want to be a teacher because then you'll have time off to spend with your kids." These types of messages can be interpreted as perhaps the most constraining on occupational choice. In fact, no men reported receiving messages encouraging them to stop work while their children were young.

Discussion

This study explored the nature of socialization messages about work and family. While research suggests that men and women are provided different messages about how their work and personal lives can be integrated, little empirical work exists to support this conclusion. This study provides both support and refutation regarding differential socialization messages provided to young adults as well as a rich description of the dialectical nature of these messages. First, this discussion will address the main themes that emerged from this analysis. We next discuss theoretical and practical implications of this study. Finally, we present related limitations and future directions for family communication research.

These findings point toward the privileging of work in daily life. The mandate to "enjoy one's work" is a late 20th-century concern (Ciulla, 2000). Perhaps born out of the desire for personal empowerment and control, men and women are crafting work lives that are personally fulfilling and professionally rewarding (Kirby et al., 2003). Or perhaps, due to the "ever expanding reach of organizations into [one's] personal life" (Kirby et al., 2003, p. 5), experiencing career fulfillment is a means of tolerating this inevitable encroachment. In fact, Kirby and colleagues (2003) concluded that work is still valued more than family, so the message to enjoy work might very well be taken as practical advice in view of the high priority work has in our society. Furthermore, underlying the parental advice to young adults to find fulfillment in one's career is the knowledge that if one does find joy in his or her work, this can in some ways trump so many other forms of success such as status, power, or monetary rewards. Indeed, the message "if you love what you do for a living, you will never work a day in your life" suggests transcending the daily grind that individuals often face at work. Thus, the advice to enjoy work and find fulfillment in a career is not simply or solely career advice but life advice as well.

The second theme, family centrality, is also a late 20th-century focus. Over the past few decades, there has been a surge of "family first" sentiments that have been borne out in new attitudes about the family as well as from the conservative backlash against feminist attempts at gender role reorganization (Douglas & Michaels, 2004; Medved & Kirby, 2005). Gregory (2001) featured the family first theme in an effort to explain how workers recommitted to family only after they could no longer count on lifetime employment as a means of self-identification. Interestingly, messages such as, "Work with your boss to figure out an alternative work schedule to accommodate family responsibilities" were not found in these data. Instead, women were told to reorganize their lives and choices and not to challenge existing work structures. Again, we see the public (or masculine) oppositional forces in tension and overriding the private (or feminine) ends of the continuum. Research conducted from the 1950s to 1980s demonstrated clear sex differences in orientations toward work (see Lueptow, 1996). Although Lueptow (1996) forecasts that these processes may be changing, the findings of the current study appear to support continued gender differentiation in terms of socializing communication between parents and young adults regarding work orientations.

Although there is ample research that concludes that work is still more highly valued than family, there is mounting evidence that this trend is changing. For example, many employees are settling for lower paying jobs and less status and power in exchange for more free time to spend with family members, and media portrayals of the "opting out" of paid labor by middle- and upper-management women for full time caregiving have added to our societal discussions (Belkin, 2003). Technology has facilitated the movement toward prioritizing family by permitting workers to complete tasks virtually (Gilbert, 1993). Furthermore, men are often advised to make family of central importance in their lives in terms of time and not only the provision of financial support. A family-first orientation is credited by Kirby and colleagues (2003) as contributing to resolved and confident decision making concerning work and family issues. Clearly, messages such as "put family first" are prevalent in discussions between young adults and their parental figures. Yet, the complexity of what this contemporary catchphrase might eventually mean to these young adults remains ambiguous in parental socialization messages. Future research needs to adopt longitudinal research strategies to investigate differential interpretations of "family first" discourses in the lives of young parents.

The third theme, rational career planning, is very integral to the prioritizing of the first two themes of enjoying work and prioritizing family. The notion that the boundaries between work and family are rhetorical rather than real (O'Keefe, 1997) highlights the importance of this memorable message theme. Young women are cautioned to plan ahead so that they can achieve a balanced state between work and family. To avoid the inevitable conflict between work and family obligations, young adults are counseled to manage their career and family through wise preparation and decision making. The serendipitous and uncontrollable elements of life such as death, divorce, or job loss were left unspoken in these data. Moreover, the assumption, although unstated, is that balance is the gold standard and that choices abound.

The combination of message pairs and themes shared with young adults by parental figures is quite informative. However, it is important to note that these recalled memorable messages are quite reflective of a privileged orientation to work and family and do not take into consideration the lack of choice many working-class people face. The very idea of choice in relation to work and family, especially the option of leaving the paid labor force for women and men, is a classist construction (Johnson, 2001). Or, at the very least, these messages are meant as pieces of advice, hopeful suggestions that parental figures share with young adults in an effort to provide wise council. Indeed, it is a luxury to enjoy work, prioritize family, and have the choice to plan a career. For example, a low-income individual working in a temporary or part-time capacity may not have the opportunity to develop long-range career goals, let alone secure steady employment or privilege family responsibilities over work.

Theoretical and Practical Implications

Studies of socialization and communication are most often conducted and presented in a contextual or bounded manner, such as distinct explorations of organizational socialization (Jablin, 2001; Smith & Turner, 1995; Stohl, 1986) or family socialization (Burleson & Kunkel, 2002; Saphir & Chaffee, 2002). That is, we often reproduce a separate-spheres orientation in our studies of socialization processes and communication; ironically, this approach represents a dualistic perspective that has been maligned in the literature as having outlived its usefulness (Kanter, 1977; Lopata, 1993). Perhaps family scholars have not significantly questioned the similar detrimental influence of perpetuating rigid boundary constructions on our theorizing and research practices. Furthermore, in everyday life, messages are not received, nor will these young adults' eventual choices be made, in isolation. We argue that applying a dialectical lens to the study of socialization and communication allows scholars to begin with assumptions of contradiction, interrelatedness, praxis, and totality (Baxter & Montgomery, 1996). The benefits of this framework for cross-fertilization of socialization studies in the field of communication abound and mark one avenue for future research that emerges from this study.

Finally, communicative practices are enactments of agency. Through our words, we reproduce particular systems of meaning and, potentially, the ideological aspects of these systems. Thus, one practical implication of this study is that of the power of everyday talk to transform the gendered structures of work and family. In her work on dual-career couples, Golden (2000) suggests that daily work and family talk should serve to remind us that balance is not only a personal responsibility but also an organizational obligation. Our findings would support and extend Golden's suggestion in that women (not men) were told to rearrange their lives and/or make particular career choices to manage family, not challenge the organization. The tendency in these data to discursively reproduce traditional gender structures supports Stohl's (1986) conclusion that "memorable messages" often reproduce conservative social values. More important, however, questioning the implicit assumptions in our own talk is essential. Parents must understand the implications of messages such as, "I couldn't imagine working when you were young," or "I felt guilty leaving work today by 6:00 p.m." The significance of this call for understanding must be underscored: The messages reported in this study are not trivial or somehow tangential to the material circumstances of work and family. Discourse recursively shapes material circumstances through actions taken by individuals making sense through particular interpretive schemes for work and family (see Ashcraft & Mumby, 2003, for an extensive discussion of discourse and material reality).

The term *balance* is laden with classism (i.e., the ability to "balance" presupposes the ability to choose or not to work in the paid labor force, a luxury not available to most lower-income families) (Kirby et al., 2003), and therefore its use in this study is a limitation. Young adults, nonetheless, are being treated to messages that do speak to the importance of career fulfillment, the centrality of family, and the need to rationally plan their lives so that they may achieve a state of balance. Future research needs to investigate the gendered nature of work-family socialization through paradoxical messages provided to women about life planning (technical rationality) and messages about stopping work or choosing particular careers laden with emotion (practical rationality). In particular, additional research must be conducted exploring the coconstruction of masculinity and femininity in work and family role socialization.

Notes

1. For extensive discussions of the historical split between the public and private spheres or what is known as the "separate-spheres" ideology, see Hays (1996), Lopata (1993), and Williams (2000).

2. This data set served as the basis for another article written by the first author. Medved et al. (2004) is currently under review at the *Journal of Family Communication*. Coding of messages conduced by Medved and colleagues was used in the analysis of data for the present study, although procedures were conducted on a subset of the original data. In the original study, an inductive coding procedure was used to organize the data. A coding scheme for each message topic (work, family, balance) was developed through a grounded coding process (Strauss & Corbin, 1998). After successive readings and iterations of coding, a final categorization scheme was decided upon, and two members of the research team completed message coding. The coding unit was a single message/sentence. Cohen's kappas for work, family, and balance message categories were .86, .83, and .79, respectively. Disagreements were resolved through discussion. When message content was difficult to place in a particular category, coders used the message interpretations provided by study participants. This allowed for an additional perspective on possible message interpretations.

3. The original data collection procedures asked participants to provide separate messages in response to three prompts: What role should family play in life? What role should work play in life? How do you balance work and family? Subsequently, messages provided in response to each of these three prompts were coded independently and resulted in 7 work, 6 family, and 8 balance categories. A reanalysis of the data revealed redundancies across categories, prompting a reorganization of the original 21 categories. Thus, the independent nature of the original coding categories was eliminated. For example, "prioritize family" emerged as a response to all three message prompts (work, family, and balance). In our reanalysis for the present study, data from the three independent "prioritize family" categories were collapsed into one overarching "prioritizing family" category. This data reduction technique resulted in 13 categories that accounted for common themes cutting across work, family, and balance message categories.

References

Ashcraft, K. L., & Mumby, D. K. (2003). *Reworking gender: A feminist communicology of organization.* Thousand Oaks, CA: Sage.

Baxter, L. A., & Montgomery, B. M. (1996). *Relating: Dialogue and dialectics.* New York: Guilford.

Belkin, L. (2003, October). The opt out revolution. *Time*, p. 22.

Burleson, B. R., & Kunkel, A. (2002). Parental and peer contributions to the emotional skills development of the child: From whom do children learn to express support? *Journal of Family Communication, 2*, 81–98.

Buzzanell, P. M. (1995). International and transracial adoption: A communication research agenda. *Journal of Family Communication, 3*, 237–253.

Buzzanell, P. M. (1997). Toward an emotion-based feminist framework for research on dual career couples. *Women and Language, 20*, 40–48.

Buzzanell, P. M. (2003). A feminist standpoint analysis of maternity and maternity leave for women with disabilities. *Women & Language, 26*, 53–65.

Buzzanell, P. M., & Goldzwig, S. (1991). Linear and nonlinear career models: Metaphors, paradigms, and ideologies. *Management Communication Quarterly, 4,* 466–505.

Cardozo, A. R. (2000). *Sequencing: A new solution for women who want marriage, career, and family.* New York: Antheneum Macmillan. (Original work published 1986)

Ciulla, J. (2000). *The working life: The promise and betrayal of modern work.* New York: Crown.

Clark, S. C. (2000). Work cultures and work/family balance. *Journal of Vocational Behavior, 58,* 348–365.

Clark, S. C. (2002). Communicating across the work/home border. *Community, Work, & Family, 1,* 23–47.

Crittenden, A. (2001). *The price of motherhood: Why the most important job in the world is still the least valued.* New York: Holt.

Douglas, S., & Michaels, M. (2004). *The mommy myth: The idealization of motherhood and how it has undermined women.* New York: Free Press.

Edley, P. (2001). Technology, employed mothers, and corporate colonization of the lifeworld: A gendered paradox of work and family balance [Electronic version]. *Women & Language, 24,* 28.

Families and Work Institute. (2004). *Generations & gender.* New York: American Business Collaboration.

Farley-Lucas, B. (2000). Communicating the (in)visibility of motherhood: Family talk and the ties to motherhood with/in the workplace. *The Electronic Journal of Communication/ La Revue Electronique de Communication, 10*(3). Retrieved from http://www .cios.org/www/ ejcrec2.htm

Ferree, M. M. (1995). Beyond separate spheres: Feminism and family research. In G. L. Bowen & J. F. Pittman (Eds.), *The work and family interface: Toward a contextual effects perspective* (pp. 122–137). Minneapolis, MN: National Council on Family Relations.

Fletcher, J. K. (1999). *Disappearing acts: Gender, power, and relational practice at work.* Cambridge: MIT Press.

Freeman, S. J. M. (1997). Parental influences on women's careers. In D. Dunn (Ed.), *Workplace/women's place: An anthology* (pp. 32–43). Los Angeles: Roxbury.

Galinsky, E. (1999). *Ask the children: What America's children really think about working parents.* New York: Morrow.

Gilbert, L. A. (1993). *Two careers/one family.* Newbury Park, CA: Sage.

Golden, A. G. (2000). What we talk about when we talk about work and family: A discourse analysis of parental accounts. *The Electronic Journal of Communication, 10*(3). Retrieved from http://www.cios.org/www/ejc/v10n3400.htm

Golden, A. G. (2002). Speaking of work and family: Spousal collaboration on defining role-identities and developing shared meanings. *Southern Communication Journal, 67,* 122–141.

Gregory, K. W. (2001). *"Don't sweat the small stuff": Employee identity in the new economy.* Unpublished doctoral dissertation, University of South Florida.

Hays, S. (1996). *The cultural contradictions of motherhood.* New Haven, CT: Yale University Press.

Heisler, J. M. (2000). *The socialization of gender roles through parental memorable message.* Unpublished doctoral dissertation, Michigan State University.

Hochschild, A. R. (1983). *The managed heart: The commercialization of human feeling.* Berkeley: University of California Press.

Hochschild, A. R. (1997). *The time bind: When work becomes home and home becomes work.* New York: Metropolitan Books.

Hochschild, A. R. (2003). *The commercialization of intimate life.* Berkeley: University of California Press.

Hymlö, A. (2004). Women, men, and changing organizations: An organizational culture examination of gendered experiences of telecommuting. In P. M. Buzzanell, H. Sterk, & L. Turner (Eds.), *Gender in applied contexts* (pp. 47–75). Thousand Oaks, CA: Sage.

Jablin, F. M. (2001). Organizational entry, assimilation, and disengagement. In L. L. Putnam & F. M. Jablin (Eds.), *The new handbook of organizational communication* (pp. 732–818). Thousand Oaks, CA: Sage.

Jefferson, D. C., & Welch, R. (2004). *Three ring circus: How real couples balance marriage, work, and family.* Seattle, WA: Seal Press.

Johnson, F. L. (2001). Ideological undercurrents in the semantic notion of "working mothers." *Women & Language, 24,* 21–27.

Jorgenson, J. (2000). Interpreting the intersections of work and family: Frame conflicts in women's work. *The Electronic Journal of Communication/La Revue Electronique de Communication, 10*(3). Retrieved from http://www.cios.org/www/ejcrec2.htm

Jorgenson, J., Gregory, K. W., & Goodier, B. C. (1997). Working the boundaries: The enfamilied self in the traditional organization. *Human Systems, 8,* 139–151.

Kanter, R. M. (1977). *Work and family in the United States: A critical review and agenda for research and policy.* New York: Russell Sage Foundation.

Kirby, E. L., Golden, A. G., Medved, C. M., Jorgenson, J., & Buzzanell, P. M. (2003). An organizational communication challenge to the discourse of work and family research: From problematics to empowerment. In P. Kalbfleisch (Ed.), *Communication yearbook 27* (pp. 1–43). Mahwah, NJ: Lawrence Erlbaum.

Knapp, M. L., Stohl, C., & Reardon, K. K. (1981). "Memorable" messages. *Journal of Communication, 31,* 27–42.

Krueger, D. L. (1986). Communication strategies and patterns in dual-career couples. *Southern Speech Communication Journal, 51,* 274–281.

Lee, D., & Lee, D. L. (1997). *Having it all, having enough: How to create a career/family balance that works for you.* New York: Amacom Books

Lopata, H. Z. (1993). The interweave of public and private: Women's challenge to American society. *Journal of Marriage and the Family, 55,* 176–190.

Lueptow, L. B. (1996). Gender and orientations toward work. In P. J. Dubeck & K. Borman (Eds.), *Women and work: A handbook* (pp. 281–283). New York: Garland.

Mains, D. R., & Hardesty, M. J. (1987). Temporality and gender: Young adults' career and family plans. *Social Forces, 66,* 102–120.

Marshall, J. (1989). Re-visioning career concepts: A feminist invitation. In M. B. Arthur, D. T. Hall, & B. S. Lawrence (Eds.), *Handbook of career theory* (pp. 275–291). Cambridge, UK: Cambridge University Press.

Mattson, M., Clair, R. C., Chapman Sanger, P. A., & Kunkel, A. D. (2000). A feminist reframing of stress: Rose's story. In P. M. Buzzanell (Ed.), *Rethinking organizational and managerial communication from feminist perspectives* (pp. 157–176). Thousand Oaks, CA: Sage.

Medved, C. E. (2004). The everyday accomplishment of work and family: Accounting for practical actions and commonsense rules in daily routines. *Communication Studies, 55,* 128–154.

Medved, C. E., Brogan, S., McClanahan, A. M., Morris, J. F., & Shepherd, G. J. (2004). *Reproducing the gendered boundaries between work and family: An analysis and critique of family socialization memorable messages.* Unpublished manuscript.

Medved, C. E., & Heisler, J. (2002). Critical student-faculty interactions: Non-traditional students manage multiple roles. *Communication Education, 51,* 105–120.

Medved, C. E., & Kirby, E. L. (2005). Family CEOs: A feminist analysis of corporate mothering discourses. *Management Communication Quarterly, 18,* 435–478.

Medved, C. E., Morrison, K., Butler-Ellis, J., Popovich, D., Heisler, J., & Johnson, A. J. (1999, November). *Describing work and family conflict situations: Sources and strategies.* Paper presented at the annual convention of the National Communication Association, Chicago.

Miller, V. D., Jablin, F. M., Casey, M. K., Lamphear-Van Horn, M., & Ethington, C. (1996). The maternity leave as a role negotiation process. *Journal of Managerial Issues, 8,* 286–309.

Mumby, D. K. (1998). Organizing men: Power, discourse and the social construction of masculinity(s) in the workplace. *Communication Theory, 8,* 164–183.

Mumby, D. K. (2000). Communication, organization, and the public sphere: A feminist perspective. In P. M. Buzzanell (Ed.), *Rethinking organizational and managerial communication from feminist perspectives* (pp. 3–23). Thousand Oaks, CA: Sage.

Mumby, D. K., & Putnam, L. L. (1992). The politics of emotion: A feminist reading of bounded rationality. *Academy of Management Review, 17,* 465–486.

Nippert-Eng, C. (1996). *Home and work: Negotiating boundaries through everyday life.* Chicago: University of Chicago Press.

O'Keefe, B. (1997). [Review of the book *Home and work: Negotiating boundaries through everyday life*]. *Communication Theory, 7,* 186–188.

Piotrkowski, C. S. (1979). *Work and the family system.* New York: Macmillan.

Piotrkowski, C. S., & Katz, M. H. (1982). Indirect socialization of children: The effect of mother's job on academic behavior. *Child Development, 53,* 1520–1529.

Piotrkowski, C. S., & Stark, E. (1987). Children and adolescents look at their parents' job. In J. H. Lewko (Ed.), *How children and adolescents view the world of work* (pp. 3–19). San Francisco: Jossey-Bass.

Rawlins, W. K. (1992). *Friendship matters: Communication, dialectics, and the life course.* New York: Walter de Gruyter.

Risman, B. J. (1998). *Gender vertigo: American families in transition.* New Haven, CT: Yale University Press.

Rosenfeld, L. B., Bowen, G. L., & Richman, J. M. (1995). Communication in three types of dual-career marriages. In M. A. Fitzpatrick & A. L. Vangelisti (Eds.), *Explaining family interactions* (pp. 257–289). Thousand Oaks, CA: Sage.

Saphir, M. N., & Chaffee, S. H. (2002). Adolescents' contributions to family communication patterns. *Human Communication Research, 28,* 86–109.

Schlessinger, L. (2001). *Stupid things parents do to mess up their kids: Don't have them if you won't raise them.* New York: Quill.

Smith, R. C., & Turner, P. K. (1995). A social constructionist reconfiguration of metaphor analysis: An application of "SCMA" to organizational socialization theorizing. *Communication Monographs, 62,* 152–181.

Stohl, C. (1986). The role of memorable messages in the process of organizational socialization. *Communication Quarterly, 34,* 231–249.

Strauss, A., & Corbin, J. (1998). *Basics of qualitative research: Techniques and procedures for developing grounded theory* (2nd ed.). Thousand Oaks, CA: Sage.

Weick, K. E. (1979). *The social psychology of organizing.* Reading, MA: Addison-Wesley.

Williams, J. (2000). *Unbending gender: Why work and family conflict and what to do about it.* New York: Oxford University Press.

Wood, J. T. (1994). *Who cares? Women, care, and culture.* Carbondale: Southern Illinois University Press.

CHAPTER 20

Relational Dynamics in Interfaith Marriage

Patrick C. Hughes

Texas Tech University

Fran C. Dickson

University of Denver

D uring the early to mid-20th century, Merton (1941) noted, "In no society is the selection of a marriage partner unregulated and indiscriminate" (p. 36). Baron (1972), examining marital trends 30 years later, also acknowledged that "all records show that in every society, historical or contemporary, primitive or modern, cultural restrictions are designed to limit the possible marriage partners available to any person" (p. 39). Yet, today, marriage patterns do not reflect these restrictions on our marriage choices.

Once considered the "last taboo" (Johnson & Warren, 1994), intermarriage—specifically, interfaith marriage—seems to be going the way of many other taboos, yet research on interfaith relationships has not kept pace with this trend. Diggs and Socha (2004) identified several areas in which family communication scholars might "explore the boundaries of diversity in family communication studies" (p. 258). Among these areas, they argue, is the need to investigate the role and influence of religion in family communication: "Theological approaches and families of various religious traditions, rather than being ignored, potentially, could be sources for culturally diverse interrogation of family communication" (Diggs & Socha, 2004, p. 259). In addition, Davidson and Widman (2002) argued that we need to investigate how religion—when combined with other cultural aspects of families—interacts. The purpose of this chapter is to shed light on the relational aspects of interfaith relationships. Specifically, we review research on rates of intermarriage, definitions of religiously mixed marriages, types of interfaith marriage, antecedents to interfaith marriage, interfaith marriage and divorce, and interfaith marriage communication. Finally, we will explore the implications for interfaith relationships.

Religion, Marriage, and Family

To better understand the relational dynamics in interfaith marriage—any marriage in which partners differ in one or more religious dimensions—it seems best to first describe the influence religion has on marriage and family in general. Second, it is necessary to discuss the sociological influences, which are attributed to bringing together people of different faiths. Finally, we discuss the historical rates of interfaith marriage.

In general, clergy and scholars alike have recognized the importance of religion in human interaction for some time (Allport, 1937, 1950, 1958; Batson, 1976a, 1976b). Allport (1960, 1963, 1966) investigated the psychosocial nature of a person's religious commitment, which suggests that a person may exhibit different orientations to his or her religion. Allport (1966) found that participants reported two different orientations toward faith: intrinsic and extrinsic. In addition to researching general orientations toward religion, Allport (1959) and Batson (1976b) explored the relationship between religious beliefs and prejudicial attitudes. At the same time they were studying religion's effects on attitudes, researchers also began looking into its effects on human relationships.

Religious community leaders and scholars have investigated the use of widows' and widowers' faiths during bereavement counseling (Carey, 1977), researched faith-based premarital counseling and clergy training (Stanley, Trathen, & Bryan, 1998), examined the faith-based counseling techniques in mental health contexts (Hulm, 1974; Mezydlo, Wauk, & Foley, 1973), and partner's faith and its relationship to marital commitment (Stanley, 1998). Finally, McQuire (1997) argued, "Religion is one of the most powerful, deeply felt, and influential forces in human society. It shap[es] people's relationships with each other, influencing family, community, economic, and political life" (p. 2).

Religion has also been investigated in the context of the family. For example, families are usually the primary means of socialization and acculturation into religious faiths and the denominations within those faiths (Lenski, 1961). These affiliations are likely to begin with religious rituals occurring at birth and infancy (i.e., Christian baptism) and continuing through childhood (i.e., Christian rituals of Confession and First Communion), adolescence (i.e., Christian ritual of Confirmation), and perhaps on through adulthood (i.e., traditional marriage ceremonies). Furthermore, religious faiths (i.e., Roman Catholicism and Judaism) in addition to other social organizations (i.e., Focus on the Family) include proscriptions or recommendations for expected family roles, behaviors, dynamics, and responsibilities (Bendroth, 1994). And according to McNamara (1992) and Mol (1978), religions and religious practices, which advocate the worship of "supernatural" forces, tend to encourage followers to free (i.e., liberate or emancipate) themselves from traditional social systems.

Religion affects marital as well as nonmarital romantic relationships. For example, Booth and White (1980) found that marital partners' strength of commitment was related to whether or not these partners contemplated divorce. Krishnan (1994) later found that religion significantly predicted women's attitudes toward divorce more than men's attitudes toward divorce. Specifically, women considered the religious implications of a divorce more than men. Religion was also found to correlate with one's marital satisfaction following an extramarital affair (Spanier & Margolis, 1983), married couples' attitudes toward sexual behavior and love (Weis, Slosnerick, Cate, & Sollie, 1986), and spouses' church activism (Wilson, Simpson, & Jackson, 1987). For example, the church activities of one spouse significantly predicted the church activities of the other spouse, suggesting that the more one's spouse participated in the activities of the church, the more likely the other spouse would also participate.

Couples who cohabited before marriage were found to have lower levels of religious commitment (Williams & Daniel, 1987). In addition, the religious commitment of parents was significantly related to romantic couples' likelihood to cohabit before marriage (Williams & Daniel, 1987). Furthermore, Huffman, Chang, Rausch, and Schaffer (1994) found that romantic partners' willingness or intent to cohabit was related to partners' reports of lower levels of religious commitment and belief. Finally, religious commitment and church attendance were found to significantly correlate with increased levels of marital dependency, self-identification, and marital homogamy (Wilson & Musick, 1996), levels of marital satisfaction (Bahr & Chadwick, 1985), and marital fidelity (Penn, Hernandez, & Bermudez, 1997).

We feel that research on marriage and religion documents the important effects religion has on personal relationships. However, research has not widely considered the impact of partners' disparate religious preferences on their personal relationships.

The following section of this chapter presents research on the divorce rates for interfaith marriages, antecedents to interfaith relationships, the incidence of interfaith relationships, a typological discussion of interfaith relationships, and interfaith marriage and divorce.

Religion and the Interfaith Marriage

Interfaith Marriage and Divorce

Interfaith marriages are more likely to end in divorce than same-faith marriages (Becker, Landes, & Robert, 1977; Lehrer & Chiswick, 1993). Bahr (1981) found that same-faith marriages are more stable than interfaith marriages. Furthermore, this divorce rate appeared to fluctuate by type of interfaith marriage, showing that the divorce rates for certain combinations of interfaith marriages are as much as nine times higher than for other combinations of interfaith marriages and than for same-faith marriages. Ortega, Whitt, and William (1988) found that Baptists, Calvinists, Fundamentalists, Lutherans, and Methodists who were married to members of their respective denominations reported higher levels of marital happiness than those who were married to members of dissimilar denominations. However, the likelihood for divorce lessened and marital satisfaction increased in interfaith marriages when the faiths of partners were similar in doctrine (Lehrer & Chiswick, 1993).

Alston, McIntosh, and Wright (1976) found that persons in religiously homogamous marriages reported higher levels of marital satisfaction, as does Glenn (1982) for males, but not for females. Catholic-Protestant couples were as much as five times as likely to divorce than marriages where the partners were either Catholic or Protestant (Reiss, 1976).

Antecedents of Interfaith Marriage

Religious endogamy is decreasingly common in the United States and Canada, and it is of less importance in mate selection than even a few decades ago (McQuire, 1997). For example, Gleckman and Streicher (1990) argued, "Religious identification is viewed as irrelevant to the choice of one's mate in modern society," and "love tends to be the driving force behind most marriages" (p. 484). In addition, Johnson (1980) suggests that same-faith marriages occur only when there are a large number of eligible religiously similar partners available. In fact, a recent poll of adults ranging in age from 18 to 35 suggests that members of many religious denominations are intermarrying at increasing levels, with many young adults reporting that it is less important to marry a person who is of the same religious background (Whitehead & Popenoe, 2001). There are several reasons for intermarriage. They include (a) proximity to people's other religious traditions (including social networks, geographical region, and immigration), (b) religion by consent, (c) education level, and (d) remarriage. We briefly explore each below.

Interfaith Marriage and Proximity

One's social network presents opportunities for interfaith relationships. Davidson and Widman (2002) found that group size influences opportunities for interaction and availability of potential marriage partners. In addition to one's social network, one's geographical location can affect interfaith marriage rates because it affects the types of religious groups and individuals available for marriage. For instance, some research suggests that in the northeastern part of the United States, where Catholics are in close proximity to mainline Protestants, interfaith relations tend to be cordial (Davidson & Widman, 2002). In the Southeast, where Catholics are in close proximity to evangelical Protestants, whose beliefs differ from each others', interfaith relations have more conflict. Although Davidson and Widman's study specifically looked at Catholics, there is a possibility that a similar effect can be found among other religious groups. In addition, migration/immigration is also considered a force forging interfaith relationships as with many other types of intermarriage, such as intercultural, interethnic, and interracial relationships (Sherkat, 2002).

Interfaith Marriage and Religion by Consent

In addition to closer proximity of people with different religious preferences and along with many young adults today declaring that religion is less important in mate selection than other qualities, there are greater numbers of minority faiths, and "the number of religious options appear to be growing" (Sarna, 1994, p. 58), suggesting that religious identity is more a matter of choice than familial descent. This may be seen most clearly in marriages in which one's ethnicity is linked to one's religious choice. For example, Irish and Italian ethnicities are almost exclusively linked to Catholicism, and German or Scandinavian ethnicities are almost exclusively linked to Protestant faiths. Where members of these faiths or people from these countries intermarry, the available choices increase. In addition, Jewish-by-choice (consent) implies less commitment to Judaism and its laws, especially those applying to marriage. Furthermore, this distinction suggests that some remain culturally Jewish but not religiously Jewish. So, those who are Jewish by consent may be more likely to intermarry than those who adopt a "Jewish-by-descent" identity. Furthermore, this analysis does not take into account religious conversion to Judaism, where one may not be culturally Jewish but chose to be religiously Jewish (consent) and may practice the religion more literally and faithfully and may not intermarry. Either way, the idea of religious consent or people deciding to have more agency over their religious identities is one explanation for the increase in interfaith marriages and is considered to be one reason why the ranks of some religions seem to be dwindling and the numbers in others seem to be increasing.

Interfaith Marriage and Educational Level

Educational level is also linked to the increase in interfaith marriage. Maxwell (1997) suggests that one's increased educational level is likely to present such opportunities as increased social and geographic mobility and likely broaden one's opportunity to meet and interact with people from different cultural and religious backgrounds—a greater variety of people. Furthermore, a high level of educational achievement may be inversely associated with value and belief systems. For example, a college education is said to cultivate more liberal attitudes in students.

Although some research has explored the impact of higher education diversity, this hypothesis has received little support. However, higher levels of education may influence one's willingness to critique one's religious background, especially as many religious doctrines may include proscriptions for traditional roles in marriage. Furthermore, higher educational levels may culminate in a redefinition and reconceptualization of one's faith. Therefore, educational level may increase the likelihood of intermarriage. Higher education creates greater career employment opportunities that may lead to geographic mobility (Mayer & Keysar, 1997).

Interfaith Marriage and Remarriage

In addition, the pattern of marriage-then-remarriage may increase the likelihood of interfaith marriage. More than 40% of all marriages are second marriages (Maxwell, 1997). Maxwell (1997) refers to this as an "in-marrying, then divorcing and out-marrying" pattern. According to Maxwell, this seems to be especially true for Jewish/non-Jewish interfaith marriages but is seen among many other faiths also. However, the impact is considered less significant since denominational switching from one denomination of Christianity to another is not as problematic as switching from one faith to another. Maxwell notes, "Huge numbers of Jewish kids of two Jewish parents . . . end up in interfaith households" (p. 43).

These four explanations for the incidence of interfaith relationships highlight how and why people with different religious preferences might meet and develop personal relationships with each other. In addition, we feel that these explanations are not likely the only ones predicting the development of interfaith relationships. Also, we feel that the incidence of interfaith relationships is best explained by these forces in combination with each other, and as proximity, education, consent, and remarriage increase, the incidence of interfaith relationships will also increase.

Rates of Interfaith Marriage

The 1957 U.S. census found, for six denominations, low levels of intermarriage. For example, the census showed that 88% of Catholics, 83% of Baptists, 81% of Lutherans, 81% of Methodists, 81% of Presbyterians, and 94% of Jews were married to members of the same denomination (Greely, 1970). Eleven years later, in 1968, a second national census survey found that 86% of Catholics, 84% of Baptists, 83% of Lutherans, 86% of Methodists, 78% of Presbyterians, and 97% of Jews were married to members of the same denomination (Greely, 1970).

Although the incidence of interfaith marriage changed for each denomination surveyed—with the incidence of interfaith marriage rising for Catholics and Presbyterians and the incidence falling for Baptists, Lutherans, Methodists, and Jews, who experienced the greatest drop among respondents—these were not significant changes (Greely, 1970). Although the incidence of interfaith marriage remained low and stable in the 1970s, research does suggest that the frequency of interfaith marriages had increased incrementally between 1930 and 1970. McCuctheon (1988) found, with measures taken at each decade between 1930 and 1970, that interfaith marriages increased by 3.8% for conservative Christians, by 20% for Methodists, by 25% for Lutherans, by 16% for Presbyterians and Episcopalians, by 25% for Catholics, and by 23% for Jews.

Current research reveals an increase in interfaith marriage. Almost 50% of marriages between all non-Hispanic Whites born in the United States are between people with no common ancestry (Alba, 1991). Kalmijn (1991) found that interfaith marriage between Protestants and Catholics increased dramatically between 1920 and 1980. In a study of married Catholics, 54% of those who were surveyed, who were 30 years old or younger, were in an interfaith marriage (Preister, 1986). Ten years later, research reported that for every 100 marriages, within the Catholic denomination, 40% to 45% were interfaith marriages (Hoge, 1990). Fishman, Rimor, Tobin, and Medding (1990) found a substantial 20-year increase in the rate of interfaith marriage. In the 1960s, every 9 of 10 Jews married Jewish spouses. In the years between 1980 and 1989, Jewish interfaith marriages increased from 10% in the 1960s to 25% and 50%, depending on the population observed. Finally, a current popular press study found that 1 in 3 Jews lives in an interfaith household. This same research also found that 21% of Catholics, 30% of Mormons, and 40% of Muslims living in the United States are in some form of interfaith marriage. In addition to the increase of interfaith marriage, these marriages, compared to same-faith marriages, are more likely to end in divorce (Hood, Spilka, Hunsberger, & Gorsuch, 1996).

This research presents a useful chronology of the consistent increase in the frequency of interfaith marriages but defines interfaith marriage as any marriage where the partners differ in their religious membership. Hood et al. (1996) observe that, "at first glance, it seems that all we need to determine [religious] intermarriage is to learn the religious preference [and membership] of the spouses, [but] few things are as simple as they appear" (p. 134). For example, couples may differ along other religious dimensions as well. The next section offers a typology of religiously mixed marriages that extends beyond the religious membership of the couples.

A Typology of Religiously Mixed Marriages

Religiously mixed marriages may be defined according to the partners' different faiths, different denominations, and different levels of commitment to those faiths. An interfaith marriage is any marriage where the marital partners differ in one or more religious dimensions (Hood et al., 1996). Marital partners may not only differ in terms of religious membership but may also differ in terms of their levels of strength of commitment—a religiously intercommitted marriage. For example, a marriage in which both partners avow a Methodist denomination but report different levels of commitment to this denomination is also considered a religiously mixed marriage in that the partners report different levels of commitment. An interchurch marriage is a marriage where the partners differ in terms of denomination but share the same faith. For example, in a marriage where one partner is Catholic and the other is Protestant, both avow Christianity but attend different religious services. Approximately one third of the marriages occurring in the United States today are considered interchurch marriages (Lawler et al., 1999). Beyond strictly individual religious differences, it could be said that each and every marriage is, on some level, an intermarriage. To highlight this idea, Falicov (1986) argued that "strictly speaking, we all intermarry, even if we marry the boy [or girl] next door" (p. 429). Our understanding of interfaith marriage dynamics, as attributed solely to denomination differences between the partners, is limited. Duck (1999) argued that explaining personal relationships in terms of demographic differences alone is at best incomplete and at worst inaccurate. However, much of the research on religion and marriage, especially on interfaith marriage, has looked to only the denominational differences when explaining the relational dynamics of interfaith relationships. In this next section, we present one approach toward understanding interfaith relational dynamics that extends beyond denominational differences: religious orientation.

Religious Orientation

Allport (1966) argued that people exhibit intrinsic and/or extrinsic orientations to their religions. Intrinsically religious persons are characterized as being strongly committed to their faith. Their religion is of primary importance to them. It helps them gain a sense of meaning in their lives. They tend to be unprejudiced and tolerant of different viewpoints, are more mature, consider their religion as a unifying principle in life and as important to mental health, and more frequently attend religious services. Extrinsically religious persons view their religion as a means to another end. For example, religion tends to be viewed as a means to a personal benefit and toward promoting social relationships with others. In addition, religiously extrinsic persons tend to be more prejudiced, dependent, in need of comfort and security, utilitarian, and irregularly attend religious services (Allport & Ross, 1967).

Religiously intrinsic persons were found to be more rhetorically sensitive—accepting a person's complexity and understanding that a person is a composite of many selves (Plante & Boccaccini, 1997). In addition, intrinsically oriented partners may be more tolerant and accepting of religious differences in others. Since religiously intrinsic persons are "typically described as individuals who seek to internalize their religious beliefs, make those beliefs a central aspect of their lives, and live out those beliefs in their lives" (Clements, 1998, p. 242) and tend to be "individualistic" toward their faith, in this case, these participants may not necessarily interfere with how others practice their faiths. Moreover, religiously intrinsic individuals espouse values related to "humility, compassion, and love thy neighbor" (Allport & Ross, 1967, p. 441), whereas religiously extrinsic individuals "are utilitarian in their religious and social attitudes and are more likely to endorse their own and their groups' concerns" (Jackson & Husberger, 1999, p. 510). Another view offered extends the intrinsic and extrinsic distinctions of religious orientation to conceptualize religious orientation as "Quest" (Batson & Ventis, 1982). Religious orientation as Quest has been described as "facing existential questions in their complexity, but recognizing that one does not know and probably will never know the truth about such matters" (Batson & Schoenrade, 1991, p. 417).

The differences between married partners' religious orientations have been shown to influence marital outcomes. For example, spouses' different levels of religious commitment and orientation affect satisfaction more than spouses' different faiths. In marriages where one partner is Jewish and the other partner is undefined, the likelihood for divorce increases by a factor of six (Ellman, 1971). In addition, Plante and Boccaccini (1997) found that respondents who reported low levels of strength of commitment were significantly more interpersonally sensitive than respondents who reported high levels of religious commitment. Looking at interfaith relationship dynamics through the lens of religious orientation can add to our understanding about these relationships as well as shed new light on the particular relational challenges interfaith partners face. In the next section, we discuss (a) communication during a religious disagreement, (b) social network composition, (c) social support as three central potential relational problematics for interfaith partners, and (d) the relationship between religious orientation and these problematics.

Interfaith Relationship Problematics

According to research, interfaith couples face more challenges than same-faith couples, particularly where religion is concerned (Gleckman & Streicher, 1990). For example, interfaith partners reported more difficulties in religious identity development (Clamar, 1992; Sousa, 1995), performance of religious-based holiday rituals (Horowitz, 1999), and the religious socialization of children (Judd, 1990; Williams & Lawler, 2000), but more recent research suggests that, in general, peers influence the religious development of children more than parents do (Gannoe & Monroe, 2002). Much of the research on the difficulties facing interfaith couples does not address the communicative and relational challenges faced by these couples or describe what communication might be like for interfaith families facing these challenges. The following sections discuss these relational and communicative dynamics of interfaith couples.

Interfaith Marriage, Social Support, and Social Networks

Social networks and social support are closely related to marital satisfaction (Burger & Milardo, 1995; Dickson-Markman & Markman, 1988; Kenny, 1996). For example, in one study, when partners seek social support from members of social groups, their spouses' reports of marital dissatisfaction increased (Julien & Markman, 1992). The lack of a shared social network can lead to spouses' reports of ambivalence toward the marriage and more problems and arguments in the marriage (Burger & Milardo, 1995). Presumably, interfaith couples are likely to have regular contact with different social networks. Interfaith partners may attend and participate in different religious services. Furthermore, different friendships may result from these different memberships. Eaton (1994) has shown that interfaith couples face challenges from family members and friends regarding their decision to religiously intermarry. Liao and Stevens (1998) found that men in interfaith marriages were more likely than men in same-faith marriages to name their wives as the first person with whom they discussed important matters. Finally, interfaith partners are more likely to lead separate lifestyles (e.g., social contacts such as visiting friends, acquaintances, and neighbors; visiting parents and siblings; visiting other family members; talking to best friends; visiting a bar or restaurant; and visiting a theater, play, concert, or the cinema) (Kalmijn & Bernasco, 2001). However, the relationship between the differences in religious dimensions among interfaith partners' social networks and social support has not been identified until recently.

Interfaith Marriage and Conflict Over Religious Issues

The research on interfaith marriage shows these marriages to be at a higher than average risk for divorce than same-faith couples. This research also shows that interfaith couples will have difficulties over such religious issues as the religious education of children, observance of religious holidays and ceremonies, and developing and maintaining different social networks. Therefore, we may draw the inference that conflict over religious issues among interfaith couples will be present in these marriages, and couples' communication processes might be strained at times. However, until recently, the religious dimensions of religion that are associated with conflict in personal relationships have not been identified.

Religious Orientation Conflict Over Religious Issues, Social Networks, and Social Support

Religious orientation has been shown to influence argumentativeness over religious issues (Stewart & Roach, 1993) as well as influence interfaith partners' communication behaviors during religious disagreements, social network composition, and perceived social support from social networks. This next section briefly summarizes these findings.

Conflict in marriage has been researched from numerous approaches (see Halford & Markman, 1997). One way scholars have operationalized conflict is as a pattern of "demand-withdraw." Caughlin and Vangelisti (1999) have shown that desire for change in one's spouse predicts this conflict pattern. While this pattern would be likely observed in most any personal relationship, interfaith relationships, where the partners report different religious orientations and disagree over religious issues, are especially vulnerable to this conflict pattern. For example, an extrinsic religious orientation is directly related to demand-withdraw, while an intrinsic religious orientation is indirectly related to demand-withdraw (Hughes & Dickson, 2005). In another study, where religious orientation was operationalized as extrinsic, intrinsic, proreligious, and nonreligious, Hughes (2004) found that extrinsic religiously oriented interfaith partners reported significantly more demand-withdraw conflict during a disagreement over a religious issue than the other orientations, with intrinsics reporting significantly less than all three other orientations.

In terms of demand-withdraw being predicted by the desire for change in a partner, it may be the case that extrinsic interfaith partners, given their preference for practicing their faiths in a social setting or as a means for relationship building, expect or *desire* more collaboration over some or all religious aspects of their marriage (i.e., worship together) from their partners, and where this expectation is resisted by the partner, the extrinsic partner might report the presence of demand-withdraw, whereas intrinsic partners tend to practice their faiths independently, might be less likely to desire this change in a partner, and therefore are less likely report demand-withdraw.

The social network and the social support from these networks are also important relational components for interfaith partners, and this influence can also be understood in terms of religious orientation and overall marital satisfaction among interfaith partners. For example, in general, interfaith partners' reports of marital satisfaction increase as their social networks grow, and the social support from these social networks increases the more one's extrinsic orientation increases (Hughes & Dickson, 2005). Also interesting is that reports of demand-withdraw conflict were inversely related to the social network composition of interfaith partners, which suggests that involvement of the social network of interfaith partners can potentially ameliorate these difficulties facing interfaith partners (Hughes & Greene, 2004).

Conclusion

Religion has long been considered a vital variable in marriage and family research, yet had not been specifically applied to interfaith marriage until recently. Today's changing demographic trends that bring people of different backgrounds together, combined with the many ways in which partners are likely to differ along religious dimensions, are important components toward understanding the increasingly complex nature of interfaith marriage. The religious orientation approach expands on the research on denominational differences and offers scholars a new way to think about the influence of religion on the relational, communication, and social dynamics of interfaith couples. Scholars need to rethink the nature of religion in interfaith marriage. Family members as members of the couples' social network need to understand that they play a pivotal role in the communication and satisfaction of these couples.

References

Alba, R. D. (1991). Intermarriage and ethnicity among European Americans. In P. Ritterband (Ed.), *Jewish intermarriage in its social context* (pp. 3–19). New York: Association for the Social Scientific Study of Jewry.

Allport, G. W. (1937). *Personality: A psychological interpretation.* New York: Holt.

Allport, G. W. (1950). *The individual and his religion.* New York: Macmillan.

Allport, G. W. (1958). *The nature of prejudice.* Garden City, NY: Doubleday.

Allport, G. W. (1959). Religion and prejudice. *The Crane Review, 2,* 1–10.

Allport, G. W. (1960). *Personality and social encounter*. Boston: Beacon.

Allport, G. W. (1963). Behavioral science, religion, and mental health. *Journal of Religion and Health, 2,* 187–197.

Allport, G. W. (1966). The religious context of prejudice. *Journal for the Scientific Study of Religion, 5,* 447–457.

Allport, G. W., & Ross, J. M. (1967). Personal religious orientation and prejudice. *Journal of Personality and Social Psychology, 5,* 432–443.

Alston, J. P., McIntosh, W. A., & Wright, L. M. (1976). Extent of interfaith marriages among White Americans. *Sociological Analysis, 37,* 261–264.

Bahr, H. M. (1981). Toward a conceptualization and treatment of interfaith marriage. *Family Therapy Collections, 25,* 71–88.

Bahr, H. M., & Chadwick, B. A. (1985). Religion and family in Middletown USA. *Journal of Marriage and the Family, 47,* 407–414.

Baron, M. L. (1972). Intergroup aspects of choosing a mate. In M. Baron (Ed.), *The blending American: Patterns of intermarriage* (pp. 39–51). Chicago: Quadrangle.

Batson, C. D. (1976a). Rational processing or rationalization? The effect of disconfirming information on stated religious belief. *Journal of Personality and Social Psychology, 32,* 176–184.

Batson, C. D. (1976b). Religion as prosocial: Agent or double agent? *Journal for the Scientific Study of Religion, 15,* 29–45.

Batson, C. D., & Ventis, W. L. (1982). *The religious experience: A social-psychological perspective*. New York: Oxford University Press.

Batson, C. D., & Schoenrade, P. A. (1991). Measuring religion as quest: Validity concerns. *Journal for the Scientific Study of Religion, 30,* 416–429.

Becker, G. S., Landes, E. M., & Robert, M. T. (1977). An economic analysis of marital instability. *Journal of Political Economy, 85,* 1141–1187.

Bendroth, M. L. (1994). *Fundamentalism and gender: 1875 to the present*. New Haven, CT: Yale University Press.

Booth, A., & White, L. (1980). Thinking about divorce. *Journal of Marriage and the Family, 42,* 605–616.

Burger, E., & Milardo, R. M. (1995). Marital interdependence and social networks. *Journal of Social and Personal Relationships, 12,* 403–415.

Carey, R. G. (1977). The widowed: A year later. *Journal of Counseling Psychology, 24,* 125–131.

Caughlin, J. P., & Vangelisti, A. L. (1999). Desire for change in one's partner as a predictor of the demand/withdraw pattern of marital communication. *Communication Monographs, 66,* 66–89.

Clamar, A. (1992). Interfaith marriage: Defining the issues, treating the problems. *Psychotherapy in Private Practice, 9,* 79–83.

Clements, R. (1998). Intrinsic religious motivation and attitudes toward death among the elderly. *Current Psychology, 17,* 237–248.

Davidson, J. D., & Widman, T. (2002). The effect of group size on interfaith marriage among Catholics. *Journal for the Scientific Study of Religion, 41,* 397–404.

Dickson-Markman, F., & Markman, H. J. (1988). The effects of others on marriage: Do they help or hurt? In P. Noller & M. A. Fitpatrick (Eds.), *Perspectives on marital interaction: Monographs in social psychology of language* (pp. 294–322). Clevedon, UK: Multilingual Matters.

Diggs, R. C., & Socha, T. J. (2004). Communication, families, and exploring the boundaries of cultural diversity. In A. L. Vangelisti (Ed.), *Handbook of family communication* (pp. 249–266). Mahwah, NJ: Lawrence Erlbaum.

Duck, S. W. (1999). *Relating to others* (2nd ed.). Philadelphia: Open University Press.

Eaton, S. C. (1994). Marriage between Jews and non-Jews: Counseling implications. *Journal of Multicultural Counseling & Development, 22,* 210–214.

Ellman, M. J. (1971). Predictors of intermarriage. *Pastoral Psychology, 22,* 35–40.

Falicov, C. J. (1986). Cross-cultural marriages. In N. S. Jacobson & A. S. Gurman (Eds.), *Clinical handbook of marital therapy* (pp. 429–450). New York: Guilford.

Fishman, S. B., Rimor, M., Tobin, G. A., & Medding, P. (1990). *Intermarriage and American Jews today: New findings and policy implications* (A summary report). Waltham, MA: Brandeis University, Maurice and Marilyn Cohen for Cohen Center for Modern Jewish Studies.

Gannoe, M. L., & Monroe, K. A. (2002). Predictors of religiosity among youth aged 17–22: A longitudinal study of the National Survey of Children. *Journal for the Scientific Study of Religion, 41,* 613–622.

Gleckman, A. D., & Streicher, P. J. (1990). The potential for difficulties with Jewish intermarriage: Interventions and implications for the mental health counselor. *Journal of Mental Health Counseling, 12,* 480–494.

Glenn, N. (1982). Interreligious marriage in the United States: Patterns and recent trends. *Journal of Marriage and the Family, 44,* 555–566.

Greely, A. M. (1970). Religious intermarriage in a denominational society. *American Journal of Sociology, 75,* 949–952.

Halford, K. W., & Markman, H. J. (Eds.). (1997). *Clinical handbook of marriage and couples interventions.* Chichester, UK: John Wiley.

Hoge, D. R. (1990). Religion in America: Catholics in the U.S.: The next generation. *Public Perspective, 2,* 11–12.

Hood, R. W., Spilka, B., Hunsberger, B., & Gorsuch, R. (1996). *The psychology of religion.* New York: Guilford.

Horowitz, J. A. (1999). Negotiating couplehood: The process of resolving the December dilemma among interfaith couples. *Family Process, 38,* 303–323.

Huffman, T., Chang, K., Rausch, P., & Schaffer, N. (1994). Gender differences and factors related to the disposition toward cohabitation. *Family Therapy, 21,* 171–184.

Hughes, P. C. (2004). The influence of religious orientation on communication during conflict in interfaith marriages. *Journal of Communication and Religion, 27,* 245–267.

Hughes, P. C., & Dickson, F. C. (2005). Keeping the faith(s): Religion, communication, and marital satisfaction in interfaith marriages. *Journal of Family Communication, 5,* 25–41.

Hughes, P. C., & Greene, R. (2004). Interfaith couples and communication about religious issues. *Family Focus: The Report of National Council on Family Relations, 48,* 16–17.

Hulm, T. S. (1974). Mental health consultation with religious leaders. *Journal of Religion and Health, 13,* 114–127.

Jackson, L. M., & Husberger, B. (1999). An intergroup perspective on religion and prejudice. *Journal for the Scientific Study of Religion, 38,* 509–523.

Johnson, R. (1980). *Religious assertive marriage in the United States.* New York: Academic Press.

Johnson, W., & Warren, D. (1994). Introduction. In W. Johnson & D. Warren (Eds.), *Inside the mixed marriage* (pp. 1–6). Lanham, MD: University Press of America.

Judd, E. (1990). Intermarriage and the maintenance of religio-ethnic identity: A case study: The Denver Jewish community. *Journal of Comparative Family Studies, 21,* 251–268.

Julien, D., & Markman, H. J. (1992). Social support and social networks as determinants of individual marital outcomes. *Journal of Social and Personal Relationships, 8,* 549–568.

Kalmijn, M. (1991). Shifting boundaries: Trends in religious and educational homogamy. *American Sociological Review, 56,* 786–800.

Kalmijn, M., & Bernasco, W. (2001). Joint and separate lifestyles in couple relationships. *Journal of Marriage and Family, 63,* 639–654.

Kenny, D. (1996). Models of non-independence in dyadic research. *Journal of Social and Personal Relationships, 13,* 279–294.

Krishnan, V. (1994). The impact of wives' employment on attitude toward divorce. *Journal of Divorce and Remarriage, 22*(1–2), 87–101.

Lawler, M. G., Graff, A. B., Graff, E. G., Markey, B., Williams, L. M., Riley, L. A., et al. (1999). *Ministry to interchurch marriages: A national study.* Omaha, NE: Crieghton University, Center for Marriage and Family.

Lehrer, E. L., & Chiswick, C. U. (1993). Religion as a determinant of marital stability. *Demography, 30,* 385–341.

Lenski, G. (1961). *The religious factor.* Garden City, NY: Doubleday.

Liao, T. F., & Stevens, G. (1998). Spouses, homogamy, and social networks. *Social Forces, 73,* 693–707.

Maxwell, N. K. (1997). If you're so smart, how come you're intermarried? *Tikkun, 21,* 42–44.

Mayer, E., & Keysar, A. (1997, September). What do rabbis think and do about intermarriage? *Jewish Outreach Institute Newsletter,* pp. 1–7.

McCuctheon, A. L. (1988). Denominations and religious intermarriage: Trends among White Americans in the twentieth century. *Review of Religious Research, 25,* 213–227.

McNamara, P. H. (1992). *Conscience first, tradition second: A study of young American Catholics.* Albany: State University of New York Press.

McQuire, M. B. (1997). *Religion: The social context* (4th ed.). Belmont, CA: Wadsworth.

Merton, R. (1941). Intermarriage and the social structure: Fact and theory. *Psychiatry, 4,* 35–42.

Mezydlo, L., Wauk, L. A., & Foley, J. M. (1973). The clergy as marriage counselors: A service revisited. *Journal of Religion and Health, 12,* 278–288.

Mol, H. (Ed.). (1978). *Identity and religion.* Beverly Hills, CA: Sage.

Ortega, S. T., Whitt, H. P., & William, J. A. (1988). Religious homogamy and marital happiness. *Journal of Family Issues, 9,* 224–239.

Penn, C. D., Hernandez, S. L., & Bermudez, M. J. (1997). Using a cross-cultural perspective to understand infidelity in couples therapy. *American Journal of Family Therapy, 25,* 169–185.

Plante, T. G., & Boccaccini, M. T. (1997). The Santa Clara strength of religious faith questionnaire. *Pastoral Psychology, 45,* 375–387.

Preister, S. (1986). Marriage, divorce, and remarriage in the United States. *New Catholic World, 229,* 9–19.

Reiss, P. J. (1976). The trend in interfaith marriages. *Journal for the Scientific Study of Religion, 5,* 64–67.

Sarna, J. D. (1994). The secret Jewish community. *Commentary, 98,* 55–59.

Sherkat, D. E. (2002). African-American religious affiliation in the late 20th century: Cohort variations and pattern switching 1973–1998. *Journal for the Scientific Study of Religion, 41,* 485–493.

Sousa, L. A. (1995). Interfaith marriage and the individual and family life cycle. *Family Therapy, 22,* 97–104.

Spanier, G. B., & Margolis, R. L. (1983). Marital separation and extramarital sexual behavior. *Journal of Sex Research, 19,* 23–48.

Stanley, S. M. (1998). *The heart of commitment.* New York: Thomas Nelson.

Stanley, S. M., Trathen, D. W., & Bryan, B. M. (1998). *A lasting promise: A Christian guide to fighting for your marriage.* San Francisco: Jossey-Bass.

Stewart, R. A., & Roach, K. D. (1993). Argumentativeness, religious orientation, and reactions to argument situations involving religious versus nonreligious issues. *Communication Quarterly, 41,* 26–39.

Weis, D. L., Slosnerick, M., Cate, R., & Sollie, D. L. (1986). A survey instrument for assessing cognitive association of sex, love, and marriage. *Journal of Sex Role Research, 22*, 206–220.

Whitehead, B. D., & Popenoe, D. (2001). *The state of our unions: The social health of marriage in America* (A summary report). Piscataway, NJ: Rutgers University, The National Marriage Project.

Williams, L. M., & Daniel, A. R. (1987). A longitudinal study of commitment and marriage. *Family Process, 28,* 250–367.

Williams, L. M., & Lawler, M. G. (2000). The challenges and rewards of interchurch marriages. *Journal of Psychology and Christianity, 19,* 205–218.

Wilson, J., & Musick, M. (1996). Religiosity and marital dependency. *Journal for the Scientific Study of Religion, 35,* 30–40.

Wilson, J., Simpson, I. H., & Jackson, D. K. (1987). Church activism among farm couples: Measuring the impact of the conjugal unit. *Journal of Marriage and the Family, 49,* 875–882.

CHAPTER 21

Women Belong in the . . . Pulpit

Family and Professional Tensions in the Lives of Southern Baptist Women Pastors

Helen Sterk

Calvin College

Rebecca Kallemeyn

Calvin College

I t is virtually impossible to escape the association of women with families. In their bodies, women bear the capacity to bring life into the world. Through their bodies, they can help babies transform themselves into children. Within the relational webs of families, women's work connects people in the basic human group of "family."

Grounded in physicality and elaborated through verbal and nonverbal languages, "family" can be a two-edged sword for women. In the name of family, women may be honored as grandmothers, mothers, daughters, and sisters. In the same name, women may be bowed into submission as "my" grandmother, mother, daughter, and sister, subject to not only the protection but also the power of the person claiming ownership. Because "family" is a socially constructed and maintained relation, even though physicality is involved, the ability to name is pivotal. When women are not included as definers of "family," even while they are implicated in the creation and maintenance of families, there is a loss, not only personally but also socially and culturally.

Within religious traditions, "family" often becomes an archetypal metaphor for church, as well as human relations. As such, the contours of the tradition's concept of "family" can drive the ways in which the church operates. When the tradition's concept of family relies heavily on patriarchal norms and practices, it impresses those norms and practices not only on individuals and families but also on the church as a social and cultural group. In such situations, women rarely are allowed a voice in what it means to be a family member, especially a dissident voice, either at home or in the church.

When religious life is considered globally, women often can be seen as the ones defined by, rather than the ones doing the defining of, domestic and religious meanings of family. In fundamentalist Islam, especially as practiced in the Middle East, women are to live in service to family and husbands. With the burka, they literally are invisible in public life. Only at home do they take on dimension (Nafisi, 2003). Given the reach of the influence of fundamentalism globally (Marty & Appleby, 1994, 1997), it is not surprising that women around the world lack a say in how they should live at home and in their churches, mosques, and temples.

Within the Southern Baptist church, there is a struggle for meaning located in the term *family*. The popular media focus on the pronouncements of the Southern Baptist convention might lead one to believe that there is a monolithic understanding of family and family values in that denomination. Pronouncements such as those made by the Conventions in 1979, 1984, and 1998, limiting the role of women in the Southern Baptist denomination, were well covered in popular mass media, leading outsiders to think that patriarchal rule governed everyone in the denomination (Kell & Camp, 2001). However, if the statements of Southern Baptist women who are seeking a new place in the family of the denomination are heard, then it becomes easier to understand why the male leaders of the denomination feel the need to lay down the law as to what family means. They are reacting to actual, not just perceived, challenges.

Southern Baptist women pastors, individually and corporately, are reinterpreting the metaphor of "family" in order to claim their authority as full partners with men in home and church. To show how these women are responding to their religious context in ways that both reinforce and challenge the Southern Baptist ethos, this chapter first will discuss how metaphors function in everyday life as shapers of people's worldviews. Next, we provide a brief explanation of the movement of women into the Southern Baptist ministry. Finally, we explore in detail how Southern Baptist women ministers honed the rhetorical meanings and uses of the metaphor of "family" through the means of *Folio,* the newsletter they publish.

From Metaphor to Worldview

Metaphor has structured understanding ever since the inception of language; this has been theorized at least as long ago as Aristotle. In the *Rhetoric,* Aristotle notes metaphor's brilliance in relation to other uses of words: "Now strange words simply puzzle us; ordinary words convey only what we know already; it is from metaphor that we can best get hold of something fresh" (Aristotle, n.d., p. 1411). Aristotle shows that metaphor allows us to use similarities and particulars in concepts to infer the universal. Centuries later, I. A. Richards called metaphor not "an *added* power of language" but "the omnipresent principle of language" (quoted in Kittay, 1987, 1–3, 17). From the time of Aristotle until now, metaphor continues to be recognized as a potent linguistic source for human understanding and, therefore, stands as a motive for action. In the name of "love," "country," "democracy," "family," and so on, people choose how to conduct their lives (see also Weaver, 1970).

Metaphor is much more than a linguistic technique. Current research in cognitive psychology supports the view that metaphor is "a process of thought rather than a product of language" (Fludernik, Freeman, & Freeman, 1999, p. 388). Kittay (1987) affirms that conceptual metaphors and their structures exist as entities outside of verbal expression. Sadock (1979) emphasizes the controlling work of thought, noting "while the intellectual faculties that are involved [in metaphor] might be *prerequisites* to speech, they are independent of it" (p. 46). Metaphor does not just affect how we talk, but because it grounds human thinking, it influences human action.

In terms of meaning, metaphors work by brushing the known up against the unknown, or the familiar against the strange, and bringing something new into being because of the interaction of the two. Hauser (1991) shows how Max Black's (1962) terminology of "frame" and "focus" clarifies the process of metaphorical meaning making. The sentence hosting the metaphor is the frame, and the focus is the word(s) in which the metaphorical connotations reside. So, the sentence "Molly is a daughter in the family of God" is the frame, and *daughter* and *family* are the foci. Note how the context of the frame brings about the connotations implied by the focus. In God's eyes, "Molly" has a place because she is a daughter in God's family. Therefore, she has a claim of intimate relation. This is an interactive view of metaphor, which holds that the relationship between the frame and the focus gives birth to the metaphor (Hauser, 1991).

Forceville (1995) has shown the necessity of analyzing the overlap between the familiar and the strange evoked by metaphor. The terms *source domain* (the familiar) and *target domain* (the strange, or new) are used to denote the two. The two transform each other. Neither remains the same in the context of the metaphor. For example, in the sentence "The church is a family," the source domain of family and the target domain of church affect each other. The metaphor primarily recharacterizes churches as places of intimate relation between people. However, all the characteristics of families that cannot transfer to churches must be discarded, such as the fact that it is not marriage between two people, physical birth, or adoption that creates the church family. The target domain has momentarily restructured the source domain, though perhaps only minimally (Forceville, 1995).

While theorists still are examining the exact mechanisms of metaphor, most agree that metaphor is central to perception and quite inextricably linked with human life. Osborn (1972) argued that metaphors of light and dark have functioned throughout human history as archetypes that encourage humans to line up that which is light with the good and dark with evil. Archetypal metaphors matter because in the name of those archetypes, humans choose to wage war, make peace, enter into trade, and so on. Lakoff and Johnson (1980) explored the links among metaphor, human thought, and culture, showing the impact of ways of speech on ways of action. While metaphors sometimes just ornament speech, in most cases, they structure thought and action, by aligning certain elements of the domains with good or evil, light or dark, and by allowing certain things to be said while silencing others. In certain religious traditions, particularly conservative American ones such as the Southern Baptist church, family is just such an archetypal, motivating metaphor.

When a religious organization routinely relies on certain metaphors to carry meaning and implicit directives for life, those metaphors become an accepted part of the tradition. Changing them, remapping the domains, is a threatening act that goes to the heart of an organization's identity. In the case of the Southern Baptists, women's reclamation of the metaphor of family has posed just such a threat. The symbolic work of the women called to ministry in Southern Baptist churches was and is seen as redefining the entire denomination in ways that have called for disciplinary retaliation by male church leaders. What the women themselves saw as speaking their minds and hearts, the leaders saw as undermining the very nature and authority of the denomination and, by extension, of God himself. Religious patriarchal authority depends on men heading the family and on God being male.

What we will find in this chapter's analysis is that the symbolic realignment of certain elements of the metaphor of family, as it applies to church in the Southern Baptist denomination, affected not only the men who run that denomination through the Southern Baptist Convention but also the women speaking. Their symbolic reappropriation of "family" in relation to a church that rejected them as pastors transformed the women from pastors into activists.

The Story of Women's Places in the Southern Baptist Denomination

Women have preached throughout Baptist history. Adult baptism is central to its theology, requiring each believer to find truth for herself or himself. Furthermore, each church may make its own decisions as to local leadership. Given these two guiding principles, from early on, women stepped up to individual pulpits, only to be pulled back by the larger group. Maeyken Wens, Anabaptist of Antwerp, was sentenced to death in 1573 for refusing to desist from preaching about Jesus. To silence her on the way to execution, her tongue was screwed to the roof of her mouth (Bellinger, 1993). The Separate Baptists allowed Martha Marshall to lead revivals with her husband in the 1750s and found themselves accused of letting women pray in public (Lynch, 1994). In 1770, a Mrs. Clay was tried for unlicensed preaching and sentenced to a public whipping. An unidentified man stepped forward, paid the fine, and saved her from public humiliation (Lynch, 1994). From 1638 to 1920, 319 women ministered to Free Will and Northern Baptists (Lynch, 1994). Unlike the Quakers, in which women ministered from the first days in harmony, the Baptists acted out a love-hate relation with women pastors.

In the 1900s, the most conservative of the Baptist denominations, the Southern Baptists, opened its seminaries, largely to train women for the mission field (a decision that smacks of ethnocentrism in that women were deemed good enough to preach to foreigners but not to Americans). Women's numbers dropped precipitously between the earlier and later years of the century. In the 1920s, the ratio of women and men in the seminaries was roughly fifty-fifty. By 1950, women made up only about one sixth of the student body in Baptist seminaries, notes historian Henry Leon McBeth (1977). Even though fewer women enrolled in seminaries, the number of women ordained as ministers in the Southern Baptist denomination has risen in the late 1900s and early 2000s. According to most accounts, in 1964, Addie Davis was the first woman to be ordained within the Southern Baptist denomination (Johnson & Pearce, 2004). The second did not follow until 1971. However, the ranks of ordained women ministers grew to 15 by 1982 and to more than 1,200 by 1997 (Anders, 1997).

While Southern Baptist seminaries and individual churches were open to women, at the denominational level, doors were closing. In 1979, the Southern Baptist Convention passed a resolution that rigidly defined family gender roles in line with its interpretation of scripture: Referring to "God's order of authority for his church and the Christian home: (1) Christ is the head of every man; (2) man the head of woman; (3) children in subjection to their parents—in the Lord" (cited in McBeth, 1979, p. 132). In 1984, the Southern Baptist Convention passed "Resolution 3," which read in part as follows: "Whereas while Paul counseled women and men alike in other roles of ministry and service (Titus 2: 1–10), he excludes women from pastoral leadership (I Tim. 2:12) to preserve a submission God required because man was the first in creation and woman was first in the Edenic fall (I Tim. 2:13 ff)" (cited in Kell & Camp, 1999, p. 79). In 1998, the Southern Baptist Convention voted to include a clause endorsing "gracious" wifely submission in the Baptist Faith and Message, a statement that comes as close to doctrine as Baptist thought allows ("50 Christian Leaders," 1998). In 2000, the Southern Baptist Convention added the prohibition of women pastors to the Baptist Faith and Message (Dilday, 2002).

Given the hostility of the Southern Baptist Convention to women pastors, outsiders to the tradition may not understand why there are *any* Southern Baptist churches left that still hire women pastors. The reason is that within the polity of the Southern Baptist church, while the Convention is made up of representatives drawn from the denomination, pronouncements that it makes are not binding on individual churches. And the Baptist denomination has splintered into several denominations, largely over the issue of women pastors. Johnson and Pearce (2004) explain,

> The statement [of 2000 prohibiting women from preaching] is not enforceable on individual Baptist congregations that continue to ordain whom they choose. American Baptist Churches, USA and newer groups like the Cooperative Baptist Fellowship and the Alliance of Baptists, formed in response to the rightward swing of the SBC [Southern Baptist Convention], are more affirming of women ministers.

Indeed, within the American Baptist church, the latest available figures put the number of women pastors in active church service at 1,069 (*American Baptist*

Women, 2003). So, while the Southern Baptist polity is not welcoming to women, women continue to be called to minister in other Baptist denominations and also in individual churches allied with Southern Baptists courageous enough to act counter to the decrees of the Convention.

Method

To study the metaphor of family within the Southern Baptist denomination, a set of stories is needed within which those metaphors are used. Just such a set exists in *Folio,* a small-circulation newsletter, continuously published since 1983 by and for Baptist women pastors. Since the denomination is large and women pastors few, the newsletter functions to unite them. *Folio* provides diverse avenues into understanding how "family" matters to these women playing out a nontraditional role. The articles talk about the women's lives, touching on all aspects of family. Through biography, literal stories of women's situated lives are presented. In the book reviews, what this conservative Christian women's group deems as important to read emerges clearly. In the news reports of the Southern Baptist Convention and denomination, stories of the larger religious context are told. Editorials provide insight into the political temperature of the times and also into the evaluative lenses that the women use to decide what to do next.

Drawing upon feminist qualitative research methodology, both first and second authors read all issues of *Folio,* published quarterly from 1983 to 2003. The second author transcribed all references to family and family roles such as mother, father, daughter, son, and the like as they occurred. The authors analyzed the transcriptions, finding the metaphors clustered naturally into literal, biblical, and personal categories. The first author drafted the analysis, and together, the authors tested out the mapping of the domains of family and church as they are developed in *Folio.*

This methodology uses a "phenomenological approach to the study of lives" (Hornstein, as quoted in Jayaratne & Stewart, 1991, p. 93). Hornstein suggests that there are three stages to a researcher's study of a large data set (as is *Folio*). First, "imaginal variation" constructs the underlying structure of an experience through comparing the presentation of the experience with alternative presentations. The second stage names categories that emerged from themes found in the first stage. It is important to let the data drive the categories rather than a priori categories suggested by preexisting theories (see also Field & Morse, 1985). Third, the researcher "attempts to describe the relationships among the various categories in order to identify the 'pattern' or 'structure' of the experience—the ways in which the elements combine to create a unified whole" (Hornstein, as quoted in Jayaratne & Stewart, 1991, p. 93). This type of grounded theory methodology requires researchers to immerse themselves in the data and to represent them as faithfully as possible (Charmaz, 1990). Through so doing, they allow the subjects to speak in their own words, tell their own stories, and create their own agendas.

Baptist Women in Ministry Transform "Family"

Susan returns to that place of her faith's beginning as home and recalls the memories of persons and personalities who touched her life immeasurably, nourishing her growth and her conviction in 'a mighty and gracious God whose presence is alive to us in the most intimate moments of our lives.' ("Profile: Susan Hull Muesse," 1983, p. 4)

The notion that God has ordained the human family as the "foundational institution of human society" is flawed biblically and theologically. . . . One is called to leave natural familial ties behind in order to live out the primacy of relationship to God with companions in faith. (Molly Marshall in "Responses to the SBC Amendment," 1998, p. 8)

In my case [where her father abused her mother physically for years], I believe the *Bible* and what it says, and yet I am ashamed to be affiliated with a [Southern Baptist] Convention that, at best, has promoted more abusive rhetoric to be used by so-called proud Baptist Men like my father who, in essence, are abusers. (Name withheld in "Responses to the SBC Amendment," 1998, p. 9)

A definite progression in understanding the two-edged nature of "family" as a structuring metaphor can be seen over the first 20 years of *Folio*'s life. Early on, in the 1980s, references to family reflect a relatively flat, unidimensional understanding of that term as referring to a warm, safe place. By the mid-1990s, *Folio* writers showed more awareness of the fact that their earlier definitions of family masked the intimate violence that had been carried out on them by leaders of the Southern Baptist Convention in the name of family. Since the mid-1990s, writers more boldly have expanded the metaphor of family, claiming God as both father and mother and charging the Convention with abuse.

The evolution of family as a metaphor can be seen in three overarching themes: as home base, as barrier to God's call, and as source of abuse.

Family as Home Base

When a Southern Baptist woman feels God calling her, answering is hard. To answer a call to ministry entails stepping out of the neatly tied box of gender identity prepared for her by the Southern Baptist Convention. That national body that speaks for the church at large, if not the churches in particular, has decreed that women should live under the protection of a husband and should support him in his work. The Baptist Statement of Faith and Message says,

A husband is to love his wife as Christ loved the church. He thus has the God-given responsibility to provide for, to protect, and to lead his family. A wife is to submit herself graciously to the servant leadership of her husband even as the church willingly submits to the headship of Christ. She, being in the image of God as is her husband and thus equal to him, has the God-given responsibility to respect her husband and to serve as his helper in managing the household and nurturing the next generation. (*The Baptist Faith and Message*, 2005)

In the family, then, the woman's role is to help her husband, to manage his home, and to bear his children. Presumably, he is the one out doing whatever professional or vocational public work should be done in the broader world. No space is named for partnership marriage, gay or lesbian families, widows, divorced people, or childless people. The same statement says the following of work in the church:

Each congregation operates under the Lordship of Christ through democratic processes. In such a congregation each member is responsible and accountable to Christ as Lord. Its scriptural officers are pastors and deacons. While both men and women are gifted for service in the church, the office of pastor is limited to men as qualified by Scripture. (*The Baptist Faith and Message*, 2005)

What, then, is to be made of women who come from Baptist families, know how they should be run, and still want to be ministers? Weren't they well trained in their families?

According to the women in *Folio*, their families-of-origin are the reasons why they chose to become pastors. For many, their father was a minister or missionary. Over and over, in the biographies of outstanding women, is the phrase, "She grew up in a pastor's family." Or a "missionary's family." Or had a close family connection with church leadership. Says one, "'My parents, grandparents, Sunday School teachers and G.A. director all played an active part in teaching and showing me a Jesus of love and forgiveness" ("Profile: Cathy Cole," 1984, p. 4). So, not only her family-of-origin but also the extended "family" of people in her local church shaped her sense of what faith is and what it demands. Says another, "I was born and raised a Baptist. With a grandfather, father, and four of my father's brothers serving as Baptist ministers, I was certainly a 'full-blooded' Southern Baptist" (Mobley, 1985, p. 6). Within that family, preaching was the norm for generations back. Not only fathers but also mothers and grandmothers provided role models and support for the women: "My calling to ministry was mid-wived by my grandmother who affirmed me and loved me," said one (Fillingim, 1994, p. 5). For some women, the strength of their family support system allowed them the luxury not to notice the pastorate was closed to them because of their sex. For Evelyn Stagg, "It never occurred to Evelyn that she could not attend seminary with Frank [her husband]. . . . The young couple could only afford one set of books, so they studied together each night, forging a partnership that still continues" (Potts, 1999, p. 7). What the church at large moved to deny them, their families granted them.

Many women, such as Evelyn Stagg, married men who affirmed their wives' ministry. In the biographies, statements such as these are familiar. Marie "spent a large portion of her adult life as mother of three children and as co-laborer in ministry with her husband, Bill Bean" (Judge-McRae, 1999, p. 8). One of the most moving was offered by Kathy Minis Findley, who said of her husband, himself a minister, "My husband Fred was always my model of compassionate, caring and selfless ministry. He put his own need for a place ministry aside and stood beside me. . . . Now that I have found more ministry than I can do, he continues to support our family and to be, at times, both mother and father to our son" ("Brotherly Support," 1994, p. 6). In their husbands' affirmation, the women found strength.

The motifs of loving parents, supportive husbands, and responsive children are archetypally light, in Osborn's (1972) terms. Family acts as a source of love, support, and inspiration for the women pastors. And until the Southern Baptist Convention prohibited women from preaching in 2000, Southern Baptist churches provided a relatively uncomplicated home for the women pastors. The combined pressures of an increasingly oppressive denominational context and increasingly complicated home contexts led to significant changes in talk about family in *Folio*.

Family as Barrier to God's Call

As the years passed, though, more and more statements appeared in *Folio* that showed diversity in family experiences and tensions in maintaining a healthy balance between family and career. In 1986, the "Resources" column quotes Virginia Ramey Mollenkott's reflections on her divorce and on the way some Christian marriage books frame the family, saying, "These books risk creating the habit of idolatry with the husband as god and also allows wives to abdicate their own spiritual responsibility" (Zimmer, 1986, p. 6). Not only divorce but also singleness, separation, and widowhood colored life more and more for *Folio* writers. Names changed, as hyphenated names of editors became single names. The requested categories of information expanded from single and married to single, married, divorced, separated, and widowed.

The darker side of family and motherhood surfaced as women shared stories of marital crisis (Campbell-Read, 1993) and of dissatisfaction with staying home and taking care of children, leading women, while enjoying caring for their children, "to inwardly resent what that reciprocates in loss of self" (Williamson, 1994, p. 1). Williamson (1994) called for new ways of understanding family: "The often unrealistic and seemingly impossible-to-reconcile explanations and definitions women adhere to of motherhood and ministry only serve to enhance their dilemma. It becomes necessary to re-think and re-evaluate from time to time" (p. 7). Statements such as these show that as the demands of career increased, stresses related to motherhood and family did, too. And by the mid-1990s, the authors of *Folio* admitted it publicly.

By the late 1990s, women were calling traditional family arrangements into question, praising partner marriage over patriarchal, in direct contradiction to the Baptist Faith and Message. Instead of emphasizing the call to "gracious submission," the women in *Folio* chose to foreground women's and men's equality before God as grounds for equality in life roles and to focus on individual choice under God's authority rather than the authority of the Southern Baptist Convention. Articles called conservative books that pushed the traditional view of marriage and family a waste of time, encouraging readers, "Rather than reading this book, however, spend your time developing the relationships that are mutually support-ive and that celebrate the gifts that God bestows on all God's children, female and male" (Allen, 2000, p. 9). In praise of a different book, the author notes "the reality that women who uphold submission of wives to husbands often end up as victims of abuse" (D. E. Keeney, 2000, p. 5). Grieb (2000) notes the prevalence of domestic violence and the fact that women are the victims of it. Because of recognition that human families were often sources of great pain as well as great comfort, as well as the realistic appraisal of the Southern Baptist Convention as a source of abuse of women leaders, the metaphor of family took on a darker archetypal meaning than it had held earlier.

Family as Source of Abuse

Framing marriage and family as problematic represents a sea change in *Folio*, from innocent to knowing. In the early days of the newsletter, and also the contemporary movement of women into active Baptist ministry, the pastors were young women, newly married, with young children. By the early 2000s, the found-ing editors and writers were older and perceived greater discrepancy between the domains of family/church and a warm, safe place than they did at the beginning. As the religious and secular culture around them changed, so too did their own families. The initially secure bonds of marriage loosened, children grew in unpre-dictable ways, and the church that welcomed them when they were children turned on them when they became adults and sought ordained positions in it. In the late 1990s and early 2000s, *Folio* writers displayed a chastened and more realistic sense of how far their denomination was from an ideal "family." As the realities around them changed, the metaphor did, too. Indeed, many began to call for women pastors to leave that denominational affiliation and find new homes. A new sense of "home" is developed in relation to the church. As the years went on, *Folio* writers turned to the idea of an abusive home situation as their metaphor for their relation with the church.

Already in the mid-1980s, *Folio* writers began to reframe their role as daughters of the church. Many had found hope and a warrant for their leadership in the prophecy of Joel 2:28 and 29, which says the Day of the Lord will come and its sign will be, "I will pour out my Spirit on all people. Your sons and daughters will prophesy . . . Even on my servants, both men and women, I will pour out my Spirit in those days." Claiming Pentecost, narrated in the biblical book of Acts, as the moment where the holy spirit was poured out on women and men, the authors of *Folio* often referred to themselves as those daughters called to prophesy. In 1986, Bellinger referred to an incident where she was called a "disobedient daughter." She called upon her sisters in ministry to be "'disobedient daughters' and to use our prophetic voices to speak to those ears that will hear" (Bellinger, 1986, p. 3). In 1987, Wright compared the church to a mother who had betrayed her child: "For years our mother the church has birthed us into faith, nurtured and suckled us at her breast, and then become our very destroyer by refusing us full entrance into her life and ministry. Why then do we stay with this sometimes rejecting and often fickle mother?" (Wright, 1987, p. 2). Metaphorically daughters, within a mother church and in relation to a Father God, how are the women pastors to live?

To thrive, they needed to refigure "home" and "family." In 1988, Bellinger compared the situation of women pastors to that of Dorothy in the *Wizard of Oz*. While Dorothy could click her heels together and go home, they could not. Their home had changed from what they thought it was. She said, "When we link home, when we link security to an institution, our foundations are shaky" (Bellinger, 1988, p. 7). If home was not the Southern Baptist denomination, what was it?

For many of the writers, their religious home was found in the sisterhood of women pastors and in the new Baptist denominations that developed out of the Southern Baptist one. They expressed deep disappointment that their home no longer had a place for them. Grieb (2000) said, "That one's suffering intensifies when the enemy is also one's Christian brother or sister is still not well understood by the church" (p. 5). The statements of the Southern Baptist Convention excluded them, and by the early 2000s, they were deciding to leave it. Bridges (2000) counseled readers, "You will find a place where women are valued, but you are going to have to leave home. Travel on, sister" (p. 12). When staying was impossible because of the abuse practiced on women leaders within the church family, the pastors did what abused women long have done. When the harm becomes too much to bear, they come to a new understanding of self and leave the situation.

Reimaging God

One of the reasons women pastors could leave such an emotionally harmful setting without losing their faith is that they began to talk about the church family differently. Locating their faith in a transcendent God, the pastors were able to recognize the wounded and wounding humanity of the Southern Baptist denomination. As Grieb (2000) recommended, "Women who read God's story wisely will know better than to trust the fickle crowd. Instead, we will put our trust where it belongs: in the God who is faithful and true, the God who vindicates us" (p. 5). This God, whom feminist theologians such as McFague (1997) argue can only be understood through metaphor, was not the God imaged in the Southern Baptist Convention. No longer was God simply a white-bearded patriarch; now, God took on the characteristics of a mother and grandmother. The metaphors for God take on the richness of both genders in later editions of *Folio*.

Within the context of a conservative Christian denomination such as Southern Baptist, these images might have seemed shocking to some of the readers. Sehested (1997) used women's bodily experience of nursing to encourage women to understand how God cares for them. She compared God to a mother whose baby is so fretful and upset that it cannot latch on to the mother's breast. That situation causes a nursing mother to ache for her child, with an ache that is eased only when the baby calms down enough to feed. "We can be anxious about so many things, that we can't quiet ourselves enough to receive the comfort and nurture that our Divine Mother longs to give us. At times, could God have aching breasts, longing to give us what we need, hoping we'll calm down enough to receive it?" (Sehested, 1997, p. 2). An entire issue (3, 1999–2000) was devoted to exploring metaphors for God, on the premise that exclusively male images limited God and constituted a kind of idolatry, where people determine God's nature rather than God determining God's nature.

Ultimately, the authors of *Folio* endorse language for God that encompasses all human experience, female and male ("BWIM Worship," 2001; Grieb, 2000; R. T. Keeney, 1999–2000; "Methodists Include 'God the Mother,'" 1999). R. T. Keeney (1999–2000) sums up how human experience joins with biblical revelation of the nature of God in ways that reflect both women and men:

> God is not really, literally, my father—my father is a human being who lives in Greenville, SC, with my mother. (God is not literally my mother, either.) God gives me, gives everyone who lives, the gift of life; loves, provides for, cares for, intimately knows and forgives and accepts me, and everyone who lives, in ways that resemble . . . a parent more than any other relationship human beings know—so, metaphorically, God is a heavenly father, my heavenly father. And my heavenly mother. What's so shocking about that? (p. 12)

The authors reconfigured family to include a broader range of Christians than just Southern Baptist and God to transcend the limits of exclusively male associations. They remapped the domains of the metaphor to make their lives as pastors possible. Without the remapping, in order to live a life that cohered with their beliefs, they would have had to give up their sense of calling and would have had to silence their own voices. Rather than do that, they changed the domains of the metaphor.

A New Sense of the Metaphor of Family

Studying the metaphor of family as situated in one fundamentalist religious institution sheds light on how metaphors work as disciplinary agents in human life. When there is agreement on the metaphor and the ways its domains fit together, people act on it without commenting on it. However, when the metaphor is contested, conflict ensues. When women first started to be ordained as ministers in Southern Baptist churches, there were only a few, and in America, the meanings of "family" were shared more widely than they are now. Nothing much needed to be said. But when more women entered church leadership, balances shifted. What once could remain unsaid now needed to be said. And the Convention said, women must submit to their husbands, and women may not be pastors. The implicit, guiding discipline of the metaphor of family as a warm, safe place turned into the explicit, ruling discipline of an angry patriarch demanding women enact roles as he defines them.

The women pastors of the Southern Baptist church could not agree to that. The tenets of their faith told them they were equal to men in the eyes of God. And they claimed the right to redefine the parameters of the metaphors they live by. Richardson (2001) says, "When the human relationships on which such metaphors rely are damaged or damaging, we must emphasize that God exceeds all humans in love, mercy, kindness, and faithfulness" (p. 4). The principle of equality before a faithful God empowered them to enter into explicit definition of the metaphor of the church as family, of God as parent, and of themselves as daughters of the church. In contesting the explicit disciplining of the men of the Southern Baptist Convention, they changed the way the entire denomination worked. When other people assented to their definition of the domains of family, the entire institution shifted. New denominations were formed in which family meant everyone— American Baptist Churches USA, the Cooperative Baptist Fellowship, and the Alliance of Baptists—and the Southern Baptist Convention was forced to retrench even more deeply. Hence, the increasingly restrictive statements about women's roles in the Statement of Faith and Message.

The far-reaching consequences of women claiming God's promises as they understood them for their own are instructive for understanding what is happening around the world in fundamentalist religions. As women see themselves as human, holding the same privileges as men in terms of defining the terms they live by, the institutions created by men are threatened. The institutional response of many fundamentalist religions is to tighten definitions of who belongs to that "family" and how they have to act to remain in good standing. Such tactics do not succeed completely over time. When people are silenced, they tend to find a way to speak, especially if they believe God holds more authority than humans. And the metaphor of family demands the existence of an authoritative parent. In the metaphor, the parent's desires for the family trump the machinations of the brothers. When a womanly space is opened up in the metaphor of the family of God, everything changes.

References

Allen, D. (2000). Book review. *Folio, 17*(4), 9.

American Baptist women in ministry report. (2003, June 5). Retrieved January 18, 2005, from http://www.abwim.org/statistics.htm

Anders, S. F. (1997). Historical record-keeping essential for WIM. *Folio, 15*(2), 6.

Aristotle. (n.d.). *Aristotle's rhetoric: Book III* (W. Rys Roberts, Trans.). Retrieved January 16, 2005, from http://www.public.iastate.edu/~honeyl/Rhetoric/index.html

The Baptist faith and message. (2005). Retrieved January 19, 2005, from http://www.sbc.net/bfm/bfm2000.asp#vi

Bellinger, E. A. (1986). Women mourners into women messengers. *Folio, 4*(2), 3.

Bellinger, E. A. (1988). Going home by a different way. *Folio, 6*(3), 6–7.

Bellinger, E. A. (1993). More hidden than revealed: The history of Southern Baptist women in ministry. In W. B. Shurden (Ed.), *The struggle for the soul of the Southern Baptist Convention: Moderate responses to the fundamentalist movement* (pp. 129–150). Macon, GA: Mercer University Press.

Black, M. (1962). *Models and metaphors.* Ithaca, NY: Cornell University Press.

Bridges, L. M. (2000). Travel on, sister. *Folio, 18*(1), 12.

Brotherly support means action according to women. (1994). *Folio, 12*(1), 6.

BWIM worship celebrates magnitude of God. (2001). *Folio, 18*(5), 1–3, 12.

Campbell-Read, E. R. (1993). Weaving a call: The thread of pastoral care. *Folio, 11*(2), 3.

Charmaz, K. (1990). Discovering chronic illness: Using grounded theory. *Social Science and Medicine, 30,* 1161–1172.

Dilday, R. H. (2002). An analysis of the Baptist faith and message 2000. *Christian Ethics Today, 8,* 40. Retrieved January 19, 2005, from www.christianethicstoday.com/Issue/040/AnAnalysisofTheBaptistFaithandMessage2000ByRusse llH.Dilday_040__.htm

Field, P. A., & Morse, J. M. (1985). *Nursing research: The application of qualitative approaches.* Rockville, MD: Aspen.50 Christian leaders affirm family statement. (1998, July 24). *Associated Baptist Press,* p. 2.

Fillingim, M. (1994). Minister and mother: Finding the intersections. *Folio, 11*(4), 5.

Fludernik, M., Freeman, D. C., & Freeman, M. H. (1999). Metaphor and beyond: An introduction. *Poetics Today, 20,* 383–396. Retrieved January 5, 2005, from www.jstor.org

Forceville, C. (1995). (A)symmetry in metaphor: The importance of extended context. *Poetics Today, 16,* 677–708. Retrieved January 13, 2005, from www.jstor.org

Grieb, A. K. (2000). Vindication. *Folio, 18*(2), 4–5.

Hauser, G. A. (1991). *Introduction to rhetorical theory.* Prospect Heights, IL: Waveland.

Jayaratne, T. E., & Stewart, A. J. (1991). Quantitative and qualitative methods in the social sciences. In M. M. Fonow & J. A. Cook (Eds.), *Beyond methodology: Feminist scholarship as lived research* (pp. 85–106). Bloomington: Indiana University Press.

Johnson, L., & Pearce, J. (2004, August 12). N.C. church marks 40th anniversary of first female Southern Baptist minister's ordination. *NC Baptist Life.* Retrieved January 16, 2005, from http://www.biblicalrecorder.org/content/life/2004/8_12_2004/bl120804nc.shtml

Judge-McRae, L. (1999). Profile: F. Sue Fitzgerald and Marie S. Bean. *Folio, 17*(2), 8–9.

Keeney, D. E. (2000). Resources. *Folio, 17*(4), 8.

Keeney, R. T. (1999–2000). Editor's column. *Folio, 17*(3), 12.

Kell, C. L., & Camp, L. R. (2001). *In the name of the father: The rhetoric of the new Southern Baptist Convention.* Carbondale: Southern Illinois University Press.

Kittay, E. F. (1987). *Metaphor: Its cognitive force and linguistic structure.* Oxford, UK: Clarendon.

Lakoff, G., & Johnson, M. (1980). *Metaphors we live by.* Chicago: University of Chicago Press.

Lynch, J. R. (1994). Baptist women in ministry through 1920. *American Baptist Quarterly, 13,* 304–318.

Marty, M. E., & Appleby, R. S. (Eds.). (1994). *Fundamentalisms observed.* Chicago: University of Chicago Press.

Marty, M. E., & Appleby, R. S. (Eds.). (1997). *Fundamentalisms and society: Reclaiming the sciences, the family, and education.* Chicago: University of Chicago Press.

McBeth, H. L. (1977). The role of women in Southern Baptist history. *Baptist History and Heritage, 12,* 3–25.

McBeth, H. L. (1979). *Women in Baptist life.* Nashville, TN: Broadman Press.

McFague, S. (1997). *Metaphorical theology: Models for God.* Minneapolis, MN: Augsburg Fortress.

Methodists include "God the Mother." (1999). *Folio, 17*(1), 5.

Mobley, J. B. (1985). One woman's story. *Folio, 2*(4), 6.

Nafisi, A. (2003). *Reading Lolita in Tehran: A memoir in books.* New York: Random House.

Osborn, M. A. (1972). Archetypal metaphor in rhetoric: The light-dark family. In R. L. Scott & B. L. Brock (Eds.), *Methods of rhetorical criticism* (pp. 383–399). New York: Harper & Row.

Potts, S. (1999). Profile: Evelyn Stagg. *Folio, 17*(1), 7, 9.

Profile: Cathy Cole. (1984). *Folio, 2*(1), 4.

Profile: Susan Hull Muesse. (1983). *Folio, 1*(2), 4.

Responses to the SBC amendment. (1998). *Folio, 16*(2), 8–9.

Richardson, P. A. (2001). Greater than: Helping children to name God. *Folio, 18*(5), 4–6.

Sadock, J. M. (1979). Figurative speech and linguistics. In A. Ortony (Ed.), *Metaphor and thought* (pp. 46–63). New York: Cambridge University Press.

Sehested, N. H. (1997). Sanctuary for body and soul—women on retreat. *Folio, 15*(1), 1–2.

Weaver, R. M. (1970). Language is sermonic. In R. L. Johannesen, R. Strickland, & R. T. Eubanks (Eds.), *Language is sermonic: Richard M. Weaver on the nature of rhetoric* (pp. 201–225). Baton Rouge: Louisiana State University Press.

Williamson, T. (1994). Motherhood and ministry: The dilemmas of two priority callings. *Folio, 11*(4), 1, 7.

Wright, S. L. (1987). Inclusive theology: The hope of women in the church. *Folio, 5*(3), 1–2.

Zimmer, M. (1986). Resources. *Folio, 3*(4), 6.

CHAPTER 22

Family-School Relationships

Theoretical Perspectives and Concerns

Pamela Cooper

University of South Carolina, Beaufort

Families send their children to school to learn the knowledge and skills needed for success in life. Schools return children to their parents, hoping that families will provide the support that children need to grow and learn. This circle of home and school sharing children is one that has been the focus of much debate and research.

Both parents and educators have a stake in the results of this debate and research. Conceptualizing and operationalizing the connections between home and school have been done in many ways by educators, researchers, and policy makers who have specific theoretical perspectives about the roles, rights, and responsibilities of participants involved in education. The research can be divided into two different, albeit related, perspectives: *between the family and the school* and *within the family*.

The *between the family and the school* perspective focuses on the way the family, as an institution, connects with the school as an institution. This perspective focuses on educational policy, administrative practice, and advice to parents. Schools are advised how to effectively communicate with parents and to entice parents to become more involved (attending parent-teacher conferences, volunteering at the school, communicating with teachers and administrators, joining the parent-teacher organization, etc.). Other literature is directed at parents with suggestions about how best to seek information from schools and to support the school's educational objectives. The body of literature on parental involvement in and with schools is reasonably focused and provides useful advice for policy makers, educators, and parents.

The *within the family* approach to examining the family-school relationship focuses on the systems of interpersonal relationships within the family and how these relationships might have an impact on the child's success, either academically or socially, in the school. Researchers and theorists seek an understanding of the social processes that affect the family-school relationship rather than on generating recommendations for policy or intervention. While the *between the family and school* literature comes primarily from scholars in the fields of educational sociology and educational policy, the *within the family* literature emanates from researchers in the fields of child development, social psychology, family sociology, family therapy, social work, and clinical psychology, among others. These various disciplines have their own research traditions. As a result, the range of family processes, parent/child characteristics, and educational outcomes that have been explored by these researchers is overwhelming. Consequently, this body of research is largely unintegrated and underused.

While the majority of the research has focused on the *between the family and school* relationship, both approaches have yielded significant data concerning the family-school relationship. These can be broadly categorized as academic achievement, social functioning, and family attitudes. See Myers, Schrodt, and Rittenour (Chapter 23, this volume) for a study that spans both approaches by focusing on communication about school in the home.

Evidence suggests that family and school relationships have an effect on student academic achievement (e.g., Fan & Chen, 1999; Ho Sui-Chu & Willms, 1996; Keith and Keith, 1993; Luchuck, 1998). Studies by Shaver and Walls (1998); Izzo, Weissberg, Kasprow, and Fendrich (1999); Faires, Nichols, and Rickelman (2000); Quigley (2000); and Chavkin, Gonzalez, and Rader (2000) all found positive impacts on reading and mathematics. Others, such as Epstein, Simon, and Salinas (1997) and Bloome, Katz, Solsken, Willett, and Wilson-Keenan (2000), have found positive effects on other subjects, such as language arts, literacy, art, science, and social studies.

Research also indicates that family-school relationships affect attendance, aspirations for postsecondary education, enrollment in challenging high school curriculum, and successful transitions from special education to regular classes. In addition, positive relationships between the family and school increase retention and reduce dropout rates among students (Miedel & Reynolds, 1999; Trusty, 1999; Yonezawa, 2000).

Not only do positive family-school relationships affect a student's academic success. Research demonstrates that a student's social functioning can be affected by family-school relationships in areas such as motivation, social competence, student behavior, language, self-help, meaningful youth-adult relationships, and positive student-teacher and peer relationships (Palenchar, Vondra, & Wilson, 2001; Sanders, 1998).

Finally, several studies have documented that family attitudes toward education and their understanding of schools improved as a result of involvement (Bauch, 2000; Sanders, Epstein, & Connors-Tadros, 1999). One study found that, when given specific opportunities to make changes, parenting styles shifted in positive ways as a result of their involvement with schools (Chrispeels & Rivero, 2000).

There are many factors that affect the family-school relationship. Researchers are beginning to measure intermediate variables such as attitude and behavior, gender, and social networks (Chrispeels & Rivero, 2000; Sanders, 1998; Walker & Hoover-Dempsey, 2001). A number of factors have been identified as mediating variables between family and school involvement:

- Parenting styles and how parents and their children interact (Chrispeels & Rivero, 2000; Cooper, Lindsay, & Nye, 2000)
- Parents' sense of their effectiveness as a parent (Bandura, as cited in Shumow & Lomax, 2001)
- Parents' idea of their appropriate role in their children's education (Cooper et al., 2000)
- Parents' own school experiences (Shumow, 2001)
- Student characteristics such as attitude toward school and behavior in school, as well as student's level of intelligence (Sanders, 1998)
- School factors such as class size and school culture and climate, including staff behavior and school policies that encourage or discourage involvement (Ho Sui-Chu, 1997)
- Social, economic, geographical, and political context in which the school operates (Yancey & Saporito, 1997)

Current research also suggests that the following factors seem to affect the level of impact that family-school relationships have on student success in more general ways:

- Demographic characteristics of students such as gender, ethnicity/race, socioeconomic status, and age (Carter & Wojkiewicz, 2000)
- Demographic characteristics of parents such as gender, ethnicity/race, socio-economic status, and education level (Feuerstein, 2000; Ho Sui-Chu, 1997)
- Policy support for parent involvement through funding and staffing decisions; accountability systems that encourage or discourage family-school relationships (Kessler-Sklar & Baker, 2000)
- School level (elementary, middle, or high school) (Adams & Christenson, 2000)
- Goal of the family-school relationship—whether it is targeted toward student success (Newman, 1995)

The body of research on family-school relationships is extensive. It is often difficult to integrate and to "make sense" of it all. This is true for several reasons that will be discussed later in this chapter. Before discussing the reasons, one needs an understanding of the theoretical approaches that have guided the research. To do this, I examine the theories of four key scholars who have investigated the family-school relationship, noting how their theory frames the relationship and thus provides implications for practice. These scholars represent diverse perspectives on the family-school relationship. They also demonstrate a progression in the way theorists and researchers examine the family-school relationship. After each theory is discussed future research and theoretical concerns are examined.

Four Key Theorists and Their Theories

Epstein's School, Family, and Community Partnerships

Epstein's (1995) framework of six types of family involvement is perhaps the most cited theoretical framework in the research on family-school relationships and has been adopted by many practitioners, most notably the National Parent Teacher Association (National PTA, 1998).

Epstein's (1995) examination of parent, teacher, and student views of and actions in education led her to develop a theoretical model of school and family partnerships. The term *partnerships* emphasizes that schools, families, and communities share responsibilities for children through various spheres of influence. These spheres can be separate (i.e., the institutions related to students share little in terms of resources, goals, or responsibility) or they can overlap (i.e., resources, goals, and responsibilities are shared, and a space of partnership is created). Epstein argues for greater overlap and therefore shared responsibility.

Epstein (1995) frames the concept of partnership as a market model whose goal is to generate capital: "We *take stock* in our partnerships; we account for our *resources* and *investments*, and we look for profits for all concerned" (Epstein, 1994, p. 40). At the center of Epstein's model are students—they are, in a sense, the profits. As Epstein suggests, "School and family partnerships do not 'produce' successful students. Rather, the partnership activities that include teachers, parents, and students engage, guide, energize, and motivate students so that *they* produce their own success" (p. 42). In other words, groups invest in the schooling of children, providing students the resources and motivational strategies to choose effective strategies.

In this model, families, schools, and communities have overlapping spheres of influence on student learning. However, schools have a primary responsibility for outreach to parents and communities.

Epstein (1995) provides an empirically generated model of six types of involvement that educators and families could use to achieve the goal of a partnership. The typology is presented below:

Type 1: Parenting—Assisting families with parenting skills and setting home conditions to support children as students, as well as assisting schools to understand families.

Type 2: Communicating—Conducting effective communications from school to home and from home to school about school programs and student progress.

Type 3: Volunteering—Organizing volunteers and audiences to support the school and students. Providing volunteer opportunities in various locations and at various times.

Type 4: Learning at Home—Involving families with their children on homework and other curriculum-related activities and decisions.

Type 5: Decision Making—Including families as participants in school decisions and developing parent leaders and representatives.

Type 6: Collaborating With the Community—Coordinating resources and services from the community for families, students, and the school and providing services to the community.

This model is a *between family and school* model. It develops a coherent vision showing the components of family and school interactions. The child is at the center of this model, which focuses on generating ideas about how families and schools can work together to improve a child's growth and education. Responsibility is shared between family and school. A large body of research has derived from this model, and most studies concur that the dimensions, or types of partnerships, are well defined and provide useful guidelines for researching these relationships. However, there are components to the family-school involvement that are not part of Epstein's (1995) model. For example, Kohl, Lengua, and McMahon (2000) point to the focus of Epstein's model on teacher- and school-initiated behaviors rather than parent-initiated involvement.

Cataloging activities within the six types is a useful step, but more work is needed to capture the variety of forms that family-school relationships can take and create a common language in the field. Stakeholders (educators, parents, community members, students) may have opposing viewpoints about what constitutes involvement and what their roles should be. For instance, Scribner, Young, and Pedroza (1999) found that teachers tend to define parent involvement differently than parents do. Teachers tended to view a parent's role solely as support for academic achievement, while parents viewed it as a means of supporting the total well-being of the child (i.e., social and moral development). Because school personnel and parents may conceptualize parent involvement activities and outcomes differently, there is a need to more fully explore teacher and parent perspectives about what constitutes appropriate collaboration and what role each can and should play in a child's education (Izzo et al., 1999).

Current research reveals that many activities connect families and schools. Although these activities may be quite different from one another, they are all grouped together as "parent involvement" or "family-school connections" or "family school relationships" or "partnerships." Some researchers emphasize activities that take place at the school in their definition of involvement, such as parental attendance at school events and participation in parent-teacher organizations (Desimone, Finn-Stevenson, & Henrich, 2000; Epstein & Dauber, 1995; Mapp, 1999). Other researchers include activities that take place in the home that support student achievement, such as parental help with homework and discussions about issues between parents and children (Faires et al., 2000; Starkey & Klein, 2000). Still other researchers include abstract concepts as well as actual involvement behaviors such as parent aspirations for a child's education in their definition (Lopez, 2001; Yonezawa, 2000). The variety of definitions of family-school relationships makes it difficult to compare studies and models of parent involvement to one another. They also make analysis of the findings of multiple studies a challenge. For practitioners, this lack of clarity may lead to difficulty in making judgments about what kinds of activities to implement, how to implement them, and what results to expect from them.

Comer's Ecological Approach

While Epstein's (1995) model focuses on what educators can do, Comer (1980, 2001) goes further in explaining the family-school relationship. He conceptualizes education as a system. His School Development Program (SDP) is a participatory program that addresses all aspects of education. Using knowledge about relationships and child growth and development, SDP's core is the activity of three teams: a parent team, which involves parents in all levels of school activity; a school planning and management team, which plans and coordinates school activities; and a student and staff support team, which addresses prevention issues and manages individual cases. Particular actions are outlined in Comer's SDP: a comprehensive school plan, which provides a systematic approach to school improvement addressing educational, social, and communication issues for students, teachers, families, and community; staff development directed by the school plan and related to the specific needs of the local school community; and assessment and modification, which generate data and provide feedback to evaluate program effectiveness. These three teams and activities are guided by three principles: consensus, collaboration, and no fault. Consensus prevents fallout from having winners and losers in negotiations, collaboration ensures that multiple points of view are appreciated, and in no fault, all participants accept responsibility for change.

Comer's (1980, 2001) model of family-school relationships works to change the system by building participation and partnership to bring about the optimal development of each child. The model is built on psychological perspectives of development and interaction. Using multiple theories and practices—field theory, human ecological theory, population adjustment model, and the social action model to disperse power and model shared decision making in all aspects of school governance and action—Comer focuses on the relational aspects of individuals involved in the educational process (Comer & Haynes, 1992). For Comer, two aspects of his model guide activities: a commitment to child development-based programming and a systems-based approach to problem solving that maximizes participation and power. Most programs designed to improve schools fail because

> they do not adequately address the developmental needs of children and the potential for conflict in the relationship between home and school, among school staff, and among staff and students. They do not consider the structural arrangements, specific skills, and conditions school people need to address in the complexity of today's schools. This is necessary to be able to cope with the kind of problems too many children present. (Comer, 1980, p. 38)

Comer (1980) focuses on strengthening relationships by promoting dialogue among relevant participants, thereby forcing attention to issues of power and engagement in education at various levels:

> Parents are more likely to support a school program in which they are partners in decision-making and welcome at times other than when their children are in trouble. Parent interest and support for the school and its staff makes it easier for youngsters to relate to and identify themselves with the goals, values, and personnel of the school, a powerful motivation to tune in and turn on to education. At the same time, parental involvement insures that their cultural values and interests are respected. (p. 70)

Comer's (1980, 2001) systems approach, in which all aspects of the program must be simultaneously functioning and a change in any part of the system affects all the other parts, forces attention to all the elements in the school-home collaboration. Thus, schools are improved by assessing needs, prompting action, and evaluating implementation. According to Comer's model, no one agenda takes precedence in the program, and no single group has more power than any other group.

Comer's (1980, 2001) model consists of individuals working within systems. The model's strength is its focus on the relational aspects of all the individuals within the system. Individuals are advanced through systems in which there is a balance of needs, voice, and power. However, two problems exist in Comer's model. First, although it seeks to build relationships between family and school, the focus is still on school-centered definitions of the family-school relationship. Schools have largely been in the position to define what a relationship with the family *is* and what the outcomes should *be*. Honig, Kahne, and McLaughlin (2001) suggest that "the focus of many school-linked services efforts has been on 'fixing' students so teachers can 'really teach' and removing barriers to learning, rather than on rethinking the learning and teaching that occurs for students—all day, in and out of school—and the conditions, resources and supports that enable it" (p. 9). Edwards and Warin (1999) agree that parent involvement efforts sometimes operate to enlist parents as agents of the schools to meet the school's needs—turning parents into "assistant teachers"—instead of using a parent's unique strengths as the child's motivator and nurturer. In general, the most important goal for schools is increased academic achievement of students. Thus, educators tend to value family relationships because of their potential for supporting this goal, sometimes at the expense of family goals.

A second problem with Comer's (1980, 2001) theoretical model is that recent research suggests that not every social and/or cultural group views child development or the connection between family and school in the ways mainstream school personnel do. For example, a study of marginalized migrant families of highly academically successful students in South Texas found that parents were not involved in the traditional involvement activities, such as volunteering at the school or attending school functions. However, they were very involved in that they instilled a strong work ethic in their children and shared their own experiences to emphasize the importance of a good education (Lopez, 2001). Other researchers

(Eunjung, 2002; Gitlin, Buendia, & Crosland, 2003; Gonzalez-Mattingly, 2002; Ho Sui-Chu, 2003; Jeynes, 2003; Jones, 2003; McKay, Atkins, Hawkints, Brown, & Lynn, 2003; Tucker & Herman, 2002; Valencia & Black, 2002) suggest the importance of examining the relationship of minority family characteristics to family involvement in schools. Instead of trying to get diverse families to adopt more dominant cultural approaches to involvement, research suggests the need to capitalize on existing cultural traditions (Peña, 2000; Scribner et al., 1999; Tapia, 2000).

Finally, this model, like Epstein's (1995) model, is a *between the family and school* model. It does not focus on the family or how what happens within the family relates to the school.

Lareau's Parents and Cultural Capital Approach

Lareau's (1989) work provides a contrast to the "one-size-fits-all" model of family-school relationships. Lareau uses the idea of "cultural capital" (defined as "high status cultural resources which influence social selection" [p. 176]) to examine the interactions between parents and school personnel in working-class and middle-class White families. In this view, parents have varying resources available to support their children's education. These resources include educational competence, income and material resources, social networks, relative class position, and so forth. Upper-middle-class families may then use these resources to advance their children's school careers in ways that are not available to working-class families. Lareau found that family-school relationships are shaped by social class, resulting in quite different forms of interaction. Working-class parents have a relationship of separateness with the school because they assume teachers are professionals who make appropriate decisions. In contrast, middle-class parents are connected to the school in ways that allow them to assert their ideas—advocating for their children and influencing the opportunities their children had by using personal and institutional resources.

By framing the nature of differences within social, institutional, and cultural matches and resources, Lareau (1989) provides a relational analysis. Activities of parents are framed in terms of both the material resources available as well as the meanings that the activities shape. Parental actions related to education result from conceptions of appropriate roles for relations between home and school, between teachers and parents, between teachers and students, and so on. The "have–have not" nature of a cultural capital analysis shifts attention from blame to accounting for the use of resources that are inequitably distributed in society.

In one respect, Lareau's (1989) model is a deficit model. The "norm" is that parents should be more involved in their children's schooling. But Lareau's research demonstrates that working-class parents are less involved. For some parents, culture dictates that resistance to unfair practices is the responsible course of action. However, in Lareau's model of family-school relationships, the cultural explanation is not accounted for. The underlying assumption is that all parents should be involved, and those who are not need to have help from others (those who are involved) to develop their involvement skills. Thus, in this model, working-class parents are seen as deficient.

Ryan and Adams's Family-School Relationship Model

The previous three theories focus on explaining the *between family and school relationship.* Although they share an interest in the child and in the child's school success, the range of family processes, parent/child characteristics, and educational outcomes that have been explored by researchers using these theories is diverse. As a consequence, this literature is largely unintegrated and underused.

In an attempt to bring some degree of order to this highly divergent literature of family-school relationships, Ryan and Adams (1995, 1999, 2000) developed the family-school relationship model. The model is aimed at accommodating virtually all variables researchers have used or could use in the study of within-the-family processes. It assumes that all processes in the family or characteristics of family members operate in bidirectional terms so that any one variable can exert some kind of influence over all other variables and be influenced by all other variables. The model also assumes that each of these processes or characteristics occupies a position along a dimension of proximity to the child's schooling outcomes, with some more intimately and closely connected to the outcome than others. The model illustrates that (a) the characteristics of a child or family that have the most immediate connection to school success also have the greatest influence, and (b) the world of the family is not a simple environment. Instead, the family's characteristics are linked together and affect each other in a chain reaction. For example, if a parent is feeling tired or anxious when the teacher sends home a note about poor grades, the parent might yell at the child, who then gets upset and does not do the homework. On the next test, the child does poorly, and so the cycle repeats. As shown in Figure 22.1 (adapted from Ryan & Adams, 1995), the model consists of a series of nested, enclosed shapes, each of which defines a particular class of variables. Each class or level is identified by a number representing the various distances from Level 0, which includes all child outcome variables, to Level 6, which includes all variables that are external to the system of family processes but affect it and, therefore, the child. In the model, the first two levels (Levels 0 and 1) are concerned with the individual child: Level 0 consists of the class of outcome variables (most usually achievement or social behavior in the school), and Level 1 variables represent the child's personal characteristics such as intelligence, frustration, tolerance, or self-esteem. Variables at this level are considered to be very closely related to the school outcome variables. Levels 2 and 3 are concerned with parent-child interactions. Level 2 designates those variables associated with school-focused parent-child interactions such as help with homework and monitoring. Level 3 is concerned with general parent-child interactions that are not focused on school activities but pertain to all of the interactions parents have with their children. With Level 4, the focus of the model shifts to the general nature of family interactions such as family warmth, cohesiveness, or hostility. Level 5 does not focus directly on any relationship involving the children. Rather, this level focuses on the parents—those variables concerned with the personal characteristics of the parents such as measures of parental depression, parents' expectations for child schooling success, and parents' attitudes toward education.

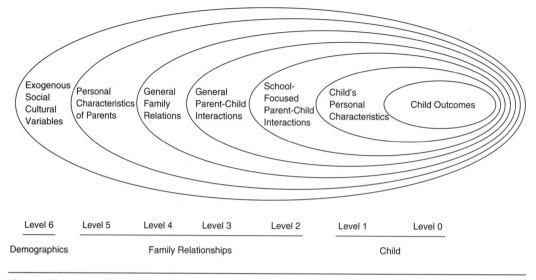

Exogenous Social Cultural Variables | Personal Characteristics of Parents | General Family Relations | General Parent-Child Interactions | School-Focused Parent-Child Interactions | Child's Personal Characteristics | Child Outcomes

Level 6 · Level 5 · Level 4 · Level 3 · Level 2 · Level 1 · Level 0

Demographics · Family Relationships · Child

Figure 22.1   Family School Relationship Model

Finally, at Level 6 are those variables outside the family that constitute the social, cultural, and economic context for the family. Level 6 variables include characteristics of the community in which the family lives, the family's socioeconomic status, or ethnic group.

The evidence to date regarding the usefulness and validity of the model is encouraging. Ryan and Adams (1995) examined 17 studies using path-analytic methods to assess the relationships between family processes and schooling outcomes for children. In 16 of the 17 studies, the observed path structures conformed very closely to what the model predicts: In these studies, the ordering of variables is consistent with the levels in the model, with the effects of variables distant from the outcomes being largely mediated by other variables closer to the outcomes. Using modestly sized, nonrandom samples of elementary school-aged children and their parents, Ketsetzis, Ryan, and Adams (1998) found that family processes and children's characteristics combined in patterns predicted by the model, with the general family processes of conflict and cohesion influencing the school-focused parent-child interactions of support and pressure. The effects on school achievement and social adjustment in the classroom of these two parent-child interactions were mediated by the child characteristics of academic effort and intellectual effectiveness. In summary, the model appears to offer a valid and useful guide to organizing multivariate analyses of family-school relationships.

Concerns for Future Theory Building

Research about the process and effects of family and school relationships is evolving but does not yet provide clear directions for practitioners. This lack of direction results from (a) unclear and overlapping definitions of the concept, its dimensions, and its measurements; (b) lack of cohesive theoretical models and frameworks that can be used to develop and test hypotheses that can inform theory; and (c) the need for a variety of research methods and designs appropriate for the types of questions that need to be explored.

Definition of Family-School Relationships

Educators, parents, community members, and students may have conflicting viewpoints about what constitutes involvement and what their roles should be. Scribner et al. (1999) found that teachers tend to define parent involvement differently than parents do. Teachers tended to view a parent's role solely as a support for academic achievement, while parents viewed it as a means of supporting the total well-being of the child (i.e., social and moral development). Because school personnel and parents may conceptualize parent involvement activities and outcomes differently, there is a need to more fully explore teacher and parent perspectives about what constitutes appropriate collaboration and what role each can and should play in a child's education (Izzo et al., 1999).

The emphasis in the field has been on school-centered definitions of family-school relationships. Many researchers, theorists, and practitioners agree that school-centered definitions do not fully express the range of connections that can and do exist (Edwards & Warin, 1999; McWilliam, Maxwell, & Sloper, 1999). A continued emphasis on school-centered connections can limit the development of the entire field and its ability to identify new directions for greater impact on student outcomes.

Much of the emerging theory and practice of family and school relationships encourages a rethinking of how children develop and how various people and contexts fit together to support that development. A new orientation is emerging in the field, from a school-centric focus toward the creation of reciprocal connections among schools, parents, and community members. These connections are mutually beneficial and reflect the shared goals of those in the field of education. Several of the authors argue for the need to develop an "asset" model, in which parents and communities are considered equal contributors to the education process and are viewed by school personnel as resources instead of as obstacles (Honig et al., 2001; Hulsebosch & Logan, 1998; Kretzmann & McKnight, 1993). They suggest there might also be a need to reconceptualize roles that various people play in the life of a child: not as positions or functions but rather as the natural product of individuals' strengths and assets, regardless of whether they are parents, teachers, community members, or religious leaders. The concept of family-centered practices represents a new way for schools to think of working with families. These family-centered practices emphasize support to families as an important goal in and of itself, not just as a means of supporting the child. In this view, families are seen as the primary decision makers for their children, they are supported as key decision makers in all aspects of school services, and their needs are also considered (McWilliam et al., 1999).

While the family-school relationships field has traditionally paid attention to cultural diversity issues, there is still more to be done to define and clarify "parent involvement" occurring within various cultural and ethnic groups. Researchers need to build understanding about how involvement varies among different cultural groups and adequately capture those experiences in new definitions of family and community connections.

Research has begun to explore the involvement patterns of parents from diverse cultural backgrounds whose children have been successful in the school system. In their study of parental involvement among low-income African American families of high and low achievers, Gutman and McLoyd (2000) concluded that both sets of families recognized the importance of their children's education but had very different strategies for helping their children reach their educational goals. Yan (1999) found that families of successful African American students possessed average or above-average social capital (measured by parent-teen interactions, parent-school interactions, parent-parent interactions, and family norms) and equal or higher levels of school contact than successful White students and nonsuccessful African American families. Scribner et al. (1999) documented some of the ways that Hispanic parents connect with schools, with positive impacts for their children. Future research can continue to build our understanding of how these families are supporting their children's success in school.

Research is also beginning to document the ways in which cultural minority parents interact with their children that support learning, yet differ from more mainstream or middle-class approaches (Cairney, 2000; Yonezawa, 2000). The strategies documented in this body of research reflect the cultural practices of the home that support success in school. Lopez (2001) explored the nontraditional ways Hispanic parents tend to be involved in their children's education, which are not necessarily recognized by educators as parent involvement. Some researchers are beginning to examine nontraditional family structures and the relationship of those structures to the family-school relationship (Mercier & Harold, 2003). More research is necessary to delve deeply into the connections that diverse and nontraditional families create that traditional indicators do not recognize and to consider the reasons why some diverse families might not be involved in the more traditional ways. Building a body of knowledge about the specific practices of various cultural groups can support the validation of those practices by school personnel and may support the sharing of effective practices across cultural groups.

There is a need to better understand different cultural groups' perceptions of appropriate involvement and to understand how these perceptions may be similar to or different from the perceptions of school personnel and majority-group parents. McCollum (1996) suggests that educators in the United States tend to believe that parents should intervene in their children's learning, while immigrant parents often come from cultures where the proper role of a concerned parent is not to intervene in the school's business or question the teacher's practices and expertise. A better understanding of the perceptions that different groups hold would support the development of appropriate outreach and involvement strategies.

Although connecting with families from diverse backgrounds has been a subject of interest, debate, and research, researchers are only beginning to understand the ways that diverse families are already involved in their children's education and how to engage them in new ways. McCollum (1996) lays out an agenda for future research that includes a careful examination of what is actually known about culturally diverse families, their attitudes regarding education, and how they support their children's education through their extended family and informal social networks.

Lack of Theories and Conceptual Frameworks

The body of research in this field that has been developed over the past three decades has not been well connected to theory. The field has greatly benefited from Epstein's (1995) model. However, the other models reviewed here have not received enough attention and have not been widely tested. When researchers have studied the family-school relationship, they have often done so without links to a theoretical framework or model. The findings are difficult to compare and interpret. In addition, they do not inform theory and do not lend themselves to building upon each other. The *between the family and school* approach has offered important initial information to help frame this issue. However, it does not yield understandings of how, why, and under what conditions these connections are linked to student outcomes. The *within the family* approach to examining family-school relationships, while seeking to answer the questions of how, why, and under what conditions, suffers from a failure to attach research questions and design to theory or models of family-school relationships. After uncovering relationships and developing theories and models, further experimental evidence needs to be collected to test those theories and give evidence of direct links of involvement to student success.

Hoover-Dempsey et al. (2001) argue that research would benefit substantially from the increasing use of theoretically based predictions about involvement, suggesting,

> Careful use of theory, the derivation of warranted hypotheses, and the design of studies enabling carefully crafted tests of hypotheses, promise considerable additions to our collective understanding, not only of what happens but also why it happens—e.g., through what mechanisms and under what conditions do specific elements of the parent involvement process influence critical student attributes and outcomes. (p. 10)

Methodological Concerns

Researchers have faced numerous methodological challenges, including choice of design, sampling, measurement, and maintaining internal/external validity. For instance, researchers often relied on measures of perceived parent involvement instead of actual involvement (Catsambis & Garland, 1997; Reynolds, 1992); others, using data from the National Education Longitudinal Study of 1988 (NELS:88), on only one perspective, usually the schools' (teachers' or principals') perception of parent involvement (Carey, Lewis, & Farris, 1998; Fantuzzo, Tighe & Childs, 2000; Izzo et al., 1999); on self-report surveys and questionnaires (Gutman & McLoyd, 2000; Sanders, Epstein, & Connors-Tadros, 1999); or on retrospective information, when surveys or interviews ask information about involvement activities in the past (Miedel & Reynolds, 1999). These data collection strategies tend to distort or bias the findings. Another challenge is the lack of large-scale data sets that are longitudinal and reflect the kinds of questions that researchers need to address as they conduct deeper and richer studies. The National Education Longitudinal Study of 1988 is the most comprehensive data set on parent involvement, including data from parents of more than 24,000 eighth-grade students across the country. However, this data set has numerous limitations that contribute to the weakness of the many studies that rely on it. It does not include information about the initiator of contact, the length of the contact, or the quality of involvement. Only one of the top six parent involvement activities that ranked as important to urban and minority parents and students (Xu, 2001) is included in NELS:88 as indicators for parent involvement. The data set is not highly generalizable beyond the middle school age group. Finally, the NELS:88 includes nonexperimental data and can only be used to determine associations between variables, not cause and effect (Simon, 2000). Epstein and Lee (1995) suggest that researchers look at other national surveys and collect focused data in local, state, and regional surveys or field studies to assess the effects of particular parent involvement practices over time.

Some researchers are beginning to make use of new advances in statistical methodology, tools, and technology that contribute to better quantitative research. Some studies (Ho Sui-Chu, 1997; McWilliam et al., 1999) have used hierarchical linear modeling, which allows researchers to look at multiple factors and outcomes simultaneously. Evaluation studies of the more formal strategies, programs, or initiatives in the field (e.g., Desimone et al., 2000) have also been a source of data on both process and outcomes.

Schorr (1997) presents at least four attributes that new approaches in methodology should have: (a) build on a strong theoretical and conceptual base, (b) emphasize shared interests between researchers and participants, (c) employ multiple methods and perspectives, and (d) offer both rigor and relevance. She comments that using theory as a starting point is in the finest tradition of social sciences, where it is important to "construct conceptual maps that link one thing to another" (Knapp, as cited in Schorr, 1997). When it comes to disentangling such complex forces as the effects of communities, families, or schools on children, parents, or school staff, the most powerful tools are not statistical but conceptual. Therefore, it is essential to ground both design and measurement in theory. Theory-based methodologies help us determine what is working in situations where statistical analysis alone cannot provide the needed answers. Combining outcome measures with an understanding of the process that produced the outcomes can shed light both on the extent of change and on how the change occurred (Schorr, 1997).

In sum, family and school relationships have been measured inconsistently across studies, and research has not yet captured the full picture of these connections and their results (Kohl et al., 2000). Although the theoretical models presented here have yielded promising information about the family-school relationship, much remains to be done. Problems of definition, theory building, and methodology must be addressed before an accurate picture of the family-school relationship will evolve. Researchers and theorists need to be precise in how they measure outcomes to avoid faulty generalizations and conclusions and to clarify the sometimes conflicting evidence about the impact of family-school relationships. To advance, the field must continue to explore new methods for capturing the processes and outcomes of these complex interactions between schools and families.

References

Adams, K. S., & Christenson, S. L. (2000). Trust and the family-school relationship: Examination of parent-teacher differences in elementary and secondary grades. *Journal of School Psychology, 38,* 477–497.

Bauch, J. P. (2000). *Parent involvement partnerships with technology: Transparent school model.* Nashville, TN: Transparent School Model.

Bloome, D., Katz, L., Solsken, J., Willett, J., & Wilson-Keenan, J. A. (2000). Interpellations of family/community and classroom literacy practices. *Journal of Educational Research, 93,* 155–163.

Cairney, T. H. (2000). Beyond the classroom walls: The rediscovery of the family and community as partners in education. *Educational Review, 52,* 163–174.

Carey, N., Lewis, L., & Farris, E. (1998). *Parent involvement in children's education: Efforts by public elementary schools* (National Center for Education Statistics, Statistical Analysis Report). Washington, DC: National Center for Education Statistics. Retrieved from http://nces.ed.gov/pubsearch/pubsinfo.asp?pubid=98032

Carter, R. S., & Wojkiewicz, R. A. (2000). Parental involvement with adolescents' education: Do daughters or sons get more help? *Adolescence, 35,* 29–44.

Catsambis, S., & Garland, J. E. (1997). *Parental involvement in students' education during middle school and high school* (CRESPAR Report 18). Baltimore, MD: Johns Hopkins University. Retrieved from http://www.csos.jhu.edu/crespar/techReports/Report18.pdf

Chavkin, N. F., Gonzalez, J., & Rader, R. (2000). A home-school program in a Texas-Mexico border school: Voices from parents, students, and school staff. *The School Community Journal, 10,* 127–137.

Chrispeels, J. H., & Rivero, E. (2000, April). *Engaging Latino families for student success: Understanding the process and impact of providing training to parents.* Paper presented at the annual convention of the American Educational Research Association, New Orleans, LA.

Comer, J. P. (1980). *School power: Implications of an intervention project.* New York: The Ress Press.

Comer, J. P. (2001, April 23). Schools that develop children. *American Prospect, 12,* 1–12.

Comer, J. P., & Haynes, N. M. (1992, June). *Summary of school development program effects.* New Haven, CT: Yale Child Study Center.

Cooper, H., Lindsay, J. J., & Nye, B. (2000). Homework in the home: How student, family, and parenting-style differences relate to the homework process. *Contemporary Educational Psychology, 25,* 464–487.

Desimone, L., Finn-Stevenson, M., & Henrich, C. (2000). Whole school reform in a low-income African American community: The effects of the CoZi Model on teachers, parents, and students. *Urban Education, 35,* 269–323.

Edwards, A., & Warin, J. (1999). Parental involvement in raising the achievement of primary school pupils: Why bother? *Oxford Review of Education, 25,* 325–341.

Epstein, J. (1994). Theory to practice: School and family partnerships lead to school improvement and student success. In C. Fagnano & B. Werber (Eds.), *School, family, and community interactions: A view from the firing lines* (pp. 30–52). Boulder, CO: Westview.

Epstein, J. L. (1995). School/family/community partnerships: Caring for the children we share. *Phi Delta Kappan, 76,* 701–712.

Epstein, J. L., & Dauber, S. L. (1995). Effects on students of an interdisciplinary program linking social studies, art, and family volunteers in the middle grades. *Journal of Early Adolescence, 15,* 114–144.

Epstein, J. L., & Lee, S. (1995). National patterns of school and family connections in the middle grades. In B. A. Ryan, G. R. Adams, T. P. Gullotta, R. P. Weissberg, & R. L. Hampton (Eds.), *The family-school connection: Theory, research, and practice* (pp. 109–154). Thousand Oaks, CA: Sage.

Epstein, J. L., Simon, B. S., & Salinas, K. C. (1997). Involving parents in homework in the middle grades. *Research Bulletin, 18,* 1–4. Retrieved from http://www.pdkintl.org/edres/resbul18.htm

Eunjung, K. (2002). The relationship between parental involvement and children's educational achievement in the Korean American family. *Dissertations Abstracts International, 62,* 3021A.

Faires, J., Nichols, W. D., & Rickelman, R. (2000). Effects of parental involvement in developing competent readers in first grade. *Reading Psychology, 21,* 195–215.

Fan, X., & Chen, M. (1999, April). *Parental involvement and students' academic achievement: A meta-analysis.* Paper presented at the annual convention of the American Educational Research Association, Montreal, Canada.

Fantuzzo, J., Tighe, E., & Childs, S. (2000). Family involvement questionnaire: A multivariate assessment of family participation in early childhood education. *Journal of Educational Psychology, 92,* 367–375.

Feuerstein, A. (2000). School characteristics and parent involvement: Influences on participation in children's schools. *Journal of Educational Research, 94,* 29–40.

Gitlin, A., Buendia, E., & Crosland, K. (2003). The production of margin and center: Welcoming-unwelcoming of immigrant students. *American Educational Research Journal, 40,* 91–122.

Gonzalez-Mattingly, N. L. (2002). When discourses collide: An ethnography of migrant children at home and in school. *Journal of Literary Research, 34,* 150–164.

Gutman, L. M., & McLoyd, V. C. (2000). Parents' management of their children's education within the home, at school, and in the community: An examination of African-American families living in poverty. *The Urban Review, 32,* 1–24.

Ho Sui-Chu, E. (1997). *Parental involvement and student performance: The contributions of economic, cultural, and social capital.* Unpublished doctoral dissertation, University of British Columbia.

Ho Sui-Chu, E. (2003). Students' self-esteem in an Asian educational system: The contribution of parental involvement and parental investment. *School Community Journal, 13,* 65–84.

Ho Sui-Chu, E., & Willms, J. D. (1996). Effects of parental involvement on eighth-grade achievement. *Sociology of Education, 69,* 126–141.

Honig, M. I., Kahne, J., & McLaughlin, M. W. (2001). School-community connections: Strengthening opportunity to learn and opportunity to teach. In V. Richardson (Ed.), *Handbook of research on teaching* (4th ed., pp. 972–1001). Washington, DC: American Educational Research Association.

Hoover-Dempsey, K. V., Battiato, A. B., Walker, J. M. T., Reed, R. P., DeJong, J. M., & Sandler, H. M. (2001). Why do parents become involved in their children's education? *Review of Educational Research, 67,* 3–42.

Hulsebosch, P., & Logan, L. (1998). Breaking it up or breaking it down: Inner-city parents as co-constructors of school improvement. *Educational Horizons, 77,* 30–36.

Izzo, C. V., Weissberg, R. P., Kasprow, W. J., & Fendrich, M. (1999). A longitudinal assessment of teacher perceptions of parent involvement in children's education and school performance. *American Journal of Community Psychology, 27,* 817–839.

Jeynes, W. H. (2003). A meta-analysis: The effects of parental involvement on minority children's academic achievement. *Education Urban Society, 35,* 202–218.

Jones, T. G. (2003). Contribution of Hispanic parents' perspectives to teacher preparation. *The School Community Journal, 13,* 73–97.

Keith, T. Z., & Keith, P. B. (1993). Does parental involvement affect eighth-grade student achievement? Structural analysis of national data. *School Psychology Review, 22,* 474–496.

Kessler-Sklar, S. L., & Baker, A. J. L. (2000). School district parent involvement policies and programs. *The Elementary School Journal, 101,* 101–118.

Ketsetzis, M., Ryan, B. A., & Adams, G. R. (1998). Family processes, parent-child interactions, and child characteristics influencing school-based social adjustment. *Journal of Marriage and the Family, 60,* 374–387.

Kohl, G. O., Lengua, L. J., & McMahon, R. J. (2000). Parent involvement in school conceptualizing multiple dimensions and their relations with family and demographic risk factors. *Journal of School Psychology, 38,* 501–523.

Kretzmann, J. P., & McKnight, J. L. (1993). *Building communities from the inside out: A path toward finding and mobilizing a community's assets.* Evanston, IL: Center for Urban Affairs and Policy Research.

Lareau, A. (1989). *Home advantage.* London: Falmer.

Lopez, G. R. (2001, March). *On whose terms? Understanding involvement through the eyes of migrant parents.* Paper presented at the annual convention of the American Educational Research Association, Seattle, WA.

Luchuck, V. L. (1998). *The effects of parent involvement on student achievement.* Unpublished master's thesis, Salem-Teikyo University.

Mapp, K. L. (1999). *Making the connection between families and schools: Why and how parents are involved in their children's education.* Unpublished doctoral dissertation, Harvard University, Cambridge, MA.

McCollum, P. (1996). Obstacles to immigrant parent participation in schools. *IDRA Newsletter, 23,* 10.

McKay, M. M., Atkins, M. S., Hawkints, T., Brown, C., & Lynn, C. J. (2003). Inner-city African American parental involvement in children's schooling: Racial socialization and social support from the parent community. *American Journal of Community Psychology, 32,* 107–114.

McWilliam, R. A., Maxwell, K. L., & Sloper, K. M. (1999). Beyond "involvement": Are elementary schools ready to be family-centered? *School Psychology Review, 28,* 378–394.

Mercier, L., & Harold, R. (2003). At the interface: Lesbian-parent families and their children's schools. *Children & Schools, 21,* 20–24.

Miedel, W. T., & Reynolds, A. J. (1999). Parent involvement in early intervention for disadvantaged children: Does it matter? *Journal of School Psychology, 37,* 379–402.

National PTA. (1998). *National standards for parent/family involvement programs.* Chicago: Author.

Newman, L. (1995). *School-agency-community partnerships: What is the early impact on student school performance?* Menlo Park: California Healthy Start.

Palenchar, D. R., Vondra, J. I., & Wilson, J. A. (2001, March). *Parental involvement and early school functioning.* Paper presented at the annual convention of the American Educational Research Association, Seattle, WA.

Peña, D. C. (2000). Parent involvement: Influencing factors and implications. *Journal of Educational Research, 94,* 42–54.

Quigley, D. D. (2000). *Parents and teachers working together to support third grade achievement: Parents as Learning Partners (PLP) findings* (CSE Technical Report 530). Los Angeles: Los Angeles Compact on Evaluation/National Center for Research on Evaluation, Standards, and Student Testing.

Reynolds, A. J. (1992). Comparing measures of parental involvement and their effects on academic achievement. *Early Childhood Research Quarterly, 7,* 441–462.

Ryan, B., & Adams, G. (1995). The family school relationship model. In B. A. Ryan, G. R. Adams, T. P. Gullotta, R. P. Weissberg, & R. L. Hampton (Eds.), *The family-school connection: Theory, research and practice* (pp. 3–28). Thousand Oaks, CA: Sage.

Ryan, B., & Adams, G. (1999). How do families affect children's success in school? *Educational Quarterly Review, 6,* 30–43.

Ryan, B., & Adams, G. (2000). The family school connection. *Transition Magazine, 30,* 12–19.

Sanders, M. G. (1998). The effects of school, family, and community support on the academic achievement of African American adolescents. *Urban Education, 33,* 385–409.

Sanders, M. G., Epstein, J. L., & Connors-Tadros, L. (1999). *Family partnerships with high schools: The parents' perspective* (CRESPAR Report 32). Baltimore: Johns Hopkins University. Retrieved from http://www.csos.jhu.edu/crespar/techReports/Report32.pdf

Schorr, L. B. (1997). *Common purpose: Strengthening families and neighborhoods to rebuild America.* New York: Doubleday.

Scribner, J. D., Young, M. D., & Pedroza, A. (1999). Building collaborative relationships with parents. In P. Reyes, J. D. Scribner, & A. Paredes-Scribner (Eds.), *Lessons from high-performing Hispanic schools: Creating learning communities* (pp. 36–60). New York: Teachers College Press.

Shaver, A. V., & Walls, R. T. (1998). Effect of Title I parent involvement on student reading and mathematics achievement. *Journal of Research and Development in Education, 31,* 90–97.

Shumow, L. (2001, March). *The task matters: Parental assistance to children doing different homework assignments.* Paper presented at the annual convention of the American Educational Research Association, Seattle, WA.

Shumow, L., & Lomax, R. (2001, March). *Parental efficacy: Predictor of parenting behavior and adolescent outcomes.* Paper presented at the annual convention of the American Educational Research Association, Seattle, WA.

Simon, B. S. (2000). *Predictors of high school and family partnerships and the influence of partnerships on student success.* Unpublished doctoral dissertation, Johns Hopkins University.

Starkey, P., & Klein, A. (2000). Fostering parental support for children's mathematical development: An intervention with Head Start families. *Early Education and Development, 11,* 659–680.

Tapia, J. (2000). Schooling and learning in U.S.-Mexican families: A case study of households. *The Urban Review, 32,* 25–44.

Trusty, J. (1999). Effects of eighth-grade parental involvement on late adolescents' educational experiences. *Journal of Research and Development in Education, 32,* 224–233.

Tucker, C. M., & Herman, K. C. (2002). Using culturally sensitive theories and research to meet the academic needs of low-income African American children. *American Psychologist, 57,* 762.

Valencia, R. R., & Black, M. S. (2002). "Mexican Americans don't value education!" The basis of the myth, mythmaking, and debunking. *Journal of Latinos & Education, 1,* 81–103.

Walker, J. M. T., & Hoover-Dempsey, K. V. (2001, March). *Age-related patterns in student invitations to parental involvement in homework.* Paper presented at the annual convention of the American Educational Research Association, Seattle, WA.

Xu, J. (2001, March). *Middle school family involvement in urban settings: Perspectives from minority students and their families.* Paper presented at the annual convention of the American Educational Research Association, Seattle, WA.

Yan, W. F. (1999). Successful African American students: The role of parental involvement. *Journal of Negro Education, 68,* 5–22.

Yancey, W. L., & Saporito, S. J. (1997). The social ecology of education: The case of Houston's inner-city public schools. In G. D. Haetel & M. C. Wang (Eds.), *Coordination, cooperation, collaboration* (pp. 136–149). Philadelphia: The Mid-Atlantic Regional Educational Laboratory at Temple University.

Yonezawa, S. S. (2000). Unpacking the black box of tracking decisions: Critical tales of families navigating the course placement process. In M. G. Sanders (Ed.), *Schooling students placed at risk: Research, policy, and practice in the education of poor and minority adolescents* (pp. 109–137). Mahwah, NJ: Lawrence Erlbaum.

CHAPTER 23

The Impact of Parents' Use of Hurtful Messages on Adult Children's Self-Esteem and Educational Motivation

Scott A. Myers

West Virginia University

Paul Schrodt

University of Kansas

Christine E. Rittenour

University of Nebraska–Lincoln

T he family plays a central role in the success and failure of children's academic performance (Alwin & Thornton, 1984; Ellis & Smith, 2004; Kandel & Lesser, 1969; see also Chapter 22, this volume). Factors such as parental education, parental income, family size, family type (e.g., stepfamily, first marriage), family environment (e.g., neighborhood, school system), and parental use of rewards and punishments are known to have an effect on students' academic aspirations (Astone & McLanahan, 1991; Crandall, Dewey, Katkovsky, & Preston, 1964; Fantuzzo, Tighe, & Childs, 2000; Hauser & Sewell, 1986; Mercy & Steelman, 1982; Rehberg & Westhy, 1967; Teachman & Paasch, 1998).

However, these factors may not be as influential as once speculated, nor are these factors as influential as the direct messages children receive from their parents about their academic performance (Hauser & Mossel, 1985; Kunz & Peterson, 1977). For many children, a common topic of conversation with their parents centers on academic performance. These topics include academic expectations (Besharat, 2003; Fan & Chen, 2001), completion of homework (Fehrmann, Keith, & Reimers, 1987; Keith & Keith, 1993), plans for higher education (Dekovic, 2002; Rehberg & Westhy, 1967), and the importance of grades (Dornbusch, Ritter, Leiderman, Roberts, & Fraleigh, 1987). When these conversations contain elements of optimism and encouragement, children report decreased test anxiety, higher grades, higher rates of homework completion, and greater educational aspirations (Besharat, 2003; Courts, 2004; Dekovic, 2002; Xu & Corno, 1998).

What is less known, however, is what happens when these conversations contain elements of pessimism, discouragement, and lowered expectations. Because students' academic success is positively correlated with parental expectations (Fan & Chen, 2001), it is likely that an indirect relationship exists between the hurtful messages adult children receive about their academic performance from their parents and their subsequent academic performance. This proposed relationship is worthy of examination for two reasons. First, Vangelisti (1992) reported that the topic of career and education is often at the root of communication problems between adolescents and their parents. Because familial relationships are differentiated from other relationships by the involuntary nature of the parent-child bond and the rich relational history that pervades the relationship (Fitzpatrick & Caughlin, 2002), the messages exchanged between parents and their adult children may contain negatively valenced emotions that seem more intense or irrational than emotions expressed in other relationships (Vangelisti, 1993). Second, most hurtful events are caused by people known to the recipient of the message (Leary & Springer, 2001), with messages occurring in family relationships being rated as more hurtful than messages occurring in nonfamily relationships (Vangelisti & Crumley, 1998). As such, in this chapter, we report on an empirical study designed specifically to explore how parents' use of hurtful messages affects adult children's academic performance.

To reach this end, this chapter is organized into four sections. In the first section, we explore the characteristics of hurtful messages and examine the forms of hurtful messages, the perceived intensity and intent of these messages, and the reactions to hurtful messages. In the second section, we identify the method by which we examined hurtful messages in the context of parents and adult children. In the third section, we provide the results obtained in our study. In the fourth section, we discuss our findings and suggest some directions for future research.

Review of Literature

A hurtful message is a message in which something is said or done to emotionally injure the recipient of the message (Vangelisti & Young, 2000). Hurt feelings, which are common across all interpersonal relationships (Leary & Springer, 2001), have several relational consequences for the recipient (Vangelisti & Sprague, 1998). These consequences include feelings of vulnerability (Vangelisti, 2001), increased relational devaluation (Leary, 2001), fear of rejection (Snapp & Leary, 2001), decreased social desirability (Leary, Springer, Negel, Ansell, & Evans, 1998), and decreased relational distance, quality, satisfaction, and closeness (Vangelisti, 1994; Vangelisti & Crumley, 1998; Vangelisti & Maguire, 2002; Vangelisti & Young, 2000). It comes as no surprise, then, that hurtful messages connote a judgment about an individual's value and importance to another person, cause feelings of emotional insecurity, and are considered negative (Mills, Nazar, & Farrell, 2002; Vangelisti & Sprague, 1998). As such, hurtful messages emerge in several forms, differ in their perceived intent and intensity, and result in one of several reactions.

Forms of Hurtful Messages

A hurtful message can emerge in several forms, although the type and topic may depend on the relational context. To date, four studies conducted on hurtful messages in the interpersonal context (i.e., romantic partners, friends) have identified several types and topics of hurtful messages. In one study, Leary et al. (1998) identified 6 types of hurtful messages, including active disassociation (i.e., when an individual is rejected or abandoned by another person), passive disassociation (i.e., when an individual is ignored or not included in activities by another person), criticism, betrayal, teasing, and feelings of being taken for granted. Among romantic partners, infidelity and deception, in addition to active disassociation, passive disassociation, and criticism, also are considered to be hurtful messages (Feeney, 2004). In earlier research, Vangelisti (1994) identified 10 types of hurtful messages, including accusations, evaluations, directives, unsolicited advice, expressed desires, informed statements, questions, threats, jokes, and lies. In addition, she classified hurtful messages into nine categories, with topics ranging from an individual's romantic or nonromantic relationships, sexual behavior, physical appearance, ability, and intelligence; to personality traits, self-worth, and use of time; to ethnicity and religion. More recently, Young and Bippus (2001) extended Vangelisti's research by adding nine additional topics, including revelations (i.e., self-disclosure), negative labels and characterizations (i.e., a negative assessment of the relational partner), idiosyncrasies and background (i.e., a negative critique of the relational partner), value as a relational partner, behavioral criticisms, third party (i.e., an evaluation of a third-party relationship), de-escalation and avoidance (i.e., a desire to minimize relational involvement), hopes and plans, and threats.

Together, the results of these studies suggest that hurtful messages can emerge in various forms. Much less is known, however, regarding the forms of hurtful messages communicated by parents to their children in the context of academic performance. In a general investigation of hurtful messages exchanged between children (i.e., 7–10 years old) and parents, Mills et al. (2002) found that children identified two general classes of hurtful messages: messages centered on discipline (e.g., yelling, denying permission) and messages of disparagement and disregard (e.g., disrespect, sibling favoritism, teasing, criticism). Given this research, it is likely there are specific forms of hurtful messages adult children receive from their parents about their academic performance. For example, educational researchers have suggested that parental expectations may be one source of hurtful messages for young adults, as Felder (1987) reported that 49% of the college students in his sample felt their parents' expectations were too high and 10% felt their parents' expectations were too low. Likewise, younger siblings typically report lower parental expectations than older siblings (Teachman, 1996; Teachman & Paasch, 1998), suggesting that parental expectations may change over time and may differ for each child. Thus, parents may communicate their expectations about academic performance in ways that are more or less hurtful to their children, yet to date, researchers have not explored the associations among parents' use of hurtful messages and adult children's educational outcomes. In this study, we consider adult children to be children who are (a) older than age 18, (b) enrolled in postsecondary studies, and (c) still dependent, to some degree, on their parents for financial support. To explore these types of messages, then, we advanced two initial research questions:

RQ1:   What are the types of hurtful messages adult children report receiving from their parents about their academic performance?

RQ2:   What is the perceived hurtfulness of each type of hurtful message?

Perceived Intensity and Intent of Hurtful Messages

A second, and perhaps more important, dimension of hurtful messages involves the relational meaning taken from such messages, as hurtful messages differ in their perceived intensity and their perceived intent. Intensity, which refers to the strength associated with a message, plays a vital role in how a hurtful message is perceived and appraised. When a hurtful message is considered to be intense, the message is generally viewed as less helpful, less comforting, and less likely to be stated out of concern (Young, 2004). Specifically in families, the frequency of hurtful messages is positively associated with the degree to which family members distance themselves from the member who said something hurtful to them and is negatively associated with forgiving the family member who uttered the hurtful message (Vangelisti & Maguire, 2002).

Intent, however, is only one of several possible motivations behind hurtful messages (Leary & Springer, 2001). In fact, hurtful messages often are uttered accidentally, under the guise of helpfulness, or out of thoughtlessness, insensitivity, or indifference

(Leary & Springer, 2001; Leary et al., 1998), with the vast majority of messages perceived as unintentional (Vangelisti, 1994). Nevertheless, when a message is perceived as intentional, the effects can be detrimental to the relationship, in part because intentionality is judged by the recipient rather than by the sender of the message (Vangelisti & Sprague, 1998). Recipients of a hurtful message who believe the message was intentional report greater relational distance, more intense hurt feelings, less relational satisfaction, and less psychological closeness than recipients of a hurtful message who believe the message was unintentional (Vangelisti & Young, 2000). By contrast, the recipient of a hurtful message is less upset when the message is perceived as accidental (Leary et al., 1998) or when the message is phrased in a humorous manner (Young & Bippus, 2001).

Given the importance of the parent-child relationship, then, the perceived intensity and intent of a hurtful message received from parents may be tied not only to their child's sense of self-worth but also to their child's academic motivation. Defined as an "individual's overall feelings of personal worth, usefulness and degree of liking of self" (Glauser, 1984, p. 117), self-esteem has commanded the attention of researchers who support the relationship between self-concept and communication (Berger, 1987; Rancer, Kosberg, & Silvestri, 1992). As Daly (1987) noted, self-concept theories posit that the self-concept is formed in large part on the basis of social interaction with others. Given that positive parental messages are positively associated with children's perceptions of global self-worth (Ellis, 2002), it stands to reason that the perceived intensity and intent of parents' hurtful messages are inversely associated with adult children's global self-esteem. To test this line of reasoning, we advanced two hypotheses:

H1:   The perceived intensity of parents' hurtful messages about academic performance is inversely associated with adult children's global self-esteem.

H2:   The perceived intent of parents' hurtful messages about academic performance is inversely associated with adult children's global self-esteem.

At the same time, it is interesting to note, theoretically, that researchers have typically investigated student self-esteem in conjunction with student motivation. Motivation has been defined as an energy or force that moves an individual to action and then directs and sustains that action (Brophy, 1983; Wlodkowski, 1978; Zorn, 1991). Although student motivation is widely recognized for its importance in the college classroom (Christophel, 1990; Christophel & Gorham, 1995; Dobos, 1996; Gorham & Millette, 1997; Jaasma & Koper, 1999), the impact of student motivation on academic achievement is still somewhat debated (Christensen & Menzel, 1998). In essence, the debate over the importance of educational motivation has tried to assess how a relatively stable personality trait is subject to situational fluctuations (Zorn, 1991). "Trait motivation is a general, enduring predisposition toward learning, while state motivation is an attitude toward a specific class" (Christophel, 1990, p. 324). In her investigation of teacher immediacy behaviors, student motivation, and learning, Christophel found that cognitive and affective learning were largely attributable to state motivation, with trait motivation at no time accounting for more than 2% of the variance. Schrodt, Wheeless, and Ptacek (2000), however, reported a negligible association among student reports of context-based motivation (i.e., motivation in the college classroom educational context) and academic performance as measured by students' self-reported grade point averages. Consequently, the impact of student motivation on student performance is somewhat dependent on whether the researcher is interested in examining specific learning outcomes or general performance indicators.

In general, educational researchers have reported positive associations among student self-esteem, motivation, and academic performance (Christophel, 1990; Murphy & Roopchand, 2003; Schrodt et al., 2000), though much less is known regarding how both student characteristics mediate the associations among parental communication behaviors, such as hurtful messages about academic performance and actual student performance. Indeed, parental messages of hurt are likely to disconfirm children, communicating to them that they are valueless and insignificant as human beings, and would thus be more likely to have a deleterious effect on their self-esteem and motivation. As such, we predicted that the perceived intensity and intent of parents' hurtful messages about academic performance would be inversely associated with adult children's educational motivation. To test this line of reasoning, we advanced two hypotheses:

H3:   The perceived intensity of parents' hurtful messages about academic performance is inversely associated with adult children's educational motivation.

H4:   The perceived intent of parents' hurtful messages about academic performance is inversely associated with adult children's educational motivation.

Reactions to Hurtful Messages

Aside from the perceived intensity and intent of a hurtful message, an individual's reaction to a hurtful message is almost always associated with an antisocial response (Leary & Springer, 2001). Vangelisti and Crumley (1998) identified three general categories of reactions to hurtful messages, including active verbal, acquiescence, and invulnerable reactions. An *active verbal* reaction is an approach reaction in which recipients respond directly to the hurtful message and includes behaviors such as attacking the individual, defending themselves, and being sarcastic. An *acquiescence* reaction is an avoidant reaction in which recipients yield to the hurtful message and includes behaviors such as crying, apologizing, and conceding. An *invulnerable* reaction is an approach reaction in which recipients respond indirectly to the hurtful message and includes behaviors such as laughing, being silent, or ignoring the message. Other ways in which individuals react to a hurtful message include expressing anger, arguing, saying something critical or nasty in response to the hurtful message, engaging in retaliatory behaviors, and seeking other relationships (Leary & Springer, 2001; Leary et al., 1998).

Undoubtedly, adult children will react in a similar manner to hurtful messages received from their parents about their academic performance, though researchers have yet to investigate these specific types of reactions. Vangelisti and Crumley

(1998) stated that a reaction to a hurtful message is shaped by the way in which the message is interpreted or appraised, which may be dependent on the type of relationship in which the message occurred. Because the parent-child relationship exerts the largest influence on children's future academic plans (Kandel & Lesser, 1969) and attitudes about school (Papanastasiou & Papanastasiou, 2004; Parsons, Adlers, & Kaczala, 1982), adult children have undoubtedly been the recipients of several messages from their parents about their academic performance. At the same time, the parent-child relationship is the longest lasting relationship adult children have had to date, and thus the relationship is bounded by a relational history containing parent-child exchanges about issues such as academic performance. To explore how adult children react specifically to hurtful messages about their academic performance, we advanced our third research question:

RQ3:   How do adult children react to the hurtful messages received from their parents about their academic performance?

Method

Participants

Participants were 231 students enrolled in an upper division communication course at a large Mid-Atlantic university. The majority of participants were European American ($n = 203$, or 88%), were currently living (when not at school) with both their mother and father ($n = 163$, or 71%), were either first or second born ($n = 159$, or 71%), and described their family-of-origin as a traditional, nuclear family ($n = 178$, or 77%). Table 23.1 contains these demographics.

Procedures and Instrumentation

Following the procedures used by Young and Bippus (2001), participants were asked to provide a "script" of a conversation that took place between themselves and their parents about their academic performance. Within the script, participants were asked to identify the hurtful message. Once the script was completed, participants completed several measures. The measures included an assessment of the perceived hurtfulness, the perceived intensity, and the perceived intentionality of the hurtful message; a measure of self-esteem; a measure of context-based motivation; and a checklist of their reactions to the hurtful message.

The *perceived hurtfulness of the message* (Young & Bippus, 2001) was assessed by asking participants the degree to which the message (a) was perceived as hurtful and (b) caused emotional pain. Responses were solicited using a 7-point Likert-type scale ranging from (a) *not at all hurtful* (1) to *extremely hurtful* (7) and (b) *it did not cause any emotional pain* (1) to *it caused a great deal of emotional pain* (7). Previous reliability coefficients of .83 and .85 (Young, 2004; Young & Bippus, 2001) have been obtained for the two-item measure. In this study, a reliability coefficient of .79 ($M = 4.22$, $SD = 1.32$) was obtained for the measure.

Table 23.1   Demographics of Respondents

Ethnicity	
European American	203
African American	11
Hispanic American	3
Native American	4
Other	10
Currently live with	
Biological or adoptive mother	44
Biological or adoptive father	6
Both mother and father	171
Mother and stepfather	8
Father and stepmother	4
Other	8
Family-of-origin	
Traditional, nuclear family	186
Stepfamily	19
Single-parent family	30
Other	5

The *perceived intensity of the message* (Young, 2004) was assessed using a three-item measure inquiring about the degree to which the message was perceived as intense. Responses were solicited using a 5-point Likert scale ranging from *strongly disagree* (1) to *strongly agree* (5). Young (2004) obtained a reliability coefficient of .85 for a five-item measure of perceived intensity. In this study, a reliability coefficient of .80 ($M = 3.10$, $SD = .94$) was obtained for the measure.

The *perceived intentionality of the message* (Young & Bippus, 2001) was assessed by asking participants the degree to which the message was (a) perceived as intentional and (b) purposefully hurtful. Responses were solicited using a 7-point Likert-type scale ranging from (a) *unintentional* (1) to *intentional* (7) and (b) *he or she did not know the statement would hurt my feelings* (1) to *he or she hurt my feelings on purpose* (7). Young and Bippus (2001) obtained a reliability coefficient of .75 for the two-item measure. In this study, a reliability coefficient of .71 ($M = 3.17$, $SD = 1.37$) was obtained for the measure.

Student self-esteem was measured using the 10-item Rosenberg Self-Esteem Scale (Rosenberg, 1965). Responses were solicited using a 5-point Likert scale ranging from *strongly disagree* (1) to *strongly agree* (5). Schrodt (2003) obtained a reliability coefficient of .86 for the scale. In this study, a reliability coefficient of .88 ($M = 3.89$, $SD = .64$) was obtained for the scale.

Student context-based motivation was measured using the 12-item Student Motivation Scale (Christophel, 1990). Responses were solicited using a 7-point semantic differential scale for 12 sets of bipolar items. The scale can measure trait-like, context-based, and state motivation based on the directions given to respondents

(Schrodt et al., 2000). In this study, context-based motivation was measured by directing participants to report their motivation for their educational experiences. Previous reliability coefficients ranging from .91 to .95 have been reported for the state motivation version of the scale (Myers, 2002; Myers & Rocca, 2000). In this study, a reliability coefficient of .90 ($M = 4.67$, $SD = .96$) was obtained for the scale.

Reactions to hurtful messages were assessed by asking participants whether (i.e., yes, no) they used each of the 10 reactions to hurtful messages identified previously by Vangelisti and Crumley (1998).

Data Analysis

The first research question was answered using analytic induction (Bulmer, 1979). Each of the 231 scripts was read separately by two of the three authors, and a preliminary categorical coding system was devised. The responses were read again, which led to a refinement of the initial categorical coding system and the subsequent development of seven categories. The 231 responses then were coded by one of the two authors (one author coded 105 scripts, one author coded 126 scripts) using the coding system, with 220 of the 231 responses falling into one of the seven deductively derived categories. (Eleven responses were coded as "other.") Following a similar procedure used by Vangelisti and Crumley (1998), the stability of the coding system was determined by having the one author code the 105 responses coded by the other author, resulting in an intercoder reliability of .85.

The second research question was answered by computing a mean perceived hurtfulness score for each of the seven categories. The four hypotheses were examined using a series of Pearson product-moment correlations. The third research question was answered by first summing and averaging the items that comprised the reaction categories (i.e., active verbal, four items; acquiescence, three items; invulnerable, three items) and then computing a series of paired t tests among the three categories.

Results

The first research question inquired about the types of hurtful messages adult children report receiving from their parents about their academic performance. Seven types of hurtful messages about adult children's academic performance emerged from the analysis (see Table 23.2).

Academic performance is a result of poor decision making on the part of the child and stems from the adult child's inability to make effective decisions about study habits, about striking a balance between academic life and social life, and about choosing a major. *Academic performance fails to meet parents' expectations* centers on the adult children's grades and how these grades are not acceptable to parents. *Academic performance will result in some form of life-altering consequence* focuses on how the adult child's poor performance will affect the potential to find worthwhile employment after college or enroll in a graduate program. *Academic performance*

Table 23.2   Types of Hurtful Messages

Academic Performance . . .	Number of Responses
Is a result of poor decision making	39
Fails to meet parents' expectations	37
Will result in some form of life-altering consequence	37
Is a result of little effort	37
Is a cause of parents' disappointment	28
Will result in some form of parental-imposed sanction	27
Pales in comparison to siblings	15

is a result of little effort on the part of the child and revolves around the adult child failing to work to his or her potential. *Academic performance is a cause of parents' disappointment* stems from parents stating that they are disappointed, in some way, about the adult child's academic performance. *Academic performance will result in some form of parental-imposed sanction* centers on how a parent will impose a punishment on the adult child due to the poor academic performance. *Academic performance pales in comparison to siblings* revolves around parents comparing the performance of the child with his or her siblings.

The second research question inquired about the perceived hurtfulness of each type of hurtful message. In descending order (by mean score), the *academic performance pales in comparison to siblings* message ($M = 4.57$, $SD = 1.07$) was perceived as the most hurtful, followed by *academic performance will result in some form of life-altering consequence* ($M = 4.50$, $SD = 1.38$), *academic performance is a result of poor decision making* ($M = 4.31$, $SD = 1.64$), *academic performance is a cause of parents' disappointment* ($M = 4.21$, $SD = 1.33$), *academic performance is a result of little effort* ($M = 4.18$, $SD = 1.26$), *academic performance will result in some form of parental-imposed sanction* ($M = 4.07$, $SD = 1.02$), and *academic performance fails to meet parents' expectations* ($M = 3.97$, $SD = 1.30$). A post hoc analysis of variance revealed no significant differences in the perceived hurtfulness of the seven types of hurtful messages, $F(7, 223) = .70$, $p = .67$, $\eta^2 = .02$.

The first hypothesis posited that the perceived intensity of parents' hurtful messages about academic performance would be inversely associated with adult children's global self-esteem. The hypothesis was not supported, $r(231) = -.08$, $p = .11$.

The second hypothesis posited that the perceived intent of parents' hurtful messages about academic performance would be inversely associated with adult children's global self-esteem. The hypothesis was not supported, $r(231) = -.07$, $p = .15$.

The third hypothesis predicted that the perceived intensity of parents' hurtful messages about academic performance would be inversely associated with adult children's educational motivation. The hypothesis was supported, $r(231) = -.12$, $p < .05$.

The fourth hypothesis predicted that the perceived intent of parents' hurtful messages about academic performance would be inversely associated with adult children's educational motivation. The hypothesis was supported, $r(231) = -.14$, $p < .01$.

The third research question inquired about how adult children react to the hurtful messages received from their parents about their academic performance. It was

Table 23.3   Reactions by Adult Children to Hurtful Messages

Reaction	Yes	No
I defended myself and my actions. (active)	184	47
I apologized. (acquiescent)	96	135
I said something sarcastic. (active)	86	145
I said something negative about my parent. (active)	82	149
I did not say a word. (invulnerable)	72	159
I told my parent I agreed with him or her. (acquiescent)	68	163
I began crying or cried later in private. (acquiescent)	63	168
I asked my parent to provide some elaboration. (active)	56	175
I ignored what my parent said. (invulnerable)	48	183
I laughed. (invulnerable)	45	186

found that adult children react using active verbal responses ($M = .44$, $SD = .25$) at a higher rate than acquiescence responses ($M = .33$, $SD = .32$), $t(230) = 3.81$, $p < .01$, or invulnerable responses ($M = .24$, $SD = .25$), $t(230) = 8.15$, $p < .01$. Adult children also react using acquiescence responses more frequently than invulnerable responses, $t(230) = 2.92$, $p < .01$. Table 23.3 reports the frequency with which adult children use each of the 10 types of reactions identified by Vangelisti and Crumley (1998).

Discussion

The goal of this chapter was to explore the types of hurtful messages adult children receive from their parents about their academic performance, specifically focusing on how such messages are associated with adult children's global self-esteem and educational motivation. Overall, our results revealed seven types of hurtful messages that were academic specific, provided minimal evidence to suggest that such hurtful messages are inversely associated with adult children's educational motivation, and indicated that adult children are most likely to react to such hurtful messages using active verbal responses.

The first finding that emerged from this study was the identification of seven types of hurtful messages that adult children report receiving from their parents about their academic performance (RQ1). These seven types of hurtful messages communicated to adult children are that poor academic performance (in descending order of frequency) (a) is a result of poor decision making, (b) fails to meet parents' expectations, (c) will result in some form of life-altering consequence, (d) is a result of little effort, (e) is a cause of parents' disappointment, (f) will result in some form of parental-imposed sanction, and (g) pales in comparison to siblings' academic performance.

The first type of hurtful message was *academic performance is a result of poor decision making* on the part of the child. This message stemmed from the adult child's inability to make effective decisions about study habits, to strike a balance between academic life and social life, and to choose a major. Respondents reported that these messages often were stated by parents in response to their engagement in activities other than studying, such as socializing and participating in extracurricular activities. For instance, one respondent stated that his father let him know that he "could be doing a lot better as long as [he worked] harder, stud[ied] more, and part[ied] less." Another respondent reported that his father said, "You should be making As and participating in academic extra-curriculars, not athletic extra-curriculars." Still other poor decisions were attributed to students' inability to select a major. One respondent commented on how her parents disagreed with her decision to switch her major from accounting to marketing:

> In my first semester as a junior I changed my mind. I wanted to major in marketing. Accounting wasn't for me; I didn't like it at all. When I told my parents they were not happy with my decision. They told me that I should stick with accounting. I told them how I didn't like it and how it was something I didn't want to do for the rest of my life. They still didn't agree with my new major. They told me that I wouldn't make as much money and it was going to be hard to find a marketing job. Then they said "we do not support you in changing your major." It is not their decision to make. I want to have a job that I enjoy.

Regardless of the topic, the message resulted in adult children feeling hurt about their ability to make a decision, particularly because the use of this message type implied the respondents were careless, indecisive, or not competent enough to make an informed decision.

The second type of hurtful message was *academic performance fails to meet parents' expectations,* which centered on the adult children's grades and how these grades were not acceptable to parents. In almost all cases, this message focused specifically on the adult child receiving any grade lower than an "A" or "B," suggesting that parents expected their adult children to perform academically at any grade better than average (i.e., "C"). For example, one respondent reported what his father said to him when he received his report card: "Look at all these As and Bs. How could you possibly get a D in calculus? That one bad grade makes all the good grades disappear." In a similar vein, several respondents were reminded by their parents that although their grades were acceptable, their grades could be better. Several respondents reported that their parents would make statements such as, "Although [your] grades were good, they needed to be better," "That [grade] is good, but could have been better," "My mom told me I could do better," and "A B isn't good enough." One respondent summarized this type of hurtful message succinctly:

> Whenever I received my report card and I didn't receive all As and Bs my parents would make me feel like I was a failure and wouldn't succeed in life. They were never just happy with what I earned. I could've worked extremely hard to get a C and not at all to get an A, but it hurts when I would get put down for it.

The third type of hurtful message was *academic performance will result in some form of life-altering consequence* and focused on how adult children's poor academic performance would affect their potential to find worthwhile employment after college or the opportunity to enroll in a graduate program. The respondents reported that parents used this message to threaten them by stating that either a negative alternative would inevitably occur or a goal or future opportunity would go unfulfilled. Many respondents were threatened with negative alternatives such as working at a gas station, supermarket, or fast-food restaurant. As one respondent noted, his father informed him that if he didn't get his act together, he would be "pumping gas for a living." Still other respondents were threatened with being transferred from the university to a community college: "My dad pretty much put me in my place and told me if I fail another class, he said I'd have to move back home and go to [Alternative] University." In other instances, respondents reported their parents informed them that their future goals, such as attending graduate school, having a successful career, or gaining admittance into a professional program, would not be accomplished if their academic performance did not improve. As one student recounted, his father's words—"How do you expect to be a doctor if you can't get an A in chemistry?"—served as a warning about his future. Although the intent behind this type of message was not always identified, many respondents reported that this message type was used as form of motivation so that they would have a better future than their own parents. One respondent stated that his father would continually remind him that if he continued to receive poor grades, he "would go nowhere in life," and another respondent stated that his father would reiterate, "I don't want you to end up cleaning toilets like your mother."

The fourth type of hurtful message was *academic performance is a result of little effort* on the part of the child and revolved around adult children failing to work to their potential.

Many respondents reported that their parents assumed that their academic performance was the result of a lack of diligence and effort on their part, coupled with parents failing to recognize that their coursework was difficult. As a result, these respondents stated that their parents would label them as stupid, lazy, or dumb. Such messages received by the adult children were "Are you stupid?" "Stop being so damn lazy and go get help with the stupid class; it can't be that hard," "I think you're just taking the easy way out so you don't have to study because you're lazy and don't want a challenge," and "My father looked at my mistake and told me I was the dumbest smart kid he had ever met." For some respondents, the perceived lack of effort was attributed to a lack of parental understanding based on the parents' educational background or occupation. For instance, one respondent said, "Both my parents have B.S. degrees where they have taken lots of science and math classes in college. My father makes comments about how my classes aren't as hard . . . because my major is a B.A." For other respondents, the perceived lack of effort was attributed to a lack of foresight on the part of the adult child. As one respondent recounted,

> After receiving a low grade on a biology exam, my parents responded by saying that I should have known better and that I needed to study harder if I wanted to make it. They implied that I didn't put any effort into studying, but in reality I had studied as much as I could. They seemed more upset about my studying than the grade itself.

The fifth type of hurtful message was *academic performance is a cause of parents' disappointment* and stemmed from parents' statements of disappointment, in some way, about the adult child's academic performance. Parents sent this type of hurtful message, either explicitly or implicitly, to convey dissatisfaction with their child. These messages were either stated directly—"My parents told me how disappointed they were when I got a 'D'"—or sensed by the adult child—"She looked very disappointed" or "I could still sense the disappointment in her voice." Furthermore, for many respondents, the content of this particular message type was perceived as far more hurtful than the manner in which the message could have been conveyed. For example, three respondents stated that being told that their parents were disappointed in them was worse than had their parents yelled at them:

> One time I got a D in a class and my mom told me that she was disappointed and knew I could do better. This was worse than her yelling at me.

> One time I got an F in my Econ class and my dad told me that he thought I [could do] better than that. And that hurt worse than him yelling at me.

> When it came time to get my report card I got a D in the class. This was the first time I did worse than a C. I was prepared to get yelled at, however my dad did not yell at all. He said, "I am extremely disappointed." This was worse than being yelled at because I could see the disappointment in his face. And letting [my parents] down sucked.

The sixth type of hurtful message was *academic performance will result in some form of parental-imposed sanction* and centered on how parents would impose a punishment on their adult child due to the poor academic performance. These sanctions involved the loss of a tangible resource or activity but not the loss of emotional support or affection. Contained within this message type was the reminder by parents that because they were financing their adult children's education, they not only expected their children to perform well academically, but all financial assistance would be halted if the academic performance did not improve. Respondents reported that their parents made statements such as "with the amount of money they spend, I should be doing much better in school" and "because of my low GPA, [my parents] threatened to pull me out for a semester, and told me if it happened again I would be pulled out for good." Moreover, adult children were threatened with having to move back home and reside with their parents. Other parental-imposed sanctions included not being allowed to study abroad, repossessing their cars, and not being allowed to engage in social activities, opportunities all made possible by parental financial support.

The seventh type of hurtful message was *academic performance pales in comparison to siblings* and revolved around parents comparing the performance of their child with siblings. Instead of (or at times in addition to) criticizing adult children for not performing well, not realizing their potential, or not working hard, parents used messages comparing their adult children's academic performance to the children's siblings such as, "Why can't you be more like your brother?" or "But your sister always maintains a 3.0." For other respondents, parents would make comments about how although their child's academic performance was not on the same level as their other children, they also did not expect the performance to be at the same level. One respondent recalled,

> This past semester I was shooting for straight As just because I want to have straight As once before I graduate. Unfortunately, I realized I have a B in one class and there was virtually no hope of getting an A. When I told my parents about this, my dad said, "I was just expecting you to graduate." This upset me because my father has never expected for me to do great in school. He always expected my older brothers to do good . . . it upset me because he assumes I will do average and doesn't think I have the ability for straight As.

At the same time, adult children (i.e., children over the age of 18 who are enrolled in postsecondary studies and are somewhat dependent on their parents for financial support) did not perceive these seven types of hurtful messages to vary in their hurtfulness. This finding may have occurred for one of two reasons. First, although all seven types of hurtful messages are rooted in some form of criticism, criticism is usually most hurtful when the message implies relational devaluation (Leary, Koch, & Hechenbleikner, 2001). Relational devaluation, which refers to the perception held by one individual about how important, close, or valued he or she is to another individual (Leary et al., 1998), may not be an issue in the parent-child relationship when it comes to hurtful messages about adult children's academic performance due to the longevity of the parent-child relationship. Second, Vangelisti, Maguire, Alexander, and Clark (2004) posited that for a family environment to be considered hurtful, hurtful messages must occur on a regular basis. Because these particular messages center only on the adult children's academic performance and constitute only one of many problematic topics (e.g., extracurricular activities, romantic relationships, behavior problems, family relationships) discussed between parents and children (Vangelisti, 1993), these hurtful messages about academic performance may arise only when the adult children's academic performance is the topic of conversation. In addition, because adult children expect their parents to comment on their academic performance regardless of the quality of the performance (Dornbusch et al., 1987; Fan & Chen, 2001), they may pay less attention to the content of the hurtful message (i.e., the seven types of hurtful messages) about their academic performance and may focus instead on the circumstance (e.g., course difficulty; competing social, work, and school demands) that resulted in the message being conveyed by their parents in the first place.

The first two hypotheses predicted that the perceived intensity (H1) and perceived intent (H2) of parents' hurtful messages about academic performance would be inversely associated with adult children's global self-esteem. Neither hypothesis was supported. Indeed, parents' hurtful messages about academic performance may have very little to do with adult children's self-esteem, though upon closer examination of the method and measures used in this report, several alternative explanations can account for these findings. For example, on a theoretical level, it might be suspected that the amount of time that has transpired since such messages were received would influence the association among hurtful messages and self-esteem. Children who receive hurtful messages from their parents about their academic performance at an earlier age are perhaps more susceptible to the deleterious effects of such messages on their self-esteem.

At the same time, adult students may become inoculated from the effects of parents' hurtful messages about academics, especially for students who no longer reside with their parents, though such speculation awaits empirical testing and comparison. A second, and perhaps more plausible, explanation involves the use of a global self-esteem measure. In the absence of a reliable and valid measure of *academic* self-esteem, we relied on the most widely used measure of global self-esteem. It stands to reason, instead, that parents' hurtful messages about academic performance may only influence the academic part of an adult child's self-esteem, a part that the child may have come to terms with much earlier in life and reconciled as having very little to do with his or her overall sense of self-worth. Consequently, a much more direct examination of the associations among parents' hurtful messages about academic performance and adult children's academic self-esteem may yield different results.

The second set of hypotheses predicted that the perceived intensity (H3) and perceived intent (H4) of parents' hurtful messages about academic performance would be inversely associated with adult children's educational motivation (i.e., context-based motivation). Contrary to the findings for self-esteem, the results provided support for both hypotheses, though the effect sizes were minimal at best. In other words, parents' hurtful messages about academic performance are inversely associated with adult children's motivation toward education in general, though the association is so small that other factors appear to have a more direct and meaningful association with context-based motivation. For example, the amount of time that has transpired since receiving hurtful messages about academic performance may mediate the negative effects of such messages on adult children outcomes. In terms of educational motivation, however, it is possible that parental communication may have less to do with the general motivation of most college students than other, more intrinsic factors such as previous academic success (or failure), perceived relevance of the course material, sense of self-efficacy, and locus of control, to name a few. At the same time, parents' hurtful messages about academic performance may actually serve as a negative reinforcement mechanism that enhances student motivation in some cases. In other words, some adult students may actually view their parents' hurtful messages as a source of motivation to continue their education and prove their parents wrong. Thus, the small, inverse associations found here may be further examined in future research by examining other variables that might soften the negative effects of parents' hurtful messages, such as resiliency, peer social support, and coping mechanisms.

The third research question explored how adult children react to parents' hurtful messages about their academic performance. It was found that adult children report using active verbal reactions at a higher rate than either acquiescence reactions or invulnerable reactions. According to Vangelisti and Crumley (1998), an active verbal reaction is one in which individuals directly respond to a hurtful message by asking for an explanation, engaging in a verbal attack, or defending their actions. For adult children, directly responding to their parents' hurtful messages is plausible for two reasons. First, by this time, adult children know how their parents communicate and undoubtedly have developed a repertoire of communication behaviors to put to use when engaging in a particular communicative episode with their parents, particularly an episode that is undoubtedly perceived as unpleasant. Second, because adult children are interested in establishing their independence, particularly at this point in their lives, they may be less likely to acquiesce or appear invulnerable to avoid appearing also immature, childish, or spoiled. Thus, for adult children, using an active verbal reaction may be the best way in which they can appear responsible or grown up.

To gain a more comprehensive picture of the role that hurtful messages about academic performance play in the parent-child relationship, future research should take two directions. First, it might prove beneficial to explore parents' perceptions of the hurtful messages they convey to their children. Leary et al. (1998) found that individuals who use hurtful messages consider their use as more accidental and less intentional yet justifiable based on the recipient's actions. Parents who use hurtful messages as a way to comment on their adult children's academic performance may view their use of these messages in the same way. The use of these messages also may be dependent on parent sex. For whatever reasons, the respondents in this study reported that the majority of hurtful messages were uttered by their fathers. Future research should strive to identify these reasons. Second, because children gather input about their academic performance from sources other than their parents, the impact of these sources should be explored. These sources include older siblings, extended family members, grandparents, and significant others (Mercy & Steelman, 1982; Pawlowski, 2004; Webb, 1985; Woelfel & Haller, 1971). Because it is possible that children receive hurtful messages from these sources, it might be fruitful to explore how these messages range in their perceived hurtfulness, intensity, and intent.

In sum, the results of this study suggest that although parents are perceived to relay hurtful messages to their adult children about their academic performance, these messages have no impact on adult children's global self-esteem and little impact on adult children's context-based educational motivation. Furthermore, when confronted with a hurtful message about their academic performance, adult children are more likely to react by actively responding to the message than by acquiescing or appearing invulnerable. Collectively, these results imply that parents' use of hurtful messages about adult children's academic performance may not have much of an effect on their adult children. As disheartening as this conclusion may sound, this effect may be more a reflection of life position than anything else. Stafford (2004) posited that by middle childhood, the family may no longer serve as the primary socialization agent. Thus, adult children's perceptions of their parents' use of hurtful messages about academic performance, the link between the perceptions of these message qualities and self-esteem and educational motivation, and the reactions to these messages may be offset in some way by other socialization agents such as the media, their peers, and their teachers.

References

Alwin, D. F., & Thornton, A. (1984). Family origins and the schooling process: Early versus late influence of parental characteristics. *American Sociological Review, 49,* 784–802.

Astone, N. M., & McLanahan, S. S. (1991). Family structure, parental practices and high school completion. *American Sociological Review, 56,* 309–320.

Berger, C. R. (1987). Self-conception and social information processing. In J. C. McCroskey & J. A. Daly (Eds.), *Personality and interpersonal communication* (pp. 275–304). Newbury Park, CA: Sage.

Besharat, M. A. (2003). Parental perfectionism and children's test anxiety. *Psychological Reports, 93,* 1049–1055.

Brophy, J. (1983). Conceptualizing student motivation. *Educational Psychologist, 37,* 122–147.

Bulmer, M. (1979). Concepts in the analysis of qualitative data. *Sociological Review, 27,* 651–677.

Christensen, L. J., & Menzel, K. E. (1998). The linear relationship between student reports of teacher immediacy behaviors and perceptions of state motivation, and of cognitive, affective, and behavioral learning. *Communication Education, 47,* 82–90.

Christophel, D. M. (1990). The relationships among teacher immediacy behaviors, student motivation, and learning. *Communication Education, 39,* 323–340.

Christophel, D. M., & Gorham, J. (1995). A test-retest analysis of student motivation, teacher immediacy, and perceived sources of motivation and demotivation in college classes. *Communication Education, 44,* 292–306.

Courts, P. M. (2004). Meanings of homework and implications for practice. *Theory Into Practice, 43,* 182–188.

Crandall, V., Dewey, R., Katkovsky, W., & Preston, A. (1964). Parents' attitudes and behaviors and grade-school children's academic achievements. *Journal of Genetic Psychology, 104,* 53–66.

Daly, J. A. (1987). Personality and interpersonal communication: Issues and directions. In J. C. McCroskey & J. A. Daly (Eds.), *Personality and interpersonal communication* (pp. 13–41). Newbury Park, CA: Sage.

Dekovic, M. (2002, April). *Discrepancies between parental and adolescent developmental expectations.* Paper presented at the biennial meeting of the Society for Research on Adolescence, New Orleans, LA.

Dobos, J. A. (1996). Collaborative learning: Effects of student expectations and communication apprehension on student motivation. *Communication Education, 45,* 118–134.

Dornbusch, S. M., Ritter, P. L., Leiderman, P. H., Roberts, D. F., & Fraleigh, M. J. (1987). The relation of parenting style to adolescent school performance. *Child Development, 58,* 1244–1257.

Ellis, J. B., & Smith, S. W. (2004). Memorable messages as guides to self-assessment of behavior: A replication and extension diary study. *Communication Monographs, 71,* 97–119.

Ellis, K. (2002). Perceived parental confirmation: Development and validation of an instrument. *Southern Communication Journal, 67,* 319–334.

Fan, X., & Chen, M. (2001). Parental involvement and students' academic achievement: A meta-analysis. *Educational Psychology Review, 13,* 1–22.

Fantuzzo, J., Tighe, E., & Childs, S. (2000). Family involvement questionnaire: A multivariate assessment of family participation in early childhood education. *Educational Psychology, 92,* 367–376.

Feeney, J. A. (2004). Hurt feelings in couple relationships: Toward integrative models of the negative effects of hurtful events. *Journal of Social and Personal Relationships, 21,* 487–508.

Fehrmann, P. G., Keith, T. Z., & Reimers, T. M. (1987). Home influence on school learning: Direct and indirect effects of parental involvement on high school grades. *Journal of Educational Research, 80,* 330–337.

Felder, L. (1987). What college students wish they could tell their parents. *Parental Concerns in College Student Mental Health, 2,* 95–107.

Fitzpatrick, M. A., & Caughlin, J. P. (2002). Interpersonal communication in family relationships. In M. L. Knapp & J. A. Daly (Eds.), *Handbook of interpersonal communication* (3rd ed., pp. 726–777). Thousand Oaks, CA: Sage.

Glauser, M. J. (1984). Self-esteem and communication tendencies: An analysis of four self-esteem/verbal dominance personality types. *The Psychological Record, 34,* 115–131.

Gorham, J., & Millette, D. M. (1997). A comparative analysis of teacher and student perceptions of sources of motivation and demotivation in college classes. *Communication Education, 46,* 245–261.

Hauser, R. M., & Mossel, P. A. (1985). Fraternal resemblance in educational attainment and occupational status. *American Journal of Sociology, 91,* 650–673.

Hauser, R. M., & Sewell, W. H. (1986). Family effects in simple models of education, occupational status, and earnings: Findings from the Wisconsin and Kalamazoo studies. *Journal of Labor Economics, 4,* S83–S115.

Jaasma, M. A., & Koper, R. L. (1999). The relationship of student-faculty out-of-class communication to instructor immediacy and trust to student motivation. *Communication Education, 48,* 41–47.

Kandel, D. B., & Lesser, G. S. (1969). Parental and peer influences on educational plans of adolescents. *American Sociological Review, 34,* 213–223.

Keith, T. Z., & Keith, P. B. (1993). Does parental involvement affect eighth-grade student achievement? Structural analysis of national data. *School Psychology Review, 22,* 474–495.

Kunz, P. R., & Peterson, E. T. (1977). Family size, birth order, and academic achievement. *Academic Achievement, 24,* 144–148.

Leary, M. R. (Ed.). (2001). *Interpersonal rejection.* New York: Oxford University Press.

Leary, M. R., Koch, E. J., & Hechenbleikner, N. R. (2001). In M. R. Leary (Ed.), *Interpersonal rejection* (pp. 145–166). New York: Oxford University Press.

Leary, M. R., & Springer, C. (2001). Hurt feelings: The neglected emotion. In R. M. Kowalski (Ed.), *Behaving badly: Aversive behaviors in interpersonal relationships* (pp. 151–175). Washington, DC: American Psychological Association.

Leary, M. R., Springer, C., Negel, L., Ansell, E., & Evans, K. (1998). The causes, phenomenology, and consequences of hurt feelings. *Journal of Personality and Social Psychology, 74,* 1225–1237.

Mercy, J. A., & Steelman, L. C. (1982). Familial influence on the intellectual attainment of children. *American Sociological Review, 47,* 532–542.

Mills, R. S. M., Nazar, J., & Farrell, H. M. (2002). Child and parent perceptions of hurtful messages. *Journal of Social and Personal Relationships, 19,* 731–754.

Murphy, H., & Roopchand, N. (2003). Intrinsic motivation and self-esteem in traditional and mature students at a post-1992 university in the northeast of England. *Educational Studies, 29,* 243–259.

Myers, S. A. (2002). Perceived aggressive instructor communication and student state motivation, learning, and satisfaction. *Communication Reports, 15,* 113–121.

Myers, S. A., & Rocca, K. A. (2000). Students' state motivation and instructors' use of verbally aggressive messages. *Psychological Reports, 87,* 292–294.

Papanastasiou, C., & Papanastasiou, E. C. (2004). Major influences on attitudes toward science. *Educational Research and Evaluation, 10,* 239–257.

Parsons, J. E., Adler, T. F., & Kaczala, C. M. (1982). Socialization of achievement attitudes and beliefs: Parental influences. *Child Development, 53,* 310–321.

Pawlowski, D. R. (2004, November). *To say or not to say: Topic avoidance in sibling relationships.* Paper presented at the annual convention of the National Communication Association, Chicago.

Rancer, A. S., Kosberg, R. L., & Silvestri, V. N. (1992). The relationship between self-esteem and aggressive communication predispositions. *Communication Research Reports, 9,* 23–32.

Rehberg, R. A., & Westhy, D. L. (1967). Parental encouragement, occupation, education and family size: Artifactual or independent determinants of adolescent educational expectation? *Social Forces, 45,* 362–374.

Rosenberg, M. (1965). *Society and the adolescent self-image.* Princeton, NJ: Princeton University Press.

Schrodt, P. (2003). Student perceptions of instructor verbal aggressiveness: The influence of student verbal aggressiveness and self-esteem. *Communication Research Reports, 20,* 240–250.

Schrodt, P., Wheeless, L. R., & Ptacek, K. (2000). Informational reception apprehension, educational motivation, and achievement. *Communication Quarterly, 48,* 60–73.

Snapp, C. M., & Leary, M. R. (2001). Hurt feelings among new acquaintances: Moderating effects of interpersonal familiarity. *Journal of Social and Personal Relationships, 18,* 315–326.

Stafford, L. (2004). Communication competencies and sociocultural priorities of middle childhood. In A. L. Vangelisti (Ed.), *Handbook of family communication* (pp. 311–332). Mahwah, NJ: Lawrence Erlbaum.

Teachman, J. (1996). Intellectual skill and academic performance: Do families bias the relationship? *Sociology of Education, 69,* 35–48.

Teachman, J. D., & Paasch, K. (1998). The family and educational aspirations. *Journal of Marriage and the Family, 60,* 704–715.

Vangelisti, A. L. (1992). Older adolescents' perceptions of communication problems with their parents. *Journal of Adolescent Research, 7,* 382–402.

Vangelisti, A. L. (1993). Communication in the family: The influence of time, relational prototypes and irrationality. *Communication Monographs, 60,* 42–54.

Vangelisti, A. L. (1994). Messages that hurt. In W. R. Cupach & B. H. Spitzberg (Eds.), *The dark side of interpersonal communication* (pp. 53–82). Hillsdale, NJ: Lawrence Erlbaum.

Vangelisti, A. L. (2001). Making sense of hurtful interactions in close relationships. In V. Manusov & J. H. Harvey (Eds.), *Attribution, communication behavior, and close relationships* (pp. 38–58). Cambridge, England: Cambridge University Press.

Vangelisti, A. L., & Crumley, L. P. (1998). Reactions to messages that hurt: The influence of relational contexts. *Communication Monographs, 65,* 173–196.

Vangelisti, A. L., & Maguire, K. (2002). Hurtful messages in family relationships: When the pain lingers. In J. H. Harvey & A. Wenzel (Eds.), *A clinician's guide to maintaining and enhancing close relationships* (pp. 43–62). Mahwah, NJ: Lawrence Erlbaum.

Vangelisti, A. L., Maguire, K. C., Alexander, A. L., & Clark, G. L. (2004, November). *Toward a message-based theory of hurtful family environments.* Paper presented at the annual convention of the National Communication Association, Chicago.

Vangelisti, A. L., & Sprague, R. J. (1998). Guilt and hurt: Similarities, distinctions, and conversational strategies. In P. A. Andersen & L. K. Guerrero (Eds.), *Handbook of communication and emotion* (pp. 123–154). San Diego: Academic Press.

Vangelisti, A. L., & Young, S. L. (2000). When words hurt: The effects of perceived intentionality on interpersonal relationships. *Journal of Social and Personal Relationships, 17,* 393–424.

Webb, L. (1985). Common topics of conversation between young adults and their grandparents. *Communication Research Reports, 2,* 156–163.

Wlodkowski, R. J. (1978). *Motivation and teaching.* Washington, DC: National Education Association.

Woelfel, J., & Haller, A. O. (1971). Significant others, the self-reflexive act and the attitude formation process. *American Sociological Review, 36,* 74–87.

Xu, J., & Corno, L. (1998). Case studies of families doing third-grade homework. *Teachers College Record, 100,* 402–436.

Young, S. L. (2004). Factors that influence recipients' appraisals of hurtful communication. *Journal of Social and Personal Relationships, 21,* 291–303.

Young, S. L., & Bippus, A. M. (2001). They hurt you in a funny way? Humorously and non-humorously phrased hurtful messages in personal relationships. *Communication Quarterly, 49,* 35–52.

Zorn, T. E. (1991). Measuring motivation-to-communicate in the classroom. *Communication Education, 40,* 385–392.

CHAPTER 24

Interrelations Between Family Communication and Health Communication

Loretta L. Pecchioni

Louisiana State University

Teresa L. Thompson

University of Dayton

Dustin J. Anderson

University of Dayton

T he death of Ronald Reagan in June 2004 provides a very public example of the many ways in which family and health issues are interwoven. Because the former president was a public figure, most people in the United States were aware that he was suffering from dementia of the Alzheimer's type for at least the last 10 years of his life. His ailment, however, did not just affect his own life but also the lives of those around him, particularly his family members. His wife, Nancy, was his primary caregiver throughout those years of "the long goodbye." His children, Maureen, Michael, Patti, and Ron Jr., were also involved to varying degrees at different times in his care, with his daughters writing publicly about the progress of the disease and their struggles with watching this man fade away from them and the toll caregiving was taking on Nancy.

Dementia is often seen as a frightening disease. As Patti Davis (2004) wrote shortly after her father's death, "Who are we if we can't recall who we have been, what we have done and learned? If we can't think back on triumphs, defeats, sad times and bright days when joy lifted us off the ground? If we can't look into the face of another and read all our history with that person?" (p. 34). This loss of identity along with memories, however, does not just affect the individual who is diagnosed with this disease. Imagine the difficulty for family members as their loved one no longer smiles with recognition when they enter the room. While dementia brings a host of problems that are absent with other illnesses and diseases, all health challenges have an impact on the patient's social support network.

This chapter examines the ways in which health and family communication intersect and influence each other, a topic further explored by Pawlowski (Chapter 25, this volume). When we experience a serious illness, we often turn to our family for support and reassurance. How does an illness affect our role in the family? How do families manage the changing dynamics of a critically or chronically ill individual? What happens when the sick person is usually the caregiver for the family? Employing a life span perspective, we examine the intersections of health and family communication by reviewing the recent literature on how families talk about health-related issues, provide care to each other, and deal with the dying and death of a loved one. We end the chapter with a brief discussion of the methods for studying family health communication and the implications that health-related issues have for broadening our understanding of the role of communication in family relationships.

The Life Span Perspective

The life span perspective assumes that people undergo change throughout their lives and that we adapt our communicative behaviors to those changes (Pecchioni, Wright, & Nussbaum, 2005). These changes, however, occur not only on the individual level but also at the relational level. The most obvious example is that of the parent-child relationship as the child matures. Inevitably, the parent and child will interact differently when the child is 2 months, 2 years, 20 years, and 60 years old. In the health arena, an infant is completely reliant on a parent or other caregiver to provide food, clothing, shelter, and other basics of life. Young children develop their attitudes toward nutrition, exercise, and other health behaviors by first observing the behaviors of their caregivers and then taking a more active role in learning about these issues by asking questions. The parent not only accompanies the child to doctor's visits but often provides more information to the doctor than the child does. As the child matures, however, he or she will begin to take charge of his or her own eating habits, exercise routines, and visits to the doctor. Throughout our adolescent and adult years, we usually visit the doctor on our own. At some point, however, the parent and child may again start visiting a doctor together, but these visits are for the parent and not the child, especially if the parent becomes frail and is widowed or divorced.

Taking a life span perspective helps us to focus on the important aspect of change over time. Individuals and relationships change over time as our knowledge and needs develop and change. During a health crisis, individuals will need different types of information and support as they come to grips with the diagnosis, manage treatment and recovery, or cope with the death of the person with the illness. Therefore, we organize our review of family and health issues based on the chronological age of individuals and the chronology of an illness.

Family Talk About Health

The family plays a central role in the development of health attitudes and behaviors and usually serves as the primary source of caregiving during a health crisis. How families talk about health-related issues reflects the relational culture established in the family regarding communication styles. Therefore, a family that generally discusses other issues openly is more likely to openly discuss health-related issues. Our review of how families talk about health issues focuses on a few key elements: establishing health attitudes and behaviors, disclosure of health concerns, family information needs during a health crisis, family caregiving, and the death and dying of a loved one and the related bereavement.

Establishing Health Attitudes and Behaviors

We first begin to learn about health in our families as we observe health-related behaviors and have discussions about health in our childhoods (Geist-Martin, Ray, & Sharf, 2003). As in other family dynamics, the lessons that are learned may be indirect. A child may observe her father feeling ill but refusing to go to a doctor. A family may have religious sanctions against certain types of health-related behavior. As discussed later in this chapter, parents may not share information with children about a family illness or talk about the death of a family member for fear that the child will not understand or be scared. All of these behaviors teach us about the role of communication in our health behaviors. Events in the life of the family may make health-related discussions more or less important at different points in time. When it comes to establishing health attitudes and behaviors, a critical time for the child is during adolescence, when young people face peer pressure to engage in potentially risky health behaviors. Despite peer pressure, active parental involvement is an important influence on adolescents' health-related behaviors. While families may talk about any number of health-related issues, we focus on how families with adolescents talk about sex and substance use as illustrations of this process.

Communication About Sex in the Family

Most of us immediately see the connection between sex and health because of the notable relationship between sex and both sexually transmitted diseases (STDs) and pregnancy. Early research on family communication about sex indicated that those families who talk more about sex generally have adolescents who engage in less premarital sexual activity (Warren, 1992). More recently, however, Wilson and Donenberg (2004) found that quality but not quantity of parent-teen communication about sex reduced sexual risk taking in adolescents in psychiatric care. In families from various ethnic backgrounds, overall communicative openness leads to increased and more comfortable talk about sex, and these conversations lead to less risky behaviors (Guzman et al., 2003; Hutchinson, Jemmott, Jemmott, Braverman, & Fong, 2003; Miller, Kotchick, Dorsey, Forehand, & Ham, 1998). When adolescents feel that their parents are monitoring their behaviors, they are more likely to delay sexual initiation, initiate condom use, use condoms, and are less likely to engage in anal sex (Romer et al., 1999).

Although comfortable and open communication between parents and adolescents about sex reduces risky behavior, the degree of comfort and specific content of these conversations often vary based on the sex combination of parent and child. For example, DiIorio, Kelley, and Hockenberry-Eaton (1999) found that male and female adolescents were more likely to talk about sex with their mothers than with their fathers, although males were more likely than females to hold such discussions with their fathers. Topics of communication were most commonly STDs, AIDS, and condom use. Females were likely to talk about menstruation with their mothers, sexual abstinence with their fathers, and sexual intercourse with their friends. Male teenagers felt less comfortable talking with mothers but more comfortable talking with fathers than did female teenagers. Consistent with the research noted above, more sex communication with the mother was related to decreased likelihood of sexual activity, although such communication with friends was related to increased sexual activity. Mothers reported feeling very comfortable talking about most sex topics. Although both male and female adolescents' attitudes about sexual behavior are related to family communication in general, parental contributions to sex education, and parental discussion of sexual values, females are more strongly influenced by family factors and males are more strongly influenced by individual factors (Werner-Wilson, 1998). In one study of minority families, the adolescents were more likely to talk to their mothers than to their fathers (Miller et al., 1998). These parents reported a greater willingness to talk about any of 10 different sex issues with a same-sex child than with child of the other sex. These discussions tended to focus on being at risk for HIV, AIDS, and STDs rather than on specific sexual behavior, contraceptive use, and physical development.

Substance Use and Abuse

In a related focus on at-risk behavior, several studies have examined families, communication, and substance abuse (including use of tobacco, alcohol, and other drugs) issues. As in the case of sexual behaviors, when parents and adolescents have open conversations about substance use, the adolescents are less likely to use substances that pose a risk to their health. This research is reviewed more thoroughly by LePoire (2004), but a few recent studies will be mentioned here.

Parents often feel at a loss for initiating conversations with their teenagers about any of these topics. In a study of parent-daughter discussions discouraging tobacco use, Argy, James, and Biglan (1999) found that such conversations could be prompted by the use of an informational pamphlet. This pamphlet facilitated conversation about the consequences of smoking, difficulty of quitting, and rules about tobacco use as well as the outcomes for breaking those rules. Not only did these families talk about issues addressed in the pamphlet, but they also initiated conversations about topics that were *not* covered in the pamphlet (e.g., attractiveness and body image, resisting peer pressure, health risks). Perhaps most important, these conversations were conducted in a nonconflictual manner.

Jackson, Henriksen, and Dickinson (1999), focusing on parenting and alcohol socialization, found that rules against alcohol use, parental communication against it, and parental responsiveness to questions were unrelated to adolescent alcohol use. Also, children who did not see their parents monitoring their use of alcohol or who paid little attention to alcohol use were more likely to drink alcohol by the seventh grade, as were those who were allowed to drink alcohol in the home. Therefore, parents cannot expect to simply set rules against the use of alcohol but must actively monitor their children's behavior to influence the age of onset of alcohol use.

Illicit drugs, of course, are an important substance abuse concern for families, and some research has examined this issue, especially the success of treatment models. For instance, Gregg and Toumbourous (2003) describe the development and testing of peer support groups for adolescents who have a sibling who uses drugs. Such adolescents are themselves at a higher risk for drug use. The adolescents participating in the group and their parents reported positive outcomes from this participation. These adolescents also demonstrated improved communication with the sibling who was using drugs. Two other relevant studies focused on involving families in rehabilitation. Liberman and Liberman (2003) discussed the benefits of using behavioral family management models that focus on changing the family's dynamics and not just the behavior of any one individual in the family. Boyd-Ball (2003) described a culturally responsive, family-enhanced intervention model for American Indian youth in rehabilitation for alcohol or substance abuse. "Standard" treatment programs have been notoriously unsuccessful with this population. By incorporating Indian legends that demonstrate culturally appropriate behaviors and attitudes, the adolescents who participated in the program were more likely to engage in prosocial behaviors and to abstain from drugs.

Other research has examined how family variables interact with adolescent personality variables to influence reactions to antidrug public service announcements (PSAs). Skinner and Slater (1995) found that family conversation openness did not influence the dependent variables of believability and persuasiveness of the PSAs. However, rebellious adolescents from authoritarian, conformity-oriented families found antidrug PSAs less believable than did nonrebellious adolescents from similar families.

Disclosure Issues

When a health crisis occurs, the patient usually receives the diagnosis from the doctor, and then the patient must decide who in the family will also be told. The disclosure of information from health care providers to patients is not the focus of this chapter, but that process may affect how and when family members are informed about an illness (see Gillotti, 2003, for a summary of the disclosure research in regard to health communication). Although disclosure of health concerns and diagnoses are frequently fairly straightforward issues, they are generally more problematic upon the delivery of bad news, especially regarding terminal illness and communication of information about genetic risk (Rosenblatt, 2004).

While patients and family members often complain about how and when bad news is delivered, they are not the only individuals who perceive problems in regard to bad news delivery. Nurses in focus groups were asked to identify what they perceived to be the key problems for the families of cancer patients (Davis, Kristjanson, & Blight, 2003). They indicated that problems with bad news delivery and the lack of clarity of treatment plans were second only to poor pain management as sources of distress for these families. Therefore, we examine the issues of when family members are told, who (the patient or the doctor) tells the family, and how that information should be shared.

While much of the research regarding the disclosure of a life-threatening illness has been experiential, Kim and Alvi (1999) surveyed cancer patients regarding family involvement in the communication of a diagnosis. Eighty-one percent of the respondents did not wish to have anyone else present at the time of the diagnostic communication. Sixty-three percent of them had further discussions with family, friends, or other physicians after the initial communication—the remaining 37% did not. Perhaps this lack of discussion helps explain the research about information needs among family members of cancer patients.

As discussed later in this chapter, social support plays an important role in how well individuals cope with illness. Because family and friends are the primary sources of social support, they must eventually be told about the illness to provide that support. Figueiredo, Fries, and Ingram (2004) studied early breast cancer patients and found that patients were more likely to confide in family and friends than mental health workers. They were most likely to talk about fears of recurrence and worries about the effects of their illness on family members but not about concerns related to body image. Those patients who did not disclose their concerns or worries perceived low social support and emotional well-being. Dismissive or distancing responses from family and friends were perceived to be unsupportive.

Although most individuals do eventually want to share this kind of information with family, cultural differences in regard to norms and expectations for disclosure of life-threatening illness are well established (Ahmann, 1998; J. L. Mitchell, 1998). Although this would be very unlikely in a culture such as the United States, in some cultures, family members are first told of a diagnosis and allowed to participate in the decision-making process regarding the telling of the patient (Akabayashi, Fetters, & Elwyn, 1999). J. L. Mitchell (1998) discusses not only these considerations but also those that affect how involved the patient would like family members to be in the reception of a diagnosis.

Because family members are eventually told about the illness, the issue arises regarding who will inform them. When a physician is the one to deliver bad news to a family, whether the physician holds junior or senior status does not affect family comprehension, satisfaction, or anxiety/depression (Moreau et al., 2004). Those family members who receive information from a junior physician, however, are more likely to feel that they have not been given enough information time and are more likely to seek information from another physician.

In some instances, individuals feel they should be the ones to share information with the family, especially in cases of genetic testing for hereditary risks because they feel a sense of responsibility toward the younger generation. For instance, interviews with individuals who have received genetic counseling for risk of hereditary breast and ovarian cancer and Huntington's disease indicate that most respondents feel that communication of risk information is a family responsibility but that disclosure patterns are influenced by family structures, dynamics, and rules as well as level of certainty of the risk information (Forrest et al., 2003).

Once the decision has been made to share information and who will be responsible for sharing this information, then the question arises about how that information should be shared. Two studies summarized by Ahmann (1998) indicated that parents being informed of a child's chronic illness or disability should be told together (in a two-parent family), in simple language, and as early as possible by an empathic supportive professional. Collectivistic cultures, however, are more likely to rely on ambiguous rather than straightforward communication of a poor diagnosis (Akabayashi et al., 1999).

Sharing information with children and adolescents, a practice that has not been common until recently, can be more difficult than sharing the same information with adults. Scott et al. (2003) attempted to review the research on interventions to facilitate such communication and subsequent coping in the children and adolescents of cancer patients. They found only five studies that had presented well-controlled, randomized studies of interventions but concluded positive benefits for the children who had participated in the interventions in terms of cancer knowledge, sibling behavior, mood and anxiety, and psychological and social problems. Barnes, Kroll, Lee, Jones, and Stein (1998) provided suggestions for communication about maternal breast cancer in families with a child with a learning disability or behavioral problem. They focus on how to communicate the information in a way that the child is likely to understand and that will facilitate coping.

An even more complicated disclosure context is presented with an HIV+ child born of an HIV-infected mother. At what point should the child be told about his or her HIV status, the nature of the illness, prognosis, transmissibility, and so forth? Experts advocate a gradual and partial communication of such information to affected children, involving continuous negotiation among caregivers (Lee & Johann-Liang, 1999). Concerns related to medication adherence, sexual exploration, the child's fears and autonomy, and treatment compliance must all be weighed as these decisions are made.

In another "take" on the disclosure research, pediatric researchers have examined the likelihood of mothers' disclosure of parenting stress and depressive symptoms with their children's pediatricians (Heneghan, Mercer, & DeLeone, 2004). Although all the mothers expressed concern for their emotional health, took responsibility for it, and felt a need to share parenting experiences, stressors, and depressive symptoms, most did not feel comfortable sharing with their children's pediatrician. They generally feared judgment or referral to child protection agencies if they initiated such discussions. This fear, however, was moderated by how well they felt they knew their children's pediatricians.

Family Information Needs

After a diagnosis has been made, the family may feel a need for information about the diagnosis, prognosis, treatment options, their roles, and so on. Families, however, often report being dissatisfied with the amount and quality of the information they receive, especially when they receive information from a number of different sources. The importance of meeting family information needs is demonstrated by such findings as those of Madigan, Donaghue, and Carpenter (1999), who concluded that the key factor determining parental dissatisfaction with care in a pediatric hospital was a lack of communication from care providers. Even when parents were satisfied with their child's overall care, they expressed dissatisfaction with communication from the child's care provider (Aitken, Mele, & Barrett, 2004). Similarly, Blackmore's (1996) study of the needs of relatives of patients in intensive care following cardiac surgery found communication fundamental to the provision of holistic care. Unfortunately, most of these studies conceptualize communication simplistically, so we do not know from these studies what kind of communication or what about communication is especially important.

Other research, however, does provide us with some insight into what patients and families want to know. Among terminally ill patients and their families, seven key concerns/information needs have been identified: expected changes in functional status or activity level; role changes; symptoms, especially pain; stress on family members; loss of control; financial burden; and the conflict between desiring information and fearing bad news (Kutner, Steiner, Corbett, Jahnigen, & Barton, 1999). Focusing on the needs of husbands of women with breast cancer, Kilpatrick, Kristjanson, Tataryn, and Fraser (1998) found a need for information about immediate care, especially in husbands whose wives were first-time cancer patients.

Patients and families report that not only do they need information but that the process, or *how* the information is shared, is just as important as the content (Kirk, Kirk, & Kristjanson, 2004). Kirk et al.'s (2004) study of families of patients receiving palliative care for cancer determined that the timing, management, and delivery of the information and the perceived attitude of the care provider played important roles at all stages of the illness. Families particularly desired information regarding their loved one's prognosis and avenues for maintaining hope. All patients in this study, which took place in Canada and Australia, wanted information fully shared with their families. Changes in communication patterns were noted over time. Most important, the communication among the family members themselves became less verbally explicit over the course of the illness. Harris (1998) reviewed relevant research on communication with the families of cancer patients, concluding that communication should be tailored to the family's educational background, cultural orientation, and level of comprehension. Patients and families differ in the degree to which they both desire information and wish to take an active role in making treatment decisions.

The family's need for information may create a burden for health care professionals who are often bombarded with questions. Noting that meeting family information needs may be a burden to ICU nursing staff, Medland and Ferras (1998) developed and tested a structured communication program. This program, which included scheduled discussion, a pamphlet, and daily telephone calls, did decrease disruptions for nursing staff while simultaneously satisfying family information needs. Another study of the families of ICU patients found that it was important to families that communication come from the same care provider across the patient's stay in intensive care (Johnson et al., 1998). In a study of fulfillment of family information needs, Fox and Jeffrey (1997) found that those needs were inconsistently met because nurses vary in their perceptions of who is responsible for this activity.

Family Caregiving and Social Support

Any review of the intersections of family and health communication must examine the family's role in caregiving. While health care professionals play an important role in diagnosing a chronic or acute illness and developing a treatment plan, the family is the most likely source of day-to-day caregiving and plays a vital role in recovery and/or adapting to long-term health-related changes. Taking care of a family member, however, is often a stressful experience. A health crisis serves as an ideal opportunity to examine family functioning and its ability to adapt to change.

Research consistently finds that people cope better with a wide range of illnesses and emotional challenges as well as life transitions when they have a strong support network (Albrecht & Adelman, 1987a; Albrecht, Burleson, & Goldsmith, 1994; Schwarzer & Leppin, 1991). When we feel that others care for us and are willing to provide us with assistance when we need it, we feel "loved, esteemed, and valued; and [have a] sense of belonging to a reciprocal network" (Sarason, Sarason, & Pierce, 1990, p. 10). Families play an important role in caregiving. They attend to the physical and emotional needs of the patient, especially when the patient has a chronic or terminal illness (Kuyper & Wester, 1998; Rabow, Hauser, & Adams, 2004). In family medicine practices, physicians focus on treating the patient within the context of his or her family because it improves the care of the patient (Cole-Kelly, Yanoshik, Campbell, & Flynn, 1998).

A basic definition of social support is the exchange of resources that assist recipients in attaining their goals (Stephens, 1990). Three types of support are commonly identified: instrumental, emotional, and informational (Albrecht & Adelman, 1987a, 1987c; Sarason et al., 1990). Instrumental support refers to tangible types of assistance. For example, when someone is sick, others may give him or her a ride to the doctor's office or bring dinner to the house. Emotional support refers to such diverse activities as listening to someone's troubles, validating someone's feelings, offering encouraging words, and simply "being there" during a time of need. Emotional support can be important during a health crisis not only for the identified patient but also for the patient's loved ones, who may be fearful of the outcomes of the illness. Informational support reflects support that shares information. When someone is ill, the individual and his or her loved ones may need information about the diagnosis and prognosis of the disease as well as coping with the emotional demands. The information needs of patients and their families are discussed in detail elsewhere in this chapter.

Social support networks are composed of individuals with strong ties, such as family members and close friends, and individuals with weak ties, such as acquaintances, clergy, neighbors, service providers (e.g., hairstylists, bartenders), or professionals (Adelman, Parks, & Albrecht, 1987; Albrecht & Adelman, 1987a; Granovetter, 1973, 1982). Especially during a health crisis, social support from family plays a critical role in well-being. Family members are more likely to provide ongoing care on a day-to-day basis. While a number of family members may be involved at various levels in providing care, typically one person is the primary caregiver. Which family member fulfills this role depends to some extent on the age and marital status of the sick individual (Nussbaum, Pecchioni, Robinson, & Thompson, 2000). When the patient is a child, one of the parents, usually the mother, is the primary caregiver. When the patient is an adult and in a committed relationship, the partner is usually the primary caregiver. If the individual is single and has at least one child, then an adult child, usually the daughter who lives geographically closest, acts as the primary caregiver.

While we know that social support has many positive aspects, the giving and receiving of support can have negative effects as well. Problems arise in seeking and giving support. We generally have a desire to present ourselves to the world as capable and competent human beings. Seeking support may challenge our self-esteem because asking for assistance may make us look weak or lacking in good judgment, making us feel vulnerable and too dependent on others (Albrecht & Adelman, 1987b). In close relationships, we have a desire for social equity and reciprocity; that is, we want to be able to return the favor when someone helps us out during times of need (Albrecht & Adelman, 1987b). In long-term relationships, we hope that, over time, the give-and-take of support will be nearly equal. A problem arises when we fear that we will not be able to provide support in return. For someone who is chronically or terminally ill, the fear of being indebted may create a barrier that makes some people reluctant to ask for help when needed.

Providing support has its costs, particularly feeling drained and generating relational conflict or strain. Providing social support uses a variety of resources, including your time and energy, tangible goods, and emotional nurturance, which may lead to emotional exhaustion and relational strain (Albrecht & Adelman, 1987b). Researchers have found that providing social support can be perceived negatively if it is associated with role obligations (Suls, 1982). For example, being a family member often carries certain role obligations and expectations along with the relationship. In other words, people may feel that it is their duty to provide support to a family member during a crisis period, regardless of whether they really want to do so.

Whether out of a sense of obligation or not, caregiving can generate considerable stress for the caregiver, resulting from the demands made on one's time to meet the patient's needs and coordinating logistics, the physical demands related to caregiving tasks, financial costs, emotional burdens and mental health risks related to concerns about the patient's health, the future, and the caregiver's own health, as well as physical health risks based on lack of sleep and social support (Kuyper & Wester, 1998; Lidell, 2002; Rabow et al., 2004). The demands of caregiving may lead to impatience or intolerance with the patient and others, a sense of lost autonomy as other roles are neglected, sleep disturbances, less time and opportunity for recreation and social contact, and anger at the situation or even the ill family member (Ellgring, 1999).

A number of factors related to the nature of the illness and its prognosis affect the amount of stress that a family experiences during caregiving. A serious chronic or terminal illness will have different consequences than will a minor, acute one. For example, caring for a child with a cold differs from caring for a child with cancer. Caregiving for individuals with dementia creates considerable risk for psychological stress and anxiety in the caregiver as the patient's disease progresses and his or her ability to assist in care and communicate declines (Ellgring, 1999). Chronic disease and illness lead to long-term demands on the family; unfortunately, these families may not receive the social support they need after initial treatment and/or rehabilitation. For example, after a traumatic brain injury, long-term family functioning is affected not only by the caregiver's perceptions of the patient's competency but also by his or her perceptions of receiving adequate social support and having effective coping strategies; however, formal ongoing support is rarely provided (Douglas & Spellacy, 1996). Another chronic illness is the physical disability associated with strokes, which may have long-lasting effects for the patient. While the patient is in a rehabilitation facility, both the patient and the family receive formal support, but when the patient is released to go home, little formal support is provided, and families have difficulty coping with the long-term problems of the stroke patient (Santos, Farrajota, Castro-Caldas, & de Sousa, 1999).

When a family member is seriously ill, family anxiety is usually quite high, which may negatively affect the well-being of all family members, with the consequences rippling throughout the family system. Because of the interwoven nature of our lives in families, family well-being is interconnected. The patient's well-being affects family anxiety, and family anxiety affects the patient's physical and psychological symptoms (Hodgson, Higginson, McDonnell, & Butters, 1997). Because discussions about stressful life events, such as a diagnosis of cancer or the death of a loved one, are intense and often unpleasant, they generate emotional distress for the listener (Albrecht & Adelman, 1987b). This distress lowers support providers' affect and may raise their own emotions related to stressful events, therefore reducing their ability to provide support. For family members, discussing potential negative prognoses may generate emotional responses that feel overwhelming. Potential support providers may avoid interactions with the individual in need of support, leading to damage to the relationship.

Providing social support can also lead to relational strain when messages of support are misinterpreted, perceived to be ineffective, or unneeded or cause conflict. Offering support may be interpreted by the receiver as a challenge to the individual's ability and competence or may generate fears in the recipient that she or he is letting the support provider down. When messages are perceived to be unsupportive, they have a negative impact on patients' well-being (Figueiredo et al., 2004). Cancer patients report that when they share their fears about recurrence of the cancer or the impact of their illness on their family members, having their fears and concerns minimized or feeling that the listener is distancing himself or herself from the patient increases the emotional problems they have with regard to dealing with their illness.

The stress of caregiving can affect family dynamics as family members attempt to adjust to the situation. All families have stresses and strengths before a health crisis, and both come into play when someone is critically injured, which adds a significant new stress to the equation (Leske & Jiricka, 1998). Having a seriously ill family member alters the ways in which family members interact with each other and the responsibilities each person takes on in the family system. Not only must families adjust to their new situation, but they also must make sense of what is happening to the sick person and to the family unit, especially if the illness is terminal (Grootenhuis & Last, 1997). If families do not deal with the emotional aspects of these demands, they function poorly, having difficulty meeting many needs within the family, not just those related to caregiving for the sick individual (Lidell, 2002). These changes in family dynamics may be long lasting. Bunzel, Laederach-Hofmann, and Schubert (1999) found that couples in which one partner had had a heart transplant felt that communication and involvement with each other declined and continued to be suppressed 5 years after the surgery. Families that seem to adapt to the stress best are those who are able to adapt to their new situation through problem-solving communication, possess effective coping strategies, and are hardy and resilient (Grootenhuis & Last, 1997; Leske & Jiricka, 1998).

Death, Dying, and Bereavement

When the prognosis for an illness is poor, those involved (i.e., health care professionals, the patient, family members) may not acknowledge the inevitable. In the United States, talk about death is often avoided or minimized. This denial about the reality of death shuts down discussions about the topic and may negatively affect both the dying person's and his or her support network's ability to cope with that death. Not talking about dying not only denies the fact of a death but also denies any feelings that are associated with that death and makes it difficult for the dying person to maintain relationships when such an important topic cannot be discussed (Fitzsimmons, 1994; Silverman, Weiner, & El Ad, 1995).

Families may particularly avoid talking about death directly with children or even when children can overhear such conversations. This avoidance usually occurs in an attempt to protect children's feelings, with the assumption that they do not have the emotional maturity to handle such serious topics. The consequence is that children develop attitudes about how to handle a loved one's death and its related emotions by what is not said as well as by what is said (Book, 1996).

When death is discussed, the use of euphemisms and metaphors helps to maintain distance from the event of death (Sexton, 1997). Saying that someone has "gone to their eternal rest" or is "lost" in some ways negates the finality of death and may continue to shut down certain emotional responses and direct other responses as more appropriate.

Most individuals who are dying do want to know that they are dying and want the opportunity to talk about a number of matters with their loved ones, although sometimes they are concerned about whether and how their family will handle the bad news, and they want to continue to have hope about their futures (Kirk et al., 2004; Kutner et al., 1999; Seale, 1991; Servaty & Hayslip, 1997). Dying individuals feel that having an opportunity to talk with family about these issues will make dying easier. This issue is addressed more fully in a later section on "a good death."

Family members also want to have information regarding an impending death, but they want to be informed in person, in private, and with sensitivity to their feelings (Seale, 1991). Family members are often frustrated by their interactions with the health care professionals who are providing services to their loved one because these professionals do not provide enough or timely information, do not listen to the family's concerns or wishes, and do not treat them or their loved one with respect.

When the patient and the family are aware of impending death, they are able to take advantage of palliative care, which is designed to help individuals and their families manage the dying process. Often, families choose to have the individual return home, if at all possible. In these cases, even when health professionals are assisting in care, families need considerable information about managing their loved one's care, especially ameliorating pain (Teno et al., 2004). In these cases, the families need physical and emotional support and encouragement in developing appropriate advance care planning (Rabow et al., 2004). The demands on families who are providing palliative care can be incredible, and the formal support providers need to provide them with emotional and informational support so that the family can continue to be of assistance to the dying patient (Hudson, Aranda, & Kristjanson, 2004).

Of course, there are times when death is sudden and the family has little or no time to prepare for the event. In these cases, as in cases in which death is imminent but has not yet occurred, the families desire to have the bad news delivered in person and with sensitivity and efforts to provide comfort (Christaki, 1998). Even when a patient is in intensive care, which is not designed for palliative care, the family can and should be included in decision making and the provision of care to the patient (Azoulay & Pochard, 2003).

In those cases in which the dying individual and the family have an awareness of and the time to discuss the impending death, several factors assist the person in having "a good death." Dying individuals want to maintain their dignity, to avoid unnecessary pain, to have an opportunity to take leave of their loved ones, to right their shortcomings with God, and to make sense of their lives and their deaths (Emanuel & Emanuel, 1998; Lynn, 1991; D. R. Mitchell, 1997). Most dying people are primarily concerned with their relationships with those to whom they are close. As a consequence, they want to discuss a number of issues with those loved ones. For the family, they want the time to be able to express their love and affection, bolster the spirits of their loved ones, express their sense of loss, and provide acts of kindness.

The death of a partner entails at least two processes: affiliation and separation. The process of affiliation entails being physically and emotionally available, while the process of separation entails realizing and talking with others about a future without the partner. These processes, however, are not mutually exclusive, so that a spouse can provide instrumental and emotional support while making plans for a future without the partner. Married couples vary in how openly they discuss the impending death of one of them. Those widows who engaged in open and honest communication with their husbands about the husband's death reported more happiness after the death, although these discussions did not help improve their ability to adjust to their new status or their daily functioning (Kramer, 1997).

Individuals typically die in the hospital but may also die in a nursing home or in their family home. In the hospital, the death may be sudden and relatively unexpected or an event that is expected, although the exact timing is never easy to predict. Comparing these different settings, dying at home with hospice care was more emotionally satisfying for both the individual and the family because they felt that they were treated with respect (Teno et al., 2004). Dying in the hospital or at home with a home health agency was in the middle, and dying in the nursing home was rated lowest for feeling that the dying person was treated with respect.

As one might expect, talking about end-of-life issues can be a particularly difficult topic when a family member is critically ill (Norton, Tilden, Tolle, Nelson, & Eggman, 2003); therefore, providing information and listening to others' wishes and desires can ease the process (Danis, 1998; Huddleston & Alexander, 1999; Kirk et al., 2004; Kutner et al., 1999; Norton et al., 2003). Patients and their families need information about the individuals' functional status and symptoms but also about role changes and the stresses of their illness on family members (Kutner et al., 1999).

Deciding when and if to end life-sustaining treatment is difficult for many families. When a loved one has not been ill for long, some families may feel that the shift from aggressive treatment to palliative care is too rapid (Norton et al., 2003). When the patient is a child, parents have a particularly difficult time making the decision to stop aggressive care, and hospital staff must be particularly sensitive to their needs and grief (Huddleston & Alexander, 1999; Pector, 2004). Although most families have not had discussions about end-of-life decisions, those who have a member in a nursing home are most likely to have these discussions and to share these discussions with the nursing home staff (Levin et al., 1999). Medical staff who must implement these end-of-life decisions must be aware that different cultures have different values for making these decisions and that, even within cultures, different individuals have different goals, wishes, and desires that should be respected (Danis, 1998; Voltz, Akabayashi, Reese, Ohi, & Sass, 1998).

The loss of a spouse is rated as the most stressful of life events, but other family members grieve as well. Adult children report the death of a parent as a major life event, and for older individuals, the death of a sibling may be particularly disturbing as they lose a long, shared, intimate history (Bower, 1997; DeVries, 1997; Gold

& Pieper, 1997). The context of the death affects the nature of the grief related to that death, including factors such as the age of the deceased person, the cause of death (e.g., an expected death from a long illness vs. an unexpected death in a car accident), and the role of the loved one in the bereaved's life (DeVries, 1997). Remember that family members are usually also important members of an individual's support network. The person who died can no longer play a vital role in that network or provide direct comfort and support. Thus, grieving for a loved one may include feelings of loss, guilt, anger, and depression. These symptoms may last for some time, but most individuals have adapted to the loss of a spouse within a year or two of the death.

The consequences of the death of a loved one radiate throughout the family and may generate greater emotional closeness or distance (Rosenblatt & Karis, 1994). Shared grief and memories may evoke happy times and lead to reconnections among family members. On the other hand, with emotions running high, long-standing conflicts and resentments may be renewed. Individual family members may express their grief in different ways, which may lead to misunderstandings.

Dealing with grief is not a simple process, even for those individuals who are trained to provide support. Often, people do not know what to say to the bereaved and therefore avoid contact, generating social isolation for the bereaved. Children and adolescents grieve differently from adults (Seager & Spencer, 1996). Even though hospice care is designed to meet the needs of the family as well as the patient, younger family members' needs are usually not fully met. Death is a common event in long-term care facilities, but most facilities do not provide grief and bereavement services to family members of their residents, nor do they make referrals or provide information regarding these issues (Murphy, Hanrahan, & Luchins, 1997).

Alternative Approaches for Studying Health in the Family Context

Because of their involvement in health-related issues, medical scholars often examine the role of communication in the health care setting. Their research, some of which is reviewed in this chapter, typically relies on traditional social scientific research methods in these studies. While this approach provides important information, as was noted previously, these scholars usually treat communication in a rather simplistic fashion. In recent years, communication scholars have adopted narrative and discursive approaches to research the lived experiences of individuals to uncover the complexity of interrelationships between health and family communication. We briefly review narrative and discursive approaches to highlight the depth of understanding that can be derived from such approaches.

Narrative Approaches

Numerous scholars have advocated examination of narratives, or stories, to facilitate both understanding and processing of communication. One also sees a discussion of narratives emerging in the literature on families and health. Several examples of the use of narratives emerged in our review of the family and health literature, including reliance on narratives as a coping mechanism during bereavement (Bosticco & Thompson, in press; Caplan, Haslett, & Burelson, 2005). Narratives are also examined to look at how people deal with and continue to function after myocardial infarction in a female spouse (Svedland & Danielson, 2004) and how families cope with chronic illness in a child (Fiese & Wamboldt, 2003). One recent study looked at narratives told by internists after the death of a patient (DelVecchio Good et al., 2004). These narratives were nuanced with assessments of the quality of end-of-life care and emphasized three major themes: time and process, medical care and treatment decisions, and communication and negotiation. The last theme focused on the effectiveness of communication with patients, families, and medical team members and the role of misunderstandings and conflict within this communication.

Discursive Approaches

Health communication scholars have recently turned to the application of various discursive approaches to the study of health-related interaction in an attempt to understand such interaction more adequately. Much of this work has focused on provider-patient interaction, but some researchers are now generating interesting insights into family communication and health. Exemplary in this area is the work of Wayne Beach (cf. Beach & Anderson, 2003), who has provided detailed analysis into the nature of such issues as the serial organization of problem narratives during a family crisis (Beach & Lockwood, 2003); the delivery and assimilation of bad news (Beach, 2002a); interaction about cancer diagnosis, treatment, and prognosis (Beach & Good, 2004); managing optimism (Beach, 2002b); and managing uncertainty about health issues (Beach, 2001). Such approaches show great promise for furthering our understanding of how families communicate about health crises.

Conclusion

Increased emphasis on research methods such as narrative and discursive analysis should certainly be encouraged in future research. In addition, all of the areas that have been surveyed in this chapter are deserving of future investigation. Although we did not have the space to review them here, promising research is being conducted on how families talk about everyday health, organ donation, family planning, depression, and a wide range of other health-related matters. Certainly, all of these areas will receive more research attention.

The bottom-line impact of health-related communication cannot be ignored—it affects both length and quality of life. Of great import is research on how family communication affects health and more in-depth analysis of just how families communicate about health. Both everyday health issues and health crises provide key contexts through which to examine family dynamics. In particular, a health crisis provides an opportunity to examine how family members manage conflict and emotions, the strengths and weaknesses that families possess that help or hinder them in coping with health-related challenges, the nature and pattern of interaction among family members, and changes that occur across the life span of individual family members and the family as a unit. Examining these events helps us to develop a greater understanding of how families communicate with each other.

References

Adelman, M. B., Parks, M. R., & Albrecht, T. L. (1987). Beyond close relationships: Support in weak ties. In T. L. Albrecht & M. B. Adelman (Eds.), *Communicating social support* (pp. 126–147). Newbury Park, CA: Sage.

Ahmann, E. (1998). Review and commentary: Two studies regarding giving "bad news." *Pediatric Nursing, 24,* 554–556.

Aitken, M. E., Mele, N., & Barrett, K. W. (2004). Recovery of injured children: Parent perspectives on family needs. *Archives of Physical Medicine and Rehabilitation, 85,* 567–573.

Akabayashi, A., Fetters, M. D., & Elwyn, T. S. (1999). Family consent, communication, and advance directives for cancer disclosure: A Japanese case and discussion. *Journal of Medical Ethics, 25,* 296–301.

Albrecht, T. L., & Adelman, M. B. (1987a). Communicating social support: A theoretical perspective. In T. L. Albrecht & M. B. Adelman (Eds.), *Communicating social support* (pp. 18–39). Newbury Park, CA: Sage.

Albrecht, T. L., & Adelman, M. B. (1987b). Dilemmas of supportive communication. In T. L. Albrecht & M. B. Adelman (Eds.), *Communicating social support* (pp. 240–254). Newbury Park, CA: Sage.

Albrecht, T. L., & Adelman, M. B. (1987c). Measurement issues in the study of support. In T. L. Albrecht & M. B. Adelman (Eds.), *Communicating social support* (pp. 64–78). Newbury Park, CA: Sage.

Albrecht, T. L., Burleson, B. R., & Goldsmith, D. (1994). Supportive communication. In M. L. Knapp & G. R. Miller (Eds.), *Handbook of interpersonal communication* (2nd ed., pp. 419–449). Newbury Park, CA: Sage.

Argy, D. V., James, L., & Biglan, A. (1999). Parent-daughter discussion to discourage tobacco use: Feasibility and content. *Adolescence, 34,* 275–282.

Azoulay, E., & Pochard, F. (2003). Communication with family members of patients dying in the intensive care unit. *Current Opinion in Critical Care, 9,* 545–550.

Barnes, J., Kroll, L., Lee, J., Jones, A., & Stein, A. (1998). Communication about parental illness with children who have learning disabilities and behavioural problems: Three case studies. *Child: Care, Health and Development, 24,* 441–456.

Beach, W. A. (2001). Stability and ambiguity: Managing uncertain moments when updating news about Mom's cancer. *Text, 21,* 221–250.

Beach, W.A. (2002a). Between dad and son: Initiating, delivering, and assimilating bad cancer news. *Health Communication, 14,* 271–298.

Beach, W.A. (2002b). Managing optimism. In J. Mandelbaum, P. Glenn, & C. LeBaron (Eds.), *Unearthing the taken-for-granted: Studies in language and social interaction* (pp. 175–194). Mahwah, NJ: Lawrence Erlbaum.

Beach, W. A., & Anderson, J. K. (2003). Communication and cancer? The noticeable absence of interactional research. *Journal of Psychosocial Oncology, 21,* 1–23.

Beach, W. A., & Good, J. S. (2004). Uncertain family trajectories: Interactional consequences of cancer diagnosis, treatment, and prognosis. *Journal of Social and Personal Relationships, 21,* 9–35.

Beach, W. A., & Lockwood, A. S. (2003). Making the case for airline compassion fares: The serial organization of problem narratives during a family crisis. *Research on Language and Social Interaction, 36,* 351–393.

Blackmore, E. (1996). The needs of relatives during the patient's stay in intensive care following routine cardiac surgery. *Nursing in Critical Care, 1,* 230–236.

Book, P. L. (1996). How does the family narrative influence the individual's ability to communicate about death? *Omega, 33,* 323–341.

Bosticco, C., & Thompson, T. L. (in press). An examination of the role of narratives and story telling in bereavement. In L. Harter, P. Japp, & C. Beck (Eds.), *Narratives in health and illness.* Mahwah, NJ: Lawrence Erlbaum.

Bower, A. R. (1997). The adult child's acceptance of parent death. *Omega, 35,* 67–96.

Boyd-Ball, A. J. (2003). A culturally responsive, family-enhanced intervention model. *Alcoholism: Clinical and Experimental Research, 27,* 1356–1360.

Bunzel, B., Laederach-Hofmann, K., & Schubert, M. T. (1999). Patients benefit—partners suffer? The impact of heart transplantation on the partner relationship. *Transplant International, 12,* 33–41.

Caplan, S., Haslett, B., & Burleson, B. R. (2005). Telling it like it is: The adaptive function of narratives in coping with loss in later life. *Health Communication, 17,* 233–251.

Christaki, K. (1998). A personal reflection on the issues surrounding the use of euphemisms following sudden death. *Nursing in Critical Care, 3,* 249–252.

Cole-Kelly, K., Yanoshik, M. K., Campbell, J., & Flynn, S. P. (1998). Integrating the family into routine patient care: A qualitative study. *Journal of Family Practice, 47,* 440–445.

Danis, M. (1998). Improving end-of-life care in the intensive care unit: What's to be learned from outcomes research? *New Horizons, 6,* 110–118.

Davis, P. (2004). "God has a plan," my dad always said. *Newsweek, 143,* 34–35.

Davis, S., Kristjanson, L. J., & Blight, J. (2003). Communicating with families of patients in an acute hospital with advanced cancer: Problems and strategies identified by nurses. *Cancer Nursing, 26,* 337–345.

DelVecchio Good, M. J., Gadmer, N. M., Ruopp, P., Lakoma, M., Sullivan, A. M., Redinbaugh, E., et al. (2004). Narrative nuances on good and bad deaths: Internists' tales from high-technology work places. *Social Science & Medicine, 58,* 939–953.

DeVries, B. (1997). Kinship bereavement in later life: Understanding variation in cause, course, and consequence. *Omega, 35,* 141–157.

DiIorio, C., Kelley, M., & Hockenberry-Eaton, M. (1999). Communication about sexual issues: Mothers, fathers, and friends. *Journal of Adolescent Health, 24,* 181–189.

Douglas, J. M., & Spellacy, F. J. (1996). Indicators of long-term family functioning following severe traumatic brain injury in adults. *Brain Injury, 10,* 819–839.

Ellgring, J. H. (1999). Depression, psychosis, and dementia: Impact on the family. *Neurology, 52,* S17–S20.

Emanuel, E. J., & Emanuel, L. L. (1998). The promise of a good death. *The Lancet, 351*(9114), S21–S29.

Fiese, B. H., & Wamboldt, F. S. (2003). Coherent accounts of coping with chronic illness: Convergences and divergences in family measurement using a narrative analysis. *Family Process, 42,* 439–451.

Figueiredo, M. I., Fries, E., & Ingram, K. M. (2004). The role of disclosure patterns and unsupported social interactions in the well-being of breast cancer patients. *Psycho-oncology, 13,* 96–105.

Fitzsimmons, E. (1994). One man's death: His family's ethnography. *Omega, 30,* 23–39.

Forrest, K., Simpson, S. A., Wilson, B. J., van Teijligen, E. R., McKee, L., Haites, N., et al. (2003). To tell or not to tell: Barriers and facilitators in family communication about genetic risk. *Clinical Genetics, 64,* 317–326.

Fox, S., & Jeffrey, J. (1997). The role of the nurse with families of patients in ICU: The nurses' perspective. *Canadian Journal of Cardiovascular Nursing, 8,* 17–23.

Geist-Martin, P., Ray, E. B., & Sharf, B. F. (2003). *Communicating health: Personal, cultural, and political complexities.* Belmont, CA: Wadsworth/Thomson Learning.

Gillotti, C. (2003). Medical disclosure and decision-making: Excavating the complexities of physician-patient information exchange. In T. Thompson, A. Dorsey, K. Miller, & R. Parrott (Eds.), *Handbook of health communication* (pp. 163–182). Mahwah, NJ: Lawrence Erlbaum.

Gold, D. T., & Pieper, C. F. (1997). Sibling bereavement in later life. *Omega, 35,* 25–42.

Granovetter, M. S. (1973). The strength of weak ties. *American Journal of Sociology, 78,* 1360–1380.

Granovetter, M. S. (1982). The strength of weak ties: A network theory revisited. In P. V. Marsden & N. Lin (Eds.), *Social structure and network analysis* (pp. 105–130). Beverly Hills, CA: Sage.

Gregg, M. E., & Toumbourous, J. W. (2003). Sibling peer support group for young people with a sibling using drugs: A pilot study. *Journal of Psychoactive Drugs, 35,* 311–319.

Grootenhuis, M. A., & Last, B. F. (1997). Adjustment and coping by parents of children with cancer: A review of the literature. *Supportive Care in Cancer, 5,* 466–484.

Guzman, B. L., Schlehofer-Sutton, M., Villanueva, C. M., Dello Stritto, M. E., Casad, B. J., & Feria, A. (2003). Let's talk about sex: How comfortable discussions about sex impact teen sexual behavior. *Journal of Health Communication, 8,* 583–598.

Harris, K. A. (1998). The informational needs of patients with cancer and their families. *Cancer Practice, 6,* 39–46.

Heneghan, A. M., Mercer, M. B., & DeLeone, N. L. (2004). Will mothers discuss parenting stress and depressive symptoms with their child's pediatrician? *Pediatrics, 113,* 460–467.

Hodgson, C., Higginson, I., McDonnell, M., & Butters, E. (1997). Family anxiety in advanced cancer: A multicentre prospective study in Ireland. *British Journal of Cancer, 76,* 1211–1214.

Huddleston, D., & Alexander, R. (1999). Communicating in end-of-life care. *Caring, 18,* 16–20.

Hudson, P. L., Aranda, S., & Kristjanson, L. J. (2004). Meeting the supportive needs of family caregivers in palliative care: Challenges for health professionals. *Journal of Palliative Medicine, 7,* 19–25.

Hutchinson, M. K., Jemmott, J. B., Jemmott, L. S., Braverman, P., & Fong, G. T. (2003). The role of mother-daughter sexual risk communication in reducing sexual risk behaviors among adolescent females: A prospective study. *Journal of Adolescent Health, 33,* 98–107.

Jackson, C., Henriksen, L., & Dickinson, D. (1999). Alcohol-specific socialization, parenting behaviors, and alcohol use by children. *Journal of Studies on Alcohol, 60,* 362–367.

Johnson, D., Wilson, M., Cavanaugh, B., Bryden, C., Gudmundson, D., & Moodley, O. (1998). Measuring the ability to meet family needs in an intensive care unit. *Critical Care Medicine, 26,* 266–271.

Kilpatrick, M. W., Kristjanson, L. J., Tataryn, D. J., & Fraser, V. H. (1998). Information needs of husbands of women with breast cancer. *Oncology Nursing Forum, 25,* 1595–1601.

Kim, M. K., & Alvi, A. (1999). Breaking the bad news: The patient's perspective. *The Laryngoscope, 109,* 1064–1067.

Kirk, P., Kirk, I., & Kristjanson, L. J. (2004). What do patients receiving palliative care for cancer and their families want to be told? A Canadian and Australian qualitative study. *British Medical Journal, 328,* 1343.

Kramer, D. (1997). How women relate to terminally ill husbands and their subsequent adjustment to bereavement. *Omega, 34,* 93–106.

Kutner, J. S., Steiner, J. F., Corbett, K. K., Jahnigen, D. W., & Barton, J. L. (1999). Information needs in terminal illness. *Social Science & Medicine, 48,* 1342–1352.

Kuyper, M. B., & Wester, F. (1998). In the shadow: The impact of chronic illness on the patient's partner. *Qualitative Health Research, 8,* 237–253.

Lee, C. L., & Johann-Liang, R. (1999). Disclosure of the diagnosis of HIV/AIDS to children born of HIV-infected mothers. *AIDS Patient Care and STDs, 13,* 41–45.

LePoire, B. (2004). The influence of drugs and alcohol on family communication: The effects that substance abuse has on family members and the effects that family members have on substance abuse. In A. L. Vangelisti (Ed.), *Handbook of family communication* (pp. 609–628). Mahwah, NJ: Lawrence Erlbaum.

Leske, J. S., & Jiricka, M. K. (1998). Impact of family demands and family strengths and capabilities on family well-being and adaptation after critical injury. *American Journal of Critical Care, 7,* 383–392.

Levin, J. R., Wenger, N. S., Ouslander, J. G., Zellman, G., Schnelle, J. F., Buchanan, J. L., et al. (1999). Life-sustaining treatment decisions for nursing home residents: Who discusses, who decides and what is decided? *Journal of the American Geriatrics Society, 47,* 82–87.

Liberman, D. B., & Liberman, R. P. (2003). Rehab rounds: Involving families in rehabilitation through behavioral family management. *Psychiatric Services, 54,* 633–635.

Lidell, E. (2002). Family support: A burden to patient and caregiver. *European Journal of Cardiovascular Nursing, 2,* 149–152.

Lynn, J. (1991). Dying well. *Generations, 15,* 69–72.

Madigan, C. K., Donaghue, D. D., & Carpenter, E. V. (1999). Development of a family liaison model during operative procedures. *American Journal of Maternal Child Nursing, 24,* 185–189.

Medland, J. J., & Ferrans, C. E. (1998). Effectiveness of a structured communication program for family members of patients in an ICU. *American Journal of Critical Care, 7,* 24–29.

Miller, K. S., Kotchick, B. A., Dorsey, S., Forehand, R., & Ham, A. Y. (1998). Family communication about sex: What are parents saying and are their adolescents listening? *Family Planning Perspectives, 30,* 218–222.

Mitchell, D. R. (1997). The "good" death: Three promises to make at the bedside. *Geriatrics, 52,* 91–92.

Mitchell, J. L. (1998). Cross-cultural issues in the disclosure of cancer. *Cancer Practice, 6,* 153–160.

Moreau, D., Goldgran-Toledano, D., Alberti, C., Jourdain, M., Adrie, C., Annane, D., et al. (2004). Junior versus senior physicians for informing families of intensive care unit patients. *American Journal of Respiratory and Critical Care Medicine, 169,* 512–517.

Murphy, K., Hanrahan, P., & Luchins, D. (1997). A survey of grief and bereavement in nursing homes: The importance of hospice grief and bereavement for the end-stage Alzheimer's disease patient and family. *Journal of the American Geriatrics Society, 45,* 1104–1107.

Norton, S. A., Tilden, V. P., Tolle, S. W., Nelson, C. A., & Eggman, S. T. (2003). Life support withdrawal: Communication and conflict. *American Journal of Critical Care, 12,* 548–555.

Nussbaum, J. F., Pecchioni, L. L., Robinson, J. D., & Thompson, T. L. (2000). *Communication and aging* (2nd ed.). Mahwah, NJ: Lawrence Erlbaum.

Pecchioni, L. L., Wright, K. B., & Nussbaum, J. F. (2005). *Life span communication.* Mahwah, NJ: Lawrence Erlbaum.

Pector, E. A. (2004). Views of bereaved multiple-birth parents on life support decisions, the dying process, and discussions surrounding death. *Journal of Perinatology, 24,* 4–10.

Rabow, M. W., Hauser, J. M., & Adams, J. (2004). Supporting family caregivers at the end of life: "They don't know what they don't know." *Journal of the American Medical Association, 291,* 483–491.

Romer, D., Stanton, B., Galbraith, J., Feigelman, S., Black, M., & Li, X. (1999). Parental influence on adolescent sexual behavior in high-poverty settings. *Archives of Pediatrics and Adolescent Medicine, 153,* 1055–1062.

Rosenblatt, P. C., & Karis, T. A. (1994). Family distancing following a fatal farm accident. *Omega, 28,* 183–200.

Rosenblatt, R. A. (2004). Getting the news. *Annals of Family Medicine, 2,* 175–176.

Santos, M. E., Farrajota, M. L., Castro-Caldas, A., & de Sousa, L. (1999). Problems of patients with chronic aphasia: Different perspectives of husbands and wives? *Brain Injury, 13,* 23–29.

Sarason, B. R., Sarason, I. G., & Pierce, G. R. (1990). *Social support: An interactional view.* New York: John Wiley.

Schwarzer, R., & Leppin, A. (1991). Social support and health: A theoretical and empirical overview. *Journal of Social and Personal Relationships, 8,* 99–127.

Scott, J. T., Prictor, M. J., Harmsen, M., Broom, A., Entwistle, V., Sowden, A., et al. (2003). Interventions for improving communication with children and adolescents about a family member's cancer. *Cochrane's Database of Systematic Reviews (Online: Update Software),* no. 4. Retrieved June 25, 2004.

Seager, K. M., & Spencer, S. C. (1996). Meeting the bereavement needs of kids in patient/families—not just playing around. *The Hospice Journal, 11,* 41–66.

Seale, C. (1991). Communication and awareness about death: A study of a random sample of dying people. *Social Science & Medicine, 32,* 943–952.

Servaty, H. L., & Hayslip, B., Jr. (1997). Death education and communication apprehension regarding dying persons. *Omega, 34,* 139–148.

Sexton, J. (1997). The semantics of death and dying: Metaphor and mortality. *ETC.: A Review of General Semantics, 54,* 333–346.

Silverman, P. R., Weiner, A., & El Ad, N. (1995). Parent-child communication in bereaved Israeli families. *Omega, 31,* 275–293.

Skinner, E. R., & Slater, M. D. (1995). Family communication patterns, rebelliousness, and adolescent reactions to anti-drug PSAs. *Journal of Drug Education, 25,* 343–355.

Stephens, M. A. P. (1990). Social relationships as coping resources in later-life families. In M. A. P. Stephens, J. H. Crowther, S. E. Hobfoll, & D. L. Tennenbaum (Eds.), *Stress and coping in later-life families* (pp. 1–20). New York: Hemisphere.

Suls, J. (1982). Social support, interpersonal relations, and health: Benefits and liabilities. In G. S. Sanders & J. Suls (Eds.), *Social psychology of health and illness* (pp. 255–277). Hillsdale, NJ: Lawrence Erlbaum.

Svedlund, M., & Danielson, E. (2004). Myocardial infarction: Narrations by afflicted women and their partners of lived experience in daily life following an acute myocardial infarction. *Journal of Clinical Nursing, 13,* 438–446.

Teno, J. M., Clarridge, B. R., Casey, V., Welch, L. C., Wetle, T., Shield, R., et al. (2004). Family perspectives on end-of-life care at the last place of care. *Journal of the American Medical Association, 291,* 88–93.

Voltz, R., Akabayashi, A., Reese, C., Ohi, G., & Sass, H. M. (1998). End-of-life decisions and advance directives in palliative care: A cross-cultural survey of patients and health-care professionals. *Journal of Pain and Symptom Management, 16,* 153–162.

Warren, C. (1992). Perspectives on international sex practices and American family sex communication relevant to teenage sexual behavior in the United States. *Health Communication, 4,* 121–136.

Werner-Wilson, R. J. (1998). Gender differences in adolescent sexual attitudes: The influence of individual and family factors. *Adolescence, 33,* 519–531.

Wilson, H. W., & Donenberg, G. (2004). Quality of parent communication about sex and its relationship to risky sexual behavior among youth in psychiatric care: A pilot study. *Journal of Child Psychology and Psychiatry and Allied Disciplines, 45,* 387–395.

CHAPTER 25

Dialectical Tensions in Families Experiencing Acute Health Issues

Stroke Survivors' Perceptions

Donna R. Pawlowski

Creighton University

Communication in every family changes in response to physical health issues or has an effect on the course of physical health problems . . . we are just beginning to understand the complex ways family interaction and physical health interact.

—Segrin and Flora (2005, p. 324)

F amilies undergo change as part of the developmental life cycle of family functioning. Issues of health and wellness are certainly aspects throughout a family's life cycle. According to Bluvol and Ford-Gilboe (2004), a family's health status refers to how family members function vis-a-vis its quality of life, satisfaction

AUTHOR'S NOTE: The author would like to thank Carol Bye for her assistance with transcription and analysis.

with family life, or ability to engage in activities of daily living. Physical health issues thus can shape family interaction and perceptions of family members in how to cope with health issues. This family health status is not only important for day-to-day healthy living but also is critical in long-term acute health situations.

Acute illness can be divided into categories of *acute onset,* such as strokes, heart attacks, and accidents, or *gradual onset,* such as progressive diseases like multiple sclerosis and diabetes (Rolland, 1999). Acute illness situations result in "rapid mobilization of crisis management skills" (Rolland, 1999, p. 244). The result of the acute illness has three trajectories: progressive (i.e., gradual worsening), constant (clear-cut limitations and semipermanent to permanent change), and relapsing/ episodic course illness (alteration of low symptomatic periods or flare-up episodes) (Rolland, 1999). Interestingly, those illnesses that are constant may also involve relapsing/episodic interludes, such as when a spinal cord injury survivor contracts an infection that requires additional medical attention or when a stroke survivor who has gall bladder surgery 2 years after the stroke has to start over with physical therapy because the muscles become atrophied from lack of exercise during surgery recovery.

While strokes are an instantaneous acute incident, the recovery process can affect a person's personal well-being and familial relationships for a lifetime as the rehabilitation process becomes a continual and permanent lifestyle. Those who have experienced acute illness experiences of strokes typically have constant and relapsing health complications. Juggling the affective, behavioral, cognitive, and communicative tensions related to these complications can be stressful for families. While some research to date examines the recovery process in the early stages of a survivor's rehabilitative life (Kvigne & Kirkevold, 2003; O'Connell et al., 2001), little is known about what happens as the survivor returns to the home, which involves "more than the basic functional capacity; it requires the active management of a self-care routine over time and social support" (Bluvol & Ford-Gilboe, 2004, p. 323).

The focus of this study involves perceptions of stroke survivors and the dialectical tensions they experience, beginning with the onset of the stroke through the rehabilitation process. In doing so, the literature review will first identify how a stroke affects family functioning and family communication. Second, research on how issues affect the survivor will be explained. Third, an examination of dialectical tension research will be delineated. Fourth, a brief rationale for a narrative approach to research will be examined. Finally, results from interview data will identify the tensions experienced by the survivors. This research extends our understanding of the recovery processes by interviewing survivors up to 12 years after the onset of the stroke and exploring how their relationships have been affected by the stroke.

Review of Literature

Throughout history, medical treatment and technology have lessened the effects of diseases, cured the sick, and extended life expectancy. While healthy living may extend one's life, no medical treatment can completely prevent one from experiencing an acute health emergency. Strokes are one such health emergency affecting someone in the United States every 45 seconds (American Stroke Association, 2004). Stroke is the leading cause of disability in the United States and the third leading cause of long-term disability and death (American Stoke Association, 2004; Murray & Lopez, 1997; Rittman et al., 2004). More than 4 million people are living with the effects of stroke, and more than 700,000 Americans suffer a stroke each year (American Heart Association, 2003). The following review examines family communication with respect to the caregiver in general, spouses as caregivers, and survivors. Additionally, the theoretical framework, dialectics, is presented as well as the methodological approach of narrative analysis.

Caregiver and Familial Functioning

Coping with uncertainties of illness can be a great challenge for caregivers and family members. Family uncertainty occurs when the illness is serious and has long-term consequences that are not easily prevented (Barbow, Hines, & Kasch, 2000). Families need to learn about the illness itself and what it does to the survivor, individuals' perceptions and feelings, and how the illness affects the communication and family functioning as a whole (Rolland, 1999). This is particularly important when the health condition is an acute situation in which the family members typically experience the worst of the situation, the sudden onset of the event (i.e., stroke, heart attack), and then learn to cope with the aftermath of the health condition. Acute illness creates unanticipated caring relationships (Brereton & Nolan, 2002). In addition, the length of stay in a rehabilitation center is also limited, which means that most stroke rehabilitation now takes place outside the hospital (Palmer, Glass, Palmer, Loo, & Wegener, 2004; Schmidt, Guo, & Scheer, 2002) and, in many cases, in the survivor's home.

When individuals undergo rehabilitation, the process is one that involves more than physical mobility. Functional, cognitive, and emotional processes are also important for the survivor's outcome. Psychosocial rehabilitation is a family process that involves the rebuilding of family systems and relationships (Palmer & Glass, 2003), which requires individuals to restructure ways of looking at the world and to develop new ways of living in it (Chick & Meleis, 1986; Parkes, 1971). This rebuilding transition within the family system includes the restructuring of roles, identities, responsibilities, communication patterns, and support systems, among others. Thus, the family's role in the care of persons with stroke-related disability has become increasingly critical to survivor outcome.

Although the survivor may have a more positive outcome from being at home, survivors and families are often unprepared for caregiving and rehabilitation therapy. As Gillotti and Applegate (2000) note, health care providers are faced with the challenges of gaining patients' and family members' understanding of complex processes under extreme anxiety, performing difficult clinical procedures while trying to comfort patients, and explaining the complexities of illness and course of treatment. According to Palmer et al. (2004), stroke survivors and their families face a *double crisis:* the physical and emotional aspects of the stroke itself and the need to create an effective health care system that requires rapid adaptation.

During the initial phases of recovery, the caregiver is focused on the patient in the hospital and less focused on his or her responsibilities and needs as the caregiver (Van der Smagt-Duijnstee, Hamers, & Huijer Adu-Saad, 2000). Once the patient returns home, many couple and caregiver dynamics need to be considered (Brereton & Nolan, 2002; Simon & Kendrick, 2002; White, Mayo, Hanley, & Wood-Dauphinee, 2003). For example, caregivers may need to help with daily living needs of the health survivor (i.e., transfers, feeding, grooming, helping with physical exercises for the patient); household responsibilities, supervision, driving, shopping, and so on may become the caregiver's sole responsibility (Hellgeth, 2002; Palmer & Glass, 2003); and caregivers may give up employment to take care of the survivor's needs (Braithwaite & McGown, 1993). Hellgeth (2002) indicates that due to these extra responsibilities, caregivers report a decrease in physical energy and health (White et al., 2003). While caregiving can be burdensome, however, many caregivers are satisfied in caring for their loved one (Bluvol & Ford-Gilboe, 2004). They feel more comfortable and are glad they are able to care for the survivor, and despite some of the negative health-related issues, many are just grateful to have their family member alive.

While it is apparent that physical issues affect the stroke survivor (i.e., from minimal paralysis to complete paralysis) and the caregiver, physical issues also affect the family system as a whole. Family members also experience physical burdens they may not have experienced prior to the acute illness. For example, many adult children help with the modification of the parent's home to make the physical setting handicap accessible, stopping by the home more frequently to help with yardwork and housework or stopping by to help with the caregiving.

Spousal Caregiver and Familial Communication

Long-term health problems challenge communication skills (Rolland, 1999) and can affect marital interactions positively or negatively (Cannon & Cavanaugh, 1998). Illness changes may alter relationships in a negative way, increasing demands placed on the spouse who is not ill. This is especially true in cases where the spouse is the caregiver for the ill spouse. Given these additional demands, communication is sensitive at the beginning as it is difficult to determine each other's perceptions and states of minds or the exact stage of the illness.

To successfully cope with situations, couples need open, sensitive, and direct communication (Rolland, 1999). Personal self-disclosure takes on a new level as issues talked about prior to the illness may drastically change after the onset of the illness. Couples need to understand and communicate about the illness and renegotiate their relationships, roles, and intimacy.

Caregivers who once could talk to the survivor about several topics may now be reserved in the topic choice and intensity of communication. Many times, caregivers do not want to worry or upset the survivor with issues regarding other family members or money; thus, they do not indulge in deep conversations about these topics. Emotional intensity arises when partners get frustrated and become angry, ambivalent, or guilty about the situation at hand (Palmer & Glass, 2003).

Caregivers and family members alike may have to change their communication strategies to adapt to the survivor's current situation. Barbow et al. (2000) argue that with more difficult illnesses in which the patient is involved in the recovery process, explanations need to be more detailed and restated to compensate for memory distortion or loss. This clarity of communication must occur at all levels: between the physicians, caregiver, survivor, and family members. Families that once were able to randomly communicate and engage in multiple functions at family gatherings may find themselves having to simplify tasks and communication patterns. This may include using shorter and more simplified sentences, avoiding any interruptions during a conversation, and using only one question or instruction at a time (Barbow et al., 2000; Segrin & Flora, 2005; Small, Gutman, Makela, & Hillhouse, 2003). Using a combination of verbal, written, and nonverbal communication or requiring complete attention from the survivor during conversations may be a drastic change of communication that takes time getting used to in the new family setting.

Regardless of these communicative efforts, frustration may occur, and the desired effects of the communication may not take place. Family members do not want to realize that emotional outbursts or irrational comments are natural given the extent of the illness. Tolerating, understanding, and forgiving each other are key to support familial communication.

Survivor Communication and Recovery Issues

Once survivors are assured stability (or survival), they are faced with the transition of managing the loss of independence of a functioning body, ushering in the onset of a transition (Bury, 1982; Schumacher & Meleis, 1994). Two salient features of the transition process follow a stroke: The process (a) occurs over time and (b) involves changes in identities, roles, behaviors, and communication patterns.

Rittman et al. (2004) interviewed stroke survivors 1 month after being at home and discovered that survivors are still very hopeful that function will return and that life will get easier. Many participants pushed themselves to test their limits of mobility and functioning. Trial and error help to determine what they can do but also help to discover who they are. According to Rittman et al., several changes take place in regard to time; as survivors experience disruption in their usually taken-for-granted daily activities, time slows down because activities take longer to accomplish. Survivors are coping with changes at multiple levels or layers of meanings. At one level is impaired functioning, at another level is slowing of time, and at another level is change in their sense of who they are as people.

Bury (1982) identifies the transition period as one of disruption, discontinuity, and stress, requiring adaptation and accommodation to the new lifestyle. The transition from the hospital to the home is more than adjusting to physical impairments. It is a multidimensional process, requiring changes in the rhythms and routines of daily life, as well as changes in one's sense of self. Issues salient in one's life include the questions of returning to work, participating in regular activities, and engaging in regular social network opportunities (O'Connell et al., 2001).

Communication issues are also relevant for survivors. Older adults, who are the stroke survivors for the most part, are more concerned with the psychosocial issues during medical interviews and daily living (Nussbaum, Pecchioni, Grant, & Folwell, 2000). Because of the physical, cognitive, and communication changes as individuals age, older patients want more explanations and perhaps need more time to absorb information. This is especially true when the physical illness has impaired the cognitive functioning at the onset; thus, interaction among the communicative partners must be productive to provide the best quality of health care for the stroke survivor.

Although research has identified short-term effects of stroke survivors, little is known about what happens as a person attempts to return and stay in the home (O'Connell et al., 2001). Research suggests that the ability to remain in the home involves more than basic functional capacity; it requires the active management of a self-care routine over time and social support. Burton (2000) argues that long-term rehabilitation programs need to be assessed as most individuals do reside in their homes after the onset of strokes. Although home caregivers do their best to aid in the rehabilitation and recovery of stroke survivors, they are not necessarily trained or equipped to assess follow-up long-term rehabilitation. Thus, more work needs to be conducted about the long-term effects of stroke survivors and the need to provide them with the necessary social and rehabilitative support.

Theoretical and Methodological Grounding

Dialectics

The dialectical approach is considered a perspective for studying interpersonal relationships (Baxter, 1988; Cupach, 1992; Duck & Pittman, 1994). Although others have studied contradictions in relationships, the main contributors to the identification of contradictions are Baxter (1988, 1990) and Baxter and Montgomery (1996). Major components of dialectics include those of contradiction, process, and interconnection (Baxter & Montgomery, 1996). Contradiction is formed whenever two tendencies or forces are interdependent yet mutually negate each other (Baxter, 1988, 1990; Cornforth, 1968; Montgomery, 1993). In general terms, it refers to the dynamic tension between opposing forces. For example, both spontaneity and predictability within a relationship may be desired.

Contradictions of relationships are normal phenomena seen as neither inherently positive nor negative—they just exist. Both poles of the opposition are assumed to possess potentially positive and negative attributes as well as to have possibly positive and negative ramifications for the relationship (Baxter & Montgomery, 1996; Montgomery, 1992a, 1992b, 1993). By realizing that inevitable forces exist and that such tensions are not unhealthy, people will better understand the process of interpersonal relationships.

Scholars from the dialectical perspective concern themselves not only with the contradictions that exist in relationships but also with the process of how contradictions produce developmental change (Baxter, 1990; Pawlowski, 1998; Wood, Dendy,

Dordek, Germany, & Varallo, 1994). Process refers to the notion that relationships involve opposing forces that are dynamic, ever changing, and continuous (Baxter, 1990; Bruess & Pearson, 1997; Conville, 1991, 1994; Cornforth, 1968; Cupach, 1992; W. K. Rawlins, 1983b; W. R. Rawlins, 1989; Werner & Baxter, 1994). Stamp (1992) claims that process implies dialectics are always present within relationships and experienced to various degrees by relationship interactants. Baxter (1994) argues that contradictions are characteristic of developmental processes, thus occurring throughout the course of relationships.

In addition to contradiction and process, several scholars identify interconnection or totality as an essential component of the dialectical perspective (Baxter, 1993; Montgomery, 1992b; W. K. Rawlins, 1983a; W. R. Rawlins, 1992; Sabourin, 1992; Werner & Baxter, 1994). Interconnection generally refers to the interdependence of the tensions such that no single contradiction can be considered in isolation of other contradictions (W. R. Rawlins, 1989; Werner & Baxter, 1994).

Initial dialectical research focused on internal and external contradictions (Baxter, 1990). Baxter's work mainly focuses on romantic relationships with three main dialectical categories: integration-separation, stability-change, and expression-privacy (Baxter, 1988, 1990, 1993, 1994; Werner & Baxter, 1994). Internal contradictions are bound to those within the dyadic social unit of study—the relationship itself, or the "interpersonal dialectical process" (Altman, 1993; Brown, Altman, & Werner, 1992). External contradictions are constituted between the social unit and the larger system in which they are embedded—the dyad in connection to outside social networks of friends, family, and the society (Brown et al., 1992; Montgomery, 1992a).

Overall, communication scholars have looked at the process of relational development using the dialectical perspective in romantic relationships (Baxter, 1990; Montgomery, 1992b; Pawlowski, 1998) and familial relationships (Conville, 1991). Other research on dialectical contradictions also investigates specific contradictions. For example, researchers have looked at autonomy-connection (Goldsmith, 1990; Montgomery, 1992b), autonomy (or differences) of couples (Wood et al., 1994), openness-closedness of relational couples and their social networks (Baxter & Widenmann, 1993), closedness in relation to taboo topics (Baxter & Wilmot, 1985), self-disclosure and privacy in terms of openness and closedness (Petronio, 1991; Petronio & Martin, 1986), and autonomy-connection and openness-closedness of marital couples (Hoppe & Ting-Toomey, 1994).

Most research to date has examined romantic, marital, and familial relationships with some focus on various family types; some recent work on various relationships includes stepfamilies (Baxter, Braithwaite, Bryant, & Wagner, 2004) and long-distance relationships (Sahlstein, 2004). In terms of the topic at hand, Kvigne and Kirkevold (2003) studied female stroke survivors who were between the onset and 2 years poststroke. Primary tensions reported by women were independence-dependence, being in and out of control, and connection-dissonance. Although these refer to short-term effects, Kvigne and Kirkevold's study appears to be one of the few studies that have examined dialectical tensions and stroke survivors.

Narrative Approach

Throughout her thorough overview of patients' needs, Thompson (2000) argues that understanding patients' concerns is critical for care providers. In order for medical practitioners to provide accurate language, examples may be most effective when presented as narratives. Thompson also states that to understand patients, asking questions in open-ended and reflective statements will allow patients to communicate emotional and content-level concerns. In order to conduct research on patients' perceptions, a similar approach is effective.

One way to tap into individuals' felt tensions is through an interpretive analysis of narratives and storytelling. Fisher (1985) argues that narratives are focused on "words and/or deeds that have sequence and meaning for those who live, create, or interpret them" (p. 82). Illness narratives can provide functions of health-related stories (Arnston & Droge, 1987; Miller & Crabtree, 1992; Sharf & Vanderford, 2003). These functions help patients use illness narratives as sense-making, asserting control, transferring identities, decision making, and community building. Health communication scholars have used illness narratives to reveal the storytellers' emotional and cognitive journeys (Sharf & Vanderford, 2003).

According to Sharf and Kahler (1996), narrative-based research allows participants to extend discussion beyond the biomedical meaning to include meanings of their illness to familial roles, identities, and social assumptions and influences. Critical to storytelling as sensemaking is the distance in time between actions and the "telling" of the story. Asking individuals to reflect upon their illnesses in retrospect helps them to interpret events and actions and make links that they could not have done in real time. In addition, narrative scholars agree that when individuals are able to tell their stories, it aids in the healing process and may help individuals reshape their identities. Stories may reflect individuals' feelings or reflect upon relationships with others, which may include support networks. Retrospective accounts are valid data because they represent what the event has come to mean to the account maker and, thus, what happened in the sense of the disheveled meaning of the event.

Research Question

As literature has demonstrated, research on stroke survivors is ample; however, much of the research is on onset or short-term recovery rehabilitation processes. As the importance of home care is a growing concern for stroke survivors, this study examines the long-term care experienced by the stroke survivors and the tensions experienced by survivors. Thus, the following research question guides this study:

RQ1: What dialectical tensions are experienced by stroke survivors during long-term recovery rehabilitation?

Method

Participants

The participants were 15 stroke survivors (13 men and 2 women) who were obtained via a purposeful network sampling method. This method is used when respondents are difficult to obtain and/or information-rich cases are needed (Creswell, 2002; Maxwell, 2005). After finding a few individuals, the researchers asked those individuals to provide names of others who experienced similar situations. In some instances, those who participated earlier in the study contacted the referral families first so as to make a personal connection and explain the project prior to the researcher's contacting the additional participants.

Participants had to meet specific criteria. First, they had to have experienced some acute health situations (e.g., stroke) at least 1 year prior to the study. Second, they had to have undergone hospitalization and rehabilitation (e.g., speech, occupational, and/or physical) therapy.

Individuals ranged from ages 53 to 78, with a mean of 64 years of age. The time frame from when individuals experienced the stroke ranged from 2 to 12 years, with the mean being 7 years prior to the study. Occupations prior to the health condition varied and included homemakers, mechanics, factory workers, construction workers, bankers, farmers, health care workers, business/salespersons, and railroad engineers. Some individuals were already retired from their professions yet still remained active in their communities or were still involved in the business at some level. All individuals had to give up their occupations or greatly reduce the capacity in which they carried out their professions, particularly in the case where the individuals were farmers or laborers in farming communities prior to the stroke and who were the primary providers for their families, regardless of age. Many individuals came from rural farming communities where the health care facilities were more than 60 miles from the survivor's residence.

All participants were married, with their primary caregiver being their spouse. Participants resided in their own homes; many of these homes needed to be adapted/remodeled for greater or safer physical mobility and accessibility. All participants currently have some permanent paralysis as a result of the health situation. In addition, while some had slight speech problems (i.e., slurring, repeating, stuttering), all individuals were cognitively adept and could comprehend the questions and respond with clear thoughts to the researcher. Finally, all survivors have had additional health-related issues such as heart surgeries, gall bladder surgery, hernias, and degenerative eye disease, among other health issues, that have created a need for the survivor to spend follow-up time in a rehabilitation center. Thus, all participants have had multiple rehabilitation visits.

Procedures and Measures

Individuals were contacted via telephone or in person and asked to participate in the study. In a few instances, participants would contact their friends and ask them to participate in the study, thus providing a familiar contact rather than the researcher imposing on individuals. All contacted participants agreed to participate in the study.

Once a meeting time was set, the researcher met in the homes of the participants—a meeting place of convenience chosen by the interviewee. Participants first completed and signed consent forms. Second, participants were asked a series of open-ended questions in an interview setting. Participants were asked to tell their stories via guided interview questions in order for the researcher to understand their experiences and perception of their health situations and the communication within the family. Interviews were used to obtain the point of view of the participants (Lincoln & Guba, 1985), thus providing survivors the opportunity to tell their stories related to the questions and to discuss any other issues they felt important to their recovery.

Based on prior research (Kvigne, Kirkevold, & Gjengedal, 2004; Reid, 2004) and personal experiences of working with family members who also have suffered from acute illnesses, interview topics were selected. Such topics included the initial onset of the acute incident, hospitalization and rehabilitation, temporary and permanent physical conditions, emotional issues, caregiving issues, communication with family members, changes in the family functioning, and difficulties and successes of their conditions, among other topics.

The interview protocol was pilot tested with three individuals to ensure accuracy and understandability of questions. Individuals in the pilot study had also experienced acute illness (i.e., accidents, strokes) and thus were similar in the project criteria of undergoing rehabilitation therapy. Pilot individuals were asked the questions in the protocol and about the clarity of questions. Based on their responses and suggestions, questions were reworded to be more listener-friendly for participants. After minor changes were made in the protocol, the 15 participants were solicited for the project; pilot-tested individuals were not used in actual data analysis.

Data Analysis

Participants were assigned an identification number and a pseudonym to protect their privacy. Taped interviews were transcribed, checked for accuracy, and edited. Interviews ranged from 45 minutes to 3 hours in length. They were audio-taped and transcribed, ranging from 35 to 97 typed pages each, with the average being 60 pages.

This study relied on inductive analysis as informed by grounded theory (Glaser, 1992; Glaser & Strauss, 1967; Strauss, 1987), which examines the identification of participants' perspectives and meanings as lived by the participants. This methodology allows the researcher to capture the essence of the participants' experiences (Creswell, 2002; Strauss & Corbin, 1990); researchers use interpretive approaches to understand, discover, describe, and give meaning to the patterns of phenomena and the unique context in which they occur.

The process of constant comparative analysis, which involves concurrent interviewing and analysis (Strauss & Corbin, 1990), leads researchers to reshape and refine themes continuously. The researcher first read transcripts while listening to the tape recordings to gather a more holistic view of the participants' experiences. The researcher then reread the transcripts but with more specific attention to discovering emergent themes and recurring dialectical tensions in the data. Using an open-coding method of content analysis for approximately half of the transcribed conversations, the researcher identified themes (tensions) in interview data.

Further analysis refined the categorization scheme by applying it to the data, and highlighted examples were taken from the data to illustrate each tension. To verify the accurateness of the identified tensions and excerpts that fit the tensions, a second coder read the transcripts to match the tensions with the highlighted excerpts. The second coder also identified any other excerpts from the transcripts that emerged as tensions or examples of the labeled tensions. Intercoder agreement was at 90%, and Cohen's kappa was .91. The researcher and coder resolved discrepancies to identify a consensus of the identified tensions.

Employing the continuation of the constant comparative method, tensions identified from remaining interview transcripts were tested against and used to reanalyze interviews conducted earlier in the research process. This mode of analysis compels researchers to revisit interpretations of early interviews through the lens of what emerges later in the research process (Creswell, 1998). It was determined that the tensions were similar, and saturation was reached within the 15 transcripts.

Results

Examining the transcripts revealed that survivors experienced seven tensions in their day-to-day functioning and in the communication with their caregiver/spouse. The tensions include success/determination—wanting to give up, isolated/loneliness—support, fear—content, independent-dependent, openness-closedness, thankfulness—frustration/anger, and reflections of past/reality of present. The following outlines the various tensions delineated in the transcripts.

Success/Determination—Wanting to Give Up

Many individuals discussed their successes with their recovery progress. Participants took great pride in being able to accomplish the small tasks and events of the day. What many take for granted are the daily struggles of stroke survivors. One individual summed it up well when he said,

> Some days I get so damn mad—one day, I tried to get my shirt buttoned and she was gone for a while. I must have spent 15 minutes trying to get it buttoned. I finally had success and got the darn thing buttoned—I was exhausted and had to sit down for a while but at least I dressed myself.

Regardless of the numbers of years since the stroke, all survivors discussed ways in which they still tried to keep strength in their weak side and increase the mobility of their muscles. One participant, whose stroke was 6 years prior, put it well as he was describing his continued determination:

> I keep working with the fingers to try to loosen them up and then if we are going to go someplace, she [wife/caregiver] gives me a glove and I work on the glove. It takes me about 25 minutes to get all my fingers in the holes that they belong in . . . when I get them in there, [as he chuckles], that is about the time we get where we are going and the wife will pull the glove off the first thing!

Not only does this show the determination of the survivor, but it also shows a glimpse of how the caregiver does not automatically "do" the work for the survivor. Many caregiver spouses were identified as giving tough love, which seemed to either frustrate the survivor or bring humor to the situation, as in the example above.

Isolated/Loneliness—Support

Since the stroke, many experienced a lack of contact with their friends and social networks. As one man states,

> I miss not having company—and I love to visit. People just don't visit with us like they used to—or when we get together [with friends] and they go for a walk—I am not able to do that. I used to play a lot of cribbage, but now I can't hold the cards so I don't play cribbage. Our daughter bought me a cardholder, but it's not the same as being able to hold the cards yourself. So many of our card players just don't come by much.

This example expresses the frustration and sadness in not being able to visit with others, as well as pride in the survivor. Friends and neighbors seldom visit the survivors and their spouses after the stroke. It is also obvious that many individuals do not want others to see them needing physical help, thus demonstrating their pride in the presentation of oneself and not wanting to look dependent. Interestingly, this notion of being abandoned is not necessarily blamed on the friends/neighbors but rather is felt as sadness that the friends do not feel comfortable in coming to the home or engaging in activities with the survivor.

This tension is also felt with the support and love received by many, and survivors are thankful for their social networks. As one man states,

> My kids and neighbors are great—one day I was trying to mow the lawn and fell on the mower. My neighbors came to help me up—they are always looking out for me when I am in the backyard. There isn't anything I could not ask them to do, and the kids have been great. The boys came to fix up the house—putting in hand rails, making the bathroom bigger, fixing stuff around the house—that I used to be able to do. I don't know what we would do without them. It used to bother me to ask them for anything but everyone just pitches in now and knows that I can't do it on my own.

In this instance, support is freely given and asked for. Overall, it appears that this tension is created by self and other induced. On some occasions, survivors create these feelings on their own; at other times, other people's behaviors generate the feelings of loneliness and comfort of support.

Fear—Content

Many talked of the uncertainty of not knowing what will happen in the future. Many are scared that they may have another stroke or perhaps are nervous and unsure of providing for the family. Others are just happy to be alive and cherish what they have in life.

I don't know if and when it will happen again—I should not have had the first one. No one knows why—I was healthy and didn't smoke or drink. It just hit me one day—so that's always on my mind. I was worried that we would not make it financially, but we have just had to live within our means since the stroke—I know I have to live life to its fullest because I don't know what tomorrow will bring and it scares me sometimes.

As demonstrated, this individual felt the back and forth of both sides of this tension—a constant flow of wondering why and accepting what happened.

Independent-Dependent

One difficult situation for stroke survivors is the loss of independence. All of the participants, regardless of age, were quite healthy at the time of the strokes; only few had health conditions or poor habits that could have contributed to the onset of the stroke, and thus individuals were used to being quite independent. Many respondents commented on how they wanted to show their independence, at least during the initial years of recovery. As one man states,

My wife thinks I don't get out enough—that I should call someone and go here or go there. I think she's probably right but I always did everything myself and I hated to ask anyone for anything—I guess I was too bull-headed and too proud. It is just hard for me to ask people to do things for me. I'm getting better at asking—I try to do what I can by myself and have come to realize it is okay to ask for things when I need it.

Many survivors experience their struggles of independence and get frustrated at their dependence on others. As one male explained,

I guess I miss the competitive things I used to do like hunting and fishing and playing ball and stuff like that. Back before my stroke—I had everything—at the drop of a hat I could go. Now before I can do stuff like that I have to try to organize it and make sure I have the right equipment—and many times am now the spectator. I guess probably more than anything, I miss the spontaneity. Now I have to plan and schedule everything.

Openness-Closedness

Many of the survivors discussed how their communication had changed as a result of the stroke. For the most part, individuals talked about the openness created in the relationship with the spouse/caregiver, identifying the amount as well as the quality of the conversations. As one younger participant stated,

We had a lot of petty arguments about who has it tougher—who has this affected the most and stuff like that. I think on the other hand—I think it got both of us more in touch with each other's feelings and more so a part of each other. I think that our marriage is stronger because of the stroke than it would have been without it.

Individuals reflected on the amount of communication that they had with their spouse/caregivers. As one woman stated,

I hardly ever saw him in our earlier years—we retired and we still had our own things so we still didn't talk much. Now that he needs to be in the house a lot to help me with things, we talk all the time—almost like two teenagers again. I guess even though I can't do much, we are having a second honeymoon and he's all sweet again.

Although many discussed the degree to which individuals became closer, struggles of not disclosing information were also stated, as another woman pointed out:

I used to talk all the time—but now I try not to bother him with my problems. He is doing enough just taking care of me and I don't think he likes to discuss things—he just likes to take it as it comes—so I try not to upset him or make him feel badly for me. I just don't complain about my bad days.

Another male talks about his involvement with his children and grandchildren after the stroke:

I never had time to go the kids' events when they were growing up—I was not home a lot and gone with my job. Now I am able to visit with them more and attend the grandkids' events—it's a blessing in disguise. Otherwise I'd still be working and miss everything at home.

Thankfulness—Frustration/Anger

One individual who suffers from a great deal of paralysis and needs assistance for most daily activities sums up his experiences and thoughts:

I guess no matter how bad things are it could always be worse. I mean I guess when I go every year for reevaluation and everything, you start to feel a little sorry for yourself, you see someone else in worse shape than you. So I mean, things could always be worse. I guess I don't know—it was goals from my dad. When I was a kid I was always playing pinochle and card games like that before I even started school—it was one of those deals where you play the hand you were dealt.

Even though individuals realize the alternative to their conditions is worse, they cannot help but reflect on the frustration of the situation at hand; as one individual stated,

Some days I just get mad—this is not the way I wanted to live my retirement and it is not the way I wanted my wife to spend her time. She raised the kids while I worked on the farm—she deserves time off from caregiving and we both wanted to travel and enjoy what we couldn't have when we were younger. I am a very faithful person—but sometimes I wonder what I did and why me?

Stroke survivors suffer great loss, but they are still able to be thankful for what they do have. Several survivors told stories about how there are others less fortunate than themselves.

I started going to stroke support groups, which was very helpful—it made me realize that I am not alone. It also made me realize that I can still share my knowledge with someone and can relate to others. I thought I was the "victim" but realize that I can help others too.

Reflections of Past/Reality of Present

Many instances identify the tension between what could be done in the past and what cannot be done in the present. In reflecting on such instances, many survivors provided advice for others, such as in this example, which includes advice from a father to his son:

I used to fill the drill on my own. I can't do that anymore. Where it involves two hands—I can't do anymore—it's just disgusting. I told that to my oldest boy one day. I said I was trying to monkey with something in the shop. And I said, "You know, I've screwed around being a mechanic." I said, "For over 40 years. I could fix anything. Now," I said, "I can't do a damn thing—be glad you can do what you can do."

Another individual discovers his limitations with his situation of the present, realizing that the past will not come back:

She [the occupational therapist] would come over every day and work my leg and arm—I was kinda still hoping I would be okay and I was going back to work next month—that's what I had on my mind. One day she says to me, "What if it does not get better?" and geez I got mad at her and said never to talk negative like that again. Then for some reason that was the day that I finally accepted the fact that maybe I wasn't going to get good again. Once I accepted it, that was the biggest step. I didn't give up or quit therapy—I just had a reality check and had to move on. She was smarter than I was and I needed that from her.

Discussion

This study examined the dialectical tensions experienced by stroke survivors. Dialectical tensions were prevalent among the survivors, and many examples demonstrated the constant flux and back and forth of feelings and emotions within the felt tensions. Various conclusions and implications can be gleaned from the tensions discovered via interpretative analysis of stroke survivors' stories.

First, individuals seem to be more reflective about life since the strokes and realize that their situations could always be worse; some concluded that they realize life is precious and needs to be embraced at all times. Many indicated that they sometimes took life for granted, but since the stroke, they live life to the fullest and remain hopeful for a satisfying lifestyle. Results are similar to those of Bluvol and Ford-Gilboe (2004), who also discovered that even though individuals are living with a disability, those who are more hopeful and place a positive value on life have a healthier family environment and a greater quality of life. Thus, regardless of the physical immobility and loss of independence, stroke survivors still see their quality of life overall as positive, despite the setbacks.

Second, stroke survivors have more open communication with and more appreciation for family relationships than prior to the stroke. More time is spent with the spousal caregivers, and although some communication was closed in nature, overall, individuals felt that their relationships were closer and that they spend more time with family members. This result is similar to Bluvol and Ford-Gilboe (2004), who discovered that stroke survivors and their caregiving spouses who are more hopeful may have greater incentives and energy to draw upon, and this may help motivate them to participate more actively in problem-solving and growth-seeking behaviors despite ongoing challenges. Although the reason for more time spent with family was not one that was anticipated or hoped for, survivors did come to the resolve that their stroke was perhaps a "blessing in disguise." Survivors realized they now had time (or perhaps were forced with the time) to spend with family that they otherwise would not have had prior to the stroke.

Third, Reid (2004) argued that little is known about long-term care for stroke survivors and that social support and active management of self-care are important to survivors' functioning in their homes. Results of this study seem to support this belief as all survivors still appear to be concerned with self-presentation and are willing to tap into social networks when necessary for daily functioning. Shortly after the stroke, survivors were hesitant in asking for help from their carer and others; currently, many now appear to be more comfortable with asking for help. More work needs to be done with long-term survivors to understand the differences between short-term and long-term recovery processes.

An implication for the dialectical perspective is that many of the tensions felt by survivors within relationships were created out of necessity rather than by choice. For example, traditional tensions of autonomy-connection, predictability-novelty, or openness-closedness (Baxter, 1988) are those tensions felt within relational members—ones that may or may not be played out physically/behaviorally. However, in the survivor and carer relationship, the independence-dependence tension appeared to be a necessity to maintain and function properly within this relationship and the recovery process. Survivors wanted the independence but required the dependence for daily living.

Length of time after the stroke also provides some interesting conclusions. First, it appears that at least 2 years after the stroke, many stroke survivors (as with this sample) have come to realize their limitations and that they probably have all the mobility that will be recovered. According to Jorgenson et al. (1995), the best time for recovery of basic self-care and mobility skills occurs within 12.5 weeks. For those in the current study, their poststroke timeframes ranged from 2 to 12 years, and thus we can assume that these individuals have more than likely reached maximum mobility. This does not mean, however, that they have given up or have discontinued their personal therapy; they have just come to accept what has happened and try to remain dedicated to keeping the best muscle elasticity possible through daily exercises or other physical activity. As with many stroke survivors, what is gained in mobility and skill can be taken away in a moment's notice with additional health-related setbacks, thus requiring additional therapy.

Another implication is the notion that stroke survivors are still an active part of society and feel like they have something to contribute. Family members and members of survivors' social networks must remember that even though survivors may not be able engage in all physical activities, they are still willing to engage in meaningful and communicative relationships. Lessons can be learned from stroke survivors and their positive outlook on life and acceptance of their situations. Most families would rather have the stoke survivor recover in their home rather than in a medical facility or nursing home. What we must remember, however, is that companionship is also necessary for one's recovery.

Hage and Powers (1999) argue that the aging process already forces individuals to redefine their roles and identities, and the role definition is more complicated when there is a disability such as a stroke. One would assume that long-term effects would become more routine and patterned. In terms of how stroke survivors experience day-to-day living, however, some long-term issues are as fresh as they are in the short term. For example, individuals still need to continue to work muscles and engage in therapy to maintain physical functioning. Many commented that each day is a new day and that they never know what they will face when they wake up. Routine is important for a stroke survivor's lifestyle. This may imply that regardless of how "routine" something may be, there are still new challenges to be confronted.

As demonstrated by many of the descriptions, tensions are created by the stroke survivors and/or felt by the survivors as a result of others' behaviors. This would suggest internal and external tensions operating within familial and social networks.

Ample research has studied social networks; however, less research has examined the dialectical tensions operating within stroke survivors and their network of relationships. Examples in this study demonstrate the tensions felt by the stroke survivors. Other areas of network research could focus on the couple's communication and functioning, the couple and their children, and the interactions among the family and health practitioners and therapists.

In addition, this study extends our knowledge and understanding of the long-term effects on the survivors. Research also needs to examine the long-term effects on spousal caregivers and other family members of the stroke survivors.

References

Altman, I. (1993). Dialectics, physical environments, and personal relationships. *Communication Monographs, 60,* 26–34.

American Heart Association. (2003). *Heart disease and stroke statistics.* Dallas, TX: Author.

American Stroke Association. (2004). *What is stroke?* Dallas, TX: Author.

Arnston, P., & Droge, D. (1987). Social support in self help groups: The role of communication in enabling perceptions of control. In T. Albrecht & M. Edelman (Eds.), *Communicating social support* (pp. 225–279). Beverly Hills, CA: Sage.

Barbow, A. S., Hines, S. C., & Kasch, C. R. (2000). Managing uncertainty in illness explanation: An application of problematic integration theory. In B. B. Whaley (Ed.), *Explaining illness: Research, theory and strategies* (pp. 41–67). Mahwah, NJ: Lawrence Erlbaum.

Baxter, L. A. (1988). A dialectical perspective on communication strategies in relational development. In S. W. Duck (Ed.), *Handbook of personal relationships: Theory, research and interventions* (pp. 257–273). New York: John Wiley.

Baxter, L. A. (1990). Dialectical contradictions in relational development. *Journal of Social and Personal Relationships, 7,* 69–88.

Baxter, L. A. (1993). The social side of personal relationships: A dialectical perspective. In S. Duck (Ed.), *Social context and relationships* (pp. 139–186). Newbury Park, CA: Sage.

Baxter, L. A. (1994). A dialogic approach to relationship maintenance. In D. J. Canary & L. Stafford (Eds.), *Communication and relational maintenance* (pp. 233–254). San Diego: Academic Press.

Baxter, L. A., Braithwaite, D. O., Bryant, L., & Wagner, A. (2004). Stepchildren's perceptions of the contradictions in communication with stepparents. *Journal of Social and Personal Relationships, 21,* 447–468.

Baxter, L. A., & Montgomery, B. M. (1996). *Relating: Dialogues and dialectics.* New York: Guilford.

Baxter, L. A., & Widenmann, S. (1993). Revealing and not revealing the status of romantic relationships to social networks. *Journal of Social and Personal Relationships, 10,* 321–337.

Baxter, L. A., & Wilmot, W. (1985). Taboo topics in close relationships. *Journal of Social and Personal Relationships, 2,* 253–269.

Bluvol, A., & Ford-Gilboe, M. (2004). Issues and innovations in nursing practice: Hope, health work and quality of life in families of stroke survivors. *Journal of Advanced Nursing, 48,* 322–332.

Braithwaite, V., & McGown, A. (1993). Caregivers' emotional well-being and their capacity to learn about strokes. *Journal of Advanced Nursing, 18,* 195–202.

Brereton, L., & Nolan, M. (2002). "Seeking": A key activity for new family carers of stroke. *Journal of Clinical Nursing, 11,* 22–32.

Brown, B. B., Altman, I., & Werner, C. M. (1992). Close relationships in the physical and social world: Dialectical and transactional analyses. In S. A. Deetz (Ed.), *Communication yearbook 15* (pp. 508–521). Newbury Park, CA: Sage.

Bruess, C., & Pearson, J. C. (1997). Interpersonal rituals in marriage and adult friendship. *Communication Monographs, 64,* 25–46.

Burton, C. R. (2000). Living with stroke: A phenomenological study. *Journal of Advanced Nursing, 32,* 301–309.

Bury, M. (1982). Chronic illness as biographical disruption. *Sociological Health, 4,* 167–182.

Cannon, C. A., & Cavanaugh, J. C. (1998). Chronic illness in the context of marriage: A systems perspective of stress and coping in chronic obstructive pulmonary disease. *Family Symptoms and Health, 16,* 401–418.

Chick, N., & Meleis, A. I. (1986). Transitions: A nursing concern. In P. L. Chinn (Ed.), *Nursing research methodology: Issues and implementation* (pp. 237–257). New York: Aspen.

Conville, R. L. (1991). *Relational transitions: The evolution of personal relationships.* New York: Praeger.

Conville, R. L. (1994). What is structure then? In R. L. Conville (Ed.), *Uses of "structure" in communication studies* (pp. 185–198). Westport, CT: Praeger.

Cornforth, M. (1968). *Materialism and the dialectical method.* New York: International Publishers.

Creswell, J. W. (1998). *Qualitative research.* Newbury Park, CA: Sage.

Creswell, J. W. (2002). *Educational research: Planning, conducting, and evaluating quantitative and qualitative research.* Upper Saddle River, NJ: Merrill Prentice Hall.

Cupach, W. R. (1992). Dialectical processes in the disengagement of interpersonal relationships. In T. L. Orbuch (Ed.), *Close relationship loss: Theoretical approaches* (pp. 128–141). New York: Springer-Verlag.

Duck, S. W., & Pittman, G. (1994). Social and personal relationships. In M. L. Knapp & G. R. Miller (Eds.), *Handbook of interpersonal communication* (2nd ed., pp. 676–695). Newbury Park, CA: Sage.

Fisher, W. R. (1985). The narrative paradigm: In the beginning. *Journal of Communication, 35,* 74–89.

Gillotti, C. M., & Applegate, J. L. (2000). Explaining illness as bad news: Individual differences in explaining illness-related information. In B. B. Whaley (Ed.), *Explaining illness: Research, theory and strategies* (pp. 101–120). Mahwah, NJ: Lawrence Erlbaum.

Glaser, B. (1992). *Basics of grounded theory analysis.* Mill Valley, CA: Sociology Press.

Glaser, B., & Strauss, A. (1967). *The discovery of grounded theory.* Chicago: Aldine de Gruyter.

Goldsmith, D. (1990). A dialectic perspective on the expression of autonomy and connection in romantic relationships. *Western Journal of Speech Communication, 54,* 537–556.

Hage, G., & Powers, C. H. (1999). *Post-industralized lives: Roles and relationships in the 21st century.* Newbury Park, CA: Sage.

Hellgeth, A. (2002). Coping with stroke: A family's perspective. *Topics in Stroke Rehabilitation, 9,* 80–84.

Hoppe, A. K., & Ting-Toomey, S. (1994, November). *Relational dialectics and management strategies in marital couples: A qualitative study.* Paper presented at the annual convention of the Speech Communication Association, New Orleans, LA.

Jorgenson, H. S., Nakayama, H., Raaschou, H. O., Vive-Larsen, J., Stoier, M., & Olson, T. S. (1995). Outcome and time course of recovery in stroke: Part II. Time course of recovery. The Copenhagen Stroke Study. *Archeology and Physiological Medical Rehabilitation, 76,* 406–412.

Kvigne, K., & Kirkevold, M. (2003). Living with bodily strangeness: Women's experiences of their changing and unpredictable body following a stroke. *Qualitative Health Research, 13,* 1291–1310.

Kvigne, K., Kirkevold, M., & Gjengedal, E. (2004). Fighting back: Struggling to continue life and preserve the self following a stroke. *Health Care for Women International, 25,* 370–387.

Lincoln, Y. S., & Guba, E. G. (1985). *Naturalistic inquiry.* Newbury Park, CA: Sage.

Maxwell, J. A. (2005). *Qualitative research design: An interactive approach.* Thousand Oaks, CA: Sage.

Miller, W. L., & Crabtree, B. E. (1992). Primary care research: A multimethod typology and qualitative roadmap. In B. E. Crabtree & W. L. Miller (Eds.), *Doing qualitative research: Research methods for primary care* (pp. 3–28). Newbury Park, CA: Sage.

Montgomery, B. M. (1992a). Communication as the interface between couples and culture. In S. A. Deetz (Ed.), *Communication yearbook 15* (pp. 475–507). Newbury Park, CA: Sage.

Montgomery, B. M. (1992b, November). *A dialectical approach to reconceptualizing familial and marital relationship maintenance.* Paper presented at the annual convention of the Speech Communication Association, Chicago.

Montgomery, B. M. (1993). Relational maintenance versus relationship change: A dialectical dilemma. *Journal of Social and Personal Relationships, 10,* 205–223.

Murray, C. J., & Lopez, A. D. (1997). Mortality by cause for eight regions of the world: Global Burden of Disease Study. *Lancet, 349,* 1269–1276.

Nussbaum, J. F., Pecchioni, L. L., Grant, J. A., & Folwell, A. (2000). Explaining illness to older adults: The complexities of the provider-patient interaction as we age. In B. B. Whaley (Ed.), *Explaining illness: Research, theory and strategies* (pp. 171–194). Mahwah, NJ: Lawrence Erlbaum.

O'Connell, B., Hanna, B., Penney, W. Y., Pearce, J., Owen, M., & Warelow, P. (2001). Recovery after stroke: A qualitative perspective. *Journal of Qualitative Clinical Practice, 21,* 120–125.

Palmer, S., & Glass, T. A. (2003). Family function and stroke recovery: A review. *Rehabilitation Psychology, 48,* 255–265.

Palmer, S., Glass, T. A., Palmer, J. B., Loo, S., & Wegener, S. T. (2004). Crisis intervention with individuals and their families following stroke: A model for psychosocial service during inpatient rehabilitation. *Rehabilitation Psychology, 49,* 338–343.

Parkes, C. M. (1971). Psycho-social transitions: A field for study. *Sociological Science Medicine, 5,* 101–115.

Pawlowski, D. R. (1998). Dialectical tensions in marital couples' accounts of their relationships. *Communication Quarterly, 46,* 396–417.

Petronio, S. (1991). Communication boundary management: A theoretical model of managing disclosure of private information between marital couples. *Communication Theory, 1,* 311–335.

Petronio, S., & Martin, J. (1986). Ramifications of revealing private information: A gender gap. *Journal of Clinical Psychology, 42,* 499–506.

Rawlins, W. K. (1983a). Negotiating close friendships: The dialectic of conjunctive freedoms. *Human Communication Research, 9,* 255–266.

Rawlins, W. K. (1983b). Openness as problematic in ongoing friendships: Two conversational dilemmas. *Communication Monographs, 50,* 1–13.

Rawlins, W. R. (1989). A dialectical analysis of the tensions, functions, and strategic challenges of communication in young adult friendships. In J. Anderson (Ed.), *Communication yearbook 12* (pp. 157–189). Newbury Park, CA: Sage.

Rawlins, W. R. (1992). *Friendship matters: Communication dialectics and the life course.* Hawthorne, NY: Aldine de Gruyter.

Reid, D. (2004). Impact of the environment on role performance in older stroke survivors living at home. *International Journal of Therapy and Rehabilitation, 11,* 567–573.

Rittman, M., Faircloth, C., Boylstein, C., Gubrium, J. F., Williams, C., Van Puymbroeck, M., & Ellis, C. (2004). The experience of time in the transition from hospital to home following stroke. *Journal of Rehabilitation Research and Development, 41,* 259–268.

Rolland, J. (1999). Parental illness and disability: A family systems framework. *Journal of Family Therapy, 21,* 242–267.

Sabourin, T. C. (1992, November). *Dialectical tensions in family life: A comparison of abusive and nonabusive families.* Paper presented at the annual convention of the Speech Communication Association, Chicago.

Sahlstein, E. M. (1994). Relating at a distance: Negotiating being together and being apart in long-distance relationships. *Journal of Social and Personal Relationships, 21,* 689–710.

Schmidt, S. M., Guo, L., & Scheer, S. J. (2002). Changes in the status of hospitalized stroke patients since inception of the prospective payment system in 1983. *Archives of Physical Medicine and Rehabilitation, 83,* 894–898.

Schumacher, K. L., & Meleis, A. I. (1994). Transitions: A central concept in nursing. *Journal of Nursing Scholarship, 26,* 119–127.

Segrin, C., & Flora, J. (2005). *Family communication.* Mahwah, NJ: Lawrence Erlbaum.

Sharf, B. F., & Kahler, J. (1996). Victims of the franchise: A culturally sensitive model for teaching patient-physician communication in the inner city. In E. R. Ray (Ed.), *Communication and the disenfranchised: Social health issues and implications* (pp. 95–115). Mahwah, NJ: Lawrence Erlbaum.

Sharf, B. F., & Vanderford, M. L. (2003). Illness narratives and the social construction of health. In T. L. Thompson, A. M. Dorsey, K. I. Miller, & R. Parrott (Eds.), *Handbook of health communication* (pp. 9–34). Mahwah, NJ: Lawrence Erlbaum.

Simon, C., & Kendrick, T. (2002). Community provision for informal live-in carers of stroke patients. *British Journal of Community Nursing, 7,* 202–298.

Small, J. A., Gutman, G., Makela, S., & Hillhouse, B. (2003). Effectiveness of communication strategies used by caregivers of persons with Alzheimer's disease during activities of daily living. *Journal of Speech, Language and Hearing Research, 46,* 353–367.

Stamp, G. H. (1992, November). *Toward generative family theory: Dialectical tensions within family life.* Paper presented at the annual convention of the Speech Communication Association, Chicago.

Strauss, A. L. (1987). *Qualitative analysis for social scientists.* Cambridge, UK: Cambridge University Press.

Strauss, A. L., & Corbin, J. (1990). *Basics of qualitative research: Grounded theory procedures and techniques.* Newbury Park, CA: Sage.

Thompson, T. L. (2000). The nature of language of illness explanations. In B. B. Whaley (Ed.), *Explaining illness: Research, theory and strategies* (pp. 3–39). Mahwah, NJ: Lawrence Erlbaum.

Van der Smagt-Duijnstee, M., Hamers, J. P. H., & Huijer Adu-Saad, H. (2000). Relatives of stroke patients: Their experiences and needs in hospitals. *Scandinavian Journal of Caring Sciences, 14,* 44–52.

Werner, C. M., & Baxter, L. A. (1994). Temporal qualities of relationships: Organismic, transactional, and dialectical views. In M. L. Knapp & G. R. Miller (Eds.), *Handbook of interpersonal communication* (2nd ed., pp. 323–379). Newbury Park, CA: Sage.

Wood, J. T., Dendy, L. L., Dordek, E., Germany, M., & Varallo, S. M. (1994). Dialectic for difference: A thematic analysis of intimates' meaning for differences. In K. Carter & M. Presnell (Eds.), *Interpretive approaches to interpersonal communication* (pp. 115–136). Albany: SUNY Press.

White, C. L., Mayo, N., Hanley, J. A., & Wood-Dauphinee, S. (2003). Evolution of the caregiving experience in the initial two years following stroke. *Research in Nursing & Health, 26,* 177–189.

Epilogue

The Future of Family Communication Theory and Research

Mary Anne Fitzpatrick

University of South Carolina

O ur editors have assembled a stellar cast of authors who have produced thought-provoking analyses of communication in families. I have read each of the chapters in this book carefully and believe there is much to be learned by a detailed study of the works of these authors. I am honored to contribute the epilogue for such a fine collection.

Epilogues have two very different meanings and functions. Both meanings have their roots in the theater. Sometimes, epilogues occur at the end of the play and tell the audience what happens to the characters in the future. At other times, epilogues function as swan songs, giving the last words of the dying central character. This chapter will serve both functions as I will point to new directions for research and theory in family communication even as I simultaneously present what will probably be some of my last words as a scholar of interpersonal communication before I disappear into full-time university administration. As I peer into the crystal ball, I will comment on what I see as three underlying themes in the book. The first centers on how we define and interpret the family; the second and third focus on theoretical and methodological considerations.

Defining Family Communication

To define family communication, a scholar needs a clear definition of the terms *family* and *communication*. Defining these terms requires a number of decisions on the part of the theorist as both terms are complex when seriously examined.

Scholars of interpersonal communication in the family have struggled with definitions of family for at least 30 years. Consider, for example, that many scholars now avoid using the term *family* in the singular and prefer the plural. The title of the *Journal of Marriage and "the" Family* has recently dropped the *the* to avoid any implication that there is a single family form. Massive cultural changes have driven the scholarly community to examine, as does the society around us, our underlying presuppositions about family. Our taken-for-granted assumptions no longer automatically work in real life or in research. In this collection, we see several ways to approach defining family provided by Galvin (Chapter 1) and Floyd, Mikkelson, and Judd (Chapter 2).

In our book, Patricia Noller and I (Noller & Fitzpatrick, 1993) settled on a transactional definition of family. Eschewing sociolegal or biological definitions of the family, we argued that family was a transactional system composed of intimates who shared an identity and a commitment to the future. In other words, if people had a close relationship (albeit not necessarily a warm one), acknowledged that they were members of a family, and had a sense of commitment to a future for the relationship, then they were a family. Members were able to define for themselves who was "in" and who was "out" of the family.

To adopt a transactional definition of the family suggests that theories and research need to be open to considering all the variations of human social forms of relating when attempting to explain communication in relationships. This commitment requires, however, not simply examining various different forms of families (e.g., single parent, stepfamily) but also thinking seriously about the underlying relationship between these large sociological classifications/types and the concepts you are exploring. Structure is not destiny as Sabourin (2003) powerfully states. Consider, for example, that married couples who are in a long-distance commuter relationship may have less in common with married couples who share the same domicile than do cohabiting couples. That is, the daily stress (as well as support) of living in the same house may have a greater and more consistent impact on patterns of communication and conflict resolution than does the fact that couples are legally married. Or not.

The transactional view of the family also places communication processes at the center of the definition. The definition of communication embedded in this view of the family includes both the interaction so eloquently discussed by Edna Rogers in the preface to this book as well as the cognitive and affective processes brought to family interactions. These cognitive and affective processes drive attention, perception, interpretation, and memory for communication messages in family. Indeed, the transactional definition not only privileges the range, diversity, and patterning of interaction important to Rogers, but also this definition includes the development of intersubjectivity (i.e., some sense of shared social reality) among family members. The mental models and associated affect that individuals and families construct about their relationships are equally important for a definition of family communication.

In my own work in marital and family communication, I have always adopted a transactional definition of the family in that I have a broad view in sampling family forms. In addition, the dimensions of interdependence, ideology, expressivity, and conformity that I investigated in my programs of research, as well as the interrelationships among these dimensions, were the central defining features in a variety of family and close interpersonal relationships forms (Koerner & Fitzpatrick, 2002). This does not mean, however, that there is the same number of different types of relationships within every sample of couples or families examined. In a sample of stepfamilies, gay marriages, single-parent households, and so on, research may predict that there will be a predominance of different types of couples or families.

Although adopting a transactional definition of the family is a satisfying solution to the definitional issue in many ways, the transactional definition demands some serious rethinking of our theoretical and methodological work.

Theoretical Considerations

A transactional definition of family brings to the fore a consideration not only of different forms but also a more serious focus on emotions in human relationships. That is, this definition allows individuals to broaden the boundaries of what constitutes a family. Families are not merely constituted in reference to legal or biological factors but can be formed through emotional ties. With some few exceptions (i.e., attachment theory), our theories of interpersonal communication in the family are fairly bloodless and without reference to the context in which family members find themselves outside of the family system.

That is, few theories of family communication capture the truly remarkable range of human emotions that occur within the family context. As we know, communication in the family can lead to some of life's most wonderful and most unbearable moments. Few of our theories deal with intense human emotions. Sillars and Weisberg (1987) reminded us that family conflict is often chaotic and unresolved over long periods of time. Jacobson and Gottman (1998) studied violent psychopaths who brutalized their wives. But curiously, the influence of those who study emotions is not as widespread as one would assume in family communication research.

I have a novel on my desk as I write this chapter. Set in Afghanistan, *The Swallows of Kabul,* written by a male Algerian army officer under a female pseudonym, tells the story of death and sacrifice in two marriages. One is an upper-middle-class love match between Zunaira and Mohsen. The other is the marriage of a poor jailor, Atiq, and his dying wife. After the war with the Russians, the streets of Kabul are rendered uninhabitable by the Taliban. Zunaira resists leaving the house as she does not want to experience directly the repressions that exist in her society. If she stays within her home and with her family, she can convince herself that life is bearable. Lured into a walk by her naive, albeit loving, husband, she witnesses too much random violence and brutality, and it kills her sense of security and her love for Mohsen. After the walk, Mohsen and Zunaira struggle, and he accidentally falls to his death. Zunaira is jailed to await her own execution for Mohsen's murder. Atiq, the jailor, falls in love with the beautiful Zunaira, but he does not even recognize the emotion. Only his frail wife, who has loved him deeply for many years, knows what emotion he is feeling. As her last act of love for her husband, Atiq's wife sacrifices herself to make it possible for him to be with Zunaira.

Few of our theories deal with these passions and the effects of context on our deepest emotions. In the novel, one woman resists the role that society forces on her and turns on the husband who cannot understand her humiliation, whereas another woman lays down her own life so that her husband can know love—even as he does not know she is taking this action. What in their patterns of interactions could predict such emotional depths?

In addition, few of our theories could answer the following question: In what ways and why did the external social context affect the deepest emotional responses that these family members had toward one another? Surely, love conquers all. The entire last section of this book struggles with the issue of context, and it is only in understanding the context in which families find themselves that we can truly develop better models and theories of family communication.

Methodological Considerations

A transactional definition of the family brings into view a consideration of different forms. In particular, our methods for studying family communication require a focus on the sampling of actors, behaviors, and contexts.

We have seen that the transactional definition broadens the number of actors who may be considered part of the family even as it makes sampling of those actors a more difficult task. Researchers who are attempting to sample actors in families, holding to the transactional definition, are on difficult terrain. Even as researchers may be committed to opening up the sample, they must always be concerned about the basic principle of empirical social science: Maximize the variation between groups and minimize the variation within groups. Although one would want to include single-parent families in a study, researchers may not have a large enough sample of these families to enable looking at their data separately. In any given study, this is a trade-off that needs to be carefully weighed. That is, scholars need to think carefully about how to draw large enough samples of diverse family types to discover the similarities and differences in their communication practices.

Once researchers have decided on which actors to sample, they need to think seriously about the behaviors they are sampling. That is, are they drawing from their participants a range of communication behaviors that will tap the phenomena in the best way? Emotional messages, for example, may more likely be communicated through nonverbal channels, and various family members may use different channels to express emotions. And gender may play a large role in certain family interactions. Gender differences are not manifest in all contexts but may be especially salient in specific family situations. Family may be a site for the development and drawing out of gender roles and gender differences. And scholars need to be careful not to cap the gender lens too soon when viewing close relationships.

Finally, the sampling of contexts also becomes important in a transactional model of the family. This book focuses on key external structural factors that interface with family processes: media, work, religion, school, and medicine. This set of frameworks is indeed comprehensive and is one set of "contextual factors" for researchers to consider. My sense of sampling of contexts, however, differs from that presented in this book. In my view, sampling contexts for understanding family communication involves shifting the frame for analysis of the family. This could take a variety of different patterns. That is, a researcher could be interested in the public/private dimension, the father present/absent dimension, the conflict/casual interaction dimension, and so forth.

These dimensions may be more psychologically real for family members and thus more likely to affect interaction patterns and the interpretation of messages.

Conclusion

Perhaps the warning note upon which I will end this epilogue is that defining your terms in a meaningful way instantiates an entire set of other decisions and choices. In my own work over the past 30 years, I have always been involved in variations on a theme. That is, I have spent my scholarly career trying to uncover patterns to describe transactional systems. Across many years and many studies, I have tried to sample actors, behaviors, and contexts to understand family communication patterns and processes. I have uncovered patterned regularities in family interaction and specific demonstrable differences in message interpretation processes. My work has always been, at base, optimistic. For as I have written about communication in family, I make the assumption that it is possible, not easy or trivial, for people to communicate with one another.

At the beginning of this chapter, I promised that I would give a sense of the future of theory and research on family communication. Clearly, the future is bright as evidenced by the thoughtful work of the authors and the editors of this volume. Optimism is alive and well in the field.

References

Jacobson, N., & Gottman, J. M. (1998). *When men batter women.* New York: Simon & Schuster.

Koerner, A., & Fitzpatrick, M. A. (2002). Toward a theory of family communication. *Communication Theory, 12,* 70–91.

Noller, P., & Fitzpatrick, M. A. (1993). *Communication in family relationships.* Englewood Cliffs, NJ: Prentice Hall.

Sabourin, T. C. (2003). *The contemporary American family.* Thousand Oaks, CA: Sage.

Sillars, A., & Weisberg, J. (1987). Conflict as a social skill. In M. Roloff & G. R. Miller (Eds.), *Interpersonal processes* (pp. 140–171). Newbury Park, CA: Sage.

Author Index

Subject Index

About the Editors

Lynn H. Turner (Ph.D., Northwestern University) is Professor of Communication Studies in the J. William and Mary Diederich College of Communication at Marquette University. Her research areas of interest include interpersonal, gendered, and family communication. She is the coauthor or coeditor of over 10 books as well as several articles and book chapters (many with Rich West). Lynn has served in a number of different positions: Director of Graduate Studies for the College of Communication at Marquette University; President of the Organization for the Study of Communication, Language, and Gender (OSCLG); President of Central States Communication Association (CSCA); and Chair of the Family Communication Division for the National Communication Association. In her free time, Lynn delights in babysitting for her grandchildren.

Richard West (Ph.D., Ohio University) is Professor in the Department of Communication & Media Studies at the University of Southern Maine. His research spans a number of different areas, including family communication, instructional practices, and classroom communication. Rich is the coauthor (with Lynn Turner) of numerous textbooks, book chapters, and research articles. Rich is the current Director of the Educational Policies Board of the National Communication Association and the Vice President of the Eastern Communication Association. He lives in Cape Elizabeth, Maine, and dedicates his free time to fixing up his 100-year-old bungalow.

About the Contributors

Alison Alexander (Ph.D., Ohio State University) is Professor and Associate Dean for Academic Affairs at the Grady College of Journalism and Mass Communication at the University of Georgia. She was editor of the *Journal of Broadcasting & Electronic Media* and is past president of the Association for Communication Administration and the Eastern Communication Association. Her work focuses on media and the family. She is the author of over 40 book chapters or journal articles and the coeditor of four books. She was named the 1998 Frank Stanton Fellow by the International Radio & Television Society for "outstanding contribution to broadcast education."

Dustin J. Anderson (M.A., English, Iowa State University; M.A., Communication, University of Dayton) is Instructor of Communication at the University of Dayton. From 2002–2006, he was the assistant editor for the journal *Health Communication*. His interests have included general message framing techniques for public communication campaigns, effects of video games and comic books on children, and health communication theory. Most recently, his work has focused on effects of various message strategies on potential organ donors.

Sharon Atkin (B.A., University of Queensland) is a graduate student in the School of Psychology at the University of Queensland. Her main interest is in the family relationships of adolescents, and she has had a lot of experience working with troubled adolescents and their families.

Deborah S. Ballard-Reisch (Ph.D., Bowling Green State University) is Professor in the School of Public Health, University of Nevada, Reno. Her research interests include family and couple communication, health and risk communication, international women's health, and narrative theory. She coedited a volume on *Communication and Sex Role Socialization,* as well as special issues of *Women and Language* and the *Journal of Family Communication.* She has served in a variety of positions: Director of Graduate Studies, Faculty Senate Chair, Assistant Director of Honors, and President of the Organization for the Study of Communication, Language, and Gender (OSCLG).

Leslie A. Baxter (Ph.D., University of Oregon) is the F. Wendell Miller Distinguished Professor of Communication Studies at the University of Iowa. She focuses her research on communication in personal and familial relationships, with a particular focus on the competing discourses that animate relating. She has published over 100 books, chapters, and articles, most recently *Engaging Theories in Family Communication: Multiple Perspectives* (with Dawn Braithwaite). She is a Past President of the Western States Communication Association. She has earned a variety of awards, including the Knower and Miller Awards from the Interpersonal Division of the National Communication Association.

Dawn O. Braithwaite (Ph.D., University of Minnesota) is Professor of Communication Studies at University of Nebraska–Lincoln. She focuses her scholarship on communication in personal and family relationships, studying relational dialectics, rituals, and social support in the context of stepfamilies, elderly couples, and people with disabilities. She has published three books and over 50 articles and chapters in scholarly books, most recently *Engaging Theories in Family Communication: Multiple Perspectives* (with Leslie Baxter). She is a Past President of the Western States Communication Association and is the current Director of the National Communication Association Research Board.

J. Alison Bryant (Ph.D., University of Southern California) is Research Director for Nickelodeon's Consumer Insights group. Her current research focuses on the role of digital media in kids' lives and the changing relationship between parents, kids, and the media. She is the editor of *The Children's Television Community* and coeditor of *Television and the American Family* (2nd ed.).

Jennings Bryant (Ph.D., Indiana University) is the CIS Distinguished Research Professor, Associate Dean for Graduate Studies, and Reagan Chair of Broadcasting in the College of Communication & Information Sciences at the University of Alabama. His research interests are in entertainment theory, media effects, media and children, and media and family. He served as President of the International Communication Association in 2002–2003 and received the University of Alabama's Blackmon-Moody Outstanding Professor Award in 2000.

Leah E. Bryant (Ph.D., University of Nebraska–Lincoln) is Assistant Professor in the Communication Department at DePaul University. She teaches undergraduate and graduate courses in interpersonal, family, gender, and small group communication as well as relational problems. Her research interests include family, relational, and instructional communication. Her current research focuses on communication in stepfamilies formed following the death of a parent. Her work has been published in the *Journal of Social and Personal Relationships, Communication Studies, Communication Research Reports*, and *Qualitative Research Reports*.

Patrice M. Buzzanell (Ph.D., Purdue University) is Professor in the Communication Department at Purdue University, where she specializes in feminist theorizing and gendered workplace processes, particularly as they relate to careers. She has published in *Communication Theory, Human Communication Research, Communication*

Monographs, Management Communication Quarterly, and *Journal of Applied Communication Research* and has (co)edited two books, *Rethinking Organizational and Managerial Communication From Feminist Perspectives* and *Gender in Applied Communication Contexts.*

Jeffrey T. Child (B.S., Wayne State College) is a Communication Graduate Teaching Assistant and Direct-to-Doctorate Ph.D. student at North Dakota State University, Fargo, North Dakota. His research interests include technology and the family, research methods, and instructional development and technology. He has published in a number of different journals, including *Communication Education, Communication Quarterly,* and *College Student Journal.*

Pamela Cooper (Ph.D., Purdue University) is Professor at the University of South Carolina, Beaufort. She taught for 25 years at Northwestern University and 2 years at the Chinese University of Hong Kong. She has published in the areas of intercultural communication, gender, classroom communication, communication education, and storytelling.

Fran C. Dickson (Ph.D., Bowling Green State University) is Associate Professor and chair of the Department of Human Communication Studies at the University of Denver. Her research interests include communication in later-life marriage and the aging process.

Steve Duck (Ph.D., University of Sheffield/UK) is Professor of Communication Studies and the Daniel and Amy Starch Research Chair at the University of Iowa. He is the founding editor of the *Journal of Social and Personal Relationships* and the editor or author of 42 books on personal relationships. In addition, he founded the International Network on Personal Relationships (now merged into the International Association for Relationship Research) and two series of international conferences on relationships.

Judith A. Feeney (Ph.D., University of Queensland) is Associate Professor in the School of Psychology at the University of Queensland. She is well known for her research on adult attachment, which she has studied across a range of contexts, including dating relationships, newlyweds, and couples going through the transition to parenthood. She has authored several books, including *Adult Attachment, Becoming Parents: Exploring the Bonds Between Mothers, Fathers and Their Infants* and *Personal Relationships Across the Lifespan.* She has also coedited *Understanding Marriage: Developments in the Study of Marital Interaction* (with Patricia Noller). She has also published extensively in journals such as *Personal Relationships* and written a number of book chapters.

Mary Anne Fitzpatrick (Ph.D., Temple University) is Dean of the College of Arts and Sciences at the University of South Carolina. The primary focus of her research has been on communication processes in marriage and the family. A past president of the International Communication Association, she received its 2001 Career Achievement Award for sustained excellence in communication research. In 1993, she was elected a Fellow of the same association. An internationally recognized authority on interpersonal communication, she is the author of over 100 articles, chapters, and books. The NIH, NIMH, and the Spencer Foundation have supported her research.

Kory Floyd (Ph.D., University of Arizona) is Associate Professor of Human Communication and Director of the Communication Sciences Laboratory at Arizona State University. His research focuses on the communication of affection in families and other personal relationships, as well as on the interplay between communication, physiology, and health. He has authored five books and over 60 journal articles and book chapters and is editor of *Journal of Family Communication.*

Megan K. Foley (M.A., University of North Carolina, Chapel Hill) is a Presidential Graduate Fellow in Communication Studies at the University of Iowa. Her research focuses on the interrelationship of the communicative act, agency, and structure. She is exploring this interest in the context of family discourse with a particular focus on intimate partner violence.

Kathleen M. Galvin (Ph.D., Northwestern University) is Professor of Communication Studies at Northwestern University. She is the senior author of *Family Communication: Cohesion and Change* (6th ed.) and developer of the PBS distance learning package in family communication. She is the author or coauthor of seven other communication books and has served on the editorial boards of a number of journals. Her current research is focused on the communicative construction of family identity as reflected in current studies on gay male parenting and international adoption. She teaches in the areas of relational communication and family communication.

Elizabeth E. Graham (Ph.D., Kent State University) is Professor of Communication Studies at Ohio University in Athens, Ohio. She teaches courses in interpersonal communication, research methods, and statistics at the undergraduate and graduate levels. In addition to being a faculty member, she also serves as the University Ombuds and has served in this position since 2002. Her research interests include communication in reconstituted families, and she is coediting a new edition of the *Communication Research Measures Sourcebook.*

Theresa L. Hest (Ph.D., North Dakota State University) is Assistant Professor of Communication Studies at Minnesota State University Moorhead. She teaches courses in interpersonal communication, family communication, communication theory, teaching methods, and gender communication. She is actively involved in academic service learning. She is a partner in a family farming operation and a mother of three.

Patrick C. Hughes (Ph.D., University of Denver) is Assistant Professor in the Department of Communication Studies at Texas Tech University. His research interests include family communication and religious and cultural influences on marital communication.

Susanne M. Jones (Ph.D., Arizona State University) is Assistant Professor in the Department of Communication Studies at the University of Minnesota. Her research interests include the study of emotional support, communication of emotion, and nonverbal communication. Her research has appeared in *Human Communication Research, Communication Monographs, Communication Research, Western Journal of Communication,* and *Sex Roles.*

Jeff Judd (B.A., Arizona State University) is a graduate student in human communication at Arizona State University (ASU). His research interests focus on emotion in friendships and on communication and physiology. At ASU, he works in the communication sciences laboratory and has coauthored papers on the relationship between affectionate communication and stress. He is the editorial assistant for *Journal of Family Communication.*

Rebecca Kallemeyn is an undergraduate at Calvin College and a National Merit scholar. She is majoring in dramaturgy and is planning on attending graduate school.

Seok Kang (Ph.D., University of Georgia) is Assistant Professor in the Department of Speech, Theatre, and Journalism at Arkansas Tech University, Russellville. His research interests focus on digital media and family communication, entertainment education, and cyber communication. He is particularly interested in the effects of the Internet and online interaction on offline behaviors, including psychosocial well-being. His works have appeared in *Public Relations Review, Journalism & Mass Communication Educator, Mass Communication & Society,* and *Journal of Asian Pacific Communication.*

Yeora Kim (Ph.D., University of Georgia) is a lecturer at Chung-Ang University in Seoul, Korea. She did postdoctoral research at Sogang University at Seoul, Korea. She studies children's media use, including new technology; family communication, including parental mediation on children's media use within the home; and health communication, specially focusing on health communication issues on the Internet.

Emily Lamb (M.S., Illinois State University) is a doctoral student in the Department of Communication Studies at the University of Nebraska–Lincoln. She serves as the Associate Director of the university's basic communication course and also teaches classes in public speaking, communication theory, and interpersonal communication. Her research interests include emotional, relational, and supportive communication in dating, marital, and familial relationships. She is an active member of the National Communication Association, the Central States Communication Association, and the International Association for Relationship Research.

Kristin M. Langellier (Ph.D., Southern Illinois University) is the Mark and Marcia Bailey Professor at the University of Maine, where she teaches communication, performance studies, and women's studies. Her research interests are narrative performance, family storytelling, and Franco American cultural identity. Her numerous publications include *Storytelling in Daily Life: Performing Narrative* (2004), coauthored with Eric E. Peterson. She is a former editor of *Text and Performance Quarterly.*

Kristen Lucas (Ph.D., Purdue University) is Assistant Professor in the Department of Communication Studies at the University of Nebraska–Lincoln. Her research interests focus on dignity in the workplace, career discourses, blue-collar organizations, and the intersection of work and technology. Her dissertation research explores how family-based, work-related communication shapes the careers of adult sons and daughters of blue-collar workers, particularly when blue-collar jobs are no longer available due to deindustrialization. She has published in *Journal of Applied Communication Research* and *Communication Research*.

Caryn E. Medved (Ph.D., University of Kansas) is Assistant Professor at Ohio University. Her research interests explore the intersections between organizational and family communication, with particular attention to issues of identity, gender, and power. Her work has appeared in outlets such as *Management Communication Quarterly, Communication Yearbook, Journal of Applied Communication, Communication Studies,* and *Journal of Family Communication.* Most recently, her research has investigated the use of corporate or managerial discourses in the communicative construction of domestic work and care labor for stay-at-home mothers.

Sandra Metts (Ph.D., University of Iowa) is Professor in the School of Communication at Illinois State University, where she teaches graduate and undergraduate classes in interpersonal communication, language, human communication and aging, and research methods. Her research interests include relationship disengagement, deception, sexual communication, emotional expression, facework, and politeness. She is the former president of the Central States Communication Association and the recipient of the University Outstanding Teacher Award and the Teaching Excellence Award of the International Association for Relationship Research. She has served as the editor of *Communication Reports* and associate editor of *Personal Relationships* and *Journal of Social and Personal Relationships,* and she also serves on several editorial boards for regional, national, and international journals.

Alan C. Mikkelson (M.A., Arizona State University) is Assistant Professor of Communication Studies at Whitworth College. He is completing his Ph.D. in human communication at Arizona State University. His research focuses on the communication of closeness among siblings and other family relationships. He has coauthored one book and several journal articles and book chapters and serves on the editorial board of *Journal of Family Communication.*

Courtney Waite Miller (Ph.D., Northwestern University) is Assistant Professor in the Communication Arts and Sciences department at Elmhurst College. She focuses her research on interpersonal communication—specifically, conflict in close relationships. She has authored or coauthored several book chapters and journal articles and has presented her research at national and international academic conferences.

Scott A. Myers (Ph.D., Kent State University) is Associate Professor and Coordinator of On-Campus Graduate Studies in the Department of Communication Studies at West Virginia University. His research focuses on the study of sibling relationships, students' motives for communicating with their instructors, and instructor aggressive communication. His work has been published in *Communication Research Reports, Communication Education, Communication Quarterly,* and *Western Journal of Communication.* He is the coauthor of *The Basics of Small Group Communication* and is the former editor of *Communication Teacher.*

Patricia Noller (Ph.D., University of Queensland) is Emeritus Professor of Psychology at the University of Queensland. For 7 years, she was Director of the University of Queensland Family Centre. She has published extensively in the area of marital and family relationships, including 12 books and over a hundred journal articles and book chapters. She is a Fellow of the Academy of the Social Sciences in Australia and of the National Council on Family Relationships (USA). She has served on a number of editorial boards and was appointed as foundation editor of *Personal Relationships: Journal of the International Society for the Study of Personal Relationships,* a position that she held from 1993 to 1997. She was president of that society from 1998 to 2000.

Alda Norris (M.A., Purdue University) is a Ph.D. student at Purdue University. Her research interests include interpersonal communication as well as sociolinguistics.

Donna R. Pawlowski (Ph.D., University of Nebraska–Lincoln) is Associate Professor in the Department of Communication Studies and a Service-Learning Faculty Development Fellow at Creighton University, where she teaches courses in theory, interpersonal communication, family, health, and managerial communication. Her research and publications focus on relational and familial communication, with an emphasis on health care and acute illness, metaphors and dialectics, and instructional communication and pedagogical implications of service learning. She has held various positions for both the Central States Communication Association and the National Communication Association. She is an editorial board member for *Communication Studies* and the *Journal of Business Communication.*

Judy C. Pearson (Ph. D., Indiana University) is Associate Dean of Arts, Humanities, and Social Sciences and Professor of Communication at North Dakota State University, Fargo, North Dakota. She is a past president of the National Communication Association, the Central States Communication Association, and the World Communication Association. She has administered and taught at Indiana University, Bradley University, Purdue University, Iowa State University, Michigan State University, Ohio University, and Virginia Tech. She is particularly proud of the work of her advisees, including Theresa Hest and Jeff Child.

Loretta L. Pecchioni (Ph.D., University of Oklahoma) is Associate Professor in the Department of Communication Studies at Louisiana State University. Her research interests focus on the development and maintenance of interpersonal relationships across the life span, as highlighted by the management of health crises within the family. Specific research projects have examined decision making related to caregiving in older mother-daughter relationships and the management of health crises by marital couples.

Candida Peterson (Ph.D., University of California, Santa Barbara) is Professor of Psychology at the University of Queensland and a Fellow of the Academy of the Social Sciences in Australia. She has been teaching life span developmental psychology at universities in the United States and Australia since 1971. Her textbook, *Looking Forward Through the Lifespan: Developmental Psychology,* guides much of this teaching and is now in its fourth edition. Her research centers on discovering how processes of communication, conversation, and conflict resolution in the family influence psychological development and social understanding, particularly at key sociocognitive turning points in the life span, including preschool and adolescence. Her recent discoveries of links between family communication and social cognition for deaf children, blind children, and those with autism raise interesting applied questions about how social and conversational experiences may relate to psychological development in the context of communication impairment.

Eric E. Peterson (Ph.D., Southern Illinois University) is Professor at the University of Maine, where he teaches in the Department of Communication and Journalism. His research and teaching interests are in narrative performance, media consumption, nonverbal communication, and communication diversity and identity. He is coauthor with Kristin M. Langellier of *Storytelling in Daily Life: Performing Narrative* (2004) and coeditor of *Public Broadcasting and the Public Interest* (2003).

Sandra Petronio (Ph.D., University of Michigan) is Professor in the Department of Communication Studies at Indiana University–Purdue University, Indianapolis; core faculty in the Indiana University Center for Bioethics in the School of Medicine; and adjunct faculty in the IU School of Nursing and the IU School of Informatics. Her research areas are in privacy, disclosure, and confidentiality. She developed communication privacy management theory, and her 2002 book on the theory, *Boundaries of Privacy: Dialectics of Disclosure,* won the Gerald R. Miller Award from the National Communication Association (2003) and the book award from the International Association of Relationship Research (2004). She commences her post as the new president of the International Association of Relationship Research in July 2006, and she is a past president of the Western States Communication Association. She has been honored with the Bernard J. Brommel Family Communication Award for outstanding scholarship and distinguished service in family communication from the National Communication Association. In 2003, she was the first recipient of the Bernard Brock Research Award bestowed by Wayne State University's Department of Communication. In June 2005, she was invited to give a congressional briefing in Washington, D.C., on issues of privacy.

Jessica J. Rack (M.A., University of Cincinnati) is a Ph.D. student at Purdue University. Her research interests include communication in marriage, family communication, language and gender, social cognition, computer-mediated communication, and communication apprehension.

Christine E. Rittenour (M.A., West Virginia University) is a doctoral student in the Department of Communication Studies at the University of Nebraska–Lincoln. Her primary research areas are family, interpersonal, and relational communication. She examines the functions of conflict, support, and commitment as well as the roles of attributions and storytelling in the construction and management of individual and relational identities. Her work has been published in the *Iowa Journal of Communication.*

L. Edna Rogers (Ph.D., Michigan State University) is Professor of Communication at the University of Utah. She is a past president of the International Communication Association and recipient of a number of distinguished teaching and research awards. Her research on interpersonal relationships focuses on the study of marital and family communication with the book, *Relational Communication: An Interactional Perspective to the Study of Process and Form* (2004), among her recent publications.

Michael E. Roloff (Ph.D., Michigan State University) is Professor of Communication Studies at Northwestern University. He researches in the area of conflict management. He wrote *Interpersonal Communication: The Social Exchange Approach* and coedited *Persuasion: New Directions in Theory and Research* (with Gerald R. Miller), *Interpersonal Processes: New Directions in Communication Research* (with Gerald R. Miller), *Social Cognition and Communication* (with Charles R. Berger), and *Communication and Negotiation* (with Linda Putnam). He has published in journals such as *Communication Monographs, Communication Research, Human Communication Research, International Journal of Conflict Management, Journal of Language and Social Psychology, Journal of Social and Personal Relationships,* and *Personal Relationships.* He is also the Senior Associate Editor of *The International Journal of Conflict Management.* He served as editor of *The Communication Yearbook* and is coeditor of *Communication Research.*

Teresa C. Sabourin (Ph.D., Purdue University) is Professor in the Department of Communication at the University of Cincinnati, where she teaches undergraduate and graduate courses in family communication, interpersonal communication, and group communication. Her research interests include relational patterns of abusive couples, verbal aggression, and dialectical management in abusive and recovering families. She is the author of *The Contemporary American Family: A Dialectical Perspective on Communication and Relationships* (2003). She is a founding member of the Family Communication Division of the National Communication Association and serves on several editorial boards for regional and national journals.

Paul Schrodt (Ph.D., University of Nebraska–Lincoln) is Assistant Professor of Communication Studies at the University of Kansas. He specializes in family and relational communication, as well as in instructional communication. His research has explored communication cognitions and behaviors that facilitate family functioning, specifically examining coparenting and stepparenting relationships in stepfamilies and the associations among family communication schemata and family functioning. His research has appeared in *Human Communication Research, Communication Monographs,* and *Communication Education.*

Xiaowei Shi (M.A., DePaul University) is a third-year doctoral student at Purdue University. Her interest focuses on persuasive message production in interpersonal and intercultural communication settings.

Thomas J. Socha (Ph.D., University of Iowa) is University Professor and Associate Professor of Communication at Old Dominion University (Norfolk, VA). In family communication, he has published two coedited books, numerous book chapters, and articles that collectively examine aspects of parent-child communication, children's communication, and family communication and ethnic culture. His current projects include a coedited book about parent-child interfacings with social systems outside the home, a study of parent-child communication among the blind, and development of positive communication theorizing.

Helen Sterk (Ph.D., University of Iowa) is Chair and Professor of Communication Arts and Sciences at Calvin College, Grand Rapids, Michigan. At Calvin, she has held the Spoelhof Teacher-Scholar Chair and is the 2006–2007 Calvin Lecturer. Her publications include, with Patrice Buzzanell and Lynn Turner, *Gender in Applied Communication Contexts* (2004) and, with Carla Hay, Alice Kehoe, Krista Ratcliffe, and Leona Vande Vusse, *Who's Having This Baby?* (2002).

Teresa L. Thompson (Ph.D., Temple University) is Professor of Communication at the University of Dayton. She has published five books and over 40 articles relating to various aspects of health communication in such outlets as *Human Communication Research, Public Opinion Quarterly,* and *Social Science and Medicine.* Her early work focused on communication and disability issues and then moved to the study of health care provider-patient interaction. She edits the international journal *Health Communication.* Her current work emphasizes organ donation issues and family communication.

Lisa Tirmenstein (M.A., Purdue University) is living and working in Ohio and applying to law schools.

Daniel J. Weigel (Ph.D., University of Nevada, Reno) is Professor with the Interdisciplinary Ph.D. Program in Social Psychology, the Department of Human Development and Family Studies, and serves as a Human Development Specialist for the University of Nevada Cooperative Extension. His research interests include family and couple relationships—especially communication, commitment, and change—as well as parent-child interaction. He has published widely in the *Journal of Social and Personal Relationships, Personal Relationships, Journal of Family Communication, Communication Reports,* and *Family Relations.* He coedited a special issue of the *Journal of Family Communication* and has written chapters in *Maintaining Relationships Through Communication* and *Handbook of Interpersonal Commitment and Relationship Stability.*

Steven R. Wilson (Ph.D., Purdue University) is Professor and Director of Graduate Studies in the Department of Communication at Purdue University. His research and teaching focus on influence and conflict processes in families, friendships, and work relationships. He is the author of *Seeking and Resisting Compliance: Why We Say What We Do When Trying to Influence Others* (2002), as well as of about 50 peer-reviewed articles and scholarly book chapters on these topics. He has served as associate editor for the interdisciplinary journal *Personal Relationships* (2001–2003), as well as chair of the interpersonal communication divisions for both the National Communication Association and the International Communication Association.